# The Journals of Claire Clairmont

# THE JOURNALS
# OF
# CLAIRE CLAIRMONT

## Edited by Marion Kingston Stocking

with the assistance of David Mackenzie Stocking

Harvard University Press
Cambridge, Massachusetts—1968

Copyright 1968 by the President and Fellows of Harvard College
All rights reserved
Distributed in Great Britain by Oxford University Press
London

Publication of this work has been aided by a grant
from The Carl and Lily Pforzheimer Foundation, Inc.

Library of Congress Catalog Card Number 68–17634

Designed by Edith Allard

Printed by Harvard University Printing Office
in the United States of America

Bound by Stanhope Bindery, Inc., Boston, Massachusetts

To the memory of Newman Ivey White

# Preface

$\mathcal{T}$he journals of Clara Mary Jane "Claire" Clairmont are one of the last—and perhaps the very last—of the major documents of the Shelley–Byron circle to be published. Although Claire is best known as the mother of Byron's Allegra, she is more important to literary history for her role in introducing the Shelleys to Byron, and the primary interest of her journals is the light they shed on the Shelley family from the time of the poet's elopement with Mary Godwin in 1814 until his death in 1822. Only the writings of the Shelleys themselves surpass Claire Clairmont's in importance for one who wishes to follow the careers of the poet and his circle. Fortunately some Shelley scholars have been able to use these journals in manuscript, transcript, or photostat, but they are now being published in full for the first time.

In preparing these manuscripts for publication I have had three sorts of readers in mind. For the general reader, with no special knowledge of the period, I have provided a biographical framework so that the book may be read as a coherent, if necessarily incomplete, account of the first thirty-two years of Claire's life. I hope that he will go on to supplement this view with the perspectives of the splendid biographies, such as that of Shelley by Newman Ivey White and Byron by Leslie Marchand, and the vivid recreation of Claire by Rosalie Glynn Grylls. And no one should forget that the biographical details derive their ultimate interest from the poems, plays, and letters of the poets themselves. I am aware, however, that most of my readers will be scholars intimately familiar with

# Preface

what has already been published; many will know the primary sources. To these readers I should like to say that they will find here a transcription of the manuscript, with minimal editing. I have put to myself the arguments against this approach: that Claire would not have been pleased to see her signs of haste (not to mention the passages she worked so hard to obliterate) displayed in type; that the quotations from her reading will interest few, if any, readers; that there are some dry stretches, particularly in the later journals; that slavish reproduction of a text is more pedantry than scholarship. I have not been able to overcome my uneasiness, however, at the prospect of omitting, editing, or paraphrasing anything. Frederick L. Jones, referring to an earlier edition of the journal of Edward Ellerker Williams, says, "One is dissatisfied to learn that anything is omitted, however insignificant the editor may consider it" (*Maria Gisborne and Edward E. Williams, Shelley's Friends: Their Journals and Letters*, p. ix), and I predict that scholars of the future, impressed by the exhaustive authority of *Shelley and His Circle*, are going to expect more, rather than less, completeness. Furthermore, unlike a poem by Shelley, which will receive many editions and benefit from the skills and wisdom of many transcribers and editors, this may well be the only edition that Claire's journals will ever see. I hope, therefore, to anticipate the needs of scholars yet to come by presenting a text so close to the original that no scholar will feel he must go back to photostats or manuscript. Though a reader may find some sections uninteresting, I do not think that Claire's informal punctuation, her corrections and omissions, as perpetuated in my text will lead to any serious obscurity or excessive difficulty for even the most casual reader. I hesitate to decide what may or may not seem important to a reader of the future, since I myself, in preparing this book, have pored through diaries, letters, histories, and travelers' accounts for details that their editors could not possibly have anticipated anyone would want. I have thus kept a third category of reader in mind: the scholar not primarily interested in Claire or the poets, coming to the journals for enlightenment about social history or music or medicine or education or some other aspect of the period.

Still, it is Claire Clairmont's book, and were it not for her relationship with Byron and Shelley her journals probably would not have been preserved, much less published. She lives on in two

# Preface

of their best-known lyrics, both of which pay tribute to her lovely singing voice. Byron's "Stanzas for Music," dated March 28 [1816], has been thought to be addressed to Claire (Byron, *Works: Poetry*, ed. Ernest Hartley Coleridge, III, 435), and although her image may be discerned in several of Shelley's poems, such as *Epipsychidion*, it is "To Constantia Singing" that assures Claire's position among the ladies who served as his muse. The version printed here is from Shelley's *Works* (the Julian edition, III, 155–156); this text is particularly appropriate because it is based on the Shelley manuscript notebook that Claire kept until her old age, when Edward A. Silsbee obtained it from her under circumstances that inspired Henry James's fictional account in *The Aspern Papers*. When Silsbee presented the notebook to the Harvard College Library he penciled a note in the margin of this poem, dating its composition from Marlow, 1817 (Shelley, *Works*, III, 328).

One of the fascinations of Claire's journals is the opportunity they provide to listen to her at first hand, to decide about her character and personality by what she writes, rather than having to rely on wildly differing accounts of others in her own day and indeed ever since. Shelley's steady friendship and Mary's recurrent irritation are true, if partial, mirrors and must not be ignored. But the journals provide another dimension: their voice is a private one, recording what she wished to remember and revealing her own inward image of herself. In taking Claire's life only up to 1830, when she was thirty-two years old and had nearly half a century still to live, I am accepting for practical purposes a break that I hope will be mended by a projected volume of her letters. These vivid letters, of which about 165 survive, either present public faces, carefully composed, and are really a substantial literary output, or they reveal intimately her private personality. In that volume, which will overlap with this one, my husband and I hope to round off the life of this talented, energetic, sometimes maddening, but always fascinating woman.

I was fortunate in arriving at Duke University in 1943, when the Graduate School of English was distinguished by a generation of scholars who were also great teachers. My deepest debt is to the late Newman Ivey White, who encouraged me to undertake the

# Preface

editing of Claire Clairmont's papers and who supported me with his friendship and advice until his untimely death in 1948. His example has continued to sustain me: as scholar, teacher, folklorist, poet and friend of aspiring poets, and as a man of quiet but effective community action. I am proud to have known him. After Professor White's death, I was fortunate in the support of two of his distinguished colleagues: the late Paull Franklin Baum, who graciously consented to see me through to my degree, and William H. Irving, then chairman of the Department of English, who lent warm and friendly encouragement. I should like also to express my gratitude to Professor Allan H. Gilbert, for his interest and instruction, and for his instrumentality in bringing to the Duke University Library the invaluable Mazzoni Collection of Italian books and pamphlets, which has been of great help to me in preparing this edition.

To those individuals who have generously granted me access to their private libraries and collections I am grateful indeed. The heirs of the Clairmont family have been especially gracious and encouraging: first the late Dr. Walter Clairmont, who allowed me unlimited access to his family papers, gave me permission to use them, and talked to me of his memories of his great-aunt Claire and her niece (his aunt) Pauline; and most recently his own niece and nephew, Mary Claire Bally-Clairmont and Christoph W. Clairmont-von Gonzenbach, who have reaffirmed this generous permission, supplied me with information, and cheered me on in my research. The Right Honorable Lord Abinger, heir to the Shelley family papers and now chairman of the Keats–Shelley Memorial Association, permitted me to microfilm his magnificently rich collection and to quote from it. Sir John Murray, K.C.V.O., D.S.O., has allowed me to study and quote from the letters from Claire to Byron. And the Farina-Cini family of San Marcello Pistoiese and Florence, heirs to Lady Mount Cashell, allowed me to consult her library, so valuable to Claire in Pisa, and to copy the Clairmont letters in their collection. I am particularly grateful to Margherita Santi-Farina for her knowledgeable assistance.

My debts to the scholars who have preceded me in the field are evident in my notes and bibliography. In addition, I should like particularly to thank those who have so generously assisted me, not only with their published works but with their conversa-

# Preface

tion and correspondence as well, over many years: Miss Rosalie Glynn Grylls (Lady Mander), Professor Herbert Huscher, Mr. Ivan Roe, Professor Lewis Patton, Miss Dorothy Hewlett, and Professor Frederick L. Jones, to whom all Shelley scholars are so deeply indebted for his pioneer work in the field. I have benefited greatly from the magnanimity, patience, and generosity of these scholars and friends.

I have been assisted in my research by the staffs of the British Museum; the Bodleian Library, Oxford; the Houghton Library of Harvard University; the State Archives of Vienna; the Rare Book Collections of the University of Texas; the Berg Collection of the New York Public Library; the Bibliothèque Nationale, Paris; the Victoria and Albert Museum, South Kensington; the Newberry Library, Chicago; the Library of the University of California at Berkeley; the Bibliothèque Nationale et Universitaire, Strasbourg; the Library of the University of Colorado; and the Beloit College Library. For very particular assistance I should like to thank Dr. Benjamin Powell, Librarian, and Dr. Mattie Russell, Curator of Manuscripts, of the Duke University Library.

For help with translations and other special problems I am grateful to Mr. Ivan Roe, biographer of Shelley; Professor Kiffin Rockwell, of Northern Illinois University; Dr. Roger Deakins, of the College of the City of New York; Professor Mary Olive Thomas, of Georgia State College in Atlanta; Professor *Emerita* Mary Elizabeth Storer, of Beloit College and Paris; and Professor Nicholas Paley, of Beloit College. I should like to thank Otto Gambs, of Ludwigshafen, West Germany, for providing information about the Gambs family, and Mrs. Ann Ray for reading this work while it was in preparation and making many valuable suggestions.

I wish to make grateful acknowledgment to the American Association of University Women for a Pennsylvania–Delaware Fellowship in 1948, and to the Alumnae Association of Mount Holyoke College for a Class of 1905 Fellowship. I wish also to thank the Duke University Library for supplying funds for the microfilming of Lord Abinger's collection, and Beloit College for granting the sabbatical leave that enabled me to complete this research.

Shelley's "To Constantia Singing" is quoted by permission of

# Preface

Ernest Benn Limited, publisher of the Julian edition of *The Works of Percy Bysshe Shelley*, edited by Roger Ingpen and Walter E. Peck. The quotations from *The Letters of Percy Bysshe Shelley*, edited by Frederick L. Jones, are by permission of the Clarendon Press, Oxford. J. A. W. Hunter's *Wallenstein: A Drama* is quoted by permission of Kegan Paul, Trench, Trubner and Co.; Louis MacNeice's translation of *Goethe's Faust*, by permission of Faber and Faber, Ltd., and Oxford University Press. I am also indebted to the University of Oklahoma Press and its director, Mr. Savoie Lottinville, for permission to make numerous citations of passages in *Mary Shelley's Journal*, edited by Frederick L. Jones.

It has been a great pleasure to work with the staff of the Harvard University Press in the final stages of this book. One of the most rewarding aspects of this period has been my association with Mrs. Archibald T. Davison, who, in the process of preparing this manuscript for the press, followed my steps with such thoroughness and raised questions of such insight that the work has been immeasurably improved. Any writer should feel rewarded to have had just one reader as attentive and sensitive as she.

My greatest debt and warmest gratitude are to my husband, David Mackenzie Stocking, Professor of English at Beloit College, without whose constant encouragement and assistance this edition could not have been completed. Much of the annotation of the journals is based on his research; his standards have strengthened it throughout.

M. K. S.

Beloit, Wisconsin
July 1, 1968

# STANZAS FOR MUSIC

## by George Gordon, Lord Byron

(thought to be addressed to Claire)

There be none of Beauty's daughters
   With a magic like thee;
And like music on the waters
   Is thy sweet voice to me:
When, as if its sound were causing
The charméd Ocean's pausing,
The waves lie still and gleaming,
And the lulled winds seem dreaming:

And the midnight Moon is weaving
   Her bright chain o'er the deep;
Whose breast is gently heaving,
   As an infant's asleep:
So the spirit bows before thee,
To listen and adore thee;
With a full but soft emotion,
Like the swell of Summer's ocean.

# TO CONSTANTIA SINGING
## by Percy Bysshe Shelley

(written for Claire)

### I

Thy voice slow rising like a Spirit, lingers
   O'ershadowing it with soft and lulling wings,
The blood and life within thy snowy fingers
   Teach witchcraft to the instrumental strings.
— My brain is wild — my breath comes quick —
   The blood is listening in my frame,
And thronging shadows, fast and thick,
   Fall on my overflowing eyes;
My heart is quivering like a flame;
   As morning dew, that in the sunbeam dies,
   I am dissolved in these consuming exstasies.

### II

I have no life, Constantia, but in thee
   Whilst, like the world-surrounding air, thy song
Flows on, and fills all things with melody:
   Now is thy voice a tempest swift and strong,
On which, as one in trance, upborne,
   Secure o'er rocks and waves I sweep,
Rejoicing, like a cloud of morn.
   Now 'tis the breath of summer's night,
Which, where the starry waters sleep,
   Round western isles, with incense-blossoms bright,
   Lingering, suspends my soul in its voluptuous flight.

# The Journals of Claire Clairmont

## III

A deep and breathless awe, like the swift change
   Of dreams unseen, but felt in youthful slumbers,
Wild, sweet, yet uncommunicably strange
   Thou breathest now in fast ascending numbers.
The cope of Heaven seems rent and cloven
   By the enchantment of thy strain,
And o'er my shoulders wings are woven
   To follow its sublime career
Beyond the mighty moons that wane
    Upon the verge of Nature's utmost sphere
    Till the world's shadowy walls are past and disappear

## IV

Cease cease — for such wild lessons madmen learn
   Long thus to sink — thus to be lost and die,
Perhaps is death indeed — Constantia turn!
   Yes! in thine eyes a power like light doth lie,
Even tho' the sounds, its voice that were
   Between thy lips, are laid to sleep —
Within thy breath, and on thy hair
Like odour, it is lingering yet —
   And from thy touch like fire doth leap.
   Even while I write, my burning cheeks are wet.
   Alas, that the torn heart can bleed, but not forget.

# Contents

# Illustrations

# Illustrations

Shelley's handwriting

*The last page of the First Journal (1814) showing the burned edge as repaired; reproduced from Ashley MS. 394 by courtesy of the British Museum*

Two pages from the Third Journal

*Entries for May 5 and 6, 1820; reproduced from Ashley MS. 2819(2) by courtesy of the British Museum*

# INTRODUCTION

# INTRODUCTION

*History of the journals.* After Claire's death in 1879, her executor, Giovanni Cosimo Cini, resigned to allow Claire's niece, Pauline, to become executrix. She sold her aunt's journals, along with other valuable papers, to Henry Roderick Newman, who was acting as agent for H. Buxton Forman, editor of Shelley and Keats and one of the original members of the Shelley Society. An inventory of these papers (now, with correspondence about the sale, in the Henry W. and Albert A. Berg Collection of the New York Public Library) lists four notebooks, 1818–1820. This must be an error, for it appears that Forman acquired five out of six journals (the sixth being the now lost Russian journal). Forman made them available to Edward Dowden, who drew on them heavily in his biography of Shelley. The journals then passed into the library of the English collector and bibliographer (and, alas, forger) Thomas J. Wise, who allowed Roger Ingpen to make transcripts of them. Ingpen used these copies in preparing the Julian edition of Shelley's works and presented them to Miss Rosalie Glynn Grylls (Lady Mander), who used them in writing her *Claire Clairmont*. Wise further permitted Newman Ivey White, while working on his definitive *Shelley*, to make photostats of the complete text, and these photostats are now in the Duke University Library. In 1937 Claire's journals went with the rest of Wise's great Ashley Library to the British Museum, which is now preparing a new catalogue of the collection. I have based my text on the original manuscripts, with some assistance from the photostats, enlargements, and infrared prints at Duke.

3

# The Journals of Claire Clairmont

Two fragments of the journal which were with the main body of the manuscript while it was in Forman's hands are now in the Carl H. Pforzheimer Library, New York City. One consists of a variant version of the first part of the 1814 journal: sixteen pages of revision and expansion of the entries for August 14 through 22. Dowden prints a long extract from this variant in his *Life of Percy Bysshe Shelley*.[1] It appears that Claire at one time planned to enlarge her journal for publication just as Shelley and Mary had reworked theirs for the *History of a Six Weeks' Tour*. This revised version, edited by Sir Gavin de Beer, will appear in *Shelley and His Circle*, volume III, edited by Kenneth Neill Cameron. The second fragment of Claire's journal in the Pforzheimer Library is the basic journal for 1818: January 17 and part of 18, and April 23 to June. Claire's second journal in the British Museum, Ashley 2819 (1), fits precisely between these two sections. There is roughly the same amount of text in the Pforzheimer and Ashley portions. My edition of the Pforzheimer section will appear in *Shelley and His Circle*, volume V, edited by Donald H. Reiman.

The sixth of Claire's journals, December 21, 1826, through February 2, 1827, once in the possession of Claire's great-niece Frau Alma Crüwell-Clairmont in Vienna, was sent with some other Clairmont treasures into the country to avoid the bombing in the Second World War and has not been recovered. Fortunately, Professor Herbert Huscher, in Vienna in the summer of 1943, had been permitted to make a transcript of this notebook ("only a very few unessential passages were omitted"), which he described and published in "Claire Clairmont's Lost Russian Journal and Some Further Glimpses of Her Later Life."[2] The text I am reproducing here, with Professor Huscher's kind permission, is that of his earlier publication, "Charles und Claire Clairmont,"[3] which according to Professor Huscher is slightly more complete and closer to the original in spelling and punctuation.

The reader may well wonder why documents of such great interest have gone so long unpublished. The explanation is that in the thirties Roger Ingpen, following the success of the Julian edition of Shelley's works, had definite plans for publishing an edition

---

[1] I, 452–453n.
[2] In *KSMB* 6:35–47 (1955).
[3] In *Englische Studien* (Leipzig), 76:55–117 (1944).

# Introduction

of Claire's journal. Among the Ingpen papers recently acquired by the Library of the University of California at Berkeley is a letter, dated February 13, 1934, to Ingpen from Desmond Flower of Cassell & Company, London, expressing a keen interest in publishing the edition. There is fortunately also in the collection a rough draft of Ingpen's reply, describing his proposed edition, which was to have had a biographical introduction, and stating "each diary will also have a introductory note which will serve to fill in any gaps." There was to have been, in addition, a conclusion, telling what was known of Claire's subsequent life. "Without destroying the value of the diaries," Ingpen explained, "it will be desirable to abridge them where necessary." Ingpen's death in 1936 prevented his proceeding with these plans, and it was in 1943 that, encouraged by Newman Ivey White, I undertook to prepare these journals for publication.

*The text.* Punctuation, spelling, abbreviations, and paragraphing are reproduced as exactly as the limitations of type will allow in an effort to eliminate ponderous textual notes as well as the intrusive *sic.* I trust the reader will not be disturbed by Claire's frequent errors — the result of haste, so usual in diaries — or by her occasional misspellings and her sublime indifference to whether an accent should be grave or acute. I have tried to keep my editorial comment at a minimum; italics within square brackets indicate editorial note and comment. Otherwise, square brackets enclose a reconstruction of missing letters (particularly in the first journal where it was damaged by fire) or, rarely, identification of a "he" or "she." In the Russian journal especially, square brackets may enclose a name indicated only by an initial. Insertions above the line are enclosed in arrows: ↑ ↓. Crossed-out passages which I have been able to read are enclosed in wide-angle brackets: ⟨ ⟩; these include Claire's minor stylistic revisions and her deletions of slips of the pen. Insignificant pen scratches, not recognizable as letters, are silently omitted. Ultraviolet and infrared photography and extreme enlargement of difficult sections have been of great help in deciphering passages which Claire tried to obliterate, and wide-angle brackets also enclose such passages. These and other unusual textual problems are dealt with in footnotes. Double-angle brackets (⟨⟨ ⟩⟩) enclose those sections where Claire went back to delete passages that already included crossed-out words. Her raised letters with a dash under them, as the <u>th</u> of a date, are lowered and the dash indicated by a period. Her quotations of poetry have been centered on the page. I have not thought it reasonable to transcribe her running heads of month, year, or both, at the top center of each page. I have made no effort to regularize Claire's spelling of Russian names; the reader may make his way through the various forms of these names by means of the index. Throughout the journals, Edward Dowden underlined in soft pencil the main references to Shelley, suggested a few identifications, and attempted to transcribe some of the crossed-out passages. I have taken little notice of these pencilings in my text unless they appear to have some special significance.

*The notes and introductions.* Even before discovering Roger Ingpen's plans for his edition I had prepared my introductory material to provide a narrative continuity before and between the journals, and in these connecting passages I have tried to keep in mind the reader who may have only a general knowledge of Byron and Shelley biography, while at the same time, by concentrating on new materials and matters of special relevance to the journals, I have tried to avoid too much recapitulation of the details familiar to readers of White's *Shelley* and Miss Grylls's *Claire Clairmont*.

Many of the notes to the text identify Claire's reading and relate it wherever possible to that of the Shelleys. I have also prepared an alphabetical list of her reading to dramatize its range and encourage comparison with Shelley's. Dates cited are not always those of first editions; I have tried to cite the edition that Claire most probably used, including the publisher only when I thought it of particular interest (as Ollier or Joseph Johnson). The reader should bear in mind that Claire's quotations are often inaccurate, as though quoted in haste and from memory, and I have not systematically called attention to the discrepancies. I have suggested translations throughout, hoping that those who find them a convenience may outnumber those for whom they may seem a condescension.

A word is perhaps in order about the main source of information running parallel to Claire's journals: the journal Mary and Shelley began to keep on July 28, 1814, the day of their departure from England. (The first entry we have in Claire's is August 14 of that year.) For eight years, with some breaks on both sides, these

# Introduction

journals complement each other, and ideally they should be read together. Mary Shelley's journal, including the entries in 1814 by Shelley, was first printed in 1882 for private circulation by Sir Percy Florence and Lady Jane Shelley as *Shelley and Mary*. The copy I have used was Dowden's (British Museum Ashley MS. 4088), heavily annotated with material from Claire Clairmont's papers which were at that time in Forman's possession. The manuscripts of the journal of Shelley and Mary have only recently been easily accessible to scholars, and the edition by Frederick L. Jones, *Mary Shelley's Journal*, was of necessity based on the earlier printed version. In 1952 Lord Abinger graciously allowed me to microfilm his Shelley collection, including the journals, and my references are to these microfilms, deposited in the Duke University Library and in the Bodleian Library, Oxford. I have relied heavily on the work of my husband and colleague, David Mackenzie Stocking, who has made a complete record of the considerable number of omissions and errors in the published version. My procedure in preparing the notes has been, whenever the entry in Shelley's and Mary's journal is essentially the same in both published and manuscript versions, to quote from the manuscript, but for the reader's convenience to note the appropriate page in the Jones edition. When, however, the manuscript has yielded any interesting new information, such as previously overlooked entries, I have incorporated this new material in my notes and cited the Abinger manuscript.

## *Description of the Journals* [4]

*First journal*: August 14 to November 9, 1814. British Museum Ashley MS. 394. 198 pages (99 leaves), in a red leather book with a broken clasp; 5½ inches wide by 4¼ inches tall. Wove paper, with a monogram watermark WT. The edges of the pages by the clasp have been damaged by fire; letters thus lost are reconstructed in square brackets in the text. The scorched edges are

[4] Earlier descriptions of these notebooks appear in Thomas J. Wise, *A Shelley Library*, pp. 98–100; R. Glynn Grylls, *Claire Clairmont*, pp. 249–253; and Lorraine Robertson, "The Journal and Notebooks of Claire Clairmont: Unpublished Passages," *KSMB* 4:45 (1952).

more clearly legible in the Duke University photostats than in the original in the British Museum, where the damaged areas have been skillfully repaired by filling in the burned-out areas with paper and securing the whole from further disintegration by an application of fine net mesh. The journal apparently first belonged to Shelley, as five pages inside what was originally the front cover are filled with his notes, in a delicate small hand. Claire appears to have turned the book over and begun using it from the back. Inside this cover are a pencil sketch of a head and another of foliage, quite certainly by Shelley. Claire's journal opens abruptly, as though continued from another volume. At least nine leaves have been torn out at various points, as indicated in the text; some passages have been scribbled over in a darker ink; some have been obliterated by having other letters written over them.

*Second journal*: January 18 to April 22, 1818. British Museum Ashley MS. 2819 (1). 32 pages (16 leaves, in two gathers of four sheets each), bound only in a folded sheet of laid paper; 4¾ inches wide by 7½ inches tall. Laid paper, watermarked with a monogram W, a liberty cap, a numeral 5, and an elaborate shield. Some passages have been scribbled over. The remaining pages of this journal are those in the Carl H. Pforzheimer Library (mentioned on page 4 above).

*Third journal*: March 7 to July 2, 1819; January 2 to August 1, 1820. British Museum Ashley MS. 2819 (2). 174 pages (87 leaves), in pink mottled paper wrapper, 4½ inches wide by 5½ inches tall. Poor quality wove paper without watermark. A leaf of laid paper has been inserted before the first leaf and after the last. Nine leaves have been torn out, as indicated in the text. Several passages have been scribbled over. Under the end papers the insides of the covers can be seen to have prints of "Pantheon di Agrippa" (front cover) and "Interno del Pantheon" (back cover).

*Fourth journal*: August 5, 1820, to April 13, 1822; September 19 and 20, 1822. British Museum Ashley MS. 2819 (3). 258 pages (129 leaves), in a soiled white vellum-covered book, 5 inches wide by 7 inches tall. Good laid paper, with a watermark V and a shield. A leaf of laid paper has been inserted before the first leaf and after the last. A recipe is fastened to the last page with four wafers. Some attempts have been made to obliterate passages by scribbling.

# Introduction

*Fifth journal*: May 12 (24), 1825, to January 2 (13) [*sic* for 14], 1826. British Museum Ashley MS. 2819 (4). 142 pages (71 leaves), plus the inner surfaces of the end papers (blank in front, written on in back), in a brown leather-bound book with gold ornamental border, 6¼ inches wide by 7¾ inches tall. Brown and blue marbled end papers, lined with white where they face the first and last leaves, with the bookplate of T. J. Wise covering a deeply-scratched area inside the front cover. Laid paper; the first leaf, tipped in, with a monogram watermark TSC below a heraldic eagle; other pages with watermark of a checkerboard shield surrounded by an elaborate scroll; still others with the Cyrillic monogram ABF 1822.

*Sixth journal*: December 21, 1826, to February 2, 1827 (with omissions). This journal, once in the possession of Claire's great-niece Frau Alma Crüwell-Clairmont, in Vienna, was lost during the Second World War; our text is from a transcript (see page 4 above).

*Two leaflets of miscellanea*: 1828 to 1830. British Museum Ashley MS. 2820 (1) and (2). (1) 48 pages (24 leaves), in a worn orange paper wrapper, stitched in green thread, 5½ inches wide by 9 inches tall. Wove paper, with no watermark. The orange wrapper is watermarked in Cyrillic characters U F A P 1820. Eleven pages have been written from one end, beginning "I am not a Mrs. Killinger"; the leaflet has been inverted and three pages written from the other end, beginning "Natalie." Thirty-four pages are left blank in the middle. See reproduction in L. Robertson, facing p. 35. (2) Originally 48 pages (24 leaves), of which 20 pages (10 leaves) remain. Leaflet headed "Anecdotes, Remembrances, &c &c," in purple paper wrapper, stitched in green thread, 5¼ inches wide by 9 inches tall. Wove paper, with no watermark. Fourteen leaves have been cut from the center of this leaflet; one to nine letters of Claire's writing remain on the cut margin of six pages. The cuts were made sometime after the journals came into Forman's possession, for some of Dowden's pencil marks remain on the edges of the vanished pages. For a discussion of these pencilings, which occur throughout the journals, see the section on the text, above.

# FIRST
# JOURNAL
## August 14, 1814, to November 9, 1814

# [1798-1814]

"Clara Maria Constantia Jane Clairmont" was the name she signed to her will in 1876.[1] No record of her birth or baptism has yet appeared, but she believed that she was born on April 27, 1798, of Swiss ancestry;[2] she was very probably illegitimate. Crabb Robinson recorded a bit of gossip about her mother: "It was said she was never married, but was kept and aban-

[1] Manuscripts in the possession of the Clairmont family, referred to hereafter as Clairmont MSS. See also Herbert Huscher, "Claire Clairmont's Lost Russian Journal and Some Further Glimpses of Her Later Life," *KSMB* 6:46–47 (1955). She was Jane or Mary Jane until late 1814, when she began to be called Clara, then Clary, Clare, and finally Claire. In old age she added the Constantia to acknowledge Shelley's poetic tribute. For consistency's sake I shall use the form Claire throughout.

[2] "Think of me in Switzerland: the land of my ancestors," Claire wrote to Byron. "Like my native mountain [*sic*] I am tranquil and ⟨like⟩ as they are tranquil so is my affection" (Grylls, *Claire Clairmont*, p. 61, printed from the manuscript in Sir John Murray's collection of Byron material. The original copies of many of Claire's letters to Byron are in this collection, referred to hereafter as Murray MSS.). See also journal entries for August 19 (with Note 12) and 29, 1814, below. When, in 1816, Shelley was defying the sentimental conventions by inscribing himself as atheist and his destination as "L'Enfer" in the visitors' book of the Hotel de Londres at Chamonix, Claire entered Clifton as her birthplace (her whole entry was later heavily crossed out, perhaps by Byron). This, the only indication of her birthplace, may have been Clifton parish in Bristol, since her brother was born in Bristol in the parish of St. Nicholas, but no birth record seems to have survived. Her second entry in the visitors' book, in which she describes herself as Irish, en route to Constantinople, certainly sounds facetious. See De Beer, "An 'Atheist' in the Alps," *KSMB* 9:10–11, and plate facing 8 (1958).

13

doned by her keeper, or, rather, left destitute at his death. She was relieved by a charitable subscription, and taken out of prison; on which she came up to town with her young children, met with Godwin at Somers Town and became certainly towards him a meritorious wife, though towards others I doubt both her sincerity and her integrity."[3] In letters to Mary Shelley in 1834 and 1835 Claire warmly defended the advantages of illegitimacy,[4] though not directly relating the argument to herself. On June 9, 1871, Claire's niece Pauline, daughter of Claire's respectably married brother Charles, noted in her journal: "One morning she [Claire] wanted to make out that my Father and Mother were never married & that we were illegitimate, counting upon my ignorance or generosity in not returning the compliment concerning *her* Mother."[5]

Crabb Robinson's story would suggest a reason for "Mrs. Clairmont's" double marriage to Godwin on December 21, 1801, first at Shoreditch Church under the name of Mary Clairmont and then an hour later at Whitechapel under the name of Mary Vial: she might have been concerned lest a marriage under an assumed name (Clairmont) might not prove binding, leaving her again destitute. A complication to the mystery appears in 1802, when a birth certificate record for her son Charles Gaulis Clairmont, on the occasion of his application for admission to Christ's Hospital, affirmed that he had been born in Bristol on June 4, 1795, to Mary Jane, daughter of Andrew Peter Devereux.[6] Today, despite the assiduous researches of Professor Herbert Huscher, the paternity of Mrs. Clairmont's first two children remains obscure. Charles and several of his descendants have borne Gaulis as a second name, in memory of Charles Abram Marc Gaulis, a Swiss merchant, born December 22, 1765, died August 23, 1796 (the year after Charles's birth, two years before Claire's). Claire apparently knew of a connection with the Gaulis family, for she took the name of Charles Gaulis' sister — Trefusis — in her

---

[3] *Henry Crabb Robinson,* I, 235.

[4] Unpublished manuscript in the collection of Lord Abinger, referred to hereafter as Abinger MSS.

[5] Clairmont MSS.

[6] Huscher, "Charles Gaulis Clairmont," *KSMB* 8:11 (1957). This article is in part superseded by the one referred to in the next footnote.

# Introduction

early notes to Byron.[7] But even if Charles Gaulis were to have been the father of his namesake — which cannot be shown — he cannot possibly have been the father of Claire. Charles Gaulis Clairmont's birth certificate record names a "Charles Clairmont" as father. Nothing further is known of him, except that Mary Jane Vial (or Devereux) had assumed his name and given it to her two children.

When Claire was three years old, and her six-year-old brother was away, probably at school, she lived with her mother in Somers Town, next door to the philosopher William Godwin. On May 5, 1801, he announced in his diary, "Meet Mrs. Clairmont."[8] Tradition says she took the initiative, but by September Godwin was in warm pursuit and reminded his friend Charles Lamb of nothing so much as Malvolio: "The Professor (Godwin) is COURTING. The Lady is a Widow[9] with green spectacles and one child, and the Professor is grown quite juvenile."[10] After two frustrating rejections by his first choices for the post, Godwin finally succeeded in finding a stepmother for his daughter, four-year-old Mary Wollstonecraft Godwin, and his stepdaughter, seven-year-old Fanny Imlay, the illegitimate daughter of Mary Wollstonecraft and Gilbert Imlay. To the four children now gathered into one family, apparently from four different fathers, a fifth child was added on March 28, 1803, when a son, William, was born.

Godwin's diary reveals the whirlwind of activity that engaged the family. In addition to caring for the children, Mrs. Godwin was hostess to a steady stream of remarkable visitors (among others

[7] Huscher, "The Clairmont Enigma," *KSMB* 11:13–20 (1960).

[8] Godwin diaries, Abinger MSS. For the story of Mrs. Clairmont's overture to her neighbor, see Paul, *Godwin*, II, 58. There is a useful map of Somers Town in *Shelley and His Circle*, I, 211.

[9] "A very disgusting woman" (Lamb's footnote in his letter).

[10] Lamb, *Letters*, I, 273. Mrs. Godwin was never more wrong than when she said that she considered Mary Shelley her greatest enemy. The top candidate for that position should have been Charles Lamb. His letters are filled with disgust at her gossiping and inquisitiveness, her staying on too late at his house, her general disagreeableness. "I will be buried with this inscription over me: — 'Here lies C. L., the Woman-hater' — I mean that hated ONE WOMAN: for the rest, God bless them" (*ibid.*, II, 70). "That damn'd infernal bitch Mrs. Godwin" found a certain painful immortality as Priscilla Pry in the "Lepus" papers. See for instance "Tom Pry's Wife," *New Times*, February 28, 1825, reprinted in *The Avon Booklet* (London, 1905), vol. III.

the playwright Thomas Holcroft and his daughter Fanny, the Irish patriot, John Philpot Curran and his daughter Amelia, Coleridge, Hazlitt, the Lambs, and later Wordsworth) who made great demands on her intelligence and good humor. Moreover, she was committed for life to a household where the finances were always to be more or less desperate.

Whatever her history, the second Mrs. Godwin was not entirely the common sort of woman that she has been made out to be. Godwin worried off and on that he was not able to give her the kind of life to which women of her birth were accustomed — the pleasure jaunts for sea bathing and the excursions to watering places.[11] Aaron Burr reported her a "sensible, amiable woman," [12] and Harriet Shelley's first impression was decidedly favorable: "The many trials that Mrs. Godwin has had to encounter makes me very much inclined to believe her a woman of great fortitude and unyielding temper of mind. There is a very great sweetness marked in her countenance. In many instances she has shown herself a woman of very great magnanimity and independence of character." [13] (One wishes Harriet had been more explicit.) Alas, her favorable impression was not to be a lasting one, since Shelley finally had to tell Godwin that Harriet called infrequently because she could not stand the company of "his darling wife." [14]

A clear picture of the period emerges from Godwin's regular and detailed diary. Though the adults' life was hectic, for the children the days must have been pleasant indeed. There were great family excursions. Sometimes the Godwins trooped, babies and all, out to dinner. A party was organized for the children's benefit to see the illuminations when peace was proclaimed in 1802. Once there was a July jaunt to Greenwich. And there was always the theater. From the age of five, Jane (she was never called Claire by her mother or by Godwin) was included in evening parties to the plays. The scheme of going on the stage which she professed

[11] Paul, *Godwin*, II, 129–130.

[12] Burr, *Correspondence*, p. 264.

[13] Harriet Shelley to Catherine Nugent (October 1812), in Shelley, *Letters*, I, 327n.

[14] Harriet Shelley to Catherine Nugent (June 22, 1813), in Shelley, *Letters*, I, 372n.

when she was trying to get to know Byron may well have been founded on a real childhood dream.[15]

In 1807 the Godwins left the house in Somers Town for an address in the very heart of the city—41 Skinner Street, a new street running directly up Snow Hill to the end of the Old Bailey. The move constituted a great improvement as far as Mrs. Godwin was concerned. In 1805 she had organized under her own name, M. J. Godwin, a "juvenile library," actually a publishing house— one of the earliest and most enterprising—to produce children's books and texts for schools. She worked hard, soliciting manuscripts, endlessly translating, and trying out the finished products on her own willing brood. In the new house the family had living quarters upstairs, and the ground floor, with its counter and its display windows low enough for children to put their noses to the panes and peer in, served as a shop. Over the entrance was a stone carving of Aesop reading his fables to a group of children.

Although Skinner Street was new, the neighborhood was inauspicious, and the very house into which they had moved was already doomed to decay. Barely one hundred yards from the door public executions were celebrated at the Old Bailey, and in the very year that the Godwins moved there the hanging of Haggerty and Halloway for the murder of a lavender merchant drew a crowd in which twenty-eight people were suffocated or trampled to death and sixty injured. It was a street of milliners, furriers, coffee dealers, oil shops, floor-cloth manufacturers, and oyster and orange warehouses—a place, eventually, to escape from if at all possible.[16] But still the interesting visitors came, despite Lamb's statement that Godwin's wife frightened off many of his cronies, and at least one of the visitors seems to have come primarily for her company. On December 1, 1808, Aaron Burr recorded in his diary: "A 8 sor. pour rendezvous de Madame G. La vû seule. Un develupment tres franc. Elle a un excellent esprit. Ses projects sur U.S. Promis de

[15] Thomas Medwin believed that had Claire satisfied her ambition she would have been a success as an actress (Medwin, *Shelley*, p. 170).

[16] Brown, "Notes on 41 Skinner Street," *MLN* 54:326–332 (May 1939). See also *Johnstone's London Commercial Guide* (1817). The construction of Holborn Viaduct in 1869 and the bombing of that section of the city in World War II have nearly obliterated the streets of the Snow Hill area. Of the buildings, only St. Sepulchre's remains.

*don. un rendez. chez moi a mon retour a* Weybridge." [17] He met her often, and the children were always glad to see "Gamp."

From August 3 to November 13 in 1808, ten-year-old Claire was at Margate, presumably in boarding school, but she had returned before Burr arrived and was at home throughout his long visit (he stayed until April 25) and through the following year as well. About once a month Godwin's diary records an outing in which she was included: a visit to the theater or to "the Pavillion," a dinner party here or there. All the Godwins were often with the Lambs, exchanging meals and sometimes going with Mary Lamb to the theater. Looking back on her childhood in Skinner Street, Claire wrote nostalgically: "Skinner Street was dull to him [Shelley], but to all others it was a lively and cheerful life that had been led there till he entered it. All the family worked hard, learning and studying: we all took the liveliest interest in the great questions of the day—common topics, gossiping, scandal, found no entrance in our circle for we had been brought up by Mr. Godwin to think it was the greatest misfortune to be fond of the world, or worldly pleasures or of luxury or money; and that there was no greater happiness than to think well of those around us, to love them, and to delight in being useful or pleasing to them." [18]

The accuracy of this picture is illustrated in Aaron Burr's diary, for by the time he paid a return visit to London in October, 1811, the children were taking an active part in entertaining the guests—singing, dancing, conducting sight-seeing tours, and serving tea. Almost immediately after Burr's arrival Charles Clairmont set sail from Miller's Wharf, bound for Scotland, where he was to be indentured in the printing office of Godwin's Edinburgh publisher, Archibald Constable. Since Mary was then boarding at Miss Petman's at Ramsgate the burden of the entertaining fell upon Claire and Fanny, and even on little William, who was just eight. Burr was seeing a great deal of Amelia Curran that winter, and both were almost daily visitors at the Godwin establishment. Sometimes they accompanied Godwin, Fanny, and Claire to hear Coleridge's

[17] Burr, *Journal*, I, 24. "At 8 left for a meeting with Madame G. Saw her alone. A very frank development. She has an excellent mind. Her projects on the U.S. Promised to meet me at my place on my return to Weybridge."

[18] In a note to Trelawny on Shelley's letter of December 30, 1816, quoted in Grylls, *Claire Clairmont*, p. 274.

# Introduction

lectures on Shakespeare and Milton, which were given at the London Philosophical Society every Monday and Thursday from November 18 to January 27.[19] The two little girls attended these lectures religiously, and when Mary returned from Ramsgate in December (looking lovely, but not strong, Burr thought), she joined them regularly. Even eight-year-old Willy went once in a while to hear his Papa's friend speak, and by February he was giving weekly lectures à la Coleridge, reading from the little pulpit specially built for him a lecture written by one of the girls. Burr was much amused at the one he heard on "The Influence of Governments on the Character of the People."[20]

Burr remained the particular friend of the girls, "les goddesses," even when he lost sleep after Claire's poisonously strong tea, and he enjoyed walking out with them to such shrines as the bust of Milton at the Church of St. Giles in Cripplegate, where the poet was buried.[21]

Throughout the spring and summer of 1812 Claire went out a great deal with her mother and Godwin to large teas and dinner parties. Then in the autumn she left London and its gay life for a boarding school kept by a French woman at Walham Green, where she was to stay off and on for about two years, supplementing the excellent education which Godwin and her mother had provided at home.

One Saturday night in October, 1812, Claire came home from Walham Green for a weekend in London.[22] On Monday, before she went back, Godwin treated her and Fanny by taking them along with him to dine with his delightful new friends, the Shelleys. The dinner party was a great success and was repeated on the occasion of her next visit home, November 7. Again as soon as the party was over she had to go back to school, this time just as Mary was coming down from Scotland, bringing along her friend

[19] For the prospectus of this series of lectures, see Gillman, *Coleridge*, I, 262. They were reported regularly in the *Courier*.

[20] Burr, *Journal*, II, 326. This subject was to be a favorite of Claire's throughout her life.

[21] *Ibid.*, II, 348, 376.

[22] The following account is based on the Godwin diaries, Abinger MSS. I have intentionally avoided using Mrs. Godwin's biased and inaccurate accounts with Claire's equally misleading emendations which are partially printed in Dowden, *Shelley*, II, appendix B, and in Grylls, *Claire Clairmont*, appendix B.

Christy Baxter, who was to stay with the Godwins until the middle of the next summer. Claire must have regretted missing the teas and dinner parties and trips to the theater, but since she was vivacious and more than usually proficient at music and languages, boarding school was probably not an ordeal for her.

At the end of May, Claire came home for the summer and had two whole holiday months with Mary and Christy. Shelley and Harriet had been in town since the first week in April, and early in the summer the Godwins had his poem *Queen Mab* fresh from the printers, with its glowing dedication to his wife at one end and the daringly radical notes at the other. They probably saw little of Harriet, for her baby Ianthe was born at the end of June, but Shelley himself was often at the shop in Skinner Street, and all the girls had an excellent opportunity to get to know him.

The youngsters of the Godwin household apparently took turns at boarding school, for at Christmas time in 1813 Claire left Walham Green for good, with her schoolgirl French in fair condition, and William, now ten, went away for the spring term. Then on May 23 Fanny went off for a visit to Pentredevy in Wales; so again for the summer months Mary and Claire were in London and seeing a great deal of Shelley. His wife was in Bath, and from June 18 to July 7 he took most of his meals in Skinner Street and walked out, sometimes with Godwin, sometimes with Marshal, Godwin's faithful literary assistant, to make arrangements with the moneylenders Nash and Ballachey for a loan to Godwin. But sometimes Shelley walked to Mary's retreat, by her mother's grave in the churchyard of St. Pancras, where she escaped for a little while from the squalid neighborhood in the city and the demands of her overworked and unsympathetic stepmother.

By July 8 Godwin had become seriously disturbed at the intimacy which had grown between Mary and Shelley, and he had a long talk with his daughter. On July 22 he felt the need of a serious talk with Claire, but all was to no avail, for at five in the morning of July 28 he discovered that both girls had fled with Shelley.

The elopement was a terrible blow to Mrs. Godwin. She followed the trio as far as Calais and begged her daughter to return, but if Claire had been as miserable and neglected on the voyage as she later gave herself out to have been, she must have recovered her high spirits very promptly, for after some deliberation and a council with Shelley she forsook her mother and went gaily off to Paris with Mary and Shelley.[23]

When Claire Clairmont left England in 1814, she had not the slightest idea of returning. Her farewell to her mother in Calais was apparently to be considered final. "As we left Dover & England's white cliffs were retiring I said to myself I shall never see these more," she wrote in her new journal (August 27, 1814). The world that opened for Claire on that trip was the world of romance made real. Her adventures had heretofore been all in her reading, and now the truth and beauty of the book world seemed everywhere to be confirmed or surpassed. Mary's account, written twelve years later, recaptures exactly the tone of the journals which she and Shelley and Claire began to keep on that first wonderful trip: "In the summer of 1814, every inconvenience was hailed as a new chapter in the romance of our travels; the worst annoyance of all, the Custom-house, was amusing as a novelty; we saw with extasy the strange costume of the French women, read with delight our own descriptions in the passport, looked with curiosity on every *plât*, fancying that the fried-leaves of artichokes were frogs; we saw shepherds in opera-hats, and post-boys in jack-boots; and (*pour comble de merveille*) heard little boys and girls talk French: it was acting a novel, being an incarnate romance." [24]

Their route can be traced in the journal which Mary and Shelley kept, and also in the book based on this journal, *History of a Six Weeks' Tour*.[25] After Calais they spent the hot night of July 30 in Boulogne, the next in Abbeville, and, after one night on the road, they arrived in Paris on August 2. That night Mary

[23] Mrs. Godwin never admitted to Lady Mount Cashell, to whom she had written detailed accounts of Mary's perversity and Claire's good character, that her daughter had undertaken such rash action of her own free will. See Dowden, *Shelley*, II, 545–547.

[24] "The English in Italy," *Westminster Review*, 6:326 (October 1826). This delightfully written review by Mary Shelley has not, to my knowledge, been reprinted in full before — see Appendix A below for the complete article.

[25] *Mary Shelley's Journal*, ed. F. L. Jones, and *History of Six Weeks' Tour through a Part of France, Switzerland, Germany, and Holland*. It is interesting to read in connection with the various accounts of the Shelley party J. R. Hale's *The Italian Journals of Samuel Rogers*. Rogers left England on August 20, 1814, and returned on May 6, 1815. Hale's introduction provides an excellent survey of the conditions of travel for the English abroad in the years just after the defeat of Napoleon.

showed Shelley the contents of the box she had brought: her own writings, letters from her father and her friends, and Shelley's letters to her. Shelley noted in their journal: "She shewed me one letter from Harriet which recommended her to write ⟨such⟩ that to me which should calm me, & enable me to subdue my love for her." [26] After several frustrating days, during which Shelley sold his watch and chain, they obtained the small sum of sixty pounds, bought an ass in the last stages of collapse, and set out on August 8, intending to walk to Uri.

The crossing of France in the wake of the allied armies confirmed what Claire had read, that "God made the country and man made the town," for the *paysage* was exciting and romantic, whereas the towns were filthy and inhospitable. To the reader of Gothic romance, the ruins which dotted the countryside, even if sometimes of recent vintage, the result of the marauding armies, were "romantic." Shelley's journal is full of horror at the devastation of war, but Claire's is uniformly enthusiastic. Mary has described Claire's reaction to the pretty town of Charenton, which they reached on August 8: "C* * * exclaimed, 'Oh! this is beautiful enough; let us live here.' This was her exclamation on every new scene, and as each surpassed the one before, she cried, 'I am glad we did not stay at Charenton, but let us live here.'" [27] After Charenton they proceeded on August 9 through Gros Brie and Brie to Guignes, where they heard that Napoleon and some of his generals had slept in the same inn, and on the next day they pushed on to Provins. On August 11 they passed through Nogent and St. Aubin, completely devastated by the Cossacks, and spent a wretched night at Trois Maisons. The next morning Mary recorded: "Jane was not able to sleep all night for the rats who as she said put their cold paws upon her face — she however rested on our bed which her four footed enemies dared not invade perhaps having overheard the threat that Shelley terrified the man with who said he would sleep with Jane." [28] At this point Shelley sprained his ankle, and they limped on through Echemine and Pavillon, depressed by the destruction and dirt, to Troyes. On August 13 they sold the mule (which had long since replaced the decrepit ass) and after a second night in Troyes proceeded by voiture to Bar-sur-Aube.

[26] Abinger MSS.
[27] *Six Weeks' Tour*, pp. 14–15.
[28] Abinger MSS.

# France 1814

Claire's journal begins in the middle of an entry for August 14; perhaps it is the continuation of a notebook since lost.

[*inside front cover*]

[*pencil sketch of a face*]

Will you try what Fortune will [do] for you?

⟨Mary Jane Clairmont⟩

August 15th 1814

Ag. 15th—20th [*in pencil and in a different hand*]

B

Barbitos

6/— [*this notation of six shillings is on its side, reading toward the top of the page, in the original*]

August.

We took a Walk in the Evening & climbed the highest of the Hills [1] —As we descended [it] a most violent storm of Rain came on &

[1] Shelley, who recorded this day in the journal, wrote: "We climbed the highest of these hills, & returned late to our Inn, wet thro with a heavy shower that had succeeded sunset. The laden clouds almost made the darkness as deep as that of midnight, but to the West, an unusual brilliant & fiery redness occupied a rent in the vapours, & added to the interest of our little expedition. The cottage lights were reflected in the tranquil river, & the dark hills behind, dimly seen, resembled vast & frowning mountains. We slept here" (Abinger MSS.). For the history of this section of the MS. see *Mary Shelley's Journal*, p. 9n. Here and elsewhere quotations from the journal of Shelley and Mary are drawn from the Duke University microfilm of the original MS. in Lord Abinger's collection. For the convenience of the reader I have provided references to the corresponding passages in *Mary Shelley's Journal*.

23

we were wet through — It was a [*a word thoroughly crossed out*]
Evening — the sky was entirely black & rain poured in torrents —
One ray of red light alone marked where the Su[n] had set — The
lights of the distant Cott[ages] were reflected in a clear & winding
s[tream] which flowed through the Valley in whic[h] this town [2]
is situated — Return to our Inn & go to Bed —

[M]onday 15th.[3] Rise ⟨earli⟩ at four — A [m]ost beautiful misty
morning & the wind [b]leak & cold — Take up a peasant to Iuzen-
[n]ecourt — where we breakfasted — Continue [our] way to Chaumont — dine there — We here saw some nuns of the order of Les
Sœurs de Charité. ⟨We passed some dull unteres[ting] Villages
& arrived at Langres about [se]ven⟩ — The approach to this town
is exquisitely beautiful — We were obliged to wind down a beautiful mountain & enter by the other side of the town as the direct
road was so extremely steep that the horse could [not] ascend it —
Rest here two hours & then set off   Reach Langres about eight —
Sup at the ta[ble] d'hôte with a numerous & vulgar set who com[e]
to the fair here — This town is extremely old [as] indeed most of
the french towns are — It stan[ds] on a hill by the side of the road
— on your [right] as you ascend is the town & on your left you
look down on a lovely valley full of trees betw[een] whose verdant
foliage you catch glimpses of a sweet stream — The Buildings which
are black from age are in the Gothic & Roman style — The town is
narrow & very dirty — Were it not for the grand ruins at its entrance
I would have it pulled down & destroyed for I observe that old towns
are always dirty —

[T]uesday ⟨17th⟩ 16th. Rise at four — Breakfast [a]t some where or
other — Dine at Cham[p]litte — Marguerite Pascal [4] — Sleep [a]t

[2] Bar-sur-Aube.

[3] Mary's entry on this date records: "We Rise at 4 and persue our journey
— We left the hills but were delighted to see one at a distance with clouds before
it. — The scenery however was not so beautiful as the day before although I
hope we have left for ever those intolerable flat torn lands — We dined at Chaumont. Shelley & Mary take a walk just outside the town — We proceed to Langres
and are obliged to sup at our inn with *tout le monde* & certainly a more disgusting
*world* I never came among" (Abinger MSS.).

[4] Mary writes: "Adventure with Marguerite Pascal — whom we would have
taken with us if her father would have allowed us & certainly I never beheld so
lovely a child" (in *Mary Shelley's Journal*, p. 9).

# France 1814

Gray — Very odd people — Little [l]imping old Woman — Shelley cooks [so]me broth all of a sudden —

Wednesday Aug. 17th. Rise at five[5] — ⟨Breakfast⟩ Rainy & very disagreeable Morning — get to some Village whose name I do not recollect wet through & uncomfortable French inhospitality — Dry ourselves & c[on]tinue our Journey[6] — Dine in another ⟨W⟩Village the name I cannot recollect   The Evening beautiful — The rainy cloud[s] fleeted fast away before the wind & lig[ht] blue summer clouds began to appear [as?] we approached Besançon the beauty of wh[ose] situation seemed as enchantment — The town is in a Valley — it is dirty & old — but Nature dear Nature more than compensates for the defects — When you have passed the town the most stupendous brown rocks [b]urst upon the eye — on the top of these rocks [sta]nds an old castle in ruins — You then pass through an immense archway cut [thr]ough the rocks under the shade of the [ju]tting & moss grown rocks it is almost dark. [No] sooner have you passed this archway than [Mou]ntains, Valleys & Rivers open on you — [A] winding road on the top of Rocks — Mountains on each side enclosing a valley verdant & smoth as velvet — among whose smooth banks was a ⟨pl⟩ pebbly & murmuring rivulet — these delight giving scenes last the whole way from Besancon to Mort a Village about a league & a half — our sulky Voiturier would remain at this dirty place   To go into such Beds as were here was impos[sible]   Perhaps never dirt was equal to the dirt we saw — We fled away & climbed some wild rocks — & sat there reading till the sun laid down to rest — I read As you like it [&] found the wild & romantic touches of this Play very accordant with the scene befor[e] me & my feeling — It was indeed a lovely Evenings — ⟨I⟩ How much is lost by those who pass their lives in cities — They are never visited by those sweet feelings which to ⟨reco⟩ recollect alone is heaven — It is fortunate [f]or them that they imagine themselves hap[py] — how boundless &

[5] Mary's journal says four. The journals frequently disagree about hours.

[6] An unpublished passage in Mary's journal for this day records: "This is the first day of rain   we are completely wet through before breakfast but as we buy an umbrella at the place where we dry ourselves we continue tolerably dry through the rest of the day — We arrived at Besançon about six & pass through the town . . . . — Passing on the *voiturier* insists on our passing the night at the village of Mort" (Abinger MSS.; cf. *Mary Shelley's Journal,* p. 9).

# First Journal

terrific would ⟨their⟩ be [th]eir surprize if they could suddenly become [p]hilosophers & view things in their true & [bea]utiful point of view. We sleep all [ni]ght by the Kitchen fire — Shelley much [di]sturbed by the creaking door, the screams [of] a poor smothered child & the fille who washed the glasses.

Thursday 18 [7] — Set off at four — The Morning balmy & refreshing — Breakfast somewhere  The road still continues beautiful — Immen[se] forests on each side of us — Reach Noë at twelve — The Postillion will stop at a m[ost] terrificly dirty inn — We go into the Wood[s] climb through a most beautiful retired glen which ascends & the pines hang [so] thickly over that it forms a deep & ne[arly] impenetrable shade — The rocks are here sometimes bare & awful & then become [*a word burned*] soft green & mossy — They rise over one another ⟨are⟩ ↑&↓ are entirely covered with Pines — Return at two to the Village find the Voiturier departed — walk to Maison Neuve. Dine there — A most detestable [s]hrill old wretch that gave one the [Hea]dach to hear her — Walk to L'Avrine [8] — the man not there — Procure a [ca]rt to Pontarlier — sup there — the Voiturier [ma]kes a thousand excuses — all falsehoods. [Sh]elley's ancle very bad all the way. [9] Go [to] bed much fatigued.

Friday 19th. [10] Set off at eight — ⟨Div⟩ The Scenery from Pontarlier most divine — Mountains on each side of us — Little bubbling rivulets pursuing their meandering courses over their pebbly & clear chan[nels.] I should take up volumes if I were to att[empt] to describe all I saw — At last we reach[ed] Les Verrieres which is

[7] Dowden published this day's entry, together with a parallel passage from Claire's revision of it from a manuscript that is now in the Pforzheimer Library (*Shelley*, I, 452–453n.).

[8] André Koszul has traced the route of this trip on modern maps and has pointed out that the worse road had been chosen, probably for its shortness and picturesqueness, since the regular road, via Ornans, was more circuitous. This would account for the unwillingness of the *voiturier*. Koszul mentions that Claire's L'Avrine is found on modern maps as La Vrine, also on the old road. Mort and Noë, similarly, would be Morre and Nodz. See "Notes and Corrections to Shelley's 'History of a Six Weeks' Tour' (1817)," *MLR* 2:61–62 (October 1906).

[9] Shelley writes: "We engaged a voiture for Pontarlier, Shelley being unable to walk" (Abinger MSS.; cf. *Mary Shelley's Journal*, p. 10).

[10] The entries for August 19 and 20 in the journal of Shelley and Mary are also in Shelley's hand.

# Switzerland 1814

considered ↑as↓ the barr[ier] of France & Switzerland — there is
an im[men]se chain suspended from a high mountain which is
thrown across the valley to the opposite mountain in time of War
— The road is most delightful & is cut through the middle of the
mountain which close in so closely that there is only room for a
clear little rivulet [to] run — The mountains are covered [w]ith
immense forests of Pine — now & then a bold, rugged, & bare rock
protrudes itself⟨s⟩ amidst ⟨the⟩ its green & woody [n]eighbours
forming a most sublime contrast. Half way to Neufchatel the Lake
is discovered — it is nine miles broad [F]irst you see ⟨three⟩ an in-
distinct line of hills that seems more like rising & uneven ground
⟨than marked⟩ & bear no marked or peculiar character, then comes
a second line still darker & more rugged & characteristic. behind
these is a third of very high dark hills, ⟨ru⟩ rude & brok[en] then
— oh then come the terrific Alp[s]   I thought they were white
flaky cloud[s]   what was my surprize when after a long & steady
examination I found them really to be the snowy Alps — yes, they
were really the Alps — Peaked broken, one jutting forward, another retreating, now the light airy clouds [r]ested a few moments
on their aspiring [fr]onts & then fled away that we might better
behold the sublimity of the scene. How much more should I have
enjoyed the [s]cene if I had been permitted to remain [in] silence
but at the village where we [d]ined we had procured a new voiturier
[&] horses & ⟨the kin⟩ in the kindness & freedom of his heart he
would talk to us — he would talk of the Brave Roi de Prusse & of
his own contentment, & where he had travelled to — all of which
at any other time I should have been delighted to hear but now it
was like discord in music — or like the ungrac[ious] scrapings of
a tuning fiddler — besid[es] his associations with the mountains
[were] those of butter & cheese — how good the pasturage was for
the cows — & then the cows yielded good milk & then the good
mi[lk] made good cheese — & so on from step to step — but however
the air of the mountains seem to have done him some good   there
was freedom in his countenance   indeed every thing seemed to
change the moment we passed from France to [Sw]itzerland —
The Cottages & people [(as] if by magic) became almost instantaneously clean & hospitable — The [c]hildren were rosy & ⟨&⟩ interesting, no [s]allow care worn looks — in France it is almost impossible to see a woman that looks under fifty — most of them bear

27

# First Journal

marks of advanced age — their cottages are in a horrible state —
dirt & ruin seem to have tak[en] up their everlasting abode with
them [11] but in Switzerland (⟨which I love [to] consider my own
country⟩)[12] you see cheerful content & smiling healthy faces. Our
Voiturier replied in answ[er] to some observations that I made
to him of this kind. Ah! it is because we have no king to fear!
when we have paid our rent to the Seigneur we have nothing to
⟨fear⟩ ↑dread↓ — we need not even take off our hats to him — we
are perfectly free ⟨till⟩ & may sit contentedly with our children
by our firesides — then we have only four Seigneurs in [a]ll the
country & we are not Roman [Ca]tholics & have no priets that
eat up [ou]r patrimony. We arrived at Neufchatel about eight —
it is a very clean neat town on the banks of the lake — We slept
at the Faucon which is the best inn we have ever yet entered. Sup
at the table d'hote with Germans.

Saturday 20th.  Get up late. Breakfast. Write my Journal — Read
in Roussea[u] Dine at five. Shelley goes in the tow[n] of the
Morning to the Banker who [kin]dly lets him have ⟨50£⟩ £50.[13] He
seeks a carriage we having sold our other to our Voiturier meaning
to h[ave] proceeded in the Diligence. He meets with a man at
the Bureau de Poste who gets him a voiture & comes home to the
Hotel. I like this Swiss very much — ⟨yet I [*a word obliterated*]
him [?] —⟩

[Sun]day August 21st. Set off at eight — Our [new?] Swiss friend

[11] The part of France through which they had been traveling had been left
in ruins by the passage of the allied armies in the preceding year.

[12] Claire referred to Switzerland as "the land of my ancestors" in a letter
to Byron (see Grylls, *Claire Clairmont*, p. 61). In speculating on the implications
of this, Herbert Huscher ("The Clairmont Enigma," KSMB 11:15 [1960])
suggests three possibilities: that Claire's mother had made her believe that she
was the daughter of Charles Gaulis, originally of Lausanne; that Claire knew
another French-Swiss, Charles Clairmont, to have been her father; or that Claire
referred to her mother's rather remote ancestors named Vial, traced near Geneva
in the eighteenth century. If the reference carried a thoroughly respectable
association, one must ask why Claire should have attempted to obliterate it when
she blotted out all indiscretions from her journal. She did not cross out the entry
of August 29, 1814 (below), in which she mentions hearing from her "very
nice" traveling companions of her relations at Geneva.

[13] Mary later says "about £38. in silver upon discount" (*Six Weeks' Tour*,
p. 45).

rides out of the town [w]ith us — Breakfast at Burée — We [there] see German Dresses for the first [ti]me — The Country is pretty & interesting rather than grand — Dine at Ar[b]erg at the table d'hote — The towns are most delightfully clean — in almost every street there are fountains which spread an air of freshness round — ⟨Shelley⟩ [*two or more words thoroughly crossed out*] [14]

[*Here one leaf at least is missing. The diary resumes on Monday, August 22.*]

Reach Murgantal about nine — Take some Bread & Butter — The Roa[d] is very woody & rather hilly — now & then the white Alps are to be dist[in]guished & they appear about half an hour's Walk although at the distance of a hundred miles — Din[e] at Zoffingen — Rest there two hours — Reach Sursee at six — It is a clean Town on the banks of the Lake Samplach & surrounded by the Alps. [S]up at the table d'hote — There [is] a miserable spinnet in the [I]nn —

[Tu]esday Aug. 23rd. Breakfast. Set off [a]t four — Reach Lucern at nine — Breakfast. Get a boat — Go down the Lake of Lucern — The first mountain is on your right Pelatus — Its shape is truly magnificent — Righi is nearly opposite to it but is far less grand — The Mountains close in upon the Lake — Micher Boden is a beauti-[ful] green promontory to your left — The trees grow on it close down to the water & are of a most beautifu[l] green — When you turn this prom[on]tory rocks entirely by themselves resembling islands suddenly present themselves — the largest of these is called Wollshtoff & has a small chapel dedicated to St. Nicholas on its top — Now & then the snowy Mountains are [to] be seen — Dine at Gersaw — Sleep at Brunnen — which [is] situated at the extremity of the Lake Lucern & opposite that of Uri. Watch the waves of the Lake which beat close before the house for some time — Most wretched beds.

Wednesday August 24th. Read Abbé Bar[ruel] [15] Talk with our

---

[14] "Shelley & Jane talk concerning J's character," writes Mary in her journal, and that evening, at Soleure, Mary and Shelley go off to visit the cathedral without her (see *Mary Shelley's Journal*, p. 11). Claire apparently defaced her diary at this point to obliterate a reference to Shelley's criticism of her.

[15] L'Abbé (Augustin) Barruel, *Mémoires pour servir à l'histoire du jacobin-*

host about living with him look over his house — Go out with
Shelley & Mary — look at lodgings — fix upon one — Sit upon the
shore for a long tim[e] the lake very much agitated — Retur[n]
& dine — M & S— go out & read Taci[tus] [16] Go to Bed early —
Very curious dreams or perhaps they were realities —

Thursday Aug— 25th. Get up late — Breakfast — Go to the large
& only boutique in Brunnen with Shelley — Remove [to] the house
on the hill — Visit from the Medecin & the Abbé. [17] Read Abbé
Barruel — Work in the Evening [as] it rains. The Clouds descended far below the Mountain tops — They seemed just to hang
over our heads & above were the black rocks with dark clouds on
their heads — The Lake is in front of our house which is on the
⟨top of⟩ declivity of a hill & on every side shut in by Mountains
some covered with trees & some bare & rugged — This would be
a most delightful residence if it were not for the amazing popu-
lousness of the country The Mountains are covered with cottages
— It is impossible to find a wild & entire solitude. In other countries the Mountains however beautiful are generally deserted —
but this being a republic & the people multiplying exceedingly no
spot is deserted for no spot in this fertile country is barren except
the very tops of the mountains — The people are rich contented &
happy. A poor beggar is never seen — The people are uninteresting
for they are most immoderately stupid & almost ugly to deformity
— The children beg the moment they see you — not from povety
but merely from habit which I suppose has descended from their
ancestors who originally begged from Poverty — Shelley begins his
Roman[ce] [18] in the Evening. Go to Bed early.

Friday August 26. Boring Morning — Project of going back to Eng-

---

*isme*, 4 vols. (London, 1797–1798); trans. R. Clifford, *Memoirs, Illustrating
the History of Jacobinism*, 4 vols. (London, 1797–1798). This work had been
a favorite of Shelley's since his undergraduate days; he owned Clifford's translation (see Shelley, *Letters*, I, 264, and *Mary Shelley's Journal*, p. 219).

[16] *Historiae.*

[17] Mary confesses that they did not treat the Abbé with proper politeness
(in *Mary Shelley's Journal*, p. 11).

[18] "The Assassins." The fragment opens with the siege of Jerusalem and
reflects Shelley's reading in Tacitus, combined with his enthusiasm for mountain
scenery and romantic ideals.

land pr[es]sed — Read Abbé Barruel. Settle to go to London — Go
to Bed early.

Saturday Aug. 27th. Get up at five    Bustle toil & trouble — Most
laughable to think of our going to England the second day after
we entered a new house for six months — All because the stove
don't suit.[19] As we left Dover & England's white cliffs were retiring I said to myself I shall never see these more — & now I am going
to England again — dear England    After having travelled & viewed
the follies of other nations my own country appears the most
reasonable & the most enlightened. It is now six o'clock    We shall
set off in a moment. What will the Abbé and the Medecin say?
I should like to know what a Pack Horse is? Shelley explains this
phenomenon at one o'clock in the boat. Set off at seven. Ra[iny]
Morning. Very uncomfortable. The clouds only just above our
head — We pass through one. Stop under a shed for half an hour
— Mont Pilate almost hid by thin white clouds. Reach Lucerne
about half after twelve — Go to the Cheval.[20] Read King Richard
III. & King Lear. Quite Horrified — [I] can't describe my feelings
for [th]e moment — when Cornwall tears [ou]t the eyes of the Duke
of Gloster — This Play is the most melancholy & produces almost
stupenduous despair on the reader — Such refinement in wickedness
& cruelty — Lear is exactly what he calls himself — "But I am a
fond foolish old Man." Jealous & anxious for the display of affection & praise — In most of Shakespeare's Plays there are generally
secondary Plots & Characters which are rather tiresome than interesting but in Lear there is not a line that does not teem with
vigour & energy & [a word thoroughly crossed out] ⟨new⟩ awakens
fresh anxiety ⟨in⟩ & horror. I think Lear treats Cordelia very ill —
"What shall poor Cordelia do — Love & be silent" — Oh [th]is is true
— Real Love will never [sh]ew itself to the eye of broad day —
[i]t courts the secret glades — ⟨Go to bed after⟩ [about five more
words thoroughly crossed out] [21] — In a fortnight we shall perhaps

[19] Shelley and Mary did not take Claire into their confidence about the
seriousness of their financial distress.

[20] The inn was "Le Cheval Blanc."

[21] Mary laconically records: "Interrupted by Janes horrors pack up" (in
Mary Shelley's Journal, p. 12). Claire, at some undetermined later date, seems
to have tried to obliterate evidence that she was rebuked by Shelley for her periodic
fits of "horrors."

# First Journal

be in London — How wild the people will think us — All because the stove did not burn rightly & there were too many Cottages.

Sunday August 28th. Rise at 5 — Breakfast — Get on board at six [22] — Nev[er] did I see such a set as were in the boat with us ⟨did never eyes behold⟩ — their mirth was [*a word thoroughly crossed out*] & loud & unmeaning — their eyes were shiny & liquid — leering ⟨pl⟩ blasphemy & horror on the beholder. There were about three out of fifty with honest Peasant faces — one old Woman I liked very much — it was rainy at intervals, & nothing could exceed her care of us [&] her generosity in the disposal of her [u]mbrella — The Scenery along the [Ri]ver is not so fine as I expected — From Lucerne we went down the Russe — which here & there has rocks which are dangerous — We flew like lightning down a chute of the River as it is here called — I dare say it was at least eight feet — that we descended — ⟨I⟩ We dined at Mettingen at the table d'hote — We staid 2/4 of an hour at Bramengen — A little past the last mentioned Village the Russe falls into the Aar a fin[e] deep rapid river the banks of whic[h] are extremely beautiful — Woody solitary & wild — Reach Dettingen about seven — Sleep there —

Monday Aug. 29th. Rise at 5. Breakfast — Get on board at six — Reach [La]uffenbourg [23] about eleven — Stay [the]re half an hour — Proceed in a [s]mall boat to Monff — Find no boats there — They tell us we ⟨ga⟩ can get one at Rhinfelldyn   Get into a Cabriole which broke down before we got a mile from the town — Walk with ⟨some four⟩ three foot travellers who carry our baggage for us to Rhinfelld[yn] Very nice companions — one of them informs me of my Relations at Geneva — Part with them Aux tro[is] Rois — Find no boat at Rhinfelldyn. Proceed to Shorf Bach [24] a quarter of a league — Great trouble — Our Companions overtake us again — another Parting. A Swiss [v]ery kind — get a boat at last — [Re]ach Basle about seven — This town stands upon the Rhine   It is finely

[22] Since funds were nearly exhausted, Shelley and Mary decided to return the whole 800 miles to England by water conveyances, the cheapest form of transportation.

[23] There is much variation in both journals in the spelling of place names. Mary spelled this name Loffenburgh, and others in the same neighborhood she spelled Mumph and Rheinfelt.

[24] Unidentified.

situated ⟨is⟩ & is large & well built — Shelley goes out to seek a boat
— The Bookseller opposite very kind to him   He procures one —
Watch the People at the Public Fountain where all sorts come to
wash Plates — Tubs & Glasses — The Banks of the Rhine are extreme[ly] beautiful — Hilly & covered with Wood of all tints &
hues — Luffenbourg stands upon the Aar & the Rhine flows round
at the back of the town — The Current of the Rhine is extremely
rapid —

Tuesday Aug 30th. Rise at five — Breakfast — Go down to the Quay
— Do not [g]et on board till ½ past seven — The morning cold &
cloudy — now & then [r]ain — The Rhine begins to get broad a few
leagues from Basle — Its banks are very beautiful — Verdantly sloping down to meet ⟨the⟩ its waves & covered with young willows —
Islands ⟨no⟩ rise on the surface of the water   they are numerous
& covered with groves — We saw a sea-mew & wonder[ed] much
how came in a place so m[any] miles from the sea — We stopt for
abou[t] an hour on a small green hill to d[ine] as we had taken
provisions — I gathered some of the most beautiful grass I ever
beheld — The Wind had been against us the whole day & was
violent — The Clouds fleeted fast away & the Sun broke forth in
the Afternoon — on both sides of the Rhine there was in the distance two high ridges of black Hills — ⟨The b⟩ About four o'clock
we [la]nded at Brisaac a town in Baden — [The] Watermen said
they could not proceed with so strong a wind against us — We were
afraid we should be obliged to delay our journey & sleep here but
in about an hour they came with the news that the wind was
changed & we hastened on Board — Shelley reads aloud the Letters
from Norway [25] — This is one of my very favorite Books — The language is so ⟨ve⟩ very flowing & Eloquent & it is altogether a beautiful Poem — We witnessed one of the finest Sun sets — The West
was a long continued strip of Yellow dying away with a lovely
pink which again mellowed itself imperceptibly into an amazing
horiz[on] of the deepest purple — The Rhine was extremely rapid
— The Waves borrowed the divine colours of the sky — Never were
tints so numerous or so perpetually varied — The undulating motion
of the waves rolling ever one over the other produced the same

[25] Mary Wollstonecraft, *Letters Written during a Short Residence in Sweden,
Norway, and Denmark* (London: J. Johnson, 1796).

effect as if snakes were creeping perpetually onwards — I now thought of Coleridge's Ancient Mariner — "Beyond the shadow of [the] ship — I watched the water snakes" — I am [c]onvinced that the descriptions contained in [t]hat Poem are ↑more↓ copied from Nature than one is at first aware of — The Rhine appeared narrow here for it ⟨was⟩ is covered with islands which produce the same effect as if you were passing through a narrow defile. The Shore on the Right were black hills — now rocky — then woody & sometimes gently declined into grassy slopes — We passed a ruined castle situated on the top of a black Hill. The ruins suited with the scene — Every thing seemed declining — the Sun had hid his beams — the trees were gaining a dar[k] hue & the mountains were receeding. We slept at Schoff Hock [26] — M's birthday — 1⟨6⟩7.

⟨W⟩Wednesday Aug. 31st. Rise at five — Our boat is changed into a most odious Canoe. Sleep a great Part of the day — Shelley reads aloud Letters from Norway — Read King Lear a second time — Reach Strasburg about eleven — ⟨The real⟩ You [en]ter by a river & pass through three Bridges. The real town is seen in the distance & is about a league off from the Bay — We stay in the Boat while Shelley seeks Provisions — The Banks of the Rhine are flat ⟨& about⟩ low & woody — The Stream is about four miles broad — Reach a beautiful little Village about Sunset ⟨which⟩ Wretched Beds

Thursday September 1st. Rise at 3 — Proceed to a little town & change Boats again — ⟨Thr⟩ Four Passengers — Shelley finishes the Letter[s] from Norway aloud — One of our Passengers of the name of Hoff very odious — The Second was neither one thing or the other — he was called Schriwtz — the third was an ideot of the name of Schneider [27] A woman & her child made up the number of our Companions — Stop at [m]any places in the course of the day [th]e names of which I do not recollect. We travel all night —

[26] The name is Shauphane in Shelley's journal entry (Abinger MSS.).

[27] In her *Six Weeks' Tour*, p. 64, Mary describes the three Strasbourg University students: Schwitz, "a rather handsome, good tempered young man"; Hoff, "a kind of shapeless animal, with a heavy, ugly, German face"; and the idiot Schneider, "on whom his companions were always playing a thousand tricks."

# Germany 1814

Friday Sept.ber 2nd. About five in the Morning we arrive at Man-
heim situated on the Banks of the Rhine—We were obliged to
wait here till seven as the Gentlemen of the Custom-House did not
rise till then—We went into the three Boys I have already mentioned and breakfast—Afterwards walk over the town which i[s]
the most noble I have ever seen—The Buildings are immensely
large ⟨&⟩ regular & clean—The Streets are wide & we now & then
found some that were paved—a comfort we had never met with
since we left England—Very near the Entrance of the town is a
large Chateau ⟨with⟩ surrounded by Pleasure Grounds [bo]th of
which are ⟨made⟩ very much [i]n the English Style—The outside
of the Cathedral is very fine—it is very old & the iron gates are
⟨ver⟩ worked in a very curious manner. The Walk from Mannheim
down to the River (about a mile) is very pretty—It is a long
Avenue—with trees on each side principally ⟨Accaccia⟩ Acaccia's
which is a very peculiar & beautiful tree—Set off about six   Continue till about eleven—Re[st] in a most lovely & woody Wilder-
n[ess.] From thence to a ⟨W⟩Village where Shelley & I seek Provisions—It was rather a Town & was called Gernsheum—The
Batelier insists upon staying till the Moon rises—When the Moon
had risen then he would stay till  he then set off & after proceeding
half a league tied the Boat to an Island & there staid till Morning.[28]

Saturday 3rd [T]he Wind was strong against us so [th]at Schriwtz
& his companion Hoff & the Boatman dragged us along the shore
to Mayntz[29] which we reached at one—Dine at Table D'hôte—
Read Memoirs[30]—Schriwtz call twice pour prendre Congé.[31] Go
to Bed at seven—The Inhabitants of Mayntz do not know to whom
they belong—They are without a government at present & have
been for some months—The town is kept in a sta[te] of strong
defence & the soldiers ⟨par⟩ parade the streets—The Russians gave
up the Seige of this town—they could only approach within six

[28] By contrast, Shelley writes: "Mary & Shelley walk for three hours: they
are alone. At eleven we depart" (see *Mary Shelley's Journal*, p. 13).
[29] Shelley spells it Mayence. Here again he writes, "M & S. are alone" (in
*Mary Shelley's Journal*, p. 13).
[30] William Godwin, *Memoirs of the Author of a Vindication of the Rights
of Woman* (London: J. Johnson, 1798).
[31] "To take leave," abbreviated *p.p.c.*, a phrase often used by Godwin in
his diary.

leagues of it for Napoleon had made it the strongest fortified town in all Europe — It is large & clean.

Sunday Sept 4th. Rise at six — Walk down to the Quay — [G]o in a Boat a league from the town to where the Diligence for Cologne is stationed — Set off about Seven — The Banks of the Rhine are very beautiful — The River itself is narrow & runs between Mountains which though not high are of every different shape & description — Ruined Castles are here very numerous & many most romanticly situated   Ruins have a fine effect & henceforth I shall hardly think any scene compl[ete] without them — I think we passed no less than twenty Castles & about 5 towns — at a small Village there is a ruind Cathedral of a fine brown colour — We dined at Bingen — Near which is a very strong Castle built in the middle of the Rhine — One Castle was built on the very top of a high & rocky Mountain — Sleep at Braubach. In our journey of to-day we passed one very dangerous place — the ⟨B⟩Bed of the Rhine is almost all Rocks — Bubbling roaring & foaming — It is a small defile — The River is only a quarter of a mile broad & complety shut in by Mountains. The Ship was steered cautiously from side ⟨to⟩ to side & we passed it in safety. We had a most horrid set on board — Nothing could surpass the ⟨licentiousness of the⟩ Manners that prevailed in the Cabin below — Drinking, smoking, singing & cracking jokes of a ⟨risque⟩ ↑dis-agreeable↓ Nature — We sat upon the deck the whole day with one or two tolerable men who smoked it is true but were brought to own it was wrong. Among these two sat talking with us [a]lmost the whole day — One was a man that pretended to something & the other [a]n Agriculturist going out to Surinam withe no pretensions to amy thing but unaffected simplicity & good Nature — We had on board besides a schoolmaster who spoke a little English — The latter & the man of Pretensions sung many German Airs which I admired very much — As we were just entering the dangerous defile the Man of Pretension turned to us & said — "Allons il faut prier le bon Dieu — We laugh[ed] — He answered — Eh! bien donc il fau[t] chanter"[32] — The Schoolmaster ⟨tei⟩ immedia[te]ly began & they sang an ⟨fine⟩ animated German Song which had a much finer effect when seconded by the breaking of the waves over the Rocks.

[32] "Come, we must pray to God." "Oh, well, then, we must sing."

# Germany 1814

Sleep at Rens. See the only beautiful girl ⟨I⟩ we have seen since we [p]arted from Paris.

Monday ⟨Aug⟩ Sept. 5th. Rise at three. Set sail without any milk — Dreadfully Cold — so dreadfully that we were reduced by dire Necessity to descend into the Cabin — Talk with the Man of Dusseldorf & a Merchant a cher ami of his  they tell us of their intention to stay at Coblentz & as they can no longer endure the Canai[lle] who snatched the meat out of their pl[ates] the Evening before at Supper — Arriv[e] at Coblentz about seven — The Man & the Agriculturist take a most tend[er] farewell — I find it is the custom for Men to kiss each other at parting — The Canaille take advantage of this & kiss each other all the day ⟨long⟩ which with their horrid leers & shine has a most loathsome effect — Never was a more disgraceful set than the Common order of people of Germany. Your soul shrinks back to its inmost recesses when by accident you cast your eye over countenances begrimmed with mental & bodily depravity — Stay half an hour at Coblentz — opposite which is a very commanding & rugged rock — The Ruins of a fortress stand upon its top[33] — Napoleon judged it dangerous that the Germans should still retain so strong a hold in their possession & therefore destroy[ed] that which ⟨was hitherto⟩ had hitherto been considered as impregnable. We saw many ruined Castles today but none so fine as those of yesterday. Dine at Trier . . . The German ⟨The Ger⟩ are really most provoking — They let the Boat entirely alone & it swims slowly round & round getting [d]own the rapid Current of the Rhine at the rate of a mile an hour. I suppose they think it goes quicker this way than straight. Get to Bonn where they intended us to sleep. We get a Voiture & proceed to Cologne much disgusted with all Water Diligences or rather Slownessess. We set out for Cologne at eight & hoped to have reach[ed] it at ten but our Postillion was a Germ[an] & went only with most excellent horses 2 miles & & ½ an hour — We did not reach till one — We staid knocking at the Montain du Rhin ½ an hour. The Postillion took everything quietly, & coolly rung gentle peals in the ears of the snoring ostler at the interval of every 5 minutes. No Beds

[33] The ruins of Ehrenbreitstein and the part of the Rhine Claire mentions in the previous entry are described by Byron in 1816, in *Childe Harold*, canto iii. Claire seems to have misunderstood some German place names, such as Trier, Glaive, and Furso (for Viersen?), that she mentions below.

there Shelley much provoked. Proceed to another. Go to Bed after writing my journal.

Teusday September 6th. Rise at four & set off in the Diligence with two other companions — Breakfast at a small Village — Dine at Glaive — There was a Roman Catholic Procession through the town in remembrance of a famous Battle which the Prussians won many years ago over the French — We found every body rejoicing going to Messe & dressed in their best. From Glaive take up a young Prussian officer — a silly fellow. Travel till one — Stop at a town to chang[e] horses — A large Room on the 1st floor wa[s] lighted up & there was music & dancing. I awoke from sleep & never did I hear so divine an air as the one that was playing — It was now like a march then became suddenly slow & afterwards animated & quick — The figures of the Company & the sound of their footsteps seemed to accord with the air — They were dancing with their hearts & Souls. Sup at a small Village — We are offered a Cabriole — ⟨Proceed till six.⟩

Wednesday Sept. 7th. Arrive at Furso about six having travelled three small leagues in the Night. Proceed to Cleves which we reach about eleven. Breakfast. Set off in a Cabriolet for Nimeguen which we reach at four — Dine there. This is the frontier town of Holland & is almost excactly like an English town but most uncommonly neat. Dine there — Set off again — Reach Trienne [34] at eight — We are hindered from proceeding by the accou[nt] we receive of the Robbers. Sup & sleep. I forgot to mention that at ⟨M⟩Nimeguen we crossed a Branch of the Rhine over a flying Bridge — [35]

Thursday September 8th. Rise at 5. Set off at six — ⟨Get⟩ Breakfast at a small Village where we again [cr]oss a river on a flying Bridge. Proceed to Rotterdam which we reach at [s]ix in the Evening — Sup & go to Bed — Holland is exactly what may termed a pretty country. We passed along narrow roads with Canals on each side — so narrow indeed that two Carriages cannot pass one another. The Country is invariably flat — We only passed one little ascent of

[34] Mary says Triel (*Mary Shelley's Journal*, p. 14). Koszul says it is properly Thiel, now Tiel.

[35] Mentioned in the letters of Lady Mary Wortley Montague, says Mary (*Six Weeks' Tour*, p. 75).

about four feet that was produced by Art as it was a Mound for the for[ti]fying the city — On every side [are] fortifications — the work of Napol[eon] who is thought to understand fortification ⟨the⟩ better than anyone that has ever yet existed — When you cast you eye over the whole face of Holland nothing is to be seen but small square ⟨patt⟩ patches of beautiful woody & green land intersected by innumerable Canals. It is the [s]ame every Where. The trees are [a]ll young straight Willows — & the [g]rass is most beautifully verdant & fertile — The Roads have trees on each side of them — They are perfectly straight & continue of the same monotonous character for Miles. The Houses stand seldom together but generally surrounded by Water & have drawbridges communicating w[ith] the Road which are generally ⟨all⟩ drawn up & give the house an [air] of individual & peculiar security. As we approached Rotterdam ⟨the hous⟩ gentlemen's country houses were scattered along the Road — These were the same as the others — the grounds were laid out untastefully — straight gravel walks with patches of grass-plots & square beds of marigolds [&] other gaudy flowers — Then at the end of the garden there are [r]ound brick summer houses sometimes without a tree to shadow them — The houses are most wonderfully neat — They have pretty green window-shutters — & the very bricks are washed down every day — We passed through Utrecht which is neatness ⟨itselft⟩ itself — The ⟨So⟩ Stones, the brick Pavements all are washed — There is a very curious tower at its Entrance & Canals with tree planted borders run through the principal Streets — I like these Canals — They spread a coolness through the Air & ⟨cot⟩ contribute no doubt much to the cleanliness of the inhabitants — Rotterdam is large clean & neat. The Dutch are sober & ⟨intell⟩ slow — They have no German licentiousness about them — They pay an unbounded [re]spect to every thing in the shape of riches — & are I doubt not a very sordid ⟨n⟩ & interested nation — They dress almost like the English & speak their language very well —

Friday September 9th. Rise at eight — Breakfast. Write my Journal. Read Sophie — Une fille lettrée ne sera jamais mariée qua[nd] il n'y aura que des hommes sensés dans le monde [36] — Sophie had

---

[36] Rousseau, *Émile: Ou de l'éducation* (1762), book v. "Every young lady that pretended to literature, would continue a maid all her life, were there none

# First Journal

never read any other book than Barreme which fell by accident into her hands & Telemachus — Sophie is the most finished ⟨&⟩ [*word thoroughly crossed out*] of Coquettes — Emile is astonished at her infidelity — "he is sure that as Sophie has proved weak there can be no truth in Woman." It is indeed partial to judge the whole sex by the conduct of one whose very education tended to fit her more for a Seraglio than the friend & equal of Man.

Dine at one — Go on Board at two — Weigh Anchor at four — The Wind west & exactly Contrary — Pass Skidam which is situated in a very pretty little Harbour — Reach Maarsluis about eight six leagues from Rotterdam [37] — Go on shore to an Inn — Our Passengers consist of a Mr. & Mrs. Turner common & vulgar people — a Dutch Gentleman who prides himself on the mountains of his Native town ⟨M⟩Nimeguen, which in reality are nothing but Mounds for fortifications & about half [a]s high as a house — Sleep at Maas-sluis — Very stormy.

Saturday Sept. 10th. Get up at eight — We cannot pursue our voyage the Wind being West & very high — ⟨Write⟩. Breakfast with our Companions — Write — Read Emile — Write a story — The Day is lowering & Windy. Our Companions except Mole-Hill go to Rotterdam. Write all day — After tea ⟨wite⟩ write the fragment of my Ideot — This has been for years a favorite Plan of mine — To develop the Workings & Improvements of a Mind which by Common People was deemed the mind of an Ideot because it conformed not to their vulgar & prejudiced views.[38] Go to Bed at ten. The Captain & ⟨our⟩ the Passengers do not return.

---

but men of sense in the world" (*Emilius: Or an Essay on Education*, trans. Nugent [London, 1763], II, 272–273).

[37] Koszul says Shelley's Maasluis, or Marsluys, should be Maarluis. Mary places it about two leagues from Rotterdam (*Six Weeks' Tour*, p. 78).

[38] At this time Shelley was continuing work on "The Assassins," while Mary began "Hate" (*Mary Shelley's Journal*, p. 14). Claire's "Ideot" sounds like the story she submitted to Byron in 1816. She described it in a letter to him as having been written "at intervals, and in scraps." Her intention was "to draw a character committing every violence against received opinion — one, educated amidst mountains and deserts, who knew no other guide than herself on the impulses arising from herself; — who, notwithstanding the apparent enormity of her actions, should however appear highly amiable, full of noble affections and sympathies; — whose sweetness and naïvete of character should draw on her the pity rather than the contumely of her readers." To the common reader,

# Holland 1814

Sunday Sept. 11th. The Wind changes from West to North East — The Captain returns from Rotterdam. We are hurried on Board — Two more Passengers both Scotchmen — sensible & Pleasant Companions — one of them is a Rousseauman ⟨& thinks Christianity & civilization have done us a great deal of harm — he⟩ thinks the more savage & uncultivated we are the better we become & the more according to Nature. The Wind blew exactly from North-East — The Dutch Packet Boats waiting in the harbour. at Maas-Sluis — did not dare venture forth the wind was so strong — but our Captain an Englishman of the name [of] Ellis said he knew well enough what he was about & he was not going to be such a Coward as the Dutchman who retorted by assuring us we should be all drowned in crossing the Bar a dangerous shoal of Sands at⟨t⟩ the Entrance on the Occean — We sailed about two hours longer on the Rhine — The Waves of the River gradually became higher & higher — Poor Mary was sick as death & was obliged to go to Bed as well as Mrs. Turner & one or two more of the Passengers most of wh[om] kept down stairs smoking [39] — Shelley & I sat upon deck & the Waves which became terribly high broke over us — We were about half an hour crossing the Bar — The face of the Captain was all anxiety — We asked him some trifling question but he said at present we must not plague him — It required much skill & [a]ttention to steer us through the Breakers — things which I have heard of before but which I could never imagine — you see them at a great distance — they are immense ridges of white foam which roll towards you with much rapidity & if not avoided break upon the ship & sometimes dash it to pieces — When we passed the Bar the Sea still continued very high but nothing to the Waves ⟨wh⟩ we had just gone throug[h]. Sit up till ten — Just before I went to Bed Henrique came & pumped about three pails of Water from the Pump — I thought that we had sprung a leak as going down the River we went a-ground — but the Scotchman told me that every ship admitted so many feet Water [&] that it was impossible to

---

the tale should seem a sermon "against extraordinary opinions," but the enlightened atheist would see it in a different light (see Byron, *Works*, III, 434–435).

[39] Shelley in his entry in the journal comments: "The sea is horribly tempestuous & Mary horidly sick nor is Shelley much better" (cf. *Mary Shelley's Journal*, p. 14).

make [o]ne without — Molehill was very sick indeed — & made me almost be washed away with laughing at him — Every one of the Passengers were sick except myself — Can't sleep in the night — The ⟨wathe⟩ weather very Squally indeed — The Boom brea[ks] in the middle of the night with a terrible crash.

Monday Sept. 12. Get up at Eight — Eat for the first time after being on Board. The Weather becomes calm & beautiful — on Rising in the Morning the Suffolk coast was to be seen very plainly. The Sea was very calm & all our Passengers got [be]tter & came on Deck. Little [M]olehill says there is a chain [of] black Hills at Maas-Sluis. In the Evening we got to the Nore. & Passed South-End & Chatham — Go to Bed at ten.

Tuesday Sept. 13th. Rise late — Find our two Scotchmen gone & Mr. & Mrs. Turner. Arrive at Gravesend about ten — Custom house officers come on Board — Row to the Custom house Cutter. Meet our Scotchm[en] again there — Get to Gravesend — Grea[t] Trouble [40] — At last get a Waterman   Delightful Row up the River — Arrive ⟨the⟩ at Blackwall at two. Get into the Stage — Arrive in Lead⟨h⟩enhall Street in about an hour — Get into a hackney Coach & drive to Martin & Call's [41] — No money there. Go to Hookham's [42] — only Edward at home — Stay a long time at the door. Drive then to Voisey's Pall Mall — Mrs. V — very indignant — Henry Voisey kind — He runs to Chapel Street while we dr⟨o⟩ive there — Shelley meets Voisey & go to Harriet's [43] — Wait there for him two hours — Gets dark   Part with our kind Boatman — Shelley returns — Drive to Stratfor[d] Hotel Oxford Street. Dine & go to Bed —

Wednesday Sept. 14th. Get up late — Write my Journal. Shelley

[40] Since the last guinea had been spent in Maarluis, Shelley had to convince the captain that he should wait until they arrived in England to receive his fare. Further funds were then needed to pay the waterman and the coachman.

[41] Shelley's bankers.

[42] Thomas Hookham, Jr., and his brother Edward published books at their father's library, 15 Old Bond Street. Thomas had arranged for the printing of *Queen Mab* and had provided financial assistance to Shelley in the past. He sympathized with Harriet and tried to act as mediator in the difficulties of 1814.

[43] Harriet was staying at her father's in Chapel Street, Grosvenor Square. Apparently Shelley obtained from her sufficient funds to discharge their debt (in *Mary Shelley's Journal*, p. 15).

visits Harriet — Her strange Behaviour — Read the Papers. Shelley gets the clothes from Hookham [44] — & writes to him. Write & send to Maria Smith's [45] — Not at home — Dine at six — Remove to lodgings in Margaret Street No⟨'s⟩ 56. [46] Go to Bed almost directly. S. gets the Recluse. [47]

Thursday Sept. 15. Rise & breakfast at nine — Send again to Maria Smith's — Letter from her. Shelley goes to Harriet. Meet Hookham there — Reconcilement  Bring him home — He writes to Voisey. Read Emile — Write i[n] my Common Place Book — Din[e] at six — ⟨Write my Ideot⟩ — till eleven — Shelley reads us the Ancient Mariner. Get our Boxes from Hookham's. Read in the Excursion — the Story of Margaret very beautiful. [48] ⟨Very good &⟩ [about three more words thoroughly crossed out]

Friday Sept. 16th. Rise at nine — Breakfast — Read Rasselas [49] — & De l'origine de l'inegalite [d]es Hommes [50] — Curious & weak letter from Harriet with Shelley's Books. S writes to Papa & Charles — Letter from Turner. [51] Hookham Dines — Just before dinner about six — Mama & Fanny pass the Window — Shelley runs out to them — They won't speak — Hookham quits us early —

[44] Shelley had maintained rooms at the Hookhams' and had left clothing and books there.

[45] A friend of the Godwins, not further identified.

[46] In Cavendish Square.

[47] Wordsworth's *Excursion, Being a Portion of the Recluse, a Poem*, just off the press. Mary comments: "We read a part much disappointed — He is a slave" (in *Mary Shelley's Journal*, p. 15).

[48] In book i of *The Excursion*.

[49] Mary took up Samuel Johnson's *The History of Rasselas, Prince of Abissinia*, 2 vols. (1759), on September 19 (in *Mary Shelley's Journals*, p. 16).

[50] Rousseau's *Discours sur l'origine de l'inégalité parmi les hommes* (1755) would have had a particular appeal to Claire, with its discussion of individualism, the nobility of the savage, and the perfectibility of man. In 1816 Shelley proclaimed, "Rousseau is indeed in my mind the greatest man the world has produced since Milton" (Shelley, *Letters*, I, 494).

[51] Thomas Turner, Godwin's friend and the husband of Shelley's Bracknell friend, Cornelia Boinville, served as an intermediary between Godwin and Shelley. In a letter dated September 16 (an error for 17), Shelley wrote to Harriet: "I have heard from Turner. Mrs. Boinville has just received intelligence of her husband's death. She is considerably affected by this circumstance, so that probably some time will elapse before I see her" (Shelley, *Letters*, I, 396).

Voisey at tea — He explains Dr. Gall'system [52] — Departs about ½ past ten — Mary retires  Shelley is writing to Papa & I am read-in[g] the notes to Queen Mab when we hear Stones at the Window — Look out & there is Charles — Joyful meeting — He stays till three in the Morning — Tells us about their Plan of putting me in a Convent — ⟨In the day time write Ideot⟩

Saturday Sept. 17th. — Rise at eleven — Breakfast — Mr. Cooper's attorney call — Shelley [g]oes to Insurance Office with him [53] — Write & read all Morning. Dine at ½ past six. ⟨W⟩Write to Charles. Shelley reads aloud the Curse of Kehama. [54] They go to Bed at ten. Sit up till one one writing ⟨the Ideot⟩. Read the Lara of Lord Byron.

Sunday Sept 18. Rise late. Read Emile. Write. Very lazy. Mr. Peacock call  he & Shell[ey] Walk he dines & goes soon after — Curious Accounts of Harriet. To Bed early.

Monday Sept. 19th. Rise late — Shelley goes to Ballechey's [55] Read the Curse of Kehama & Emile. Hookham calls at dinner time. he goes early — Read the [S]orcerer & Political Justice. [56] Admire the Sorcerer very much —

[52] According to an advertisement in the *Courier*, Johann Caspar Spurzheim's *The Physiognomical System of Drs. Gall and Spurzheim* (London, 1814) had just appeared. Franz Joseph Gall (1758–1828) and his disciple, Spurzheim, were physicians in Vienna, studying the localization of the functions of the brain. Dr. Gall was known for his work in training deaf and dumb children, but the system referred to here is probably that which led to the pseudo science of phrenology. Gall had visited England earlier in the century, and his lectures had been interdicted as dangerous to religion. Dr. Gall seems to be the prototype of Mr. Cranium, satirically sketched by Thomas Love Peacock in *Headlong Hall* (1816), particularly in chap. xii.

[53] Shelley wrote to Harriet: "This morning Cooke's [*probably copyist's error for* Cooper's] Attorney called on me & I appeared at the Insurance Office. I feel that my personal safety is endangered by your imprudence in sending him hither" (Shelley, *Letters*, I, 395). Thus this letter, dated September 16 in the copy in the Public Record Office, was almost certainly written on the seventeenth, when, as Mary's journal notes, "PBS out on business."

[54] By Robert Southey (1810).

[55] G. B. Ballachey was the bond broker or moneylender through whom Shelley hoped to auction a post-obit bond; he was a member of the firm of Ballachey and Bridges (White, *Shelley*, I, 369, 685).

[56] Veit Weber [pseud. of George Philipp Waechter], *The Sorcerer: A Tale from the German* [trans. Robert Huish?] (London: J. Johnson, 1795); William

Tuesday Sept. 20th. Rise late. Shelley goes to Ballachey's   Read
Emile — Write also. Dine at Seven — Shelley reads aloud Thalaba
till Bed time.[57]

Wednesday Sept. 21st. Rise late — Shelley goes with Hookham to
the Sale [58] — ⟨No⟩ Obliged to buy the Reversion etc. — Write &
learn Gre[ek] Characters. Hookham dines. Goes Early. Write
Greek again.

Thursday Sept 22nd. After Breakfast walk out with M & S — Search
for drawings. Return at ⟨2⟩ 4. Read Greek. Letter from Harriet.
Mean & worldly [59] — ⟨Re⟩ Sit up till one reading the Monk.[60]

Friday Sept. 23rd. Finish the Monk. Walk after breakfast with
M & S — Go to Hookham's. & Priestly's in Holborn [61] — Buy a
Greek Anacreon. & the ⟨pr⟩ Life of Johanna Southcott.[62] When
we get home find a letter from Papa. ⟨Very prejudiced &⟩ [*two
more words thoroughly crossed out*] — Read Greek — Hookham
dines — Shelley reads Thalaba aloud in the Evening. Write a
little Gre[ek] & learn four tenses of the Verb to strike —

Saturday Sept. 24th. Shelley & Mary to Ballachey's. Learn ειμι [63]
— Read Lewis Tales of Wonder & Delight.[64] Shelley reads aloud

Godwin, *An Enquiry Concerning the Principles of Political Justice, and Its Influence on General Virtue and Happiness*, 2 vols. (London: G. G. J. and J.
Robinson, 1793).

[57] Robert Southey, *Thalaba the Destroyer*, 2 vols. (1801).

[58] "No bidder at the sale" (in *Mary Shelley's Journal*, p. 16).

[59] See *Mary Shelley's Journal*, p. 16.

[60] By Matthew Gregory Lewis (1796), also read at this time by Shelley and
Mary.

[61] From a bookseller, probably Priestly, they bought a guinea's worth of
books (in *Mary Shelley's Journal*, p. 16).

[62] Both Mary and Claire were studying Greek with Shelley at this time.
The entry "Read two odes of Anacreon before breakfast" in the Shelleys'
journal for September 25 is in Mary's hand (Abinger MSS.). *The Life of Joanna Southcott, the Prophetess: Containing an Impartial Account of Her Wonderful . . .
Writings, Her Miraculous Conception, . . .* (London, 1814). There were at
least a dozen editions in this year.

[63] The verb "to be."

[64] Matthew Gregory Lewis, *Tales of Wonder* [in verse], 2 vols. (London,
1801). Claire may have had on her mind the subtitle of Lady Mount Cashell's
*Stories of Old Daniel: Or Tales of Wonder and Delight*, published by Mrs.
Godwin's Juvenile Library in 1807.

Thalaba in the Evening finishes it. Write Greek — Read Smellie.[65]

Sunday Sept. 25th. Write Greek. Read Smellie Philosophy [o]f Natural History. Mr. Peacock dines. Shelley & he go to Mr. Warre's [66] in Norfolk Street.

Monday Sept. 26th. Read the Empire of the Nairs [67] & Smellie. Mr. Peacock at breakfast. Do no Greek — Letter from Amory — Shelley writes to him & Harriet.[68] — Read the Empir[e] of the Nairs —

Tuesday Sept. 27th. Read Smellie. Pack up all Morning. Remove about five o'clock to ⟨St⟩ Pancrass.[69] Read Smellie in the Evening.

Wednesday Sept. 28th. Read Smellie. Walk to Margaret Street.[70] Peacock at breakfast. Hookham call. Read Smellie. Walk again to Russell Square. Mary Shelley & Peacock go to Ballachey's. P— at tea — Mr. Finnis call.[71]

Thursday Sept. 29th. Walk to Hookham's. Call in Margaret Street. Shelley goes to Westminster Insurance Office. Read Smellie.

Friday September ⟨2⟩ 30. Walk to Hampstead heath — with M. & S — Most beautiful ⟨P⟩Promenade Project the plan of carrying off poor [E]liza & Helen — Return. Peacock calls — Shelley takes him out tells him the plan — I go to Margaret Street — meet Mr Corsi. Peacock likes our plan — he dines.[72]

[65] William Smellie, *The Philosophy of Natural History*, 2 vols. (Edinburgh, 1790, 1799).

[66] Warry's (in *Mary Shelley's Journal*, p. 16).

[67] Sir James Henry Lawrence ("Chevalier Lawrence"), *The Empire of the Nairs; or, the Rights of Women*, 4 vols. (London: Edward and Thomas Hookham, 1811).

[68] The letter to Harriet is in Shelley, *Letters*, I, 396–397.

[69] At Mrs. Page's, 5 Church Terrace, Somers Town (in *Mary Shelley's Journal*, p. 16, and White, *Shelley*, I, 368).

[70] But "Jane goes to Hookham" (in *Mary Shelley's Journal*, p. 17).

[71] A moneylender.

[72] Shelley alludes to the plan in the journal: "Discuss the possibility of converting & liberating two heiresses. Arrange a plan on this subject . . . .Peacock calls. Talk with him concerning the heiresses & Marianne Arrange his marriage" (in *Mary Shelley's Journal*, p. 17, and White, *Shelley*, I, 371–372). Shelley's sisters, Eliza and Hellen, were in Mrs. Hugford's school at Hackney. Marianne de St. Croix's relationship with Peacock is summarized by F. L. Jones, in Mary Shelley, *Letters*, I, 67–68n.

# London 1814

Saturday ⟨Sept.⟩ October 1st. Peacock at breakfast — Walk with him Mary & Shelley to Hackey — cal[l] at Mrs. Hugford's — see Eliza Helen & Anne — Return home without Peacock who ⟨dines⟩ joins us at dinner. — Talk over our Plan the whole Evening — Letter from Tavernier.[73] Hookham calls.

Sunday Oct. 2nd. Peacock at breakfast — We all go to a Pond past Primrose Hill & make Paper Boats & sail them — Talk over our Plan the whole day — Mary very tired & goes to bed early — We talk a long time about our plan with Peacock after whose departure

[*one leaf torn out*]

⟨& perfectly⟩ natural & perfectly ⟨in⟩ [*a word thoroughly crossed out*] well sustained through the whole — ⟨In Pri⟩ melancholy parts [*a word thoroughly crossed out*] are[?] written in a strain ↑of↓ poetry & deep feeling.[74]

Tuesday Oct. 4th. Shelley early to Finnis's & Ballachey's. Read Alexy ⟨Humi⟩ Haimatoff twice through — more delighted with it — Mary writes to Isabel[75] — Shelley to Hogg[76] & I to Tavernier — In the Evening read Political Justice — Sit up till twelve. Shelley makes chemical experiments.

Wednesday Oct 5th. Peacock at Breakfast — Talk of Pigault Le Brun & his detestable Works.[77] Go with Mary & Shelley to Primrose Hill Pond & sail fire Boats — Return to Dinner. Read Political Justice    Shelley reads aloud the Ancient Mariner. & Mad ⟨Mother⟩

[73] Tavernier was probably a lawyer or moneylender. He had produced £60 for the party in Paris in August, had dined with them, and conducted them about town (in *Mary Shelley's Journal*, pp. 5–6). In March of 1815 he was seeing Godwin (diaries of William Godwin, Abinger MSS.).

[74] Possibly a comment on Thomas Jefferson Hogg's *Memoirs of Prince Alexy Haimatoff*, by "John Brown" (London: Hookham, 1813).

[75] Isabel Baxter, Mary's school friend, later Mrs. David Booth. See entry for November 3, 1814, and Note 17, below.

[76] Shelley's letter acquaints Hogg with the history of his separation from Harriet and the new contentment and integrity he has found with Mary (Shelley, *Letters*, I, 401–403).

[77] Pigault-Lebrun was a novelist of the Revolution, whose works are permeated with his hatred of priestcraft and tyranny. It is difficult to see why they were "detestable" at this time. Peacock wrote of them later in "French Comic Romances," *London Review*, 2:69–84 (July 1835).

Mother. Mary goes early to Bed — Sit up till one over the fire ⟨talking with Shelley — he writes an answer to Harriet⟩ [78]

Thursday Oct. 6th. Peacock at breakfast — Read a little of Political Justice — Walk out by myself to Kentish Town — ⟨See a funeral⟩ — Run after Patty & Eliza — Peacock stays wearying us all the morning — Dine at six. Shelley writes to Mrs. Hugford ⟨&⟩ After dinner he reads part of St Godwin aloud — terrible nonsense [79] — ⟨How did the author dare to paraphrase such a Book as St Leon⟩ — ⟨Even the Ideot would with his sacrilegeous hand refrain from polluting Beauties he could not imagine.⟩ Hookham call . . . . Read some of Mary Wollstonecraft's letters in the Evening.

Friday Oct. 7th. Peacock at Breakfast — Read Political Justice. Shelley Mary & Peacock walk out in the fields — I go by myself in the Squares — Dine at six. Peacock goes at eight — Mary goes to Bed — Shelley & myself sit over the fire — we talk of making an Association of philosophical people [80] — of Eliza & Helen — of Hogg & Harriet — at one the conversation turned upon those unaccountable & mysterious feelings ↑about supernatural things↓ that we are sometime subject to — Shelley looks beyond all passing strange — a look of impressive deep & melancholy awe — I cannot describe it I well know how I felt it — I ran upstairs to bed — I placed the candle on the drawers & stood looking at a pillow that lay in the very middle of the Bed — I turned my head round to the window & then back again to the Bed — the pillow was no longer there — it had been removed to the chair — I stood thinking for two mo-

---

[78] "The Mad Mother" is one of the poems by Wordsworth in *Lyrical Ballads* (1798). The letter to Harriet is in Shelley, *Letters*, I, 404–405.

[79] Claire's original sentence order, which she corrected, was: "After dinner Shelley writes to Mrs. Hugford ⟨&⟩ he reads part of St Godwin aloud." The parody was *St. Godwin: A Tale of the Sixteenth, Seventeenth, and Eighteenth Century*, by "Count Reginald De St. Leon" [Edward du Bois] (London, 1800).

[80] Shelley's entry says, "Jane states her conception of the subterraneous community of women" (in *Mary Shelley's Journal*, p. 18). This may have been inspired by a reading of Ludvig Holberg's *A Journey to the World Under-Ground. By Nicholas Klimius* (London, 1742), which describes the underground province of Cocklecu, where the "Order of Nature" is reversed, and the females behave like males, "in Possession of all Honours and Employments sacred, civil, or military" (p. 119).

ments—how did this come? Was it possible that I had deluded myself so far as to place it there myself & then forget the action? This was not likely—Every passed at it w⟨h⟩ere in a moment—I ran down stairs—Shelley heard me & came out of his room—He gives the most horrible description of my counte-tenance—I did not feel in the way he thinks I did—We sat up all night—I was ill—At day break we examined the room & found every thing in the State I described—[81]

Saturday Oct 8th. Rise at twelve—Not well—Walk with Shelley & Mary into the fields—Sit by the fire all day in a melancholy mood—Go to Bed at nine.

Sunday Oct—9th—Rise late—Read Political Justice—Hookham calls—⟨Want to send him the wrong way to⟩ [*a word thoroughly crossed out*]—Peacock tell him our horrors—he laughs at us—Shelley reads aloud part of Abbé Barruel about the Illuminati—⟨Mary⟩ ↑We↓ goes to bed at eight—⟨sit up with Shelley over the fire⟩—get rather in a horrid mood—⟨go to bed at eleven⟩ ↑thinking of ghosts↓ cannot sleep all night.

Monday Oct—10th. Read Political Justice—Walk with Shelley & Mary to Oxford Street—Buy shoes S—calls at Finnis's. Come home by the Regent's Park—They walk farther I come home & read Political Justice—Peacock calls—Alarming letter from Harriet—S— & P go to Dr Sims[82]—not at home—Peacock goes at five—After dinner we set out with the intention of my seeing Harriet. Call at Dr. Sims—not at home—Miss Sims knows nothing—proceed a little further & then change our intention & return home—I go over the fields to find a messenger—Send to Harriet & Dr. Sims—They go to Bed—sit up till twelve when the messenger returns with a letter from Dr. Sims assuring us ⟨of⟩ that Harriet's danger is not very considerable. Read through Zastrozzi—by Shelley.

Tuesday Oct. 11th. Read Political Justice—Peacock all morning

[81] For Shelley's detailed account of this attack of horrors, see *Mary Shelley's Journal*, pp. 18–19.

[82] Harriet wrote "of what she imagines a dangerous illness" (in *Mary Shelley's Journal*, p. 19). Dr. J. Sims of 67 Guilford Street was her physician (Shelley, *Letters*, I, 400n., 406).

# First Journal

& at dinner. Walk by myself in the Squares — Peacock goes early — Shelley reads [a]loud Abbe Barruel — the Illuminati — Letter from Harriet — cheerful — from Mrs. Boinville — very sneering [83] — ⟨Mary goes to bed early⟩ — read Political Justice & talk with Shelley over the fire till — 12 o'clock

Wednesday Oct. 12 — Rise late — Note from Marshal [84] — Write to him — Go to him — Long talk — Fanny Holcroft comes while I am there [85] — Return about two — Go with Mary & Shelley to Finnis's & an auctioneer's in Newgate St — Return to dinner at six. Read Abbé Barruel. To bed at ten.

Thursday — 13th. Read Political Justice. Walk with Shelley to Southampton Buildings [86] — Meet Peacock & St Croix — Peacock returns with us — Long talk about removing — Dine at four — Set out for Drury Lane — call on Peacock — We go to the Boxes — he goes to Covent Garden — Kean in Hamlet — all every thing very detestable — come away at the End of the second act [87] — Return to Pancras — we don't like the house [88] — get a Coach & sleep at the Stratford Hotel — In the Morning see Mama in Holborn.

⟨Thursday⟩ Friday Oct. 14 — Get up late — Go down in a very ill humour — Quarrel with Shelley [89] — But to know one's faults is to mend them — perhaps this morning though productive of very painful feelings has in reality been of more essential benefit to me than any I ever yet passed — How hateful it is to quarrel — to

[83] Madame de Boinville's coldness must have come as a blow to Shelley, who had just written Hogg about his two months with her in the spring of 1814 as "probably the happiest of my life" (Shelley, *Letters*, I, 401). Her letter marks the formal end of their relationship.

[84] Godwin's old friend. See Paul, *Godwin*, I, 47.

[85] The daughter of Godwin's good friend Thomas Holcroft. See Paul, *Godwin*, II, 110–115.

[86] Peacock's residence.

[87] Edmund Kean was making a "progress through the circle of Shakespeare's characters" at Drury Lane. The *Courier* (October 14, 1814) found his performance uneven, with a "stop-watch" reading of "To be, or not to be" which merited no applause.

[88] For some account of the panics and alarms of this week, see *Mary Shelley's Journal*, pp. 19–21. The entry for October 13 is in Shelley's hand.

[89] Shelley records his despair at "Janes insensibility & incapacity for the slightest degree of friendship" and his skeptical amusement at her latest hallucinations (in *Mary Shelley's Journal*, pp. 20–21).

say a thousand unkind things — meaning none — things produced by the bitterness of disappointment — ⟨I hate these feelings⟩ — Walk home through the Regent's Park — Leave them & go home by myself. Peacock calls — Laughs at us — Good news of Eliza — Shelley comes into my room & thinks he was to blame — but I don't — how I like good kind explaining people — S & P go to the Pond — Walk out a little by myself. Peacock goes after tea — Read St. Leon [90] — go to bed at ⟨ten⟩ nine — About ½ after ten Shelley comes up & ⟨makes⟩ I go down & sleep with Mary because I groan — ⟨can't think what the deuce is the matter with me — "I weep yet never know why — I sigh yet feel no pain."⟩[91] Go to sleep at ½ past two.

Saturday Oct. 15. Shelley goes about his money & with Peacock to Homerton — Copy the letter to the Dutchess of York — Write to Marshall — Letter to me from Papa — Walk out in the fields with Mary anxiously waiting the return of Shelley — They return about six. Write a refusal — Peacock goes after tea — Go to bed early — Don't sleep at all — Note from Marshal

Sunday Oct 16. Peacock at breakfast — Hookham calls — Walk with S— & M— to Kentish Town — very uncomfortable Walk Peacock dines — He goes after tea — ⟨Mary goes to Bed⟩—⟨Shelley explains he thought I despised him⟩—⟨We talk till near one⟩— [92]

Monday Oct — 17 — Breakfast in Southampton Buildings — Shelley goes about his money affairs — Disappointed — Dine — Hookham at tea — Sleep in Southhampton Buildings — Read Memoires de Voltaire by Himself [93] — Letter from Hogg. very cold — [94]

Tuesday Oct — 18 Rise at nine — breakfast ensemble — Peacock & Shelley to Ballachey's  Disappointed — the glorious uncertainty of

[90] Godwin's *St. Leon: A Tale of the Sixteenth Century*, 3 vols. (London, 1799).

[91] Claire did her very best to obliterate this passage, which is legible in infrared enlargements.

[92] Another passage assiduously crossed out.

[93] Possibly *Mémoires de M. de Voltaire écrits par lui-même*, bound together with its translation, *Memoirs of the Life of Voltaire. Written by Himself* (London, 1784).

[94] "Letter from Hogg. — cold & unfriendly. Few friendly spirits in the world," writes Mary (cf. *Mary Shelley's Journal*, p. 21).

the law — Mary & I walk to Pancras — Very rainy — We borrow an umbrella — return to Southampton Buildings after resting half an hour — find ⟨that⟩ Shelley gone to Pancras in search of us — He returns soon — Dine ⟨with Mr⟩ ensemble — Return in a coach to Pancras about nine. ⟨Mary goes to Bed⟩ — ⟨Talk with Shelley⟩ ↑Talk↓ over the fire till two[95] — Hogg — his letter — friendship — Dante — Tasso & various other subjects. Eliza's birthday.[96]

Wednesday Oct 19th. Rise late — Read Prince Alexy Haimatoff again — read also Political Justice — Shelley all morning at Ballachey's — Disappointment about the money — Walk to Turnstile in Holborn by myself ⟨al⟩ look at some shawls — Very rainy morning — Mary says things which I construe into unkindness — I was wrong — We soon become friends but I felt deeply ⟨at⟩ the imaginary cruelties I conjured up — In the Evening read Memoires of Voltaire by himself.

Thursday Oct — 20th Rise at eight. Shelley to Ballachey with Peacock who returns & spends the morning — S— had seen Bramley who gave him some hope — Read Political Justice — About four o'clock take a walk in the squares by myself — Peacock had called upon Papa this morning — he will hear nothing from any friend [of] Mr. Shelley's — Let him send his Attorney — Dine at six — Peacock goes — After dinner read Political Justice — Shelley & Mary to Bed early — read Memoires of Voltaire — & the Life of Alfieri till late — [97] [one leaf torn out] I am much delighted with Alfieri — He seems to have possessed much genius & enthusiasm — but certainly he was never very far from raving Mad — the anecdotes of his infancy are delightful — an attentive & philosophical person would surely have observed in them the first traits of genius — He was a detirmined republican but he seems to have appropriated his fortune entirely to the procuring an endless variety of delights. Hookham calls in the morning — tells us about Ringer ⟨I in a fit of fury

[95] Mary's comment: "I go to bed soon — but Shelley and Jane sit up and for a wonder do not frighten themselves" (in *Mary Shelley's Journal*, p. 21).
[96] Since Shelley's sister's birthday was in May (White, *Shelley*, I, 564), the Eliza of this reference, and perhaps of the October 6 reference, may well be an unidentified friend in London.
[97] *Memoirs of the Life and Writings of Victor Alfieri: Written by Himself*, 2 vols. (London: Henry Colburn, 1810).

write a letter to Mama but do not send it⟩ — ⟨It may only irritate them with us   it were better this should be avoided — It is certainly very⟩[98]

[one leaf torn out]

till she returns — tell her — she rejoices — Go out again by myself to the top of Piccadilly — When I get home find Mr. Starling just going away — He had obliged Shelley to give him a Bill at a month — Dine at six — When the cloth was removed the servant enters with a letter which a little boy said a lady waiting in the opposite field [h]ad sent him with. It was from Fanny [99]   Shelley & I hasten to the field — I catch hold of her — She foolishly screams & runs away — She escapes — Shelley & I hasten to Skinner St. We watch through the window   we see Papa, Mama, & Charles — Step into Wallis's & write Charles a little note — Take it into the shop myself — I request a moment's interview — Charles after much deliberation grants it — He comes out — I ask him everything about the Hookham's — He denies knowing anything in such a voice that I thought him sincere — We return — call at Peacock's. only his mother at home — We go to Auber's in Everitt St. for him — Tell him every thing — Return to Pancrass about nine — We consult write a note to Fanny — To bed at twelve —

Sunday Oct 23 — Get up at six — Mary, Shelley, & I go to Skinner St — Watch till the Shutters are opened — Ring at the Bell — Fanny opens it — Talk to her — Surprizing treachery of the Hookham'[s]   I find Charles deceived me last night   After 5 minutes conversation with Fanny we return. ⟨to⟩ call in our way back at South hampton Buildings — Breakfast there — Mary & I return to Pancrass by ourselves — Shelley & Peacock to Hookham & Tahourdin.[1] Hookham not at home — the little sly rascal got out of the Way — Shelley returns alone about one — Consult how to raise fifty Pounds for Chartres[2] — In the course of which Consultation

[98] After attempting to obliterate what she had written, Claire tore out a leaf. The next entry is Saturday, October 22.

[99] The note from Fanny Imlay was to warn them of the supposed treachery of the Hookhams. See Shelley, *Letters*, I, 408n., for Jones's summary of this crisis and his suggestion that Hookham's offense was probably in revealing Shelley's address to his creditors.

[1] Shelley's lawyer.

[2] Thomas Charters (or Chartres), the coachmaker, was one of the chief

we all quarrel — Shelley makes all right again in his usual Way —
Peacock comes — Set out by myself for Chapel St — Write a letter
to Harriet — bear one from Shelley — drop the letters — wait up
& down Park Lane call again — Receive a letter ⟨from⟩ for S—
Return about six — Have tea — Peacock & Shelley set off about ½
past eight[3] — Sleep with Mary — Harriet promises to raise money
for Chartres —

Monday Oct. 24th. Rise at eight — Breakfast — Write my Journal
— M. reads aloud She stoops to [C]onquer — She sets out to see
Shelley at eleven — I stay at home & read Political Justice — Go about
one to Mrs. Peacock's — Mary comes   she has not seen Shelley[4] —
She goes home — I return & stay in Fleet St till 3 — o'clock — come
back to Peacock's — Maryann there — Go home to Pancras — I find
M set out for London ⟨g⟩ again. Suspicious men been in my absence[5] — Set out again for Southampton Buildings — find only
poor old Mrs. P. at home — have some grumbling Conversation with
her — most luckily M. comes in search of P — she had been to the
Coffeehous[e] & seen Shelley — I go out to him in Holborn — we
go to Harris's the optician — he won't have our miscroscope — I go
to Peacock fetch him & the microscope — He talks to Shelley a little
while in Holborn   S— & I go to Davison's in Skinner St. We are
sent away for half an hour — Walk up & down Chatham Place
though we are both so tired we can hardly stand — I am so hungry
for I had had nothing since Breakfast & it was now six o'clock —
Return again to Davison's   get 5 Pounds — for our microscope[6] —
In my absence Peacock had gone all the way to Pancras we were
not at home — he sees the waiter of St Jame's Hotel there — much
frightened & returns home — Part with S in Holborn — Send Peacock to him — Have some dinner in Southhampton St. Return with

---

creditors threatening Shelley at this time. For a summary of the financial puzzle,
see White, *Shelley*, I, 687–688.

[3] From this night until November 9 Shelley was in hiding from the bailiffs.

[4] See Shelley's explanation (Shelley, *Letters*, I, 408).

[5] "I suppose bailiffs," says Mary (in *Mary Shelley's Journal*, p. 22).

[6] Shortly after this Shelley wrote to Harriet: "We have even now sold all
that we have to buy bread. I am with a friend who supplies me with food &
lodging, but I think you will shudder to hear that before I could sell the last
valuable Mary & her sister near[ly] perished with hunger" (Shelley, *Letters*, I,
410).

# London 1814

M. in a Coach about ½ past eight[7] — Find that a gentleman (I suppose Charles) had been with a letter from Fanny to me in our absence — that the extraordinary way he had knocked at the door had almos[t] frightened the children in to fainting fits. Fanny requests an interview at Marshall's tomorrow — To bed at nine.

Tuesday Oct. 25 — Rise late. Go to Marshall's at ½ past eleven — Meet Fanny — talk with her till three[8] — Walk home with her to Brownlow St — Return to Mary   dine — We go to Peacocks — Go to Holborn & meet Shelley — Walk up & down Bartlett's Buildings. Go into a Pastry-Cook's — Shelley comes with us to Southampton Buildings. We return to Pancrass at ten in a Coach. Patrickson's death.[9]

Wednesday Oct. 26th Visit from the Bailiffs — They are much disappointed — Mary goes to meet Shelley at St Pauls — We read in the Evening.

Thursday Oct. 27. Fanny calls early & leaves a letter from herself & Charles — Mary goes to Shelley   She takes the letters to him. I answer Fanny's letter — I walk about Kentish Town fields — Mary returns at six — Read & sleep in the Evening.

Friday Oct. 28th. ⟨Go⟩ I receive two letters from Shelley[10] Read — I have ↑spent↓ three very idle inactive days — Fit of enthusiasm. I remember what Shelley said in Margaret St. & I make new vows

[7] See Mary's account (Mary Shelley, *Letters*, I, 3–4).

[8] Mary records on this day the desire of the Godwins for Claire to go into a family (*Mary Shelley's Journals*, p. 22). On November 8 Godwin wrote to his friend Taylor of Norwich that they had proposed first that she go as a governess; when she declined, they suggested that she go as a visitor in some family. She offered to comply on two conditions: "That she should in all situations openly proclaim and earnestly support, a total contempt for the laws and institutions of society, and that no restraint should be imposed upon her correspondence and intercourse with those from whom she was separated" (Ingpen, *Shelley in England*, pp. 641–642).

[9] P. Patrickson had been Godwin's protégé since 1810. His morbid letters from Cambridge during the following three years had reflected a growing paranoia, and after composing a gloomy suicide note to Godwin he shot himself on August 10, 1814 (Paul, *Godwin*, II, 192–200). For Mary's grim comment see *Mary Shelley's Journal*, p. 22.

[10] One had been written in a feigned hand to surprise her (Shelley, *Letters*, I, 413).

# First Journal

— These shall not be ⟨br⟩ broken — I think he'll find himself mistaken — What a divine Pleasure — Mary goes to Shelley    I walk out by myself about Kentish Town — Read Comus. Mary returns to dinner at six. A letter to her from Mama.[11] Go to bed at nine.

Saturday — 29th. Get up late. Have a letter from Shelley. Read Comus. & Prince Alexy Haimatoff — Mary goes to Shelley. I write a long letter to him. Walk a little although it rains — Mary returns to dinner at six. Read after dinner. Walk up & down till half past twelve when Shelley comes.[12] Go to bed soon after.

Sunday Oct 30th. Rise at nine — Breakfast — write my Journal — Hookham calls — He stays an hour & then departs — We talk & dispute about Peacock — We [d]iscuss about Mary's going with Shelley — We talk over Harriet's Plan of ruining Papa — [*a word or two thoroughly crossed out*] Dine at four. Read Comus. Shelley & Mary sleep till eight. M. dresses & packs up — S. & M go away in a coach at ½ past 8 — Shelley very nervous & sleepy — Sit up till ten reading Queen Mab —

Monday Oct. 31st Get up at nine. Breakfast. Read a Canto of Queen Mab & Louvet's Memoirs.[13] I am much interested for Louvet — but like all French men he is so intolerably full of himself & never lets the reader find out the merit he may possess — but praises his own actions in the grossest way — he forsees — he plans — he would direct — but his prognostications are not attended to — his plans are neglected & his directions unobeyed — he then shews how much Injury ⟨to⟩ the cause of Republicanism suffered from Condorcet & Brissot's want of his penetration & judgement — Surely this could not have been the case — A man of Condorcet's wonderful genius must have seen deeper into thing than Louvet — by whose account Condorcet's weakness was the cause of Robespierre's maintaining his situation & of his numerous Massacres — Mrs. Page [14] wants some money — Set out in search ⟨in⟩ of Shelley & Mary — Go to Aldersgate St. see Mama in Charlton St. they are

[11] For Mary's reaction of hatred for Mrs. Godwin, see *Mary Shelley's Journal*, p. 23; and Mary Shelley, *Letters*, I, 4.

[12] Debtors were exempt from arrest on Sundays.

[13] Jean-Baptiste Louvet de Couvray, *Narrative of the Dangers to Which I Have Been Exposed, since the 31st of May, 1793* (London: J. Johnson, 1795).

[14] The landlady.

not at the Castle & Falcon — search for them call twice at Peacock's — find them at the Cross-Keys Keys St John Street.[15] Very detestable situation. Dine with them — Shelley walks home with me as far as Peacock's. — When I get home find a letter from Mary & that Charles has been — Sit up till eleven reading Louvet's Memoirs. I never remember be more interested in any book — So many fine instances of individual republican spirits displayed — so many generous Women — such constancy in misfortune.

Tuesday Nov. 1st. Letter from Shelley. Breakfast. Read Louvet's Memoirs. Set out for Cross Keys — Write to Fanny there — gone out — Impertinence from the Master of the Tavern — Set out in a Coach for Hookham's  See him — Return to Cross Keys. Set out for home — Write a Note to Charles — Send it by the daughter of the Woodman — Note from him that he will come — Call at Peacock — Send a note to them — Auber there. Return to Pancrass about six — Charles comes — Takes tea — Walk with him to Peacock's  Shelley there — find Mary gone home — Get into a coach & reach home at ten — find Mary's Coach at the door.

Wednesday Nov. 2nd. Get up at nine. Write my Journal — Take a Walk with Mary to High Holborn. Read Political Justice. Chapter on Necessity. Go to Sommers town for some Plays. Letter from Shelley to Mary [16] — Dine at four. Read & sleep in the Evening. Go to bed at ten.

Thursday Nov — 3rd. Rise at nine. Read Political Justice. Go to Mrs. Peacock's — Shelley & her Son out. Letter to Mary from David Booth [17] — Dine at four — Read after dinner some Plays.

[15] Mary had spent the night there with Shelley.

[16] See Shelley, *Letters*, I, 415–416.

[17] David Booth (1766–1846), brewer and lexicographer, had married Margaret Baxter and after her death married illegally, in 1814, his deceased wife's sister, Isabella, Mary's childhood friend. Mary had spent long visits with the Baxters in Dundee in 1812 and 1813 and described Isabella as adoring the shade of Mary Wollstonecraft (see Mary Shelley, *Letters*, I, 5, and n.). Thus Booth's severing of relations between his new, but illegal, wife and Mary came as a depressing blow. In her journal for November 3 she wrote: "Receive a letter from Mr. Booth — so all my hopes are over there — ah Isabel I did not think you would act thus" (in *Mary Shelley's Journal*, p. 24). Since Baxter was suffering some persecution about his own "unlawful marriage" at this time, his unexpected conservatism no doubt stemmed from the necessity of avoiding

# First Journal

Have a small note from Shelley in which ⟨he is suspicious⟩ he ⟨th⟩ says he is unhappy — ⟨God in heaven⟩ what has he to be unhappy about! Go to Bed at ten.

Friday Nov. 4th. Rise at nine. Finish a novel called Manfroné or the one handed monk by Mrs. Radcliffe.[18] this is the morning when S— will receive money — If he does not I know not what we shall do — Dine at one — Go with Mary to Gray's Inn Gardens to meet Shelley — Walk about with him till four — Return home. Work & read all Evening. I am much disappointed in Shelley to-day — I thought him uniformly kind & considerate but I find him act as weakly as other people —

Saturday Nov. 5th. Rise late. Work all morning. Very rainy — take a Walk for all that to South hampton Buildings — A letter from Shelley — putting all the fault of yesterday's Interview on me — Dine at four — About six Mary proposes that we should go for Shelley in a Coach — We do so — He won't come — Return home — M. sleeps on the Sofa  Write a scene in Gertrude. Very shocking. S— comes home at ½ past twelve.

Sunday Nov. 6th. Rise at nine — Talk all Morning — Read Prince Alexy Haimatoff & King Richard III. Shelley writes many letters. Dine at four. Mary & Shelley & I sleep all Evening — S goes at ten — Very philosophical Way of spending the day — To sleep & talk — why this is merely vegetating —

Monday Nov. 7th. Rise at nine — Work. Read Political Justice — Mary dines at one & goes to Shelley. Read King Richard the Third — Dine by myself at four. Mary returns at six — Talk with her. & read some miscellaneous poetry — Hogg is going to drink tea with

---

any further damage to his respectability. See the *Dundee Courier*, July 8, 1922, quoted in *Shelley and His Circle*, II, 558–559. Another attempt by the Shelleys to reopen this relationship failed in 1817 (see Mary Shelley, *Letters*, I, 30, and n.). Mary continued to cherish the memory of her childhood friend, but when they did finally meet on December 1, 1830, the encounter was disenchanting, and Mary could only exclaim in her journal: "Good heavens is this the being I adored" (Abinger MSS.).

[18] Mary-Anne Radcliffe, *Manfroné; or, the One-handed Monk* (London, 1809). A follower of Mary Wollstonecraft, Mrs. Radcliffe, who also wrote on the subject of the rights of women, should not be confused with Ann Radcliffe, author of *The Italian* and *The Mysteries of Udolpho*.

# London 1814

Shelley to-night — Shelley had seen ⟨C⟩ Charles & Lambert [19] — the last is playing a double part — but I think ⟨we will⟩ we shall not suffer him to deceive us — Lambert is worth £300,000 & he oppresses & insults Godwin for the paltry sum of a hundred & fifty — pretending at the same time to admire his energy & talent — And it is for these people that Godwin has sacrificed his happiness & well-being — that he refuses to see his daughter & Shelley — the two people he loves best in the World.

Tuesday Nov. 8th. Rise at nine — Read through the Man of Feeling who would have just suited Fanny for a husband.[20] Mary writes to Isabel [Baxter]. I copy the letter for her. She dines at two & goes to meet Shelley — violent storm of thunder & lightning — one clap was the loudest I ever heard — Read Political Justice. Mary re[turns] about six. Shelley had seen Charles in the morning who had taken Hogan [21] the £ 10 — Hogg had ⟨M⟩ been with him the Evening before & asked him after his *two Wives*. He joked all the time & talked of the Pleasures of Hunting — It [f]ills me with surprize that the Author of Prince Alexy Haimatoff should delight in Sporting & Hunting — Human Nature is a Composition of Contradictions. Read Paul & Virginia [22] — in the Evening. I admire the descriptions [*one leaf torn out, with* Skin *and* We *legible at the beginnings of the two bottom lines on the edge*] [of] this beautiful Country. The Story is ⟨int⟩ in itself trifling & uninteresting — the speeches and Characters are inflated & unnatural. Go to bed at nine — Talk with Mary till eleven — who tells me about Moving tomorrow.[23]

Wednesday Nov. 9th. Rise at nine. Spend the morning [in] Packing up. Dine at one — Send [f]or a Coach at three — Great plague with the Coachman & ⟨pac⟩ putting in the Trunks. Drive to Southampton Building. Take up Shelley — Proceed to Nelsons Square — The way stopped by [*next three leaves torn out, with*

---

[19] See Shelley, *Letters*, I, 416.

[20] Henry MacKenzie, *The Man of Feeling* (Edinburgh, 1771). The hero represents an extreme of tenderheartedness.

[21] Like Lambert, one of Godwin's creditors.

[22] Jacques Henri Bernardin de Saint-Pierre, *Paul and Virginia*, trans. Helen Maria Williams (London, 1795).

[23] Shelley suggested that Mary discuss Pimlico or Sloane Street with Claire (Shelley, *Letters*, I, 420).

# First Journal

wa   Ski *and* We *legible on the first of the three remaining scraps
and*   I won   -un   who *and* observ   *legible on the second*] [24]

Rigi [25]
Micherboden
Blamire
Meheux
Matravers.


Ultra montanis [26]
U              montanis
I have nothing left to do but to frolic [?] in the Sun for your Amusement

Murgantalle                    Zoffingen

*[Claire's entries stop here; the rest of the writing is in Shelley's
hand]* [27]

[24] Claire's reason for tearing out the last entries of her journal may be guessed from Mary's entry on this day: "Jane very gloomy — she is very sullen with Shelley." On the following day, November 10, Mary for the first time refers to her as Clara: "Clara is not well & does not speak the whole day. . . . Shelley & Clara sit up till 12 — talking — S talks C. into a good humour" (cf. *Mary Shelley's Journal*, p. 25).

[25] Claire listed these place names sideways on the page (as if the right margin were the top of the page). They relate to the visit to Switzerland, Rigi, for example, being a mountain seen from Lake Lucerne, and Micherboden a promontory in that lake. Following this are five pages in Shelley's hand (see Note 27 below).

[26] These few notes, in Claire's hand, appear on the inside of the back cover. Murgantalle and Zoffingen (visited on August 23) seem to begin the list of Swiss place names continued above (see Note 25).

[27] The five pages of Shelley's notes and compositions are here transcribed in the order in which they appear to have been written. Apparently Shelley handed over to Claire this notebook which he had started to use, and she turned it upside down, beginning her entries from the other end. Thus, in transcribing Shelley's writing, I am starting with the first page inside the back cover and working back toward the point at which Claire had finished. Others who have described these pages and transcribed them in part are Ingpen (quoted in Grylls, *Claire Clairmont*, pp. 249–250), White (*Shelley*, I, 702–703), and Robertson ("Unpublished Verses by Shelley," *MLR* 48:181–184 [April 1953]). Their readings differ from each other, and my reading differs from theirs in some details. I tend to agree with Miss Robertson that both internal and external evidence suggests

# London 1814

Gallica Encyclopedia non obliviscenda!.[28]

Lasciate ogni Speranza, voi ché intrate.[29]

Basia labris impressit! Subito omne terrestre vestitur coloribus eternis coeli. Adhuc vivo . . . adhuc maestum lumen adspicio! Terribili solitud[ine] contempli amoris sicut captivus miser content[*a few letters burned*] Sum adhuc vivere! Suscitabam somnis neg[*a few letters burned*] libitium deliciosum — Cur sordidum vener[*a few letters burned*] vitalis poculi [?] imbibo? Cessatur spumare felicat[*a letter or two burned*] et immortalitate

Lecto me brachiis tenebat, delisio voluptatis peue deliquio cecidi. Basies mutes vitae reclamabunt delecta labia! Timores quiescebat.[30]

---

Nondum amabam, sed amare amabam, quiesebar quid amarem amans amare.[31]

---

[Tr]ue knowledge leads to love. The meanest of our [fel]low

that these entries were made in 1814 before the notebook was turned over to Claire.

[28] Apropos of Shelley's hope that the French encyclopedia not be forgotten, see his enquiries about it to Thomas Hookham, December 1812 — January 1813 (Shelley, *Letters*, I, 342, 350).

[29] "Abandon hope, all ye who enter here" (Dante, *Inferno*, canto iii, l. 9). Quoted by Shelley to describe his union with Harriet, in a letter to Hogg, October 4, 1814 (Shelley, *Letters*, I, 401–402). In 1816 Claire quoted it in a letter to Byron, adding, "I think it is a most admirable description of marriage" (Byron, *Works*, III, 433). The last phrase should have been "voi ch'entrate."

[30] This passage in Latin may be Shelley's own composition. Handwriting experts consulted by Newman Ivey White agreed that it was in Shelley's hand. However, Professor Kiffin Rockwell, who has suggested the following translation, finds it hard to believe that Shelley would write such imperfect Latin.
"He pressed kisses upon my lips! Suddenly all the world is clad in the eternal colors of heaven. Still I live . . . still I behold the sad light! In terrible solitude I looked on love like a wretched captive, content. I am yet to live! I was awakening from dreams, ignorant of [?] delicious desire. — Why do I drink the filthy cup of life-giving desire? It ceases to foam with happiness and immortality.
"He was holding me in his arms in the bed. I almost died of madness and delight. Beloved lips were again seeking mutual kisses of life. My fears were giving way; he calmed my fears."

[31] "Not yet did I love, but [and] I loved to love, I sought what I should love loving to love." This passage from St. Augustine's *Confessions* (book III, chap. i) appears in the "Advertisement" of "Poems to Mary" (1810), in *The Esdaile Notebook*, pp. 115 and 245, and also as the epigraph to *Alastor*. Here

beings contains qualities, ⟨if⟩ which if developed [we] must
admire & adore. The selfish, the [ho]llow, & the base alone de-
spise & hate. [To them] I have erred [?] much.[32]

[Q]uam nequerimus[?] amare quia nunquam miser est.[33]

> Ma s'a conoscer la prima radice
> Del nostro amor tu hai cotanto affetto
> Faro come colui que piange e dice.
> Noi leggiamo un giorno per diletto
> Di Lancilotto come amor lo strinse
> Soli eravamo e senze alcun sospetto
> Per piu fiate glie occhi ci sospinse
> Quella lettura, e scollorocci'l viso
> Mo solo un punto fu quel che ci vinse
> Quando leggemmo il disiato riso
> Esser [*several words burned*] cotanto amate
> Ques [*several words burned*] fia diviso
> La bo[*several words burned*]utto tremante,
> Galeotto fu'l libro e che lo scrisse
> Quel giorno piu non vi legemmo avante
> > *Inferno   Canto V.*[34]

> — The thoughts of my past life
> Rise like the ghosts of an unquiet dream
> Blackening the cheerful morn.

---

Shelley has written *sed* for *et,* and a scribble of something like *quiesebar* for
*quaerebam.*

[32] H. Buxton Forman has transcribed this passage, or one nearly identical,
from Shelley's notebook containing the "Notes on Sculpture" (see his note,
*Prose Works of Percy Bysshe Shelley,* III, 79). I have leaned heavily on his
published transcription, since this page is badly burned in Claire's journal.

[33] Professor Rockwell translates this: "How have we been unable to love?
Because he is never unhappy."

[34] *Inferno,* canto v, lines 124–138, from the account of Paolo and Francesca:
"But if thou art so eager to learn the starting-point of our love, I will do as he
doth who weeps and speaks withal. We were reading for pleasure one day of
Lancelot, how love mastered him; we were alone and devoid of all fear. Many
a time did that reading impel our eyes to meet, and take the colour from our
cheeks, but one point only was that which overpowered us. When we read how
by that noble lover the longed-for smile was kissed, this one, who never shall
be severed from me, kissed me on the lips all trembling. The book and its author
played the part of Gallehault: that day we read no further therein" (Tozer's
translation).

Shelley had resumed his study of Italian in March, while staying with the
Boinvilles and Cornelia Turner in Bracknell (see Shelley, *Letters,* I, 384).

# London 1814

Now the dark boughs of the eolian pine
Swing to the sweeping wind, & the light clouds
And the blue sky beyond so deep & still
Commigles like a sympathy of sight
With the sweet music!

*[one leaf torn out]*

How beautiful it sails
Along the silent & serene expanse
Blending its sober & aerial tints
With the pale sky — now an extingushd moon
The frail dim spectre of some quenched orb
Beamless & broad on the still air upheld
It hangs in Heavens deep azure. like a flame
Sphered by the hand of some belated gnome
That chides for its delay the pausing blush
Where the red light of evenings solemn smile
Hangs on the skirts of the exhausted storm
Or where the embattled clouds of orient day
Allow short respite to the waning stars.
Now the eo⟨al⟩lian chords within yon bower
Most like a moth that mocks the wandering fire [?]
When mill [*the rest of this word and several other
words burned*] ray moons
Troop [?] [*more words burned*] feverish dream [35]

[35] For a discussion of these lines of blank verse by Shelley, see White, *Shelley*, I, 702–703, and Robertson, "Unpublished Verses by Shelley," *MLR* 48:181–184 (April 1953).

# SECOND
# JOURNAL
## January 18, 1818, to April 20, 1818

# [1814-1817]

$\mathcal{B}$y the end of 1814 Claire had firmly established for herself the position in the Shelley household that she was to maintain, with a few interruptions, to the end of the poet's life. She was different in temperament from both Shelley and Mary; restless and whimsical, she was always a disturbing force in the household, constantly rubbing Mary the wrong way. In the Shelleys' journal for the winter of 1814–1815 the situation is clear: Mary records the miseries of a particularly uncomfortable pregnancy; while she is indisposed, Claire is always ready to walk out with Shelley, to talk to him, to entertain him, and to play her role of the promising and responsive pupil. A typical entry suggests not jealousy or resentment but a wistful, unresigned self-pity: "Very unwell. Shelley and Clara walk out, as usual, to heaps of places."[1] "As usual" echoes repeatedly through Mary's journal of her miserable winter.

The first sign of serious irritation on Mary's part was on March 12, 1815, a week after her baby had died: "Not well, but better. Very quiet all the morning, and happy, for Clara does not get up till 4."[2] Clearly it was Claire's very presence that was upsetting Mary in her weakened condition, and she and Shelley talked of her leaving, but with no idea of where she might go, since the door in Skinner Street was shut to her. Claire advertised under the initials "A. Z." for a position as a companion, but no suitable offer

[1] December 6, 1814; in *Mary Shelley's Journal*, p. 28.
[2] *Ibid.*, p. 40.

67

appeared.[3] She lingered through the spring, with many a walk and Italian lesson and game of chess with Shelley. Finally it was settled that she should go to Lynmouth, where Shelley and Harriet had been so happy in 1812, and only on the day before she was to leave did Mary let loose in her journal some of her pent-up feeling: "Shelley and the lady walk out. After tea, talk; write Greek characters. Shelley and his friend have a last conversation."[4] On May 13 she was gone, and Mary inscribed firmly: "I begin a new Journal with our regeneration."[5]

It was in a sense a period of regeneration for Claire too. In her letter to Fanny from Lynmouth she sounded nearly as sententiously uplifting as Jane Austen's Mary Bennet: "You may learn Wisdom & Fortitude in adversity & in Prosperity you may relieve & soothe — I feel anxious to be wise — to be capable of knowing the best — of following resolutely — however painful what Nature & serious thought may prescribe & of acquiring a prompt & vigorous Judgement & powers capable of Execution. What are you reading?"[6] Claire herself was submerged in a book world, and saw her rural retreat through the eyes of Rousseau and Wordsworth, Coleridge and Gray. Whether she went into Devonshire as a companion to her mother's friend Mrs. Bicknell or whether, as is more probable, she was boarded there at Shelley's expense, it appears from the tone and content of her letter to Fanny that she was genuinely contented in proving to herself, as well as to her family and friends, that she could be happy when alone.[7] Nevertheless, twenty years later, looking back on this period, Claire found it impossible to be-

[3] *Ibid.*, p. 41. See also White, *Shelley*, I, 694.

[4] *Mary Shelley's Journal*, p. 46.

[5] *Ibid.*, p. 47. No doubt more important in the Shelleys' "regeneration" than Claire's departure was the settlement with Sir Timothy which relieved them from the immediate bondage of debt and consequent danger of arrest (White, *Shelley*, I, 404).

[6] Abinger MSS., May 28, 1815. Published in Marshall, *Mary Shelley*, I, 117–119. Cf. Shelley's dedication to Mary in *Laon and Cythna* (1817), lines 31–33:

> I will be wise,
> And just, and free, and mild, if in me lies
> Such power.

[7] Mrs. Godwin is responsible for the story about Mrs. Bicknell (see White, *Shelley*, I, 404, 695). There is no supporting evidence; perhaps Mrs. Godwin invented the companion to make her daughter's retreat seem more responsible.

# Introduction

lieve that she had been anything but miserable: "Hatred and persecution let loose their destroying hounds upon me in the very dawn of life; but a mere child I was driven from all I loved into a solitary spot, without a friend to soothe my affliction, without even an acquaintance with whom to exchange a word, day after day I sat companionless upon that unfrequented sea-shore, mentally exclaiming, a life of sixteen years is already too much for me to bear."[8] This letter, written to Mary from an abyss of melancholy at the death of Lady Mount Cashell, can hardly be taken as a balanced recollection, but there is little question that among the delights of the Lynmouth retreat the chilly idea must have haunted her that she had been sent away against her own preference, even if with her own consent.

While away from the Shelleys Claire was an erratic letter writer. In July, Mary, having received no word from her for some time, suspected that she might have heard that Shelley was in London and come to town to see him.[9] In October Claire was in Ireland, where her brother Charles was investigating the distillery business.[10] And on January 5, 1816, she was back in London, with extended visits to Skinner Street, ready for a new adventure.[11]

Although Shelley was providing the money for Claire to live in London, he could not be asked to do so indefinitely.[12] She wanted to avoid the drudgery and the sacrifice of freedom involved in the life of a governess or a companion. Country life, *rusticans sed non rusticus*, was bound to become the "merely vegetating" that she abhorred. Indeed the opportunities for a well-educated but impecunious young lady were limited. Mary was the only person she knew who had found a way of life exactly to her liking: Claire's entire social and intellectual training seemed to have suited her for one position — companion to a poet. And in mid-January of 1816 England's most glamorous poet, whose work had the sanc-

[8] Abinger MSS., June 2, 1835.
[9] Mary Shelley, *Letters*, I, 8. There is no evidence that she saw either Shelley or Mary that summer, but it is reasonable to assume that when they were traveling on the Devon coast they stopped to visit her.
[10] Shelley, *Letters*, I, 434. Shelley sent £10 to her there.
[11] Godwin's diary, Abinger MSS.
[12] As far back as January 1814 Francis Place had been of the opinion that Godwin ought to make his grownup girls maintain themselves (White, *Shelley*, I, 706).

tion of vigorous praise from Shelley, was separated from his wife. It must have appeared to Claire like the story of Shelley and Harriet all over again, except that for Byron there was nobody to console him and inspire him and, in short, play Mary Shelley to him. Claire was ready to step into the role: she had understudied it for two years.

Her very first letter to Byron shows her still attempting to transfer her vicarious experience obtained from books directly into her everyday living. As yet she had not been seriously disillusioned. Her acquaintance with Shelley had gone a long way to convince her that to love the man and to love his poems were the same thing. She wrote to Byron to confess the love she had borne him many years.[13] Her expectation of his kindness in return betrays the naïveté of the girl still not eighteen at the same time that it pays an indirect compliment to the love which Mary had received from Shelley.

The story of Claire's pursuit and brief capture of her poet is too familiar to need detailed repetition; it is common knowledge that she attracted his attention first with her theatrical and then with her literary projects, and finally with the story of her life (which Byron was inclined not to believe until she produced as evidence some letters and then Mary Shelley herself). She saw almost at once that he did not care for her, and she soon came to anticipate the Byronic sneer,[14] but she had great faith in the power of patient and faithful devotion. It is clear that she had in mind the same concept of ideal unselfish love which had brought Mary, the year before, to try her best to please Hogg that they might make physical intimacy the final seal on the intellectual community of philosophical spirits.[15] Claire denied to Byron that she was drawn to him by physical passion, and she expressed the hope and ex-

[13] Claire's letters to Byron are in the Murray MSS. Excerpts from these letters and occasionally entire letters have been published in Grylls, *Claire Clairmont*; Byron, *Works*, III, 429–437; Paston and Quennell, *"To Lord Byron"*; *Shelley and Mary*; and Marchand, *Byron*.

[14] In the first of her letters to Byron in Switzerland she said, "Were I to float by your window drowned all you would say would be: 'Ah, voilà'" (Paston and Quennell, *"To Lord Byron,"* p. 212).

[15] In January 1815 Mary wrote to Hogg that when she came to love him "we shall be happier, I do think, than the angels who sing for ever & ever, the lovers of Jane's world of perfection" (Scott, *Harriet and Mary*, p. 46).

pectation that Byron would fall in love with Mary (indeed they got along very well). The evidence of Claire's later life appears as witness to the sincerity of her statement to him in 1816: "I have no passion; I had ten times rather be your male companion than your mistress."[16]

In mid-April Byron waited only for the separation papers to be signed before leaving England for Switzerland. Shelley awaited the outcome of a lawsuit relative to the disposal of the family estate, planning, when the affair was settled, to move to Cumberland or Scotland, or perhaps Italy, to avoid the neglect and hostility that oppressed him and his family.[17] At this juncture Claire wrote cryptically to Byron: "I steal a moment to write to you to know whether you go tomorrow. It is not through selfishness that I pray something may prevent your departure. But tomorrow Shelley's chancery suit will be decided & so much of my fate depends on the decision; besides, tomorrow will inform me whether I should be able to offer you *that* which it has long been the passionate wish of my heart to offer you."[18] Perhaps it was herself she wished to offer, and she anticipated an opportunity to steal away for a night. Perhaps — though it seems almost too early — her *"that"* was a baby. At any rate, Claire did offer herself to Byron and was — briefly — accepted. The chancery suit went against Shelley, as expected, and there was nothing to keep them any longer in England.

The Shelleys yielded to Claire's "pressing solicitations," she told Byron, to follow him to Geneva.[19] On May 3, 1816, they set out, with Claire and their baby William, planning to remain abroad "perhaps forever."[20] The summer for Claire was a bittersweet one;

[16] Murray MSS.; printed in Paston and Quennell, "To Lord Byron," pp. 210–211.

[17] Shelley, Letters, I, 453.

[18] Murray MSS. (ca. April 22, 1816); printed in Marchand, Byron, II, 604.

[19] Murray MSS.; printed in Shelley and Mary, I, 91.

[20] Shelley, Letters, I, 471–473. I have no new evidence as to when Shelley and Mary discovered the nature of Claire's liaison. That they changed their plans at the last minute and left Hogg behind might suggest that Shelley knew before they left, but there are other plausible explanations. The fact that Claire, on arrival at Geneva, made elaborate arrangements to bring Byron to her room without his being discovered by Shelley might imply that she still kept her secret, but this evidence too is inconclusive. At any rate, the opportunity of seeing Byron would have been enough to bring them to Geneva without Claire's

her affection for Byron and her realization that he cared nothing at all for her deepened simultaneously. She saw only enough of his gentle and unstoical side to confirm the "eternal love" to which she had pledged herself. Her pregnancy, which she recognized while she was in Switzerland, committed her inescapably to that love. Before she left England she had been able to write of the possibility of never seeing Byron again, but the promise of the baby nourished her hope.

Shelley and Mary knew better. They realized that Claire had forced her attention on Byron, that he had accepted her advances reluctantly. Byron never took seriously the idea of her being in love. A decade later Claire looked back on this period and wrote of it to Jane Williams:

> A happy attachment that has seen its end leaves a void that nothing can fill up, therefore I counsel the timorous and the prudent to take the greatest care always to have an unhappy attachment, because with it you can veer about like a weather-cock to every point of life. . . . a happy passion like death has *finis* written in such large characters in its face, there is no hoping for any possibility of a change. You will allow me to talk upon this subject for I am unhappily the victim of a *happy passion*; I had one like all things perfect in its kind, it was fleeting and mine only lasted ten minutes but these ten minutes have discomposed the rest of my life; The passion God knows for what cause, from no fault of mine however disappeared leaving no trace whatever behind it except my heart wasted and ruined as if it had been scorched by a thousand lightnings.[21]

After her return to England in September Claire continued to write voluminously to Byron.[22] Her letters are interesting as the productions of a teen-age girl, and one perceives that had she not been so awkwardly on the defensive they might have been gay and charming. They are coy, flirtatious, and self-consciously calculated

---

making the disclosure. In one letter, for example, Claire told Byron that Mary had entreated her in private to obtain his address abroad so that they might renew their acquaintance (Murray MSS., quoted by Paston and Quennell, "To Lord Byron," p. 208).

[21] Abinger MSS., postmarked January 22, 1827, printed in Marshall, *Mary Shelley*, II, 159–160.

[22] Letters in the Murray MSS.

to please. But it is quite obvious that she had no real notion of the kind of man she was writing to. The effect of her tactlessness on Byron is painful to contemplate. She wrote catty and scornful remarks about the other women in his life and even of his male friends, such as Douglas Kinnaird; she revealed herself as a little reformer by imploring him to avoid excesses in wine; she begged unendingly for letters from him. He read hers and put them away, sometimes crushed as though he had only just resisted the impulse to hurl them into the fire. His summary of the affair in a letter to Kinnaird reveals how vast was the gulf between them:

> You know and I believe saw once, that odd-headed girl, who introduced herself to me shortly before I left England; but you also know that I found her with Shelley and her sister at Geneva. I never loved nor pretended to love her, but a man is a man, and if a girl of eighteen comes prancing to you at all hours, there is but one way – the suite of all this is that she was with *child* – and returned to England to assist in peopling that desolate island. Whether this impregnation took place before I left England or since I do not know; the (carnal) connection had commenced previously to my setting out – but by or about this time she is about to produce – the next question is, is the brat mine? I have reasons to think so, for I know as much as one can know such a thing – that she had *not lived* with S. during the time of our acquaintance – and that she had a good deal of that same with me.[23]

On the return to England Shelley found lodgings in Bath so that he and Mary might be near Claire to see her through her child-bearing and avoid the curiosity of the Godwins. Claire took a room apart from the Shelleys and assumed for a while the title of Mrs. Clairmont.[24] There was no real alternative to this arrangement, but for Mary there was again the old tension of the day in, day out, presence of Claire's disturbing influence. Shelley was often away in London, and Mary's letters to him suggest that Claire's presence was harder for her to stand when he was away; her much-

[23] Marchand, *Byron*, II, 681.

[24] The Shelleys, with little William and the Genevan nurse Elise, lived at 5 Abbey Churchyard, whereas Claire lived at 12 New Bond Street. For Claire's elaborate joke with Elise about her double identity as Mrs. Clairmont and her unmarried sister Claire, see Mary Shelley, *Letters*, I, 34.

quoted plea for *"absentia Clariæ"* was made at this time.[25] Mary had good reason to wish her away; there is no doubt that Claire was tactless. Just when Mary was looking forward most longingly to the possible arrival of "darling Ianthe and Charles," Shelley's children by Harriet, Claire was thoughtlessly planting the seeds of discontent by continually reminding William that he was going to "lose his pre-eminence as oldest and be helped third at table." [26]

The affectionate friendship between Shelley and Claire continued, but even here there was a new tension, since it was Shelley's duty to make clear to the deluded girl the truth that she was loath to face — that she was not to expect letters or visits from Byron. Shelley's realistic attitude toward Claire's relation with Byron is clear from his letters. He had suffered himself from her importunate enthusiasms and adolescent effusions, if not in the same manner or degree. "Clare is about to enjoin me some messages which are better conceived than expressed," he asserted in a letter to Byron, candidly but not unkindly.[27]

The domestic problems complicated by Claire were relatively minor, however, compared to the serious blows 1816 still had in store. On October 9 the first disaster struck: Fanny Imlay committed suicide. She was twenty-two years old, four years older than Mary and Claire, and older sister to both of them practically from their birth. In the midst of an excessively long but generally representative letter to Byron, Claire took stock retrospectively of her relationship with the girl:

> Are you angry with me now dearest that I have told you all the news I can to please you. If you are forget all the complaining in the first sheet perhaps it is my health that makes me so melancholy and peevish I suffer from Rheumatism. Then I live in such an extreme solitude that I do nothing but think on my disquietudes till perhaps I get cross. Add to this the unhappy death of that poor girl. I passed the first fourteen years of my life with her & though I cannot say I had so great an affection for her as might be expected yet she is the first person of my acquaintance who has died & her death so horrible too. Now if I tell you all my thoughts dearest you mustn't bring

[25] *Ibid.*, I, 14.
[26] *Ibid.*, I, 16.
[27] Shelley, *Letters*, I, 504.

them against me to make me look foolish as you did that hateful novel thing I wrote.[28] Do you know, dearest, I do not like to be the object of pity & nothing makes me so angry as when M[ary] & S[helley] tell me not to expect to hear from you.[29]

It is hardly strange that Claire and Fanny were not close friends. In any situation Claire would play the rebel, whereas Fanny would behave, in Mary's word, "slavishly." When Mary came back from the six weeks' tour in 1814, Godwin threatened never to speak to Fanny again if she saw Mary, and Mrs. Godwin, a month later, refused to let twenty-year-old Fanny come down to dinner because she had received a lock of Mary's hair.[30] Claire considered her stepsister excessively sentimental and thought Henry MacKenzie's "man of feeling" would make her a perfect husband.[31]

Mrs. Godwin did little to promote a happy relationship between the girls, and with her notorious tactlessness, some of which was inherited by her daughter, she played them against each other. "I understand from Mamma that I am your laughing-stock & the constant beacon of your satire," wrote Fanny unhappily to Mary on May 29, 1816; and exactly two months later she was so upset by the depression in England, the widespread unemployment, and her own lack of independence, particularly financial, that she wrote to Mary, "I am not well — my mind always keeps my body in a fever." One of her last thoughts had been for Claire's happiness, for on September 26, only a little more than a week before her death, she had written Mary, saying, "I am very glad you have got Jane a pianoforte; if anything can do her good and restore her to industry, it is music. I think I gave her all the music here; however, I will look again for what I can find." [32]

The second severe shock for the Shelleys was Harriet's suicide: her body was found two months to the day after Fanny's death. Then followed the prolonged and desperate struggle for

[28] In one of her early letters to Byron, Claire had asked him to read the rough draft of a novel she had started and to advise her as to her fitness for a literary career. The outline of the novel is incorporated in that letter (Byron, *Works*, III, 434–435).

[29] Murray MSS., October 27, 1816. The passage quoted here is unpublished. Two sentences of it are in *Shelley and Mary*, I, 150–151.

[30] *Mary Shelley's Journal*, pp. 25, 30.

[31] See entry for November 8, 1814, above.

[32] Abinger MSS., quoted in *Shelley and Mary*, I, 140–142.

the custody of Harriet's children, which caused Shelley to be away from Mary (and from Claire, who also protested) for extended periods of time. On December 30 Shelley and Mary were married, with the immediate effect of mitigating Godwin's oppressive animosity, but the "respectability" achieved by the marriage was insufficient to sway the court, and on March 25, 1817, Lord Eldon decided that Shelley was unfit to have custody of Charles and Ianthe.

On January 12, 1817, Claire's baby was born, a beautiful little girl called first Alba (an echo of Byron's nickname Albé), then Clara, and finally Allegra.[33] On February 18 Claire left the child with the nurse Élise and went to London with William Shelley. The Godwins never suspected anything of her liaison with Byron and, indeed, were still having trouble believing it more than three years later.[34] On March 18 the Shelleys moved from Bath to Albion House in Marlow, and Claire and Allegra stayed for a time with Leigh and Marianne Hunt in Hampstead while Shelley and Mary enjoyed the quiet of their new home. As soon as Claire was away Mary could genuinely sympathize with her: "Poor girl she *must* be lonely," she wrote to the Hunts.[35] At the end of March Claire rejoined the Shelleys and was with them when Godwin came for one of his several visits to Marlow, from April 2 to 6.[36] In May the

[33] Byron's nickname Albé may have been derived from "Albanian" or from his initials, L. B., or from a combination of these. Perhaps a third influence was the title of Madame Sophie Cottin's popular epistolary novel *Claire d'Albe* (1798; trans. as *Clara; a Novel* [London 1808]), composed largely of letters from the virtuous Claire, as she succumbs to a guilty passion, addressed to her confidante Elise. The Shelleys unquestionably knew the book, since it had been one of Harriet Shelley's favorites, and the triple coincidence of the names cannot possibly have escaped them. See Rieger, "Lord Byron as 'Albè'," *KSJ* 14:6–7 (Winter 1965). Byron chose the name Allegra, "a Venetian name" (letter to Douglas Kinnaird, January 13, 1818, *Lord Byron's Correspondence*, II, 65, ed. J. Murray, quoted in Marchand, *Byron*, II, 719).

[34] Maria Gisborne's journal, August 28, 1820, in Gisborne and Williams, *Journals*, p. 48. I cannot agree with the editor that because Godwin was still incredulous that Byron was the father he must therefore have considered Shelley as the only other candidate for the honor.

[35] Mary Shelley, *Letters*, I, 23. But no sooner were they together again than Mary had to make a conscious effort to get on with her. She then wrote to Shelley, "Claire is forever wearying with her idle & childish complaints" (*ibid.*, I, 45).

[36] Godwin diaries, Abinger MSS.

# Introduction

Hunt children — John, Mary, and Swynburne — came for a long visit, accompanied by Marianne Hunt's talented sister, Bessie Kent.[37] For part of their visit Mary was in London and Claire took over the role of hostess.

By 1817 Claire had developed into a very attractive young lady of nineteen. She had begun to take an interest in her appearance, and even Godwin was enough impressed to write to his wife, "You will, I believe, be pleased to hear that Jane is taking to new habits: she wears stays, and dresses herself every day becomingly and with care: this at the entreaty of Shelley and Mary."[38] Thornton Hunt, the eldest son of Leigh, first came to know her at this time, when he was seven, and he later described her as "a girl of great ability, strong feelings, lively temper, and, though not regularly handsome, of brilliant appearance."[39] At Marlow she spent many hours playing with her child, walking about the countryside, reading Latin and Italian, and finding time to write, for by October Shelley was unsuccessfully offering her book to London publishers.[40]

There was much music at Marlow, and here Claire was in her

[37] Elizabeth Kent was the author of *Flora Domestica, or the Portable Flower-Garden; with Directions for the Treatment of Plants in Pots; and Illustrations from the Works of the Poets* (London, 1823). After a long preface devoted to a discussion of great men who had enjoyed flowers, including the sketches of Shelley and Mavrocordato with which she had been helped by her brother-in-law, she listed each plant that could be reared in a pot or tub, giving its botanical name and its common name in French and Italian, its description, hints on care and feeding, and copious quotations from authors, both classic and modern, who had written about it. In 1825 the work went into a second edition, and she published a similar work, *Sylvan Sketches; or, a Companion to the Park and the Shrubbery; with Illustrations from the Works of the Poets* (London, 1825). See Thornton Hunt's note in *The Correspondence of Leigh Hunt*, I, 5–6.

[38] Paul, *Godwin*, II, 250. On the other hand, shortly after this, Mary was trying to convince Marianne Hunt to leave off her stays (Mary Shelley, *Letters*, I, 28).

[39] Thornton Hunt, "Shelley: By One Who Knew Him," *Atlantic Monthly*, 11:187 (February 1863).

[40] Shelley, *Letters*, I, 561. This is all that is known of this work. It is doubtful that after Byron's merciless scorn she would have continued the novel she had showed to him. It is more probable that contrary to what has been generally assumed Claire went ahead and finished the tale of terror which she had undertaken at the same time that Mary began *Frankenstein*.

glory. All who knew her were enchanted with her voice, and she was considered among her friends as an authority on music. On April 17 Shelley commissioned Vincent Novello to obtain a cabinet grand piano, and five days later it arrived. It was to this calm and contented Claire that Shelley addressed his lines "To Constantia Singing" which have immortalized her at her best.[41]

Late in September and again in November Shelley and Claire traveled to London together.[42] By October Shelley had made up his mind to go to Italy, but it was to be five months before the ménage was actually on its way. Because the presence of Allegra in the family was a constant threat to Shelley's reputation, and because as the daughter of a peer she would have advantages which the Shelleys could never offer, it was decided to send the child to Byron. But to "send" a baby to Italy was no simple matter. In fact, as Mary understood, "Clare although she in a blind kind of manner sees the necessity of it, does not wish her to go and will instinctively place all kind of difficulties in the way of our as it is very difficult task."[43]

Claire was, indeed, deeply happy with her child. She now had an object on which she could lavish her affection and attention, and she no longer needed to demand so much attention for herself. When the baby was just a year old she took great delight in describing her to Byron, with her "pretty eyes of a deep dazzling blue,"[44] the curls which made the back of her head look quite divine, and the "little square chin divided in the middle like your own." She tried to visualize her darling with her father: "My affections are few & therefore strong — the extreme solitude in which I live has concentrated them to one point and that point is my lovely child. I study her pleasure all day long — she is so fond of me that I hold her in my arms till I am nearly falling on purpose to delight her. We sleep together and if you knew the extreme happiness I feel when she nestles close to me, in listening to our regular breathing together, I could tear my flesh in twenty thousand

[41] Neville Rogers reconstructs the Shelleys' life at this period and sensitively discusses the impact of Claire's musical talents on Shelley's poetry, including *Prometheus Unbound*, in "Music at Marlow," *KSMB* 5:20–25 (1953).

[42] Godwin diaries, Abinger MSS. From November 21 to 24 the two of them were daily at Skinner Street.

[43] Mary Shelley, *Letters*, I, 36.

[44] This has been misread "day-time" blue (Grylls, *Claire Clairmont*, p. 89).

different directions to ensure her good and when I fear for her residing with you it is not the dread I have to commence the long series of painful anxiety I know I shall have to endure it is lest I should behold her sickly & wasted with improper management lest I should live to hear that *you* neglected her. My dearest friend if all this while your feelings are good and gentle then have I done you an irreparable harm in thus suspecting you." [45]

*[January 17 and part of January 18 in the Pforzheimer Library]* [1]

like a savage beast for blood; he had blood & may it lie like lead on his soul! The poor husband was shot dead in the meeting! The wife was left with her children starving & desolate & the poor Sister went instantly mad and has been ever since ⟨in⟩ confined   But their miseries are nothing   Do we ⟨kn⟩ not know that the Brother had blood? Shortly after this "blood-hunter" was canvassing for some office or other at one of the Universities & he won it because so many people admired this *"noble generous action"* of his.

Monday Jany. 19th. Hogg goes after breakfast. Walk to Wycombe. Learn an Italian Dialogue. Copy part of Verses to *Constantia*.[2] Read three of Cobbett's Registers. In one of these he mentions Mr.

[45] Murray MSS. Parts of this letter, not including the passage quoted, have been published in Paston and Quennell, *"To Lord Byron,"* pp. 230–233, and Grylls, *Claire Clairmont*, pp. 89–91.

[1] The beginning of Hogg's story in the MS. now in the Pforzheimer collection was printed in the sales catalogue of the Harry B. Smith collection and reprinted in Grylls, *Claire Clairmont*, pp. 250–251, as follows: "January, 1818. Hogg tell [*sic*] us a curious story very descriptive of the Christian virtues. A gentleman of fortune lived very happily with his wife. Her sister fell in love with him and as the Sisters loved each other this made no difference in their happiness. Unhappily, both the love and the consequences came to the knowledge of the family of the Sisters and then began the persecution. The Husband though a man of immense wealth possessed his estates only for life; he was therefore very averse to accept the Challenge of the irritated Brother as they were pleased to call him. These three people went abroad; they tried every means to avoid a meeting but the Brother followed thirsting . . ."

[2] Shelley's recently completed "To Constantia Singing." On Claire as Constantia, see White, *Shelley*, I, 731–732, and Shelley, *Works*, III, 328.

# Second Journal

W— Friend as a very able, firm, & worthy Man.³ Mr. Francis relates this story of Cobbett. Mr. F many many years ago was standing near Somerset House talking to *Frend*. Cobbett, then a Sarjeant ⟨on duty⟩ came up & asked me why he talked with that levelling, jacobin rascal adding much more abuse. Mr. Francis begged to be permitted to chuse his own associates & after much violence on the part of Cobbett he retired. Some time afterwards as Francis was passing thro' Spring Gardens there arose some dispute about the passage & Cobbett as I understood being on duty behaved with with ⟨a⟩ the most insolent assumption. Francis persisted & Cobbett drew his hanger, cut at him & wounded F in the ⟨breat⟩ breast which scar he now shews — F avoided further wounds by breaking his hanger & putting one half in his pocket. [*two or three letters crossed out*]

Tuesday Jany. 20th. Learn an Italian Dialogue. Walk upon the Reading Road & see *La grande Chasse*. Godwin & Will arrive.⁴ Peacock in the Evening.

Wednesday Jany 21st. William teazes me all day. He is a strange Creature. We walk together in the Woods. In the Evening play at Chess.

Thursday Jany. 22nd. Read an article in the Edinburgh Review. Meroigne Thericourt a poissade in the time of the Revolution now raving mad.⁵ I cannot but think there exists an intimate & close connexion between Madness & Brutality. Walk towards Maidenhead — ⟨Play with the Darling who who throws at me the chalk. Naughty Child⟩.⁶ Read some Latin & Anacharsis. Curious syllogism of Ebulis of Megara. "Epimenides said that the Cretans were all liars: now he was a Cretan himself so he lied & consequently the Cretans

---

³ *Cobbett's Weekly Political Register*, 33:col. 12 (January 3, 1818).

⁴ William Godwin, Jr., son of Godwin and Claire's mother, was in his fifteenth year.

⁵ "Among them, though better off than the others, was the famous Theroigne de Mericourt, one of the most sanguinary of the Poissards [fishwives], who distinguished herself for acts of cruelty in the beginning of the Revolution" ("Lunatic Asylums," *Edinburgh Review* 28:450 [August 1817]).

⁶ References to Allegra (at this time called Alba), like many references to Byron, have been inked out but are today quite legible in the MS., owing to the fading of the inks.

are not liars; or Epimenides did not lie & the Cretans are liars."
Euclid of Megara used to steal away of a night to Athens in the
disguise of a Woman to talk with his master Socrates, though it
was death for a Megarese to be found in the Athenian Territories.[7]
⟨L.B.'s Birthday. 30⟩ —

Friday Jany. 23rd. ⟨I⟩ Walk towards Seymour's Court. Rainy &
Stormy. Shelley is attacked again with bad eyes. Do an Italian
exercise & read some of Moore's Anacreon.[8] Peacock dines. Read
Anarcharsis. Beautiful History of Periander, tyrant of Corinth &
of Clisthenes of ⟨Scyone⟩ Sicyon⟨e⟩.[9]

Saturday Jany. 24th. Little Will's birthday. 2 yrs. Rainy do not
walk. Read Anarcharsis. Do an Italian exercise & learn an Italian
Dialogue. ⟨Aft⟩ Do not dine below for Peacock is there. ⟨Read Bg⟩
Begin Goldsmith's History of Greece p. 40.[10] Play in the Evening.

Sunday Jany. 25th. — Walk on the Wycombe Road. When I come
home find the House Sold. Great Rejoicing. Peacock dines & spends
the Evening.

Monday Jany. 26th. Walk. Peacock dines.

Tuesday Jany 27 — Walk — Read — Repose.

Wednesday Jany 28 — Walk on the Reading Road    Read Anarcharsis.

Thursday Jany. 29th. Go up to Town in the Carrige with Shelley
& Peacock. Spend my time at Hunt's very agreably.[11] Go to the

[7] [Abbé Jean Jacques Barthélemy], *Voyage du jeune Anacharsis en Grèce,
dans le milieu du quatrième siècle avant l'ère vulgaire*, 5 vols. (Paris, 1788), II,
354–355, 352.
[8] Thomas Moore, *Odes of Anacreon, Translated into English Verse, with
Notes* (London, 1800).
[9] *Anacharsis*, II, 366–373.
[10] Oliver Goldsmith, *The History of Greece, from the Earliest State, to the
Death of Alexander the Great*, 2 vols. (11th ed.; London: J. Rivington, J.
Johnson, et al., 1812). There is an account of the sexual freedom of the Spartan
women in I, 30.
[11] Claire's first mention of James Henry Leigh Hunt (1784–1859) and his
wife Marianne. Since December 1816 the relationship between the two family
groups had been very warm.

Opera with Hogg — Shelley Peacock & the Hunts — Both [?] La Molinara. Walk about Visit the British Institution and the Last Supper by Leonardi Da Vinci [12] ⟨Alba looks — odd.⟩ [?]

Thursday Feb. 5th. Return to Marlow. ⟨My Da not well⟩.

Friday. Feb 6th. Look at Work. Read Rob Roy.[13]

Saturday. Feb. 7th. Prepare. Bustle — Shelley goes up again to London. Finish Rob. Roy.

Sunday Feb. 8. Busy all day. Read Helen Monteagle by A. Lefanu [14] Stupid foolish Book.

Monday Feb 9th. Go up to London with ⟨Alba &⟩ Milly.[15] Reach there at Eleven. Drive to New Hummums Family Hotel.[16] Go with Peacock to the ⟨Appo⟩ Apollonicon [17] and to the British Museum. Elgin & Townley Marbles & Terra-cottas. Dine. Sleep in the Evening.

[12] Mozart's *Le Nozze di Figaro* had just opened at Covent Garden. Paisiello's *opera buffa, La Molinara,* had recently been presented with some of the same cast. The British Institution was a gallery displaying the work of British painters, such as Alston, Westall, and Wilkie (see the *Examiner,* no. 528, pp. 91–92 [February 8, 1818], and subsequent numbers). The *Examiner* comments on the copy of "The Last Supper" on display in London in no. 503, pp. 524–525 (August 17, 1817). At the end of this entry is a crude sketch of a tree.

[13] Mary was also reading Scott's novel, just published, at this time (*Mary Shelley's Journal*, p. 91).

[14] Alicia Lefanu, *Helen Monteagle,* 3 vols. (1818); also read this week by Mary (*Mary Shelley's Journal*, p. 92).

[15] Amelia (Milly) Shields was a Marlow girl who remained with the Shelleys to the end of 1819.

[16] Peacock's residence.

[17] "A magnificent musical machine, constructed upon the principle of the organ; the sound being produced by a current of air urged by bellows through several series of vertical pipes, so as closely to imitate all the most admired wind instruments, with the effect of a full orchestra. It is the invention of Messrs. Flight and Robson, who spent five years in its completion. There are about 250 keys, upwards of 1900 pipes, 45 draw-stops, and 2 kettle-drums: the largest double-diapason pedal-pipe is twenty-four feet long and twenty-three inches square, being eight feet longer than the corresponding pipe in the great organ at Haarlem. The mechanism is enclosed in a case twenty-four feet high, embellished with pilasters and paintings of Apollo, Clio, and Erato. The Appollonicon was first exhibited at the inventor's house, 101 St. Martin's Lane, in June 1817" (John Timbs, *Curiosities of London* [London, 1855], pp. 16–17).

# London 1818

Teusday Feb. 10th. Sublimi Shelley — Cantor di verdade, Sorge Queen Mab a ristorar il mondo." [18] Go with Peacock ⟨&⟩ a shopping. Mary & the Babes come. We all go to the Opera in the Evening. Il Don Giovanni & Acis et Galathe. Remove to 119 Great Russel Street Bloomsbury Square. Mr. Bramsen calls.[19]

Wednesday Feb. 11th. Read Il Barbiere di Seviglia.[20] Spend the Evening at Hunts. Peacock, Hogg & Keats. Music.

Thursday Feb. 12th. We go with Peacock in the Morning to visit the India House Library. Curiosities. See the Panorama of Rome. In the Evening not well. Hogg & Peacock dine.

Friday Feb. 13th. Finish Il Barbiere di Seviglia. Mr. Madocks calls.[21]

Saturday. Feb. 14. Go with Shelley to Ollier's.[22] Death of Sir Richard Croft.[23] Mary spends the day at Hunt's. Go to the Opera with S— Peacock & Hogg. Il Don Giovanni. Mr. Madocks calls.

[18] "Sublime Shelley — Singer of truth, May Queen Mab arise to restore the world." Thomas Love Peacock quotes these lines, somewhat differently spelled, from a sonnet by a young Brazilian medical student named Baptista (Joachimo Baptista Pereira), who in 1814 became a disciple of Shelley and undertook to translate *Queen Mab* into Portuguese (see Peacock, *Memoirs*, II, 334–335).

[19] Mozart's opera and Favier's ballet. For the *Examiner*'s mention of the ballet (no. 531, pp. 138–139 [March 2, 1818]) see Appendix B. The Mr. Bramsen mentioned has not been identified. Mary spelled it Bransen (*Mary Shelley's Journal*, p. 92).

[20] Mary's journal for March 2 says "Read Italian operas" (Abinger MSS.). Looking ahead, we find Peacock's account of March 10, 1818, the night before the Shelleys left England: "The evening was a remarkable one, as being that of the first performance of an opera of Rossini in England, and of the first appearance here of Malibran's father, Garcia. He performed Count Almaviva in the *Barbiere di Siviglia*. Fodor was Rosina; Naldi, Figaro; Ambrogetti, Bartolo; and Angrisani, Basilio. I supped with Shelley and his traveling companions after the opera" (Peacock, *Memoirs*, II, 349–350). Leigh Hunt's review in the *Examiner*, no. 534, p. 188 (March 22, 1818), is reprinted in *Leigh Hunt's Dramatic Criticism, 1808–1831*, ed. Houtchens, pp. 188–189.

[21] One of Shelley's creditors, from Marlow.

[22] Shelley's publisher.

[23] Sir Richard Croft, M. D., aged 57, while attending a Mrs. Thackeray in childbirth, retired to another room and, taking a pistol in each hand, discharged both at his head. The inquest was held on February 13 and was reported in the *Courier* on the following day. He had been despondent ever since the death in childbirth (in 1817) of Princess Charlotte, heiress to the throne, whom he had

# Second Journal

Sunday Feb. 15. Read le Mariage de Figaro. Peacock, Hogg & Mr Bramsen dine.

Monday Feb. 16   Go with Shelley to Ollier's & several places. Very unwell. Peacock dines. We all go to Covent Garden. The tragedy of Fazio & the Pantomime of Harlequin Gulliver.[24] Very ill. Miss M. A de St Croix calls.

Tuesday Feb. 17th. Better. Walk a little. Hogg dines & spends the Evening.

Wednesday Feb. 18th. Walk with Il Pavone.[25] Visit the Exhibition of Painted Glass. Mary spends the day at Hunts. Hogg & Peacock dine. We all go to Hunts in the Evening. Music.

Thursday Feb. 19th. Walk with Peacock to Bond St. Visit Canova Casts from Phidias of Castor & Melpomene. ⟨M. S. & Peacock dine at Ho⟩ Call on Hunt. M. S— & Peacock dine at Horace Smith's.[26] The following Epigram was written by an Italian on the Colonnade of Carlton House. He addresses them thus.

Care Colonne, che fate là?

To which they reply

Non lo sapiamo, in verità! [27]

---

attended. Mrs. Thackeray was having difficult, protracted labor, and he feared, erroneously, that she too would not survive.

[24] Henry Hart Milman's *Fazio* (Oxford, 1815) starred Miss O'Neill as Bianca. Peacock records Shelley's absorbed attention (*Memoirs*, II, 330). *Harlequin Gulliver; or, the Flying Island* was part of Covent Garden's standard repertoire at the time. For a colorful description in the *Examiner*, no. 524, p. 26 (January 12, 1818), see Appendix B.

[25] Peacock. Mr. Backler's pictures painted on glass were described by Leigh Hunt in the *Examiner*, no. 500, p. 475 (July 27, 1817). They were exhibited by daylight and by firelight and consisted of copies of such well-known pictures as West's "King Lear in the Storm" and Lonsdale's "King John Signing Magna Charta."

[26] Horace Smith (1779–1849) referred to himself in a letter to Shelley as "a rhyming Stockbroker" (Abinger MSS.). As a member of the stock exchange he was so successful that he was able to retire in 1820. With his brother James he wrote the famous *Rejected Addresses, or the New Theatrum Poetarum* (1812), a group of parodies of such writers of the day as Scott, Crabbe, Southey, and Cobbett.

[27] Since 1783 Carlton House had been the residence of the Prince Regent, whose architect Holland had added a Corinthian portico and a screen of Ionic

Friday Feb — 20th Get up late not well. Walk with Peacock in Bond Street & in the Parck. Hogg & ⟨Pea⟩ Peacock dine. Visit Pidcock's see the Lioness & her cubs.

Saturday Feb. 21st. ⟨A shopping with my Darling⟩. Go with Peacock to the ⟨Appollonicn⟩ Appollonicon. Hogg & Peacock dine. We all go to the Opera — Il Don Giovanni & the new Ballet — Le Retour du Prinptems. Beautiful Dancing.[28]

Sunday Feb. 22. M & S. spend the day at Hunts. ⟨Stay at home & play with A & Willy⟩. Read Berrington's History of the Middle Ages.[29]

Monday Feb. 23rd. Walk with Shelley to Long Acre to see the Carriage. Peacock & Hogg dine. They go to Drury Lane to Bride of Abydos. ⟨Stay at home with my Darling.⟩

Tuesday Feb. 24th. Walk about in the Mornin   Hogg & Peacock dine. All go to the Opera in the Evening Il Don Giovanni & Le Retour du Primptems. Meet Mr. & Mrs. Hunt.

Wednesday Feb. 25. Go with Peacock to the Appollonicon. Mr. & Mrs. Hunt Hogg & Peacock dine. Very pleasant Evening.

Thursday Feb. 26th. Read the Opera of Cosi Fan Tutte. Walk in Bond St with Peacock. They go to the Appollonicon in the Evening.

---

columns facing Pall Mall. In 1827 the house was removed and the portico transferred to the National Gallery, but years later Bonomi's epigram was quoted in guide books, with a translation by Prince Hoare:

Dear little columns, all in a row,
What *do* you do there?
Indeed we don't know.

(Timbs, *Curiosities of London*, pp. 64–65.) See Shelley's scornful account of a fete at Carlton House in a letter to Elizabeth Hitchener, June 20, 1811 (Shelley, *Letters*, I, 110).

[28] *Zephyr: Or, the Return of Spring*, by Duport, opened on this night. The dancing of the prima ballerina Mlle. Milanie had an enormous impact on Shelley (see Dowden, *Shelley*, II, 116 and n.; also Claire's journal for April 8, below). For reviews that provide a clear record of the ballet and its reception, see Appendix B.

[29] Rev. Joseph Berington, *A Literary History of the Middle Ages* (London, 1814).

# Second Journal

Friday Feb. 27th. Walk — Read Tristram Shandy.[30] Hogg & Peacock dine

Saturday Feb. 28th. Mr. Carter & Mr. Wright call.[31] Walk with Peacock in Bond Street. We all go to the Opera. Griselda[32] et Le Retour du Primptems.

Sunday Feb. 29th. Rainy. Walk over the Strand Bridge. Peacock dines — M. & S— spend the Evening at Hunts.

Monday ⟨Feb. 2⟩ March 1st. Ride with Shelley into the City. Call on Mr. Baxter.[33] Miss Kent calls[34] —
From this Monday till the next I was employed nearly in the same Way. We saw a good deal of the Hunts. The Children were Christened.[35] We went to the Opera.[36] Miss M. Lambe pays us a Visit.[37]

Wednesday March 11. Set out for Dover. Breakfast at Dartford. Chatham. Ospringe Canterbury. & Dover. I admire the Entrance to Dover. We come at night & it looks almost like a fairy city from the multitude of ⟨lik⟩ lights that are sprinkled here & there over the hills. We stay at York House.

Thursday March 12th. Walk upon the Beach. ⟨Bathe my Darling⟩. Discussion whether we shall go. Major & Mrs. Hare. We do go in the Lady Castlereagh with Major & Mrs. Hare & some other ladies. The brine is very stormy. The Waves Mountains high. But the Wind⟨ow⟩ was favorable & blew us in two hours & forty minutes into Calais. Mrs. Hare was much frightened & repeated the Lord's

[30] Mary was also reading Sterne's novel this year (*Mary Shelley's Journal,* p. 91).

[31] Probably from Marlow. See Mary Shelley, *Letters,* I, 44.

[32] Opera by Ferdinando Paër.

[33] William Thomas Baxter was the father of Mary's friend, Isabel Baxter Booth.

[34] Elizabeth (Bessie) Kent, Marianne Hunt's sister. See Note 37, p. 77.

[35] At St. Giles-in-the-Fields, on March 9. "Alba" became Clara Allegra; her baptismal certificate is printed in Origo, *A Measure of Love,* p. 28.

[36] See Note 20 to the entry of February 11, above, for Peacock's account of this evening.

[37] Mary writes on March 10: "Mary Lamb calls" (in *Mary Shelley's Journal,* p. 93). F. L. Jones presents convincing evidence from Dorothy Hewlett that this was the daughter of Dr. William Lambe, physician and vegetarian (Shelley, *Letters,* II, 15n.).

Prayer in her Distress. every now & then requesting her Servant to go on with it as she was prevented by Sickness. Nothing can be more delightful than Calais. The people are so agreeable & the the town is airy & agreeable. We stay Au grand Cerf. Detant. Go to Bed Early.

Friday March 13. Walk about Calais. Buy a Carriage.

---

⟨Wednesday April 8th.⟩ [*remainder of page left blank*] [38]

Milan. Wednesday April 8th. 1818. We arrived at Milan last Saturday April 4th. Locande Reale. We went through Artois from Calais to Lyons. without visiting Paris. We passed through the Towns of St Omer, Bethune  Douai to Cambray ⟨We see nothing⟩ The English soldiers are quartered in this province. The Post House at Cambray ⟨is⟩ was once a Convent. Here there is likewise a most Magnificent Cathedral. From Cambray to St Quentin & thence to a miserable town called La Fere where we sleep. Next day we get to Rheims but through such Roads by Berry le Bac that every instant the Carriage was in Danger of being overturned. Laon where we breakfasted is finely situated on a steep hill The Inn was once a Convent. The Cathedral is partly in ⟨Ruins from⟩ Ruins. From Rheims to ⟨Cal⟩ Chalons sur Seine, Chaumont &c to Dijon — le Chapeau Rouge. from thence to Macon and then to Lyons — l'hôtel de l'Europe. Lyons is a most Beautiful City. but its ⟨most⟩ best parts are all the work of Napoleon. We go to the Theatre. L'homme Gris et le Physiognomiste. We ride along the River side to L'ile de Barbe where there is a fete. Go and see the confluence of the Saone & the Rhone. We engage two Voituriers to take us to Milan. After a stay of four days we set off. The first day we sleep at Tour le Pin.[39] The second at Chambery, which is

[38] The party which moved across France to Italy in the spring of 1818 consisted of five adults and three children: Mary and Shelley with their William and Clara; Claire with her Allegra; and two servants, Elise, the Swiss servant, and Amelia (Milly) Shields. The day-by-day itinerary may be traced in Shelley's and Mary's MS. journal, which has been misleadingly punctuated in the printing (cf. *Mary Shelley's Journal*, p. 93): on Friday, March 13, they were at St. Omer; March 14, Douay; March 15, La Fere; March 16, Rheims; March 17, St. Dizier; March 18, Langres; March 19, Dijon; March 20, Mâcon; and March 21 (a Saturday), Lyons.

[39] Wednesday, March 25.

the capital of Savoie.[40] We entered Savoy at Pont Beau Voisin —
a bridge most romantically situated. Curious scene. The French
soldiers ⟨on⟩ at one end of the Bridge & the Piedmontese at the
other. Our Carriage stands on the middle of the Bridge nearly an
hour before Passports, impots &c could be settled. It rained all day
at Chambery. Shelley is teized with his Books. He meets with a
Canon who helps him & who knew his father at the Duke of Norfolk's. Monsieur et madame Romieux et la petite Aimèe.[41] We
enter the most beautiful Vallies on our departure from Cham-
berry. The snowy Alps are above & green fertile Valleys ⟨below⟩
issuing one out of another & watered by mountain torrents. The
plains are covered with trellice works which in a few months will
appear as bowers of vines. We dine at Aigue-belle & sleep at St
Jean le Maurienne.[42] there the snow lies in heaps above the town
& the ascent of Mt Cenis may be said to begin   From St Jean de
Maurienne we continually ascend by the side of the Mountain
River to Lans le ⟨Burg⟩ Bourg ⟨a l⟩ a village at the very foot of
Cenis. Our road ⟨lies⟩ lay through deep snow — One pass was very
difficult about ½ a mile from Modêne. The snow at the edges was
as ⟨deep a⟩ high as the Carriage. We sleep at Lans le Bourg.[43]
Next Morning we begin the ascent of Mont Cenis. ⟨singing all
the way⟩ and Shelley sung all the way

> "Now Heaven neglected is by Men
> And Gods are hung upon every tree
> But not the more for loss of them
> Shall this fair world unhappy be.

and assert⟨ing⟩ed that the Mountains are God's *Corps de Ballet*
⟨and the⟩ of which the Jung fraue is Mademoiselle ⟨Milanie⟩ Milanie.[44] We dine on the top of Cenis & bless Napoleon for the pas-

[40] See Shelley's detailed account of this day, *Mary Shelley's Journal*, pp.
94–95.

[41] Mary writes: "Remain at Chambery all day   it rains — Elise's Mother —
father-in-law, and little girl come to see her" (in *Mary Shelley's Journal*, p. 95).
See also Mary Shelley, *Letters*, I, 49. By "father-in-law" Mary probably meant
stepfather.

[42] Saturday, March 28.

[43] Sunday, March 29.

[44] See Note 28 to the entry of February 21, 1818, above. On April 20 Shelley wrote to Peacock, "Clare requests you to write a history of Mademoiselle
Millani" (Shelley, *Letters*, II, 9).

sage must have been dreadful before the new Road was made. We see Cascades of Ice hanging in ⟨imme⟩ immense & frozen Masses from the top to the Bottom of Precipices. A sight I shall never forget was a flowing stream between two snowy Banks. We passed some Alpine Bridges. The Descent is most beautiful — The road is wide & smooth & turns so often upon itself that the decclivity is ⟨sarce⟩ scarcely felt. The Snow is gone and both above & below one looks upon green sunny declivities separated by clumps of trees & ⟨cl⟩ glades. The primroses ⟨shine as brightly⟩ are scattered everywhere. The fruit trees covered with the richest blossoms which scented the ⟨wind⟩ air as we passed. A sky without one cloud — every thing bright & serene — the cloudless Sky of Italy — the bright & the beautiful. We reach Susa about six o'clock. It is ⟨a⟩ delightfully clean and very romantically situated between mountains. The next day we travel along a fertile plain; & reach Turin at six.[45] Torino is nobly built. We stay a day & go to the Opera. of which I neither could get at its tit⟨t⟩le nor make out a single word of what it was all about; there was however ⟨be⟩ in it some beautiful airs. The only light in the house is that which the stage affords. I could not even perceive the faces of those who Sat in the loge next to our's. In ⟨two⟩ three days more we get to Milan. The route is not very interesting — rural country with cornfields & orchards. We pass many Bridges of Boats built over the Beds of the Torrents which pour down from the snowy Mountains when the Sun is up & awakes the Waterfalls. We lodge at the Locande Reale at Milan. Go to the Opera. A most magnificent Ballet Pantomime of ⟨Othello⟩ the story of Othello.[46]

Thursday April 9th M & S— set off for the Lake of Como. Read

[45] Tuesday, March 31. See Mary's description in a letter to the Hunts (Mary Shelley, *Letters*, I, 47–49).

[46] *Otello ossia il moro di Venezia*, a *ballet d'action* by the Italian composer and choreographer Salvator Viganò. Claire's description of a later performance, in the section of the journal now in the Pforzheimer Library, is quoted by Dowden as follows: "The Venetian dance embodies the idea I had formed of the ancient dances of the bacchantes. It is full of mad and intoxicating joy, which nevertheless is accompanied by voluptuousness. Maria Pallerini, the Desdemona, is a lovely creature. Her walk is more like the sweepings of the wind than the steps of a mortal, and her attitudes are pictures" (Dowden, *Shelley*, II, 194–195). Shelley described the ballet to Peacock as "the most splendid spectacle I ever saw" (Shelley, *Letters*, II, 4).

# Second Journal

George Dandin  L'avare, M. ⟨Pour⟩ Porceaugnac, Le Tartuffe of Moliere  The following lines as descriptive of the doctrines of Christinity & Those of the Tartuffe are admirable

> Qui suit ses leçons, goute un paix profonde
> Et comme du fumier regarde tout le monde.

> Oui je deviens tout autre avec son entretien;
> Il m'enseigne a n'avoir affection pour rien.

> De toutes amities il detache mon âme;
> Et je verrois mourir frere, enfans, mere et femme;
> Que je m'en soucierois autant de cela.

> CLEANTE.
> Les sentimens humains, mon frere, que voilà! [47]

⟨Take a ride with my child in the Afternoon round Il Corso.⟩ The Cathedral here is something wonderful. I can conceive of no building that partakes more perfectly of the nature of air & heaven. The carved pinnacles whiter than snow rise into the cloud⟨e⟩. The dazzling white of the marble and the immensity of the work impress one with the belief of the aid of some supernatural power. We went up it. There is a winding staircase, the steps of marble confined on each side by ⟨a⟩ slight irons running horizontally; it rises from the body of the Building & seems to ascend to the clouds. This is the work also of Napoleon. ⟨Take a Ride in the afternoon⟩

Friday April 10th. Read Le Bourgeois Gentilhomme, Le Mariage forcè, Le Festin de Pierre, L'Amour Medecin, Les Fourberies de Scapin de Moliere. In the Evening take a ride round Il Corso. Read a page or two of the Life of Tasso.[48]

---

[47] "[Orgon:] Whoever follows his [Tartuffe's] lessons savors a profound peace and regards all the world as smoke. Yes, I have become another person under his instruction; he teaches me to be attached to nothing. He detaches my soul from all friendships; and I could see brother, child, mother and wife die without becoming upset about it.
"Cleante: What humane sentiments, brother!"
Mary Shelley began reading Molière at about this time and listed "Oeuvres de Moliere" in her 1818 reading list (*Mary Shelley's Journal*, p. 114). The lines Claire quotes are from Act I of *Le Tartuffe*.
[48] On May 11 Shelley was reading Giovanni B. Manso's *Vita di Torquato*

# Italy 1818

Saturday April 11th. Read the Life of Tasso—Read Le Malade imaginaire, Le Medecin malgrè lui, La comtess D'Escarbargnas of Moliere. In the Evening ride on the Corso ⟨with my child⟩.

Sunday April 12th. M & S return. Talk of the Lake of Como. Curious adventure. When they were at Como S thought he would take a walk to some solitary place that he might fire off his pistol which had been loaded during our whole Journey. In walking he observed two men to follow him & when he had got pretty far he stopped till they came up to him. They said they were Police & must take him into Custody as it was forbidden to any one to be carrying Arms about as he was. He expostulated but they persisted in carrying him before the ⟨Pre fact⟩ Prefect. This gentleman when he heard that Shelley was an Englishman and his intention with regard to the pistol behaved with the greatest politeness but said he should keep the pistol safe in his custody till he had heard from Madame Shelley that her husband had no intention of shooting himself through the head. Mary having certified this—the Pistol was rendered. In the Evening we ride round the Corso. Play at Chess with Shelley in the Evening.

Monday April 13th. Walk in the Morning. In the Evening go to the Theatre of the Marionetti. Play at Chess. Read L'Etourdi of Moliere. X [49]

Tuesday April 14th. Sit at home all day. Read the Life of Tasso and L'Étourdi of Moliere. Play at Chess with Shelley in the Evening. Longinus said that the Odyssey was indeed the work of an old Man but of Homer old. [50]

Wednesday April 15th. Read the Life of Tasso. Read Le Depit Amoureux of Moliere—The plot & intrigue of this play is excellent. Play at Chess.

---

*Tasso* (Venice, 1619) (*Mary Shelley's Journal,* p. 98), but Claire on April 20 mentions reading the life by Marcantonio Serassi—actually Pietro Antonio Serassi, *La Vita di Torquato Tasso* (Rome, 1785).

[49] Claire's mark for her menstrual period. See Kessel, "The Mark of X in Claire Clairmont's Journals," *PMLA* 66:1180–1183, esp. 1182n. (December 1951). The recognition of the obvious significance of the monthly mark has not helped Shelley's biographers solve any of their problems.

[50] Serassi, p. 102.

Thursday April 16. Finish the Depit Amoureux   read Les precieuses ridicules. Also part of Clarissa Harlowe.[51] Play at Chess.

Friday April 17th. Read Clarissa Harlowe and Amphitryon of Moliere. Play at Chess.

Saturday April 18. Read the Life of Tasso. Shelley reads aloud Hamlet. Read Lear. Letter from Peacock. Play at Chess.

Sunday April 19th. In the Morning walk with Shelley in the public gardens with "itty Ba."[52] In the Evening ride with M. round the Environs of Milan and round the Corso. Play at Chess.

Monday April 20th. Read the Life of Tasso by Marcantonio Serassi. Walk in the Public Gardens with the Darling.

Tuesday April 21st. Letter from Albè. Nothing but Discomfort.[53] Walk in the Public Gardens. S— & M go to the Opera.

Wednesday April 22. Write to Albè. Mr. Merryweather calls. Walk in the Evening. Read Clarissa Harlowe.

*[April 23 to June in the Pforzheimer Library]*

[51] Samuel Richardson, *Clarissa; or, the History of a Young Lady*, 7 vols. (1747–1748).

[52] Another of Claire's many nicknames for Allegra.

[53] Shelley's answer says: "You write as if from the instant of its departure all future intercourse were to cease between Clare and her child" (see Shelley, *Letters*, II, 9–13).

# THIRD
# JOURNAL
## March 7, 1819, to August 1, 1820

# [1818-1819]

On April 24, 1818, Shelley, walking out to the post office in Milan, met a Venetian full of gossip and bad news about Byron's life in Venice. "Albe Albe everywhere" wrote Mary,[1] but after the receipt of his letter of April 28 Elise set out with Allegra for Venice, in defiance of the evil omens, on the day after Claire's twentieth birthday.

Claire's letters of this period show that she was far from being resigned to a permanent separation from Byron. She always called him "my dearest friend," and obsequiously bent herself to beg of him the small favors of a kind word or a lock of her little girl's hair. Despite Shelley's firm and patient warnings, she sealed her eyes to the gulf which separated her from Byron and blindly wrote: "Yet, my dear friend, why should my presence tease you? Why might not the father and mother of a child whom both so tenderly love meet as friends?"[2] Her passionate attachment to Allegra kept her fighting the battle long after it had been lost.

In May the Shelley party came down to Pisa, stayed two days, and moved on to Leghorn, where they looked up the old friend of Godwin and Mary Wollstonecraft, Maria Gisborne, with her husband John and her son by a former marriage, the engineer Henry Reveley.[3] The six of them made a congenial party, and they took

[1] In *Mary Shelley's Journal*, p. 97.

[2] Murray MSS.; partially printed in Paston and Quennell, "*To Lord Byron*," p. 235.

[3] For Henry Reveley, see Appendix C. The name is sometimes spelled "Reeveley," both by Godwin (a notoriously bad speller) and by Claire and the Shelleys. This can probably be taken as a clue to the pronunciation.

long daily walks and visited constantly together until on June 11 the Shelley party moved into Signor Chiappa's house, Casa Bertini, at the popular Bagni di Lucca.

At Bagni di Lucca the three adults took up horseback riding, a sport popular with the numerous English at that resort. Apparently Claire threw herself into the new pastime with her usual nervous enthusiasm, for she was the one who took the bad falls, one of which was serious enough to injure her knee and incapacitate her for some time.[4] All the activity and the company at the resort were not enough to tranquilize Claire's mind, and once having extracted the promise from Byron that she was to be allowed to see Allegra, she was not content until finally, on August 17, Shelley consented to accompany her to Venice. They began the hard journey immediately, bumping over the rough roads to Florence in a nearly springless cabriolet and then pushing on for three more days of heavy traveling during which they covered sixty miles a day.[5]

It is not necessary here to enter into the details of this visit: Claire's happy days with Allegra at Este, the arrival of Mary, the death of little Clara, and the kindness of the British consul general, Richard Belgrave Hoppner, and his wife. Byron was very reasonable about Allegra, as long as he did not have to see Claire, and he was delighted to have Shelley's company. Even the servants got along well; it was here that the Shelleys' dishonest but temporarily useful factotum Paolo Foggi, who had accompanied Shelley from Bagni di Lucca, met for the first time their Swiss maid Elise, whom he later married. When the Shelleys and Claire left Este on November 5 to travel to Naples by way of Florence and Rome, they took their own horses, with Paolo to drive, and were accompanied by Elise and Milly Shields.[6]

When they arrived in Naples on December 1 Mary was completely exhausted by the wearying trip (her journal reveals her constantly tired) and was suffering a deep depression caused by the loss of her child. Claire, as usual, was little help, being indeed unwell herself part of the time, though not enough to keep her from the strenuous sight-seeing excursions — to Herculaneum, Vesuvius, the Bay of Baiae, Pompeii, Paestum, and a half a dozen more. On

[4] Mary Shelley, *Letters*, I, 56.
[5] Shelley, *Letters*, II, 32–34.
[6] Mary Shelley, *Letters*, I, 60.

# Introduction

February 27, 1819, Shelley went before a magistrate to sign a statement that on December 27, 1818, Elena Adelaide Shelley had been born to him and Mary. Whoever the parents really were, Shelley by this act exposed himself to threats of blackmail by Paolo and damaging gossip by Elise, who later told the Hoppners that Shelley had smuggled his child by Claire into the Naples foundling hospital. It seems clear that Elise's story was a fabric of falsehood, but the episode still remains obscure.[7]

On the last day of February Claire and the Shelleys departed for Rome, and on March 5 they saw the Coliseum again. In Rome Claire resumed her journal, Mary felt that she had begun to live again, and Shelley's letters — some of the best travel letters ever written — testify to his own revitalization. He immediately started writing poetry: 1819 was his *annus mirabilis*. A music master was

[7] Elena Adelaide Shelley still remains a "Neapolitan mystery." After the publication of his *Shelley*, White never ceased his investigation of Neapolitan sources. He examined the files of the Ospedale Annunziata, the only foundling hospital in Naples at the time Shelley was there (copies of the files are in the library of Duke University), and came to agree with the officials of the hospital that no child was deposited there or withdrawn by Shelley. With the addition of this last piece of evidence, inconclusive in itself except as it disproves a part of Elise's story, both Dr. White and Count Riccardo Filangieri, superintendent of the Archivo di Stato di Napoli, were convinced that the investigation had been carried as far as possible in Naples.

Apologists for Byron have always choked on his ready acceptance of Elise's story. Nevertheless, his attitude is not inconsistent with his known readiness to spread slanderous and patently untrue stories about Claire (inexcusable, but understandable as an attempt to justify to others, and probably to himself as well, his callousness towards Claire and his eventual cruelty). As early as September 29, 1816, for example, Claire wrote to Byron: "Kinnaird says you told him I was an atheist and a murderer. You see the stupidity of people, so be chary of my name. A fine character I shall have among you all, when I am nothing more than an innocent, quiet little woman, very fond of Albé" (Murray MSS.; partially published in Paston and Quennell, "To Lord Byron," p. 222).

I do not think that a sexual union between Claire and Shelley would have been inconsistent with their principles, provided that they had been genuinely and deeply in love. I can find, however, no evidence that they were.

Ursula Orange has reviewed the evidence in her "Elise: Nursemaid to the Shelleys," *KSMB* 6:24–34 (1955), and asserts the "probability" that Elena Adelaide was the daughter of Elise and Shelley. There is no new evidence. My only conclusion from a review of the evidence is that it seems to support the "strong possibility" proposed by White that, after the death of Clara, Shelley undertook to adopt a child, hoping eventually to console Mary, and that he hoped to avoid legal complications by registering the child as his and Mary's (White, *Shelley*, II, 78–83).

# Third Journal

engaged for Claire, and Mary took up painting. On April 9 Mary wrote to Maria Gisborne that they would spend the summer in Rome and return to the vicinity of Naples in the autumn so that she could have the attendance there of Dr. Bell, the eminent British surgeon, for the baby she was now expecting.[8] This plan was abandoned when Dr. Bell, himself in failing health, moved elsewhere.[9]

[inside front cover]
Gratze, Soldi — Bajocci — Grani —
Lira, Paoli, Carlini, Piastra, Francesconi
Centisimi, Pezzi.          Ducati.
Quattrini[1]
Guardi [erased]

Ne le me voglie ognor stringe e rafferme
A cenni altrui; ne tra speme e timore
Misero in vecchia e più miser si muore.[2]

On the country of Italy.
On the Manners & Customs
including those of the Country & those of the town.
On the ⟨Belle Arts⟩ ↑Pictures & Statues↓.
On the Music and the State of the Opera.[3]

[8] Jones, "Mary Shelley to Maria Gisborne," SP 52:50 (January 1955).

[9] See John Bell, *Observations on Italy* (London, 1825). This volume, posthumously published, was written in 1817 and describes much of the route and many of the spots visited by the Shelleys. See also Note 10 to the entry of March 20, 1819, below.

[1] Italian coins. *Francesconi* (or *scudi*) were then worth about five shillings (the equivalent of about a pound today); a *paul* (*paoli*), sixpence; *lira*, ninepence; *gratze* (or *crazia*), one-eighth *paul*; *quattrino*, one-fifth *crazia*; *soldo*, three *quattrini*, etc.

[2] I have not found the source of these lines, which may be translated: "In my desires I am always pulled to and fro by someone else; the result is that between hope and fear one is wretched in old age and dies even more wretchedly."

[3] From April 5, 1820, to the end of July (below) Claire records writing her

# Rome 1819

Letter for Bologna
Passport
Blk. Silk Stockings & Shoes
Ivy Leaves

Palazzo Verospi
Al Corso Roma

Sunday March 7—1819 Remove from La Villa di Parigi to Palazzo Verospi upon the Corso[4]—Read the Edinburgh & Quaterly Reviews.

Monday March 8—Visit St Peters—& the Museum of the Vatican.

Tuesday March 9th. Walk in the public gardens—Go to the ⟨P⟩ Fontana di Trevis and to the Pantheon now called La Rotunda—Walk with Shelley to the Capitol, to the Forum & the Coliseum—A beautiful & mild Spring Evening—After dinner pay a Visit to the Signora Marianna Dionigi[5]—then go to the Pantheon to see it by Moonlight—

Wednesday March 10th. Go to the Capitol and visit the gallery of Statues there. Read Voyage de Constantinople by a frenchman.[6] In the Evening pay a visit to the Signora Marianna Dionigi.

Thursday March 11th. Walk to the Capitol—the Forum & the Coliseum—Read Vie de Mademoiselle Montpensiers ecrite par elle meme[7]—In the Evening visit the Signora Marianna Dionigi.

---

"Letters from Italy." This seems to be a table of contents for that work, which has not survived.

[4] 300 Corso. Although very narrow, the Corso, running from the Porto del Popolo to the Piazza Venezia, along the side of the Campus Martius, next to the ancient city, was the busiest, handsomest, and gayest street in Rome. It was the center of festivities during carnival, and the street where the nobility drove up and down every evening in fine weather, displaying their equipages.

[5] For Marianna Candida Dionigi, see Appendix C.

[6] Probably either [Charles-Marie d'Irumberry], *Voyage à Constantinople, en Italie et aux îles de l'Archipel . . .* (Paris, 1799), or [Abbé Guillaume Martin], *Voyage à Constantinople, fait à l'occasion de l'ambassade de M. le Comte de Choiseul-Gouffier à la Porte ottomane* (Paris, 1819).

[7] *Mémoires de Mademoiselle de Montpensier, fille de M. Gaston d'Orléans, frère de Louis XIII . . .* , 6 vols. (Paris, 1728).

# Third Journal

Friday March 12th. Go to St Peters with the Signora Dionigi — hear Mass and a Sermon from the Padre Pacifico  The voice of the Padre is his chiefest excellence — powerful & musical — his Italian is perfect   The music of the Mass is divine and the voices of the Singing Boys sounded ⟨like⟩ in this vast edifice like flutes. We saw the Pope Pius VII a poor old man upon the brink of the Grave and many cardinals almost as old and trembling. In the afternoon go to the Capitol and visit the Statues.

Saturday March 13. Read Cobbett, which is a strange book to read with one's head full of the ruins of Rome. We visit the Palazzo Doria and its gallery of pictures which are some of them extremely beautiful particularly two or three landscapes by Claude Lorraine — Two pictures by Salvator Rosa one ⟨the death⟩ Cain killing Abel and the other Belisairius suffering from a violent storm are most magnificent works. We go also ⟨to the Capitol⟩ across the Capitol to the Forum — the Arch of Constantine   the Coliseum — Then skirting the Palatine Mount we went to the Baths of Antoninus Caracalla — As we came home we met the Pope who had descended from his carriage to walk — We visited also the Arch of Janus Quadrifrons — and the ruins of the golden house of Nero on the Palatine.

Sunday March 14th. Read Cobbett — Go to the Capitol and the Coliseum — We range over every part — along the narrow grassy walks on the tops of the arches — above us on the nodding ruins grew the wall-flowers in abundance — the Coliseum resembles a mountain, its arches and recesses appear as so many caves, and here & there are ⟨p⟩ spread as in the most favoured of Nature's spots, grassy platforms with a scattered ⟨fruit⟩ fruit or thorn tree in blossom — I think there can be nothing more delightful than a daily walk over the Capitol ⟨w⟩ to visit the ruins of the Forum. In ancient times the Forum was to a city what the soul is to the Body — the place in which concentered all the most powerful and the best — In the evening I go there again with S— and see it under the grey eye of twilight —

Monday March 15th. In the morning go ⟨th⟩ to the Gardens of the Villa Borghese where there is a beautiful lake and an ancient temple dedicated to Esculapius the Saviour — here then I caught a glimpse of the ancients so rose their temples like the one before us — on the brink of a clear lake a pillared edifice of white marble of the most ⟨ea⟩ aerial form around groves of the dark Ilex and Laurel trees — These gardens are extensive with a variety of green shady nooks, with fountains and statues.

Tuesday March 16th. Go in the Morning to the Gardens of the Villa Borghese — sit on the steps of the temple of Esculapius and read Wordsworth — Go to the church of St Stefano Rotondo, et St Giovanni et Paolo.

Wednesday March 17th. Walk in the Gardens of the Villa Borghese — ⟨read Vie de Ninon de L'Enclos⟩[8]  Go to the Baths of Titus — to Porta Maggiore — the Aquduct of ⟨Claudia⟩ ↑Aurelian↓ — the Temple of Minerva Medica, the ⟨family⟩ tomb of the Aruntian family and Monte Cavallo — Take a drive in the Borghese Gardens — After dinner visit the Signora Marianna Dionigi —

Thursday March 18th. Walk in the Gardens of the Villa Borghese — Il Signor Amorone calls — in the afternoon ride in the Giardini Borghese.

Friday March 19th. Today is the festa of San Giuseppe — Walk in the Gardens of the Villa Borghese — Read the second Volume of ⟨Schel⟩ Schlegel's Criti⟨s⟩cism[9] — Go to the Villa Doria Pampfili outside the ⟨B⟩ Porta Pancrazio — The inside of the Palace is shabby and there are no statues of any worth but the outside is very beautifully ornamented with statues and Bas-reliefs — There is a curious fountain in the Garden which begins playing to music and if it does nothing else at least surprizes one. Ride in the Borghese Gardens — In the Evening M— somebody a music master comes —

[8] [Antoine Bret], *Mémoires sur la vie de Mademoiselle de Lenclos*, 2 vols. (Amsterdam, 1750-1751). Claire at some later date crossed out references to reading that might be considered improper (see references to Madame de Pompadour and Boccaccio, below, for other instances).

[9] Mary lists "Schlegel on the Drama" in her 1818 reading list, and according to the journal Shelley read Schlegel aloud on the trip through France in March (*Mary Shelley's Journal*, pp. 93, 114). This was probably August Wilhelm von Schlegel, *A Course of Lectures on Dramatic Art and Literature*, trans. John Black, 2 vols. (London, 1815). Mary lent their copy to the Gisbornes, and on July 26, 1818, she wrote to Maria: "How do you like Schlegel? I suppose

# Third Journal

Saturday March 20th. A lesson in Music — Call with S— in the Carriage at several places — at Doctor Bell's[10] and the Villa de Paris — We go to the Palazzo Ruspigliosi — in this palace we see La bella Aurora da Guido Reni and six other other fine heads by the same painter also his Andromeda bound on the rock a picture of great beauty — the beautiful whiteness of her skin seems to cast a light ⟨on the rock⟩ around her — David with the head of Goliath by Domenichino — and Sampson pulling down the temple on the heads of the Phillistines by Caracci — We drive to Monte Cavallo and admire the fountain and the horses of Castor and Pollux for some time — In the Evening visit the Signora Marianna Dionigi —

Sunday March 21st. Go to the Palazzo di Spada — See the statue of Pompey at the base of which Caesar fell — Both the face and figure are extremely fine — two pictures by Guido Reni delighted me — Judith holding the head of Holofernes in one hand and a bloody sword in the other — Lucretia stabbing herself. I saw also a beautiful Magdelaine by Luc Cambiasi — We drive in the Borghese Gardens — In the Evening visit the Signora Marianna Dionigi —

X Monday March — 22nd A lesson in Music — Mr. Bell calls — Go to the Farnesina where there are two ceilings painted in fresco by Raffaello — Also to the Villa Lanti where is nothing but a fine view — It belongs to the Prince Borghese who is never there but always at Florence — Call on Milani the painter — ⟨Read Memoires de Madame de Pompadour⟩[11] —

Tuesday March 23rd. ⟨Read Memoires de Madame de Pompadour⟩ — Go to St Peters ⟨et⟩ and La Rotunda[12] and the Borghese Gardens —

---

you have finished it — how much finer a view does he take of the tragic poets than that Frenchman Barthelemy, who, if he could without an anachronism in his work, would, I doubt not, have prefered Racine to Sophocles" (Jones, "Mary Shelley to Maria Gisborne," *SP* 52:45 [January 1955]).

[10] Dr. John Bell, described by Claire in a letter written for Mary as "reckoned even in London one of the first English Surgeons" (Mary Shelley, *Letters*, I, 72). He attended both Shelley and little William.

[11] *Mémoires de Madame la Marquise de Pompadour . . . écrits par elle-même* [or rather by an unknown writer], 2 vols. (Liège, 1766).

[12] The Pantheon. Shelley's magnificent letter to Peacock on this day should be read (Shelley, *Letters*, II, 83–90).

# Rome 1819

Wednesday March 24th. A lesson in Music — Go to the Museum of the Vatican and the Borghese Gardens —

Thursday March 25th. Festa of the Annunziata in our language Lady-day — Go to the church Santa Maria sopra Minerva. See the Pope and the Cardinals. Walk in the Borghese Gardens — Go to the Palazzo Giustiniani where there are some very fine statues — Go to the Gardens of Villa Borghese — In the Evening to the Signora Dionigi's — & S— to Torlonia's [13] — an old Moldavian there who said he saw Christ in every thing —

Friday March 26th. ⟨Read Memoires of Madame de Pompadour⟩ — Walk to the Coliseum and about the Forum.

Saturday March 27th. A lesson in Music — Read Schlegel Criticism — Go to Canova's — and the Gardens of the Villa Borghese — In the Evening to the Signora Marianna Dionigi — See the Duchess of Clermont-Tonnerre there — a most beautiful Woman [14]

Sunday March 28th. Mr. & Mrs. Bell call — Walk with S— to the Capitol & the Coliseum — It is a most bright and beautiful day — Drive in the Borghese Gardens and sit on the steps of the divine temple to Esculapius the Saviour I see many priests walking about it — In the Evening go to the ⟨Con⟩ Conversazione of the Signora Marianna Dionigi where there is a Cardinal and many unfortunate Englishmen who ↑after having↓ crossed their legs & said nothing the whole Evening, rose all up at once, made their bows & filed off — [15]

[13] This wealthy banker, whom Napoleon had made a duke, was well known for his hospitality and good services to strangers in Rome — particularly the English. He was Keats's banker as well as Shelley's.

[14] Antonio Canova (1757-1822), distinguished sculptor, had his atelier at 16 Via S. Giacomo. Thomas Medwin visited him in the spring of 1822, at which time, he later wrote, "It would have been considered little short of sacrilege to have doubted the infallibility of Canova, or the faultlessness of any work of his; a pilgrim to Delphi might as well have denied the divinity of Apollo in the zenith of his power" ("Canova: Leaves from the Autobiography of an Amateur," *Fraser's Magazine*, 20:370 [September 1839]). The Duchess was Anne de Carvoisin d'Achy.

[15] B. Ducos, who arrived in Rome in November of this year, defined a *conversazione* as what would be called a *soiré* in Paris, a *rout* in London, and, as far as he was concerned, *boredom* in any language (*Itinéraire et souvenirs d'un voyage en Italie en 1819 et 1820* [Paris, 1829], II, 122).

# Third Journal

Monday March — 29th. ⟨W⟩ A lesson in music — ⟨Go to the⟩ Walk with M— ⟨to⟩ across the Capitol to the Forum and Coliseum — Go to Palazzo Borghese where there is a large collection but only one or two good pictures — one is the Sybil of Domenichino in the ⟨act⟩ moment of inspiration — it is an exquisite picture — She is very beautiful both in face and form and her headress & drapery are arranged with the utmost taste   In the Evening go with the Signora Marianna to a friend of hers where we hear sung the Celebrated ⟨Misere⟩ *Miserere* — Nothing was ever so beautiful — Words can never express it for ⟨could⟩ they could only do so by turning to Music ⟨itself⟩ themselves — Nothing but itself can be its parellel —

Tuesday March 30th. Walk to the Campidoglio — Finish Schlegel's Critiscism — Drive in the Borghese Gardens — ⟨Sh⟩ S— goes to hear the Miserere which delights him —

Wednesday March 31st. A lesson in Music — Drive in the Borghese Gardens — Walk to the Campidoglio  the Forum & the Coliseum —

Thursday ⟨Mar⟩ April 1st. Walk with M— to the Capitol and the Forum — then again with Signor Ottavio Dionigi — then to Monte Cavallo — In the Evening ⟨read Lettres de Madame de Pompadour⟩ —

Friday April 2nd. Go to Ponte Molle formerly Milow to see the Pavillion prepared for the Emperor ⟨— the arrive⟩ of Austria — he arrives in Rome at four o'clock in the afternoon.[16] Drive to the Borghese Gardens. A letter from Elise.

Saturday April 3rd. A lesson in Music — Walk to the Capitol — Go to St Peters —

---

[16] On April 9, 1819, Mary wrote to Maria Gisborne: "We are delighted with Rome, and nothing but the Malaria would drive us from it for many months. It is very busy now with the funzioni of the holy week, and the arrival of the Emperor of Austria, who goes about to see these things preceded by an officer, who rudely pushes the people back with a drawn sword, a curious thing that a fellow, whose power only s[ubs]ists through the supposed conveniences of the state, of the complaisance of his subjects, should be thus insolent — Of course, we keep out of his track, for our English blood would, I am afraid boil over at such insolence" (Jones, "Mary Shelley to Maria Gisborne," *SP* 52:50–51 [January 1955]).

Sunday April 4th. ⟨Finish Letters de Madame de Pompadour⟩ — Go to St Peters — Il Signor Delicati calls[17] — ⟨Walk⟩ Drive in the Borghese Gardens After dinner walk to the Capitol & Coliseum. ⟨W⟩ Visit the Signora Dionigi

Monday April 5th. A lesson from il Signor Bandelloni[18] — Drive in the Gardens of the Villa Borghese — Visit the pictures of Raffaello in the Vatican. In the Evening visit the Signora Dionigi. Letters from Hunt & Peacock.

Tuesday April 6th. Il Signor Delicati calls — Drive in the Borghese Gardens.

Wednesday April 7th. A lesson in Music — Write to Mrs. Hoppner — Drive in the Borghese — Go to the Vatican

Thursday April 8th. Holy Thursday — Drive in the Borghese Gardens — In the Evening go with the Signora Dionigi to see the Illumination of the cross in St Peters and the Paoline Chapel.[19] See the Benediction also. Mr Bell calls.

Friday April 9th. Good Friday — Walk — meet Signor Chiappa[20] — In the afternoon — hear part of a Miserere by Guglielmi[21] — See the Illumination of the Cross and the ⟨P⟩ Washing & Supping of the Pellegrini.

Saturday April 10th A lesson in Music — ⟨Rea⟩ Read Tour by Forsyth[22] — Drive in the Borghese Gardens — Visit the Vatican.

[17] Signor Delicati, an artist, was a frequent visitor during April; on April 6 Mary sat to him (*Mary Shelley's Journal*, p. 119). The letters that Claire read on April 1 and 4 were *Lettres de Madame la Marquise de Pompadour; depuis 1753 jusqu'à 1762 inclusivement . . .* , 2 vols. (London, 1771), a fictitious correspondence attributed to the Marquis F. de Barbé-Marbois or to Prosper Jolyot de Crébillon.

[18] Claire's music master (see Mary Shelley, *Letters*, I, 79).

[19] On April 9 Mary wrote to Maria Gisborne, "We saw the illuminated cross in St. Peter's last night, which is very beautiful; but how much more beautiful is the Pantheon by moonlight!" (Jones, "Mary Shelley to Maria Gisborne," SP 52:51 [January 1955]).

[20] Signor G. B. del Chiappa was the owner of Shelley's house, Casa Bertini, at Bagni di Lucca (June 1818). Mary called him "a stupid fellow" (Mary Shelley, *Letters*, I, 53).

[21] Pietro Guglielmi (1728–1804), best known for his operas, was *maestro di cappella* of St. Peter's in the Vatican from 1793.

[22] Joseph Forsyth, *Remarks on Antiquities, Arts, and Letters during an Ex-

# Third Journal

Sunday April 11th Easter Sunday — Go to St Peters with Mr. Davies and hear the funzioni [23] — Afterwards see the Benediction — In the Evening We see the Illumination of St Peters and the Girandola at the Castle St Angelo [24] at the Loggia of the Signora Marianna Dionigi.

Monday April 12th. No lesson in Music — ⟨Dis⟩ Letter from Mrs. Hoppner concerning Mrs. Vavassour [25] — Drive in the Bor-

cursion in Italy in the Years 1802 and 1803 (London, 1813). Read by Mary on April 8 and 9 (Mary Shelley's Journal, p. 119) and recommended by Shelley to Peacock (Shelley, Letters, II, 89).

[23] Ducos (Itinéraire, II, 106–109) describes in detail the funzione at St. Peter's, which were attended by as many foreigners as Romans. According to his account, the base of the spectacle was a high mass. The Cardinal was the center of a magnificent pageant of pomp and veneration, with several changes of vestments and a succession of different miters, the entire ceremony climaxed by Gregorian chant, followed by orchestral music and hymns of joy, with priests dramatically displaying holy relics illuminated by a shaft of light from the opening of a window high in the cupola, and the whole terminating in clouds of incense. See also Mariana Starke's excellent Travels on the Continent (London, 1820), p. 382.

[24] The following account is from Starke, Travels, pp. 382–383: "About six in the evening commences the first Illumination of the outside of S. Peter's; which is effected by means of four thousand four hundred paper lanthorns, lighted by men suspended on the outside of the edifice by ropes, and drawn up and down by persons stationed within: but the service is so imminently dangerous that these lamp-lighters receive the sacrament before they begin their labour. The lamps which compose this first Illumination cast a light somewhat resembling that of the moon: but, at seven o'clock, literally in one moment, the whole scene changes, and presents the most brilliant spectacle imaginable; as every part of the Church, to the very summit of the cross on the cupola, appears one blaze of fire. The materials which compose this second Illumination are pitch, wood-shavings, and eighty-four flambeaux, so wonderfully managed that the effect is perfection. About eight o'clock commence the Fireworks of the Castle of S. Angelo: for seeing which to advantage it is needful to secure a balcony, or a window, in the opposite Piazza. This magnificent display of fireworks begins with an explosion, called the Girandola; and produced by four thousand five hundred rockets, so arranged as to represent an eruption of Vesuvius. A variety of beautiful changes then take place; and exhibit the Tiara, the Keys of S. Peter, the Pope's Name, blazing super-eminently amidst more sombre fire, and the Statue of the Arch-Angel Michael encompassed with resplendent rays of glory. Wheels, Fountains, Roman candles, &c. are likewise exhibited; and the whole closes with a second Girandola that appears to convert the very Tiber into flames; and throws reflected light upon the majestic dome of S. Peter's, which shines brilliantly amidst the seeming conflagration."

[25] Mrs. Vavassour was a wealthy and childless English widow who had

ghese Gardens. In the Evening go to the Conversazione of the Signora Dionigi — Music by two from Arpino[26] — Mr. Davies and the Principessa Belvidera —

Tuesday April 13th. Arrange some little matters — Signor Chiappa call. Drive in the Borghese. Walk to the Campi d'oglio. In the Evening Mr. Davies calls.

Wednesday April 14th. A lesson in Music. Read S—'s translation of Plato's Symposium.[27] Go to Monte Cavallo — Drive in the Borghese Gardens. In the Evening go to the Signora Marianna Dionigi —

Thursday April 15th. Practise. Read Plato's Symposium. Drive in the Borghese Gardens. In the Evening Visit the Signora M— Dionigi. Music by two from ⟨Arppino⟩ Arpino —

Friday April 16 — Finish the Symposium of Plato — The fanelli of Arpino call — In the Evening Practise —

Saturday April 17th. A lesson in Music — Read La Fleur des Batailles a history of Chivalry[28] — Drive in the Borghese ⟨Vis⟩ gardens —

Sunday April 18th. Read Regner Lodborg a history of Chivalry[29] — Go to the Vatican   Meet there the two from Arpino — Drive in the Borghese. In the Evening at the Conversazione of the Signora Marianna — The 2 from Arpino called Fanelli two Irish Ladies & Mr. Davies

X Monday April 19th. A lesson in Music. Drive beyond Porta

offered to adopt Allegra if Byron would relinquish all parental authority, but nothing came of the plan (see Marchand, *Byron*, II, 803).

[26] Musicians called Fanelli (linnets).

[27] Shelley made his translation July 9–20, 1818, during an otherwise unproductive period at Bagni di Lucca (*Mary Shelley's Journal*, pp. 101–102, and Mary Shelley, *Letters*, I, 56). It is published in Shelley, *Works*, VII, 165–220.

[28] Both Mary and Claire were reading in *Bibliothèque universelle des dames*, section five: novels, 20 vols. (Paris, 1785–1788). "La Fleur des Batailles" is in vol. XI (1787). Mary's journal references to "Romans Chevaleresques" (May 1) and "Bib de Chevalerie" (May 3) are doubtless to this series (in *Mary Shelley's Journal*, p. 120).

[29] "Histoire de Rigda et de Regner Lodbrog," in *Bibliothèque universelle*, vol. XI.

# Third Journal

Salaria—Visit Villa Albani  Also in the Borghese—See the trying of the Ponies for the approaching corso in Piazza Navona—Dr Bell calls and the Signor Delicati—In the Evening visit the Sig. Dionigi—The Avocato Galimberti & his Wife.

Tuesday April 20th. Read Huon de Bordeaux[30]—Mr. Davies calls & Signor Delicati—Drive in the Borghese— In the Evening go to the grand festa ⟨in⟩ at the Capitol with M— & Mr. Davies. Meet Mr. & Mrs. Bell.

Wednesday April 21st. Read 1 Canto of Ricciardetto[31]—Drive in Villa Borghese. A lesson in Music—

Thursday April 22nd. Finish Huon de Bordeaux—Visit Palazzo Colonna—See the Portrait of Beatrice Cenci—Drive in the Borghese. Visit the Signora D— Sir W Drummond calls.[32]

Friday April 23rd. Read Guerin de Montglave[33]—and 2nd Canto of Ricciardetto—Drive in the Borghese—We think we see Miss Curran.[34] In the Evening go to the Signora D— the 2 from Arpino & La Ricqueta—

[30] *Bibliothèque universelle*, vol. XII (1787). Mary writes (April 15), "Read Huon de Bourdeaux, a Roman de la Chevalerie" (*Mary Shelley's Journal*, p. 119).

[31] [Niccolò Forteguerri], *Il Ricciardetto di Niccolò Carteromaco* ([Venice], 1738), consisting of thirty cantos of more than one hundred ottava-rima stanzas each, parodying Italian Renaissance epics. Shelley, who read it aloud June 26, 1820 (*Mary Shelley's Journal*, p. 135), found it "admirable" (Shelley, *Letters*, II, 207).

[32] Shelley had mentioned Sir William Drummond's *Academical Questions* (1805) with admiration in the preface to *The Revolt of Islam*. Drummond was at this time British Minister to Naples and had undertaken excavations at Herculaneum. On November 3, 1819, Shelley wrote to Hunt: "Has not Sir William Drummond, the most acute metaphysical critic of the age, a man of profound learning, high employments in the state & unblemished integrity of character, controverted Christianity in a manner no less undisguised & bold than Mr. Paine?" (Shelley, *Letters*, II, 142.)

[33] In *Bibliothèque universelle*, vol. XII.

[34] Amelia Curran, daughter of the witty and eloquent Irish patriot, John Philpot Curran. Aaron Burr described her in 1812, the year Shelley first met her, as having "all the genius and eloquence of her father, and the vivacity, the ingenuousness, and the sensibility of her sex and her country" (Burr, *Correspondence*, p. 333). Lady Sydney Morgan found her living like a hermit in Rome in February 1820, but judged her "full of talent and intellect, pleasant, interesting, and original; and she paints like an artist" (*Lady Morgan's Memoirs*,

# Rome 1819

Saturday April 24th. Lesson in Music. Read 3rd. & 4th. Canto of Ricciardetto. Leave a Card at Miss Curran's. Drive in the Borghese. Mr. Bell calls  In the Evening music by the 2 from Arpino — La Ricqueta the Cavaliere de Piedmont, & one or two others.

Sunday April 25th. Read 5th. & 6th. Canto of Ricciardetto — Mr. Bell calls — In the Evening at the Signora D— Meet that very particular friend of Lord B's ⟨Colo⟩ the Rev. Col. Finch[35] — a painter, La Ricquetta & two Prelates — Signor Delicati calls —

Monday April 26th. A lesson in Music — Read 7th. Canto of Ricciardetto — Rainy all the day —

Tuesday April 27th. Read 8th & 9th. Canto of Ricciardetto — Miss Curran calls — Go with her & M. to the Capitol to the German Exhibition — Call in Via Sistina[36] and chat there two hours — In the Evening visit the Signora D p. p. c.

Wednesday April 28th. A lesson in Music — Read the tenth Canto of Ricciardetto —

Thursday April 29th. Read 11th. Canto of Ricciardetto  Call on Miss Curran — We drive with her to the Borghese and to the Capitol and the Forum.

Friday April 30th. Read the 12th. Canto of Ricciardetto and read no further. I find it so stupid — Call on Miss Curran & drive in the Borghese. The Signor Delicati calls.

---

II, 130). She lived at 64 Via Sistina and painted portraits of Mary, Claire, William, and Shelley. A letter from Mary to Amelia (June 20, 1820) makes it clear that Claire did not like her portrait, and the postscript of Mary's letter to Amelia on September 25, 1820, reveals that relations were still strained between Claire and the artist: "Claire desires (not remembrances — if they are not pleasant) however she sends a proper message & says she w[oul]d be obliged to you if you let her have her picture" (Mary Shelley, *Letters*, I, 111, 114). The portrait is now at Newstead Abbey. There is considerably more warmth and vitality in the likeness than the familiar black-and-white reproductions convey.

[35] Robert Finch, called "Calicot" Finch by the Shelleys, after Biddy Fudge's lover in Thomas Moore's *The Fudge Family in Paris* (1818). See Mary's high-spirited description of the encounter in her letter to Maria Gisborne, April 26, 1819 (Mary Shelley, *Letters*, I, 68–69). See also E. Nitchie, *The Reverend Colonel Finch* (1940).

[36] Amelia Curran's lodging.

# Third Journal

Saturday ⟨April 3⟩ ↑May↓ 1st. A lesson in Music — Read 1st. Canto of Dante's Paradiso —

Sunday May ⟨1st⟩ 2nd Rainy — Read Floris & Fleur Blanche — Cleomades et Clarimonde et Pierre de Provence et la Belle Maguelone [37] — Also 1st Chapter of Winkelmann — [38]

Monday May ⟨2nd.⟩ 3rd  A lesson in Music — Read Petrarch. Walk out to the Capitol — Meet Mr. Bell & Signor Bandelloni. In the Evening the Canonico Dionigi calls — He complains of the weight of the taxes which amount in the Roman State to between three & four million a year and are much higher now than under the french.

Tuesday May ⟨3rd.⟩ 4th. Read Petit Jehan de Saintrè [39] — Miss Curran calls — Drive with her in the Borghese —

Wednesday May ⟨4th.⟩ ↑5th↓  A lesson in Music — Go with S— to Miss Curran — Sit for my portrait — Drive in the Borghese. M.P. [40]

Thursday May ⟨5th.⟩ 6th  Go to Miss Curran's and sit for my portrait — Read Corinne — S—'s adventure at the Post Office. [41] Signor Delicati calls.

Friday May ⟨6th.⟩ 7th  S— sits for his portrait to Miss Curran. Read Les Visions de Quevedo [42] — & Mon Bonnet de Nuit de Mercier. [43] Move from 300 Corso to 65 Via Sistina L'Ultima Casa sulla Trinita dei Monti. [44] In the Evening Walk on the Trinita with S & Mr. Bell.

[37] "Flores et Blanche-fleur," "Cléomades et Claremonde," and "Pierre de Provence et la belle Maguelone, Fille du Roi de Naples," in *Bibliothèque universelle*, vol. IX (1786).

[38] Johann Joachim Winckelmann, *Histoire de l'art chez les anciens*, trans. from the German by H. J. Jansen, 2 vols. (Paris, 1790, 1803). Shelley read Winckelmann aloud in December 1818, January and March 1819 (*Mary Shelley's Journal*, pp. 114–117).

[39] In *Bibliothèque universelle*, vol. XIV (1787).

[40] I have not been able to discover the significance of these initials.

[41] Madame de Staël, *Corinne; ou, l'Italie*, 2 vols. (Paris, 1807). For some versions of what this adventure may have been like, see White, *Shelley*, II, 178, and 589, n. 6.

[42] Francisco Gómez de Quevedo y Villegas, *Les Visions* [*Sueños*] (1627). Mary was reading it on May 6 (*Mary Shelley's Journal*, p. 121).

[43] Louis Sébastien Mercier, *Mon Bonnet de nuit*, 2 vols. (Neuchâtel, 1784).

[44] Next door to Amelia Curran.

# Rome 1819

Saturday May ⟨7th⟩ 8th. Walk out — Miss Curran calls — Shelley sits for his portrait — A lesson in Music

Sunday May 9th. The English Vice Consul — Mr. Cary calls — Miss Curran calls. We walk with her on the Banks of the Tyber beyond the Porto del Popolo.

Monday May 10th. A lesson in Music — Miss Curran calls — ⟨Read Boccaccio[45] — among others⟩ the tale of Guiscardo & Ghismonda which is very beautiful.

Tuesday. May 11th. Walk in the Gardens of the Trinity — Miss Curran calls. Read again the story of Guiscardo & Ghismonda — & half 1 Chapter of Winkelmann.

Wednesday May 12th. A Lesson in Music — Miss Curran calls — Walk in the Gardens of the Trinità. Miss C— spends the Evening —

Thursday May 13th We go to Tivoli with Miss Curran  We see the Cascades & the temple of the Sybil — The day then comes on Rainy & we return to Rome. This I shall ever remember as one of the pleasantest of my life and one as only Italy can give —

Friday May 14th. Read Manuscript of the Cenci Family[46] — Practise. Walk in the Gardens of the Trinita — Meet Mr. & Mrs. Bell. We go to Miss Curran's to see Will's Portrait. A discussion concerning Jealousy.

X Saturday May 15th. A lesson in Music — Read 1 Canto of Dante's Purgatorio. Miss Curran calls. Write to Mrs. Hoppner⟨r⟩. Walk on the Gardens of the Trinità.

[45] Mary's journal records her reading of Boccaccio, specifically the *Decameron*, from May 7 to 22 (*Mary Shelley's Journal*, p. 121). On September 27, 1819, Shelley wrote at length to Leigh Hunt about his enthusiasm on recently reading "this most divine writer" (Shelley, *Letters*, II, 121-122).

[46] On this day Mary records: "S writes his Tragedy [*The Cenci*]" (in *Mary Shelley's Journal*, p. 121). On the following day Claire wrote to Byron the first letter in which she allowed him to see the violent resentment that she was to nurse toward him for the rest of her life (partially printed in Paston and Quennell, "*To Lord Byron*," pp. 241-242). In an unpublished passage in the letter she writes: "Did you ever read the history of the Cenci's a most frightful & horrible story?" She then wrote and crossed out: "I am sorely afraid to say that in the elder Cenci you may behold yourself in twenty years [*one word illegible*] but if I live Allegra shall never be a Beatrice" (Murray MSS.).

# Third Journal

Sunday May 16th. Read 4 Canto's of Dante's Purgatorio. Miss Curran calls — Walk in the Gardens of the Trinita —

Monday May 17th. A lesson in Music — Read 5th. 6th 7th. & 8 Canto of Dante's Purgatorio. Walk in the Gardens of the Trinita Miss Curran calls —

Tuesday May 18th. Walk before Breakfast on the *Trinity*. Read Alfieri's Tragedy of Mirra [47] — Write a letter to Albè [48] — Read 9 & 10th Canto of Purgatorio.

Wednesday May 19th. A lesson in Music — Miss Curran calls. Read 11th. & 12th Cantos of Purgatorio — Walk in the Gardens of Trinità — ⟨read a few tales of Boccaccio⟩ —

Thursday May 20th. Read 13th. 14th. 15th. & 16th. Cantos of Dante's Purgatorio. Walk in the gardens of the Trinità  Miss Curran calls — A grand festa being the Ascenscion of the Virgin

Friday May 21st. Practise 7 — hours — Walk on the Trinità — ⟨Read a few of the tales of Boccaccio⟩.

Saturday May 22nd. A lesson in Music — ⟨Read a few of the tales of Boccaccio⟩. Miss Curran calls. Walk on the Trinita

Sunday May 23rd. Practise. ⟨Read Boccaccio⟩. S— goes to Albano. Walk on the Trinità.

Monday May 24th. A lesson in Music — Walk with S— on the Trinità dei Monti. Read The Infernal Quixote. [49]

Tuesday May 25th. Practise — ⟨Read Boccaccio⟩ — Walk in the Gardens of the Trinità. Miss Curran calls.

Wednesday May 26th. ⟨Read Boccaccio⟩ — A lesson in Music. Walk on the Trinità — William ill.

[47] *Myrrha,* in *The Tragedies of Alfieri,* trans. C. Lloyd (London, 1815), vol. III. Alfieri's play was one of Shelley's precedents for the subject of *The Cenci* (see Shelley, *Letters,* II, 200, and Peacock's note quoted in Shelley, *Works,* X, 82n.).

[48] Perhaps she finished on this day the letter that she dated May 15.

[49] Charles Lucas, *The Infernal Quixote: A Tale of the Day,* 4 vols. (London: Minerva Press, 1801), a novel about a young woman corrupted by Mary Wollstonecraft's *A Vindication of the Rights of Woman* (London: J. Johnson, 1792).

# Rome 1819

Thursday May 27th. William ill — Dr Bell calls — Also Miss C— In the Evening go with S— to an Accademia of Music at Zerletti's in Piazza di Spagna. Hear the Salmi of Marcello.[50] See ⟨Thurlvansen⟩ ↑Thorwaldsen↓ the famous German Sculptor.[51]

Friday May 28th. Dr. Bell calls also Miss Curran William ill. Walk on the Gardens of the Trinità.

Saturday May 29th. Mr. Bell calls also Miss C. William better. Read Tableau de Societè de P— ⟨Le Braun⟩ ↑Le Baune↓.[52] A lesson in Music.

Sunday May 30th. Mr. Bell calls — curious story of the consultations of Italian physicians at Naples. ⟨Read Boccaccio⟩. Miss C— calls   Walk on the Trinità —

Monday May 31st. A lesson in Music. Call in several places in Rome. William better   Mr. Bell calls. ⟨Read Boccaccio⟩.

Tuesday June 1st. Mr. Bell calls — ⟨Read Boccaccio⟩ — Miss Curran calls

Wednesday June 2nd. William very ill — Mr. Bell calls three times — Miss Curran calls. A lesson in Music. I sit up with Willy. Read ⟨Le petit Charles ou Neveu de Mon Oncle⟩.[53]

Thursday June 3rd.[54]

Monday June 7 — at noon-day [55]

Thursday June 10th. set out from Rome for Livorno   We visit

---

[50] Benedetto Marcello, whose settings of fifty psalms appeared in Venice from 1724 to 1726 and were considered by the Italians of Shelley's day to be masterpieces of their kind, although Burney in his *History* disagreed (see *Grove's Dictionary of Music and Musicians*, V, 564; *Louis Spohr's Autobiography* [1865], I, 300).

[51] Actually Danish. Bertel Thorwaldsen did a bust of Byron.

[52] Charles Antoine Guillaume Pigault-Lebrun, "Tableaux de société," in *Œuvres complètes* (Paris, 1822–1824), vol. XVI.

[53] Not identified.

[54] On June 3 Mary made her last journal entry until August 4: "William is very ill but gets better towards the evening. Miss C calls" (in *Mary Shelley's Journal*, p. 122). See Claire's note to Maria Gisborne, June 3, 1819, in Mary Shelley, *Letters*, I, 72.

[55] William Shelley died. He was buried in the Protestant cemetery.

# Third Journal

the waterfall of Terni once again    We see also the Lake of Thrasimene now called the Lake of Perugia. Arrive at Livorno Aquila Nera Thursday 17th. Stay there a week. See the Gisborne's.[56] Remove to Villetta Valsovano near Monte nero    Read Cobbett's Journal in America    Birbeck's Notes on the Illinois Nightmare Abbey & the Heart of MidLothian by Walter Scott.[57]

Thursday July 1st. A lesson in Music from Signor Squillone — Mr. & Mrs. Gisborne call. Practise. Read the Spectator.

Friday July 2nd. Walk to Livorno with S & Mr Gisborne. Practise.

*[remainder of this page and all of the following page blank]*

[1820]

⟨Saturday⟩ ↑ Sunday↓ Jan. 2nd. 1820 Florence [58] Read a little Spanish — Los Cabellos de ⟨Calderon⟩ Absalon de Calderon de la Barca.[59] Go to Church with Mr. & Mrs. Meadows.[60] Call on Mrs.

[56] Shelley's first impression of Maria Gisborne, formerly a close friend of Godwin, was of a "very amiable & accomplished Lady" (Shelley, *Letters,* II, 18), living in Leghorn with her husband and her son by a former marriage, the engineer Henry Reveley. He described John Gisborne, in August 1819: "Her husband a man with little thin lips receding forehead & a prodigious nose is an excessive bore. His nose is something quite Slawkenburgian" (*ibid.,* II, 114).

[57] This refers to the crop of new books that had arrived in June from Peacock (Shelley, *Letters,* II, 98–99): William Cobbett, *A Year's Residence in the United States of America* (London, 1818), and eight numbers of the *Register;* Morris Birkbeck, *Notes on a Journey in America, from the Coast of Virginia to the Territory of Illinois* (London, 1818), and *Letters from Illinois* (London, 1818); Thomas Love Peacock, *Nightmare Abbey* (London, 1818); and Sir Walter Scott, *Tales of My Landlord,* second series (Edinburgh, 1818), containing *The Heart of Midlothian.* See Peacock, *Letters,* p. 80. The books were sent on November 29, 1818.

[58] On September 4, 1819, Charles Clairmont had arrived from a fifteen-month tour of Spain, and early in October the Shelleys, with Charles and Claire, moved to the Palazzo Marini, Via Valfonda 4395, in Florence. Their landlady was Madame Merveilleux du Plantis, who, with her daughters Zoide and Louise, had called on them in Leghorn just after arriving from England and visits to Godwin (see Nitchie, *Finch,* pp. 48–49, for an account of the colorful background of this woman). On November 10 Charles had departed for Vienna, two days before the birth of Percy Florence Shelley.

[59] In July Shelley had learned enough Spanish from Maria Gisborne to be reading Calderón (Shelley, *Letters,* II, 105), and the arrival of Charles from Spain had given fresh impetus to the "Calderonizing." *Los Cabellos de Absalón*

114

# Florence 1820

Pollok & Miss Sherlock. Dine at Madame Merveilleux with Mr. & Mrs. Harding and their Children. Mr. & Mrs. Meadows, Mr. Pidwell Mrs. Dalton & Mrs. Baxter   Il Capitano & Signora Mutii in the Evening.

Monday Jany. 3rd. A lesson from Pelleschi.[61] Practise. Mrs. Pollok & her children call. Read Don Juan.[62] Read the Life of Plutarch.[63]

Tuesday Jany. 4th. Call with Zoide du Plantis on Mrs. Pollok. Call on Pelleschi at the Scuola delle belle Arti. Mr. Tomkyns.[64] Dine at Casa Gerini with many Italians — the Signora Marianna & Giovanino Fabri — the Doltons Fabrils — The Polloks.

Wednesday Jany — 5th. A lesson from Pelleschi. Practise — Read the Life of Theseus.[65] Pelleschi comes in the Evening & sings. Read Mazeppa.[66]

Thursday Jany 6. The feast of the ⟨Ephi⟩ Epiphany. ⟨Re⟩ Finish reading los Cabellos de Absalon of Calderon. Read the Life of Theseus. Mrs. Tomkyns calls.

Friday Jany. 7th. A lesson from Pelleschi. Mr. Tomkyns takes

---

particularly interested Shelley because of its poetical treatment of incest (*ibid.,* II, 154).

[60] Mary, in summarizing the last months of 1819, says: "We have seen a good deal of Mr. & Mrs. Meadows" (in *Mary Shelley's Journal,* p. 126).

[61] Claire's new singing teacher, Gaspero Pelleschi, was also a composer (see "L'Ombra di Dante: Cantata di Francesco Gonnella, posta in musica dal Maestro Gaspero Pelleschi," in Giuseppe Gonnelli, *Elogio di Lorenzo Ghiberti* [Florence, 1822]).

[62] Cantos i and ii of Byron's poem.

[63] John and William Langhorne, *Plutarch's Lives,* translated from the original Greek, with notes critical and historical, and a new life of Plutarch, 6 vols. (London, 1770). She had written to Byron, January 12, 1818: "Alone, I study *Plutarch's Lives,* wherein I find nothing but incitement to virtue and abstinence" (Paston and Quennell, *"To Lord Byron,"* p. 232).

[64] See Dowden's note (*Shelley,* II, 312) on Mr. Tomkins, an amateur portrait painter also staying at the house in the Via Valfonda.

[65] In Plutarch, which she continued to read, with occasional passages transcribed in her journal, through January 21.

[66] By Byron (1819).

# Third Journal

Shelley's likeness. Read — the Auto of La Vida es Sueño de Calderon. Finish the Life of Theseus. S— is ill in the Evening.[67]

Saturday — Jan. 8th. Read the Auto of Vida es Sueño — Begin the Life of Romulus. A letter from Madame Hoppner — The Hero is gone to Ravenna.[68] Mr. Tomkyns calls. Work in the Evening while Shelley reads the Gospel of Mathew aloud. A ⟨letter from⟩ lesson from Pelleschi.

Sunday Jany. 9th. Mr. Tomkyns calls to take S—'s likeness. Read the Auto of Vida es Sueño — Very severe frost — ⟨Read the⟩ Finish the Life of Romulus and half that of Lycurgus.

Monday Jany. 10th. A lesson from Pelleschi. Drive with Mrs. Harding and the two Duplantis to Palazzo Pitti — Meet there Mr. Meadows & Mrs. Harding and a nephew of Captain Mutii — Examine the Gallery of Pictures — A Cleopatra by Guido applying the asp to her breast is of exquisite delicacy in the Colouring — Also a masterpiece of Raphael — the Virgin Mother presenting Jesus an infant to the aged Elizabeth — with Anna the prophetess & a young St John.  two Magdalens one by Domenichino who have nothing beautiful but their long & flowing ↑hair↓. A large & fine picture by Rubens — Mars between Bellona & Venus. Two large landscapes by Salvator Rosa. Spend the Evening with Mrs. Pollak — the Cavaliere Gerini & his Wife — her Cavaliere Servente Bertini — Mr. Greaves & Mrs. Macdonald — A very very severe frost —

⟨Monday Jany 11th⟩ Tuesday Jany. 11th. Finish the Life of Lycurgus — Begin that of Numa — Pythagoras ⟨ordered⟩ says when you sacrifice to the celestial Gods let it be with an odd number & when to the terrestial — with an even — "for the odd number is most perfect because it cannot be divided into two equal parts as the even number may which is therefore the symbol of division"  Let

[67] On January 12, 1820, Mary wrote to Maria Gisborne, "Besides all pains in the side, of which Shelley has plenty, he had an attack last Friday of fever, just like, only more severe, the one he had on returning from Leghorn to Florence [September 25]. Wind! Frost! Snow! How can England be worse?" (Jones, "Mary Shelley to Maria Gisborne," SP 52:54 [January 1955]).

[68] On Christmas Eve, 1819, Byron had gone to Ravenna as Teresa Guiccioli's acknowledged *cavalier servente.* Allegra was with him, the pet of Teresa and the servants.

this rule be applied to marriage and we shall find the cause of its unhappy querulous state.

It snows all day — Letter from Miss Stacey [69] — A lesson from Pelleschi in the Evening. Mr. Tomkyns calls.

Wednesday Jany 12th. A lesson from Pelleschi — ⟨3 — Birthday⟩.[70] Read & finish the Life of Numa — Begin Solon — also made a law by which a citizen who should remain neuter during a sedition was punished with Death — Romulus ordered ⟨that⟩ the Punishment of Death to woman who should be found drunk — The Grecian Women were much freer than the Romans, altho' they were earlier — the Romans full of superstitious religion — half Numa's care seems to have been employed in ordering the religious ceremonies whereas Lycurgus's whole thoughts were devoted to the education both moral & physical of his Spartans.

Thursday Jany. 13th. Finish the Life of Solon — — Mr. Tomkyns calls — Mr. & Mrs. Meadows drink tea with us. Play at Snow Balls with the ⟨Tow⟩ Two Duplantis & the little Hardings. A lesson from Pelleschi.

Friday Jany. 14th. Read the Life of Poplicola — A lesson from Pelleschi. Play at Snow Balls with the Hardings and the 2 Du Plantis. Mr. & Mrs. Meadows drink tea.

Saturday Jany. 15th. Finish the Life of Poplicola. The thaw begins — Mr. & Mrs. Meadows drink tea with us. Mr. Tomkyns calls.

Sunday Jany. 16th. Very great Thaw. Pelleschi says there has not been so severe a Winter in Florence for 70 years. Read the Life of Themistocles which a beautiful monument to the glory & virtue of the Athenians. Notwithstanding they were sometimes cruel for in a difference of opinion concerning an old oracle which ran thus "Divine Salamin thou wilt destroy the children of Women" Themistocles said that it was in their favour since by the Children of Women the Persians were meant on account of their softness & effeminacy but Cyrsilus an orator who maintained a

[69] Sophia Stacey, a ward of the Mr. Parker who had married Sir Timothy Shelley's sister, visited the Shelleys in Florence in December 1819 (see Angeli, *Shelley and His Friends in Italy*, pp. 95-105).

[70] Allegra's third birthday.

contrary opinion was stoned by the Athenians and their wives stoned his Wife. They also stoned the Ambassador who coming from Xerxes demanded Earth & Water for his Master. The Lacedemonians conducted themselves in this war extremely ill  they thought of nothing else but securing their dear Sparta from the Persians.

Monday Jany. 17th. Read the Life of Camillus — A lesson from Pelleschi — Mr. Tomkyns calls. Work all day.

Tuesday Jany. 18th. Work — Finish the Life of Camillus.

Wednesday Jany. 19 Work. Mrs. Meadows drinks tea with — Casa Lozzi comes into my head.

Thursday Jany. 20th. M. writes to Madame Hoppner.[71] Work all day. S reads Henry 4th. to us.

Friday Jany. 21st. Begin Life of Pericles. Work all day.

Saturday Jan 22nd. Work all day — Mrs. Pollok calls.

Sunday Jany. 23rd. Elise calls.[72] Take a short Walk — Spend the Evening at Mrs. Pollok's with Zoide. Meet Mr. Tomkyns & Mr. Shepherd there.

Monday Jan 24th. A lesson from Pelleschi — Walk with Shelley to Mrs. Pollok's — Then in many places about town. Work. We talk of going to Pisa.

X Tuesday Jany. 25th. Walk on several commissions about Florence with Zoide Du Plantis — Pack up. Call upon Miss Sherlock in Borgo ogni Santi — In the Evening — our little babe is half baptized by the name of Percy Florence by Mr. Harding —

Wednesday Jany. 26th. Set off at eight — Mr. & Mrs. Meadows & Zoide walk with us to the rill of the Arno where we begin our navigation — The weather was at first very severe — a keen wind blowing all the time — The Banks of the Arno are very beautiful somewhat like those of the Rhine but of a much softer character. ⟨The hills are seen the whole length of the⟩ We see Hills the whole length of our course — now hanging over the River and now

[71] This letter seems not to have survived.
[72] Elise Foggi.

receeding in long green Vallies to meet others — We arrived at
Empoli about two having done 30 miles in 5 hours — Here we
landed and took a carriage for Pisa — which city we reached about
5 — at night — We lodge at the Tre Donzelle.

Thursday Jany 27th. Walk with — S— about the town seeking
Lodgings. Call on Mrs. Mason and the pretty Laurette [73] — The
Weather most exquisitely warm & sunny — Read an Irish pam-
phlet [74] — Horrid dream about Skinner Street & apoplectic fits

Friday Jany 28th. Rainy — Read Irish Pamphlet & Travels before
the Flood [75] — Also two chapters in Schlegel's Dramactic Criticism

[73] "Mrs. Mason" was Margaret Jane King Moore, second Countess Mount
Cashell (1773–1835), separated from her husband and living in Pisa in Casa
Silva, in the Via Mala Gonella, on the south side of the Arno, as the common-
law wife of George William Tighe (known to the Shelleys as "Tatty," *never*
as Mr. Mason). They had two daughters, Anna Laura Georgina (Laurette or
"Tetta"), born July 19, 1809, and Catherine Elizabeth Louisa ("Nerina"),
born June 20, 1815. Mary Wollstonecraft had been governess to Lady Mount
Cashell in Ireland, and after Mary's death her protégée had continued her friendship with Godwin and his sprawling family. As Mrs. Mason, she became Claire's
"Minerva," and she was the center of Shelley's Pisan circle, where he was at
home for the rest of his life. (See E. McAleer, *The Sensitive Plant: A Life of
Lady Mount Cashell* [1958].) Shelley wrote of her to Leigh Hunt (April 5,
1820): "We see no one but an Irish lady and her husband, who are settled here.
She is everything that is amiable and wise, and he is very agreeable. You will
think it my fate either to find or to imagine some lady of 45, very unprejudiced
and philosophical, who has entered deeply into the best and selectest spirit of
the age, with enchanting manners, and a disposition rather to like me, in every
town that I inhabit. But certainly such this lady is" (Shelley, *Letters*, II, 180).
[74] Lady Mount Cashell had been an active member of the United Irish
movement, which culminated disastrously in what Shelley called "the liberti-
cide war" of 1798. The Irish pamphlets which Claire and the Shelleys were
reading at this time may have included the three ascribed to Lady Mount Cashell
in the National Library in Dublin: *A Few Words in Favour of Ireland by Way
of Reply to a Pamphlet Called "An Impartial View of the Causes Leading This
Country to the Necessity of an UNION,"* by No Lawyer (Dublin, Printed, and
Sold by the Book-sellers, 1799); *Reply to a Ministerial Pamphlet, Entitled "Considerations upon the State of Public Affairs in the Year 1799, Ireland,"* By a
Philanthropist (Dublin: Printed and Sold by the Booksellers, 1799) [the "ministerial pamphlet" was by T. R. Bentley]; and *A Hint to the Inhabitants of Ireland by a Native* (Dublin, 1800).
[75] Friedrich Maximilian von Klinger, *Reisen vor der Sündfluth* (1794),
appeared anonymously in English as *Travels before the Flood. An Interesting
Oriental Record of Men and Manners in the Antidiluvian* [sic] *World; Inter-*

# Third Journal

Saturday Jany 29th. Call at Mad. Mason's. Zanetti calls [76] — Remove to Casa Frasi Lung' Arno. Read another Irish Pamphlet — also one of Chateaubriand's — De Buonaparte et des Bourbons — He says that the men raised for the army by Conscription were nick-named *matiere essentielle chair a canon* [77]

Sunday Jany 30th. Read Rousseau sur Les Arts & Les Sciences [78] — a piece of most extraordinary Prejudice and envious wailing — It had better have been entitled a Disquisition on the Military Art since it teaches the way to make good Soldiers but not ⟨Philo⟩ Philosophers. Letter from Mrs. Pollok. Drink tea at Madame Mason who tells us some very amusing stories of English Prudery. Of a Lady who "mounts her Chastity and rides over us all."

Monday Jany. 31st. Mad. Mason and her Children call. Walk with Lauretta — Write to Mrs. Pollok — Read Common Sense by Paine and two numbers of the Crisis a Paper which he published during the American War. [79] Shelley goes to Livorno —

Tuesday February 1st. A lesson from Zanetti — Mad. Mason calls. Walk with Laurette on the Argine — Read Paine — The Spaniards have this proverb — That he who lives in a glass-house

---

preted in *Fourteen Evening Conversations between the Caliph of Bagdad and His Court*, trans. from the Arabic, 2 vols. (London, 1796). It was read by both Shelley and Mary in 1820 (*Mary Shelley's Journal*, p. 143). The quotations in Claire's entry of February 5, below, are from vol. II, between pp. 110 and 185.

[76] Signor Zanetti was a music teacher.

[77] François René de Chateaubriand, *De Buonaparte, des Bourbons, et de la nécessité de se rallier à nos princes légitimes* . . . (Paris, 1814). "Essential matter — cannon fodder."

[78] *Discours qui a remporté le prix à l'Académie de Dijon, en l'année 1750: . . . si le rétablissement des sciences et des arts a contribué à épurer les moeurs* (1750). Subsequent editions carried the refutations. Shelley had ordered this work in 1815 (Shelley, *Letters*, I, 433) and again in 1817, when he specified the edition "avec les Reponses" (*ibid.*, I, 585).

[79] Claire's reading of Thomas Paine was doubtless inspired by Lady Mount Cashell, who, as a great admirer of revolutionaries, had made a visit to Paine in Paris in 1802. For an account of the visit, see Wilmot, *An Irish Peer on the Continent* (1801–1803), pp. 56–57. Miss Wilmot was Lady Mount Cashell's traveling companion, and her detailed and lively journal gives a valuable picture of the rich literary and political background of the woman who was to be Shelley's Mrs. Mason.

should not begin by throwing stones — In Paine I find an account of the English cruelties in America and India — In the latter General Clive used to destroy his prisoners by shooting them from the mouth of the canon [80] — Hints for Don J — which appears to me a soliloquy upon his own ill-luck — Ungraceful & selfish — like a beggar hawking his own sores about and which create disgust instead of Pity. [81]

Wednesday Feb. 2nd. Mad— Mason calls. Walk a little with Laurette — Read Paine's Works. Shelley comes home in the Evening from Livorno —

Thursday Feb. 3rd. Walk with Shelley on the Argine — The Hills are beautifully blue which we see — The River smooth & flowing and a pretty planted plain around. We dine at Madame Mason's — She talks to us of her Sisters Caroline & Lady Diana di Richi — [82]

Friday Feb. 4th Read Paine. In the American War the Amount of the taxes paid by the English (not including Ireland & Scotland) was £11,642,653 — which makes 1 pound 13 shillings & three pence per head per annum. 5 million of this went to discharge the interest of the national debt — the ⟨o⟩ rest to defray government expences — To begin the American War ⟨th⟩ & to continue it England borrowed about 10 million sterling per annum to pay the increased interest of which she raised new taxes to the amount of 40 shillings per annum upon every head Women & children included. America had a population of three millions of Souls. The whole expence of the War & of the Government did not amount to more than two millions sterling which on an average is thirteen Shilling & four pence per head Women & Children included per Annum. Paine's says "if the War ceases we shall not then pay more than an annual tax of five shillings per head." [83]

[80] The Spanish proverb is in *The American Crisis* (1776–1783), no. 7; the English cruelties are referred to in no. 3.

[81] Notes for a critique, or perhaps a parody, of Byron's poem — and Byron the man — appear regularly in Claire's journal through November 28, 1821.

[82] Caroline married Major General Edmund Morrison; Jane Diana married first Herman, Count Wentringerade, and second General John Robert Augustus di Ricci (McAleer, *The Sensitive Plant*, p. 19).

[83] In *The American Crisis*, no. 10.

# Third Journal

Walk with Laurette on the Argine — Finish Paine's Crisis — The last number which congratulates the Americans on the conclusion of the War is fine — A lesson from Zanetti

Saturday Feb. 5th. A letter from Charles. Practise. Walk with Laurette and call in Casa Silva   Vaccà calls & says I am scrofulous and I say he is ridiculous [84] — M. & S drink tea at Casa Silva. Answer Charles letter — Read Paine's Letter to the Abbè Raynal. Read Travels before the Flood which I like much. The Copts who have a thinking sultan discharge God as superfluous — the Sullahers keep him on account of his ⟨use in poetry⟩ being a grand, mysterious poetical subject. In the Alcoran are these words speaking of Poets — Bereft of their senses they run about in the Vallies and talk what they do not perform." An ambassador of St Louis King of france met a Woman in the streets of Damascus carrying water in one hand & fire in the other. The Ambassador asking the reason of so singular an appearance she answered "With the fire I will burn Paradise — with the water extinguish the fire of Hell that men may worship God for his own sake and not as mercenary labourers."

Sunday Feb. 6th. Walk with Laurette on the Argine and the Banks of the Arno. ⟨W⟩ Vaccà calls. Drive with Nerina & Laurette on the Lung' Arno after dinner to see the Mascherata — Drink tea in Casa Silva. Letter from Charles to Mary.

Monday Feb 7th. A lesson from Zanetti — The Day is rainy — Read and finish Paine's Letter to the Abbè Raynal   the feeling of this letter I admire exceedingly — it is truly cosmopolitan — Finish the travels before the Flood.

Tuesday Feb 8th. Read Paine's Rights of Man. Laurette calls. Practise. Write to L— Du Plantis.[85] In the Evening go to the Opera with Laurette Shelley and Signor Zanetti. La Cenerentola di Rossini. Many Masks.

[84] See journal entry and Note 98 for January 1, 1821, below, and Appendix C.

[85] Charles Clairmont was much in love with Louisa du Plantis when he left Italy for Vienna, and one can only guess at the contents of Claire's letter by its repercussions. Perhaps she had told Louisa that if she really loved Charles she would set out after him. At any rate, in a letter to Mary written February 26 and sent on by her to Claire, who received it on March 8 (see below), Charles reported receiving a furious letter from Madame du Plantis: "First she says

# Pisa 1820

Wednesday Feb 9th. A lesson from Zanetti. Walk with Laurette. Read Rights of Man first part — "It is the faculty of the human mind to become what it contemplates and to act in unison with its object". A Greek author says. "A bad wife is like Winter in a house"

Thursday Feb 10th. Practise. Walk with Laurette on the Argine. Call in Casa Silva. Finish the first part of Rights of Man. Ride in the Mascherata with the Children.

> Di tanti fiaschi
> Tutti ben pieni
> Pene, pensieri
> Lungi da me
> Tu m'escerai
> Io venerò
> Affanni, guai,
> Più non avrò [86]

Friday Feb 11th. A lesson from Zanetti. Practise. ⟨Read⟩ Begin La Cisma de Ingalaterra de Calderon della Barca. Walk with Laurette on the Argine. Impertinent letter from Madame Du Plantis concerning Chiroplast. Write her an answer. Newspapers containing the death of the Duke of Kent on Jany 23, 1820. In the Evening read ⟨Pai⟩ the second part of Paine's Rights of Man. ⟨Simple⟩ Account of the simple and sensible manner in which the

---

Claire has written a most indecent letter to her daughter, from which her virtuous Child turned with horror, & foreswore every alliance with the Author; next says she, independently of this, 'circumstances of another nature, respecting yourself have reached our ears, which render it necessary to break off all correspondence with you.'" She then proceeded "to dash Claire in a most furious manner, vowing, (which is very wicked if it be true) that Claire has taken away her Chiroplast, CASE AND ALL!" (Charles Clairmont to Mary Shelley, February 26, 1820, from Austria; Bodleian MS. Shelley Adds. d. 5) Claire mentions receiving "an impertinent letter from Madame Du Plantis concerning Chiroplast" and answering her, in the entry for February 11, below. For the story of the "Chiroplast," a mechanical device invented by Johann Bernhard Logier to assist the young pianist in the correct positioning of the hands, see Kingston, "Notes on Three Shelley Letters," *KSMB* 6:13-15 (1955).

[86] These verses, which I have not been able to identify, may be translated: "Out of so many failures [flasks], all brimming over; out of sufferings; out of long thoughts you will be born of me. I shall worship, and I shall have no more weariness and woe."

# Third Journal

Americans constituted their government⟨s⟩ — Paine's writings are a monument to their glory which they repaid by refusing him Burial in any of their Church-Yards. Whenever such examples fall in my way I remember Southey's apostrophe. "Man is the worst of all animals and it is a disgrace to the Oran Outang to be compared with him." [87]

Saturday Feb 12th. Write to Mrs. Pollok. Practise. Call in Casa Silva — The weather becomes rainy. Read La Cisma de Ingalaterra de Calderon de la Barca. Finish the second part of Paine's Rights of Man. Burke calls the House of Commons a pillar of security to the landed interest — very true and a pillar of such strength that the tax upon brewing small beer amounted at that time to nearly as much as the whole of the land tax — and to infinitely more if the tax upon malt & hops should be added. These are but three articles of consumption — if we remember that all articles of consumption are almost as much taxed we can have some notion of the selfishness of the house of Commons, for the tax upon ⟨brew⟩ beer does not fall on those who can brew in their own houses, but upon the most miserable of the poor who purchase it by retail.

Sunday Feb 13th. Begin Locke's essay on the Understanding [88] Drink tea in Casa Silva — Curious stories of Lady Mountcashell. When she was young being a great admirer of freedom and an united Irishwoman she had a great passion for seeing all the extraordinary men of the day — She was in London at the trial of Hardy and the other eleven men for conspiracy to overturn the government.[89] They were acquitted and shortly afterwards she

[87] "But man is a Beast, and an ugly Beast, and Monboddo libels the Oran-outangs, by suspecting them to be of the same family" (Robert Southey, *Letters Written during a Short Residence in Spain and Portugal* [Bristol and London, 1797], p. 63). James Burnett, Lord Monboddo, adopted his notion of the kinship between man and the anthropoid apes from Rousseau. He was the object of gentle satire by Peacock, who introduced Sir Oran Haut-ton, an orangutan who stands for Parliament, into his novel *Melincourt* (1817), written while he was closely associated with Claire and the Shelleys at Marlow.

[88] John Locke, *An Essay Concerning Human Understanding*, 2 vols. (19th. ed.; London, 1793).

[89] Thomas Hardy, shoemaker, founder and secretary of the London Corresponding Society, was arrested for high treason on May 12, 1794. John Horne Tooke, John Thelwall, and eight others followed him to the Tower within the week. William Godwin produced a pamphlet widely circulated before the trials

walked into the city to Hardy's shop — She found only his wife there to whom she said that she came to order a pair of shoes ⟨and⟩ as she had a great curiosity to see the man who had been acquitted on a charge of high treason. The wife said he would come presently and knocking Lady M on the ⟨ha⟩ arm she whispered, pointing to a little vulgar dirty man ⟨in⟩ "there's another of them." When Hardy entered she ⟨told⟩ said — "Are you not one of those who were committed to the Tower"? to which he replied with great calmness — "Yes I had that honor." This answer pleased her as daring to justify what he had dared to do — and she found him a good, strait forward man with great firmness & ⟨much⟩ some understanding. She ordered a pair of shoes which she called for herself but she found them shockingly made pinching & galling her dreadfully so much that she took a hackney coach to his house. When she saw him she said — "Mr. Hardy I am very sorry for it but my feet are democratical and your shoes are aristocratical and they d'on't agree at all — Pray have the kindness to put them on the last for me." To this he agreed and when she returned for her shoes she found he had made her a new pair which tho' bad shoes did not hurt her in the wearing. Hardy would never receive any payment for either of the pairs and he was the more pleased at her frank acceptance of his present when on asking her name he found her to be a Countess.

She asked Holcroft to recommend her a governess for her daughters and he proposed his own child Fanny — whom she believing to be accomplished received.[90] But Fanny was of that kind which goes by the name of *"luckless."* She could not take anything into her hands but she let it fall — she thought herself handsome tho' a very plain girl and her dress & affectations excited the ridicule of the whole house. She attended nothing to her pupils but was for ever writing poetry. Did a great man enter the house she wrote Poetry — a little one? — she wrote poetry — was there a party to

---

which was credited with saving the lives of the accused, whose acquittal was hailed as a glorious victory for reform (Brown, *Life of William Godwin*, pp. 90ff., and Woodcock, *William Godwin*, pp. 111–112).

[90] Fanny was the daughter of Godwin's good friend Thomas Holcroft. For the whole background of Lady Mount Cashell's story, see Paul, *Godwin*, II, 110–115. The luckless Fanny eventually achieved some repute as a novelist and translator.

dinner she wrote poetry — Was there no party to dinner? ⟨she⟩ still she wrote poetry — and such poetry! She was called down by one of the servants on the arrival of a party of strangers — she rushed into the room breathless and with a pen in her hand. Ah! my God!" said she — "have the kindness to excuse me I have left my heroine in my hero's arms and I must fly to relieve them" — so saying she disappeared to the great astonishment of all the company. She was found missing one morning — sought for and pursued — She had run away with a gentleman and all the account she could give of him was that he wore a *green coat* — yet with all this she was the best creature in the world, of a sweet and equable temper and very generous disposition

As we walked to Casa Silva we met the Revd. Colonel Finch — a sight I did hope never ↑to↓ see more. A Letter from Miss Stacey, who is at Naples.

Monday Feb. 14th. This is St Valentine's day. Practise. Begin 1st part of Paine's age of Reason. Also read part of his trial for that publication.[91] Ride with Laurette and Nerina to see the Mascherata. In the middle ages Vergilius was condemned to be burnt for asserting the Antipodes or in other words that the Earth was a globe and habitable in every part where there was land.

Tuesday Feb ⟨15th.⟩ 15th. Practise. Walk on the Argine with Laurette. This is the last day of the Carnival — Drive on the Lung' Arno with the Children masked. Finish 1st part of Paine's Age of Reason and begin the second.

Wednesday Feb 16th. Practise. Walk on the Argine with Laurette. A lesson from Zanetti. News of the Death of King George who died the 29th. of January. Read a little of La Cisma de Ingalaterra. Instance of false ⟨ph⟩ prophecy in ⟨Isaaih⟩ Isaiah — The Kings of Syria and of Israel marched against Ahaz King of Judah — He being frightened Isaiah to reassure him ⟨phrophe⟩ prophesied that a "Virgin should conceive and bare a child" and that ⟨the two kings should quit his territory before this same child⟩ before this child shall know to refuse the evil and choose the good, the land which thou

[91] *The Age of Reason* (1794-1795) and *The Trial of Thomas Paine, for Certain False, Wicked, Scandalous and Seditious Libels Inserted in the Second Part of the Rights of Man* (4th. ed.; London, n.d.). The passage about Vergilius, mentioned below, is from *The Age of Reason*, part i.

dreadest (viz Syria and Israel) shall be forsaken of both her kings."
but it is related in the ↑28 C— of the↓ 2nd Book of Chronicles
that Ahaz was defeated and destroyed; an hundred & twenty
thousand of his people killed—Jerusalem plundered and 200,000
people made captives.[92]

Thursday Feb 17th. Practise—Walk with Laurette. Read 1st.
Chapter of Locke's Essay. Write to Mrs. Pollok. Finish the 2nd
part of Paine's Age of Reason.

Friday Feb 18th. Practise. A lesson from Zanetti—Story of the
pretty Laurette. It was necessary to have one of her teeth drawn
but her Mamma and *Tatty* could not resolve to give her the Pain—
She, understanding this, sent secretly for the dentist suffered the
operation and then told them of it. This happened this afternoon.
Read Locke. At the end of the IIId. Chapter—19 Edition   No
Innate Practical Principles—"Who is hardy enough to contend
with the reproach which is every where prepared for those who
dare venture to dissent from the received opinions of their Country
or Party? And Where is the Man to be found that can patiently
prepare himself to bear the name of Whimsical, Sceptical, or
Atheist which he is sure to meet with who does in the least scruple
any of the Common opinions?"

Saturday Feb 19th. Read 1 Scene in the Cisma de Ingalaterra.
Begin Davanzati's Tacitus.[93] Rainy Weather—Mrs. M. has the
power of shutting up her nose so that she need not smell bad
odours. ⟨W⟩ Vaccà thinks it is the muscle which prevents the food
from going from the mouth to the nose which she closes tight.
Madame ⟨W⟩ Vaccà by long practise has acquired also this facility
—so at least she says.

Sunday Feb. 20th. Write to Albè and Madame Hoppner.[94] Call
in Casa Silva.

Monday Feb 21st. A lesson from Zanetti. Read La Cisma de
Ingalaterra. Also a little of Davanzati's Tacitus. Walk with Laurette
—⟨Mr⟩ Il Signor Gianetti calls in the Evening—Read Locke.

[92] In *The Age of Reason*, part ii.
[93] Bernardo Davanzati Bostichi, *Tacito volgarizzato*, 3 vols. (Paris, 1804).
[94] These letters seem not to have survived.

# Third Journal

He distinguishes Ideas in two distinct orders. The 1st. which are produced in the mind from External Substances & the 2nd. from the Perception we have of the Operations of the mind — such as Thinking (examination of an impression) Doubting (⟨arising⟩ state arising from an imperfect impression) Believing (Confidence reposed in our impressions)   Reasoning (the comparing of two Ideas) Knowing (the certainty arrived at by comparison) Willing (the directing of the powers towards the attainment of an object). Some people do never attain a clear idea of the three latter operations — for their sensations are so fleeting that they leave not time for the understanding to turn inwards and examine and make them more peculiarly its own.

Hypothesis drawn from this in explanation of Genius — Acute senses receiving profound Impressions — long contemplated by the Understanding which grows ⟨at⟩ like the body by Exercise. ⟨⟨*Creation* the peculiar attribute of Genius   the work of Judgement consisting in the just and proportionned ⟨adaptat⟩ adaptation⟩⟩ [95] of ⟨one force⟩ impressions ⟨till it creates⟩ untill also like the ⟨body⟩ creation of the body into height and stature   the mind creates & generates. ⟨⟨If so, the irritation so common to people of Genius ought to be generally allowed, in favour of the advantages which Genius procures to us.⟩⟩ This is no argument in favour of the "genus irritabile" ⟨which⟩ of which this sect are accused, since if their perceptions of pain are strong, so must equally ↑be↓ their ideas of the faultiness in giving way.

Teusday Feb 22nd. Practise. Walk with Laurette to the convent of Santa Chiara to pay a visit to Betsy an English Nun.[96] Read Davazati's Tacitus.

X Wednesday Feb. 23rd. Practise. Walk with Laurette by the Back of Scota's Garden & ⟨on⟩ outside the Florence Gate. Read La Cisma de Ingalaterra — in which the Queen Cattarine tells Henry that ⟨the⟩ Jane Seymour can sing, Ana Bolena dance and the

[95] In this and the following section Claire has cast about for the proper wording of her reading notes. Her first drafts, lightly crossed through, are enclosed in double-angle brackets.

[96] Claire made four more recorded trips to see Betsy, or "Suora Ancilla." Then on August 7 Madame Tantini called and had the nun with her. These are the only references to her in all of Claire's journals, which are reasonably complete for the period of 1820 through the summer of 1822. See Appendix C.

# Pisa 1820

Infanta Maria knows the elements of Moral Philosophy — Drink tea in Casa Silva. Talk over a Plan of Capuccini for Madame Du Plantis. Much Laughter. A letter from Mrs. Pollok.

Thursday Feb. 24th. Practise. Read Cisma de Ingalaterra — Walk a little with Lauretta — but it rains. Read Davanzati's Tacitus. Also a little of Locke.

Friday Feb. 25th. A lesson from Zanetti. Call in Casa Silva. ⟨A le⟩ Hear the news of the assasination of the Duc de Berri.[97] Walk with Laurette. Read Cisma de Ingalaterra. Letter from Horace Smith. Il Signor Vaccà ⟨ad⟩ et Gianetti call. Finish the 1st. Book of Tacitus.

Saturday Feb 26th. Practise. Walk with Laurette on the Argine. Read a little but very little of Tacitus. Drink tea in Casa Silva. Anecdote of Lord Edward Fitzgerald[98] — When he was eighteen he was sent with the English Army to America — Some of his friends complimented him on the gallant manner in which he behaved being the first battle he was ever in — he said Ah! how much better I should have fought had I been on the other side!

Sunday Feb 27th. Walk with S— in the Cascini — Dine in Casa Silva — Lady Oxford used always to travel with an English doctor in her suite — She said one day ⟨in⟩ to a large ⟨pr⟩ party —

[97] Charles Ferdinand de Bourbon, Duc de Berry, was assassinated on February 13, 1820, by a fanatic at the door of the Opera House in Paris. For a detailed account, see Mary Berry, *Extracts of the Journals and Correspondence of Miss Berry from the Year 1783–1852*, ed. Lewis, III, 207–215.

[98] Lord Edward (1763–1798), one of the great Irish revolutionary heroes, killed in the United Irish rebellion. He was to Shelley one of the martyrs "to the swinish multitude, to the undiscriminating million" (Shelley, *Letters*, I, 294). See Thomas Moore's *Life and Death of Lord Edward Fitzgerald*, which reveals Lady Mount Cashell as a friend of the family. On May 18, 1798, Lady Mount Cashell's father, Viscount Kingsborough, second earl of Kingston, was on trial before his peers for murder. According to W. E. H. Lecky, Lord Edward, military leader of the United Irishmen, suggested at a secret meeting that the Chancellor and peers might be attacked while they were all under one roof at the trial and the government taken over at once. The plan was rejected by one vote; by the next night Lord Edward had been apprehended (Lecky, *History of England in the Eighteenth Century*, VIII, 40–41, and note). After riding with Lady Mount Cashell on March 10, 1820, Mary writes: "Conspiracy to kill all the English ministers," clearly an allusion to Lord Edward's plot (in *Mary Shelley's Journal*, p. 130).

# Third Journal

"Well I do not know what I should have done last night — I was so thirsty had not Bickerstaff my doctor who slept in my room got me a glass of water I should have perished!" When she was at Vienna she used on the pretence of delicate health to make this Bickerstaff carry her to & from her carriage in his arms and she always danced with him which astonished the Germans who thought it "tres drôle que Miladi dansoit toujours avec son accoucheur." [99]

Read Davanzati's Tacitus — When Germanicus entered Athens he was attended by only one lictor to shew his respect for this ancient & wise city. He visits ⟨Ital⟩ Egypt — which was contrary to a law of Augustus — that no patrician could visit Egypt without permission — as it was so easy with a few troops to prevent any communication with this key of land — by which stoppage Italy would suffer a famine — [1]

Write to Mrs. Pollok et Madame Hoppner.

Monday Feb. 28th. Call in Casa Silva — N—a [Nerina] is ill — Mr. & Mrs. Gisborne spend the day with us. Chat in the Evening with Mad. M — Meet Vaccà and Tantini [2] I do nothing of reading all day

Tuesday Feb. 29th. This is Leap-Year — Call in Casa Silva — N—a better. A lesson from Zanetti — There is a report that the English ships sent out under Captain Parry have found the N.W.

[99] "Very droll that milady should always dance with her accoucheur." Jane Elizabeth Scott, countess of Oxford, is now best known for her association with Byron.

[1] *Annals,* book ii, in Davanzati, I, 105.

[2] Francesco Tantini (1779–1831), a disciple of Francesco Vaccà and friend of his son Andrea, was the second distinguished physician in Lady Mount Cashell's circle. In the Cini family library there was (in 1952) a copy of his work, *Opuscoli scientifici,* 3 vols. (Pisa, 1812–1830), presented to "M. — M." "d'alta stima. Pisa 10 Gennajo 1823." The Reverend Colonel Finch described him in 1817, in Italian leaving something to be desired, as "professore di medecina, un uomo garbato, a che è bravo per la litteratura," which may be translated, "professor of medicine, a graceful man, and enthusiastic about literature" (Bodleian MS. Finch d. 21). Mary wrote to Maria Gisborne on March 26, 1820: "The Rev. Colonel [Finch] has been impudent to Mad[a]me Tantini & is dismissed" (Mary Shelley, *Letters,* I, 103). La Tantini was born Cecilia Liebrecht, in Hamburg, 1772 (see Francesco Tantini, *Pensieri, reminiscenze ed elogj del Professore Francesco Tantini* [Hamburg, 1833]).

# Pisa 1820

Passage. In the Evening go to an Accademia of Music — Many buffa songs by a Priest.[3]

Wednesday March 1st. Practise — Call in Casa Silva — Nerina ill of the measles — Read Davanzati   Begin translating De la Servitude Volontaire d'Etienne de la Boëtie — [4]

Thursday March 2nd. Call in Casa Silva — ⟨Mr⟩ Nerina better. Il Signor Vaccà calls. Walk about with S— Call at the Convent of Santa Chiara to see Betsy or Suora Ancilla — our Catarina is sent there. Read Davanzati's Tacitus. Letter to Mrs. Hoppner.

Friday March 3rd. Call in casa Silva — S— goes to Livorno. Call at the Convent Santa Chiara — Read Davanzati's Tacitus — ⟨Begin⟩ Translate Etienne de la Boëtie —
  Tacitus calls the days of Tiberius putrid times so great ⟨w⟩ and ⟨deb⟩ pervading was the base flattery of the Senate — Tiberius used to say in Greek when he came out of the Senate — *O Homines ad Servitutem paratos!* [5]

Saturday March 4th. Call in Casa Silva — A lesson from Zanetti — Call at the Convent. Read Davanzati's Tacitus — Death of Junia the sister of Brutus and wife of Cassius — She leaves her riches to the principal people of Rome excepting Tiberius — At her⟨s⟩ funeral the statues of 20 of the principal families were carried but Tacitus says those of Brutus and Cassius shone the more because they were not there.[6]

Sunday March 5th. Call in Casa Silva — Letter from Miss Stacey — Read Davanzati's Tacitus — Practise. Translate Etienne de la Boëtie —

[3] An *accademia* was a literary or musical entertainment, held in a theater or a private residence, often with an admission charge or a collection at the door to raise funds for the artist or for charity. For an account of one by Sgricci, see Mary Shelley, *Letters*, I, 132–133.
   [4] Étienne de La Boétie, *Discours de la servitude volontaire* (ca. 1553) (also known as *Le Contre-un*). The author was a friend of Montaigne.
   [5] "Oh men, ripe for servitude!" *Annals*, book iii. Davanzati quotes this line in Italian, which suggests that along with his translation Claire was reading Adolph J. C. A. Dureau de La Malle's *Tacite*, 6 vols. (Paris, 1818), a new translation with the Latin text facing that included notes, a life of Tacitus, and Gabriel Brotier's supplements as translated by Dotteville.
   [6] *Annals*, book iii.

# Third Journal

Monday March 6th. Call in Casa Silva — Call at the Convent — Lesson from Zanetti — Shelley comes home from Livorno.

Tuesday March 7th. Call in Casa Silva — Read Davanzati.

Wednesday March 8th. Letter from C— at Wien[7] — and Mrs. Meadows at Rome. Drive with Mad. M. on the Lucca Road.

Geist — Ghost — *Heilige Geist* the Holy Ghost — *Ach! Er ist ein geist"* Oh! he is a very Ghost! "Eine geistliche frau" is a witty woman. *"Ein Geistlicher"* or the person of Ghost means a clergyman. *Geistlichkeit* is the thing of Ghost, that is the clergy & Geistreick or rich in Ghostliness is the quality of a very spirituous Wine of a witty man or Woman, or a devout parson and *Geistseher* a Ghost seer.

*Ein bild* is a picture. *sich einbilden* to immagine — *Fahren* is to drive a coach; the participle ⟨gefuhrt⟩ geführt driven — so *angeführt werden* to become conducted by a person or duped. *Laufen* is to run, *nach* is after, consequently to *nachlaufen* a lady is to be in love with her. Schuld is guilt and beschuldigen is to guiltify or accuse. *Fertig* is ready and *fertigen* to make ready and *rechfertigen* to prepare the right of a thing or person, that is to justify. *Kraft* is force & *bekräftigen* to give force or confirm. *Ja* is yes & *bejahen* to affirm. *Nein* is No and *verneinen* is to say no or deny. *Ent* is out & *entschuldigen* is to put out of guilt or excuse. *Lieb* is Love; *kosen* to chatter *liebkosen* to caress. Adventure of Col. Finch — & Blacksmith.[8]

Thursday March 9th. Our little Percy has the measles. Vaccà calls. A lesson from Zanetti. Call in Casa Silva —

Friday March 10th. Practise. Read Davanzati's Tacitus — Translate Étienne de la Boëtie —

Saturday March 11th. Walk with Laurette — No lesson from Zanetti — In the Evening go to the Opera with Lauretta ⟨L⟩ and

[7] The letter from Charles in Vienna, written February 26, 1820, was addressed to Claire and Mary (Bodleian MS. Shelley Adds. d. 5). The notes on the German language are extracted from this letter. See also Note 86 to Claire's journal entry of February 8, 1820, above.

[8] This episode is described by Mary in a letter to Maria Gisborne, March 11, 1820 (Mary Shelley, *Letters*, I, 101).

# Pisa 1820

Z ⟨a⟩ et la Sua Signora — Aureliano in Palmira — Prima donna Adelina Catalani[9] seconda La Mosea.

Sunday March 12th. Meet Pappino who gives me a letter from Mrs. Pollok. Call in Casa Silva — Read Davanzati's Tacitus —

Monday March 13th. Call in Casa Silva — L — ta ill of a cough. Read Dramatic Biography[10] — Of an Author so fond of conviviality that he makes so many feasts in his play that before the third act is over, the actors are all drunk and can proceed no farther. Thophilus Cibber, son of Colley, born in a great storm and drowned in one. Addison's Cato had immense success at his time — The Whigs thought it a ⟨pat⟩ party piece and gave it their warmest support — as also did the Tories who were determined not to take it as a reflection on their administration — so far did the latter party carry it that they one night made a collection in the Boxes of 50 Guineas to present to Mr. Booth who represented Cato which were delivered to him with this message — That it was a slight acknowledgement *for his honest opposition to a perpetual dictator and his dying so bravely in the cause of liberty.* Life of Booth — Story of Shakespeare being the father of Sir William D'Avenant. Betsy Thoughtless — the first novel that was published in England written by Mrs. Heywood a lady whom Pope has put into his Dunciad as one of the prizes to be run for at the inauguration of the Monarch Dulness.

Tuesday March 14th. We move from the Mezzanino to the 330[3rd?] Piano of Casa Frassi.[11] Call in Casa Silva — Read Dramatic Biography —

[9] Probably Angelica Catalani, who sang in England from 1806 to 1814 before returning to Italy to continue her career. The opera was by Rossini.

[10] David Erskine Baker, *Biographia dramatica; or, a Companion to the Playhouse: Containing Historical and Critical Memoirs, and Original Anecdotes, of British and Irish Dramatic Writers* . . . , "Originally compiled, to the year 1764, by David Erskine Baker. Continued thence to 1782, by Isaac Reed, F. A. S. And brought down to the End of November 1811 . . . by Stephen Jones," 3 vols. (London, 1812). The anecdotes recorded here are all from vol. I, part i.

[11] On April 5, 1820, Shelley wrote to Leigh Hunt: "We have pleasant apartments on the Arno, at the top of a house, where we just begin to feel our strength, for we have been cooped up in narrow rooms all this severe winter, and I have been irritated to death for want of a study" (Shelley, *Letters*, II, 180).

# Third Journal

Wednesday March 15th. A letter from Mad. Hoppner — Read Davanzati's Tacitus — Translate Etienne de la Boetie — Talk with Madame M. of the Prusic Acid distilled from Laurel leaves which kills without pain in a few minutes [12] of Jackson in the Irish Rebellion a conspirator who tho' he might have escaped from prison, refused because it would have involved the safety of others — He knew he should be condemned, and therefore he swallowed a strong poison and expired in torture before his judges. See W— Curran's life of John P— Curran.[13] A lesson from Zanetti. Report that the Insurgents of Spain have twice defeated the troops under General Freyre. and are now called ⟨nat⟩ armèe nationale.

Thursday March 16th. Take a lesson in dancing. call at Casa Silva — Read the life of Adam Smith [14] he was ⟨t⟩ stolen in his infancy from his Mother's door by a troop of gipsies — his uncle goes after them and recovers the Boy — In one of Hume's letters to Adam Smith I find the following which tho' a well know & hacknied truth will have weight coming from him. "A Wise man's kingdom is in his own breast, or, if he ever looks further it will only be to the judgement of a select few who are free from prejudices and capable of examining his work. Nothing indeed can be a stronger presumption of falsehood than the approbation of the multitude and ⟨M⟩ Phocion you know always suspected himself of some blunder when he was attended with the applauses of the multitude."

In Smith's Treatise concerning the Imitative Arts I find the following. "The Minuet, where the Lady passes & repasses the Gentleman, then gives him one hand and then another, and at last both, is supposed to be a⟨n Eastern⟩ Moorish dance emblematic of the passion of love." So little did our prudish grandmother's know what they were about.

[12] On June 18, 1822, Shelley wrote to Trelawny asking for some highly concentrated prussic acid, saying, "I have no intention of suicide at present, — but I confess it would be a comfort to me to hold in my possession that golden key to the chamber of perpetual rest" (Shelley, *Letters*, II, 433).

[13] This refers to the Reverend William Jackson, described in William Henry Curran, *The Life of the Right Honourable John Philpot Curran, Late Master of the Rolls in Ireland* (London, 1819), I, 321–335.

[14] Adam Smith, *Essays on Philosophical Subjects* (London, 1795), to which is prefixed an account of the life and writings of the author by Dugald Stewart. The first two passages cited below are from Stewart's introduction, pp. x and xlviii; the third is on p. 175.

# Pisa 1820

Translate Etienne de la Boëtie — Answer Madame Hoppner.[15] Spend the Evening with Laurette who is ill of the measles.

Friday March 17th. Take a dancing lesson. A lesson from Zanetti. Call in Casa Silva. Translate Etienne de la Boëtie. Read Dauvanzati's Tacitus and the Play of Beggar's Bush.[16] Caligula seems to have been a wild beast — turned silly — he adores his horses he ·hides some of his own men in the woods on the Banks of the Rhine, falls on them & defeats them, then the Provinces & Rome ring with the fame of his victory. He goes to Britain and pretends to have conquered it making his soldiers fill their helmets with shells. He farms the public games to the best bidders then ⟨pois⟩ poisons the already sold gladiators that ⟨then⟩ he may supply the public demand with new ones. The Deaths & proscriptions are innumerable. Titus Rufus among others for saying that the Senate did not speak what they thought. He is killed by ⟨Cherea⟩ Chaerea after reigning four years being 29 yrs old.[17]

Saturday March 18th. Call in Casa Silva — A lesson in dancing. Practise. Read the Woman Hater of Beaumont & Fletcher.[18] Excellent Spy scene which would apply to the present ministers. Translate Étienne de la Boëtie. Write Beggar's Bush. Read a little of Davanzati's Tacitus.

Sunday March 19th. A letter from Bessy and Captain Medwin [19] at Geneva.

> Now Phingari doth gleam o'er the gardens of Sul
> And the Alsous resounds to the pleasant Bul-bul
> Ravle on [?]

Translate Etienne de la Boetie   read Davanzati's Tacitus. Finish

---

[15] The letter was to Byron, forwarded through Mrs. Hoppner, and asked Byron to bring Allegra to see her in Pisa (Paston and Quennell, "To Lord Byron," pp. 244–245).

[16] By Fletcher, probably with Massinger.

[17] This account is in Brotier's supplement to book v of the *Annals* of Tacitus.

[18] *The Woman Hater* is by Beaumont.

[19] Thomas Medwin (1788–1869), Shelley's cousin, who in July 1819, after service with the Twenty-fourth Light Dragoons in India, had been retired on half pay with the rank of captain. See E. J. Lovell, *Captain Medwin* (1963), for a detailed and sympathetic biography. The "Bessy" referred to is probably Bessie Kent (see Note 37, p. 77, above). The two lines below are no doubt from Medwin's letter.

Woman-Hater of Beaumont & Fletcher. ⟨I am to L-r-ta what a valet dè chambre is to her.⟩[20]

Monday March 20th. A lesson in Dancing. A lesson ⟨fr⟩ from Zanetti. Translate Etienne de la Boëtie. Spend the Evening in Casa Silva.

Tuesday March 21st. A lesson in dancing. Translate Etienne de la Boëtie. Call in Casa Silva. Read Tacitus. Anecdote of Sir Richard Steele[21] — Some bailiffs came to his house to arrest him he was going to give a dinner-party and he ⟨prevat⟩ prevailed on them to dress themselves in the livery of ⟨th⟩ his servants and to wait at table — all went very well till speaking to one of the bailiff servants too harshly he in resentment threw up his employment and seized Sir Richard to the great astonishment of the Company.

Wednesday March 22nd. Very great storm of wind. Read Tacitus. Finish translating Etienne de la Boëtie — Some one said after reading Otway's Orphan — "Oh! what an infinite deal of mischief would a farthing rushlight have prevented!" This tragedy was never a favorite of mine — There is a ⟨pever⟩ perversity about its heroes who determine to be unhappy because they are in a play.[22]

X Thursday March 23rd  A lesson in dancing — Call in Casa Silva. Letter from Mad. Du Plantis & the impudent Louise.[23]

Friday March 24th. Call in Casa Silva — Begin transcribing Etienne de la Boëtie. Read Tacitus.

Saturday March 25th. Festa della Santissima Annunziata. "Non Epicuri schola sed stoa, veteres Respublicas perturbavit says Bacon. de Augm. ⟨Scientar⟩ Scientiar[24] — Read Tacitus — Transcribe. Thunder at Night.

Sunday March 26th  Call in Casa Silva. Ride with Mad. M. on the Lucca Road — Signor Vaccà Berlinghieri calls. Begin Con-

[20] Claire had been sitting with ten-year-old Laurette, who had the measles.
[21] In Baker, *Biographia dramatica*, I, part ii, 687.
[22] *Ibid.*, III, 105.
[23] See Note 85 to entry of February 8, 1820, above.
[24] "It is not the Epicureans but the stoics who disturb established States." Attributed by Claire to Francis Bacon, *De augmentis scientiarum* (1623).

dorcet's Life of Voltaire [25]  On the tragedy of Alzire  was first represented so great was the enthusiasm of the audience they insisted upon Voltaire coming forward — which he did in the box of the Marechale de Villars — not content with this they made the young Duchess de Villars in the same box 〈wh〉 with him embrace him. Read Tacitus.

Monday March 27th. Call in Casa Silva. Transcribe Etienne de la Boëtie. Read Tacitus.

Tuesday March 28th. Call in Casa Silva. A lesson in dancing. A lesson from Zanetti. Transcribe. Read Tacitus.

Wednesday March 29th. Call in Casa Silva — A lesson in dancing — Read Condorcet's life of Voltaire — Transcribe. Read Tacitus —

Thursday March 30th. Holy Thursday. 〈Cat〉 They had cattle about the streets in a procession, their horns painted and their heads crowned with 〈olive〉 branches of olive and laurel. Call in Casa Silva — A lesson in dancing. A lesson from Zanetti. Transcribe. Read Tacitus.

Friday March 31st. Good Friday which here they do not keep in the same solemn way we do 〈at〉 in England. Call in Casa Silva — A lesson in dancing. Transcribe   Read Tacitus. Il Signor Tantini calls. Write to Mrs. Pollok.

Saturday April 1st. Call in Casa Silva. Transcribe   Read Tacitus.

Sunday April 2nd. Easter Sunday. Transcribe. Read Tacitus. Call in Casa Silva.

Monday April 3rd Call in Casa Silva. Finish transcribing Etienne de la Boetie. Read Tacitus. Account of the Lake Asphaltites — it is the colour of the Sea, with a horrible smell — lead will float on it — Its bitumen 〈takes out〉 makes stains of blood disappear from cloth.
 Account also of the Jews who were the lepers of Egypt col-

[25] *Vie de Voltaire par le Marquis de Condorcet; suivie des mémoires de Voltaire, écrits par lui-même*, vol. LXX (1789) of *Œuvres complètes de Voltaire* ([Kehl], 1785–1789), Eng. trans., 2 vols. (London, 1790). Read by Mary on March 27 and 31, and by Shelley on April 2, 1820 (*Mary Shelley's Journal*, p. 131).

lected into a body and sent thence into the deserts, they wandered for a long while sustained by the courage of Moses (also a leper) till being pleased with the situation of Jerusalem they drove away its scattered inhabitants & built that city. It grew by being like Rome made a sanctuary for all the vagabonds and villains of the surrounding provinces. They hated their parent country for ⟨their⟩ its desertion of them hence their customs concerning certain animals. They sacrifice the Bull which in Egypt was the most sacred of all animals — they will not intermarry with foreign women — they circumcised themselves that it might be a mutual ⟨cement⟩ band of union in their infant state.[26]

Tuesday April 4th. A lesson from Zanetti — Call in Casa Silva. Begin writing Letters from Italy. Read Tacitus and finish his history which ends with the 5 Book. Read Chronological Supplement by Brotier.

Wednesday April 5th. Call in Casa Silva — A lesson in dancing. Write Letters from Italy — Read Brotier Chronological Supplement. Read Memoires of Voltaire written by himself — Sekendorff was sent embassador from Charles VI of Germany to ⟨Fede Fre⟩ the father of Frederic of ⟨P⟩ Prussia to prevent the latter's head being cut off. Frederic afterwards wrote his portrait and very frightfully upon which Voltaire remarks "Apres cela servez les princes et empechez qu'on leur coupe la ⟨tat⟩ tête —"[27]
  I see *Tatty* & Madame Tantini.

Thursday April 6th. Call in Casa Silva — A lesson in dancing. A lesson from Zanetti. Write Letters from Italy. Read Brotier's Chronological supplement.

Friday April 7th. Rainy all day. Write & read a little. Thoughts concerning Reviewers — 1st they write for sale — 2nd they ⟨generally⟩ criticise in half an hour what has perhaps taken its author three years to consider. Reviewers ⟨have gone⟩ are generally disappointed authors; they retire to the bridge of Criticism and their endeavours go to catch every passing author & ⟨throw⟩ by throwing him into the deep & rapid river of abuse that flows below to destroy him &

[26] *Histories*, book v, in Dureau de La Malle, *Tacite*, V, 351.
[27] "After that serve princes and prevent their decapitation." In Condorcet, *Vie de Voltaire*, p. 270.

his ⟨mortality⟩ immortality — *Job* their first parent who in the bitterness of his disappointment cried out *Oh! that mine enemy had written a book!* Moral Procusteses who measure every man by their own ⟨height⟩ Grub-street Bed, and what is wanting they will stretch him too, ⟨if he is⟩ what exceeds they cut off ⟨and th⟩ & thus disabled they dismiss their *protegès* to limp through the world.[28]

⟨⟨Estimate of *Morality* — Paris is called an immoral city because ⟨they there are only⟩ it contains but 8,000 prostitutes — London a very moral one because it possesses one hundred thousand of these poor wretches.⟩⟩[29]

Saturday April 8th. System of Sir Humphrey Davy concerning the earth that it is composed of the rust of metal & oxygen ⟨gass⟩ ↑gas↓. ⟨Round⟩ the other planets ⟨there are no doubt⟩ have no doubt other elements than our's — for ⟨if air could⟩ if a sufficient degree of cold could be applied to air it would freeze to a white mist but a little way above the earth — ⟨Thus⟩ This would no doubt be the case round Saturn where the cold is so intense — in the same way iron which with us is the hardest metal would there be ↑the softest↓ ⟨sensible enough to⟩ ↑& would↓ serve in a thermometer as quicksilver does here. Some believe the Sun not to be a body of fire but a property which when mixed with others produces heat.[30]

[28] Reviews of *The Cenci* began to appear in the middle of March, but there is no evidence that Shelley had received word of them. Claire is probably reacting to the *Quarterly*'s attack on *The Revolt of Islam* in the preceding year. Shelley had used the quotation from Job in *Peter Bell the Third*, part vi.

[29] This passage, which Claire was at pains to cross out, is similar to one in Thomas Holcroft, *Travels from Hamburg* . . . , 2 vols. (London, 1804), II, 125.

[30] I have not found this material nor that in the entry for April 10, just below, in any of the volumes Claire or Shelley is known to have read. Claire's new concern with scientific matters doubtless reflects the interests of Tighe, who achieved some degree of fame for his agricultural writings. Among the publications of this transplanted Irishman are "Memoria intorno a una nuova varietà di patata con alcune esperienze riguardo alla coltura ed all' uso delle patate in generale," four articles, in *Giornale agrario toscano*, nos. 11–14 (Florence, 1829–1830). Perhaps his nickname "Tatty" derived from his interest in *gli patate*; on May 5, 1820 (below), Claire refers to him as putting "potatoes in Pots." It was under his influence that Shelley reported to the Gisbornes, April 13, "I have been thinking & talking & reading Agriculture this last week" (Shelley, *Letters*, II, 182).

# Third Journal

Write Letters from Italy — A lesson from Zanetti. I see to-day ⟨streaks⟩ that the Arno is streaked with lines of white foam which floats down with inconceivable quickness. This the Italians say is foam from the mountain torrent ⟨ge⟩ agitated by the late high wind. Drink tea in Casa Silva.

Sunday April 9. Walk with Laurette — Read ⟨Taci Tacitus⟩ Brotier's Chronological Supplement which I shall not finish for its dullness. Begin the Germany of Tacitus. Read Les Chevaliers des Sept Montagnes by Baron Bock — When a franc-juge wanted to warn a friend to be gone who was followed by the secret tribunal he said "On mange ailleurs d'aussi bon pain qu'ici." [31] One of the similes of this book. "Otho betook himself to solitude as a worm retreats to his hole after having traversed the globe tired of his humanity resolving to die."

Monday April 10th. Salt is composed of ↑the↓ metal Sodium & of a green air called Clorine. It is possible to procure an ⟨inficient &⟩ efficient manure by digging in the stalks & leaves of plants; ⟨not⟩ which is better than the aid of beasts. Soda is composed of the metal Sodium & oxygen gas.

A lesson in dancing. Call in Casa Silva — Write Letters from Italy. Read the Germania of Tacitus & begin his Life of Agricola.

Tuesday April 11th. A lesson in dancing. Call in Casa Silva. Write letters from Italy. ⟨Read⟩ Finish the Life of Agricola by Tacitus Begin his De Oratoribus.

Wednesday April 12th. A lesson from Zanetti. A lesson in dancing. Call in Casa Silva. Finish *De Oratoribus* of Tacitus. Finish the Life of Voltaire by Condorcet. To Madelle. Dusmenil acting his Merope with tamness he reproached her and she said Il faudroit avoir le diable au corps pour arriver au ton que vous voulez me faire prendre! Eh bien! oui Mademoiselle said he c'est le diable qu'il faut avoir au corps pour exceller dans tous les arts." [32]

[31] "They eat elsewhere as good bread as here." Baron Félix de Bock, *Les Chevaliers des sept montagnes, ou aventures arrivées dans le XIIIe siècle, du temps où le tribunal secret avait sa plus grande influence, avec une notice sur l'état ancien et actuel de ce tribunal,* trans. from the German, 3 vols. (Paris, 1800).

[32] "One would have to have the devil in one's flesh to achieve the tone you want from me." "Just so, Mademoiselle. One must have the devil in one's

# Pisa 1820

Thursday April 13th. A lesson from Legerino[33] — Write only a little. Call in Casa Silva. Read Farquhar's Love & a Bottle.[34]

Friday April 14th. Call in Casa Silva. A lesson in dancing & Giovane. A lesson from Zanetti. Write Letters from Italy. ⟨Read⟩ Begin Locke's on the Understanding.[35]

⟨Ca⟩ Saturday April 15th. Call in Casa Silva. A lesson from Legerino. Il Signore & la Signora Tantini call. Read Locke — The laws are passed in france for the restriction of the press. So straw is put before the door of a dying man that he may not hear the rolling of the carriages never the less the carriages roll & he dies so these laws are the straws which hide to the ⟨monar⟩ king his departing ⟨re⟩ monarchy, nevertheless Liberty rolls along & monarchy must die.

Sunday April 16th. Dine in Casa Silva. Read the fall of Sejanus — [36]

Primus in orbe, deos fecit timor
⟨Petronius Arbiter⟩

Monday April ⟨16⟩ 17th Call in Casa Silva — A lesson from Legerino. A lesson from Zanetti. Write a few pages of letters from Italy. Read Locke. Pay Legerino

Tuesday April 18th. Call in Casa Silva. A lesson from Legerino. Read Locke & fall of Sejanus.

Wednesday April ⟨18th.⟩ 19   Call in Casa Silva   a lesson from Legerino. A lesson from Zanetti. Read Locke. Write Letters from Italy. Finish the fall of Sejanus of Ben Jonson   begin The Woman's prize or the Tamer tam'd by Beaumont & Fletcher.[37]

---

flesh to excell in all the arts." This episode by Abbé du Vernet is in "Choix de pièces justificatives pour la vie de Voltaire," an appendix to Condorcet's *Vie de Voltaire*, p. 249.

[33] Probably her dancing master.

[34] George Farquhar's *Love and a Bottle* was produced in 1698.

[35] Claire had begun this essay once before, on February 13.

[36] By Ben Jonson (1605). Shelley read from it aloud, March 11 (*Mary Shelley's Journal*, p. 130). The line just below from Petronius is Jonson's source for a line of a speech by Sejanus, Act II, scene 2: "'Twas only fear first in the world made gods."

[37] By Fletcher after the death of Beaumont.

# Third Journal

Lady M— told Volney[38] ⟨wha⟩ how happy she was to see ⟨him⟩ the author of the Ruins of Empire — He said Never wish to see an author, ⟨be⟩ content yourself with his book & be assured it is the best part about him — And the manners of Volney were so rude & rough that she was tempted to say *Ecce signum*. What he said is very true  there is scarcely an author who does not prejudice the ⟨p⟩ opinion of his work by being known.

Thursday April 2⟨1⟩oth. Letter from Horace Smith in which he says there must be a financial convulsion in England. A lesson from Legerino. Call in Casa Silva. Mr. & Mrs. Gisborne arrive from Livorno.

When the Spanish Consul heard of the successful turn of the politics of Spain he almost broke the table in two with thumping so vehement was his joy & so violent his anger against Ferdinand VII.[39]

Friday April 21st. Vaccà calls — ⟨we have⟩ a very profound & atheistical conversation between him & ⟨Shelley⟩ ↑S——↓ La Signora Maria & il Signor Giovanni [Gisborne] not unmixed with joy at an interview after ⟨after⟩ ten-years absence with his old & liberal friends.

In the evening they set out for Livorno carrying S— along with them. ⟨We⟩ Drink tea in Casa Silva.

Mr. Johnson coming from Pisa to Livorno called upon Mr. G— they asked him after the health of Madame Tantini — he said I called upon that lady before I set out. I found her in floods of tears ⟨which⟩ whose cause I in vain entreated her to tell me; after many sobs she at last told me that she was weeping for the death of one of her husbands friends who died 3 years before & whom she had never seen. "This said" Mr. Johnson "is what the Germans call SCHWÄRMEREI."

[38] For the occasion of her meeting with Constantin Volney (1757-1820), see Wilmot, *An Irish Peer*, p. 46.

[39] The two insurgent victories mentioned by Claire on March 15 (above) prompted Mary to write to Maria Gisborne: "The Inquisition is abolished — The dungeons opened & the Patriots pouring out — This is good. I sh[oul]d like to be in Madrid now" (Mary Shelley, *Letters*, I, 104). Shelley in his enthusiasm considered going there (Shelley, *Letters*, II, 180), and the "glorious events" inspired him to write his "Ode to Liberty."

# Pisa 1820

Mrs. M. also told a very droll story. Giunto-tardi a Roman friend of her's came to her one morning & informed that an old priest one of their friends had just lost his mistress and was in extreme distress ⟨upon⟩ about it. She was not in very good spirits but as it was a sorrowful errand felt less objection to go. ⟨The⟩ They entered the room. she Giunto-tardi & the Signor Tighe who also accompanied them; they found the old priest ⟨in⟩ shaking in a cold room & holding in his shrivelled hands a little pot of fire. They condoled & he told how grieved he was for the loss of *"una fresca donna di sessant' anni."* Giunto-tardi was in an agony but when he saw the Signora Contessa hiding ⟨both⟩ her face with both her hands ⟨in⟩ to hide the violence of her laughter & the Signor Tighe ⟨givin⟩ give way to an *"eclat de rire"* he could hold no longer to the great surprize of the priest who beheld his polite condolers fail in the very tenderest part of his story.[40]

Motto for the Bible Society – If thy son ask for bread wilt thou give him a stone and if for ↑a↓ fish . . . . . . . Letter from Peacock   tell us ⟨with⟩ of his marriage with Jane Griffiths of ↑Festiniog↓ [41]

X Saturday April 22nd. Read Woman's Prize or Tamer tam'd Wit at several weapons also Wit without money of Beaumont & Fletcher.[42] Read Locke.

[40] Giunto-tardi was considered the best language master in Rome (Starke, *Travels on the Continent*, appendix, p. 110). "A sweet young lady of sixty years." "A burst of laughter."

[41] Nine years earlier Peacock had described Jane Gryffyth as "the most innocent, the most amiable, the most beautiful girl in existence" (*Letters to Hookham*, p. 42). Dowden saw a notebook in which Claire wrote of herself: "In 1818 she refused an offer of marriage from P—; he knew her whole history" (Shelley, *Works*, X, 252n.). Although it is true that Claire avoided him in London at that time (see entry for January 24, 1818, above), she thought highly of him in her old age: "I have a great esteem and admiration for Peacock – he is a rare specimen of noble humanity – and so generous and unselfish – May he flourish many years!" (unpublished letter to Dina Williams Hunt in the library of the University of Texas, December 31, 1862). Lady Mount Cashell wrote to Mary, August 22, 1824, "How often I regret her not having married Mr. P.," and on August 20, 1832, Maria Gisborne wrote, "How much suffering she might have been spared had she married Peacock – It is an advantage that both of them have lost" (Abinger MSS.).

[42] *Wit at Several Weapons* was probably a revision by Rowley and Middle-

# Third Journal

Sunday April 23rd. Write to Albè.[43] Laurette calls. Read Brydone's Letters ⟨in⟩ from Sicily.[44] S— comes home from Livorno.

Monday April 24 Call in Casa Silva. A lesson from Zanetti. Read Brydone's letters from Sicily & Malta which are most delightfully interesting.
    Drink tea in Casa Silva.

Tuesday April 25th. Read Brydone's Letters.

Wednesday April 26th. A lesson from Zanetti. Write to Mad— Hoppner. Call in Casa Silva — Finish Brydone's Letters from Sicily & Malta. ⟨Letters⟩
Letters from two Irish Kings —
Pay me tribute or if you don't ————
                                                    *O'Donnel*
⟨I⟩ Answer. I owe you no tribute or if I did ————
                                                    *O'Neil.*

Thursday April 27th. Birthday 22 — Read Noble Gentleman of Beaumont & Fletcher.[45] Thunder all night.

Friday April 28th. M. & S. go to Livorno to take leave of Mr. & Mrs. G— Read the Encyclopedia[46] — Drink tea in Casa Silva. See Tatty who has a very agreeable countenance.

Saturday April 29th. A lesson from Zanetti. A lesson from Legerino. Read Locke. Call in Casa Silva.

---

ton of an early play by Beaumont and Fletcher; *Wit without Money* was by Fletcher before the death of Beaumont.

[43] A long excerpt from this letter is in Paston and Quennell, *"To Lord Byron,"* pp. 245–246. In it she expresses concern for Allegra's health in the heat of Ravenna and announces that unless the child is sent to her she will set out on the third of May to pick her up.

[44] Patrick Brydone, *A Tour through Sicily and Malta. In a Series of Letters to William Beckford . . .* , 2 vols. (London, 1773). Mary finished it on April 24 (*Mary Shelley's Journal*, p. 132).

[45] By Fletcher and Massinger.

[46] The Gisbornes and Henry Reveley were leaving for England, and Mary had asked if they might borrow Henry's set of the encyclopedia in their absence (Mary Shelley, *Letters*, I, 106). This was probably the *Encyclopaedia Britannica*, 20 vols. (5th ed.; Edinburgh, 1814–1817).

# Pisa 1820

Sunday April 30th. A letter from Mad— Hoppner concerning green fruit & God — strange Jumble.[47] Drink tea in Casa Silva. Read Elder Brother — [48]

> "A couple of the world's fools met together
> To raise up dirt & dunghills

Monday ⟨April⟩ May 1st. A lesson from Legerino. I spend the day in cogitation ⟨and I write to *my damn'd Brute*⟩ [49]

Tuesday May 2nd. Send letter to Madame Hoppner with an enclosure ⟨for Ravenna⟩. A lesson from Zanetti. Call in Casa Silva.

Wednesday May 3rd. A letter from Albè. ⟨Call in⟩ Breakfast in Casa Silva. A lesson from Legerino. Read Agnes de Lilien by the sister in law of Schiller which seems to me to be a stupid Book.[50] Drink tea in Casa Silva.

*Conversation between Lord Kingston & Miss Johnstone walking on the Promenade of St Stephen's Green by Moonlight.*[51]

Ld. K.   What a fine night to run away with another man's Wife in —

Miss J.   And why not with another man's daughter.

Ld K   Will you?

Miss J   Yes.

Lrd. K   Done then. (taking her hand)

Miss J.   Done. (Giving her hand.

And they ran away that very night without further courtship.

[47] On April 22, 1820, Byron had written to Hoppner of Allegra's good health and the Shelleys' bad fortune in the rearing of children: "The Child shall not quit me again to perish of Starvation, and green fruit, or be taught to believe that there is no Deity" (Byron, *Works*, V, 14–15).

[48] By Fletcher, with Massinger. The quoted lines are from Act II, scene I.

[49] The longest excerpt from this letter is in Paston, "New Light on Byron's Loves. VI. Claire Clairmont: The Struggle for Allegra," *Cornhill Magazine*, 150:269 (September 1934). In it Claire very calmly answers each of Byron's taunts and objections.

[50] Mme. Caroline Wohlzogen, *Agnès de Lilien*, trans. from the German (Paris, 1802).

[51] Lady Mount Cashell's eldest brother, George, who ran away with the forward Miss Johnstone to the British West Indies, where they had three children. He returned to Ireland in 1794 to marry the sister of Lord Mount Cashell (McAleer, *The Sensitive Plant*, p. 64).

# Third Journal

Thursday May 4th. Write to Albè.[52] Call in Casa Silva   Read
Agnes de Lilien.

Friday May 5th. Finish Agnes de Lilien. Breakfast in Casa Silva.
A lesson from Legerino. Account of the *odd* English at present in
Pisa. Walter Savage Landor who will not see a single English person says he is glad the country produces people of worth but he
will have nothing to do with them.[53] Shelley who walks about ⟨w⟩
reading a great quarto Encyclopedia with another volume under
his arm.[54] ⟨Mr⟩ *Tatty* who sets potatoes in Pots,[55] & a Mr. Dolby
who is rejoicing that he is escaped from England at last although
he is 70 some say 80 yrs of age —   he is short & thick & goes about
with his pockets stuffed out with books, singing, & a pair of spectacles hung by a gold chain round his neck. He is learned & tells
every one that he would put on a better coat to visit them in if
he had another in the world besides the one he wears. A letter
from Miss Stacey.

Saturday May 6th. Rainy. Work. Read a little of De la Virgen
del Sagrario de Don Pedro Calderon de la Barca.

>No entiendo de argumentos, pero entiendo
>de *estacas*, y con esta
>tengo de dar a tu opinion respuesta.[56]

Read Memoires of the ↑last↓ Revolution at Naples[57] — When the
Patriots yielded upon a treaty that they should be allowed to ⟨lv⟩
live in peace on their properties they were however all seized in
defiance of the solemn compact and the trials began. One of them

[52] Perhaps this is the letter quoted by Dowden from a copy, since disappeared, in Claire's hand (Dowden, *Shelley*, II, 329–330).

[53] Landor had been in Pisa a year before the Shelleys arrived, but, as he
explained to Mary years later when he met her in London, a disgraceful story
about Shelley's treatment of Harriet had caused him to refuse a meeting. On
Mary's explaining that the story was "a most infamous falsehood," Landor assured her "I never could forgive myself for crediting a slander that had prevented
me from knowing Shelley" (Field, "Last Days of Walter Savage Landor,"
*Atlantic Monthly*, 17:543 [May 1866]).

[54] See Note 46 to the entry of April 28, above.

[55] See Note 30 to the entry of April 8, above.

[56] "I don't understand about arguments, but I do understand about *cudgels*,
and with this understanding I will answer you" (*La Virgen del Sagrario*, Act I).

[57] Vincenzo Cuoco, *Saggio storico sulla rivoluzione di Napoli*, 3 vols. (Milan,
1800).

interrogated according to the law concerning his name & profession replied. ⟨My n⟩ "I am called Domenichino Cirillo; under the despotism I was a physician, under the republic, a deputy, & now I am a hero" His death as well as all the other Patriots was noble.

Sunday May 7–th. Call in Casa Silva. Read De la Virgen del Sagrario. Drink tea in Casa Silva.

Monday May 8th. Breakfast in Casa Silva. A lesson from Legerino. Read Virgen del Sagrario. Old Sky-Ball & young Sky-Ball.

Teusday May 9th. Breakfast in Casa Silva. A lesson from Legerino. Read Locke & a little of Virgen del Sagrario. Call in the Evening with Laurette & Nerina upon Madame Tantini.

Wednesday May 10th. Breakfast in Casa Silva. A lesson from Legerino. Read Women Pleased and tragedy of Thierry & Theodoret of Beaumont & Fletcher. Read Virgen del Sagrario de Calderon. Of Grief.

> Cuchillo, que a romper vida tan corta
> Parece que se afila en lo que corta.[58]

Thursday May 11th. Festa of the Ascension. Read La Virgen del Sagrario. Call in Casa Silva. A lesson from Legerino.

Friday May 12th. Read Procès Fualdes.[59] Breakfast in Casa Silva. A lesson from Legerino

Saturday May 13th. Read Procès Fualdes. Tatty goes to Casciano. A lesson from Legerino

---

[58] *Woman Pleased* is by Fletcher; *The Tragedy of Thierry King of France, and His Brother Theodoret* is by Fletcher revised by Massinger. Shelley read the latter aloud to Mary May 9–10 (*Mary Shelley's Journal*, p. 132).

"Oh knife, as you break a life so short it seems that you are sharpened by the very shortness of life" (*La Virgen del Sagrario*, Act II).

[59] The stenographic report of the most famous of the criminal trials in France during the restoration of the Bourbons (*Cause célèbre: Procès des prévenus de l'assassinat de M.* [Antoine Bernardin] *Fualdès . . . accompagné d'une notice historique sur les principaux personnages* [Madame Manson and others] *qui figurent dans cette affaire* [Paris, 1817]). Godwin recorded in his diary for April 3, 1812, "Meet Fualdes" (Abinger MSS.). On July 5, 1818, Peacock had sent the Shelleys a copy of the *Procès*, at their request (see Mary Shelley, *Letters*, I, 50, and Peacock, *Letters to Hookham*, p. 68).

# Third Journal

Sunday May 14th. Spend the day in Casa Silva ⟨L⟩ Library in order.

Monday May 15th. Breakfast in Casa Silva A lesson from Legerino. Bathe & have a bad headach. In the Evening call with the children on Madame Tantini. A lesson from Sforzi.

Tuesday May 16th. Bad Head-ach all day — Bathe — Read Plays by Farquhar.[60] Call in Casa Silva in the Evening.

Wednesday May 17th. Severe Head-ach all day. A lesson from Sforzi — Read Vanburgh Plays. Read the account of the execution of Thistlewood, Brunt Ings, Davidson & Tidd for high treason which affects me much.[61]

Thursday May 18th. Breakfast in Casa Silva — Put the Library in order. Dine there. Severe Headach. Pay Legerino.

X Friday May 19th. A lesson from Sforzi. A Brutal letter from Albè [62] — Call in Casa Silva.

Saturday May 20th. Read History of the Revolution at Naples. Severe Head-ach

Sunday May 21st. Dine in Casa Silva. Put the Library in order.

Monday May 22nd. A lesson from Sforzi. Shelley goes to Casciano —

Tuesday May 23rd. Breakfast in Casa Silva. Read Boswell's Life of Johnson. Finish ⟨b⟩ putting the Library in order. Laurette drinks tea with us.

Wednesday May 24th. Read Boswell's Life of Johnson. Unwell all day with Headach — A lesson from Sforzi.

[60] *The Works of George Farquhar*, 3 vols. (Dublin, 1775).

[61] Sir John Vanbrugh, *Plays*, 2 vols. (London, 1719). Arthur Thistlewood, J. T. Brunt, J. Ings, W. Davidson, R. Tidd, and others were tried and executed for high treason (the "Cato Street Conspiracy"). Thistlewood was executed on May 1, 1820. See Byron's letter to Murray, June 7, 1820 (Byron, *Works*, V, 39, and note); also journal entry below for October 29, 1821.

[62] This letter was to Shelley, but Claire saw all such correspondence. In reply Shelley wrote on May 26 urging Byron to be more moderate in writing about Claire. He added, "I do not say — I do not think — that your resolutions are unwise; only express them mildly — and pray don't *quote me*" (Shelley, *Letters*, II, 198).

# Pisa 1820

Thursday May 25th. Read Boswell. S— returns from Casciano.

Friday May 26th. Read Boswell. A lesson from Sforzi. Call in Casa Silva where we drink tea

Saturday May 27 Read Boswell. Bathe. Drive with Madame M— ⟨on ↑in↓ the⟩ beyond the Porta Piaggi to Casa Aquinta.

Sunday May 28th. Bathe. Read Boswell — Write to Albè. Walk in the Evening with Laurette & Gigia [63] to the Convent of the Cappuccini.

Monday May 29th. Signor Tantini calls. A lesson from Sforzi. Letter from Vienna [64] & from Mr. Gisborne. In the Evening drive with Madame M. on the florence road. We are caught in a thunder storm. Read Rights of Woman.[65] Letter from Madame Hoppner.

Teusday May 30th  A lesson from Zanetti. Bathe. Call in Casa Silva. Read Rights of Woman.

Wednesday May 31st A lesson from Sforzi. Arrival of Miss Mathilda Field.[66] Call in Casa Silva — Meet Tantini. Read Rights of Woman

Thursday ⟨May⟩ June 1st. This is Corpus Domini day. Go with Laurette to the Duomo & hear the funzione in the Morning. Call in Casa Silva. *Tatty* from Casciano  In the Evening go with the Children to Gigia's to see the Procession. Read Letters from Norway.[67]

Friday   June 2nd. The Signor Tantini calls. A lesson from Sforzi. *Tatty* calls. Read Rights of Woman & Letters from Norway. Bathe.

Saturday June 3rd. Signor Tantini Calls. A lesson from Sforzi. Bathe. Read Rights of Woman.

Sunday June 4th. Bathe. Finish Letters from Norway & Rights of Woman. Call in Casa Silva. Signor Tantini calls.

[63] Lady Mount Cashell's servant.
[64] From Charles.
[65] Mary Wollstonecraft, *A Vindication of the Rights of Woman*. Mary was rereading it on May 21 (*Mary Shelley's Journal*, p. 133).
[66] An English schoolmistress who stayed for a year with Lady Mount Cashell (see Shelley, *Letters*, II, 291).
[67] By Mary Wollstonecraft. See entry above for August 30, 1814.

149

# Third Journal

Monday June 5th. Read Saggio ⟨I⟩ storico sulla Rivoluzione di Napoli. Bathe. A lesson from Sforzi. Call in Casa Silva.

Teusday June 6th. A lesson from Zanetti. Bathe. Read Saggio Storico di Napoli — Call in Casa Silva & on Madame Tantini — We talk about Sandt who was beheaded the 20th. of May — the spectators dipped their handkerchiefs in his blood to preserve as relics & all tried to ⟨be⟩ possessed themselves of a lock of his hair.[68]

Wednesday June 7th. A lesson from Sforzi. Read Saggio Storico. The circulation of money is slower in an agricultural country than in a commercial one. Call in Casa Silva.

Thursday June 8th.[69] Set off at Seven in the morning with Gigia & Laurette to Pugnano where we spend the day in walking about the hills of this delightful place. Visit Villa Roncione. & Casa ⟨Posck⟩ Poschi. Dring tea in Casa Silva. Read 1st Vol of Ivanhoe by Walter Scott.[70]

Friday June 9th. A lesson from Sforzi — Read Ivanhoe — Cobbett's Registers & Examiners.[71] Bathe

Saturday June 10th. Bathe. A lesson from Zanetti   Mad— M calls. S— goes to Casciano to see Tatty. Finish Ivanhoe. "He who keeps his grief within his own breast, is a cannibal of his heart."

Sunday June 11th. Read Edinburgh Reviews & Quarterly. Bathe. Drink tea in Casa Silva with Mad— M & Miss Field.

Monday June 12th. Sforzi calls. Letters from Miss Stacey & Mr. Gisborne. Then Bother & Confusion with packing up. — We sleep in Casa Silva. Oh Bother.[72]

[68] Charles Sandt, who had assassinated Kotzebue at Mannheim on March 23, 1819, thinking him a Russian spy, was executed May 20, 1820 (see Byron, *Works*, V, 39, and note).

[69] The tensions of this period are reflected in Mary's journal entry (later crossed out): "A Better day than most days & good reason for it though Shelley is not well. C. away at Pugnano" (in *Mary Shelley's Journal*, p. 134).

[70] As soon as Claire finished *Ivanhoe* (1819), Mary began to read it (*ibid.*, p. 134).

[71] Leigh Hunt was editor of the *Examiner*.

[72] On this day Mary wrote simply "Paolo," followed by a crude drawing of a crescent moon. This was the distressing period of Paolo Foggi's blackmail attempt (*Mary Shelley's Journal*, p. 134).

# Leghorn 1820

Teusday June 13th. Breakfast in Casa Silva — S— goes to Livorno — We return to our own house
>"The king of England with all his merry men
>Marched up a hill & ↑then marched↓ down again"

Read Quarterly Review.

Wednesday June 14th. Tatty comes from Casciano. Read the Reviews & Cobbett.

Thursday June 15th. Call in Casa Silva. Go in a Calesse to Casa Ricci at Livorno.[73] Read Vicar of Wakefield[74] S— & M. arrive at night —

Friday June 16th. Little Babe ill of diarrhœa.[75] Dr. Palloni calls. Read Bride of Lammermoor.[76]

Saturday June 17th. Little Babe ill — Dr. Palloni calls. Read A Legend of Montrose.
All this Week employed in unpacking & arranging —[77]

Sunday June 25th. Practise. Read Edinburgh Review. Walk out with S— in the Evening. Write to Tetta. Read a History of England, written in french by a Jew after the manner of the Bible "Ou les faits du Roi Henri; les lamproies qu'il mangea & les enfans qu'il engendra, ne sont-ils pas ecrits dans le livre de Baker l'historien?
Of the miracles performed at Becket's tomb.
Que celui qui croit ces choses, continue de les croire ! & que celui, qui en doute, reste dans son Incredulitè, et soit damnè.
Of James 1st
Ou, le reste des faits du Roi Jacques, sa haute sagesse, son profond savoir, et tous les livres qu'il a ecrite, voila vous pouvez les trouvez

[73] The house of the Gisbornes, who were in London.

[74] Mary read Oliver Goldsmith's *Vicar of Wakefield*, 2 vols. (1766) on June 14 (*Mary Shelley's Journal*, p. 134).

[75] For Shelley's account of the devastating effect of Percy Florence's illness, see Shelley to Godwin, August 7 (Shelley, *Letters*, II, 227).

[76] Mary had just finished this novel by Scott and his *Legend of Montrose*, both published in 1819 (*Mary Shelley's Journal*, p. 134).

[77] On June 17 Mary wrote "Babe unwell — We are unhappy & discontented," but by the next day the baby was better, and Mary wrote a sprightly letter to Maria Gisborne (in *Mary Shelley's Journal*, p. 134, and Mary Shelley, *Letters*, I, 108–111).

dans les boutiques des Epiciers, ou chez la Beurriere jusqu'a ce jour.[78]

Monday June 26th. Practise — Finish writing to Tetta. Read Newspapers — The standing army of England is encreased 11,000 men; in 92 the⟨re were⟩ regiment of guards consisted of 692 men now it is augmented to 1,530 each guard man costing £ 140 per annum.

Teusday June 27th. Practise. Read Edinburg Review. Begin a letter to Madame Hoppner — Bathe. Begin also Latin which I pray I may continue.

Wednesday June 28th. Bathe — Write a Latin Exercise — Begin Nicholson's Natural Philosophy[79] — Read Saggio Istorico della rivoluzione di Napoli. The author affirms that all the people of the middling class & all the nobles were republicans and that so far from the revolution failing from a want of patriotic feeling it fell as it were through the overpowering virtue of the republicans. Finish letter to Madame Hoppner.

Thursday June 29 Festa of San Pietro and San Paolo. I am ill all day —

> ⟨Nonne me memenisti
> Quod mihi dixisti
>     In Corpore Christi⟩
> Nonne memenisti
> Quod mihi dixisti
> De Corpore Christi
>     Crede quod vedes et vedes
> Ita tibi dico
> De tuo Palfrido
>     Crede quod habes et habes.[80]

[78] I have not been able to identify this work. The quoted passages may be translated thus: "Or the deeds of King Henry; of the lampreys that he ate & the children he engendered, is it not written in the book of Baker the historian? . . . . Let those who believe these things, continue to believe them! & let those, who doubt, continue in their Incredulity, and be damned . . . . Or, the rest of the deeds of King James, his lofty wisdom, his profound knowledge, and all the books that he has written, how you can find them in the grocery shops, or at the dairy until this very day."

[79] William Nicholson, *An Introduction to Natural Philosophy*, 2 vols. (London: J. Johnson, 1782).

[80] These verses, which I have not been able to identify, may be translated:

# Leghorn 1820

Read Saggio Istorico della Rivoluzione di Napoli.

one thing for the people to remember — that they can do very well without a king but there was ↑never↓ heard of a king without a people."

Friday June 30th. Read the life of Xenophon by Diogenes Laertius [81] — I am ill all day. ⟨Read a few tales of Boccaccio⟩. Definition of a Courtizan from the Greek. That she sold for hire the things of ↑Venus.↓

Saturday July 1st. Write to Mrs. Gisborne — I am ill. Walk with S— to Livorno in the Evening.

Sunday July 2nd. Do a latin Excercise. Read a little of the ⟨Enead⟩ Enead.

Tantae molis erat Romanorum condere gentum,[82]
So huge a work of weight it was to build of Rome the line.

Monday July 3rd. Bathe. Write to Madame Mason. "Better than a sop to Cerberus or the music of Orpheus to the furies is a £ 100 to a philosopher!! An english philosopher however it would seem to mean since Alciabiades tells us that he had thoughts of trying to seduce Socrates by gold but he knew him to be more invulnerable to that, than was Achilles to ⟨still⟩ steel." [83] Read Saggio Istorico della Rivoluzione di Napoli.

Tuesday July 4th.
"Heigh — ho the Clare & the Ma
Find something to fight about every day —"

_____

Don't you remember
What you said to me
About the Body of Christ
   Believe in what you see, and you shall see it
This I say to you
About your Palfred
   Believe in what you have and you shall have it.

[81] *Diogenes Laertii de vitis, dogmatibus et apophthegmatibus clarorum philosophorum libri decem, graece et latine* (Leipzig, 1759). Shelley's copy survives; see Male and Notopoulos, "Shelley's Copy of Diogenes Laertius," *MLR* 54:10–21 (January 1959). Since Claire was studying Latin at this time, she may well have been reading in Shelley's own copy.

[82] *Aeneid*, Book i, l. 33. It should be *Romanam* and *gentem*.

[83] Perhaps the most distressing of all the Shelleys' troubles at this time were Godwin's financial agonies and impositions.

# Third Journal

January 5th. 1820 the amount of the unfunded debt was 836, 916,923 £ of which the total annual interest is 49,592,152 £ and the revenue of the British Empire is 49 millions which all goes to pay the interest of the debt.

In Spain the King has ceded a great part of the Royal domains only reserving the principal residences of the Court & their dependencies — The late ministers of his iniquitous Government are left in peace & obscurity. This is as it should be!

Bathe. Do Latin Exercise. Read Virgil — Lines 100. Read Aristippe by Wieland.[84]

Wednesday July 5th. Bathe. Copy Letters from Italy. Do a Latin exercise — Read 40 lines of Virgil and Aristippe and Saggio Istorico di Napoli.

Thursday July 6th. Bathe. Copy Letters. Read Virgil. Do Latin Exercise & read Aristippe and Saggio Istorico.

Friday July 7th. Bathe. Copy Letters. Do Latin Exercise — Read Virgil & Saggio Istorico. A letter from Mr. Gisborne from London. Walk out in the Evening with S—

Saturday July 8th. Bathe — Copy Letters. Do a Latin Exercise — Read Virgil, Aristippe & Saggio Istorico della Revoluzione di Napoli. In the Evening walk in the *Podere* with the ⟨Signor⟩ Signorine Ricci.[85]

Sunday July 9th. Bathe. Copy Letters. A letter from Medwin — Read Virgil & Aristippe.
Swift wrote an epigram on two famous ⟨muscians of⟩ musicians of his day whose partizans disputed much about their merit —.

> Strange! such difference there shouldst be
> ⟨'Twixt Twedeldum⟩
> 'Twixt Tweedledum & Tweedledee.

---

[84] Christoph Martin Wieland, *Aristipp und einige seiner Zeitgenossen*, 4 vols. (Vienna, 1812). Shelley read it in an Italian translation and recommended it to Hogg in 1818 as "very Greek, though perhaps not religious enough for a true Pagan" (Shelley, *Letters*, II, 15).

[85] Mary described a *podere*, a sort of glorified kitchen garden, in a letter to Hunt (Mary Shelley, *Letters*, I, 76). Appollonia and Carlotta Ricci were the daughters of the Gisbornes' Livornese landlord. Mary teased Henry Reveley about Appollonia's pining away in his absence (*ibid.*, I, 109, 110, 112).

so ⟨the only difference⟩ ⟨⟨I find it strange that such a hatred should exist between Christians & Atheists when the whole difference of their creed consists in the first believing ⟨man⟩ God made man after his own Image whilst the other that Man made God after his own image⟩⟩.[86]

Monday July 10th. Bathe. Copy Letters. Read Virgil & Aristippe. Do a latin Exercise.

Tuesday July 11th. Bathe Copy Letters — Read Virgil & Aristippe & Saggio Istorico. Do a Latin Exercise. Walk with S in the Evening.

Wednesday July 12th. Bathe. Copy Letters. Read Virgil. Do a Latin exercise. Read Aristippe — Letter from Zambelli at Ravenna.[87]

Translation of Anacreon's Ode to the Cicala.[88]
"How happy are you sweet Cicala! sitting upon the tops of the trees, and drinking dew & singing. Kings might envy your free life! All that the fields b⟨are⟩↑ear↓ and all that the Seasons bring⟨s⟩ is your's. You hurt nothing & so the farmer loves you; you are the delight of all men, the prophet of summer! The Muses love you & Apollo in his love for you has given you that melodious voice. Old age harms thee not. Child of earth. wise, musical passionless creature, not made of flesh & blood you are almost equal to the Gods."

[86] The epigram is by John Byrom (not Swift): "Epigram on the Feuds between Handel and Bononcini," in *Miscellaneous Poems,* I, 343–344. The passage beginning "I find it strange" Claire worked particularly hard to obliterate. It has been read with the assistance of infrared photographs and suggests that Byron's taunts about her religion were not unjustified at this time (see Byron, *Works,* V, 15).

[87] Lega Zambelli had been Count Guiccioli's steward. By about this time he had passed into Lord Byron's service, and it was he who prepared the regular reports on Allegra which Shelley always passed on to Claire. Byron usually referred slightingly to him and to his mistress (and Teresa's confidante) Fanny Silvestrini: "Lega (my *secretary,* an Italianism for steward or chief servant)" (Byron, *Works,* V, 161). See also Origo, *The Last Attachment, passim.* After Byron's death Zambelli and Frederick William Fletcher, Byron's valet, settled in London and established a spaghetti-manufacturing business. See Appendix C.

[88] Mary referred to the insect and the ode (Mary Shelley, *Letters,* I, 76) and in a letter of July 19 to Maria Gisborne said: "The country wants rain and the Cicalas sing in the trees, I suppose, entreating for dew, and telling the Gods that the dry leaves hurt the sweetness of their merry song. With this exception, the season is promising" (Jones, "Mary Shelley to Maria Gisborne," *SP* 52:63–64 [January 1955]).

# Third Journal

Thursday July 13th. The Italians say to those who threaten to take the law, "Cantate cantate, e poi farete come la Cicala, scoppiarete." which alludes to the Cicala singing louder & louder if his stomach is rubbed untill it finally bursts.[89]
Bathe. Write Letters from Italy. Walk with S— in the Evening — to Livorno.

Friday July 14th. Bathe    Read Aristippe. & Virgil. Letter from Mad. Mason. ⟨Write a scene of Don Juan⟩.

X Saturday July 15th. Write to Mad. M. Go to Livorno with the Signorine Ricci. S— goes to Pisa. I am ill all day & do nothing.

Sunday July 16th. Ill all day — A letter from Mad. M. enclosing H M. W's letter from Paris.[90] Write an answer. Read Barber of Seville & Jerome Pointu.[91] Report of the Revolution at Naples; the people assembled round the palace demanding a Constitution; the King ordered his troops to fire ⟨upon them⟩ & disperse the crowd, they refused, and he has now promised a Constitution. The head of them is the Duke of Campo Chiaro. This is glorious & is produced by the Revolution in Spain.[92]

Monday July 17th. Ill all day — S returns from Pisa —

Tuesday July 18th. At five in the morning set out for Pisa. Arrive at Casa Silva by ½ past seven. Miss Field, Madame M. & Tatty. In the Evening ride out on the Lucca road with Mad— M— See

[89] On June 15 the Shelleys had transplanted themselves to Leghorn to consult a lawyer, Federico del Rosso, about how to cope with Paolo's blackmail. The proverb says, "Sing, sing, and then like the cicala you'll burst."

[90] Helen Maria Williams, friend of Godwin and Mary Wollstonecraft, who had been imprisoned by Robespierre for her advocacy of the Girondists. On their first trip to Paris in 1814 Claire and the Shelleys had called on her, but she had been out of the country (*Mary Shelley's Journal*, pp. 5–6). She was the author of ten volumes of verse, a novel, four volumes of letters about the Revolution, and several volumes of translations. Lady Mount Cashell had seen a great deal of her in 1802, at her brilliant soirees in Paris (Wilmot, *An Irish Peer*, pp. 38–41, 75–77).

[91] Probably *Le Barbier de Séville* (1775) by Beaumarchais. *Jérome Pointu: Comédie* (1781) is by De Beaunoir (pseudonym for Alexandre L. B. Robineau).

[92] See Mary's account in Jones, "Mary Shelley to Maria Gisborne," *SP* 52:65 (January 1955).

# Leghorn 1820

Tantini & Zanetti & old Sforzi. Read Continuation of the Stories of Old Daniel.[93]

Wednesday July 19th. Tetta's Birthday — She is 11 yrs. Ride out with Mad. M at five in the morning. Read Comic Dramas by Miss Edgeworth[94] — In the Evening call on Madame Tantini & ride on the Capucini Road. Read Essay on Irish Bulls.[95]

Thursday July 20th. At 5 in the morning Tetta, Mad M. & Miss Field & myself set out for Livorno. ⟨A⟩ where we arrive at ½ past seven. They spend the day with us. Tetta I & Miss F— ride all over ⟨Liv⟩ Livorno and along the sea shore as far as the Lazzarettos. They depart taking S— with them about six in the Evening for Pisa.

Friday July 21st. Finish Essay on Irish Bulls — Begin Edward by Dr Moore.[96] Bathe.

Saturday July 22nd. Finish Edward by Dr. Moore. Bathe. In the evening go with the Signorine Ricci to see the founding of a Cylinder for the steam boat at the Molino.[97] It was at nine in the evening. The building was composed of ⟨m⟩ massy walls with holes cut for windows; the floor was of earth and many opening led to apartments of the same kind which ⟨we⟩ seemed however buried in darkness — The whole place had the appearance of the recesses of some cavernous mountain for on the ⟨walls above⟩ broken & unequal surface of the walls above the weeds were shaking in

[93] Lady Mount Cashell's own *Continuation of the Stories of Old Daniel: Or Tales of Wonder and Delight. Containing Narratives of Foreign Countries and Manners, and Designed as an Introduction to the Study of Voyages, Travels, and History in General* (London: M. J. Godwin and Co. at the City Juvenile Library, no. 41 Skinner Street, 1820). The first volume of *The Stories of Old Daniel* (1807) had proved highly successful and was regularly reprinted until the middle of the century.

[94] Maria Edgeworth, *Comic Dramas, in Three Acts* (London, 1817).

[95] Maria Edgeworth and Richard Lovell Edgeworth, *Essay on Irish Bulls* (London: J. Johnson, 1802).

[96] Dr. John Moore, *Edward: Various Views of Human Nature, Taken from Life and Manners, Chiefly in England*, 2 vols. (London, 1796).

[97] Henry Reveley describes the casting of earlier cylinders for his steamboat in a letter to Shelley, November 10-13, 1819, in Gisborne and Williams, *Journals*, pp. 55-57; see Shelley's reply, Shelley, *Letters*, II, 157-158.

the night air. Only a small space was illumined by the furnace ⟨which⟩ from a small aperture of which flames of golden air seemed to issue for the fire was of wood & it produces this effect when heated to any extraordinary degree. In the middle of the flames the liquid metal lay like a lake over which ⟨the wind is hov⟩ misty clouds hover — ⟨bright⟩ red-bright, glowing with ⟨intense⟩ intensity of colour when it was allowed to run into the form it ⟨apun⟩ appeared like one of the brightest lava rivers of Vesuvius. I was extremely delighted — The flames enlightened the countenances of the workman & such others as came like myself ⟨to⟩ a spectator. The ⟨dark & pr⟩ muscular forms & the dark hair & skin of the Italians ⟨did not⟩ looked picturesque seen by the intermitting burst of flame. Close to me a Jew was leaning ⟨W⟩ against ⟨the⟩ a projection of broken wall — his short features with the peculiar cast of the ⟨Jew⟩ Jewish eye I saw by fits — The director of the foundery was a Priest who every now & then stirred the ⟨fire with⟩ liquid metal with large brands of wood upon which the Jew observed "Such will be his employment in Hell, replenishing the fire under the souls of the dammed. On my other side was a ↑little↓ french woman who in a soft voice excused herself from coming forward to see the progress of the founding by saying that "ce n'etoit pas pour voir qu'elle venoit mais pour la ⟨compagnie⟩ ↑societé↓." [98]

Sunday July 23rd. Read Florence Macarthy all day by Lady Morgan which I finish. The Italians say of Massa on account of its being surrounded by the Maremma.

Massa
Salute e passa
Chi troppo ci sta
La pelle ci lascia [99]

Monday July 24th. Bathe. Write a little. ⟨R⟩ Translate an exercise from Latin. Read Saggio Istorico.

[98] "She hadn't come for the sights, but for the society."
[99] Lady Sydney Morgan, *Florence Macarthy: An Irish Tale*, 4 vols. (London, 1818).

> Greet us and pass on your way
> Whoever stays too long
> Dies here

The town of Massa was surrounded by a marshy and malarial region called the Maremma.

# Leghorn 1820

Tuesday July 25th. S— returns from Pisa. A letter from Horace Smith. Write a little of Italian Letters. ⟨Re⟩ Do a latin Ex⟨c⟩ercise. The Signor Puccini calls.[1] He talks of the Neapolitan revolution — The exiled Patriots headed by the Duke of Campo Chiaro sailed into the bay of Naples from Palermo having on board their fleet an army of 20,000 men; they were joined by the citizens, landed & forced the King to sign the Constitution which he did as Bankers sign their Bills.

Wednesday July 26th Bathe. Write Italian Letters. Read 1 Book of Pope's Homer's Iliad. In the Evening go with S— to Livorno, & Villa Webb.[2] We meet Puccini. Read Saggio Istorico.
> Whose limbs unbury'd on the naked shore
> Devouring dogs & hungry vultures tore.

---

> O Monster! mix⟨e⟩'d ⟨in⟩ of insolence & fear
> Thou dog in forehead, but in heart a deer!

> To heap the shores with copious dead, & bring
> The Greeks to know the curse of such a king.
> Pope's Iliad.[3]

Thursday July 27th. Bathe. Copy Letters from Italy. Do ⟨an Italian⟩ ↑a Latin↓ exercise. Read a little of Virgil. Read Saggio Istorico. In the evening walk with the Signorine Ricci to villa Busnach; the Jew Montefiore & his daughter. in the gardens Busnach all the Pergolas are made of wood of the Scipio english man of war which sunk in the harbour and was afterwards brought up & bought for that purpose.

Friday July 28th. Go with S— to town in the Morning. He goes to Pisa. A letter from Tetta. Read 2 Books of Pope's Homer's Iliad. Translate Latin Speeches of Demosthenes.
> Unhappy Paris! but to women brave!
> So fairly form⟨e⟩'d, and only to deceive!

---

[1] Possibly Cavaliere Puccini, friend of Governor Niccolò Viviani, father of Shelley's Theresa Emilia. Viviani Della Robbia, *Vita di una donna*, p. 170.

[2] Where Zoide du Plantis had tried out as a governess (Mary Shelley, *Letters*, I, 90, 92).

[3] All three couplets from book i. "Dead" should be "death."

So firmly proof to all the ⟨shlo⟩ shocks of fate
Thy force like steel a temper'd hardness shows
Still edg'd to wound, & still untired with blows!

---

But, when he speaks what elocution flows!
Soft as the fleeces of descending snows,
The copious accents fall with easy art;
Melting they fall, & sink into the heart.

Book III.

Saturday July 29th. Bathe. Copy Letters. Read Book IV of Iliad.
⟨Re⟩ Finish the first Book of Virgil. Read Saggio Istorico.

> Discord! dire sister of the slaughtering power,
> Small at her birth, but rising every hour.[4]

In the evening walk to Livorno with M.

Sunday July 30th. Bathe. Copy Letters from Italy. Read Virgil &
half the V Book of the Iliad.

> Unnumber'd woes mankind from us sustain
> And men with woes afflict the Gods again!
>
> Speech of Dione   Book V 2470.

Walk with the Ricci to Villa Parenti & Regina

Monday ⟨August 1st⟩ July 31st. Bathe. Copy Letters. Finish the
V Book of the Iliad. Translate Demosthenes.

Tuesday August 1st. Bathe. S— returns from Pisa. Copy Letters
from Italy. In the Evening go with the Ricci to the Coral manufactories in Livorno.

*[the next page has only ⟨Augu⟩ at the top; it is followed by one leaf
blank on both sides; then by a page blank except for two columns
headed respectively* Received *and* Paid]

| Received[5] | Paid — | | | |
|---|---|---|---|---|
| August 1 | | S— | P— | C— |
| 43–4.4 | Clasp ................... | 0 .. | 5 .. | 0 |
| | Shoes ................... | 1 .. | 4 .. | 0 |
| | Ties ................... | 0 .. | 1 .. | 4 |

[4] Book iv.
[5] This list of payments is written upside down on the page.

# Leghorn 1820

| | | | |
|---|---|---|---|
| Ricci ...................... | 3 .. | 0 .. | 0 |
| Muslin ..................... | 0 .. | 3 .. | 0 |
| Muslin ..................... | 0 .. | 4 .. | 0 |
| Gown ...................... | 8 .. | 0 .. | 0 |
| Silk handchief ......... | 1 .. | 0 .. | 0 |
| Nonna ..................... | 1 .. | 0 .. | 0 |

*[two leaves torn out, with blank edges remaining, and three more leaves missing from the middle of the gathering at this point]*

Translation of a Greek epigram written by Antiphilus a Byzantium, upon Julius Agricola.[6]

It is between a traveller & a fountain.

T. Fons tua quo fugiens delapsa est lympha? quid undis
Tot factum? quonam est ustus abe igne liquor?

F. In lacrimas abii totus: quodcumque liquoris
Mi fuit, omne hausit jam cinis Agricola.

The selfish & the dark contend ↑rebel↓ in vain
Slaves by their own ⟨compulsion⟩ ↑compulsion↓; in mad game
They break their manacles & wear the name
of Freedom graven on a heavier chain.[7]

Aristotle's definition of Comedy that it is a picture of Human Nature worse & more deformed than the original.

Aetherial air, and ye swift winged winds
Ye rivers springing from fresh founts, ye waves
That o'er th⟨e⟩' interminable oceean wreath
Your crisped smiles, thou all producing Earth,
And thee, bright Sun, I call, whose flaming orb
Views the wide world beneath.[8]

[6] These lines of Antiphilus of Byzantium, freely translated into Latin, are from the *Anthologia Palatina*, IX, 549: "A. Ye streams of the fountain, why have ye fled? Where is all the water gone? What fiery sun has exhausted the ever-running spring? B. We are exhausted by tears for Agricola; his thirsty dust has absorbed all the drink we had to give" (*The Greek Anthology*, 5 vols., trans. W. R. Paton [Loeb Classical Library], III, 305).

[7] From Coleridge's "France: An Ode" (1798). Claire is quoting from memory, with her usual inaccuracies. She writes "selfish" for "sensual," "break" for "burst," and omits Coleridge's capitals and exclamation points.

[8] These six lines are a rendering of the three lines of Greek transcribed immediately below, from Aeschylus, *Prometheus Bound*, lines 88–90. Though

# Third Journal

Ο διος αιθηρ και ταχυπτεροι πνοαι
Ποταμωντε πηγαι ποντιωντε κυματων
Ανηριθμον γελασμα

Immortal beauty, majesty and grace,
Blend in his form and on his aspect glow;
Celestial glory beaming from his face
He sees his triumph o'er the scaly foe.[9]

*[following one blank page, two leaves have been torn out and a
third left blank, after which a sheet of laid paper has been inserted;
the following has been written inside the back cover (items super-
imposed on one another in the manuscript have been separated in
the transcription)]*

Palazzo ⟨W⟩ Verospi        300 Corso [10]

Giorgio Vasari
    The car.
    The Castor & Pollox
    The Bas-reliefs both Baccantes & the Battle of
        the Assyrians
  Camicia da Notte
  1 de di Giorno
  1 Camicino
  1 Pezzuola

                Dispute between Nature & Art concerning Man.

                Soler

|  |  | S— | P— |
|---|---|---|---|
| 2 .. 2 | William | 2 .. | 2— |
| 1 .. 0 | Woman | 1 .. | 3— |
| 4 .. 0 | ⟨N⟩ | 1 .. | 1 |

the handwriting is Claire's, she may be transcribing Shelley's translation. In
omitting the Greek accents she follows Shelley's practice.

[9] I have not been able to identify these lines.

[10] The address of the Shelleys in Rome. The rest of the cover is a palimpsest
of a shopping or laundry list, two lists of accounts — probably in shillings and
pence — and miscellaneous jottings.

# Leghorn 1820

```
4 .. 0
3 .. 0
0 .. 8
1 .. 4
4 .. 8
────────
   .. 0

    18
```

⟨Coachman ........ 4 .. 0⟩
⟨Shelley .............. 1 .. 4⟩
G— L—        1— 0 .. 0
M ..............⟨4⟩.... 4 .. 0
M ...................... 4 .. 0
S ........................ 8 .. 8
S ........................ 3 .. 4
S— Letters ........ 1 .. 0    ⟨tri⟩
M ...................... 0 .. 8    tricôt
Vincenzo  .......... 0 .. 1
Woman   .......... 0 .. 6
Scuffie M  ......... 1 .. 4
Woman   .......... 1 .. 4

# FOURTH
# JOURNAL

August 5, 1820, to April 13, 1822
September 19-20, 1822

*[inside front cover]*
Madame Colonel Target   26 Rue des Moulins near the Palais
Royale.

54 1
Chocolate for Madame Mason.
Der Kampf mit dem Drachen [*in German script*]
La Signora Maddalena Bianchi [1]
Casa Giacour


Anna Marie [*upside down*]

24 Allsops Buildings
    New Road
       Mary le bone
          London.

$$
\begin{array}{ccc}
1 & .. & 3 \\
1 & .. & 1 \\
3 & .. & 0 \\
1 & .. & 0 \\
1 & .. & 1 \\
2 & .. & 2 \\
0 & .. & 4 \\
1 & .. & 2 \\
\hline
1 .. & 4 & .. 3
\end{array}
$$

*[the following is written sideways bottom to top along the outside edge of the page]*

[1] On February 2, 1821 (below), Claire attended an "Accademia of Music" in Casa Bianchi in Florence, and on February 9 recorded a lesson from Bianchi.

167

# Fourth Journal

Casa Baldini

Casa

    Via del Giglio
        Passato Santa Maria Maggiore
Inghilterra


Saturday August 5th. Pack up & remove from Livorno to Baths of Pisa Casa Prinni where we arrive at five in the Evening.[2]

Sunday August 6th. Bathe. Employed in unpacking. In the Evening call with M— upon Madame Tantini.

Monday August 7th. Bathe. S— goes to Pisa. Read old English Baron.[3] Madame Tantini calls & Betsy the Nun. S— returns in the evening with Tatty.

Teusday August 8th. Ill all day. ↑I dream I see a ghost↓ Bathe. Read Castle of Otranto & Caleb Williams.[4]

Wednesday August 9th. Ill all day — Read Caleb Williams. In the Evening walk with M. & S on the Lucca Road — Meet Madam Tantini.

Thursday August 10th. Finish Caleb Williams — Read Symposion.[5] Letter from ⟨Bob⟩ Southey.[6] Mad— M— comes to the Baths in the Morning. In the Evening call on Madame Tantini. Translate Demosthenes. Read Saggio Istorico. "For Women — I imagine it would be of little use for their lords & governors that they should be disciplined to lofty thoughts and to the union and

[2] No lawsuit evolved out of their troubles with Paolo, so the Shelleys left for the Bagni di Pisa (also called Bagni di San Giuliano), where Mary and Shelley were to remain until October 29. They were within visiting distance of Pisa (only four miles away), Lucca, and Leghorn.

[3] Clara Reeve, *The Old English Baron: A Gothic Story,* bound together with Horace Walpole's *The Castle of Otranto* (London: J. Walker, J. Johnson, et al., 1808).

[4] William Godwin, *Things as They Are: Or, the Adventures of Caleb Williams,* 3 vols. (London, 1794).

[5] Claire may have been rereading Shelley's translation. See Note 27 to entry of April 14, 1819, above.

[6] This letter, and Shelley's answer dated August 17, are in *Correspondence of Robert Southey,* pp. 359–363.

# Baths of Pisa 1820

community of stedfast friendship which demands for its foundation ⟨nay cannot have a beginning but from⟩ equality, nay cannot have a beginning but in Liberty.

Friday August 11th. Read Symposion. Write a little. In the Evening we all go to Lucca — Sleep at the Croce di Malta.

Saturday August 12th. S— goes to Monte San Pellegrino — Walk with M. about Lucca. We ⟨mont a⟩ mount a Tower from which we examine the situation of Lucca and the surrounding country which is beautiful. We visit the Duomo, San Francesco & San Fridiano and we ⟨dr⟩ drive round the walls of Lucca. We return to the Baths passing through Ripa frata & Pugnano. In Lucca we see the palazzi Guinigi on one of which there remains an ancient tower with trees growing on its roof — That powerful family quarrelled and divided ⟨w⟩ itself into two parties, the Bianchi & the Neri — They ↑joined to↓ build a church (now in the ⟨slam⟩ same street as the two palaces) ⟨placing a white stone⟩ whose door is ⟨white on one side⟩ of white marble on one side & ↑of↓ black on the other — ⟨to⟩ In the church of San Francesco we see the tablet raised over the grave of Castruccio.[7]

Castruccio Antelmenillio. Gherii F. Lucens.
Imperatori fortissimo felicissimoque
Qui totum [totam] aut domuit armis aut agitabit Etruriam
Patriamq. suam fere cum Atheniensi et
Romana urbe se cive adaequavit
Quod Castracanis Fanensibus antel⟨l⟩minilliorum agnatis
Senatorius ordo ob nobilitatem generis
Redditus ex S.C. fuerit
Memoriam gentilis decus veteris patriae
Beneficium Senatus illustrare cupientes
Com. Castruccius et Alexander Castracanii. R.
Et Angelus Castruccii F.
Patricii Fanenses et Lucenses

[7] For Mary's account of this day, see *Mary Shelley's Journal*, pp. 136–137. On the tomb of Castruccio, see Mary to Leigh Hunt, August 7, 1823 (Mary Shelley, *Letters*, I, 245–246). In March Mary had begun work on her novel about Castruccio, published as *Valperga: Or, the Life and Adventures of Castruccio, Prince of Lucca*, 3 vols. (London: G. and W. B. Whittaker, 1823).

# Fourth Journal

Antiquissimum Sepulcrum Maximo conditum duci
    Sibimet ipsis et posteris vindicare curarunt.
        An. CDDCCXLIX [8]

Underneath this tablet is another which is the ⟨one erected⟩ original one inscribed to Castruccio.

        En vivo Vivamque
        Fama rerum gestarum
        Italiae Militiae splen
        dor Lucensium
        decus Etruriae
        Ornamentum Cas
        truccius Gerii An
        telmineorum ⟨stri⟩ stirpe
        Vixi — Peccavi — Dolui
        Cessi Naturae indigen
        ti animae↑e↓ piae↑e↓ benevoli
        succurrite brevi memo
        res suos morituros. [9]

                       Without date.

[8]   To Castruccio Castracani degli Antelminelli, son of Gerio,
      Most courageous and victorious general
Who subdued or waged war in all parts of Tuscany and Italy,
Who made his city equal in glory almost to Athens and Rome.
Because to the family of the Castracani Antelminelli of Fano
      the Senatorial Dignity has been restored
[*i.e., enrollment among the senatorial families of Lucca*]
By public decree of the Council of Lucca, in honor of
      the ancient nobility of the Castracani,
The Counts Castruccio and Alessandro Castracani R
      and Angelo, son of Castruccio,
Patricians of Fano and Lucca,
Desiring to commemorate the glory of their ancestral city
      and their gratitude for the honor conferred upon them,
Have restored this ancient sepulcher, founded for the very great
      commander, for themselves and their descendants.
                  The Year 1749
 [9] "Behold, I live and shall live by the fame of my deeds, splendor of Italy's arms, and of Lucca's, glory of Tuscany. Castruccio, son of Gerio, ornament of the family of the Antelminelli. I lived, I sinned, I suffered, and paid my debt to nature with a calm mind, in love of God and man. Attend and be mindful that you too are soon to die." (I am indebted to Professor Kiffin Rockwell for the translation of these two inscriptions.) Mary Shelley ended *Valperga* by quoting this inscription, commenting: "The antient tombstone is still seen on

# Baths of Pisa 1820

Sunday August 13th. Read the Life of Castruccio by Nicalao Tegrimi.[10] S— returns from ⟨Mole⟩ Monte San Pellegrino. In the Evening call upon Madame Tantini — & the Signor Francesco.

**X** Monday August 14th. Ill all day. Walk in the Buboli  Walk before Breakfast. Read the Symposion. Translate Demosthenes.

Tuesday August 15. Festa of the Assunta. Ill all day.

Wednesday August 16th. Write to Albè — ⟨Write a little of Don Juan⟩ — Read Christabel [11] & the Saggio Storico. A letter from Miss Stacey.

Thursday August 17th. A letter from Mr. Gisborne. ⟨Write Don Juan⟩ Weather intolerably warm  In the Evening walk with S— in the road to Asciano. Call upon Mad— ⟨Tat⟩ Tantini — A Lucchese recommended his brother to her ⟨as⟩ calling him a bravo giovane — "hà dato già tre coltellatè ed ha appena vent' anni" [12]

Friday August 18th. Translate Demosthenes. Walk before Breakfast on the Lucca Road. ⟨Write a little of Don Juan⟩.

Saturday August 19th. Tetta calls. Read Parents Offering [13] — Thunder Storm — Bathe. the Water of an icy Coldness. Do a Latin exercise from the Odyssey. Walk with M— in the Evening on the road to Asciano.

Sunday August 20th. Thunder Storm. Read Swiss ↑Family↓ Robinson Crusoe.[14] Latin from Odyssey — Copy S— letter to Southey. Il Signor & La Signora Tantini call.

---

the walls of the church; and its inscription may serve for the moral and conclusion of this tale" (III, 269).

[10] Niccolò Tegrimi, *Vita di Castruccio Castracani de gl' Antelmi nelli principe di Lucca* (Modena, 1496). In her preface to *Valperga* Mary acknowledges "Tegrino's [sic] *Life of Castruccio*" among her sources (I, iii).

[11] By Samuel Taylor Coleridge.

[12] "A brave lad — 'has already given three knife wounds and is scarcely twenty years old.'" Edward Williams heard this story from Claire over a year later and recorded it in his journal (Gisborne and Williams, *Journals*, p. 104).

[13] Mrs. Caroline Barnard, *The Parent's Offering; or Tales for Children*, 2 vols. (London: M. J. Godwin, 1813).

[14] Johann David Wyss, *The Family Robinson Crusoe: Or, Journal of a Father Shipwrecked, with His Wife and Children, on an Uninhabited Island*, trans. from the German, 2 vols. (London: M. J. Godwin, 1814). One of Mrs. Godwin's happiest publishing ventures, known today as *The Swiss Family Robinson*.

# Fourth Journal

On Monday August 21st. I went to Pisa & staid there untill Thursday the 24th which day ⟨the⟩ Mad. M. with her Children & Miss Field ⟨ca returned⟩ spent with us at the Baths it being the fair of St Bartolommeo [15] — Zanetti & his wife call — Call ⟨in⟩ on Madame Tantini   Horse races in the Evening.

Wednesday August 30th. ⟨Write Juan⟩. Bathe. Walk on the road to Asciano   A letter from Ravenna.

Thursday August 31st. Go with S— to Pisa — Call in Casa Silva — Then continue to Livorno where we arrive at 6 in the Evening — [16]

Friday Sept. 1st. Read Ormond.[17] Mr. Jackson calls.[18] Walk in the Podere.

Saturday Sept. 2nd. Play — Go to Livorno with S— Call upon Peter & Giavelli — Report from Naples ⟨the⟩ that the Carbonari have ⟨taken a secure possession⟩ possessed themselves of the ⟨per⟩ persons of the royal family & have informed the Emperor of Austria that on his first hostile movement they shall think them selves bound to execute every single royal individual. Reports from Paris that the people are besieging the Tuileries & from England that Albè arrived there with dispatches for the Queen.[19]

[15] On this market day Shelley's attempt to read aloud his "Ode to Liberty" to Lady Mount Cashell was nearly drowned out by the grunting of the pigs brought to market to the fair. He compared it to the chorus of frogs in Aristophanes, "and it being an hour of merriment, and one ludicrous situation suggesting another, he imagined a political satirical drama on the circumstances of the day, to which the pigs would serve as chorus" (note by Mary Shelley to *Oedipus Tyrannus; or, Swellfoot the Tyrant* in Shelley, *Works*, II, 350).

[16] Claire spent the next month pretty much by herself in Leghorn, sea bathing for her health.

[17] Probably Charles Brockden Brown's *Ormond; or, the Secret Witness* (New York, 1799). Shelley almost certainly drew his name of Constantia for Claire from the heroine of this novel, Constantia Dudley, who, as Peacock says, "held one of the highest places, if not the very highest place, in Shelley's idealities of female character" (*Memoirs*, II, 328).

[18] Shelley mentions in a letter to Mary (September 1, 1820) a Mr. Jackson's drinking tea at Casa Ricci with Claire and himself (Shelley, *Letters*, II, 234).

[19] Shelley's letters to Mary from Leghorn (September 1) and to Byron (September 17) cast considerable light on the rumors rampant at this time. It appeared that all Europe was on the brink of a revolutionary conflagration (Shelley, *Letters*, II, 234–236).

# Leghorn 1820

Sunday Sept. 3rd. Hint for Don Juan.
> I'll kiss the lips & break the Pate
> Of the maid I love & the man I hate [20]

─────

> for freemen mightier grow
> And slaves more feeble, gazing on their foe. [21]

S— returns — ↑to Pisa↓ Read Clarissa Harlowe.

Monday Sept. 4th. Read Clarissa — Take a ⟨bariette⟩ Barchetto & row to a Barracca & bathe. Practise. Write to Madame Mason.

Tuesday Sept. 5th. Go to the Bath of Regina and Bathe. Read Clarissa Harlowe — Go to Livorno in the Evening.

Wednesday Sept. 6th. Go to the Bath of the Regina & Bathe. Practise & read Clarissa Harlowe  Thunder storm in the Afternoon. A letter from Madame M. & Mary

Thursday Sept. 7th. Bathe in the Bath of the Regina. Practise & read Clarissa Harlowe. Eclipse of the Sun from two 'oclock of the fore noon untill four.

To pretend to *convince* a man who knows in his heart he is doing wrong!

Lovelace.

Another jiggeting rascal called Biron.

Idem. [22]

X Friday Sept 8th. Go to Pisa with Appollonia Ricci then to the Baths.

Saturday Sept 9th. Read Philosophical Survey of the South of Ireland written as it is said by one Campbell. [23]

Sunday Sept. 10th. Read Survey of the South of Ireland. Walk with S— in the Buboli [24]

[20] See entry for November 8, 1820, below.
[21] Shelley's "Ode to Naples," lines 87–88, which he had written at the Baths of Pisa a week or two earlier.
[22] From *Clarissa Harlowe*.
[23] Thomas Campbell, *A Philosophical Survey of the South of Ireland, in a Series of Letters to John Watkinson, M. D.* (London, 1777).
[24] Not to be confused with the gardens of the same name in Florence. The Florentine Buboli (or Boboli) Gardens, extending along the side of the hill behind the Pitti Palace, were the largest evergreen gardens in Italy and on certain days were open to the public. They appealed more to the contemplative

# Fourth Journal

Monday Sept. 11th. Return to Pisa — Breakfast in Casa Silva then return to Livorno.

Tuesday Sept. 12th Bathe. Read Philosophical Survey's & Clarissa Harlowe.

Wednesday Sept. 13th. Go to the Bath of La Regina & Bathe. Read Clarissa Harlowe.

Thursday Sept 14th. Go to the Bath of La Regina & Bathe. Finish Clarissa Harlowe.

Friday Sept 15th. Go & bathe in the Bath of the Regina. Read Irish Poetry translated by Miss Brooke [25]

Saturday Sept. 16th. Go & bathe in the Bath of the Regina Afterwards to Livorno. Caterina [26] from the Bagni. Letter from M & Madame Mason.

Sunday Sept. 17th. Bathe in the Bathe of the Regina — Write to Madame Mason & M— Begin Earl of Castlehaven's Memoirs. [27]

Monday Sept. 18th. Bathe in the Bath of the Regina. Practise. A letter from Charles at Wien. [28]

A florin silber geld is worth about 2s/1d sterling — but this is confined almost entirely to the language of Bankers. The paper florins were first issued during the war with France & were originally substitutes for Silber geld florins & of course of the same value. The Austrian government was however imprudent enough

---

than to the fashionable stroller, and men and women with books were often seen walking among the ilex, cypress, bay, laurel, and fir. The heart of the gardens was the harpsichord-shaped formal garden, adjacent to the palace, with its Egyptian obelisk, rather in the style of Versailles. Beyond this stretched the woods of the Boboli, with alleys leading to bowers, grottoes, and labyrinths, adorned with statues, fountains, and temples and commanding a view of the whole city, the Val d'Arno, Fiesole, and the Apennines.

[25] Charlotte Brooke, *Reliques of Irish Poetry: Consisting of Heroic Poems, Odes, Elegies and Songs, Translated into English Verse* . . . (Dublin, 1789).

[26] The Shelleys' servant.

[27] James Touchet, Lord Audley, third earl of Castlehaven, *The Memoir's of James Lord Audley Earl of Castlehaven, His Engagements and Carriage in the Wars of Ireland, from the Year 1642 to the Year 1651* (London, 1680).

[28] This letter from Austria, July 29, 1820, is in the Bodleian Library (MS. Shelley Adds. d. 5). The rest of this day's entry is obviously drawn from it.

to issue them in such quantities that they soon began to lose credit & fell suddenly to one 1/6 of their ↑first↓ value; consequently all persons who had taken them in any quantity, lost a vast deal of their property. After the Peace the finances took a better turn; large quantities of this paper were called in and burnt by Government; not at its true price but *at the then current standard of 1/6th*. So that where the Government had borrowed one shilling it repaid its debt with 2d — Judge of the enormous sum thus stolen out of the people's pocket. These burnings have now been going on for 5 or 6 yrs. at the rate of 2d. or 3d. in the shilling: and never less than 4 or 5 millions at a time, thus the paper florins at length began to fetch a better price in the market, & would of course in proportion to the dim↑i↓nution of the overwhelming flood have at last reached their real value: so about 3 months ago Government seeing there was no chance of a further diminution & fearing a rise which might force them to buy in the remaining paper at the price they received for it, finally fixed the Exchange at 250 per Cent — above which it never can rise; so now a Government Creditor who lent 1000 fl — must pay in, in paper 2600 to receive his money back again. Thus those persons who may have been in sufficiently easy circumstances not to need to use ⟨this paper⟩ their paper & have laid it by in hopes of a final rise to its true value are at once debarred all hopes of ever regaining their property & must submit to the tyranical alternative of making the Emperor a present of 2/3rds of his debt to them, or very nearly so, for the paper florin is worth about 10d sterling and the silver one about 2s/1d as I before said.

The Germans call God *grossen Herrn* which is literally the great Gentleman.

Teusday Sept. 19th. Bathe in the Bath of the Regina — An ⟨very⟩ extremely high wind — the Ocean worked into waves with white sharp edges, dashing among the rocks. A letter from Mad. M— M. & S— & the Signora Dionigi — Thunder storm at Night.

Wednesday Sept. 20th. I am not well & do not bathe. Walk to Livorno after dinner with Charlotte. Read Miss Brooke's Irish poetry.

# Fourth Journal

⟨Vallancey's Irish Grammar at the end of which is printed an old Irish Manuscript entitled Lessons for a Prince⟩[29]
In the Evening go to town on commissions.

Sunday Sept. 24th. I dreamt this night that ⟨my Allegra⟩ Elise & Fletcher[30] came to tell me that Allegra was on the road from Ravenna to visit me.

Bathe at the Bagnetti. Do some Latin, practise & finish Miss Brooke's Irish poetry

> Before our host the beauteous stranger bowed
> And, thrown to earth, her eyes their glories shroud.[31]

---

> Again at gentle Love's command
> Reach forth thy snowy hand!
> Soft into mine its whiteness steal
> And its dear pressure let me feel!
> Unveil the bashful radiance of thine eyes
> (Bright trembling gems) & let me see them rise.
> Lift the fair lids where their soft glories roll
> And send their secret glances to my soul![32]

Translation of an Irish Song by ⟨End⟩ Edmond ⟨Ryan⟩ Ryan, chief of the *Rapparees* an unhappy multitude of Irish soldiers who turned Banditti after the Battle of the Boyne.

> Ah! what woes are mine to bear
> Life's fair morn with clouds o'ercasting!
> Doom'ed the ⟨vic⟩ victim of Despair!
> Youth's gay bloom, pale sorrow blasting!

---

> Sad the bird that sings alone
> Flies to wilds, unseen to languish,
> Pours unheard the ceaseless moan
> And wastes on desart air its ⟨l⟩ anguish!

---

[29] Charles Vallancey, *A Grammar of the Iberno-Celtic, or Irish Language* (Dublin, 1773).

[30] William Fletcher was Byron's servant. See Note 87 to entry of July 12, 1820, above.

[31] "Moira Borb: A Poem," Brooke, *Reliques*, p. 123.

[32] "Elegy to the Daughter of Owen," *ibid.*, p. 194.

# Leghorn 1820

Mine oh hapless bird! thy fate
    The plundered nest, — the lonely sorrow! —
The lost-loved-harmonious mate!
    The wailing night, the cheerless morrow.

---

O thou dear hoard of treasur'd love!
    Though these fond arms should n'eer possess thee
Still — still my heart its faith shall prove
    And its last sighs shall breath to bless thee! [33]

---

O might I call thee now my own!
    No added rapture joy could borrow:
'Twould be, like Heav'n, when Life is flown
    To cheer the soul ⟨d⟩ & heal its sorrow.

See thy falsehood cruel maid
    See my cheek no longer glowing;
Strength departed, health decayed
    Life in tears of sorrow flowing!

O Sickness, past⟨,⟩ all med⟨i⟩'cine's art!
O Sorrow, every grief exceeding!
O wound! that in my breaking heart!
Cureless, deep, to death art bleeding!

                          Ibid

Carolan describing the beauty of Mable Kelly

    Ev⟨e⟩'n he whose hapless eyes no ray
    Admit from Beauty's cheering day
    Yet though he cannot *see* the light
    He feels it warm & knows it bright [34]

Monday Sept. 25th. Go to town in the Morning with Signora Giulia. I see a beggar sitting at his post yawning with *ennui* — another crawling on all fours politely saluting a young washerwoman a bundle on her head & bare footed ⟨and⟩ with *mi rincresce che La Mamma e ammalata;* [35] Greeks ⟨crossed⟩ with legs folded

[33] "Elegy" by Edmond Ryan, *ibid.,* pp. 205–207. The section following is from pp. 211–212.
[34] "Song for Mable Kelly. By Carolan," *ibid.,* p. 253.
[35] "I'm sorry your mother is sick."

under them sitting upon the parapets ⟨w⟩ & gazing stupidly upon the muddy current of the canal below — Further I met persons ⟨with⟩ of every country & every costume — and numerous old women ugly hag-ridden beldams rich in nothing but deformities — here men burning coffee before their doors, & there others beating the flock of mattrⁱaˡesses; violins squeaking, & women singing — Life every where but like ⟨to⟩ the life which is engendered of putrefaction creeping crawling worms not that ⟨of the⟩ wholesome ⟨breathing country or of Liberty⟩ strength of an agricultural product or that animation which is the child of Liberty.

Practise — do some Latin.

Teusday Sept. 26th. Bathe at the ⟨Bgnetti⟩ Bagnetti. Rain all day — Write to M. & Mad— Mason. Do some Latin. Read Keats' Endymion.

Wednesday Sept. 27th. Do some Latin from Virgil. Rain all day. Practise — Finish Keats' Endymion.

Shortly afterwards — S— came to fetch me from Livorno. Go with him to the Baths — then return to Casa Silva where I stay — ⟨untill⟩ [36]

Friday October 13 — Call upon Miss Field — Read Memoirs of O'Connor [37] — Go in the Barrocino to the Bagni and return. M— & S— call with little Babe — A lesson from Legerino

Saturday October 14th. Walk before breakfast with Tetta out of the Porta Nuova round to the Porta Lucca home. Practise — A letter from Ravenna.

Sunday October 15th. Walk before breakfast with Tetta upon the Argine. Read the Isabella or Pot of Basil by Keats.

> Parting they seem'd to tread upon the air
> Twin roses by the Zephyr blown apart

---

[36] On October 1 Mary wrote in her journal: "S. goes to Leghorn & returns" (in *Mary Shelley's Journal*, pp. 138-139). As usual, Claire is not named, but a small sketch of a sun with rays appears here and subsequently as a symbol for Claire (see Note 49 below).

[37] Arthur (afterwards Condorcet) O'Connor, T. A. Emmett, and W. J. McNevin, *Memoir on the Objects of the Societies of United Irishmen* (London [1798]).

# Florence 1820

Only to meet again more close, and share
The inward fragrance of each other's heart.[38]

Monday October 16th. S— comes. Walk about with him looking for lodgings. Walk with Tetta from the Porta di Mare to the Porta Fiorentina. A letter from Mrs. Gisborne.[39] Mary arrives from Livorno in the Evening.

Teusday October 17th. Walk with Tetta before breakfast — We are caught in the rain. Call upon Miss Field & the Signora Bronzoli and Appollonia. S— calls & goes to Livorno.

Wednesday October 18th. Rain all day — Prepare —

Thursday October 19th. Call on Miss Field & on Appollonia — S & M. come from the Bagni. Pack up & prepare. Mr. Reeveley calls in the evening.[40]

Friday October 20th. Set out with S— at six in the morning  We arrive at Florence about six in the Evening — Sleep at the Fontana. Whoever does a benefit to another buys so much envy, malice, hatred and all uncharitableness from him.[41]

Saturday October 21st. Il Signor Tantini calls. Go with him to La Signora Cecilia [42] — then to Casa Bojti — opposite Palazzo Pitti. Unpack my things. Shelley takes leave of me in the Evening.

[38] "Isabella," stanza 10.

[39] The Gisbornes, on their return from England, deeply offended the Shelleys by failing to call. For Mary's letter of October 16, 1820, in reply to Maria's, and for Jones's conjectures about the source of strain between the two families, see Shelley, *Letters*, II, 238n.

[40] For Henry Reveley, see Appendix C.

[41] On November 20, 1844, Claire wrote to Mary: "Thus much I have learned that what Shelley once wrote to me in a letter is true — 'that to do a kindness to the unworthy is to purchase a large dose of hatred, calumny and all uncharitableness'" (Abinger MSS.). Probably this outburst was inspired by the behavior of the Gisbornes (see Shelley's letter of October 11, Shelley, *Letters*, II, 237; and Mary Shelley, *Letters*, I, 114–115, and note).

[42] His wife. The Tantinis introduced Claire to the Bojtis, in whose home Claire stayed as a paying guest for a trial month. See Appendix C. Dr. Bojti was 42 when Claire came into his home. He had several little girls, the oldest of whom, Annina and Louisa (Luisa), spent a great deal of time with Claire. There was also a grandmother, the "nonna" or "grossmutter," and a small boy, "the Bimbo."

# Fourth Journal

Sunday October 22nd. Rain in torrents. The Signor Tantini calls — Unpack my Boxes —

Monday October 23rd. Do a fable and a half of Phaedrus.[43] Begin to learn the German verb *Ich bin*.[44] In the Evening go with Madame Bojti to the house of Madame Tantini — the Signori Tonelli[45] & Giannini.

Teusday October — 24th. Do 5 and a half fables from Phaedrus. Read a little of Bolingbroke's Political Works.[46] Learn part of a German verb. The Signori Tantini call in the Evening.

Wednesday October 25th. Write to Madame Mason, Tetta & S— Work — After dinner walk out with Madame Bojti in the town.

Thursday October 26th. Write from Phaedrus. Learn some German — Walk in the Buboli Gardens with Louisa & Annina.

Friday October 27th. Do Latin from Phaedrus. Begin Istoria Civile di Napoli da Giannone.[47] Learn some German. Walk out after dinner.

Saturday October 28th. Translate from Phaedrus — Walk out in the Town. Learn German.

Sunday October 29th. I am not well today — Work. Walk in the Buboli. First ⟨chaber⟩ chamber-man's Wife & wife of the ⟨che⟩ cleaner of the Plate. Die grosmutter at dinner. ⟨Im⟩ Think of thyself as a stranger & traveller ⟨in this world⟩, on the earth, to whom none of the many affairs of this world, belong and who has no permanent township on the globe.

[43] Phaedrus' Latin fables are derived largely from those of Aesop.
[44] Claire's German studies suggest that she was contemplating joining her brother in Austria.
[45] Tonelli was a pianist of considerable repute. The Shelleys had had some dealings with him or his wife in 1819 (see Gisborne and Williams, *Journals*, p. 61).
[46] *The Works of the Late Right Honourable Henry St. John, Lord Viscount Bolingbroke*, 7 vols. (London, 1754–1798), or perhaps *A Collection of Political Tracts*, "By the Author of the Dissertation upon Parties" (London, 1788).
[47] Pietro Giannone, *Dell' Istoria civile del regno di Napoli*, 4 vols. (Naples, 1723).

# Florence 1820

Monday October 30th.

⟨⟨You may mistake the misgivings of your ↑town↓ heart for the voice of reason, you have my ⟨leave to babble about⟩ & frightened, bid warn others with the coming ↑blowing↓ of the "last trump"; or more innocent still, you may look⟩⟩ ↑usefully↓ ⟨⟨employ yourself in finding out & pointing out to the edification of the world, proper spots for men to look up to* —

---

Vide 4 Canto Child H.          * There let him stay [*lay* ?])⟩⟩ [48]

Do some fables from Phaedrus — a lesson in dancing. Write to Shelley & Madame Mason.

Teusday October 31st. Fables from Phaedrus. Work. Walk with Madame Bojti in the town. Rainy day. A letter from S— [49]

Wednesday ⟨O⟩ November 1st. All Saint's day. ⟨⟨The words for piety, decorum, behavior, respect for the opinions of the world are nothing but the coverings people put upon their souls when like

[48] The asterisk and its note are Claire's. I have had to guess at the last three words before the asterisk. In her attacks on Byron, written in the form of critiques of his poetry, she several times alludes to the "last trump" passage in *Childe Harold*, canto iii, stanza 31, in which the poet meditates on those fallen on the field of Waterloo:

> The Archangel's trump, not Glory's, must awake
> Those whom they thirst for; though the sound of Fame
> May for a moment soothe, it cannot slake
> The fever of vain longing, and the name
> So honoured but assumes a stronger, bitterer claim.

Claire had served as Byron's copyist in June and July of 1816, and one of her tasks had been to make a transcription of his first copy of this canto (*Works of Lord Byron*, ed. E. H. Coleridge, II, 211). One may guess that Claire recalled this particular passage with such bitterness for reasons suggested by the caricature of the poet in the entry for November 8, below. See also her entry for April 15, 1821.

[49] Shelley's letter of October 29, in which he says that he has seen the Tantinis who confirm her letter: "They tell me you looked very melancholy and disconsolate, which they impute to the weather. You must indeed be very uncomfortable for it to become visible to them" (see Shelley, *Letters*, II, 241–244). In summarizing the week of October 26 to November 4, Mary mentions in her journal, "Letters from ☀ complaining of dullness" (Abinger MSS.). Mary's symbol for Claire (a sun with rays) has the sarcastic effect of "Letters from Miss Sunshine."

# Fourth Journal

Adam & Eve ⟨decking⟩ placing the fig leaf they are ashamed of its deformity⟩⟩.[50] Work. Do some German Excercises.

Thursday November 2nd. Write to Shelley & do some German. Go after dinner to visit the chapel of the Vicario of Florence. Work.

Friday November 3rd. Write to Madame M— Do German Excercise — Read Giannone. After dinner walk with Luisa & Annina on the Lung Arno. Work.

Saturday November 4th. Do some German excercises. Write to Mary. Read Giannone. After dinner walk to the Post — ⟨N⟩ a letter from S— In the evening play with the children & their friends —

X Sunday November 5th. Do some German excersises — Walk upon the Terrace.

Monday November 6th. Do German Excercises — Read Giannone — A few Lines of Latin. In the Evening the Marchesa Rosalis & her son call. —

Teusday November 7th. Write to Mary — Do some German Excercises. Walk to the Post. Do a fable from Phaedrus. In the Evening go with Madame B. to the theatre of the Cocomero.[51] Benefit of the Prima Donna, La Signora Teghil; 1st. act of Corradino, by Rossini, Ballo, Il pittore per Amore, and the 1st act of Barbiere di Seviglia, music by Mozart.[52]

Wednesday Nov. 8th. Caricatures for Albè.[53] He, sitting ⟨at⟩

[50] Another passage that she tried to obliterate.

[51] So called from its ensign — a bomb — which people took for a watermelon.

[52] Claire seems to have been mistaken about the composers. Professor Nino Pirrotta of the Department of Music, Harvard University, has explained in a letter that Rossini's *Matilde di Shabran* (also presented as *Corradino*) was not yet begun, and that it seems likely Claire saw a *Corradino* by Francesco Morlacchi, which *was* performed in the autumn season at the Cocomero in 1820. While the *Barbiere* could have been Morlacchi's (composed 1816) or Rossini's (composed 1817), Professor Pirrotta has found no mention of the ballet *Il Pittore per amore*, nor of a singer named "Signora Teghil."

[53] An example of the type of caricature envisioned by Claire may be seen in *KSMB* 7:facing 27 (1956).

# Florence 1820

writing poetry, the words *Oh! faithless Woman*; round the room, hearts are strewed, ⟨insert⟩ inscribed, *We died for love of you.* Another — he catching a lady by her waist, his face turned towards her, his other hand extended holding a club stick in the act of giving a blow to a man who is escaping. From his mouth

> The maid I love, the man I hate —
> I'll kiss her lips & break his Pate.

Three more to be called Lord Byron's Morning, Noon & Night. the first he looking at the sky, a sun brightly shining — saying ⟨come I feel quite bold & cheerful — there is no God⟩ the second towards evening, a grey tint spread over the face of Nature, the sun behind a cloud — ↑a shower of rain falling↓ ⟨he⟩ a dinner table in the distance covered with a profusion of dishes, he ⟨with a Wallup⟩ says — ⟨What a change I feel in me after dinner; where we see design we suppose a designer; I'll be ⟨a Deist⟩ I am a Deist.⟩ The third — evening — candles just lighted, all dark without the windows ⟨whose⟩ ⟨a cup of green tea on the table⟩: and trees agitated much by wind beating against the panes, also thunder & lightning. He says ⟨God bless me! suppose there should be a God — it is as well to stand in his good graces. ⟨Let me say prayers⟩ I'll say my prayers to night, & ⟨put in a touch about the last trump⟩ write to Murray to put in a touch concerning ↑blowing of the↓ the last Trump.⟩ [54] Pistols are on the table, also daggers. — bulluts turkish scymitars . . . .

Another to be called Lord Byron↑'s↓ receipt for writing pathetic Poetry. He sitting drinking spirits, playing with his white mustachios. His mistress, the Fornara opposite him Drinking coffee. Fumes coming from her mouth, over which is written garlich; these curling direct themselves towards his English footman who is just then entering the room & he is knocked backward — Lord B. is writing he says, Imprimis to be a great pathetic poet. 1st. Prepare a small colony, then dispatch the mother by worrying & cruelty to her grave afterwards to neglect & ill treat the children — to have as many & as dirty ↑mistresses↓ as can be found; ⟨⟨to be covered with ⟨a⟩ horrible diseases⟩⟩ from their embraces to catch horrible diseases, thus a tolerable quantity of discontent & remorse being prepared to give it vent on paper, & to remember particularly to

[54] For an amusing parallel to Claire's satire of Byron's orthodoxy, see his *Don Juan,* canto xi, stanzas 5–6.

rail against learned women. This is ⟨an⟩ my infallible receipt by which I have made so much money.

The last his Death. ⟨Ex⟩ He dead extended on his bed, covered all but his breast, which many wigged doctors are cutting open to find out (as one may be saying) what was the extraordinary disease of which this great man died — His heart laid bare, they find an ⟨immen⟩ immense capital *I* ⟨la⟩ grown on its ⟨face⟩ surface — and which had begun to peirce the breast — ⟨A⟩ They are all astonishment. One says. (A new disease. Another. (I never had a case of this kind before) A third (What medicines would ↑have↓ been proper) the fourth holding up his finger (A desert island.)

Caricature for poor ⟨dear⟩ S. He looking very sweet & smiling. a little ⟨child playing⟩ Jesus Christ playing about the room    He says. Then grasping a ⟨sm⟩ small knife & looking mild

⟨I'll quietly kill that little child⟩

I will quietly murder that little child.

Another. Himself & God Almighty. He says If you please God Almighty, I'⟨d⟩ had rather be dammed with Plato & Lord Bacon than go to Heaven with Paley & Malthus. God Almighty. It shall be quite as you please, pray don't stand upon ceremony. Shelley's three aversions. God Almighty, Lord Chancellor & didactic Poetry.[55]

------

The french so polite they call a robber un amateur de ce qu↑e↓⟨'il⟩ ne lui appartient pas.[56]

------

Work. Read Giannone. Do some German Excercises. A letter from S—   Read Lamia by Keats.

Thursday Nov. 9th. Work— Do German Excercises. Read Giannone. Translate from Phaedrus.

Friday Nov. 10th.

Nel quinto mistero si contempla La Vergine Maria, avendo perso il suo ⟨fig⟩ santissimo figlio, dopo tre giorni lo trovo in tempio che disputava coi dottori.

*da Vulgo*

Nel quinto mistero, si scontempla, & non si scontempla, la Vergine

[55] Based on the preface to *Prometheus Unbound*. Claire had just received her copy.

[56] "An enthusiast of what doesn't belong to him."

# Florence 1820

Maria avendo perso il suo figliuolo, al di quaè e al di la è lo tro-
vorno dopo tre giorni in un Bigonciolo che ⟨sputavan⟩ sputava in
faccia i dottori.[57]
Rain all day — I work. Read Hyperion of Keats

Saturday Nov. 11th. Do some German Excercises. A letter from
Mary — walk upon the Terrace. Read the 1st. act of Prometheus unbound.

Sunday Nov. 12th. Do some German Excercises. Write to Madame
M—. Madame Werner dines. I After dinner walk with the Doctor
& his Wife to the Fortress of the Cascina.

Monday Nov. 13th. Il solo nome di Christiano gli faceva esosi ed
abominevoli, e per rendergli più esecrandi, gli accagionavan di
molti delitti e scelleraggini: ch'essi fossero omicidi, aggiugnendo
che ammazzassero gl'infanti, & ci cibassero delle loro carni: che
fossero incestuosi, e che nelle loro notturne ⟨assemb⟩ assemblee
mischiati, con esecrande libidini si contaminassero. Ed a coloro
che per la manifesta lor probità non potevan imputar queste scel-
leratezze, rendevano presso agl⟨i⟩' Imperadori, come disprezzatori
del culto degl'Iddii; che defraudassero gl'Imperadori del lor onore
mettessero ⟨soto⟩ sottosopra le leggi Romani ed i lor costumi, e tutta
la natura non volendo invocar gl'Iddii ne degnando di render loro
i Sacrifizj laonde venivan chiamati *Atei* Pertubatori dello Stato,
e dei costumi e pestilenza eterna del genero umano e della natura;
poichè col disprezzo che i C⟨h⟩ristiani facevan dei loro Dii ne sti-
molavan l'ira alla vendetta tanto che presso dei gentili passò per
comune & perpetuà querela che i Cristiani fossero cagione di tutti
i loro mali. Giannone Storia di Napoli ↑vol 1st↓ Lib I. C— II p. 58 [58]

---

[57] "In the fifth mystery we see the Virgin Mary, who having lost her most
holy Child, after three days found him in the Temple in disputation with the
learned men. In the Vernacular: In the fifth mystery we see and then we don't
see. The Virgin Mary having lost her little lad, went here and there and then
found him after three days on a Soapbox spitting in the faces of the doctors."

[58] Claire has made her usual minor errors and omissions in transcribing.
The passage as published may be translated as follows, with words omitted by
Claire in square brackets.

The mere title of Christian made a man odious and abominable,
and to make him even more execrated they accused him of many crimes
and rascalities: said that the Christians were murderers, adding that
they killed children, and fed on their flesh: that they were incestuous,

# Fourth Journal

↑Is not this ⟨was⟩ what is now↓ said against the ⟨Atheists⟩ ↑liberals↓? and shall they not like the Christian martyrs, establish their creed with their blood & suffering, in spite of persecution.
Do some German exercises. Read Giannone. Translate a fable from Phaedrus. Walk upon the Terrace.

Teusday Nov. 14th. Write to Shelley. Read Giannone. Walk upon the Terrace. Do 2 fables from Phaedrus.

Wednesday Nov 15th. Not well. Work.

Thursday Nov. 16th. A Rettel morf ⟨A⟩ Yellehs [59] — Od emos Namreg Sesicrexe. Osla ⟨a Elbaf⟩ Selbaf morf Surdeahp.

Friday Nov 17th. Od emos Namreg Sesicrexe. Osla Selbaf morf Surdeahp. Ni eth ⟨gineve⟩ Gnineve Li Rongis Inailug semoc.

Saturday Nov 18th. A Rettel morf Yellehs — Klaw tuo htiw Ani- loap ot *aiggop* ⟨er⟩*elairepmi*.[60] Krow lla yad.

---

and that they defiled themselves with horrible License at their mixed nocturnal meetings. And those whose obvious uprightness put them above the imputation of such wickedness were made [detestable] in the eyes of the Emperors as people contemptuous of the cult of the Gods; that they robbed the Emperors of their dignity, turned topsy-turvy the Roman laws and customs and upset the whole of nature, not being willing to worship the gods and disdaining to make Sacrifices to them; whence they came to be called *Atheists*, [*infidels*,] Disturbers of the State and of the established order — the eternal plague of the human race and of nature; since the Christians' scorn for the Gods gave rise to an angry desire for vengeance, [which in turn led to many evils] among men and in the nation, it was accepted by the heathens, and became a permanent grievance, that the Christians were the cause of all their ills.

[59] Perhaps to confuse or to amuse the Bojti childen, or to satisfy some whim of her own, Claire spelled each word backward for a few days. Mary's journal employs the same device on February 22, 1821, where "il oloviad inaihccaP" represents Pacchiani (cf. *Mary Shelley's Journal*, p. 148). The letter from Shelley is probably the long detailed one in which he advises her that if she feels she must leave the Bojtis she should leave on the friendliest terms, but before the twentieth, since after that date she is obliged for three months more. She should leave herself a loophole so that she might return if necessary (Shelley, *Letters*, II, 247–250). Claire did, indeed, return to the Bojtis after her month in Pisa.

[60] The Poggio Imperiale (Imperial Hill), built by Cosimo di Medici, was a very popular promenade, at the end of a long, dark avenue of cypress and larch, beyond the Porta Romana.

# Pisa 1820

Sunday Nov 19th. Klaw no eth Lung'Arno dna Cascina. daer Conversazione da Bondi.[61]

Monday Nov. 20th. Pack up.

Teusday Nov 21st. Get up at six—Walk out of the Gate with Madame Bojti—Go in the Diligence to Pisa where I arrive about five o'clock.[62]

Wednesday Nov 22nd. Call upon Madame Mason & Tetta. In the evening see Rm. Niwdem[63]

Thursday Nov. 23rd. Call with M. upon Madame Mason. After dinner walk with Miss Field & call upon Madame Tantini—non c'è.[64]

Friday Nov. 24th. Read Newspapers. Rainy day—⟨in P⟩ Pacchiani[65] spends the Evening. News that the Queen is acquitted by the Ministers giving up the point.

[61] Clemente Bondi, "Le Conversazioni: Poemetto," *Poemetti italiani,* 12 vols. (Turin, 1797), VIII, 138–199.

[62] Mary drew her little sun-symbol for Claire in her diary at this point.

[63] Captain Thomas Medwin had been with the Shelleys since October 22. He soon became a great bore—a *seccatura*. On January 14, 1821, Mary was to write to Claire: "S[helley] does nothing but conjugate the verb seccare & twist & turn Seccatura in all possible ways. He is Common Place personified" (Mary Shelley, *Letters*, I, 129–130). Had Claire been able to anticipate the garbled account of her liaison with Byron that Medwin was to write in his biography of Shelley, amused irritation would have become outrage. Nevertheless, the reader today is grateful for his vignette of her at this time, living *en pension* in Florence, though he recalls her as being 26 or 27, when she was, in fact, only 22:

> She might have been mistaken for an Italian, for she was a *brunette* with very dark hair and eyes. . . . As she possessed considerable accomplishments—spoke French and Italian, particularly the latter, with all its *nuances* and niceties—she was much courted by the Russian coterie, a numerous and fashionable one in that city. Though not strictly handsome at that time, for she had had much to struggle with, and mind makes its ravages in the fairest, most, she was engaging and pleasing, and possessed an *esprit de société* rare among our countrywomen. From her personal appearance at that time, I should conceive, that when Byron formed an intimacy with her at Geneva in 1816, she must have been strikingly handsome (Medwin, *Shelley,* pp. 169–170).

[64] "Not there."

[65] The general outline of the life of Professor Francesco Pacchiani may be found in Medwin, *Shelley,* pp. 273–277, and Viviani Della Robbia, *Vita di*

# Fourth Journal

Saturday Nov. 25th. Go to Livorno with S— Return at nine in the Evening very tired.

Sunday Nov. 26th. Call upon Madame M. Ride with Tetta. Call upon Miss Field. Il Professore Pacchiani & Zoppo [66] spends the Evening.

Monday Nov. 27th. Walk with M. and Tetta upon the Argine. Call upon Madame M. S— goes to the Collini — Write to Madame Bojti.

Teusday Nov 28th. Walk with M. from Porta Nuova to Porta Lucca. Drink tea with Miss Field. Pacchiani & Esopo to supper. The picture of posterity is like a barrel of wine — you shake the dregs the lightest rise to the top, ⟨&⟩ the heaviest fall to the bottom — so the favourite authors of the day ⟨float⟩ because light and of little value float on the surface of the multitude whilst the profound ⟨sink heavily⟩ are borne by their weight through the depth

---

*una donna,* pp. 45–51. Shelley's first reaction to him was of delight, but by the time Mary wrote to Claire in January 1821 he had become "our Black Genius," a hypocritical avaricious tyrant (Mary Shelley, *Letters,* I, 130–133). His whole life followed the pattern of his association with the Shelleys: great promise, never fulfilled. Born in 1771 in Prato, he was ordained *canonico,* or rather rector, of a chapter of the cathedral, and throughout his life continued as confessor to certain noble families, among them that of the governor of Pisa, Niccolò Viviani. By 1801 he held the chairs of logic and metaphysics at the University of Pisa and encouraged by Humboldt, Gay-Lussac, and Cuvier seemed about to distinguish himself as a physicist and chemist (see Tipaldo, *Biografia,* VI, 67–71). The Reverend Colonel Finch reported in his journal on December 12, 1817, during a visit to Pisa: "The Professors reputed by the students to give the best lectures are Savi, professor of Botany, and the mad Pacchiani, professor of theoretical physics. It is extraordinary that the latter who never opens a book, and lives in unremitted habits of idleness and distraction should be able to conduct the most profound demonstrations in sublime mathematics" (Bodleian MS. Finch. d. 21). When the Shelleys knew him his promise had failed; he had by a flamboyant bon mot sacrificed his chair at the University, so that he was living by his sharp tongue — an amusing conversationalist but a formidable enemy. Mary included him in *Valperga* (II, 104) as Benedetto Pepi, "half a buffoon, and half a madman."

The trial of Queen Caroline for adultery was abandoned on November 10.

[66] Esopo Campetti. For Mary's account of Pacchiani's exploitation of this young teacher, see her letter to Claire, January 23, 1821 (Mary Shelley, *Letters,* 131–132).

# Pisa 1820

of ages. Pacchiani calls his priests cap a Tartuffeometro — ⟨becau⟩ or measure for hypocrisy. Mr. Taaffe [67] calls.

Wednesday Nov 29th. Go with M. to a funzione in the church of San Niccolo. Pacchiani Fudge [68] & Campbells. ⟨Miss⟩ Then with Pacchiani to the Convent of St. Anna. The beautiful Teresa Viviani,[69] Madame Aust & Bassanti. Call upon Madame Mason see

[67] John Taaffe. An Irish adventurer, Knight Commander of the Order of St. John of Jerusalem, translator and annotator of Dante, and "poet laureate of Pisa," he was to the Shelleys a great bore. See Mary Shelley, *Letters*, I, 161ff.; Shelley, *Letters*, II, 292; Medwin, *Shelley*, pp. 249-250; and for his later role in the Masi incident, Cline, *Byron, Shelley and Their Pisan Circle*. An unpublished letter (Bodleian MS. Finch. d. 9) from a Captain Hely, in Rome, to the Reverend Colonel Finch, in Pisa, January 21, 1820, refers to him thus:

*Largo Sostenuto*

As to my Brother Officer, Colonel ⎧ Ta - a - a - a - a - ffe
I am inclined to think he had better by ⎩ Ha - a - a - a - lf
"mozzle" his Muse and let my poor dear Dante alone. He is, probably, unapprized that his countryman, Boyd, has already *munster-ized*, & *monster-ized* the great Florentine. But, as Homer, and Virgil have been travestied, and maccaronated, we must add this attempt to our former shudderings.

[68] Dowden says "Fudge" is Claire's nickname for Foggi (*Shelley*, II, 370). The Foggi she refers to is Ferdinando Foggi, professor of law at the University of Pisa. He was known to the Gisbornes and Lady Mount Cashell as a useful sort of person who would carry parcels between friends on his trips between Florence and Pisa and who would on occasion give language lessons. References to him in Mary's letters indicate that she knew him in these capacities before he became a sporadic visitor in Casa Galetti at this time. The Reverend Colonel Finch, who had met him through the Gisbornes, described him as "a smug little old man in a wig" and added later: "Der herr Ferdinand Foggi ist ein dichter, und die wissenschaft der mathematiken gefallene habe [*sic*]" (Bodleian MS. Finch. d. 21).

[69] Teresa Emilia Viviani was the daughter of Niccolò Viviani, governor of Pisa, who had placed her in the convent school of St. Anna, where she felt herself to be virtually a prisoner. She immediately absorbed the interest and sympathy of the Shelleys and Claire and provided the inspiration for Shelley's *Epipsychidion*. Medwin's description of her when he and Shelley first visited her at the convent helps to explain her intense appeal:

> Her profuse black hair, tied in the most simple knot, after the manner of a Greek Muse in the Florence gallery, displayed to its full height her brow, fair as that of the marble of which I speak. She was also of about the same height as the antique. Her features possessed a rare faultlessness, and almost Grecian contour, the nose and forehead making a straight line, — a style of face so rare, that I remember Bartolini's telling Byron that he had scarcely an instance of such in the numerous casts of busts which his studio contained. Her eyes had

189

# Fourth Journal

Madame Vaccà. then with Miss F upon Madame Tantini. In the evening go upstairs — Esopo calls.

Thursday Nov. 30th. Call upon Madame M. Walk with Tetta fuori Porta Mare to Porta firenze. Call in Convent St Anna upon Theresa Emilia Viviani — A letter from the same. Esopo & Pacchiani sup. Read the ⟨Mo Novollell⟩ Novella of Belfegor da Macchiavelli.[70]

Friday Dec. 1st. Call with Pacchiani upon the Greek Archbishop and the Princess Argiropoli.[71] Call upon Madame M. and Miss Field — Meet Foggi. ⟨In the Evenin⟩ Pacchiani, Sgricci[72] and Esopo sup. Sgricci improvisava upon the future independance of Italy — ⟨News of damm'd Brute⟩. Sgricci imitates him & his friend Eliseo. Call with M. upon the Viviani.

Saturday Dec. 2nd. Call with Pacchiani upon the Countess Pecori[73]

---

> the sleepy voluptuousness, if not the colour of Beatrice Cenci's. They had indeed no definite colour, changing with the changing feeling, to dark or light, as the soul animated them. Her cheek was pale, too, as marble, owing to her confinement and want of air, or perhaps "to thought." There was a lark in the *parloir*, that had lately been caught. "Poor prisoner," said she, looking at it compassionately, "you will die of grief! How I pity thee! What must thou suffer, when thou hearest in the clouds, the songs of thy parent birds, or some flocks of thy kind on the wing, in search of other skies — of new fields — of new delights! But like me, thou wilt be forced to remain here always — to wear out thy miserable existence here. Why can I not release thee?" (Medwin, *Shelley*, p. 279.)

See the accounts of her in Shelley's and Mary's letters and her biography by Viviani Della Robbia, *Vita di una donna*.

[70] First published as *Novella piacevolissima* (1545).

[71] This is the first introduction to the group of Greek patriots who so enlivened the Shelley circle. The Princess Ralou Argiropoli (properly Argyropoulo) was the daughter of Prince Caradja, former hospodar of Wallachia. She was married to George Argyropoulo, not strictly speaking a prince. There is an unpublished letter from Ralou d'Argyropoulo to Mary Shelley, September 5, 1822, thanking her for a copy of *Hellas* and offering sympathy on the death of Shelley (Abinger MSS.). For a wealth of information on the Argyropoulo and Mavrocordato families, see Huscher, "Alexander Mavrocordato," *KSMB* 16:29–38 (1965).

[72] Tommaso Sgricci (1789–1836), the most celebrated *improvvisatore* of his day. See Appendix C.

[73] Probably the wife of Guglielmo Pecori-Giraldi, squire to Elisa Bonaparte Bacciocchi (see Note 79 to entry for May 5, below).

and upon the Signora Tadioli[74] — Call upon Madame M. meet Madame and the Signor Tantini. Write to the Viviani, a letter from her. Read English with Esopo. The Prince Mauro Cordato[75] calls. Read 1 Canto of Purgatorio.

Sunday Dec. 3rd. Write to Albè. The Prince & Princess Argiropoli call. After dinner call with M. & S upon the Viviani and upon M. Mason   Mr. Taafe in the Evening.

X Monday Dec 4th Go and see the Viviani. Call upon Madame M. and Miss Field.

Teusday Dec. 5th. Call ⟨wi⟩ upon the Viviani — M. & S and Mr. Medwin call to see her. Ride with M & S— upon the Lucca Road — Then with Tetta — Call upon Madame M— in the Evening with S— Esopo in the Evening — Write to Madame Bojti —

Wednesday Dec 6th. Call upon the Viviani — and upon Madame M.   Read a Canto of Purgatorio.

Thursday Dec 7th. The Signor Tantini calls. Call with M. upon the Princess Argiropoli. ⟨Sg⟩ Scricci dines. Call upon the Viviani.

[74] Signora Elena Taddeoli, a friend of Emilia Viviani (see White, *Shelley*, II, 476–477).

[75] Prince Alexander Mavrocordato (1791–1865), a cousin of the Princess Argyropoulo, and the leader of the group of Greek patriots. See Huscher, "Alexander Mavrocordato," *KSMB* 16:29–38 (1965). Throughout Shelley's acquaintance with him the Prince was a hero, the living embodiment of the freedom-loving spirit of the ancient Greeks, and it is to him that Shelley dedicated his *Hellas* (see Mary's notes to that poem, Shelley, *Works*, III, 63–64; and Dowden, *Shelley*, II, 361–363). In the back of Mary's 1819–1821 diary she copied the following notice from the *Constitutionel*, November 12, 1821, four months after he assumed leadership in the Greek revolution: "Alexandre Mavrocordato rèunit a la persèvèrance et à la fermetè de caractere l'exterieur le plus doux et le plus affable. Il a tout sacrifiè pour la cause de sa Nation; sa fortune toute entiere a ètè employèe a faire des preparatifs de guerre, et son seul but semble etre la libertè de sa patrie. Aussi jouit il dejà de l'estime genèrale des chèfs et toute l'affections des troupes Suliotes" (Abinger MSS.; the French is as Mary copied it and may be translated: "Alexander combines perseverance and strength of character with the most gentle and affable exterior. He has sacrified everything for the cause of his nation; his entire fortune has been used in preparation for war, and his sole aim seems to be the liberty of his country. Furthermore he enjoys already the general esteem of the leaders and the entire devotion of the Suliote troops"). For a lengthy description which deserves to be better known, see Appendix C.

# Fourth Journal

A letter from Madame Bojti. ⟨There is a stren⟩ Foggi spends the Evening. 1st. Toast at the Indian Mess. A bloody war, a sickly season, and a field officer's Corpse.

---

⟨⟨There is a strength in truth ⟨for⟩ ↑to↓ every one but you, ⟨whose⟩ ↑but your↓ unhappy fate ⟨it seems has destined you⟩ makes you to know ⟨no⟩ no others than crime and evil.⟩⟩ There is a strength in truth which ⟨carries⟩ forces ↑⟨a⟩↓ conviction, and men are happy to ⟨have⟩ have arrived at a just point ⟨where they which⟩ from which they act securely, but the dullness of your senses has forbidden this ever to be known to you, and I fear that your constant companions will be as they ever have been, evil and error.[76]

Friday Dec. 8th. Call upon the Viviani and upon Madame M. In the evening a letter and flowers from Emilia and go to the play with Tetta and Mary. *Il Ciarlatano*[77] which is not bad. A letter from Ravenna. The English are ⟨the aristocrats⟩ not only *aristocrats* but *des aristocrats enragés*.

Saturday ⟨Nov.⟩ Dec. 9th. "It is time to nourish my feet with flight stronger than tempest footed horses."[78] Call upon Madame Mason. We talk a long while. Play at Chess in the Evening    Esopo in the Evening. "Io non piangeva si dentro ⟨m⟩ impietrai — as Dante says in Ugolino.[79] Madame Tantini calls — she relates of Pacchiani that once he sent for Tantini in the middle of the night: who thinking him to be ill, got up in all haste, cursing the sickness which called him from his warm bed and hastened grumbling to the Professor who received him very warmly saying ⟨he had [?]⟩ that finding he could not sleep he had sent for him to hold a little pleasant conversation. Pacchiani also came to them one night and begged a bed, as from some cause or other he could not find one — They agreed and he going away they prepared ⟨one agan⟩ a cham-

[76] Lovell is confident that the toast was reported by Medwin (*Captain Medwin*, p. 74). Claire's character analysis might well apply to him, as Lovell believes, or it might be one more of her characteristic attacks on Byron.

[77] Either Carlo Goldoni's *melodramma giocoso*, with music by Giuseppe Scolari (1759), or the farce by L. G. Buonavoglia, with music by Giacomo Cordella (1805).

[78] Sophocles, *Oedipus Rex*, second chorus, strophe A.

[79] "I did not weep, so stony I grew within" (*Inferno*, canto xxxiii, l. 49).

ber against his return. He never returned nor did they see him again for four years.

Sunday Dec. 10th. Call upon the Viviani — Prince Mauro Cordado and the Princess Argiropoli & her brother call. After dinner go with M. to Madame Mason — Mr. Taaffe in the Evening.

Monday Dec. 11th. Begin the Observations of Macchiavelli upon the Decades of Livy.[80] Pacchiani calls on his return from Florence. After dinner call upon the Viviani and stay till eight — Walk home with Gasperino. Pacchiani sups and shews us the reverse of the medal that is to say an inquisitive and indelicate character. Write to Albè & Madame Bojti. Also a letter from her.

Teusday Dec. 12th. Rain all day: write to Emilia who sends me a present of a drawing. In the evening, the Signor Vaccà and Scricci call. Read Indicators by Hunt — Hints for Don Juan. "Your will is driven mad by the power it has had of indulging itself — and like that *"household fiend,"* temper, you work your wretched pleasure in tormenting me the only person you can worry; ⟨The this makes deformity⟩ the deformity of your mind surpasses all that may be imagined of ⟨monstrous⟩ monstrous but ⟨already⟩ in your birth Nature had set her warning mark upon you, unheeding that, by my own blindness have I fallen.
Beware of still water, because that it is deep —. The gushing spring, that with noise & foams ⟨lengthens through man⟩ ↑flows↓ ⟨lengtheni⟩ ⟨⟨lengthening through the country, with banks of every character, now rocky, ⟨now⟩ and cavernous, now ⟨smot⟩ smooth ⟨as⟩ with grassy plains,⟩⟩ ⟨ever⟩ into a prolonging length, has a shallow bottom that may be seen; ⟨wan⟩ we wander in its course and in the ever changing character of its banks we ⟨may⟩ ↑shall find↓ our ⟨wan⟩ appropriate spot, ↑but↓ The tranquil surface, tempts us to gaze & then to plunge, drowning with the ⟨sh⟩ waves closing above our heads we are lost in its depth. This is the explication of Calderon's *Badate del Agua Mansa*[81] and applies to human life with perfect aptness.

⟨Allegra⟩.
O! vanity, human weakness, I am never weary of admiring my own

[80] *Discorsi . . . sopra la prima deca di Tito Livio* (1531).
[81] *Guárdate del agua mansa* (1649).

work: I am intoxicated with self love, I adore myself in that which I have made. (Rousseaus Pygmalion).[82]

Address of an injured yet beautiful mind to Nature.[83]

O! ye green and happy woods, breathing like sleep! O safe and quiet population of these leafy places, dying brief deaths! Oh! Sea, O earth! Oh! heavens, never uttering syllable to man! Is there no way to make known the meaning of your gentle silence, of your long basking pleasures and brief pains? And must the want of what is beautiful and kind from others, ever remain different from what is beautiful & kind in itself? And must form obscure essence? And human confidence in good from within, never be bolder than suspicion of evil from without? O! ye large looking & grand benignities of creation, is it that we are atoms in a dream; or that your largeness & benignity are in those only who see them, and that it is for us to hang over you till we make you into a voice with our kisses? I yearn to be made beautiful with one kind action, and beauty itself will not believe me!

Wednesday Dec. 13th. Rain all day. Read Indicators — After dinner call upon the Viviani. Pacchiani in the Evening.

Thursday Dec 14th. Rainy. Dine at Mrs. Mason's — Pacchiani in the Evening. He is indecent.[84] Esopo calls.

A great Poet resembles Nature — he is a Creator and a destroyer; he presides over the birth & death of images, the prototypes of things — the torrent of his sentiments should flow like waves one after the other, each distinctly formed and visible yet ⟨to in⟩ linked ⟨to⟩ between its predecessor and its follower as ⟨if to form in com-

---

[82] *Pigmalion: Scène lyrique*, opening speech, quoted by Leigh Hunt in his *Indicator*, 1:243 (May 10, 1820).

[83] The speaker is an enchanted lady, transformed into the Serpent of Cos, in Leigh Hunt, "The Daughter of Hippocrates," *Indicator*, 1:284 (June 14, 1820).

[84] Mary Shelley wrote to Maria Gisborne at about this time: "Pacchiani is no great favourite of ours. He disgusted Shelley by telling a dirty story. So much for him" (Mary Shelley, *Letters*, I, 121). In the remainder of her entry for this day Claire wrote in her journal as though she were preparing an essay — perhaps inspired by her reading of the *Indicators*. Lorraine Robertson has commented on the similarity between Claire's ideas on the nature of poets and poetry and Shelley's in "A Defence of Poetry," written in February 1821 ("The Journal and Notebooks of Claire Clairmont," *KSMB* 4:46–47 [1952]).

mon with them a lengthened chain⟩ ↑to form↓ ⟨and⟩ between them ⟨an⟩ ↑both by beauty & necessity↓ an indissoluble connection. He requires also to possess that power of harmony ⟨which⟩ which like the fire of Vesta should burn perpetually ⟨altho' in fits adaptin⟩ bursting by fits into flame & strength according to the subjects.

---

One of Madame M's rules, to consider a prejudiced person as one labouring under a serious illness.

---

I read today some Sonnets of Petrarch in an old edition — Not the least attention was there paid to the concord of the gender & number of the substantive with the article, besides (as in Dante) many other grammatical errors in the persons & cases of Verbs. But so it is — Liberty is essential to the nature of Poetry; ⟨the first writers of a⟩ so that it is to be observed the first & the last writers of a country are the best Poets; the first are grand, sublime, ⟨and ressemble Nature, who is without restraint⟩ — and ⟨natural because⟩ natural, because like Nature they ⟨have been the creators of the laws⟩ create their own laws — ⟨⟨the second have the appearance of Liberty those who follow imitate their predecessors and taking themselves a master as the Jews did a king ↑and ⟨and affect nothing being bound⟩↓ are lost & suffocated by the evil can do nothing. With ⟨the⟩ luxury Civilization gradually increases ⟨and ↑fictitious↓ licence is the⟩ ↑liberty is wanted &↓ introduced ↑called licence↓ ⟨as a substitute for Liberty, which⟩ ↑because real Liberty↓ never ⟨will⟩ can exist but with simplicity. Thus the ⟨younger⟩ latest Poets of a nation, exhibit the true character of their times, strange fantastic and distorted, they abound in ⟨licentious⟩ the wildest caperings & freaks, the children of licence, and ⟨like⟩ ↑with↓ her, as ⟨far removed from⟩ ↑unlike↓ the ↑free &↓ natural movements of Liberty as the east is removed from the West.⟩⟩
those who follow ⟨them⟩, imitate their predecessors and taking to themselves a master as the Jews did a King are lost and suffocated by the evil. Language is tied by laws, its native plastic powers are lost, and stiffened it yields no more to the hand of the modeller. As Civilization increases, luxury is produced restraints are found irksome and *licence* the step daughter of liberty is introduced, because the latter cannot exist but with simplicity. Thus the latest poets of a nation exhibit the true character of their times; they have

thrown aside the restraints of the middle age, but they cannot ⟨attan⟩ attain to the great productions of the first authors; strange ⟨fat⟩ fantastic and distorted, they have all the gloss & finery which licence can give, as ⟨unlike⟩ ↑far from↓ the free & natural movements of liberty as the East is removed from the West, ⟨yet⟩ although both are visited by the sun and upon each he sheds his glories giving to the first the promise of a long bright day, but to the last only the splendour of his farewell smile ere he is to be covered by the blackness of Night.

Friday Dec. 15th. Read the Indicators. Rain in torrents all day. Mr. Taaffe calls in the Evening — Shelley is magnetised — he begs them not to ask him more questions because he shall say what he ought not. Major Pittman said he once magnetised a child through its mother who answered the questions of what was its disease and what the cure. When she awoke & was told of this, she would not believe it. Magnetism is much tho' secretly used in France, and they explain ⟨with it⟩, the miracles which Hume speaks of as being well attested done at a french Bishop's Tomb, by a magnetic chain. To be a magnetiser it requires, a profound belief, a capacity of intense application to the act of volition and they assert, pure motives, for if he should attempt to magnetise a person upon one outward motive, with another internal & discordant, the experiment will fail.[85]

---

Mr. Taaffe gives a bad account of Naples — whose King has published the invitation or rather the command he has received from the allied powers to meet them at Troppau. The Carbonari have imprisoned the wives & daughters of many of the Cortes or Parliament, to forfeit their lives if the King shall be allowed to go. By a private letter it said, that assassinations were frightfully common, and that ⟨an⟩ anarchy and massacre were hourly expected to succeed.

Saturday Dec. ⟨17th.⟩ 16th. A letter from Emilia. — Read indicators

[85] See Medwin, *Shelley*, pp. 269–270, for his account of his hypnotizing of Shelley. Mary's diary says simply "Magnet" (Abinger MSS.). The passage in Hume is from section x, "Of Miracles," in "An Enquiry Concerning Human Understanding," *Essays and Treatises on Several Subjects*, 2 vols. (Edinburgh, 1809), II, 131, close to the passage Shelley quotes in his notes to *Queen Mab*.

—Pacchiani in the Evening. "Rather wise because it loves much than because it knows much.[86] Write to Emelia.

Sunday Dec. ⟨18th.⟩ 17th. Call upon the Viviani.—Rainy day Read Cox's Guide to Italy[87]—Mary reads aloud 1st Canto of Tasso[88] "My heart has been made wise through love, not by knowledge, and ⟨suffering⟩ by suffering has made a path to Wisdom.
D. Juan. You fill up the gaps of your ignorance with general assertions.
D. Juan. God ill by me not well has done! Has he not welded me ⟨to an inseparable⟩ to myself — ⟨a⟩ body & soul connected by a ⟨lik⟩ link more mysterious, & more inseperable than that of the Trinity! Stamped with a mark by Nature in my birth from which disgrace I can never escape! Every where I am myself, that fiend ⟨from⟩ who never leaves me! ⟨⟨Death only can dissolve this ↑on↓ earth ⟨invincible⟩ matrimony. I must resign ⟨Every⟩ a black atmosphere ⟨flows around me⟩ is ingendered from my being and continually waits upon me, as vapours upon a parent marsh informing Man, the heavens, and all the earth of the ↑hideous↓ presence it conceals!⟩⟩
As black vapours hover over their parent marsh and are imbued with hereditary pestilence, so does my being waiting ever upon me, inherit deformity informing myself and man, and the pure air of the hideous soul it interprets. My actions are monsters, the children of my soul, who drag to light and mimic with frightful preciseness the hidden deformities of their father.

Monday Dec. ⟨19th.⟩ 18th. Call upon Madame Mason. After dinner upon Emilia. Play chess in the Evening.

Teusday Dec 19th. La Signora Elena Tadeoli calls. Visit Emilia with S— In the Evening play at Chess. ⟨Sh⟩ Mr. Taaffe & Esopo in the Evening.

[86] Claire, writing to Byron, March 24, 1821, says: " 'My heart,' to use the words of an author, 'is rather wise because it loves much than because it knows much' " (Byron, *Works*, V, 500).
[87] Henry Coxe, *Picture of Italy: Being a Guide to the Antiquities and Curiosities of That Classical and Interesting Country* . . . (London, 1815).
[88] *La Gerusalemme liberata.*

# Fourth Journal

Wednesday. Dec 20th.[89] Visit Emilia. Walk with the Signora Taddeoli. Dine ⟨at⟩ in Casa Silva. Call upon Madame Tantini & walk with Miss Field. Report that the King of Naples is arrived at Livorno.

In the foldings of the many bosomed hills.

A tyrant or *master* newly ruling is ever rough says Eschylus.[90]

Thursday Dec. 21st.[91] Call upon Madame Mason & Mad— Tantini. ↑and upon the Princess Argiropoli. Non c'e↓ After dinner play 2 games of chess with S. ⟨Thr⟩ Prince Mauro Cordato calls. Spend two hours with Emilia then to the theatre to hear ⟨Sg⟩ Scricci — He improvisa's a Canzone upon Pyramus & Thisbe then a tragedy, Iphegenia in Tauris⟨s⟩. Wonderfully fine; ⟨he seemed⟩ it seemed not the work of a human mind, but as if he were the instrument ⟨of the passion⟩ interpreting ↑played upon by↓ the superhuman inspirations of a God;[92] the impression was so strong & fresh, a feature which belongs peculiarly to the art of the Improvisare. Of Iphegenia in grief he said — ⟨her forehead appears

---

[89] Mary's diary for December 20 says: "Greek — C. dines at M. M." (Abinger MSS.).

[90] *Prometheus Bound*, first speech of Hephaestus.

[91] Mary's diary for December 21 says: "Greek — call on the Princess Argiropolis & Emilia — Prince Mavrocodarto calls & Pacchiani — Go to the theatre & hear the Improvise of Sgricci — A most wonderful & delightful exhibition — He poured forth a torrent of poetry clothed in the most beautiful language" (Abinger MSS.; cf. *Mary Shelley's Journal*, p. 142; the two days, December 20 and 21, had been run together in *Shelley and Mary*). This is the performance described by Shelley to Byron, as reported by Medwin (who confused Pisa with Lucca):

> "But Sgricci! To extemporize a whole tragedy seems a miraculous gift."
>
> "I heard him improvise a five-act play at Lucca," said Shelley, "on the subject of the '*Iphigenia in Tauris*,' and never was more interested. He put one of the finest speeches into the mouth of Iphigenia I ever heard. She compared her brother Orestes to the sole remaining pillar on which a temple hung tottering, in the act of ruin. The idea, it is true, is from Euripides, but he made it his own."

(Medwin, *Conversations of Lord Byron*, ed. Lovell, p. 137.)

[92] Notopoulos cites this passage (as quoted by Dowden) as evidence for placing Shelley's translation of Plato's *Ion* in 1820, since "the thought and phrase here clearly reflect the influence of the *Ion* which she must have read in Shelley's translation" ("New Texts of Shelley's Plato," *KSJ* 15:110 [Winter 1966]).

clear〉 her clear fair forehead appears like a star in the morning mist.

---

Pacchiani & Mr. Taaffe at the theatre.   the first had seen the King of Naples at Livorno, who had exclaimed the moment he got on board the English ship in the bay of Naples "Eccommi al fine in Paradiso, dopo due mesi in Inferno.[93] He was received at Livorno in perfect silence, no solitary voice exclaiming *Viva!*

Friday Dec 22nd. Pack up. Dine at Mad. Mason's. Sgricci & Pacchiani sup. Go to the convent and take leave of Emilia. Prince Mauro Cordato calls.

Saturday Dec. 23rd. Esōpo calls. Set out with Pacchiani at twelve o'clock for Florence. and the little boy Balzani. We arrive about ½ past eight. Go to Casa Bojti sup and go to Bed. Empoli. Locanda delle 27th.

A Bon Mot of Pacchiani's Di femmini ha Italia molte e 〈grassiassi〉 ↑graziosissime↓ Ma donne Signor Mio pochissime.[94]

Sunday Dec. 24th. Unpack. Pacchiani calls—. Ride with him in the Cascina — He calls again in the Evening.

Monday Dec 25th. Xmas day. The Nonna dines. — Pacchiani calls. In the Evening 〈M〉 the Signora Martini 〈fetches〉 calls. Go with her to the Marchesa Orlandini. from thence with the Marchesa Madame Martini & Fabbrini l'Auditore to an Accademia in Casa dori.[95] I am not well.

Teusday Dec. 26th. Write to M— M. to Mary & Emilia. Pacchiani calls. Signor Pucci at dinner & the childrens friends in the Evening. Very unwell. Read Allemagne by Madame de Staël. Volney raconte que des français emigres vouloient, pendant la revolution,

---

[93] "Here I am at last in Paradise, after two months in Hell."

[94] "Italy has a great many very agreeable females. But Lord very few real women." This bon mot is quoted "in its imperfection" by Forman in Medwin's *Shelley*, p. 275n.

[95] On this day Claire entered into a wider group of Florentine society: Madame Martini, the mother of Sgricci; the Marchesa Orlandini, one of his early patronesses, an elderly lady well known for her delightful parties; Judge Fabbrini, his wife Maddalena, and their children Clorinda and Francesco; and a host of others whom I have not been able to identify.

etablir une colonie et defricher des terres en Amerique; mais de temps en temps ils quittoient toutes leurs occupations pour aller, disoient ils, *causer a la ⟨wi⟩ ville*; et cette ville, la Nouvelle Or-leans, etoit a six cents lieues de leur demeure.[96]

Hint for Don Juan. Quand la vanite se montre elle est bien veil-lante; quand elle se cache la crainte d'etre decouverte la rend amere, et elle affecte l'indifference, la satiétè enfin tous tout ce qui peut persuader aux autres qu'elle ⟨m⟩ n'a pas besoin d'eux — ⟨Vanity⟩ Pride is concealed Vanity and that is what makes it so odious. Two examples ⟨wh ve⟩ we have in Albè and Hunt.

————

In france the universal desire is to do ↑& think↓ what others do. On a fait la revolution de France en 1789 en envoyant un courrier, d'un village a l'autre, qui crioit: *armez vous car le village voisin s'est armè*, et tout le monde se trouva levé contra tout le monde, ou plutôt contre personne.

Wednesday Dec. 27th. Ill all day. Read L'Allemagne. A little German. Nonna dines. Pacchiani calls.

Thursday Dec 28th. Very unwell. Write to Emilia & Mary. Pacchi-ani calls in the Evening   Read L'Allemagne.

Friday Dec 29th Very unwell. Read L'Allemagne & study Ger-man. In the Evening Pacchiani calls. L'Acqua cheta rompe il ponte.[97]

[96] *De l'Allemagne*, 3 vols. (Paris, 1810). This and the two following quota-tions are from vol. I, part 1, chap. xi, "De l'esprit de conversation." In the English ed., *Germany*, 3 vols. (London, 1813), they are translated as follows:

> Volney relates, that some French emigrants began, during the revolution, to establish a colony and clear some lands in America; but they were con-tinually quitting their work to go and talk, as they said, in town — and this town, New Orleans, was distant six hundred leagues from their place of residence (I, 102).

> When vanity displays herself, she is good-natured; when she hides herself, the fear of being discovered renders her sour, and she affects indifference, satiety, in short, all that can persuade other men that she has no need of them (I, 109).

> The French revolution in 1789, was effected by sending a courier from village to village to cry, "Arm yourselves: for the neighbouring village is in arms already;" and so all the world found itself risen up against all the world, or rather against nobody (I, 114).

[97] "Standing water breaks the bridge."

# Florence 1821

Saturday Dec. 30th. Unwell. Do nothing all day. Letters from M. Emilia & Mad. M.

Sunday Dec 31st. Unwell. Madame Martini calls.

[1821]

Monday Jan. 1st. New⟨s⟩ year's day. ⟨I⟩ My gland is opened.[98] I am ill all the day.

X Teusday Jany 2nd  Ill all day. Pacchiani calls p.p.c for Pisa. Write to Mary & Emilia

Wednesday Jany 3rd. Ill. Read German and Allemagne by Mad. de Staël.

Thursday Jany 4th. Better. Write to M. & Madame M. A letter from Mary & Madame Mason. Read German

Friday Jany 5th. Ill all day. Study German. Read L'Allemagne. In the Evening the Contessine Maria ed Elena Buterlin[99] call and Miss Clarke

[98] On February 5, 1820, Claire had entered in her journal, "Vaccà calls & says I am scrofulous and I say he is ridiculous." Shelley wrote on January 2, 1821, "You ought to be aware that if this gland should be scrofulous, no small portion of the disease consists in the dejection of spirits and inactivity of mind attached to it; it is at once a cause and an effect of it; for which the best remedy is society and amusement, and for which even bustle and occupation would be a palliation" (Shelley, *Letters*, II, 255).

[99] This was Claire's introduction to the distinguished Russian and Polish colony in Florence. For more than a year she was a regular visitor in Casa Boutourlin (also spelled Butterlin, Buturlin, and Buterlin) and at Villa Parenti, the Boutourlin summer residence in Leghorn. The head of the family was Count Dmitri Boutourlin (1763–1829), son of Count Peter-Jonas Boutourlin (1735–1787), who had been senator and governor-general of Moscow. Count Dmitri's mother was born Maria Waronzoff (on the connection between the Waronzoffs and the Boutourlins, see Note 20 to entry of February 18, below).

After a military education, Dmitri became aide-de-camp to Prince Potemkin; he then went into the ministry for foreign affairs, from which he resigned in 1793 to settle in Moscow and devote himself to the creation of his famous library. He gained international fame as a bibliophile and a man of encyclopedic knowledge, and after the destruction of his library (by then one of the greatest in Russia) in the 1812 Fire of Moscow he dauntlessly began to assemble a second great collection. He moved to St. Petersburg as director of music at the Hermitage

# Fourth Journal

Saturday ⟨Sunday⟩ Jany ⟨12⟩ 6th. ⟨18⟩ Ill all day. Madame Martini calls. Letters from Emilia & Mary. Read German.

Sunday Jany 7th. Ill. Read German. In the Evening the Conte ↑Oppizzoni↓ ⟨Pizzoni⟩ calls. Write to Emilia.

Monday Jany 8th. Ill. Read German.

Teusday Jany. 9th. A letter from Madame M. Write to her & to Mary. Read German.

Wednesday Jany 10th. Better — Study German. Read Sintram by Baron de la Motte Fouquè.[1]
Hint for Don Juan. Poets talk of "Weeds of Glorious Feature" and verily I believe they mean such ones as you, who fatten to hideousness upon the corruptions of the soil, and raise themselves by Impudence above their brothers, oppressing the few flowers the world affords, with a longer Shadow. You are dead to every thing beautiful, whether of shape or essence; you rot and are corrupted, while the light of Truth is upon you, as a Corpse which putrifies in the rays of the Sun, to every thing besides the parent of Life.

Thursday Jany 11th. Better. A letter from Mary. Study German.

Friday Jany 12th. Allegra's Birthday. 4. In the Morning Call upon

---

and remained there until 1817, when poor health obliged him to go to Florence, where he continued the accumulation of his library. On March 16, 1818, Mary Berry, an English tourist, went to his house there to look at a library of about 6,500 volumes that he had just purchased from an estate (*Journals and Correspondence of Miss Berry*, ed. Lewis, III, 156). After his death in 1829 his second library was dispersed at an auction sale in Paris. (Information on Dmitri Boutourlin from Fitzlyon, *Memoirs of Princess Dashkov*, p. 295, and Nesselrode, *Lettres*, VI, 74n.; the Chancellor's letters are a good source of information about members of the distinguished Russian circle in Italy.)

In 1843 a Madame Boutourlin was in Florence and inquired after Claire (Mary Shelley, *Letters*, II, 181).

[1] Friedrich Heinrich Karl, Baron de La Motte-Fouqué, *Sintram and His Companions: A Romance*, trans. from the German by Julius C. Hare (London: C. and J. Ollier, 1820). Mary had read it December 24 (*Mary Shelley's Journal*, p. 143), and Shelley mentions sending it to Claire (Shelley, *Letters*, II, 254). See Note 12 to entry of January 26, below.

the Princess Montemileto.[2] In the Evening in Casa Butterlin & Schwaloff.[3]

Saturday Jany 13th. Walk with Luisa & Annina to the Cascina [4] and the Gallery. Write to M. to S. and to Madame M. Study German.

Sunday Jany 14th. Rain all day. Write German Excercises. The Princess ⟨Montemittel⟩ Montemiletto Caraffa calls. Read German.

Monday Jany 15th. In the morning walk with Luisa & Annina in the Gallery. Read German and write Exercises.

[2] Shelley had written to Claire in November, when she was painfully depressed, that Lady Mount Cashell had spoken to him of introducing Claire to the Princess Montemiletto, "which introduction, if it could be carried into effect, would certainly place you in a situation to require no other. But as she has not seen or heard from the Princess for 16 years, we cannot be sure of the reception her recommendation would meet" (Shelley, *Letters*, II, 248). On January 2 he wrote: "Do not on any account neglect, if possible, to present the letter to the Princess Montimilitti, taking especial care to specify *who* is the writer" (*ibid.*, II, 255). Lady Mount Cashell had met the Princess Montemiletto Caraffa in Florence in December of 1802, during her tour of the continent after the peace of Amiens. Catherine Wilmot describes her thus:

> I must give you some idea of this charming little Neapolitan. . . . She is highly educated, accomplish'd, and very sensible, with the reputation of a Belle Esprit, but totally without any of its pretensions. During the horrors of Naples, circumstances threw her into the publick notice, and amongst the conflict of Parties, she narrowly escaped being torn to pieces by the Lazzaroni. Disgusted therefore with the miseries to which she was witness, and by which she lost some of her nearest relations, Florence became a temporary retreat, and her society is so much esteem'd, that everybody yields her the homage of goodness, amiableness, wit, beauty and accomplishments (*An Irish Peer*, p. 128).

The Princess was probably in her fifties when Lady Mount Cashell broke the long silence of her anonymity to introduce Claire, and for more than a year Claire climbed nearly every evening to her lovely villa higher than the Villa Strozzi, with its magnificent view of Florence below and Fiesole in the distance.

[3] On this evening Claire expanded her Russian acquaintance. Lady Murray mentions "Countess Schouwaloff" and her husband as being among the agreeable Russian and Polish families in Florence (Lady Murray, *A Journal of a Tour in Italy*, IV, 265).

[4] The Cascina was an extensive wood a short distance from town, along the bank of the Arno. It was a popular promenade, and on warm evenings carriages congregated around a small square, as in Hyde Park. Several alleys ran through the wood, and in the fall of 1819 the Cascina provided some of Shelley's pleasantest solitary walks. It was here that his "Ode to the West Wind" was conceived and chiefly written.

# Fourth Journal

⟨Saturday⟩. Teusday Jany 16th ⟨St. Antony's day⟩ Write German. A letter from Madame M. & Tetta. Madame Martini calls. After dinner walk with Louisa. Read German.

Wednesday Jany 17th. St Antony's day. Walk with Paolina to the Cascina. Write to Emilia & Tetta. The Abate Pucci, and Coveri, and ⟨Mr⟩ Mr. & Mrs. ⟨Reate⟩ ↑Read↓ to dinner. In the Evening go with Madame Martini to Casa Orlandini. Conte Bagnese. Then to the Princess ⟨Montemittel⟩ Montemiletto Caraffa. Contessa Bagnese and Miss Farrell.[5]

Thursday Jany 18th. Go to the Convent. A letter from M. & S.[6] Write to M & Mad. M. Walk with Annina after dinner — Study German. A letter from Elise.

Friday Jany. 19th. In the Morning walk with Mad. B. on the Lung'Arno — ⟨I⟩ Write German exercises. In the Evening go to Casa Orlandini. ⟨Go with the Marchesa an⟩ Contessa Bagnese. ⟨Go⟩ and Madame Martini. Go with the Marchesa, and Signor Fabbrini to the Pergola[7] — the Opera miserable. Ballet of ⟨Cyn⟩ Agamemnon with the ⟨phr⟩ prophesying of Cassandra beautiful.

Saturday Jany 20th. Walk in the Morning with Luisa ed Annina from the Pisan Gate to the Roman and to Poggia Imperiale. Study German. Letters from Emilia Madame M. and Mary. Write to them.

Sunday Jany 21st. Read and study German. Walk in the Buboli and on the Lung'Arno.

Monday Jany 22nd. Write to Madame Mason. Walk to Poggia Imperiale. Read German. La Signora Orlandini calls.

[5] Probably Miss Farhill.

[6] See Mary Shelley, *Letters*, I, 126–130; Shelley, *Letters*, II, 256–257.

[7] The theater of the Pergola was the largest in Florence. While Claire was there it played principally operas by Rossini, the prima donna being Mlle. Mombelli. There were six tiers of boxes, varied by curtains of different colored silks, and seats for all the pit spectators. Étienne de Jouy, in Florence at about this time, tells that there was much conversation in the boxes, except during favorite arias, with much eating and drinking everywhere but in the pit, so that the smell of meat and wine was unpleasant. During carnival, maskers ran from box to box, and ladies in disguise rushed about plaguing the men, while even those on stage occasionally joined in (*The Hermit in Italy*, II, 177ff.).

# Florence 1821

Teusday Jany 23rd. A letter from Madame Martini. Answer it. A letter from S. Write to him and Albè. In the Evening go to Casa Buterlin. Magnelli there.[8]

Wednesday Jany 24th. Study German.

Thursday Jany 25th. Study German. A letter from Emilia. Walk with the Bojtis to the Convent of San Matèo — The Nun Suora Gesualda — See 2 Cappanuccia. Madame Martini and her nephew call in the Evening. Go to Casa Baldini — Miss Farrell. Italian proverb. e il sasso ritorna sopra colui che la rotola from the proverbs of Solomon   Et qui volvit lapidem revertetur ad eum.[9]

Friday Jany 26th. Go to Casa Orlandini. Ride with the ⟨Marces⟩ Marchesa and the Avvocato Boldi in the Cascina. A parcel from Pisa via Sgricci which contains a letter from Ravenna. Read newspapers and Reviews.[10]
"All her excellencies stand in her so silently, as if they had stolen upon her without her knowledge." Sir Thomas Overbury's Characters.[11] "Scepticism, says Frederic Schlegel, proceeds always along this scale: first the Devil is attacked, then the Holy Ghost, then our Lord Christ and last of all God the father." [12]

[8] H. R. Angeli reports that Sophia Stacey studied music with him ("le maître de la Cour") in Florence (*Shelley and His Friends in Italy*, p. 98).

[9] "And the rock comes back upon him who rolls it."

[10] There was also a letter from Mary (Mary Shelley, *Letters*, I, 130–133). The newspapers and reviews included *Olliers Literary Miscellany in Prose and Verse*, no. 1 (London: C. and J. Ollier, 1820), and the *Retrospective Review*, vol. II (1820), with "all the quotations from old books" that so pleased Shelley (see his letter to Ollier, January 20, 1821 [Shelley, *Letters*, II, 257–259]).

[11] Overbury's character of "A Fair and Happy Milkmaid" is reprinted in the *Retrospective Review*, vol. II, part 1, p. 96.

[12] Shelley, in his letter to Ollier (Shelley, *Letters*, II, 258) says: "I was immeasurably amused by the quotation from Schlegel about the way in which the popular faith is destroyed — first the Devil, then the Holy Ghost, then God the Father. I had written a Lucianic essay to prove the same thing." The fact that Claire noted in her journal the very passages that Shelley responded to and mentioned to Ollier suggests that he had marked the books and periodicals that he sent on to her. Even when no evidence survives of the influence of Shelley on her reading, one must always entertain the strong possibility that Claire's reading is a reflection of Shelley's. The passage from Friedrich Schlegel is quoted in "On the German Drama: No. 1, Oehlenschlaeger," *Olliers Literary Miscellany*, No. 1, pp. 120–121n. Shelley asked Ollier who had written this article,

# Fourth Journal

Saturday Jany 27th. Study German. A letter from M. & S— Write to both and Mrs. Mason. Madame Martini calls.

Sunday Jany 28th. Read Reviews — Madame Martini calls. Walk in the Boboli.
"Eagles, we see, fly alone, and they are but sheep which always herd together." Sir P. S. Arcadia. Also says the good old Kalander, "too much thinking doth consume the spirits & oft it falls out, that while one thinks too much of his doing, he leaves to do the affect of his thinking." Idem.[13]

Monday Jany 29th. In the Morning call in Casa Orlandini. Miss Latin. Walk with the Marchesa to Madame Martini & Sgricci. Write German Exercises.

X Teusday Jany 30 Walk with Madame Bojti to the Spedale of San Mateo and the Convent of Sant Ambrogio. A letter from Mary & Mad— M. Write to them. In the Evening Pacchiani calls. Go with Mad. B and Madame Ceresa to the Pergola — Academia of the little Baron Sigismund ⟨Brauer⟩ ↑Brown↓. A letter from Emilia.

Wednesday Jany 31st. In the Morning call ⟨upon⟩ in Casa Orlandini — Ride with the Marchesa in the Cascina. Write a letter

---

and later Lady Shelley, in *Shelley Memorials* (p. 136n.), identified the author as Archdeacon Julius Charles Hare, "who, despite his orthodoxy, was a great admirer of Shelley's genius." (Shelley had only recently read Hare's translation of La Motte-Fouqué's *Sintram*; see Note 1 to the entry of January 10, above). This article appears to contain (p. 149) the "review" of *The Cenci* about which Shelley also questioned Ollier. More a passing tribute than a review, it is worth quoting in its entirety:

> Shakespeare accordingly has made all his evil characters, Edmund, Iago, Richard, all more or less self-reflective. In the words of a great modern poet, whose genius, when he has bowed down his neck and received into himself the purifying and sanctifying influence of the Spirit, if such be his earthly fate, must assuredly prove a cherisher of innocent thoughts and a kindler of noble thoughts unto many:
> "It is their trick
> To analyse their own and other minds.
> Such self-anatomy doth teach the will
> Dangerous secrets. For it tempts our powers,
> Knowing what must be thought, and may be done,
> Into the depth of darkest purposes.
> *(Cenci*, Act II. Scene II.)

[13] *Retrospective Review*, vol. II, part 1, pp. 9–10.

to Emilia—In the evening to to the Princess Montemiletto's—Miss Farrell.

A man with one eye on the 1st. floor and the other on the second. Lean horses are fond of their master, for as they cannot shew him their heart they do their ribs.

Virtues are still more enhanced in a person who displays them naturally and as if unknowingly—like the Sun who shines and yet sees not.

Thursday ⟨Jany⟩ Feb. 1st. Walk with Mad. B. in the Morning. Letters from S— & M. Write to M. In the Evening Mad. M. calls.

Friday Feb. 2nd. In the Morning go to Casa Orlandini—Pacchiani, Torrigiani, Boldi  Fabbrini and Madame Martini. Go to an Accademia of Music in Casa Bianchi—In the Evening Sgricci calls—

Saturday Feb. 3rd. Walk with Paolina to the Cascina—A letter from Mary.

Sunday Feb. 4th. Rainy day—Write to M. & S. and Madame M—Study German.

Monday Feb. 5th. Rainy day. Work. In the Evening go with the Bojti's to the theatre in Borgo Ogni Santo to see Stenterello[14] and a Ballet performed by children.

Teusday Feb. 6th. Work. Sgricci calls. He says the Neapolitans—

[14] The little theater in the Borgo d'Ogni Santi specialized in melodrama, and admission was four *crazie* (about threepence). Stendhal has left the following account of the *stenterello*: "C'est l'homme le plus mince et de la figure la plus sèche que vous ayez jamais vu. Il arrange avec toute l'élégance possible son habit troué; le principal fondement de sa cuisine, ce sont des tranches de concombres à la glace; du reste, vaniteux comme un Castillan, peu lui emporte de mourir de faim, pourvu qu'on ne le sache pas. . . . Surtout il est beau parleur, et se pique de ne s'exprimer que dans les termes les plus toscans. Il lui faut trois phrases pour vous demander quelle heur il est." ("He is the most withered meagre skeleton figure ever seen. He arranges his ragged coat with all the elegance possible; and slices of cucumber iced are the principal objects that ever grace his table, yet he is proud as a Castilian; he cares not whether he may die with hunger, provided it is not known. . . . above all he piques himself upon his oratory and never speaking but in the truest Tuscan phraseology; he cannot ask *what's o'clock* in less than three well-rounded phrases.") Stendhal, *Rome, Naples et Florence, en 1817*, p. 174; English trans. from the London edition of 1818, p. 170.

those few who were for the Constitution cried Viva la Costerna-zione instead of ⟨Constr⟩ Costituzione. In the Evening Pacchiani calls. Go to the Princess Montemil⟨l⟩etto's — Miss Farrell and Monsieur & Madame Aloi — The Scotch & french philosophic system of ⟨all⟩ personal interest is called in Germany Empiric philosophy — Kant has had fifty Commentators each of whom has explained his system in a different ⟨wa⟩ manner. Reasoning by Syllogism bad because in the very first beginning it supposes a thing as true ⟨which⟩ before it has been decided by argument —
A letter from Madame Mason.

Wednesday Feb. 7th. In the Morning call with Madame Bojti in Casa Orlandini — Work. Madame Martini calls in the Evening.

Thursday Feb. 8th. Go with the Doctor and his wife to Casa ⟨Mazzei⟩ Mazzei [15] ⟨where⟩ to hear Madame Mazzei improvisare which she did upon Liberty, love, Agrippina returning with the ashes of Germanicus, whether love was aristocratical or demo-cratical, a Scene between Helen and Hecuba, and a Canzone of the Matron of Ephesus, a Song which were [?]⟨w⟩ of the Eyes or Mouth was most expressive — Meet Madame Orlandini there and Fabbrini and the lawyer ⟨Baldi⟩ Boldi — A letter from M — Emilia and from Ravenna. Write to M—

Friday Feb. 9th. Work. Read Das Geheimniss one of Schiller's minor Poems. A lesson from Bianchi —

[15] The Signora Lucretia Mazzei, celebrated *improvvisatrice*, was of an illustrious and ancient family. Her virtuosity was in her command of verse forms: the octaves of Tasso, the tercets of Dante, the "loose and unconstrained numbers" of Metastasio (*Rambles in Italy: In the Years 1816 . . . 17*, "by an American," pp. 283–284). Lady Murray was one of those invited to Signora Mazzei's own house on the morning Claire describes, and she has left an account: "Whether love is aristocratic or democratic? (she pronounced in favor of the latter); whether the eyes or the mouth are most powerful in love? (the answer to this question was given in twelve lines, expressing some beautiful ideas)." Earlier Lady Murray had heard her at Madame Orlandini's and described the Signora herself: "She appeared about forty; her face plain and pale, blue eyes, and rather a flat nose. She wore a black hat and feathers, with a mob-cap tied under her chin, a high black velvet spencer, and a grey silk petticoat: her waist was remarkably thick." But the moment she began to improvise, her plainness was forgotten, and her melodious voice, her ease and animation of speech gave her "an air of inspiration totally independent of her exterior" (Lady Murray, *Journal*, IV, 270–272). Madame de Staël modeled the heroine of her *Corinne* on Signora Mazzei.

# Florence 1821

Gross zwar nenn' ich den Mann, der sein eigner
      Bildner und Schöpfer
Durch das Tugend gewalt selber die Parze
      bezwingt.[16]

Saturday Feb. 10th. Walk with Paolina to the Cascina — A letter from Mary — Write to Madame Mason. Read Das Gluck a poem by Schiller.

Sunday Feb. 11th. Walk on the Lung'Arno with the family — Write part of letters to Mary & Emilia. Read Das Lied von der Glocke by Schiller.

Monday Feb. 12th. Entry of 11,000 Austrian troops into Florence.[17] In the Morning call upon Madame Orlandini — the Signora Luisa Mugnai [18] — In the Evening go to Casa ⟨Butterlin⟩ Buterlin.

Teusday Feb. 13th. Walk to the Convent. A letter from S— Emilia and Mad. M. Write to ⟨Emil⟩ Emilia and Mary — Translate Das Lied der Glocke by Schiller —

Wednesday Feb. 14th. In the morning call in Casa Orlandini. The grand-children of Madame Orlandini [19] & the Signora Luisa Mugnaj. In the Evening Madame Martini calls & go to the Princess

---

[16] Great must I call the man, who, his own creator and sculptor,
    Vanquishes even the fates, by his strong virtue alone.

The quotation is from Schiller's "Das Gluck," lines 9–10 (trans. E. A. Bowring, *The Poems of Schiller*). Starting on this day, most of Claire's German is written in script.

[17] Lady Murray reported: "We were at Florence in 1821, when the Austrian troops, sent to quell the Neapolitan insurrection, arrived, and saw nine thousand men, under the command of General Frimont, march into the town. Some of the infantry regiments were composed of Hungarians, tall and hardy-looking men, with very dark complexions. . . . The squares of Florence were filled with baggage-wagons, and the cavalry-horses bivouacked in the field adjoining the Cascina. I believe the number of troops exceeded thirty thousand. The masks were forbidden to use drums during their stay" (Lady Murray, *Journal*, IV, 274).

[18] Probably the wife of the advocate Mugnai. She gave Claire lessons of some sort.

[19] Madame Orlandini's two granddaughters, one seven and one nine, performed a pantomime at a party attended by Lady Murray, who commented, "There was a degree of grace and sentiment in their action which would have been admired on any stage" (Lady Murray, *Journal*, IV, 269).

# Fourth Journal

Montemiletto. The Signor & Signora Fabbroni and Monsieur Pallard. To day 10,000 Austrian troops pass through the Roman Gate out of Florence & 16,000 enter from Bologna by the Porta San Gallo.

Thursday Feb. 15th. Write to Shelley & Madame M— Call with Madame B— at the Post—meet the Signori Ferdinando & Giulia Orlandini—Read Das Lied von der Glocke. After dinner walk with Paolina to the Post & in Boboli. A divine day.

Friday Feb 16th. Walk with ⟨the wife⟩ my hostess about town— Call upon Madame Orlandini. Entry of 16,000 Austrians by Porta San Gallo. Translate Das Lied von der Glocke—

Saturday Feb. 17th. Letters from M. S. and Madame M— Walk with the Bimbo upon the Lung'Arno—The Grandmother at dinner.

Sunday Feb. 18th. In the Morning walk with the family on the Lung'Arno. After dinner drive in the Cascina with the Orlandini & Fabbrini & La Luisa Campi. In the Evening in Casa Schwaloff—The ⟨Comt⟩ Countess Waronzoff & Buterlin & their niece Annette.[20]

Monday Feb. 19th. Call upon the Signora Orlandini—Study German. Walk with the Children upon Lung'Arno—

Teusday Feb 20th. A letter from S—[21] and Emilia—Write to Mary—Work. In the Evening ⟨to⟩ go to the theatre Goldoni ↑with the mother & 2 daughters↓—a comedy and aftewards the Veglioncino.[22] Dr. Pherson there.

[20] The Boutourlins were related to the Waronzoffs (also spelled Varontzoff, Vorontsov) through the marriage of Count Peter Boutourlin (father of Dmitri; see Note 99 to January 5, above) to Maria Waronzoff, sister of Princess Catherine Dashkov (1743–1810), and Simon Waronzoff (1744–1832), Russian ambassador in London (Fitzlyon, *Memoirs of Princess Dashkov*, table I, p. 9).

[21] On February 18 Shelley wrote to Claire congratulating her on her "Germanizing" and commenting on her plan of going as a *dame de compagnie* with some German lady of rank to her own country (Shelley, *Letters*, II, 265–268).

[22] The Teatro Goldoni, very small and prettily decorated, with four tiers of boxes, usually played comedies and melodramas. Lady Murray explains that "towards the end of the Carnival there are masquerades at the theatres. Those expected to be small are called Veglioncino, and those on a greater scale Veglione;

# Florence 1821

Wednesday Feb. 21st. In the Morning call upon Madame Orlandini and at the Bankers. also at Court to enquire after the Grand Duke — In the Evening go to the Princess Montemiletto — Miss Farrell & Signor Pietro [23] — Interesting conversation upon Politics — Bitter cold weather.

Thursday Feb. 22nd. Go to the convent in the Morning. A visit from the Fabbrini's. Mother & daughter. Write some German Exercises. Pay the B—s. [24]

Friday Feb. 23rd. Walk to the Convent — Call upon the Signora Orlandini — Read a Magazine called Bibliotheque Universelle de Gênève [25] — Spend the Evening in Casa Buterlin where I meet Madame Calamaj — [26]

Saturday Feb. 24th. A letter ⟨fr⟩ from Mary. Write to Emilia & M. Write German exercises. In the Evening go with the Fabbrinis' to Casa Majotti. Music & Dancing.

Sunday Feb. 25th. Write German Exercises. ⟨In the aftern⟩ Go with the Fabbrini's & the Bojti's to an Accademia in the house of the priest Allegri. In the afternoon drive with the Signora Orlandini, & Luisa Cambi & Fabbrini on the Corso. [27] In the evening mask with the Fabbrini's & Mad. B— we go to the theatre Santa

they are beautifully lighted. The women wear black dominos, hoods, and masks, and the amusement is to plague the men, who are all unmasked; but there appears great want of spirit." In the streets, masks of all descriptions were seen (Lady Murray, *Journal*, IV, 260–261).

[23] Claire mentions a "Signor Pietro" regularly during the following two months and then on April 29 records news of the death of Signor Pietro Stoppione.

[24] On February 16 Shelley had sent Claire a check for two months (Shelley, *Letters*, II, 264). This explains her trip to the banker on the preceding day.

[25] *Bibliothèque universelle des sciences, belles-lettres, et arts*, literature, 60 vols., sciences and arts, 60 vols. (Geneva, 1816–1835).

[26] Probably the wife or mother of Luigi Calamai (1800–1851). See G. Negri, *Luigi Calamai* (Florence, 1932).

[27] "Another amusement at the end of the Carnival is the *Corso*, which extends from the Piazza Santa Croce to the end of the Via della Scala. There were on one occasion above three hundred carriages. . . . Prince Borghese had seven equipages in the string, and the liveries were covered with gold lace. The Marchese Torrigiani drove four horses abreast, with two leaders" (Lady Murray, *Journal*, IV, 261).

# Fourth Journal

Maria & see part of a comedy in the box of the Ceresa — then to the theatre Santa Maria Novella ⟨to⟩ where there is a veglione. The Signori Tolomei[28] — Miccale, Pasta, Zanobbi Ricci, besides English & German.

Monday Feb. 26th. Write German. Read Prose Campestri da Pindemonte.[29]

Teusday Feb. 27th. Write German. Read Hyperion of Keats. In the Evening a visit from ⟨the⟩ Marietta Moselle and Clorinda Fabbrini. A ridiculous anonymous love letter from Pisa.[30]

Wednesday Feb. 28th. Rainy day  Write German. A visit from Clorinda Fabbrini. In the Evening go with Madame Orlandini to the Pergola. Miserable Opera of Emilia by ↑the Marchese↓ Sampieri[31] and a bad ballet of the three Gobbi. Fabbrini there and the Marchesa Grimaldi — a french Baronessa and the Comte de ⟨Chateua⟩ Chateau — the Countess Bochdann a greek from Pisa. the Marchese Feroni and the Count & Countess Bagnese & Ferdinando Orlandini.

Thursday ⟨Feb. 29th.⟩ March 1st. A letter from Mad M. & Tetta. Visit from the Fabbrini's — Go with them in the Evening to the *Veglione* at the Pergola. Masked as a Turk. English & Germans. Zanobbi Ricci the Countess ⟨Sw⟩ Schwaloff & ⟨Holckm Folchm Folckmann.⟩ Volkmann.

X Friday March 2nd. A visit from Captain Medwin. Letter from Mary & Papers. The Count Oppizzoni calls. Read Newspapers.

Saturday March 3rd. Write to Madame M. A visit from the Fabbrini's — Walk after dinner on the Lung'Arno with the family. In the Evening go with the Fabbrini's to Casa Majotti — Count

[28] The Marchese Neri Tolomei married Fulvia Bernardo (born 1770), Claire's Countess Tolomei, and they lived in Florence at Casa Seratti dietro San Remigi. Claire frequently saw them and their three daughters, Nera, Angiola (Gangia), and Signora Alberti.

[29] *Le Prose e poesie campestri d'Ippolito Pindemonte* (Verona, 1817).

[30] See entry and Note 43 for March 17, below.

[31] Marchese Francesco Sampieri (1790–1863). Lady Murray heard *Emilia o la vestale*, which had "excited much interest, from its author being one of the fashionable members of society, and it was consequently much applauded" (Lady Murray, *Journal*, IV, 259).

Cicognara[32] & Cavaliere Pitti there—the 2 Fontebuoni—Dancing. Spend two hour's with the Princess Montemiletto & Signor Pietro—Conversation on politics—News of one of Lady Oxford's daughters at ⟨Geneva⟩ Genoa and Mr. Harvey Aston.

Sunday March 4th. Rainy day. In the Evening the Fabbrinis call. Go with them to the Veglione at the ⟨Opera⟩ Pergola.

Monday March 5th. Read ⟨Poes⟩ Poesie Campestre. by Pindemonti[33] In the Morning walk under the Uffizi with the Bojti's. Meet the Buterlins, Countess Schwaloff, the Princess Montemiletto Miss Farrell Signor Pietro & the Fabbrini's. In the Evening go with the Bojti's & Fabbrini's to theatre Borgo ogni Santo to see Stenterello and a ballet performed by Children of the Italians in Algiers.

Teusday March 6th. In the Morning call upon the Signora Orlandini. Count Bagnese there. Walk with her under ⟨Uffiji⟩ Uffizi. Meet the fabbrinis & Cavaliere Pallicci. After dinner drive on the Corso with the Signora Orlandini & the Signora ⟨Luisa⟩ Theresa Cambi. At ten at night go with the Signora Theresa and the Marchese Bartolini[34] to the Veglione at the Pergola. Meet Mr. Medwin there & the Signor Tempestini also Marchese Riccardi & Colonel Ricci. Return at three in the Morning. This the last day of Carnival.[35]

Wednesday March. 7th. 1st. day of Lent. Call upon the Signora Orlandini Go to mass with her & drive in the Cascina where there is a cricket match between the English.

*Inno di Guerra* by A Neapolitan.

Chi minaccia le nostre Contrade?

L'Innocenza chi ardisce assalir?

Cittadini snudiamo le spade:

Pria si cada, che ceppi soffrir.

[32] Count Leopoldo Cicognara, president of the Academy of the Fine Arts in Venice and author of the important *Storia della scultura*, 3 vols. (Venice, 1813–1818), and many other works on art. He had been exiled as a revolutionary leader but was later repatriated. See Stendhal, *Journal d'Italie*, p. 344n.

[33] See Note 29 to February 26, above.

[34] This could be Lorenzo Bartolini, the principal sculptor in Florence; Bartolino Bartolini, the banker; or Professor Antonio Bartolini.

[35] Shelley wrote to Peacock, March 21, 1821, "Clare has passed the carnival at Florence & has been preternaturally gay" (Shelley, *Letters*, II, 276).

# Fourth Journal

Vecchio Padre, che tema ti rode?
  A che muto mi guardi così?
  Piangerai sulla tomba del Prode
  Non sul onta del Vil, che fuggi.
O Straniero che guerra ci porti
  Chi t'offese? Quell'Ira perchè?
  Va; rispetta la terra de' Forti
  È servile, è profano quel piè.
Ma sprezzante l'Iniquo c'invade
  Stà di Sangue nell'occhio il desir:
  Cittadini tocchiamo le spade,
  Qui si giuri svenarlo, o morir.
Ombri bieche degl'Avi possenti
  Deh! squarciate de'Nuvoli il Vel:
  E la strage del estero Genti
  Rimirate dai nembi ⟨del⟩ del Ciel.
Libertà, libertà si difende
  Si difende la gloria e la fè
  Già gl'allori, Giustizia ci stende
  Viva, viva la Patria ed il Rè.[36]

[36] Shelley discussed the spirit of the Neapolitans in a letter to Claire, February 18, 1821 (Shelley, *Letters*, II, 266-267).

### Battle Hymn

Who is threatening our streets?
  Who dares to assail innocence?
  Citizens, let us bare our blades:
  Better that one should fall than endure fetters.
Old Father, what fear is gnawing at you?
  Why do you look at me as if you were dumb?
  You will weep on the Hero's tomb
  Not over the shame of the Coward who runs away.
O Stranger who is bringing war to us
  Who did you any injury? Why that wrath?
  Go; respect the homeland of the Valiant
  The foot you place on it is servile and profane.
But shatteringly the Wicked invade us
  Red-eyed with desire:
  Citizens, draw your swords,
  Here we are sworn to kill, or die.
Grim specters of our powerful Ancestors,
  For pity's sake rend the Veil from the Clouds:
  And the havoc wrought by the Foreigners
  Behold from the black clouds of Heaven.

# Florence 1821

Luigi Cornaro ⟨ste⟩ says of Venice, le sue fortissime e sante mure ed i suoi lidi, che sono una sua seconda muraglia, fatta non già di pietre, ne di altre materia frale, ma di due perpetui elementi acqua e terra.[37]

Thursday March 8th. Rainy day. Finish Poesie Campestre by Pindemonti. Captain Medwin calls p.p.c. pour Rome. Write to Mary and Emilia. Spend the Evening in Casa But⟨t⟩erlin.

Friday March. 9th. Call upon the Signora Orlandini. Arrival of the King of Naples.[38] Work & write some German Exercises.

Saturday March. 10th. Call in Casa Orlandini—Go with the Signora to call upon Miss Latin. Non c'è. Spend the Evening in Casa Montemiletto. Colonel Ricci Miss Farrell, Signor Pietro. News from the ⟨Aut⟩ Austrian Army of a victory near Rieti but the news is suspicious.

Sunday March 11th. Go with the Signora Fabbrini to the Duomo and to an accademia in Casa Allegri   After dinner ⟨to⟩ with Clorinda [*Fabbrini*] to Casa Giorgi. News that a body of 5000 Austrians have put to flight one of 14,000 Neapolitains

Monday March 12th. Rainy day. Work.   read & write German Exercises.

Teusday March 13th. Write to Madame M. After dinner walk to the Post with Frederiga. Meet the Fabbrini's. In the Evening read Das Lied von der Glocke [39] and begin the History of the Crusades by Michaud.[40] Stille Wassers gründen Tief.[41]

---

Liberty, liberty is what we are defending
We defend glory and the faith
Already the laurels, Justice, spread before us
Long live the Fatherland and the King.

[37] "Her powerful and holy walls and her shores, which are her second fortification, made not indeed of stones, nor of any other fragile material, but of two eternal elements, water and earth." Cornaro, a Venetian writer, lived from 1467–1566 and was famous for his tracts on how to live healthily to be over a hundred. I have looked through them for this quotation but have not found it.

[38] One hundred and one guns were fired on his entering Florence.

[39] By Schiller.

[40] Joseph François Michaud, *Histoire des croisades*, 7 vols. (Paris, 1819–1822).

[41] "Still waters run deep." On March 15 she varies the proverb: "Still waters are very deep."

# Fourth Journal

Wednesday March. 14th. Beautiful warm day. Call upon Madame Orlandini — Non c'e. She calls upon me. Walk to the Convent. After dinner walk in the Garden of the Specora with the children — In the Evening read & finish Das Lied von der Glocke, by Schiller — News from the Austrian Camp that the Avant Guard ⟨are⟩ advanced ⟨through⟩ ↑to Antrodocco↓ ⟨the defile of the Madonna della Grotta past Antrodocco to the city of Aquila which received them with open arms   Also that General Pepè is fled.⟩

Thursday March. 15th. Rainy day. Letters from Emilia Shelley & Mary with enclosures from Ravenna. The child in the convent of Bagnacavallo.[42] Spend a miserable day. Begin the Hero & Leander of Schiller. News from the Austrians who are advanced through the defile of ↑the↓ Madonna della Grotta to the city of Aquila which was evacuated by the Neapolitan troops and were received by its inhabitants with open arms. Stille Wassers sind gerne Tief.

Friday March. 16 In the Morning call upon Madame Orlandini — Sgricci, Abate Nuova casa Monsieur Blarnis & the Signora Luisa Mugnai there. In the Evening Clorinda Fabbrini calls. News that the troops at Turino have demanded a Constitution and that the King has retired to Alessandria leaving the Principe Cariquano as Regent.

Saturday March 17th. Write. A letter from M— & Madame M— A second anonymous love letter from Pisa.[43] Arrival of General Fardelli from Naples ⟨to⟩ who brings an act of submission & respect from the Parliament & troops to the King. In the Evening go to the Princess Montemi⟨l⟩letto who exclaimed — Vous savez, vous savez que tout est fini[44] — Miss Farrell, Signor Pietro &

[42] See Byron's letter about placing Allegra, now four years old, in the convent (Byron, *Works*, V, 262–265).

[43] See February 27, above. Claire accused Shelley of sending these letters, but he replied, "Pray don't imagine that the trees upon the letter sent to Mary are my manufacture — I disclaim such daubs, and I had hoped that you knew my style too well to impute them to me. The love-letters themselves do not seem to have been meant for you" (Shelley, *Letters*, II, 279–280).

[44] "You know, you know, all is lost." Lady Murray reports that the news of the submission of the Neapolitans "was a cruel mortification to the liberals of Florence, who had predicted a glorious resistance, and affected to pity the Austrians sent to restore order" (Lady Murray, *Journal*, IV, 275).

Signor Benvenuti, Prince & Princess Scilla Ruffo, the late ⟨Ambassador⟩ Neapolitan Ambassador in Spain and nephew to the Archbishop of Naples. Talk with the Princess about my own situation

Sunday March. 18th. Read. Hero und Leander von Schiller Walk with Madame B— and the two eldest — After dinner ride with Madame Orlandini  La Signora Luisa Cambi, Marchese Bartolini & the Signora Luisa Mugnaj to the fiera [45] at Porta San Gallo. In the Evening go with the Bojti's & the Fabbrini's to the teatro Goldoni — Play of Luisa de la Valliere.[46]

Monday March 19th. Call upon the Signora Orlandini — non cè — Work. Clorinda Fabbrini spends the Evening —

Teusday March. 20th. A letter from S— Write to him & Albè — Rainy day.

Wednesday March 21st. Walk with Madame Bojti, ⟨a hll⟩ we return because it rains — On the 17th. of March the Austrians had advanced to Volturno by L— Germano & Ceprano. News that the Duke del Genevese has published a proclamation refusing the Constitution, also of an attempt ⟨at⟩ ↑to↓ revolt at Porta Ferrajo in the island of Elba now belonging to the Grand Duke of Tuscany. Finish the Hero und Leander von Schiller — He says when at the break of morning the body of Leander is brought by the waves to the feet of Hero

> Ja er ist's, der auch entseelet
> Seinem heil'gen Schwur nicht fehlet! [47]

Thursday March 22nd. Rainy day. Write a letter to Albè. Read the Milanese Gazettes. In the Evening go to teatro Goldoni with Madame Bojti & Clorinda. Play of the Cavaliere Wender. the scene of which is placed in England.[48]

Friday March 23rd. Work — Read Der Gang nach dem ⟨E⟩ Eisenhammer — von Schiller.

[45] Fair.
[46] Ippolito Tito d'Aste, *Luigia de la Valliere.*
[47]             Ah, 'tis he who, even now,
                Keeps in death his solemn vow!
Schiller, *Hero und Leander*, lines 241–242, trans. Bowring.
[48] Simone Sografi, *Il Cavalier Woender* (1816).

# Fourth Journal

Saturday March. 24th. Send letter to Albè.[49] Spend the afternoon with the Fabbrini's. The Evening in Casa Montemiletto & Majotti . . . . Bulletin that the Austrians have entered Capua & advance towards Aversa. A letter from Madame M.

Sunday March 25th. Write German Exercises. Walk after dinner with the Bojti's in the Cascina. Clorinda Fabbrini spends the Evening. Criti⟨s⟩cism of the Neapolitans upon the King & Queen of Naples & their favourite Acton, an Englishman, written in or about the year⟨99⟩. 1799.

> Hic Regina, haec Rex,
> Hic et haec, et hoc Acton.[50]

Monday, March 26th. Write a German Exercise. Walk with the Fabbrini's to their villa at St Paolo fuori le Mura, or Belsquardo. Call with them upon the Signor & Signora Nuti and Padre Puccini. After dinner walk about on commissions — Read Der Gang nach ⟨dem⟩ dem Eisenhammer von Schiller.

Teusday March 27th. Write to Madame M. & Emilia. Work and finish Schiller's Der Gang nach dem Eisenhammer.

Wednesday March 28th. Write German Exercises. Work. The Austrians entered Naples 23rd. of March. Every thing there is quiet.

Thursday March 29th. Write German Exercises. Walk after dinner Madame Martini calls. Read L'Avaro Fastoso di Goldoni.[51]

Friday March. 30th. Call upon the Signora Orlandini — Signori Sgricci & Demetrio Lorenzi there & Signor Fabbrini. Walk after ⟨dinner⟩ dinner in Boboli with the Doctor. Clorinda Fabbrini calls. Go to teatro Goldoni with Madame B & Louisa. La Clemenza di

---

[49] Claire's letter, begging that Allegra be placed, at her expense, in an English boarding school, is printed in full in Byron, *Works*, V, 498–500.

[50]
> He's the Queen
> And she's the King
> Acton's he and she, and it.

For an account of John Acton, see Morgan, *Italy*, II, 366–368. (Claire read this book beginning September 1, below.)

[51] Carlo Goldoni (1707–1793). Claire read sixteen of his three-act prose comedies during the following year.

# Florence 1821

Tito [52] and a farce which ⟨cons⟩ is the trying to put a Man out of humour who had never been so for thirty years.

Saturday March 31st. Rainy day. Write to Mary & Emilia. In the Evening go to Casa Orlandini and then with the Signora to Casa Marucelli where there is an Accademia, and the Signora Mazzei improvisava. 1st. Acis & Galatea, 2d. the Rape of Prosperpine. & 3rd. Whether Infidelity or Constancy was most amusing in Love, but the Question however she did not settle.

X Sunday April 1st. Walk with the Fabbrini's, fuori della Porta Romana ⟨round⟩ to the Cascina. Go with the Signora Orlandini, Signor Demetrio Lorenzi & Signor Fabbrini to the fiera in the Cascina. In the Evening with the Fabbrini's to Casa Grilli.

Monday April 2nd. Write German Exercises. Call upon the Signora Orlandini. ⟨W⟩ Call with her & Signor Fabbrini upon La Luisa Mugnaj. Read Der Ring des Polycrates.[53]

Teusday April 3rd. A letter from M. & S.[54] Write to S— Call upon the Signora Mugnaj. In the Evening in Casa Orlandini   Go with the Signora to the Box of ispezione at the Pergola   Signor & Signora Fabbrini, Countess Bochdamm, Signora Laura Bartolini, Marchese ⟨Feroni⟩ Ferroni, Conte Bagnese, Lino Novelluccia & Demetrio Lorenzi.   The Opera Mosè music by Rossini beautiful.[55] News that Greece has declared its independance   Ipselanti, a Greek general in the service of Russia, has collected together 10,000 Greeks & entered Wallachia declaring the liberty of his country. The Morea, Servia, are in revolt.

Wednesday April 4th. Call in Casa Orlandini. Write German Exercises. In the Evening in Casa Montemilleto — Miss Farrell, Signor Benvenuti, & Signor Giuseppe Baldi & Signor Pietro.

Thursday April 5th. Call upon the Mugnaj in borgo Pinti — First lesson in German. Letter from Emilia which incloses a letter written to her from her *Amico Amante* and a chain of hair. Letter

[52] By Pietro Metastasio.
[53] By Schiller.
[54] See the letter from Shelley and Mary about the declaration of Ipselanti (Mary Shelley, *Letters*, I, 136–137; Shelley, *Letters*, II, 278–280).
[55] *Mosè in Egitto* (1818).

also from Mary & Madame M. ⟨After⟩ Write to Emilia, M. & Mad M. After ⟨dinn⟩ dinner, take a trotatta with Clorinda and la Gatteschi[56] to the Villa Fabbrini. Call in the Evening in Casa Butterlin. Non c'erano. Begin Der Kampf mit dem Drachen von Schiller.

Friday April 6th. Write German Exercises. After dinner call upon Clorinda. ⟨In the⟩

Saturday April 7th. Call in Borgo Pinti. A lesson in German Begin a book by ⟨Carl⟩ Carolina Pichler. Call upon Clorinda —

[56] The name Gatteschi occurs at three points in the history of the Shelley circle. The first is in the journal of the Reverend Colonel Robert Finch (Bodleian MS. Finch. d. 21), in the autumn of 1817, when Finch was in Pisa, visiting John and Maria Gisborne and Henry Reveley. Professor Gatteschi lectured on chemistry and physics at the University of Pisa and was a friend of the physician Tantini, a colleague of Pacchiani. On December 27, 1817, Finch recorded: "Professor Gatteschi married his wife on account of her being a fine poetess. She has translated my verses on Delphi." Finch read the third canto of *Childe Harold* to them, and Henry Reveley delighted the professor by making a model of his steam engine for him. Finch included them as "Gatteschi, Professor, Countess. Pisa" in his manuscript list of his Italian acquaintance, but alas he provided no first names. One can only guess that these were the same people whom Claire knew in Florence several years later. Claire records the death of "la Gatteschi" in Casa Fabbrini on May 17, 1821 (below). The second shadow of a Gatteschi falls across Claire's life in the 1840's, when a handsome adventurer named Ferdinand Gatteschi assisted Mary Shelley in preparing her *Rambles in Germany and Italy in 1840, 1842, and 1843*, 2 vols. (London, 1844). Claire's letters of 1844 portray him as a glamorous scandalous adventurer, living off the favors of women and finally attaching himself to Lady Sussex as her lover. By 1845 this Gatteschi was writing threatening letters to Mary Shelley, attempting blackmail (see Mary Shelley, *Letters*, II, 193–194n.). This cannot be the Gatteschi referred to by Claire in her journal, but it might well be his son. There is no doubt that he is the same Gatteschi (variously referred to as Luigi, L. F. Gatteschi, and F. G.) who called at Claire's house in Florence in 1872 and met her niece and companion Pauline. Pauline recorded the call in her journal (Clairmont MSS.) and added on May 11, 1875, that he was at the house of Lady Sussex, a member of Claire's Florentine circle. In Pauline's words: "After dinner came F. G. a most fascinating man — old now & fat with a pancia [*paunch*] & rather deaf — but clever! — amiable & cultivated — — When Aunt heard of it she went into a regular fit of rage — she grew livid with anger — It is all a plot she cried to entrap you — I won't have it — you shall choose between the G's and me. If you go to their house you shall never enter mine again — — — Somebody observed that most likely G. knew secrets of Aunt's that she would dread to have revealled — & G has an excellent memory."

also in Casa illerahc.[57] After dinner walk to Piazza S— Firenze &
read Der Kampf mit dem Drachen. Spend the Evening in Casa
Buterlin. Music & singing with Magnelli.

Sunday April 8. Write German Exercises. Read Der Kampf mit
dem Drachen.

Monday April 9th. Write German Exercises. Finish Der Kampf
mit dem Drachen. In the Evening write a letter to Mad. Mason.

Teusday April 10th. Call in Borgo Pinti. A lesson in German. A
letter from M & Mad. Mason. In the Evening call with Madame
Bojti in Casa Fabbrini.

Wednesday April 11th. In the Morning call upon the Signora
Orlandini. Begin Avventure ed Osservazioni di Filippo Pananti
sopra le coste di Barberia.[58] Write German Exercises. Spend the
Evening in Casa Montemilletto. Miss Farrell, Signor Pietro, Signor
Giuseppe Baldi.

Thursday April. 12th. Call in Borgo Pinti. A lesson in German. A
letter from M. inclosing letters from Albè. News of the stopping
of Shelley's income.[59] Very unhappy all day. Read Pananti's
travels.[60]
The fool, says a chinese proverb, the ⟨fa⟩ fool asks of others the
cause of his misfortune, the wise man asks it of himself.
Another chinese proverb. The wise man fears a calm: but intrepid
he would ⟨ride throu meet to⟩ pass the waves & the wind.
Seneca said to Nero. The limits of your power finish there where
Justice terminates.
In the *Ania* a Hindoo book are the following sentences. A good
man ought not only to pardon but also to wish good to his enemy.
He should ressemble the Sandal tree which ⟨at⟩ in the very mo-

[57] Charelli, for Sciarelli. I have not been able to identify this family, whose
name is generally spelled backwards.
[58] Filippo Pananti, *Avventure e osservazione sopra le coste di Barberia*, 2 vols.
(Florence, 1817).
[59] Shelley wrote to Claire on Friday morning (April 13?) to explain the
false alarm and to promise her money directly for the ensuing month (Shelley,
*Letters*, II, 281–282 and note).
[60] All of Claire's notes on this day are drawn from Pananti. It is significant
that many of the passages she records are clearly related to her personal problems
and her own outlook on life.

ment of its fall ⟨covers with⟩ sheds its perfume upon the ⟨ace⟩ axe which strikes it. Learn says the Persian Poet Hafiz, learn from the shell of the ocean to fill with pearls the hand which wounds thee. ⟨See⟩ Behold that tree, assaulted by a shower of stones. In return it lets fall upon those who threw them, delicious fruits & flowers. Pievano Boschi said   Ah my life will be my death! ⟨will be the death of me.⟩.

Of my fortune I say with Dante. ⟨della bolgia del Inferno

Oscura era profonda, nebulosa

Tanto che ancor ch'io ficchi l'occhio a fonda

Non vi potea distinguer niuna cosa.

Che facevate voi sotto quelle ampie ruine? Fu domandato alla duchessa di Popoli rimasta tre giorni in vita sotto le volte d'un gran palazzo diruto nei terremoti delle Calabrie?

Ella rispose: *io aspettava*.[61]

Camoens in a great tempest, saved himself by swimming; with one hand he divided the agitated waves, in the other he bore the book of his fame. When the Divina Commedia ⟨wa⟩ after being lost in the troubles of the civil war, was found & brought to Dante he pressed it to his heart and ex↑c↓laimed; it appears to me as if I had recovered my lost immortality. ⟨So would it be to me if I recovered Allegra as if I had come back to the ⟨warnt⟩ warmth ↑warm ease↓ of life after the cold⟨ness &⟩ stiffness of the grave: so cordially ↑cheerily↓ would my feelings flow in their hitherto choked channels.

Ogni cosa perdei; ma ancor mi avanza

E il maggior mi restò la mia costanza.[62]

[61] The passage is from Dante's *Inferno*, canto iv, lines 10–12: "So dark it was and deep and misty, that, peer as I would into the depths, I could distinguish nothing there" (trans. Tozer, p. 15).

The next passage says: "What were you doing beneath those wide ruins? Had it been demanded of the Duchess of Popoli to remain living three days under the vaults of a great palace ruined in the Calabrian Earthquakes? She replied: *I was waiting*."

This may have been the story Claire recalled when she wrote to Jane Williams (letter postmarked January 22, 1827): "If you ask me what I shall do, I can only answer you as did the Princess Montimiletto when buried under the ruins of her villa by an earth quake. 'I await my fate in silence'" (Abinger MSS., printed in Marshall, *Mary Shelley*, II, 159).

[62]           I lost everything; but still I went on
             And the greater remained to me my constancy.

# Florence 1821

In Pananti I read a beautiful description of the Palm-tree. The beauty of its form, raised majestically towards heaven, a foliage yielding in the sultry climate ⟨shade⟩ a deep shade, and used also by the natives as roofs to their cabines, ⟨the the dates on⟩ its fruit the date sweet & nutritious, its stem yields a liquor, like to Champaigne but weaker and extremely refreshing. Its bark & boughs are used in various works useful and elegant. It lives sixty years. It yields the wine about two months, a bottle full every twenty four hours, ⟨will⟩ and then dies & contrary to the general nature of plants which do not flourish where a similar plant has perished, a new palm grows vigourously in the place of the destroyed one.

The tuscan Traveller Mariti believes the ancient fable of the Phoenix to be founded upon this particularity, ⟨par⟩ especially as the Palm tree like the Phoenix is called the tree of the Sun and that in the Hebrew & Phenician languages the Palm tree is called Phoenix.

---

The Arabians call the Camel their ship of the desert.

Friday April 13th. Call upon the Signora Orlandini — She is ill — Call at the fabbrica Ginora to buy a Stove for Madame M.[63] After dinner walk in Boboli — I mounted the hill & sat an hour at the foot of the statue of Ceres. Below the groves of evergreens were shaken by a high wind, and the noise ressembled the dashing of ⟨the⟩ waves on the sea-shore. Being alone there, with such a sound brought to my mind the many solitary hours of Lymouth: [64] since that time five years are past, ⟨each⟩ ↑every↓ hour of which has ⟨been⟩ brought its misfortune, each worse than the ⟨hor⟩ other.

In the Evening call upon Clorinda, & with her upon the Du Fabris. Finish Travels of Pananti.

Tu proverai come sa di sale
Lo pane altrui.[65]

[63] This is probably not the stove referred to by Mary in her letter of January 14 (Mary Shelley, Letters, I, 130). It may well be the one sent off to Pisa on May 18 (see below).

[64] In May of 1815 Claire had gone off alone to Lynmouth when her presence had become irritating to Mary. In retrospect, this period, like her sojourn in Florence, seemed to Claire more and more an enforced exile from the Shelleys with whom she would have preferred to live.

[65] "Thou wilt learn by experience how bitter is the taste of another's bread."

# Fourth Journal

The ⟨Jo⟩ joy of a wise person is seen not heard.[66]
Osservazione di Necker sulle parole ch'ei chiama *parasite,* cioè quelle parole, che si hanno quasi sempre in bocca e di cui uno si è fatto una specie d'intercalare. Osservava che si ha quasi sempre il carattere opposto al senso di quella favorita ⟨espr⟩ espressione, perchè l'uomo, che ha conosciuto il suo difetto, o il suo debole, usa più spesso quell'espressione per ingannar gli altri, e ancor se medesimo, come si fa per celare anco i difetti del corpo.

A german poet says. He who possesses four women is happy; he who possesses only one is a Demi God.

Saturday ⟨Mar⟩ April 14th.
> O Konigen, du weckst der alten Wunde
> Unnenbar Schmerzliches Gefühl!

Read Die Zerstörung von Troja, freie ⟨Ubersess⟩ Ubersetsung der zweiten Buchs der Aeneide.[67] A letter from M. & S. & Mad. M. Write to S. & Mad. M. Walk after dinner with Annina to Piazza San Lorenzi — then in Buboli. Spend the Evening in Casa Buterlin. "I cannot" says Lord Bacon call riches better than the baggage of virtue; the Roman word is better impedimenta; for as baggage is to an army so is riches to virtue; it cannot be spared nor left behind, but it hindereth the march." [68] No one had better reason to know this truth than Lord Bacon; possessed of a sufficing wisdom and every ↑⟨every⟩↓ favourable disposition he could never arrive at virtue because he was rich.

These lines (Dante, *Paradiso,* canto xvii, lines 58–59, trans. Tozer) are quoted by Pananti and struck a responsive chord in Claire in her "exile." She quotes the same passage at greater length on February 2, 1827 (below), and Trelawny alluded to it in a letter: "Does the bread of strangers please you better?" (Trelawny, *Letters,* ed. Forman, p. 49.)

[66] This and the passage following are also from Pananti. The quotation from Necker may be translated: "Remarks of Necker on the words which he calls *parasites,* that is, those words that people almost always have on their lips and of which one has become a sort of refrain. He was observing that one almost always has the attribute which is the reverse of the one signified by that favorite expression, because the man who has recognized his defect or his weakness most often uses that expression to deceive others, and even himself, as is done to conceal physical defects also."

[67] "O Queen, you open the inexpressible painful feeling of an old wound" (Schiller, *Die Zerstörung von Troja* [free trans. of the second book of the *Aeneid*], lines 3–4).

[68] "Of Riches," in *The Essayes or Counsels, Civill and Morall* (1625).

# Florence 1821

⟨⟨"He n⟨'⟩e"er is crown'd⟩⟩    He ne'er is crown'd
    With immortality who fears to follow
    Where airy voices lead."

H   Keats [69]

Sunday April 15th. Walk with the children in Boboli. Write in the Evening some German Exercises.
               He ne'er is crown'd
    With immortality who fears to follow
    Where airy voices lead.

It is for this reason that I think L.B.'s poetry will not immortalize him; it is so entirely divested of any thing pertaining to the ⟨aethe⟩ aerial voice of imagination, so sensual, so tangible that like every thing corporeal, it must die. His song is woven of the commonest & grossest elements of our Nature; desire, hatred revenge, a proneness to mischief spoliation & cruelty, ↑the description of↓ these animal appetites, interspersed here and there with an appeal to freedom which however a marked animosity to philosophy & virtue renders null & void ⟨form the materials of which of this poet's fabrics⟩ form both the groundwork & superstructure of this Poets works. They are ⟨a⟩ pictures of animal life ⟨in h its⟩ of the sensations which ⟨that might be supposed⟩ belong to the robust body of a savage whose senses ⟨bore⟩ ↑bear↓ a most immoderate preponderance in the sum total of his being. It is a measurement of the body of Man; there is so much of leg & so much of thigh, hands feet &&c in proportion without a sign of the lord & master of the mansion, the soul. This poet's hand seems to heavy to paint the subtle motions of the invisible inhabitant whose etherial emanations create the grace and the poetry of life. Again we repeat his poetry is the poetry of the body and the poetry of the body is to the ⟨poetry⟩ ↑poesy↓ of the soul, what prose is by the side of poetry. Prose is the language of every day life: it is used by lawyers, cooks, dancing masters & courtiers: it expresses our wants, our sicknesses, our crimes & our follies: it is dedicated to the service of that part of us which ⟨the⟩ is destined to the grave. Poetry however has been throughout the ⟨world⟩ long age of the world, the ornament, the

[69] *Endymion*, book ii, lines 211–213. The "H," followed by a tiny scribble, suggests that it is a false start on the word "Keats," which Claire neglected to delete.

225

song, the music of humanity: it has more particularly been the handmaid of the ⟨soul, the im⟩ immortal sojourner on Earth the soul, waiting to celebrate the inspirations of this mysterious power which to become visible to man assume the shapes of noble actions, as the mute Eolian strings wait for the breathing wind ere they swell into music; so poetry bursts into harmony inspired by mental perfection. Nature which ⟨I⟩ is the ⟨ins⟩ unsubstantial food ⟨which⟩ on which the soul feeds is ↑as↓ equally neglected by this poet: except one or two passages in a style ↑so↓ totally different that we wonder how they came there; he looks upon her fair adorned breast, not as ⟨the⟩ if it were the bosom of beauty, the pillow upon which the golden locks of poetry should repose, but as so much space alloted for the ⟨commission⟩ completion of his desires. Religion too with him becomes earthly: she bears him not to the heavenly spaces informing them with beneficence & promises of eternal happiness; he turns her into a demon; the fit companion of his savage heroes, bending to all their purposes; the ⟨Jat⟩ Jack Ketch of ↑the↓ Almighty blowing the last trump as a signal to to execute an eternal doom of suffering upon criminal myriads: such are his praise offerings to the Creator of ⟨the⟩ Beauty & Goodness: the possessor of never ending beneficence.

Monday April 16th. Rain in torrents. Read I Piffari di Montagna a pamphlet upon the Carbonari.[70] Write German Exercises.

Tuesday April 17th. Rainy day. A letter from Madame M. about the Ellice's & Monte nero. Write to her & M.  Professore Bagnoli at dinner.[71] He talks about Pietro Aretino whose ⟨tongue⟩ ↑satire↓ was so much feared that he was pensioned by ⟨m⟩ most of the European Kings to be silent ⟨m⟩ concerning them. Charles V of Germany having made a very ⟨ill⟩ silly & unsuccessful enterprize upon the algerines sent a gold collar (collari) to ⟨P⟩ Aretino begging him to be quiet — He took it in his hand ⟨&⟩ as if weighing

---

[70] I Piffari di montagna, ossia cenno estemporaneo sulla congiura del principe di Canosa, é sopra i carbonari (Dublin, 1820).

[71] Pietro Bagnoli, professor of classical studies at the University of Pisa, was just then publishing his epic in twenty cantos on the siege of Thebes, Il Cadmo, the major work upon which his reputation rests (see G. Delli, Un Poetica dimenticato [1919]).

The Italian just below may be translated, "Yes, yes, I'll hold my peace; but it's a bit light for such a jest."

it & then said Si, si tacquerò, ma è un po leggiero per un tale min-
chionerìa. This Aretino devised a book of an indecent nature he
wrote the verses, which consisted of fourteen sonnets (I believe
the first sonnets that were ever written) Julio Romano drew appropriate sketches & some engraver was found to engrave the plates.
This book was so infamous that ⟨the Pope⟩ Julio Romano & the
engraver fled from Rome, but Aretino ⟨remained⟩ not only remained but presented himself to the Pope to ⟨beg beg the⟩ inter-
cede for his fellow workmen. Julio Romano retired to Mantua
which by this accident became ⟨the pope⟩ adorned by most of his
works.

---

"I have not lived by the length of life but by its breadth so much
have I seen & suffered."

Wednesday April 18th. Beautiful warm, sunny day. Read Die
Zerstörung von Troja von Schiller.

> Da floss in Trauer hin mein unbemerktes Leben
> Und der verhalt'nen Rache Schmerz
> Zernagte still mein wundes Herz.[72]

A note from the Princess Montemiletto. Spend the Evening with
her. Miss Farrell, Signor Pietro Signor Giuseppe Baldi.

Thursday April 19th. Holy Thursday. In the morning call in
Casa Montemiletto. ⟨Later⟩ See Baron Schuhbard. A letter from
Emilia. After dinner go with the Bojti's to ↑hear↓ the Music in the
⟨chapel Cou⟩ Court chapel. Then visit the sepulcres at three
churches.

Good Friday April 20th. Call upon the Signora Orlandini. Signora
Mugnaj & Contessa Tolomei there also Ferdinando Orlandini.
After dinner go to the Funzioni in the Court Chapel. Divine music.
Spend the Evening in Casa Fabbrini. Singing with the Prete
Allegri.

Saturday April 21st. I dreamed this night that Tatty had been to
⟨Bagnacallo⟩ Bagnacavallo and had returned ⟨with⟩ bringing Allegra to me. He said Mr. Hobhouse was at Ravenna but had de-

[72] "My obscure life flows away in sadness, and the pain of unfulfilled revenge
gnaws at my wounded heart" (lines 118–120).

clined interfering — a Miss O'Neill there had threatened Albè who then allowed Allegra to come on a visit to me. I rejoiced said to S— now she shall never go back again.

Call in Borgo Pinti — A lesson in German. A letter from ⟨A⟩ M & S— News of the death of Keats who died in Rome.[73] Thus has been extinguished the brightest promise of genius which England had seen for many days: which would have needed the utmost tenderness to develope: no wonder that it was withered by the poison of calumny.

Write to M. Emilia & Mad. M. Read Die Zerstörung von Troja.

Easter. Sunday April 22nd. Read Die Zerstörung von Troja. After dinner walk in Boboli with the children. Delightful warm day.

Monday April 23rd. Read ⟨De⟩ Die Zerstörung von Troja & write German Exercises. Walk with the Bojti's to the Cascina. Very warm day. Spend the Evening in Casa Buterlin. Madame Calamaj there.

Teusday April 24th. Call in Borgo Pinti. Walk with the Bojti's to St Ambrogio. A letter from Mad M. After dinner walk in Boboli where I watch the Ants on the pedistal of the statue of Ceres. A visit from Miss Lattin. Read a little of Die Zerstörung von Troja.

Wednesday April 25th. Call at the Post for money, upon the Signora Orlandini whom I find going to Court & upon Miss Lattin 2084 Piazza San Spirito. Meet Mad. Olivieri there. Spend the Evening in Casa Montemiletto. Miss Farrell and the Signora Baccocchi.[74]

Thursday April 26th. Call in Borgo Pinti: a lesson in German. Call at the fabbricca Ginori in San Lorenzo. A letter from Emilia. Write to S & Mad— M.

Friday April 27th. Birthday 23. Call upon the Signora Orlandini. Sgricci there. Because it is my Birthday I amuse myself ⟨but it⟩ lest the day should appear too odious to me so I read Goldoni. La Vedova Scaltra e la famiglia dell' Antiquario.

[73] Keats had died on February 23.
[74] See Note 79 to entry of May 5, below.

# Florence 1821

Saturday April 28th. Call in Borgo Pinti. A lesson in German. Read Goldoni.

X Sunday April 29th. Bad Headach. Read La ⟨Camier⟩ Cameriera Brillante by Goldoni. After dinner ride with Madame Orlandini to the Cascina with La Signora Teresa Cambi & Signor Fabbrini. Contessa Bochdamm & Mr. Fraser. News of the death of Signor Pietro Stoppione.

Monday April 30th. Call upon the Signora Orlandini. Signor Ferdinando there & Signor Demetrio Lorenzi. Read La Moglie Saggia ed Il Feudataria[75] da Goldoni. I suffer low spirits.

Teusday ⟨A⟩ May 1st. Call in Borgo Pinti. A letter from Mad M. S. and Emilia. Write to E & Madame M. Very low spirits & suffer from Headach.

> und des eingeschränkten Wirküngs kreis
> dich von allen Seiten Schmerz hast drücket.[76]

Wednesday May 2nd. Write German Exercises. Read La Buona Moglie di Goldoni. Write to S. Call upon Clorinda Fabbrini and La illeraics.

Thursday May 3rd. Call in Borgo Pinti and upon the Signora Orlandini. After dinner upon Miss Farrell in Casa Capponi Via dei Bondi. The Signor Avvocato Biondi[77] calls also Signor Sgricci.

Friday May 4th. Write German Exercises. A note from Miss Farrill. Entry of Austrian troops after dinner from Naples. Spend the Evening in Casa Butterlin. Lady Charleville there & Miss Tisdale ⟨Dismall ↑Disdale or Disdell↓⟩ her daughter.

---

[75] Two plays, the second, properly, *Il Feudatario*.

[76] "And the misery of a shrunken sphere of activity has oppressed you from all sides." I have not been able to identify this quotation. Its content would appeal strongly to Claire at this point, when she felt painfully restricted in her sphere of operations. The letter from Shelley received on this day reports long and serious conversations with Lady Mount Cashell about Claire's prospects (Shelley, *Letters*, II, 287–288).

[77] The *avvocato* (lawyer) Carlo Biondi was the brother of the Luigi Biondi who married Emilia Viviani on September 8, 1821. They were sons of Francesco Biondi, former president of the Buon Governo (Good Government) and councillor of state, of Pomerance, and Maria Bertolini (Viviani Della Robbia, *Vita di una donna*, p. 133).

# Fourth Journal

Saturday May 5th. Call in Borgo Pinti. A letter from Mary. Write to her & Emilia. Begin Reise durch Italien von J.J. Garning.[78] Spend the Evening in Casa ⟨A⟩ Montemiletto. Monsieur & Madame ⟨Bascocchi⟩ ↑Baciocchi↓,[79] the Swedish Minister.

⟨Satui⟩ Sunday May 6th. Read Reise ⟨von⟩ durch Italien. Marriage of the Grand Duke to the Princess ↑Maria Ferdinanda↓ ⟨Amelia⟩ of Saxony which takes place at six in the Evening. Afterwards fire works from the tower of Palazzo Vecchio.

Monday May 7th. Call upon the Signora Orlandini. ⟨La⟩ Read Reise durch Italien. After dinner call upon La Martini. See Sgricci. Then go with the Doctor & his wife to the Palco di Corte Piazza Santa Maria Novella Vecchia to ⟨the⟩ see the Palio ⟨ai⟩ ↑dei↓ Cocchj.[80]

Teusday May 8th. Call in Borgo Pinti. Pay the Mugnaj. A letter from Emilia & Mad. M. Write to her & S— In very low spirits all day.

Wednesday May 9th. Call in Casa Orlandini. Contessa Bagnese there. Miss Farrell calls and the Signor Avvocato Biondi. Spend the Evening in Casa Montemiletto. Miss ⟨Farrell⟩ ↑Farhill↓, ⟨S⟩ Cavaliere ⟨Gino Capponi⟩ ↑del Tocco↓ and the Abate Parigi.

Thursday May 10th. Call in borgo Pinti. A lesson in German. The Avvocato Biondi calls. Write to Emilia & Mary [81] & Madame M. Read Reise in Italien.

[78] Johann Isaac von Gerning, *Reise durch Oesterreich und Italien*, 3 vols. (Frankfort on Main, 1802).

[79] Elisa Bonaparte (1777–1820), eldest sister of Napoleon, had married into the Bacciocchi family. In 1842 Mary wrote to Claire: "Have you seen Bacciochi he is in Paris — & will be a great resource to you I should think" (Mary Shelley, *Letters*, II, 155). This is probably Conte Felice Bacciocchi (see *Storia genealogica delle famiglie illustri italiane*, I, 292). I have not been able to identify the various Bacciocchis (variously spelled Baccocchi, Baciocchi, Basciocchi) to whom Claire refers.

[80] On the vigil of the Feast of St. John, the patron saint of Florence, this traditional chariot race was run. Although the chariots were of rather clumsy modern design, the charioteers wore ancient costume.

[81] This was probably the letter to which Mary and Shelley framed so long and thoughtful a reply, from Bagni di Pisa, about May 11 (Mary Shelley, *Letters*, I, 139–142). In it they tried to reconcile Claire to doing nothing about Allegra's staying for the time being in the convent at Bagnacavallo.

Friday May 11th. Write German Exercises. Miss Lattin calls. Walk after dinner. Read Reise von Italien.

Saturday May 12th. Call in Borgo Pinti. A letter from Madame M. & Mary. Write to them. I am in very bad spirits & do nothing all day.

Sunday May 13th. Bad Spirits all day. Read Le donne Puntigliose, il Tutore ed Gli innamorati [82] di Goldoni.

Monday May 14th. Translate Goldoni into German. Call upon Miss Farhill — non c'e. A lesson in German from Signor Edoardo Auspitz.

Teusday May 15th. Call in Borgo Pinti. A letter from Emilia & S. [83] Write to M. Dreadfully out of Spirits. In the Evening call upon the Princess Montemiletto but she is in the country.

Wednesday May 16th. Call upon the Signora Orlandini — Sgricci and the Canonico Cambi there. Begin Seitenstuck zum Flussgott Niemen von Kotzebue. [84] Spend the Evening in Casa ⟨Butte⟩ Buterlin. Countess Drojinsky and her daughter.

Thursday May 17th. A letter from Mad. M. ⟨& S. Write⟩ & Emilia. Write to them. Death of la Gatteschi in Casa Fabbrini. In the Evening go to teatro Goldoni with Madame Orlandini. La sposa fedele music by Pascini [85] — bad — the ballet good. the story is — A King having ⟨fallen in lov⟩ profaned the mysteries of Bachus, is ⟨struck⟩ inspired by the God⟨s⟩ with a passion for his own daughter — in the end he kills himself. Signora Laura Bartolini, Conte Bagnese, Avvocato Boldi there.

Friday May 18th. Call upon Madame Orlandini. After dinner pack off a stove for Pisa & call upon the Fabbrini's. Read the Donna Volubile by Goldoni.

[82] Three plays, the first, properly, *Le Femmine puntigliose*.

[83] No doubt the letter dated May 14?, 1821, by Jones (Shelley, *Letters*, II, 291–292). For some new insight into Shelley's "M. A. in the art of Love," see Huscher, "A New Viviani Letter," *KSMB* 14:30–33 (1963).

[84] August Friedrich Ferdinand von Kotzebue, *Possen, die Zeit beachtend, bey Gelegenheit des Rückzugs der Franzosen. Seitenstück zum Flussgott Nieman . . .* (Leipzig, 1813).

[85] Giovanni Pacini, *La Sposa fedele* (1819), libretto by Rossi.

# Fourth Journal

Saturday May 19th. Call in Borgo Pinti. A letter from S— After dinner Miss ⟨Farrell⟩ ↑Farhill↓ calls. I am in low Spirits.

Sunday May 20th. Read L'Adulatore, di Goldoni. Finish Possen von ⟨Kotzebe⟩ Kotzebue. Clorinda Fabbrini spends the Evening.

Monday May 21st. Call upon the Signora Orlandini and upon Miss Farhill. ⟨Spe⟩ The Signor Read dines. Spend the Evening in Casa Fabbrini.
Mich erhebt die Tugend allein, sie giebt mir selige freuden.[86]

Teusday May 22nd. Call in Borgo Pinti. A letter from M. & Emilia. Write to M— Read the life of Mozart in Reise von Italien. This amiable man buried a bird in his garden, and raised a tomb with an epitaph to its memory, yet no stone commemorates where the bones of this great genius are buried. The Avvocato Biondi calls. Spend the Evening in Casa Monte⟨milet⟩miletto. Miss ⟨Farrell⟩ ↑Farhill↓ & Cavaliere del Tocco, and Abate Parigi there.

Wednesday May 23rd. A packet from Pisa containing Papers. Read them. ⟨B⟩ Pay the B—'s.

Thursday May 24th. Call in Borgo Pinti. Miss Latin & Henry Reeveley call. Call ⟨wi⟩ in ⟨C⟩ Casa Orlandini. Write to M. inclosing a letter for E. from the Avvocato Biondi.
Be assured ⟨tha the⟩ my child inherits a nature wherein his could take no part: nothing but discord could come between two such contrary dispositions — I therefore have been at much pains to separate them that she may return to that ⟨w⟩ from which she is sprung, and may find peace in ⟨the association⟩ living with what she ressembles.

Friday May 25th. Write a letter to S. Call upon Miss Lattin — non c'è. and upon Mrs. illeraics. Walk after dinner with the Bojti's to ⟨the⟩ Via del Arancio to ⟨the⟩ see the chapel of the Vicar General of Florence. See 2 young Tortoises in his garden. To day is the festa of San Zanobbi one of the patron Saints of Florence. Spend the Evening in Casa ⟨Montenill⟩ Montemiletto. Miss Farhill there, Cavaliere del Tocco & Signor Benci.

[86] "Virtue alone exalts me, it gives me blessed joy." Quoted in Gerning, Reise, I, 81. In the next entry (May 22), the Mozart reference is in Reise, I, 77.

Saturday May 26th. A letter from Mary with inclosures from Ravenna. Write to S— & Mad M. Miss Lattin calls. After dinner call upon the s'illeraics. Long Conversation. Spend the Evening in Casa Fabbrini.

X Sunday May 27th. Ill all day. The Signor Giuliani at dinner. Read Congrès de Vienne de M. Pradt.[87]

Monday May 28th. Call upon the Signora Orlandini and Miss Lattin. Meet ⟨there⟩ at Miss Lattin's Monsieur & Madame Ivanhoff.[88] Then call upon the illeraics. Conversation with Mr Iniressap.[89] Read Congrès de Vienne.

Teusday May 29th. Call in Borgo Pinti. Read the 1st Letter in Leiden von Werther.[90] ⟨A⟩ Letters from M. S— and Mad. M. The latter relates the departure of Miss Field. Write to Mad— M. and Emilia — I am in bad Spirits.

Wednesday May 30th. Call upon the Signora Orlandini. Baronessa ⟨Sim⟩ Semplere from Goritia and Signor Demetrio there. Then upon Miss Lattin meet there Monsieur & Madame Ivanhoff. After dinner call upon the illeraics to talk with Mr. Iniressap. Also in Casa Fabbrini.

Thursday ⟨June 1st⟩ May 31st. The feast of the ⟨Ascension Asension⟩ Ascencion. Go at seven in the Morning with Mad. Orlandini, the Baronessa Semplere Signora Laura Bartolini, Contessa Bagnese, Conte Tolomei, Signor Francesco Fabbrini, Marchese D'Ony, Avvocato Boldi, Capitano Pannatieri and Signor Demetrio Lorenzi to the Cascina where we breakfast on the grass in the wood. Read a little of Werter. A letter from Mad. M. & S. After dinner Clorinda Fabbrini calls. Spend the Evening ⟨with⟩ at Miss Lattin's. Meet Mons— & Mad. Ivanhoff there.

Friday June ⟨2nd.⟩ 1st Captain Medwin calls— Call upon Miss Farhill and Miss Lattin. Read a little of Werther. Spend the Eve-

[87] Dominique Dufour de Pradt, Du Congrès de Vienne, 2 vols. (Paris, 1815).
[88] The Ivanhoffs (or Ivanoffs) were to be friends of Claire for many years. In 1843 their son Alexy was vice-consul in Paris and of friendly service to both Mary and Claire.
[89] Cavaliere Passerini — possibly Luigi Passerini, one of the outstanding professors at the University of Pisa.
[90] Johann Wolfgang von Goethe, Die Leiden des jungen Werther (1774).

ning at the Princess Montemiletto's. Miss Farhill, Cavaliere del Tocco, Signor Santarelli, Signor & Signora ⟨Baccocchi⟩ ↑Baciocchi↓, and Monsieur & Madame Lageswerth there.

Saturday June ⟨3rd.⟩ 2nd Call in Borgo Pinti. Read Werther.

Sunday June ⟨4th.⟩ 3rd. Read Werther. Finish Congres de Vienne par M. de Pradt. Signor & Signora Read at dinner.

Monday June ⟨5th.⟩ 4th Call upon the Signora Orlandini. After dinner upon the illeraics — meet there Mr. Iniressap. Then upon Clorinda Fabbrini — then upon Miss Lattin. The Marchese D'Ony there. Read Werther.

Teusday June ⟨6th.⟩ 5th. Rain & thunder all day. Read Werther and begin Emile de Rousseau.

Wednesday June ⟨7th.⟩ 6th. Call upon the Signora Orlandini. The Contessa Tolomei and Bagnese, and Cavaliere Pallici there. Then upon Marietta Moselle. Clorinda & Frederigo there. After dinner upon Miss Lattin p. d. A.[91] At six the Signora Orlandini calls for me — Ride with her & La Cambi in the Cascina. Then to the Pergola ⟨with⟩ in the box of Fabbrini, cavaliere d'Ispezioni — ⟨the⟩ the Opera of Rossini — Ricciardo & Zoraide  David sings divinely — He said before appearing to some one behind the scenes Stasera voglio far pentir quelli che sono andati al teatro Goldoni.[92] ⟨Madame⟩ Meet Madame Falconriri, Laura Bartolini, Maddalena Fabbrini & her Son, Cavaliere Pitti, Count & Countess Bagnese, La principessa Ghigi and many other people whose names I did

---

[91] *Pour dire adieu* (to say good-by).

[92] "Tonight I want to make everyone who went to the Teatro Goldoni sorry." Giovanni Davide (1789–c. 1851) was a distinguished Italian tenor. Mary described his singing in Milan in a letter to the Hunts (May 13, 1818): "He has a tenor voice and sing[s] in a softer & sweeter way than you ever hear in England — In Italy except the first night or two you can never hear any thing of the opera except some favourite airs — for the people make it a visiting place & play cards and sup in the boxes so you may guess that the murmur of their voices rises far above the efforts of the singers — but they become silent to hear some of David's songs which hardly at all accompanied — stole upon the ear like a murmur of waters while Mad. Camporeri ran up the octaves beside him in a far different manner" (Mary Shelley, *Letters*, I, 51). On February 14, 1831, Mary heard him again in London and noted that although his voice had lost some of its mellowness, his style was perfect (in *Mary Shelley's Journal*, p. 201).

not hear. Miss Farhill and L'Avvocato Biondi call but I am not at home. I have forgot that towards Wednesday Morning I had a most distressing dream — that I received a letter which said Allegra was ill and not likely to live. The dreadful grief I felt, made awaking appear to me the most delightful sensation of ease in the world. Just so I think must the wearied soul⟨s⟩ feel ⟨whe⟩ when ⟨they⟩ ↑it↓ finds ⟨themselves⟩ ↑itself↓ in Paradise, released from the ⟨an⟩ troubling anguishes of the world.

Thursday ⟨July 8th.⟩ June 7th Call in Borgi Pinti. Read Emile & Werther.

Friday ⟨July⟩ June ⟨9th.⟩ 8th. Read Emile. Walk with Madame Bojti to buy some artificial flowers. Spend the Evening in Casa Montemi⟨l⟩letto   Miss Farhill there, Cavaliere del Tocco, Signor Giuseppe Baldi, Signor Benci.

Saturday June ⟨10th.⟩ 9th. Read Emile. A letter from S— & Madame M.   Mr. Taaffe sent two guinea pigs to Mary, and said at the end of his letter — Ah! that I were one of those guinea pigs that I might see you this Morning![93] Read Werther.

Sunday June 10th. Read Werther. Spend the Evening in Casa Fabbrini. Clorinda ill in bed.
Rousseau says.   children fed upon meat & soup are much more subject to colic and worms than children nourished upon vegetables. Cela n'est guère étonnant, puisque la substance animale en putrefaction fourmille de vers: ce qui n'arrive pas de même a la substance vegetale. Le lait bien qu'élaboré dans le corps de l'animal, est une substance vègètale; son analyse le demontre⟨nt⟩; il tourne facilement a l'acide; et loin de donner aucun vestige d'alkali volatil comme font les substances animales, il donne comme les plantes, un sel neutre essentiel.

———————

Il faut que le corps ait de la vigueur pour obeir a l'âme: un bon serviteur doit être robuste. Plus le corps est faible, plus il commande: plus il est fort, plus il obeit⟨;⟩. Toutes les passions sensuelles

[93] Shelley's letter was written June 8 (Shelley, *Letters*, II, 296–297). In it he also said that Madame Mason discouraged Claire from taking lodgings in Leghorn for the sea bathing, where she would be alone or in "odious" society.

# Fourth Journal

logent dans ces corps effèminés; il s'en irrite d'autant plus qu'ils peuvent moins les satisfaire.[94]

Monday June ⟨12th.⟩ 11th. Call upon the Signora Orlandini — The Signora Martini & Signor Demetrio Lorenzi there. Call upon the Signora Moselle & go to Mass in the church of Santa Trinita with her. Spend the Evening in Casa Buterlin. Madame Aufer, a Scotch lady, and Mademoiselle Pauline & Olga Gerepshoff there.

Teusday June ⟨13th.⟩ 12th Call upon the Signora Orlandini & go with her to the Banker Orsi — Then upon the Signora Moselle — Go a shopping with her & Clorinda. The Signora Werner dines. Go at six with all the Bojti's to a garden ⟨where we have a m⟩ in Via Chiara where we have a merenda.[95] A beautiful girl there with her lover. Then with my host and his wife and two daughters to the theatre Goldoni the Opera of Frederic the 2nd. music by Pacini,[96] the ballet of Cyanippe & his daughter good. Meet there the ⟨Fuontebonn⟩ Fontebuoni's — the Signora Orlandini, Laura Bartolini, the Signor Francesco Fabbrini &c.

Wednesday June ⟨14th.⟩ 13th Rainy all day. and I do nothing all day.

Thursday June 14 ⟨15th.⟩ Walk with Mad B. to Lord Burghersh's[97] in Borgo Pinti to get a passport — We call upon the Signora Mugnaj. Then upon the Signora Orlandini & the Signora Moselle. After dinner call upon the illeraics — Spend the Evening with the Fabbrini's in Casa Moselle. The Signor Gatteschi there.[98]

[94] Both passages are from *Émile*, book i. "This is not at all surprizing, since we see that putrid animal substances swarm with worms, which never is the case with respect to vegetables. Milk, though elaborated in the animal frame, is a vegetable substance, as its analysis sheweth; it easily turns acid, and, instead of having the least tincture of a volatile alkali, like the animal substances, it affords, like plants, an essential neutral salt" (Rousseau, *Emilius*, trans. Nugent, I, 40–41).
"The body must be vigorous, to obey the soul; a good servant ought to be robust. . . . The weaker the body, the more it commands; the stronger, the more it obeys. All the sensual passions lodge in effeminate men; and the irritation is greater, as they are less able to indulge them" (*ibid.*, I, 33).
[95] Light luncheon.
[96] *Il Falegname di Livonia* (1819).
[97] British minister to the ducal court.
[98] This is the only mention of the Signor Gatteschi. See Note 56 to April 5, above.

236

Friday June 15th. Call upon the Signora Moselle & upon Miss Farhill. Spend the Evening in Casa Montemiletto — Miss Farhill there, and Cavaliere del Tocco, Signor Giuseppe Baldi and Signor ⟨Basscocchi⟩ ↑Baciocchi↓ Signor ⟨Bascocchi⟩ ↑Baciocchi↓ said — he delighted so much in the singing of David, he would leave counting money to hear him.

Saturday June 16th. Call in Casa Moselle. Meet Miss Farhill — walk with her to Madame Orlandini's. There I write a letter to the Countess Tolomei. After dinner Clorinda calls. Spend the Evening in Casa Buterlin p. d. a.

Sunday June 17. ⟨the⟩ Pack up. The Fabbrini's spend the Evening. Go with Mad & Doctor B & Clorinda in the Afternoon to the theatre of the Arena.

Monday June 18th. Pack up. The Fabbrini's call. Read the Cavaliere del Buon Gusto da Goldoni.

Teusday June 19th. Rise at five and set out in the Diligence, with one woman, going to bathe at Livorno for an Aneurism of the heart. I arrive at Pisa about four o'clock.

Wednesday June 20th. The birthday of Nerina — 6 yrs old. Shelley spends the day. Call with him upon Emilia — then walk round the walls. M. & Mad Tantini dine. After dinner I call upon Emilia again.

Thursday June 21st. Rainy cold weather — Go to the Baths of San Giuliano & spend the day with Mary.[99] Return at night to Pisa.

Friday June 22nd. Call upon Madame Tantini — she is ill in Bed. ⟨After⟩ Mary dines with the little Percy. After dinner call upon Emilia where I find Shelley.

Saturday June 23rd. Go with Shelley and Mr. Williams[1] to Livorno — call upon Emilia before leaving Pisa — Arrive at no 91

[99] Claire had been in the wrong in a recent quarrel with Mary and had not been writing to her. This meeting was something of a reconciliation. Mary's journal says "⊙ dines with us," the circle with a dot in the center replacing her usual sunburst as a symbol for Claire (Abinger MSS.).

[1] Edward Ellerker Williams, who, with Jane, had been with the Shelleys since mid-January.

# Fourth Journal

Via Grande about one o'clock.[2] The Miss Brandi's spend the Evening and Shelley calls.

Sunday June 24th. Ill with a bad headach all day—Very heavy dark weather. Read the Abbot by Walter Scott[3]—Shelley calls in the Evening.

X Monday June 25th. Not well all day. Read Melincourt[4] Write to Mad— M. Ride in the Evening with my companions to the Bagni of St. Jacopo.

Teusday June 26th. Ill all day—Walk in the town with Nera— After dinner we row to the Baths outside the harbour & about the Bay.

Wednesday June 27th. Translate Geschichten von Kotzebue. A lesson in German from C. A. Vanzon. Walk after dinner with Nera and Gangia to ⟨Nuro⟩ Muro Rotto fuori Porta Pisa.

Thursday June 28th. ⟨Transl⟩ Walk about shopping with the Tolomei's—Translate German. In the Evening write to Mrs. G— Sk. St.[5] and begin a letter to Mad. Bojti.

Friday June 29th. Festa of San Pietro & San Paulo. Translate German. Go ⟨&⟩ to the Baths of San Jacopo & bathe. A lesson from ⟨Signor⟩ Mein Herr C. A. Vanzon. Read the Quarterly. Review of Southey's Life of Wesley.[6] The following are a few anecdotes given by the Reviewer who is however professedly favorable to— Wesley. "He went out as chaplain to Georgia—there among his other intolerancies—he refused to read the burial service over the body of a Dissenter & repelled from the communion one of the

---

[2] Claire spent her summer in Leghorn, as did the Countess Tolomei and her daughters Nera and Angiola (Gangia). Although the sea bathing within the sea wall was a bit muddy and tame, Claire enjoyed it, and it seemed to have a good effect on her health.

[3] Mary had read *The Abbot* on January 14 (*Mary Shelley's Journal*, p. 145).

[4] By Thomas Love Peacock (1817).

[5] Mrs. Godwin, Skinner Street.

[6] Robert Southey's *The Life of Wesley; and the Rise and Progress of Methodism*, 2 vols. (2nd ed.; London, 1820), was the subject of the leading review in the *Quarterly Review*, 24:1–55 (October 1820).

most pious men of the ⟨com⟩ colony, because he had been brought up a non-conformist, and would not submit to be rebaptized by an episcopally ordained minister. But what gave most offence of all was his making his sermons so many satires on particular persons. All the quarrels of the town were at length imputed to his intermeddling conduct.

Wesley offered his hand to a young lady of the colony, who rejected him and afterwards married another. Wesley however still continued to watch over her spiritual welfare till after some little quarrels in consequence of his advice being rejected, he repelled her from the communion untill she should openly declare herself to have repented of certain faults which, without publickly stating them, he professed to have observed in her conduct.

Wesley complained of the Moravians, chiefly on account of the supremacy exercised over them by Zinzendorf their head, a supremacy says the Reviewer which Wesley was likely to brook in no man though he afterwards, in his own person was guilty of the very fault, he reprobated in another.

George Whitefield describes himself as having all sensible comforts withdrawn from him, overwhelmed with a horrible fearfulness & dread, all power of thinking or even meditation, taken away, his memory ↑2↓ gone, his ↑3↓ whole soul ↑1↓ barren and dry, & his sensations as he imagined like those of a man locked up in an iron armour. How very desirable ⟨is⟩ Religion appears to be.

When Wesley preached, violent outcries, howling, gnashing of teeth, frightful convulsions, frenzy, ⟨blashe⟩ blasphemy, epileptic and apopleptic symptoms were excited in turn on different individuals in the Methodist congregations. Wesley declared they were produced either by the holy ghost or the agency of evil spirits. He spoke slightingly of Newton & contemptuously of Locke.

Hint for Don J — ⟨As much as one can love who⟩ As much as one can love, who hates himself —

Saturday June 30th. Translate German. Bathe at San Jacopo. Write to Emilia. After dinner walk on the Mole with the Tolomei's and Signor Moriconi a Siennese surveyor.

Sunday July 1st. ⟨Write to Miss Farhill & send her books. Translate German. Bathe⟩

# Fourth Journal

Rise at four & row out to the fanale[7] — Then walk to the english Campo Santo.[8] Write to Miss Farhill & send her books. Translate German.

Monday July 2nd. Translate German. Go & bathe at the Bagnetti in the harbour — A lesson from Carlo Antonio Vanzon. After dinner walk upon the Molo with the Tolomei's & Signor Moriconi — ⟨Then⟩ Go to the converzatione of the Signora ⟨Ricardi⟩ Ricciardi.

Teusday July 3rd. Translate from french into German. Go to Bathe at the Bagnetti in the harbour. After dinner walk to the English Church yard with Gangia. The Signor Moriconi, the Signor Felisciati and the Count Fricavalli.

Wednesday July 4th. Translate french into German. ⟨W⟩ Go to bathe at the Bagnetti in the harbour. Write to ⟨Mand⟩ Madame Bojti. After dinner walk with Gangia from Porta Colonella to Porta Pisa & on the road to Pisa. Conversation in the Evening with the Signor Felisciati, the Conte Frecavalli, Signori Brandi & Moriconi Signor Paulo Ragn↑i↓one and Signor Ducci.

Thursday July 5th. Write to Tetta. Bathe in the ⟨ar⟩ harbour take my first lesson in swimming. A lesson from Herr C. A. Vanzon. After dinner walk with Gangia (Angiola) from Porta Colonella to Porta Pisa. Then all together with the Count Frecavalli & Signor Felisciati to the caffè.

Friday July 6th. Write to Madame M. Bathe at the Bagnetti. Second lesson in Swimming. After dinner walk with Gangia. Then to the Caffe with Conte Freycavalli, Signor Felisciat⟨t⟩i and Cavaliere Esandieri.

Saturday July 7th. Translate German. bathe at the Bagnetti. A lesson from K. A. Vanzon.

Sunday July 8th. Rainy day. A note from the Countess Marie Buterlin. Dine and spend the afternoon at Villa Parenti. Mrs. Beauclerc[9] & her daughter[10] there. Go with the Tolomei's in the Evening to the Conversation in Casa Spannocchi.

[7] Lighthouse.
[8] Smollett was buried in this churchyard.
[9] A daughter of the Duchess of Leinster by her second marriage, and half sister to Lord Edward Fitzgerald, Mrs. Beauclerc was a former neighbor of Shelley's family in Sussex (Dowden, *Shelley*, II, 447n.). Shelley wrote on December

# Leghorn 1821

Monday July 9th. Bathe at the Bagnetti. A letter from Mad. Bojti & ↑from↓ M enclosing one from Charles at Vienna. A lesson from K. ⟨A. A. A.⟩ A Vanzon. Walk with Nera and Signor Brandi after dinner to ⟨M Mu⟩ Muro Rotto in the rain. The Signori Duci, Sabbattini, and Felisciati in the Evening.

Teusday July 10th. Go to the church of ⟨Mon⟩ the Madonna at Montenero in the morning with Gangia. Madame Orlandini arrives. I call upon her. Walk after dinner with the Countess & Signor Brandi & Felisciati to the Caffè della Costanza. The Signora Orlandini & Avvocato Boldi & ⟨Cap⟩ Signor Sabbatino in the Evening.

Wednesday July 11th. Read Edgeworth's Memoirs [11] — Go to bathe in the Barracca. After dinner walk on the Molo with Gangia and Nera. Write to Madame Bojti.

---

31, 1821, to enquire whether Claire knew her; she had embraced Shelley effusively but had not called on Mary (Shelley, *Letters*, II, 371 and note).

[10] One daughter of Mrs. Beauclerc and Charles George Beauclerc was Georgianna, who became a close friend of Mary Shelley in London. On October 10, 1826, Georgianna, the "Gee" of Mary's journal (see *Mary Shelley's Journal*, p. 201), married Sir John Dean Paul. Sir John and his wife lived at 218 Strand, next door to Sir John's bank, and had one child, Aubrey. Mary saw much of them, and in her journal on November 10, 1831, she wrote: "After a good deal of discomfort and uncertainty I have learnt the meaning of the strange occurrences at the Strand — Poor Gee is sent to Norwood [?] — her child torn from her — cast away & deserted — My first impulse is to befriend a woman — I will do her all the good I can." Then on February 27, 1832, "My attention — time & feelings have been absorbed by poor Gee's misfortunes I am happy to think that I have done her good — though her fate is sufficiently sad. She signed the act of separation before me on 6 Feb — the 9th. she departed for Ardglass & her Grandfather with her child." On April 3, 1832, "Lady Paul has been singularly kind since I befriended Gee — which shews a ladylikeness — a generosity or refinement of feeling — of which her family has shewn itself devoid" (Abinger MSS.). Mary continued in correspondence with "Gee," and after her death in 1847 Mary wrote: "She shed a charm over my life by the lively and affectionate interest she took in all that belonged to me that I shall miss at every hour, in every act" (Mary Shelley, *Letters*, II, 311). In 1960 Huscher noted that the surname of this close friend of Mary's was still unknown ("The Clairmont Enigma," *KSMB* 11:16–17 [1960]).

[11] *Memoirs of Richard Lovell Edgeworth, Esq. Begun by Himself and Concluded by His Daughter, Maria Edgeworth*, 2 vols. (London, 1820). Read by Mary July 1–2, 1821 (*Mary Shelley's Journal*, p. 157).

# Fourth Journal

Thursday July 12th. Translate french into German. A letter from Mad. M. Read Life of Edgeworth — I think their system seems to aim at making the mind satisfied with little. Bathe in the Barracca — Take a lesson in swimming.

Friday July 13th. Translate french into German. Bathe at the Bagnetti. A lesson in swimming  A lesson from Vanzon. Copy out Oh, Cara Memoria. Write to M. S. & Emilia.

Saturday July 14th. Work. ⟨Bol⟩ Avvocato Boldi calls.  go with him to the Signora Orlandini. Bathe at the Barracca, a very high wind so that with two men we could scarcely row past the Bocca. A lesson in swimming. Departure of Angiola for Genova. Walk with Nera from Porta Pisa to Porta Colonnella then on the ⟨M⟩ Molo. Signori Duci, Sabbatino, Felisciati, & Boldi and the Signora Orlandini spend the Evening. An old Italian poet says of Livorno that

       Non c'è un viso che viso ha di viso [12]

and this applies equally well at present.

Sunday July 15th. Bathe at the Barracca. A lesson in swimming. The waves extremely high — The waves jump down my throat. Walk after dinner on the ⟨No⟩ Molo with the Countess & Nera and the Signor Camassei.

Monday July 16th. Rainy windy day. Work. A lesson from Vanzon. Walk after dinner on the Molo with the Countess, Nera, Felisciati Brandi and Avocato Boldi. The Signor Duci comes in the Evening & relates the arrival of official intelligence that Buonaparte died of ⟨dropsy⟩ ↑cancer in the stomach↓ on the ⟨6th.⟩ ↑5th↓ of last May; the same disease which destroyed his father.

Teusday July 17th. Go to bathe in the Barracca with the Signora Caterina Finetti. After dinner we ride to the Ardenza with the Signor Camassei. The Signora Orlandini and the Marchesa L'Antinori spend the Evening.

Wednesday July 18th. Work. Bathe at the Barracca. After dinner call upon La Calovolo. Meet M. & Madame Ivanhoff. Row with them in the Harbour. The Avvocato Boldi & the Signor Brandi spend the Evening.

[12] "There is no face that can look at itself."

# Leghorn 1821

Thursday July 19th. Work. Bathe in the Harbour — Take a Lesson in Swimming. ⟨Af⟩ Spend the Evening with the Ivanhoff's. A letter from Mary inclosing one from Ravenna.

Friday July 20th. Work. Bathe in the Harbour. ⟨H⟩ A note from Miss Boutourlin Write an answer. The Count Frey Cavalli calls.

X Saturday July 21st. Head ache. Conte Freycavalli calls  Dine with the Boutourlins at Villa Parenti. Return at five and set out for Pisa. Arrive at Casa Silva about ½ past Seven.

Sunday July 22nd. Ride before breakfast — Then walk with Tetta to the Rat's hole and the Poderè. Shelley dines. Drive with him ⟨p⟩ almost to the Baths. ⟨home⟩ [?].

Monday July 23rd. Ride before breakfast to the Baths. Spend the day with M-ary. Come home at six. Emilia says that she prays always to a Saint, and every time she changes her lover, she changes her Saint, adopting the one of her lover. A man, said to Mr. Williams — how ⟨what⟩ how happy the Genevese republic would be if they had the 36,000 thousand a year of Sir John St Aubyn, who lives on its banks. and added he wondered what they would do with it — what they would do with it — said Williams  Why they would copper bottom their lake.

Teusday July 24th. Shelley comes to breakfast. Read Adonais. Walk with him to the Post and the Banker's — we saw his daughter for the first time and she related us a long story concerning the corking up of her *utero* by Vaccà. After dinner Ride out in the Charaban and pay a Visit to the Eusta in the Convent of St. Anna and go with Tetta and Signor Zanetti to see the Jugglers at the theatre.

Wednesday July 25th. Play on the Piano forte. Read Sandford and Merton.[13] Mary dines — Go to the Baths with her in the Evening. See Madame Tantini. Return to Pisa at seven.

Thursday July 26th. Tetta goes to Crespina. Ride before breakfast with Madame M. Then after dinner to the Villa of Count Arquinto. Tetta returns in the Evening.

[13] Thomas Day, *The History of Sandford and Merton*, 3 vols. (London, 1783–1789). Mary read it May 15–22, 1820 (*Mary Shelley's Journal*, p. 133).

# Fourth Journal

Friday July 27th. Set out at ½ past five and arrive at Livorno at eight. Go to No. 1188 Via San Francesco. Call upon the Countess Tolomei. Bathe with her ⟨at⟩ the ⟨Bagne⟩ in the harbour. Call upon the Ivanhoffs.

Saturday July 28th. Bathe in the harbour with the Tolomei's. Walk after dinner with the Ivanhoff's and go to see a lesson in dancing at a french school.

Sunday July 29th. Festa of San Jacopo. Read Tom Crib's Memorial to Congress.[14] After dinner walk with the Ivanhoffs to the Bagni of San Jacopo. We see the foam of the sea dashing up in the distance over the rocks and it looked like ⟨masss⟩ masses of white cloud⟨s⟩ upon the horizon.

Monday July 30th. Write to Madame Bojti and Mad. M. Bath with Rosina at six in the morning in the harbour. The Countess Tolomei & her daughter Nera call in the Evening.

Teusday July 31st. Write some German Exercises. Bath with the Countess & Flavina Cambi in the harbour. After dinner drive to Villa Parenti to see the Boutourlins. Meet the Misse's Beauclercs there. Spend the Evening with La Signora Cambi. Meet there the Marchese Bartolini & La Signora Mozzi.

Wednesday ⟨Ju⟩ August 1st. Copy Music. Write to S. Bathe with the Countess T— and Flavina Cambi in the harbour. Swim by myself. Ride in the Evening to the Ardenza with the Ivanhoffs. Meet Mr. Sloane & Michael Boutourlin.

Thursday August 2nd. Copy Music. ↑Walk before breakfast to Muro Rotto↓ Bathe in the Harbour with the Countess, Nera and Flavina. See the Conte Freycavalli & Principe Bel ⟨Gui⟩ Goijoso di Milano. Call in the Evening upon the Signora Cambi — Marchese Bartolini & the Marchesa Mozzi there   Then upon Madame Ivanhoff. A lesson from M. Vanzon. A letter from Madame M.

Friday August 3rd. Work. Lucrezia & Flavina Cambi call. Bathe with the Countess, Nera and Flavina. Swim. M. Vanzon calls. Spend the Evening with the Countess Tolomei — Count Freyca-

14 Thomas Moore, *Tom Crib's Memorial to Congress* (London, 1819).

valli ⟨and⟩ Principe Bel Jojoso, and the Captain Sabbattini there. When I return find Shelley is arrived.[15]

Saturday August 4th. S's Birthday 29 yrs. Rise at five — Row in the Harbour with S— Then call upon the Countess Tolomei. Then we sail out into the sea. A very fine warm day. ⟨wh⟩ the white sails of ships upon the horizon looked like doves ⟨sailing⟩ ↑stooping over↓ ⟨on⟩ the water. Dine at the Giardinetto. S— goes at two. A lesson from M. Vanzon. In the Evening call upon La Signora Cambi — Marchese Bartolini there & Cavaliere Esandieri. M. & Madame Ivanhoff & Alexy & Alexander spend from nine untill ten.

Sunday August 5th. Unwell.[16] Bathe with Nera & swim. Begin Cabale und Liebe of Schiller.

Monday August 6th. Unwell. Read Cabale und Liebe von Schiller. Accompany Nerina to the Bath. In the Evening ride with the Signora Cambi il Cavaliere ⟨C⟩ Esandieri and his two daughters to the Ardenza. ⟨Then⟩ Marchese Bartolini, the Marchesa ⟨Monte Catin⟩ Monte Catini, and Tempi. Then spend an hour with the Ivanhoffs.

Teusday August 7th. Get up at six & go to bathe & swim. Lucrezia & Flavina spend from ten till twelve with me. A lesson from Vanzon Read Mrs. Hutchinson.[17] Unwell in the Evening. Mrs. H speaking of the hatred which ignorant people bear to the wise says —"hating that light which ⟨reproves⟩ reprooved their darkness."

Wednesday August 8th. Rise early and go with the Countess Tolomei to buy linen for M. Then call upon the Ivanhoffs — At ½ past

[15] Shelley's letter beginning "I slept at Empoli last night" (Shelley, *Letters*, II, 313–314) was almost certainly written on August 5, 1821, and should be read in connection with this visit to Claire in Leghorn. See Kingston, "Notes on Three Shelley Letters," *KSMB* 6:16–17 (1955), for the background to this hectic period, which appears so calm in Claire's journal.

[16] A pain in her stomach was troubling Claire at this time (see Shelley, *Letters*, II, 314).

[17] *Memoirs of the Life of Colonel Hutchinson . . . Written by His Widow Lucy . . . Now First Published from the Original Manuscript by the Rev. Julius Hutchinson, &c. &c. to Which Is Prefixed the Life of Mrs. Hutchinson, Written by Herself, a Fragment* (London, 1806), read by Mary, July 15–17 (*Mary Shelley's Journal*, p. 158).

one go to Villa Parenti and dine — ⟨return⟩ the Countess Caterina Waronzoff there. return at the ⟨vell⟩ ventiquattro. Spend an hour with the Ivanhoffs. A letter from Mad. M.

Thursday August 9th. Rise at six and ⟨walk to Mure Rotto⟩ ↑go to Bathe & swim↓. The Ivanhoffs call. Call upon the Countess Tolomei. ⟨Read⟩ A lesson from Vanzon. A letter from Madame & Luisa Bojti. A letter from S— [18]

Friday August 10th. ⟨Write to⟩ Rise at six and walk to Muro Rotto. Write to Madame M. The Ivanhoffs call. Call upon the Countess. Read Cabale und Liebe.

Saturday August 11th. Rise at six — Go to bathe & swim. Read Cabale und Liebe. Lucrezia & Flavina call. After dinner call upon the Cambi to take leave — Spend the Evening with the Countess Tolomei We walk with the Capitano Sabbatini & Signor Felisciati & Brandi from la Porta Pisa. Then spend an hour with the Ivanhoffs.

Sunday August 12th. Rise at six. Walk from Porta Pisa to Porta Colonella. The whole sky is dark with clouds — and from nine untill two nothing but violent rain with vivid & continued lightnings. Sit at home all day & read Cabale und Liebe.

Monday August 13th. Rise at six — Bathing and swimming The water of an icy coldness. Write a note to Shelley. Spend the morning with Monsieur & Madame Ivanhoff Call upon the Countess Tolomei — Signor Camassei there — he takes leave for Perugia — Read Cabale und Liebe Spend from nine untill ten in the Evening with the Ivanhoffs —

Teusday August 14th. Rise at six. Walk to St. Jacopo Call upon the Countess Tolomei. A lesson from Vanzon. A letter from Mary & Mad M inclosing one from Skinner St. Write to them. Spend from nine untill ten with the Ivanhoffs.

Wednesday August 15th. Festa of the Assunta. Rise at six and go to bathe & swim. Read Mrs. Hutchinson ⟨At two go⟩ A letter from S— and Clorinda Fabbrini — At two go to Villa Parenti Dine there. The Cavaliere Esandieri and his two daughters call. Go to

---

[18] In Shelley, *Letters*, II, 313–314.

# Leghorn 1821

Vespers in the little chapel ⟨M⟩ and return at the ventiquattro —
Go ⟨to the⟩ with the Countess Tolomei and Nera to the theatre —
Opera of the Barber of Seville music by Rossini and a Comic
⟨theatr⟩ ballet. Signori Paulo Ragnione Felisciati, Brandi Sproni
⟨and⟩ & Duci and Conte Freycavalli.

Thursday August 16th. Rise at ½ past seven. Call upon the Countess Tolomei — Capitano Sabbatini & Felisciati there. After dinner
walk to the Rica matova's fuori Porta Pisa. The Ivanhoffs call in
the Evening.

X Friday August 17   Bathe and swim. At twelve o'clock Mary &
the William's arrive [19] — They dine and we ⟨m⟩ set out for the
Baths of Pisa at five — we reach them at nine — I ⟨spent⟩ staid at
the Baths untill Monday August the 27th. when I returned to Pisa
spent the day in Casa Silva & then returned in the Evening to
Livorno — In this time Shelley returned from *Ravenna* — Very
unexpected news of Albè ⟨an⟩ near arrival.

Teusday August 28th. Read Kenilworth [20] — Call upon the Countess Tolomei — Count Pepoli of Bologna there and upon the
Ivanhoffs

Wednesday August 29th. Read Kenilworth. Call upon the Ivanhoffs.

Thursday August 30th. Finish Kenilworth. Begin Anastasius.[21]
⟨Wh⟩

Friday August 31st. Read Anastasius. Walk about shopping. Meet
the Signor Felisciati ⟨At two⟩ Write to Mary. At two go to Villa

[19] Mary summarizes the period of August 6 to August 31 as follows: "S.
goes to Ravenna — read 2 books of Homer; X [*Claire*] here some days — S.
returns — go often to Pugnano [*where the Williamses are staying*] — E[dward].
with us every morning — The Guiccioli arrives      see her — my portrait painted
— S.'s began — walk to meet E[dward]. every morning at 6 — Copy C[astruccio].
P[rince]. of L[ucca]." (Abinger MSS.)

[20] Mary finished Scott's *Kenilworth* September 6 (*Mary Shelley's Journal*,
p. 160).

[21] Thomas Hope, *Anastasius: Or, Memoirs of a Greek*, 3 vols. (London,
1819). For Shelley's high commendation of this novel, see his letter to Mary,
August 11, 1821 (Shelley, *Letters*, II, 332). For its impact on Byron, see Blessington, *Conversations of Lord Byron*, p. 74.

# Fourth Journal

Parenti — Dine there   Mademoiselle Pauline & Olga Gerepsoff there. Return at eight

Saturday September 1st. Bathe at six and swim. Call upon the Countess Tolomei — Finish Anastasius and begin Lady Morgan's Italy [22]

Sunday Sept — 2nd. Walk before breakfast from Porta Pisa to Porta Colonnella. Read Lady Morgan's Italy — In Anastasius I find the following description of Venice — "The fat and torpid oyster of the Lagunas —

Monday Sept. 3rd. Finish ⟨La⟩ 1st. Vol. Lady Morgan's Italy — At two go to Villa Parenti — dine there with Doctor Palloni,[23] ⟨Sig⟩ & Signori Guerazzi and Puccini. The Countess brings me back in the Evening. Go with the Tolomei and Nera, to the theatre del Giardinetto — where we see a comedy. Signori Brandi Keefenti, ⟨and⟩ Joyce and Tausch there.

Teusday Sept. 4th. A letter from Mary and Madame Bojti   The Ivanhoffs call. Go at one with the Countess & Nera to bathe and swim. The next day I went to the Baths of Pisa and in a day or two afterwards with M & S—[24] we set out for the Gulph of Spezia, we spend two days there and return by Carrara and Massa to the Baths — I return shortly ↑after↓ to Livorno where I am occupied in buying furniture from Mary.[25] The Countess Tolomei departs and I make the acquaintance of an American Lady who lives next door to me.

Sunday Sept. 30th. Rise at six — Walk to San Jacopo and bathe at Cavallegeri   Work. Mr. and Mad. Ivanoff in the Evening —

[22] Her two volumes include excellent site-by-site descriptions of the cities of Italy as Claire and the Shelleys saw them.

[23] Shelley had recommended that Claire consult Palloni about the pain in her stomach, since Vaccà did not always attend when he thought the illness slight (Shelley, *Letters*, II, 314).

[24] Mary noted Claire's arrival at the baths of San Giuliano on September 5. Her symbol this time is a circle with a cross in it. She recorded that on September 8 they went to Spezzia, and on September 14, "Claire & Shelley go to Pisa." On September 15 she marked "O—," which probably indicates Claire's return to Leghorn (Abinger MSS.; in *Mary Shelley's Journal*, p. 160).

[25] Mary skipped all of October in her diary and summarized: "We are at the baths occupied with furnishing our house, copying my novel — &c &c" (in *Mary Shelley's Journal*, p. 160).

# Pisa–Pugnano 1821

Monday ⟨Sept. 31st.⟩ ↑Oct 1st.↓ Work all day. In the Evening walk to Cavallegeri and call upon the Ivanoffs. Write to Miss Boutourlin.

Teusday Oct. 2   Letters from M. enclosing one from Ravenna and from S. Work all day. M. and Mad. Ivanoff and the Children and Madame Nutzolini drink tea.

Wednesday Oct 3rd. Work all day. After dinner walk with the Ivanoffs and spend the Evening there. Letter from Shelley that Allegra is not coming.

Thursday Oct 4th. Work all day. Letter from M. & Mrs. Mason. The Ivanoffs call. Finish Ivanhoe.

Friday Oct. 5th. Work all day. Write to M. Drink tea with the Ivanhoffs. S— arrives in the Evening.

Saturday Oct 6th. Work. The Ivanoffs call. Begin Johanna D'Arc von Schiller.[26] Thunder & Lightning all night.

Sunday Oct 7th. Rain all day. Read Johanna D Arc von Schiller.

Monday Oct 8th   Read Johanna ⟨von⟩ D Arc — ⟨G⟩ Call upon the Ivanoffs   Drink tea with S— at the Nutzolini's.

Teusday Oct. 9th. Pack up all day — The Ivanoffs call. At three set out with Shelley for the Baths where we arrive about eight.

Wednesday Oct 10th. Go to Pisa with S— and spend the day ⟨w⟩ in Casa Silva.

Thursday Oct. 11th. Read Johanna D Arc with S—   Then we go to Pugnano. M. & S go away in the Evening.

Friday Oct. 12th. Get up at six. We go to the Baths to breakfast, where we spend the day, and return to Pugnano in the Evening.

Saturday Oct. 13th. Get up at six and go to the Baths   Read Johanna D Arc with S— Return to Pugnano in the Evening.

[26] As the entry for October 11 shows, Shelley and Claire read German together. On October 22 Shelley wrote to John Gisborne, "I have read since I saw you the Jungfrau von Orleans by Schiller — a fine play, if the 5th Act did not fall off" (Shelley, *Letters*, II, 364). On December 11 he wrote to Claire, "What are you doing in German? I have read none since we met, nor probably till we meet again — should that ever be — shall I read it" (Shelley, *Letters*, II, 368).

# Fourth Journal

Sunday Oct 14    Play and walk in the Garden. S— comes to dinner. We go to walk to the Serchio in the Evening. Thunder & Lightning all Night.

Monday Oct. 15th. Get up at six and go to the Baths where we breakfast — then to Pisa to look for furniture — Rain all day. Return through the rain to Pugnano at Night. Finish Johanna D/Arc.

Teusday Oct ⟨15th.⟩ 16    I daudle all the Morning away. After dinner go with Mrs. W—[27] to Pisa in a Barroccio — Return at eight.

Wednesday Oct. ⟨16th.⟩ 17th. Work all the Morning. S and M come to dinner. Return with them to the Baths. Begin Faust by Goëthe —

> Die wenigen, die was davon erkannt
> Die töricht g'nug ihr volles Herz nicht warten
> Dem Pobel ihr gefühl, ihr Schauen offenbarten
> Hat man von je, gekreuzigt und verbrannt.
>
> ———
>
> Wir nur dem Kopf nicht alle Hoffnung schwindet
> Der immerfort an schalem Zeuge klebt
> Mit gier'ger Hand nach Schätzen gräbt
> Und froh ist, wenn er Regenwürmer findet.
>                    Mephistopheles
> Ich bin der Geist der stets verneint!
>
> ———
>
> Nur mit Entsetzen wach'ich Morgens auf
> Ich möchte bittre Tränen weinen
> Den Tag zu sehen, der mit in seinem Lauf
> Nicht einen Wunsch erfüllen wird, nicht einen.[28]

[27] Jane Williams.

[28] The passages quoted are all from part i, published in 1808 (trans. Macneice [1951]). The speaker, except for Mephistopheles in line 1339, is Faust.

> The few who have known anything about it,
> Whose hearts unwisely overbrimmed and spoke,
> Who showed the mob their feelings and their visions,
> Have ended on the cross or at the stake.
>                    (lines 590–593)
> To think this head should still bring hope to birth
> Sticking like glue to hackneyed rags and tags,
> Delving with greedy hand for treasure
> And glad when it finds an earthworm in the earth!
>                    (lines 602–605)

# Pisa – Pugnano 1821

Thursday Oct. ⟨17th.⟩ 18th. Rain all day. Read Faust.

Friday Oct. ⟨18th.⟩ 19th Fine day. Read Faust. At twelve go to Pisa to Casa Silva where I dine and spend the day. Write to Madame Bojti. Return to the Bagni at Night. Mary at Pugnano.

Saturday Oct ⟨19th.⟩ 20th M. and Mr. W. come to Breakfast. Mrs. W. has fallen and hurt herself. We all go to Pugnano in the Evening.

Sunday Oct. 21th. Fine Sunny day. S— comes to Breakfast. Read Faust all day — M. comes after dinner.

Monday Oct. 22st. Rain all day. Work and play.[29]

Teusday Oct. 23rd. Fine Morning. M. comes at two and I go to the Baths with her. Read a little of Faust. The W's come in the Evening and we return to Pugnano at ten.

> Ihm hat das Schicksal einen Geist gegeben
> Der ungebändigt immer vorwärts dringt
> Und dessen übereiltes Streben
> Der Erde Freuden überspringt.[30]

A letter from the Countess M. Boutourlin and Mad. Ivanoff.

Wednesday Oct 24th   Rain all day. I make a Cap. Write to the Countess M. Boutourlin.

Thursday Oct. 25th. Get up and directly after breakfast walk with the W's to the Baths[31] — find Mary removing to Pisa where they

---

> I am the Spirit which always denies.
> (line 1339)
> I wake in the morning only to feel appalled,
> My eyes with bitter tears could run
> To see the day which in its course
> Will not fulfil a wish for me, not one.
> (lines 1554–1557)

[29] Edward Williams records in his journal a lesson in Italian from Claire (Gisborne and Williams, *Journals*, p. 104).

[30]
> Fate has given this man a spirit
> Which is always pressing onwards, beyond control,
> And whose mad striving overleaps
> All joys of the earth between pole and pole.

*Faust*, part i, lines 1856–1859 (trans. Macneice). The speaker is Mephistopheles.

[31] Williams recounts a vivid incident from this walk (Gisborne and Williams, *Journals*, p. 105), in which a ragged, wild-looking man attempted to force on them a paper presumably carrying an infection.

251

all go.[32] I return about three by myself to Pugnano — A delightful Walk. Play all the Evening. The W—s return about Eight. A letter from Mad. B— and the Ivanoffs.

Friday Oct 26th. ⟨W⟩ Very fine day. Copy out Music all day. After dinner we all walk in Roncione's Garden.

Saturday Oct. 27th. Get up and breakfast. Afterwards walk with M. and Mad. W to the Baths where we get Pancani and go on to Pisa to the tre Palazzi di Chiesa — the Guiccioli calls and Lega Zambelli.[33] After dinner ⟨w⟩ call upon Mad. M. Then we return to Pugnano.

Sunday Oct. 28th. Copy Music. Walk in the Garden because it is a divine day. M. comes to dinner and goes away at seven in the Evening.

> Be hush'd my dark spirit! for wisdom condemns
> When the faint and the feeble deplore;
> Be strong as the rock of the ocean that stems,
> A thousand wild waves on the shore!
> Through the perils of chance & scowl of disdain,
> May thy front be unaltéréd, thy courage elate!
> Yea! even the name I have worship⟨p⟩'d in vain
> Shall awake not the sigh of remembrance again;
> To bear is to conquer our fate.
>
> Campbell.[34]

Monday Oct. 29th. Divine day — Walk in the Garden all day. Play and write music. The following passage is from Thistlewood's Defence

A few hours hence and I shall be no more; but the nightly breeze which will whistle over the silent grave that shall protect me from its keenness, will bear to your restless pillow the memory

---

[32] The Shelleys moved into an apartment at the top of the Tre Palazzi di Chiesa.

[33] Unfortunately one cannot judge from this entry whether Claire and Teresa Guiccioli actually met on this occasion.

[34] Thomas Campbell, the final stanza of "Lines Written on Visiting a Scene in Argyleshire" (1800), in Complete Poetical Works (London, 1907), pp. 242–243.

of one who lived but for his country — and died when liberty and justice had been driven from its confines by a set of wretches.[35]

Teusday Oct 30th. Beautiful weather — Walk in the garden. Copy music. After dinner pack up take leave of Pugnano and go in a Calisse with Pancani to Casa Silva  Pisa where I arrive about seven. Mrs. M. and Tetta.

Wednesday Oct 31st.[36] After breakfast Mary comes. She stays till dinner time. About six in the Evening Mr. W comes to fetch me — We go to ⟨Casa⟩ I tre Palazzi — Mrs. W there. Shelley returns with me to Casa Silva at ten.

Thursday November 1st. Festa di Ogni Santo. Get up at six and at ½ past set out with the Signor and Signora Durrazzini of Sienna for Florence. The weather was very beautiful. Just before Empoli ⟨I think Lo⟩ we passed Lord B— and his travelling train.[37] As we approached Florence we entered also a thick white fog so that the Signora Durrazzini said Par che i cieli cascin addosso.[38] Arrive at Casa Bojti Florence at Eight in the Evening.

Friday Novr. 2nd   Unpack in the Morning — Write to Mad. M. Spend the Evening ⟨wi⟩ in Casa Ivanoff —

Saturday Nov. 3rd. In the Morning call in Casa Boutourlin. Then walk to Mercato Nuovo. After dinner write to M— Then ⟨read⟩ begin Wieland's novel of Menander & Glycera.[39]

Sunday Nov 4th. Translate Wielands Menander & Glycera. ⟨spend⟩ p. 31. Spend the Evening in Casa Ivanoff.

[35] On this day Williams also copied this passage into his journal (Gisborne and Williams, *Journals*, p. 107). See Claire's entry for May 17, 1820, above. The passage quoted is from *The Trials of Arthur Thistlewood, James Ings, John Thomas Brunt, Richard Tidd, William Davidson and Others, for High Treason . . . with the Antecedent Proceedings*. Taken in short-hand by William Brodie Gurney, 2 vols. (London, 1820), II, 627.

[36] Claire's letter to Mary written on this day is printed in Marshall, *Mary Shelley*, I, 310–311.

[37] Of course Claire's departure for Florence was designed to correspond with Byron's arrival in Pisa.

[38] "It is as if the skies were about to fall on you."

[39] Christoph Martin Wieland, *Menander und Glycerion* (Vienna, 1812).

Monday November 5th. Rain in torrents. Translate Wieland p. 39. and work.

Stobeus has preserved the following lines from ⟨the⟩ Menander's Arrephoren.

A.  Nein, du heirathest nicht so lange du
Bey Sinnen bleibt. Ich selbst heirathe vordem
Drum eben rath' ich dir, heirathe nicht.
B.  Es ist ⟨bes⟩ beschlossen, freund; die Würfel mögen
Nun fallen, wie sie konnen!
                    A.  Gut, so bleib' es denn
Dabey und wohl bekomm' es dir! Genug du wirst
Dich in ein Meer von schlimmen Händeln stürzen; nicht
Ins Lybische, noch ins Aegermeer,
Noch ins Aegyptische, wo unter dreyssig Schiffen
Nicht drey zu Grunde gehen, indess von denen, die
Sich in den Ehstand stürzen noch nicht Einer
Mit völlig heiler Haut davon gekommen ist.[40]

Teusday November 6th. High Wind. Translate Menander and Glycera p. 45. A letter from Madame M. Call in Casa Boutourlin. Non ci sono. Meet M. and Mad. Ivanoff. Work in the Evening.

Wednesday Nov. 7th After breakfast call upon the Buterlins Meet there ⟨Sign⟩ M. Demidoff an old Russian [41] and Miss Torrigiani and Mad. Perrin. A lesson in dancing from Mad Benini. Afterwards call upon the Ivanoffs. When I return find that Miss

[40]    A.  No, you will not marry, so long as you remain in your right mind. I myself was married once, and for that very reason let me advise you: don't marry.
B.  It is all arranged, friend; let the dice fall as they may!
A.  Well, so be it, and much good may it do you! Bad enough to plunge yourself into a sea of evil quarrels; not into the Libyan, nor into the Aegean, nor into the Egyptian sea, where out of thirty ships not three go to the bottom, while of those who plunge into matrimony, not one has yet emerged unscathed.
Stobäus, in a note to *Menander und Glycerion*, p. 30.

[41] Niccolò Demidoff, called by Lady Blessington "the Russian Croesus" (*Literary Life and Correspondence*, I, 117). His house was a rendezvous for foreigners, where, with grotesque ostentation, he gave soirées, spectacles, and balls. Though old and crippled with sciatica, he was still getting around in 1827 (Potocka, "Voyage d'Italie (1826–1827)," *La Revue hebdomadaire*, 6:472–473 [May 28, 1898]).

# Florence 1821

Farhill has called upon me. In the Evening spend an hour with the Princess Montemilleto. Miss Farhill there.

**X** Thursday Nov 8th. Work and read a little of Wieland. A letter from M. Clorinda calls in the Evening.

Friday Nov. 9th. A note from Mad. Ivanoff. Call upon her. Then go ⟨in⟩ to Bello Squardo where I spend the day with Clorinda — The Signor Passerini there and Miss Bani.

Saturday Nov. 10th. Call upon Miss Farhill — non c'era. Call in Casa Boutourlin — Call upon the Ivanoffs. A letter from Mad. M. ⟨reproching⟩ reproaching me with affecting singularity in dress. Spend the Evening with the Ivanoffs. Write to Mad M. and Mary.

Sunday Nov. 11th. Fine cold day. The Thermometer 2 degrees below freezing point. The Signor Galli and the Nonna to dinner. Spend the Evening with the Ivanoffs.

Monday Nov 12th. Fine warm day. Note from the Countess Maria Boutourlin. Call upon Miss Farhill Mr. Austin there. Miss F. related to me that being one night at Mad. Passerini's she observed Mad. Mancini an Italian lady making love at the same time to three different Gentleman, an Italian a Spaniard and an Englishman — upon which she observed to a frenchman a Mons. Guilliaume — Il ne lui ⟨manque⟩ manque que le français, pour la rendre l'hotêl des quatres nations. He replied, Vous, vous trompez, Mademoiselle, les français ne se laissent pas prendre aussi facilement.[42] She was so uncomfortable there that when she entered her own house, which was without doors, windows or even a bed to lie on she thought herself in Paradise.

In the Evening call upon the Ivanoffs — The Piano forte comes and I spend the rest of the Evening in playing on it.[43]

Teusday Nov. 13th. Fine Weather. Clorinda and La Sciarelli call. Go at twelve to walk with the Countess Maria. We go to Poggia

[42] "All she needs is a Frenchman to qualify as a hotel of four nations." He replied, "You are mistaken, Mademoiselle; the French are not so easily taken in." The hotel of the *Quatri Nazione* was one of the most popular tourist hotels in Florence.

[43] Perhaps the Gisbornes' piano, which they had tried to sell before leaving for England.

# Fourth Journal

Imperiale and home round by the walls. We meet Mr. Sloane, James and Michael. I dine in Casa Boutourlin and spend the Evening there. Story of Lord Weymouth son of the Earl of Bath, who married a woman of the town because his father prevented him from marrying the object of his attachment.

Wednesday Nov. ⟨15th.⟩ 14th. Call upon the Ivanoffs. We go to the Petit Schneider and call upon the Princess ⟨Koutouz⟩ Koutou-zoff. Her daughter Madame Heitroff there and Madame Marchatti. Play upon my Piano. Spend the Evening with the Ivanoffs.

Thursday Nov 15th. Practise. Call upon the Signora Anna Orlandini. Meet there the Signor Demetrio Lorenzi and Signora Martini. A letter from Mad M. Low spirits. Spend the Evening with the Ivanoffs.

Friday Nov 16th. Practise. Low spirits — Walk to Mercato Nuovo to buy a bonnet. The Princess Montemilleto calls while I am out. I dine and spend untill seven in the Evening with the Ivanoffs. Then I return and dress and go with the Princess Montemilleto to the teatro del Cocomero — Opera of Edoardo e Cristina music by Rosini. Tacchinardi and ↑La↓ Bonini the primo uomo and prima donna.

Saturday Nov. 17th. Call upon the Princess Koutouzoff. Non c'era. Call upon the Ivanoffs and in Casa Boutourlin. Practise. A letter from M. Write to the Countess Tolomei. Spend from after dinner untill seven with the Ivanoffs as a farewell visit. ⟨T⟩ Madame Ivanoff told me the following history of her Cousin Count Tolstoi a Russian. When a⟨t⟩ boy at college of about thirteen he shut his tutor up in a Case in which however there was no danger of his perishing since he was surrounded by rooms inhabited ⟨ed⟩ and could make himself be heard, and jumping out of the window entered a carriage ready prepared and made the best of his way to his Uncle's house. When a man ⟨he⟩ with much difficulty he ⟨got⟩ procured to be allowed to go in the ship which the Emperor had fitted out for a voyage of discovery to the North Pole but when set out he tormented the whole crew so dreadfully by his tricks that they resolved to get rid of him, and after disembarking him and his trunk upon the shore of Kamschatcha proceeded on their way — Here he passed himself off upon the savages for the Grand

# Florence 1821

Duke Constantine, the brother of the Emperor[44] and played his part so well, that he was always attended by a train of three or four hundred and made war upon and harassed the Governors of the neighbouring districts. From this place he wrote to a friend at Petersburg: I have planted the standard of revolt and hope before long to be Emperor of all the Russias — if Bonaparte from a simple individual became King of France why should I not also succeed." But shortly afterwards being somewhat unsuccessful, he abandoned his enterprize and set out on foot for ⟨Per⟩ Petersbourg, where he arrived after infinite fatigues and hardships. Although his whole conduct was know to the Emperor no notice was taken of him and he retired to live *en philosophe* sometime afterward, having ⟨made⟩ gained a very comfortable fortune by gaming. I must add that when the conspiracy was made to assassinate the Emperor Paul,[45] one of its members came to *Tolstoi* the Evening before the Night fixed upon for ⟨its ex⟩ the execution of the plot and asked if he would make one of the body of conspirators — Yes, said Tolstoi, to kill all of them, but not to kill only one. His friend left him to join his companions and the assassination was happily achieved. Tolstoi went to bed and was awoke early the next morning by his servant to get up and proceed to the parade as was usual every morning. I know by your face says Tolstoi that the Emperor Paul is dead — the servant much astonished confirmed the news and added the whole town was in commotion. Naturally then, replied his master, there will be no parade ⟨then⟩ this morning, and turning on his side composed himself again to sleep.

The Night before the Emperor Paul was killed, he signed an order for the exile of eleven hundred persons to Siberia, to take place the first thing in the Morning — He was killed a coup de poing so that no mark ⟨be⟩ might be seen and his body exposed next morning to the people ⟨who⟩ and it was reported that he had died of apoplexy his face being previously painted to assume such an appearance. Such was his tyranny that for the smallest fault on

[44] "Count Feodor Ivanovich Tolstoy (1782–1846), well-known gambler, rake, and roisterer, called 'the American' because he had visited the Aleutian Islands (then Russian America) and often dressed in Aleutian costume. He was an enemy [1821], later a friend of Pushkin's" (Shaw, *Letters of Alexander Pushkin*, I, 122). The Grand Duke Constantine (1779–1831) was brother to Alexander I (1777–1825), czar of Russia 1801–1825.

[45] Paul I (1754–1801), czar of Russia 1796–1801.

parade he would order the offender into Exile where he most probably was never more heard of — so that the officers previous to such a day used to embrace all their relations as if for the last time ⟨and⟩ no one ever feeling sure that ⟨the⟩ he should not be chosen as the next object of sacrifice. The exiles were chained two by two and placed in a carriage from whence they were never allowed to get out untill the Journey was at an end — It happened frequently that one of these unhappy people died from Sorrow or from Suffering in this most terrible Journey and his body remained by the side of his still more wretched companion, putrefying in his sight sometimes for weeks untill he arrived ⟨at his⟩ ↑in↓ Siberia.

Sunday Nov. 18th. Practise. Low Spirits — The Signora Orlandini calls. The Miss Nasi's spend the Evening. The Ivanoffs go to Rome.

> But Pleasures are like poppies spread
> You seize the flower — the bloom is sped
> Or like the snowfalls in the river
> A moment white — then fled forever.
> Or like the borealis race
> That flit ere you can point the place
> Or like the rainbow's lovely form
> Evanishing amid the Storm.[46]

---

> ⟨The mother may forget the child
> Who smiles so sweetly frae her knee⟩
> The bridgroom may forget the Bride
>> Was made his wedded Wife yestreen
>> The monarch may forget his crown
>> That on his head an hour ⟨th⟩ hath been
> ⟨But I'll remember thee, Glencairn
> And all thou hast done for me.⟩
>> The mother may forget the child
>> Who smiles so sweetly frae her knee
> But I'll remember thee Glencairn
> And all thou hast done for me.[47]

[46] From Robert Burns, "Tam O'Shanter." Shelley quoted the first half in a letter to Hogg, March 16, 1814 (Shelley, *Letters*, I, 383).
[47] From Burns, "Lament for James Earl of Glencairn."

# Florence 1821

Monday Nov 19th. The Bojti's go to Pisa. Call upon the Princess Koutouzoff. Non c'era  Walk with the Countess Maria in Giardino Torregiani.[48] Dine. Then walk to Borelli's in Porta Rossa. Meet the Countess Elizabeth and Mad. Le Roy — In Borelli's there were two Englishman ordering a supper because as they said — Nous avons besoin pour ce soir d'un tres joli *soupire* pour trente personnes.[49] A lesson from the Abate Pucci in the Evening. Write to Mad. M. and M.

Teusday Nov 20th. Practise. Clorinda and La Sciarelli call — Dine and spend the Evening in Casa Boutourlin — Miss Reboul there a Genevese. Return at Eight — Clorinda spends untill ten with me.

Wednesday Nov 21st. Practise. After dinner walk to the German Shoemakers at L'Arco di San Piero  A lesson from Abate Pucci in the Evening.

Thursday Nov. 22nd. Practise. Two letters from S— Write to him and Mad. Ivanoff. After dinner walk to the Post and then call in Casa Sciarelli — Spend the Evening there and in Casa Moselle with Clorinda.

Friday Nov 23rd. Call upon Miss Farhill. Non c'é. Call upon the Princess Koutouzoff with whom I spend an hour. Walk ↑with↓ the Countess Maria Boutourlin all over Buboli — The sky is covered with clouds and though warm there was not a ray of Sun. Practise in the Evening  A lesson from the Abate Pucci — and read a few pages of Menander and Glycera.

Saturday Nov 24th. Fine Warm day so that I leave off my flannel garment and am not incommoded by the cold. Walk with the Countess Maria to Poggia Imperiale.

Sunday November 25th. Showers. Practise and read a little of Menander and Glycera, in which I find the following description of the face of a Woman called Nannion.

[48] The Torrigiani Garden, near the Roman Gate, was in the English style. All of the grounds could be seen from a tower. Cows were kept in a stable painted like a Swiss farmhouse, and the building opposite was painted like a church, complete with funeral inscriptions (Lady Murray, *Journal*, IV, 280).

[49] "This evening we need a very nice *sigh* [*soupire*, sigh, for *souper*, supper] for thirty people."

# Fourth Journal

Beym ersten ⟨Blick⟩ Anblick scheinen alle Züge ⟨is⟩ ihres Gesichts in einem allgemeinen Aufstand gegen einander begriffen; keiner passt recht zum andern; nichts ist in seinem gehörigen Ebenmass; aber ⟨is⟩ ihr grosses feuersprühendes Auge herrscht wie ein Gott in diesem Chaos, und zwingt die widerspenstigen Elemente ihres Gesichts zu einer Art von seltsamer aber gefälliger Einigung.[50]

The Sciarelli and Clorinda and the Signor Passerini call in the Evening and we all go to Casa Moselle. A letter from Mad. B.[51]

Monday Nov. 26th. Practise. The Princess Montemilleto calls. Write to Madame B. A lesson from the Abate Pucci. Call in the Evening in Casa Montemilleto — Contessa Pandelfini   Signor Benci, Signor Francesco Carradori   Signor Giuseppe Baldi and Miss Farhill there. Come away at ten and spend untill eleven in Casa Moselle.

Teusday November 27th. Get up at seven — Walk from Porta San Fridiano to Porta Romana. Practise. A letter from Madame M. Spend from five untill Nine in the Evening in Casa Boutourlin. Mrs. Beauclerc and her daughter. the Duchess Strozzi and her Sister, Magnelli and a man who plays divinely on the harp there.

Wednesday Nov. 28th. I dreamt this Night that Mrs. Williams having said something imprudent against the Ministers was tried for high treason and found guilty and beheaded. I read all this in the Newspapers which represented her conduct throughout the whole as most noble and interesting. I then saw Mr. Williams at Pisa who was inconsolable. I afterwards dreamt that a child fell into a Well and that when I thought all hope was lost of getting him I turned round and found that Mary had picked him out — he was insensible and I took him in my Arms and we recovered him by ⟨lik⟩ licking his stomach.

   Get up at seven. Walk from Porta San Fridiano to Porta Romana. Practise. A lesson from Signor Pucci. Spend the Evening

---

[50] "At first glance all her features seem to be contending against each other; no one harmonizes with the others; nothing is in its due symmetry; but her large fire-sparkling eyes reign like a God in this chaos, and compel the rebellious elements of her countenance to a kind of strange but pleasing unity" (*Menander und Glycerion*, pp. 68–69).

[51] Bojti, who was at this time away from Florence.

in Casa Montemilleto — The Signor Francesco Carradori, Signor Giuseppe Baldi, Signora Basciocchi and Abate Buoncompagni there.

> Will't thou teach her to say father
> Tho'⟨u⟩ his care she must forego.
>
> ———
>
> Will't thou teach her to say tyger
> Tho' his claw she must forego.[52]

Thursday Nov. 29th. Practise — Write Music. A letter from Shelley. Write to Madame M. Spend the Evening with Clorinda partly in Casa Fabbrini and partly in Casa Moselle. Il Signor Passerini there. I found myself ill and very nearly fainted but why I do not know.

Friday Nov 30th. Go in the Morning with Clorinda and the Signor Passerini and La Sciarelli and Penelope to the Bankers Bartolini for Money. Then with Clorinda to the Specula which the Signor Passerini shews us. Clorinda spends the Evening with me. Festa of Saint Andrea.

Saturday Dec. 1st. Letter from M.[53] She relates that Patras has fallen into the hands of the Greeks with the slaughter of 10,000 Turks. Prince Mavro Cordato it is said led the Greeks to the assault of Tripolizza which ⟨fell⟩ yielded to them with all its treasures, after ⟨the⟩ the slaughter of 22,000 Turks
Low spirits all the Morning. Write to S— Foggy dismal weather. Spend from 6 untill eight in Casa Boutourlin   Miss Lanz a Swiss there and Miss Annette Staucher a Russian girl. Clorinda fetches me and we go to Casa Moselle where I ⟨p⟩ spend a very disagreeable Evening. The Signor Pietro Grilli there and Signor Carlino Passerini.

Sunday Dec 2nd. Foggy wet weather though it does not rain. Read Julius Caesar of Shakespeare. Brutus says advising the battle of Philippi

> There is a tide in the affairs of men,
> Which taken at the flood leads on to fortune;

---

[52] A bitter parody of Byron's lines from "Fare Thee Well."
[53] Mary records writing to Claire on November 29 (*Mary Shelley's Journal*, p. 161).

# Fourth Journal

Omitted, all the voyage of their life ⟨is b⟩
Is bound in shallows and in miseries.[54]

---

One Sin I know another doth provoke
Murder's as near to lust, as flame to Smoke.
                                    Pericles [55]

Monday December 3rd. Wet weather — Transpose Music. A lesson from the Abate Pucci. Spend the Evening in Casa Boutourlin. The Countess Maria Waronzoff the Duchess Strozzi and her Sister and Mrs Aufrere there.

Teusday December 4th. Practise all day. A letter from S— from Madame Ivanoff and from Mad. M. Write to Mary. Spend the Evening in Casa Boutourlin. A Russian Gentleman Magnelli, the Countess Waronzoff, Miss Annette and Miss Lanz there.

Wednesday Dec. 5th. Practise. Call upon Miss Farhill. Colonel Austin her Cousin there. Then Call in Casa Boutourlin we all go and call upon the Countess Waronzoff and Miss Lanz and Annette go with us to Mercato Nuovo and Jacchereggia — Meet Signor Sgricci and Mr. Sloane and Michael riding. Dine in Casa Boutourlin — Return home at seven — The Princess Montemilleto comes and takes me to the Cocomero The Play L'Abbè de l'Epèe and a farce concerning a *Bacchettona*.[56] Signor Giuseppe Baldi, Signor Basciocchi, Signor Castracani, ⟨this gentleman says he is a descendant of Castruccio of Lucca, the upper part of his face is good but his mouth has a smile which looks as if it had once been one but was now faded or withered it is so very faint. ↑it had all the length of a smile but none of its fullness.↓⟩ and a Roman gentleman an exile from Faenza there.

Thursday Dec 6th. Write to Madame Bojti — Go at twelve to the Princess Montemilleto and we walk untill four — out of Porta San

[54] Act IV, scene 3.
[55] Shakespeare, *Pericles, Prince of Tyre*, Act I, scene 1.
[56] *L'Abbé de l'épée, comedie historique* (Paris, 1800), by Jean Nicolas Bouilly, a melodrama, based on a work by Kotzebue, dealing with the predecessor of the Abbé Sicard at the *institution des sourd muets*. It had enjoyed a success in London in 1801 as *Deaf and Dumb: Or, the Orphan Protected*.
*Bacchettona* is religious bigot or devotee.

frediano to her house near Bello Squardo, over the hills and home by the Porta Romana. We meet the children of Principe Nero Corsini — Very tired — Practise in the Evening

Friday Dec. 7th. Fine Weather Read some of Wieland's Glycera and Menander. Practise. A lesson from Abate Pucci in the Evening. Then write to Mad. M. of a female dancer Menader says.

Man⟨n⟩ kann nichts geschmeidigers und gewandters, k⟨l⟩einen leichtern und zierlichen Anstand, keine schönere harmonie aller Glieder zu sehen verlangen. Der Blick vermag ihr kaum schnell genug zu folgen ⟨a⟩ und man wünscht sich alle hundert Augen des Argus, um alles was sie auf einmahl darstellt, zugleich auffassen zu können; denn etwas geht immer verloren, da es kaum möglich ist, auf die kraftvolle Sprache ihrer Augen und Gesichtszüge, ⟨an⟩ und auf die eben so sprechenden Bewegungen ihrer Arme und hände und übrigen Glieder zugleich scharf genug Acht zu geben, dass Einem nichts entwische.[57]

Saturday Dec 8th. Festa of the Madonna. Write to Madame Ivanoff — Practise — Clorinda M. Passerini and La Sciarelli call in the Evening. Finish Wieland's Menander and Glycera.

Sunday Dec 9th. Fine day. Begin the Life of Joseph Mendez Pinto.[58] Spend the Evening in Casa Boutourlin — The Ducchess Strozzi and her Sister there and a Russian Lady of the name of Mazimsky. Bring home with me Lady Morgan's Italy.

Monday Dec. 10th. X Stay at home all day although the Weather is divine. Read Lady Morgan's Italy — In the Evening a lesson from the Abate Pucci and afterwards practise.

Teusday December 11th. Fine day. Call upon the Princess Kou-

[57] "One cannot desire to see anything more lithe and nimble, with more light and elegant manners, more beautiful harmony of all limbs. The eye is scarcely quick enough to follow, and one wishes he had all the hundred eyes of Argus, to be able to take in equally all that she displays at once; for something is always lost, since it is scarcely possible to pay attention to the powerful speech of her eyes and features, to the equally expressive movement of her arms, hands and other limbs, enough so that nothing escape one" (*Menander und Glycerion*, p. 77).

[58] Probably the sixteenth-century Portuguese Jesuit Fernando Mendes Pinto, whose *Peregrinção* had been frequently translated — for example as *Voyages and Adventures of Fernand Mendez Pinto* (London, 1653).

touzoff — A letter from M. Write to her. Spend the Evening in Casa Boutourlin. The Countess Maria Waronzoff, Miss Annette and Miss Lanz Magnelli, the Signor Ma↑n↓nucci and another Italian Gentleman there. Divine singing — the ⟨sa⟩ psalms of Marcello and Mi Manca La Voce.[59]

Wednesday Dec. 12th. Get up at Seven and walk from Porta San Frediano to Porta Romana. The white frost lays on the ground. Afterwards it is a very fine day. Practise — read Lady Morgan's Italy — A lesson from the Abate Pucci in the Evening.

Thursday December 13th. Festa of Santa Lucia. Fine Sunny day First lesson from M. Plich.[60] A letter from S—[61] Write to him to Mad— M and to Charles. After dinner walk to the Post — Call for a quarter of an hour upon Clorinda and spend the Evening in Casa Boutourlin. Miss Annette and Miss Caroline Lanz Miss Reboul, a Russian Gentleman and the Ducchess Strozzi and the Ducchess Beaufort her Sister there.[62]

Friday Dec. 14th Get up at seven — Walk to Poggia Imperiale — Breakfast — Practise. At twelve walk ⟨the⟩ with the Countess Maria Boutourlin fuori le Mura where we see the entry of some Austrian troops returning from Naples. Read Lady Morgans France.[63] A lesson from the Abbè Pucci in the Evening.

Saturday Dec. 15th. Very cold Weather. After Breakfast a lesson from M. Plich. Practise all day. Read Lady Morgan's ⟨France⟩. Italy. ⟨After⟩ at twenty-three o'clock a white fog covers the whole city so thickly that objects at five paces distance are not visible. Notwithstanding I go to the Princess Montemilleto's — Signor Leo-

---

[59] The quartet from Rossini's *Mosè in Egitto.*

[60] Claire's spelling wavers between Plich and Plick.

[61] Shelley's letter of December 11, in which he reassures her: "Do not think that my affection & anxiety for you ever cease, or that I ever love you less although that love has been & still must be a source of disquietude to me" (Shelley, *Letters*, II, 367–368).

[62] Claire has referred three times (November 27, December 3, and December 9, above) to the "Duchess Strozzi and her Sister." As Charlotte Sophia, duchess of Beaufort (1771–1854), was not related to any Duchess Strozzi (whom I have been unable to identify), Claire appears to have been mistaken about their relationship.

[63] While *France* (London, 1817) was in its fourth edition by 1818, this is doubtless Claire's error for *Italy.*

poldo Fabbroni, Signor Giuseppe Baldi, Signor Francesco Carradori, Abate Panni, and a Cavaliere whose name I do not recollect there. Return at ten.

Sunday Dec 16th. Get up at Seven — Walk to Marignolle — When I return I find I am locked out — Sit with a Man who lives opposite in Palazzo Tosi untill ⟨th⟩ another Key is found — Read a little of Joseph Mendez Pinto — but I am in low spirits and do nothing all day.

---

The country walk of the Morning was curious — as the path mounted through the hills the country below appeared glimmering through a dense mist — the solitude, the bareness of the trees and the dark hue of the earth through the ⟨whule⟩ white fog made a picture of desolation — the heavens were also lowering and grey and the air was cold with damp. Not a bird twittered nor a blade of glass was stirred. I heard nothing but the ⟨clocks⟩ bells of the distant city which itself was hid sounding to Mass. Winter is the death of Nature — all is discoloured lifeless and melancholy — this season is pleasant to sufferers who live as it were entombed and the noisy magnificence and pomp of summer with its ceaceless sounds is a too unpleasing contrast.

Monday Dec 17th. I dream many dreams this night — or rather I continued my life of yesterday without that usual and pleasant interregnum sleep. I dreamt the Ducchess of Wirtemberg was dead — then I dreamt that I had gone to Pisa and that the weather was unusually dark and turbid and that some violent commotion of Nature such as Earthquake was expected — I then was told that Mrs. William's little Boy Medwin had died of a Worm fever and that she had removed to Florence — I was much discomforted by this news and attributed it as usual to my unlucky fortune to arrive in a place just as the people I wished to see ⟨were⟩ ↑had↓ quitted it. I practise all day. And in the Evening read a little of Joseph Mendez Pinto —

Teusday Dec. 18th. Practise. A lesson from M. Plich — A letter from S. — Spend the Evening in Casa Boutourlin. Lord Guildford there.[64] Go to the Novena in Chiesa San Felice. Magnelli there

[64] He had called on the Shelleys in Rome, March 13, 1819 (*Mary Shelley's Journal*, p. 117).

also ↑M. Charrière↓ a Gentleman of the Suite of the Duke of Wirtemberg. Today the weather changes from cold dry weather to soft rainy airs.

Wednesday Dec. 19th. Rain in torrents. Practise. Read a little of Joseph Mendez Pinto — After dinner walk on the terrace. A lesson from the Abate Pucci whom I pay.

Thursday Dec. 20th. Rain. Practise. A lesson from M. Plich   Read a little of Ferdinand Mendez Pinto. Walk on the terrace after dinner. A letter from Mad. M.

Friday December 21st. Practise. Rain. Read a little. ⟨In the Evening a lesson from Abate Pucci⟩ In the Evening write to Mad. M. and Shelley.

Saturday Dec. 22nd. A lesson from M. Plich. Practise. In the Evening a lesson from the Abate Pucci. Read the tragedy of Gabrielle de Vergy by Belloi[65] and False Delicacy an English Comedy translated into French.[66]

Sunday Dec 23rd. Rain always. Practise — and transpose Languir per una Bella from L'Italiana in Algieri.[67]

Monday Dec. 24th. Fine day. Practise. Call in the Evening in Casa Boutourlin — the Countess Maria Varontzoff there. Then go to the Princess M's. Miss Farhill, Monsieur & Madame Lagesward Signor Santarelli Signor Benvenuti, Abate Panni and Mr. Biddulph there.

Teusday Dec. 25th. Xmas day — Practise all day. Torrents of rain intermixed with gleams of passing Sunshine — Two flashes of lightning. Walk upon the Terrace   Read Lady Morgan's Italy. Send letter to Shelley and Mad. M. A letter from M and Madame Ivanoff.

Wednesday Dec. 26th. Practise. Walk upon the Terrace. Spend the Evening in Casa Boutourlin. We go to see two *Cappanne*[68]

[65] Pierre-Laurent Buirette de Belloy, *Gabrielle de Vergy*, tragédie (Paris, 1770).

[66] Hugh Kelly, *False Delicacy, ou La Fausse Délicatesse*, comedy, trans. Marie Jeanne Riccoboni in vol. VI of her *Oeuvres complètes*, 6 vols. (Paris, 1818).

[67] By Rossini (1813).

[68] *Capanna* is hut — in this case crèche. See Appendix A, p. 455, below.

one in Via dei Caldaj and the second a very pretty one in Casa
Frilli Via Chiara. The Countess Maria Varontzoff, Miss Annette
Miss Lanz   Countess Pecori, and Madame Du Chateau there.

Thursday Dec 27th. Rain in torrents all day. A lesson from M.
Plich. Practise. Walk upon the terrace. Read Lady Morgan's Italy.

Friday Dec. 28th. Rain. Practise. Write to Madame B— Finish
Lady Morgan's Italy.

Saturday Dec. 29th. Rain in torrents accompanied by Thunder
and Lightning. A lesson from M. Plick. Walk upon the Terrace.
Read Hypermnestre ↑a tragedy↓ by M. le Mierre and Rhadamiste
et Zenobie by I. Crebillon.[69]

  Non c'è Patria, ne Altar ne causa Santa
  Ma passa Schiavo in Babilonìa e canta.[70]

Sunday Dec 30th. Rain in Torrents. Stay at Home all day. Read
Cymbeline Titus Andronicus and 1st. and 2nd. part of Henry IV.

Monday Dec 31st. Rain in torrents. Practise. walk upon the Terrace. Begin Ditmar von Aarenstein.[71]

[1822]

Teusday Jany. 1st. Fine Sunny day after so much rainy foggy
weather   it shone like a ray of light across a cave. Practise. Spend
the Evening in Casa Boutourlin. The Princess Suwarrow Miss
Reboul The Countess Varontzoff — Miss Annette and Miss Lanz
and a Polish Gentleman and an Abbè there.

Wednesday Jany. 2nd. Practise. A letter from S.[72] Read Ditmar
von Aarenstein. In the Evening a lesson from Abate Pucci   The
Rain begins again in torrents at two o'clock. P.M.

[69] Antoine Marin Lemierre, *Hypermnestre*, tragedy in five acts, in *Théâtre
des auteurs du second ordre. Tragédies* (Paris, 1808), vol. IV; Prosper Jolyot de
Crébillon, *Rhadamisthe et Zénobie*, tragedy in five acts, in *Oeuvres complètes de
Crébillon* (Paris, 1824), vol. I.

[70] I have not found the source of this couplet: "There is no country, faith
or sacred cause but passes eventually into Babylonian slavery, and wails."

[71] Not identified. Possibly Benedict David Arnstein (or Arnsteiner), whose
*Dramatische Versuche* (Vienna, 1787) I have not found.

[72] His letter of December 31 in which he comments on the effects of the
dramatically foul weather (Shelley, *Letters*, II, 370–371).

# Fourth Journal

Thursday Jany. 3rd. A lesson from M. Plich. Fine day. Practise. Write to M. Read Ditmar von Aarenstein. Spend the Evening in Casa Boutourlin. Singing with Magnelli. Little Marguerite Dillon Countess Maria Varontzoff, Miss Lanz, Annette and a Polish Gentleman there.

Friday Jany. 4th. Fine Sunny day. Write music. Call in Casa Orlandini — Signor Demetrio Lorenzi there and the Countess L'Antinori. Then in Casa Seratti dietro San Remigi upon the Countess Tolomei. Her daughter La Signora Alberti. Dine   Walk upon the Terrace — A lesson from Abate Pucci — Practise.

Saturday Jany. 5th. Rain. A lesson from M. Plich. Practise. It is the feast of the Epiphany and in the Evening there are a quantity of processions going about with trumpets and lights   A letter from Mad. M. ↑Write to Mad. Ivanoff↓ News of the death of Prince Clement of Saxony at Pisa.

X Sunday Jany 6th. Practise. Rainy Weather. Walk upon the Terrace. Clorinda La Sciarelli and il Signor Passerini call for a moment in the Evening.

Monday Jany. 7th. Practise. Read Shakespeare. Walk upon the Terrace. Spend the Evening in Casa Boutourlin. M. de la Charrière there.

Teusday Jany. 8th. A lesson from M. Plich. Practise. A lesson from Abate Pucci in the Evening.

Wednesday Jany. 9th. Practise. Walk upon the Terrace. A lesson from Abate Pucci in the Evening. Read a page or two of Ditmar von Aarenstein.

Thursday Jany. 10   A lesson from M. Plich. Begin the Overture by Mozart to the Clemenza di Tito. A letter from Madame Ivanoff announcing their departure to Naples. Practise. Write to M.

Friday Jany 11th. Fine frosty day. Practise — Call in Casa Boutourlin. Meet the Signora Fabbrini we walk to Casa Moselle and then to Mercato Nuovo. Meet Michael James and M. Boning. Dine   Practise. A lesson from Abbè Pucci — Practise.

Claire Clairmont at twenty-one
Oil painting by Amelia Curran, 1819

Percy Bysshe Shelley at twenty-nine
Watercolor by Edward Ellerker Williams, 1821 or 1822

Mary Shelley
Portrait by Richard Rothwell, 1841

George Noel Gordon, Lord Byron, at thirty
Portrait by James Holmes, 1818

Charles Clairmont, about 1835
Artist unknown

*Clairmont family archives*

Edward John Trelawny
Pen-and-ink sketch
by Joseph Severn, 1838

*National Portrait Gallery*

William Godwin at seventy-six
Previously unpublished watercolor by Sophia Gent, 1832

October 1820

Saturday October 28th

Translate from Phædrus — Walk out in the Town. Learn German.

Sunday October 29th

I am not well today — Work. Walk in the Ruboli. First chamber chamber-maid's wife & wife of the cleaner of the Plate. Die grosmutter at dinner. For think of thyself as a stranger & traveller in this world, on the earth, to whom none of the many affairs of this world, belong and who has no permanent township on the globe.

Monday October 30th

[crossed out / illegible lines]

A page from the Fourth Journal

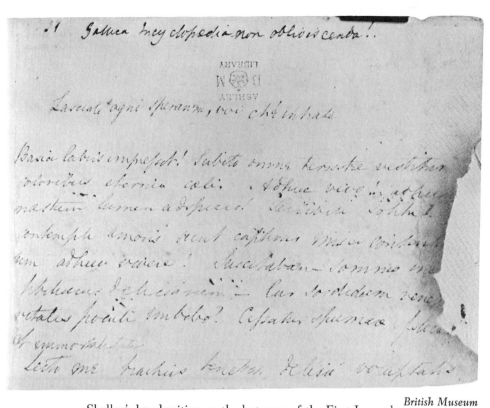

Shelley's handwriting on the last page of the First Journal

*British Museum*

Two pages from the Third Journal

*British Museum*

# Florence 1822

Saturday Jany 12. Birthday 5th.[73] A lesson from M. Plich. Practise. Call after dinner in Casa Fabbrini. Il Signor Passerini makes a scene. Then in Casa Montemilleto But the Princess is not there. Pay M. Plick. A letter from Wien.[74] Write to Mad. M. and Mad B.

Sunday Jany. 13th. Practise. In low Spirits. After dinner the Countess Alberti and Nera and Gangia Tolomei call. Finish Ditmar von Aarenstein.

Monday Jany. 14th. Low spirits all day. In the Evening Go with the Princess Montemilleto and Miss Farhill to the Cocomero. the Play of ⟨L'impostore L'Am⟩ L'Amante e L'Impostore and the farce of the Pa↑p↓pagalli.[75] Signor Giuseppe Baldi, Signor e Signora Basciocchi Signor Castracani and Signor Conte Colombani di Forlì and ⟨a Venetian Cavaliere there⟩ Conte Antonelli there.

Teusday Jany. 15th. A lesson from M. Plick. Practise. Miss Farhill calls. Write to Vienna. A letter from Mad M. Spend the Evening in Casa Boutourlin — The Countess Maria Varontzoff Miss Annette and Miss Caroline Lanz and the Sardinian Minister there. Disagreeable questioning.

Wednesday Jany 16th. Low spirits all day. Do little else but practise and that badly. A lesson from Abbe Pucci in the Evening.

Thursday Jany. 17th. Fine frosty weather. A lesson from M. Plick. Spend from 5 to Seven in the Evening in Casa Fabbrini — M. Passerini there. Then Practise. Read King Lear.

> These miserable gentry make
> The proverb good at once
> That learning has for enemy
> No creature but a dunce.

In the reign of Charlemagne a student of the name of Loup Ferrieres was much persecuted by the clergy on its being detected of admiring Homer and of applying himself seriously to the Art of writing well, and still later under the reign of Philip Augustus

[73] Allegra's.

[74] From Charles Clairmont.

[75] *L'Amante e l'impostore,* a comedy in four acts by Felice Romani. *Pappagalli* are parrots.

# Fourth Journal

Poetry was inserted in a list officially published by the clergy of "futile & criminal Arts."[76]

> Le temps a quitèe son Manteau
> De vent, de froideur, et de pluie
> Et s'est vetu de Broiderie
> De soleil luisant, clair et beau.
> Il n'y a ni bête ni oiseau
> Qu'en son jargon ne chante et crie
> Le temps a quittèe son manteau
> De vent, de froidure, et de pluie.
>
> Rondeau by Charles of Orleans.[77]

---

> Alors qu'on parlera de Cesar et de Rome
> Qu'on se souvienne aussi qu'il a été un homme
> Un Brute, le vengeur de tout cruauté
> Qui auroit d'un seul coup gagnè la liberté.
> Quand on dira. — Cesar fut maitre de l'empire
> Qu'on sache quand et quand Brute le eut occire!
> Quand on dira — Cesar fut premier Empereur
> Qu'on dira quand et quand Brute en fut le Vengeur!
>
> Greoin, Mort de Cesar.[78]

---

[76] I have not found the source of this information or of the quatrain before it.

[77]
> The season's shed his overcoat
> Of wind, of cold, and rain
> And put on his embroidery
> Of bright, clear, shining sun.
> And there's no animal or bird
> But sings in his own tongue
> The season's shed his overcoat
> Of wind, of cold, and rain.

Perhaps Claire quoted from memory or from a friend's copy book. One finds *laissie* for *quitèe* and *raiant* for *luisant* in *Poësies de Charles d'Orléans* (Grenoble, 1803), p. 257.

[78]
> When they come to speak of Caesar and of Rome
> Let them remember too that there was a man
> A Brutus, the avenger of all cruelty,
> Who would have gained liberty with a single blow.
> When they say. — Caesar was head of the empire
> Let them know all the same that Brutus killed him!
> When they say — Caesar was the first Emperor
> Let them say all the same Brutus took vengeance upon him!

Jacques Grévin, *La Mort de César* (1560). Here too there are differences in spelling and wording from published texts.

# Florence 1822

Lear. You do me wrong to take me out o' the grave —
Thou art a soul in bliss; but I am bound ⟨upon a wheel⟩
Upon a wheel of fire, that mine own tears
Do scald like molten lead.

Through tatter'd ⟨robes⟩ clothes small vices do appear
Robes and furr'd Gowns hide all.

Lear. Then let them anatomize Regan; see what breeds about her heart: Is there any cause in Nature, that makes these hard hearts?[79]

Friday Jany 18th. Practise. Clorinda and Marietta Moselle call for me  we go to Palazzo Pitti to see the guarda roba of the Grand-Ducchess which is shewn to us by the Balestrucci and La ⟨Francesh⟩ Franceschini. then we call upon the Tolomeis and they walk home with us. A letter from Mad. B. A lesson from Abbè Pucci in the Evening.

Saturday Jany. 19th. Practise. A lesson from M. Plich. A letter from Mad. M. Write to her and Mad. Ivanoff. ⟨In the Evening go with⟩ Call upon Miss Farhill — Non c'è. She comes with the Abate Panni and we go to the Princess Montemilleto's — La Signora Pallavicini Conte Basciocchi, Signor Francesco Carradori and a Neapolitan and Cavaliere Medici L'Ex Minister of Naples there. the latter talking of physicians quoted the following description of them from Voltaire. Un medico è un uomo che ⟨sa⟩ sta accanto al letto d'un ammalato col bastone in mano; da delle colpe, se coglie il male guarisce l'uomo, se la natura, muore.[80]

Sunday Jany. 20th. Walk upon the Terrace. Practise. La Sciarelli and Penelope call. Go after dinner to her house. Meet there the famiglia Allodi. Then Practise.

Monday Jany. 21st. Practise. Write to Madame B. Spend the Evening in Casa Boutourlin. A russian Artist there. Disagreeable talk about a German woman whom they mean for Mary Wollstonecraft.

Tuesday Jany. 22nd. A lesson from M. Plich. A letter from M.

[79] *King Lear,* Act IV, scene 7; IV, 6; III, 6.
[80] "A doctor is a man who stands at a sick man's bedside with a stick in his hands. If the blows he delivers strike what is wrong with a man, he gets better; but if they hit what is right with the patient, he dies."

271

# Fourth Journal

enclosing one from Mrs. Gisborne. The following are extracts from it. During the greater part of the year in this city (London) sea coal is a substitute for the Sun, and its mephitic exhalations for its bright beams. The umbrella is the constant companion of the pedestrian. ⟨Leave⟩ Letter from. G.[81] to her. Dear Madam I had the favour of a Note from you more than a fortnight since which has lain on my table hitherto unanswered. The distance at which you reside is unexpectedly great, the chance of my being so fortunate ↑as↓ to find you at home is extremely precarious. Under these circumstances, my growing infirmities, and various ⟨embass⟩ embarass⟨ments⟩↑ting↓ particulars not ⟨worth⟩ necessary to be entered into, compel me to say that I know not when it will be in my power to accept your obliging overture. Thus it is that the remorseless hand of time interrupts or dissolves intimacies which under other circumstances could not have expired but with the last breath of my Existence. With the kindest recollections believe me to remain ever sincerely. Your's. W.G.

Coleridge's opinion of Calderon. Take from Shakespear his philosophy and his deep individual knowledge of the human heart and Calderon is his equal. What any other man labours and toils to effect, Calderon accomplishes by unpremeditated instantaneous flashes. His region is that of the imagination when he establishes himself there he never deviates, consequently his work forms a perfect whole. Fancy has other counters to play with she generally presents one thing to you for another &c. &c.[82]

Coleridge is at present employed after twenty years of preparation in writing an assertion (not defense) of the Christian Religion; he takes an opposite course to Paley and Grotius; for he does not prove the religion by the miracles but the miracles by the truth of the religion.

Wednesday Jany 23rd. Practise.

Thursday Jany. 24th. A lesson from M. Plich. A letter from Mad M. Write to her. Practise all the Evening.

[81] Godwin.
[82] This opinion is recorded in Maria's journal for August 1, 1820 (Gisborne and Williams, *Journals,* p. 41). The news of Coleridge is probably from her letter. Henry Crabb Robinson records a conversation in which Coleridge gave a similar opinion on November 24, 1811 (*Henry Crabb Robinson,* I, 52).

Friday Jany. 25th. Practise. Walk upon the Terrace. Write to M. in the Evening.

Saturday Jany. 26th. A lesson from M. Plich. A letter from Madame M. ⟨W⟩ Spend the Evening in Casa Montemilleto. Il Signor Radi, Giuseppe Baldi, Francesco Carradori, Miss Farhill, Abate Panni, Monsieur Lagesward, Signor Giovanni, Signor Leopoldo and Signora Fabbroni and Signor Benvenuti and Signor Benci 'there. A Poet wrote under a statue of Louis Quinze who was represented upon horseback ⟨un⟩ on a pedestal upon which was sculptured ⟨the fi⟩ at each ⟨con⟩ corner ↑the figure of a↓ ⟨four⟩ virtue⟨s⟩ —

        Beau statue — belle piedestal
        Les Virtues vont a pied — le Vice a cheval.[83]

Sunday Jany. 27th. High wind. La Sciarelli and Penelope call. also Miss Farhill. Practice all day. Walk upon the terrace. The Clown in All's well that ends well⟨e⟩ says, I am for the ⟨narrow⟩ house with the narrow gate, which I take it is too little for pomp to enter.[84]

Monday Jany 28th. Practise. Walk upon the Terrace. Write to the Countess Boutourlin and Mad. B.

Teusday Jany 29th. A lesson from M. Plich — Send letter to the Countess. A letter from Mad. M. Write to her. After dinner go⟨t⟩ to Casa Seratti. Il cavaliere Pecci  il Cavaliere Pitti and Camilla Pitti there.

Wednesday Jany. 30th. Practise. Call upon Miss Farhill — Non c'è. A letter from the Countess Boutourlin. The Princess Montemilleto calls. Spend the Prima Sera in Casa Boutourlin — Miss Lanz and Miss Annette there. Then go to the Cocomero with the Princess and Miss Farhill — The Play of the Sacente.[85]

Thursday Jany 31st. A lesson from M. Plick. A letter from Madame Ivanoff and from M. & S with money. Write to Madame M. Spend from five till ten in Casa Seratti — Mr. Harris there.

[83]      Beautiful statue — beautiful pedestal
        The Virtues are on foot — Vice on horseback.
[84] Act IV, scene 5.
[85] Perhaps Lacente. I have not been able to identify it.

# Fourth Journal

Friday February 1st. Call at Molini's and on Madame Orlandini who was not at home and at Lorenzi's. After dinner I am not well.

Saturday February 2nd. Practise. Festa of the Purification of the Virgin. Letters from Mad M enclosing one from Sk. St. and from Mad. Ivanoff — Write to Mad. I—

Sunday Feb. 3rd. Walk on the Terrace. Practise.

Monday Feb. 4th. Practise. At four o'clock the Bojti's return from Pisa. The Abate Pucci and Signor Puliti call.
A lesson from M. Plick. A letter from Mad M. and M. Write to M.

Wednesday Feb. 6th. Practise. Call upon Miss Farhill — La non C'era. And ⟨up⟩ in Casa Moselle whose little Girl is ill. The Doctor Bojti returns at three in the afternoon — Practise. A lesson from Herr Auspitz in the Evening.

X Thursday Feb. ⟨6th.⟩ 7th  No lesson from Signor Plich — Call upon Miss Farhill — Non C'è. Upon Marietta Moselle whose child is dead. A letter from S— M and Mrs. Williams. Write to Mad. M. Read Southey's and Lord B's squabble in Galignani [86] — Spend the Evening in Casa Boutourlin. Meet there Elise.[87]

Friday Feb. 8th. Practise. Call after dinner upon the Countess Tolomei. Mr. Harris there. In the Evening a lesson from Auspitz.

Saturday Feb. ⟨8th.⟩ 9th. A lesson from M. Plich. Practise. Spend the Evening in Casa Montemilleto. Miss Farhill, Signor Radi, Francesco Carradori, Benvenuti and Abate Panni there.

Sunday Feb. ⟨9th.⟩ 10th. Practise. La Sciarelli and Penelope call. Also Elise. Practise in the Evening. ⟨E's report of Naples and me⟩ [?] [88]

[86] On February 4 Mary wrote in her journal, "Southeys letter concerning L. B. Write to Claire" (in *Mary Shelley's Journal*, p. 166). Southey's letter (see Byron, *Works*, VI, 389–392) provoked Byron to offer a challenge through Douglas Kinnaird, who did not communicate it. Mary apparently sent on to Claire *Galignani's Messenger*, a Paris newspaper published in English to which the Shelleys subscribed.

[87] Elise Foggi, whose scandalous gossip to the Hoppners had caused so much distress to Mary and Shelley in August of 1821. Apparently Claire was not told about Elise's story but discovered it for herself from Elise on February 10.

[88] Claire worked extraordinarily hard to obliterate this line, by the very

# Florence 1822

Monday Feb. 11th. Spend a very unhappy day. La Sciarelli and Elise call. A lesson from Auspitz in the Evening.

Teusday Feb. 12th. A lesson from Plick. The Signora Orlandini calls. Letters from Vienna, M. and Mad M. Write to S— and Mad. M. Pay Plick.

Wednesday Feb ⟨12th.⟩ 13th Practise. The Bojti's dine at the Allodi's — In the Evening a lesson from Auspitz.

Thursday Feb. ⟨13th.⟩ 14th. A lesson from M. Plick. Write to my Mother. A letter from S. and Mad M. Spend the Evening in Casa Boutourlin — The Conte Velo of Vincenza there.

Friday Feb. ⟨14th.⟩ 15th. Practise. The Princess Montemilleto calls. In the Evening go with her ⟨to the C⟩ and Miss Farhill to the teatro del Cocomero. The Play of the Il Viaggio d'una donna di Spirite and an afterpiece called ⟨the⟩ Orfanello.[89] Signor Giuseppe Baldi and the Signor Giorgi there. Miss F— said — there were three ugly sisters to whom they gave the name of Battle, Murder and Sudden Death, and three others who were ⟨nick na⟩ nicknamed Plague, Pestilence and Famine.

Saturday Feb. 16th. No lesson from Plick. No letters. ⟨I stay in terrible anxiety all day.⟩

Sunday Feb. ⟨16th.⟩ 17th ⟨At nine o'clock⟩ a letter from S— [*one word thoroughly crossed out*] ⟨is too [?] slowly [?] gone.⟩[90] I spend a most wretched day. La Sciarelli and Penelope call.

Monday Feb. ⟨17th.⟩ 18th Miserable day. After dinner the Countess Tolomei calls with Nera and Gangia. Write to Albè.[91] No lesson from Auspitz.

---

efficient method of writing meaningless letters over her crossing out. I am fairly certain of my reading of all but the last word, which looks like *bini* and *guama* written over *me*. Infrared enlargements have been of some help.

[89] Giacomo Bonfio's one-act comedy. The afterpiece may have been Zinelli's *L'Orfanello* (1801).

[90] Presumably the messenger carrying Shelley's letter to her came too slowly, so that she sat in an agony of anticipation all day Saturday. I should guess that her anxiety was over how to cope with the news of Elise's gossip to the Hoppners, although it is possible that it is concerned with Allegra.

[91] This letter is printed by Dowden (*Shelley*, II, 484–486) from a rough draft in Claire's hand (now in the British Museum, Ashley 4752). In it she

# Fourth Journal

Teusday Feb. ⟨18th.⟩ 19th. No lesson from Plich — Send letter to Charles, Albè, S— Mad. M. and M.[92] Spend a miserable day.

Wednesday Feb. ⟨19th⟩ 20th. Call in Casa Boutourlin. Return and read Goldoni. Spend the Evening there. Packing up for Rome.[93] The Countess Varontzoff, Miss Lanz, Annette, the Countess Filippi, the Count and Countess Stackelberg, Conte Velo, Signor Benvenuti, Monsieur Svertckkopff, and Signor Grilli there.
When I return find Domenico Bini[94] arrived ⟨to fetch⟩ from Pisa to fetch me.

Thursday Feb. 21st. Set out for Pisa at ½ past eight where I arrive at six. See the Williams'es.

Friday Feb. 22nd. Fine bright Sunny day. Talk with M. all the morning. We dine at two. Mr. Medwin dines with us. At six go with Mr. Williams to Mad Mason's where I stay untill nine. Finish the Evening in Casa Williams. Mr. Trelawny there.[95]

Saturday Feb. 23rd. Fine Warm day. The Williams Mrs.[96] Medwin and Mr. Trelawny dine. Afterwards go with S— to Mrs. Mason's. Zanetti there.

Sunday Feb. 24th. Spend the Morning with the William's — Dine there with Mr. T. and Mr. M. Spend the Evening in Casa Silva.

---

expresses her desperate longing to see Allegra: "I assure you I can no longer resist the internal inexplicable feeling which haunts me that I shall never see her any more." She announces that she is shortly to leave Italy "for a new country to enter upon a disagreeable and precarious course of life; I yield in this not to my own wishes, but to the advice of a friend whose head is wiser than mine" (presumably Lady Mount Cashell).

[92] All of these letters no doubt announced her plan of going to Vienna. Mary's astonished answer tells Claire to come straight to Pisa the next morning (Mary Shelley, *Letters*, I, 157).

[93] A puzzle. Perhaps Claire was to meet a traveling companion in Rome. Perhaps some of her friends were packing for Rome.

[94] Dowden suggests that this is the Domenic of Shelley's "The Boat on the Serchio" (*Shelley*, II, 407n.). He carried Mary's letter to Claire.

[95] This is Claire's first meeting with Edward John Trelawny (1792–1881), with whom she was to enjoy a close relationship — sometimes affectionate, sometimes querulous — for the rest of her life.

[96] Claire's error for "Mr."

# Florence 1822

Monday Feb. 25th. Set off for Florence.[97] Arrive in Casa Bojti at six in the Evening. Dr. King a German there p.p.c pour Dresden.

Teusday Feb. 26th. Walk about seeking Mad. Watheld. Elise spends the Evening.

Wednesday Feb. 27th. Practise — Marietta and Clorinda call. After dinner call upon Madame Watheld or Whately. Elise calls in the Evening. I am not well.

Thursday Feb. 28th. Practise. Unwell all day. A lesson from Auspitz in the Evening. A letter from Mad. M   Write to S—

Friday ⟨February 29th.⟩ March 1st. Mrs. Whately ↑Watley↓, Miss Farhill call. After dinner the Tolomei's call. Practise. Spend the Evening in Casa Montemilleto. Miss Farhill, Signor Giuseppe Baldi, Count Antonelli, Signor Benci and Abate Panni there.

Saturday March 2nd. Fine day. Write to my mother — Elise calls. ⟨In⟩ A letter from Mary. In the Evening a lesson from Auspitz. and a note from the Princess ⟨Montemille⟩ Montemiletto Caraffa.

Sunday March 3rd. Call upon Miss Farhill — Go with her and the Abate Pagni and a young Italian Gentleman to Palazzo Borghese — There we meet the Princess M. and Signor Giuseppe Baldi — We see the Palace. Return at two. Elise spends the Evening. Read Hamlet.

Monday March 4th. Miss Farhill calls — also Elise — Spend the Evening in Casa Seratti.

Teusday March 5th. Send letters to Sk. St. and Charles. Call upon Elise and Mrs. Watley. After dinner write to M, and Mad. Ivanoff. Call in Casa Inirazzal and in Casa Fabbrini — A lesson from Auspitz. Pay the Bojti's.

Wednesday March 6th. Write German Exercises. Clorinda spends the morning. Spend the Evening in Casa Montemilletto — Signor Giuseppe Baldi, Signor Benci, and Conte Bagnese there.

X Thursday March 7th. Spend the Morning with Miss Farhill — Meet there the Abate Pagni and Signor Benci. A letter from Mad

[97] Her long talks with Mary and her friends seem to have reconciled her to returning to the Bojtis.

# Fourth Journal

M. and Mary. Write to S— and Madame M. Call upon Elise. A lesson from Auspitz. My spirits weak all day.

> In quoque littoribus nostris Enia nutrix
> Aeternam morieus famam Cajeta dedisti.[98]

Friday March 8th. Rainy day. Read Shakespeare. In the Evening Dr. Gonsani and Fabbrini call. Write German Exercises. Write to M. and Madame M.

Saturday March 9th. Fine day though some showers fall. Translate ⟨W⟩ a little of the life of Goethe.[99] Spend the Evening in Casa Fabbrini — Elise calls. — Miserable spirits all day.

Sunday March 10th. Clorinda spends the Morning. Read Romeo and Juliet.

> Shake the yoke of inauspicious stars
> From this world wearied flesh.[1]

Elise calls in the Evening. ⟨Give the Naples commission to her Husband.⟩[2] Miserable spirits.

[98] "On these our shores died Cajeta, nurse of Aeneas, which has given them eternal fame" (*Aeneid*, book vii, lines 1-2).

[99] Medwin quotes Byron as saying: "I have a great curiosity about every thing relating to Goethe, and please myself with thinking there is some analogy between our characters and writings. So much interest do I take in him, that I offered to give 100 *l.* to any person who would translate his 'Memoirs' for my own reading. Shelley has sometimes explained part of them to me" (*Conversations of Lord Byron*, ed. Lovell, p. 261). Goethe's *Aus meinem Leben: Dichtung und Wahrheit* appeared between 1811 and 1822 in Tübingen and Stuttgart. Claire undertook the translation for Byron, in circumstances made clear by Shelley's letter to her on March 24, 1822: "I am much pleased with yr. translation of Goethe which cannot fail to succeed if finished as begun — Lord B. thinks I have sent it to Paris to be translated & therefore does not yet expect copy. I shall of course have it copied out for him, & preserve your's to be sent to England" (Shelley, *Letters*, II, 401). On March 31 Shelley followed this with a letter in which he said: "Your translation of 'Goethe' is excellent. — I did not understand from you that your name was to be told to Lord B., and I must now adhere to the story already told. I am sure you will gain a great deal by it — if you go on as you have begun" (*ibid.*, II, 403; see also Mary Shelley, *Letters*, I, 192). By 1824 Henry Colburn in London had brought out a two-volume *Memoirs of Goethe: Written by Himself*, a paraphrase and abridgement of a French translation of the previous year. No more became of Claire's translation, though for several years her friends urged her to continue with it.

[1] Act V, scene 3.

[2] This passage was nearly obliterated. The suggested reading is not absolutely certain, and if it is correct its exact significance is still not clear to me.

# Florence 1822

Monday March 11th. Write from Goëthe — Call upon La Signora Orlandini, and in Piazza San Lorenzo, ↑also↓ upon Mrs. Watheld. Non c'era. After dinner call upon Mrs. Waltheld and spend an hour with her and her husband. Return at seven and go to the Princess Monte⟨ml ml⟩milletto's. Miss Farhill, Signor Giuseppe Baldi, Francesco Carradori, Abate Pagni, and Signor Benci there.

Teusday March 12th. Translate Göthe. La Signora Orlandini calls — Call with her upon Mrs. Watheld. The Signor Bianchi dines. A letter from S— and Mad M. ⟨Wa⟩ Elise calls. A lesson from Auspitz.

Wednesday March 13th. ⟨W⟩ Write German Exercises. Clorinda calls — Go with her a shopping all the Morning. After dinner Translate Goethe.

Thursday March 14th. A note from Miss Farhill. ⟨Write⟩ Translate Göthe. After dinner Mrs. Watheld calls. also Elise. A lesson from Auspitz in the Evening. Write to M. Send 1st. sheet of Göthe.

Friday March 15th. Translate Göthe. Call with Mrs. Watheld upon the Orlandini. ⟨Then⟩ Returning I meet the Tolomei's and go with them to the Princess Argyropoulo's ⟨Bo⟩ Casa Peruzzi, Borgo dei Greci. Translate Göthe in the Evening.

Saturday March 16th. Translate Göthe. A letter from M. Write to her. A lesson from Auspitz. Very bad Spirits.

Sunday March 17th. Clorinda spends the Morning. Translate Göthe.

Monday March 18th. ↑A lesson from Auspitz.↓ Translate Göthe. Elise spends the Evening — She writes to Mad Hoppner.[3]

Teusday March 19th. Festa of San Giuseppe. Clorinda spends the

[3] Claire and Mary wished Elise to write to Mrs. Hoppner denying that she had told her what, indeed, she must have told her about Shelley and Claire. One purpose of such a letter would be to avert any possible future blackmail. On April 12 (below) Claire was still trying to get the letter written, having written on April 9 to ask Mary: "I wish you would write me back what you wish Elise to say to you and what she is to say to Mad. H[oppner]. I have tried in vain to compose it" (printed in *Shelley and Mary*, III, 778). Elise's two notes of denial are dated April 12 and have been printed by John Murray in *Lord Byron's Correspondence*, II, 190–191.

# Fourth Journal

Morning. A letter from M. enclosing one from Mrs. Gisborne.[4] Write to M. Dine at the Fabbrini's. Signor Passerini, Marietta Moselle, Signora Salucci [Tolmei?] there.

Wednesday March 20th. A lesson from Auspitz. Call upon Elise and Miss Farhill. ⟨Call⟩ As I walk home meet the Signora Luisa Fabbrini. After dinner call upon Mrs. Watheld — Non c'era. At eight Miss Farhill calls for me. We go to the Princess's. She is not well. Conte Bagnese, Signor Carradori, Abate Pagni and Signor Benci there. The two latter walk home with us.

Thursday March 21st. Translate Göthe. A letter from M. & S— Write a long letter to M. At four o'clock Miss F— calls. We walk ⟨to⟩ by Poggia Imperiale to the Cascina dei Ricci — where we drink Milk and then home by Santa Margherita and Porta San Niccolo — We arrive at her house at ½ past seven. Drink tea there and then ↑I↓ return home. The ⟨Bob⟩ Bojti children sick of the measles.

Friday March 22nd. A lesson from Auspitz. Pay him down to this day. Translate Göthe. After dinner Elise calls. I have a violent tooth-ache in the Evening.

Saturday ⟨March⟩ March 23rd. Translate and send 2nd Sheet of Göthe. ⟨Miss⟩ Write a note to Mad. Watheld. Miss Farhill calls. High wind all day. ⟨A⟩ letter from M. Write to her and Mad M. Spend the Evening in Casa ⟨Montemilleto⟩ Montemiletto. The Princess not well. ⟨Si⟩ Miss Farhill, Signor Giuseppe Baldi, Signor Francesco Carradori, Signor Santarelli and Abate Pagni there.

Sunday March 24th. Clorinda calls. Also Mr⟨s⟩. and Mrs. Watheld. After dinner there is the corso from Porta Romana to Ponte St. Trinita. Translate a little of Göthe.

Monday March 25th. Festa of the Santissima Annunziata. Clorinda spends the Morning. Translate Göthe. Spend the Evening with Mr. and Mrs. Watheld.

Teusday March 26th. Finish copying Göthe. A letter from M. S—[5]

[4] Mary's journal for Sunday, March 17, records: "Walk with Jane — Write to Claire — dine at the W's. very weary" (Abinger MSS.). The entry given for that date in *Mary Shelley's Journal*, p. 174, corresponds to Mary's entry for March 18 in the MSS.

[5] This is an answer to a letter outlining a wild scheme for abducting Allegra

and Mad M. An Account of a fuss at the Gate of the Porta delle Spiazze — Write to M and send 3rd sheet of Göthe. Read in the Evening I Mercanti[6] and Le Donne Curiose di Goldoni.

Wednesday March 27th. No lesson from Auspitz. Call ⟨in V⟩ on the Banker Wolff.[7] ⟨Sp⟩ Spend the Day in Casa Tolomei. Read Mad. de la Valliere by Mad. Du Genlis.[8] We go to the Pergola. The farce of the Astrologer and the Play of Il Matrimonio per Concourso.[9]

Thursday March 28th. A letter from M. Write to her. Spend the Evening in Casa Fabbrini. The Signor Carlo Passerini there and Miss Bani. Clorinda ill with a frignolo.[10]

Friday March 29th. Read Il Poeta Fanatico di Goldoni. I am very idle all day. Spend the Evening in Casa ⟨Mote⟩ Montemiletto. M. & Madame Wolff and Mad. Müller (Swiss), Abate Pagni and Signor Francesco Carradori there. Abate Pagni walks home with me. Luisa ed Annina sick with the measles.

Saturday March 30th. Call upon Miss Farhill. "A man's beauty is ⟨hl⟩ all hill and dale and the country about Brighton." A letter from M. Write to her and Mad. M. Mrs. Watheld calls in the Evening. Also Doctor Bojti.

(see Shelley, Letters, II, 399–401). Shelley expressed himself as "shocked at the thoughtless violence of your designs," which would have involved a forged letter and probably a duel with Byron. He tentatively encouraged her plan to go to Vienna and offered her excellent advice: "Give up this idle pursuit after shadows, & temper yourself to the season; seek in the daily & affectionate intercourse of friends a respite from these perpetual & irritating projects. Live from day to day, attend to your health, cultivate literature & liberal ideas to a certain extent, & expect that from time & change which no exertions of your own can give you." At the same time as Shelley's letter, Claire received one from Mary recounting the affair with the dragoon which Claire mentions in the next sentence (the episode is fully treated in Cline, Byron, Shelley and Their Pisan Circle).

[6] I Due Pantaloni o i mercatanti.

[7] Shelley had just sent her sixty francesconi, six more than her income (Shelley, Letters, II, 401).

[8] Stéphanie Félicité Brulart de Genlis, La Duchesse de la Vallière, 2 vols. (London, 1804).

[9] By Goldoni.

[10] Frignolo = fignolo, a boil or tumor.

# Fourth Journal

Sunday March 31st. Read Il Matrimonio per Concorso di Goldoni. The weather changes to cold and rain. Nurse the Children.

Monday ⟨March⟩ April 1st. Black windy Day—and very cold. Call upon Miss Farhill with Doctor B. Then shop in Mercato Nuovo and Vacchereccia After dinner work—at six Miss F. calls and we walk to the Villa of the Princess M—beyond Bello Squardo where we spend untill ten and then return. Signor Giuseppe Baldi there. A clergyman in his Sermon defended the character of Solomon saying he was a libertine upon a principle of Enquiry.

Teusday April 2nd. A letter from M. S—[11] Mad M. and Miss Boutourlin. The weather still cold. Write to M.

Wednesday April 3rd. Translate Göthe all day. Call upon Elise. The weather is very bleak. Write to Mad. Ivanoff.

X Thursday April 4th. Holy Thursday. Bitter bleak weather. The Tolomei's call. I am unwell with a cough and do nothing all day. A letter from S—

Friday April 5th. Good Friday. Pay the Bojti's.
> Cada L'indigno, e miri
> Fra gli ultimi sospiri
> La man che lo svenò.
> Mora; ne poi mi duole
> Che a me tramonti il sole
> Se il giorno a lui mancò.[12]

Call upon Miss Farhill. Story of Mrs. Bodwin and Signor Tonelli. After dinner upon Mrs. Watheld. Captain Henning there. Mrs. W— walks home with me.

Saturday April 6th. Warm weather. Unwell with a cough. Mrs. Watheld calls about four. Spend the Evening in Casa Fabbrini Marietta Moselle and Signor Passerini there.

Sunday April 7th. Easter Sunday. Rain all day. I am unwell with a cough. Translate Göthe. Elise calls for a moment.

[11] See Shelley, *Letters*, II, 402–403.
[12] "Let the unworthy one fall, and during the final sighs let the hand that killed him take aim. Let him die; but then it pains me that for me the sun should set when his light has been put out." I have not identified these lines.

# Florence 1822

Chi ha il neo in collo
E figlio d'un rompicollo,
Chi ha il neo e non lo vede
E bello e non lo crede [13]

Monday April 8th. Rainy weather. A lesson from Auspitz. Copy and Translate the fourth sheet of Göthe. Elise calls in the Evening. Low spirits.

Teusday April 9th. Low spirits. Send Göthe—Write to M.[14] Clorinda and her mother and the Bani call. The Doctor calls in the Evening.

Wednesday April 10th. Pay Rosa. A lesson from Auspitz. It rains all day—Go notwithstanding with Geppina Geloni to buy a gown in Mercato Nuovo. Read Göthe.

Thursday April 11th. A letter from M & S.[15] Write to them. Clorinda and the Bani call. Mr. & Mrs. Watheld spend from four to six.

Friday April 12th. Call upon Elise—to write the letter to Madame H.[16] Call upon Clorinda. Spend the Evening with Mrs. Watheld. Monsieur Aimè Revoire there. We play at Cards. No lesson from Auspitz.

Saturday April 13th. Write to Madame Ivanoff and Miss Boutourlin. Walk to the Post. After dinner a shopping with my hostess. At the ventiquattro the Misericordia come to fetch Vincenzio who is ill of a mal di petto.[17] Then I go to Casa Montemiletto with the Fabbrini's. Signor G. Baldi, Carradori Abate Pagni, Signor San-

---

[13]     He who has a mole on his neck
         Is the son of a rash fellow,
         He who has a mole and can't see it
         Is handsome, but doesn't believe it
I have not identified these lines.

[14] Her letter says that she wishes to come to Pisa, now that the worst gossips (Mrs. Beauclerc and Medwin) have left there (*Shelley and Mary*, III, 776–778).

[15] Shelley's letter invited Claire to join them for the summer (Shelley, *Letters*, II, 403–404).

[16] See Note 3 to entry of March 18, above.

[17] Chest ailment (usually tuberculosis).

tarelli & Miss Farhill there. Walk home with Miss F and Abate Pagni. ⟨Learn that Albè is arrived in Florence.⟩ [18]

Friday the 6th. of September.[19]

[18] She was mistaken, as the journal of Edward Williams shows. The rest of this page is blank except for Dowden's transcription of the crossed-out line and his addition of the words "Allegra ob. 20 Apr. 1822" in brackets.

On April 15 Claire went to Pisa and on April 23 set off with the Williamses to find a house on the Gulf of Spezzia. While they were gone the Shelleys heard that Allegra had died at the Convent of Bagnacavallo on April 19. To delay breaking the news they rushed both families to Spezzia, but on May 2, by Williams' account, Claire had guessed the worst. Her first spasms of grief gave way to a new tranquility, and on May 21 she returned to Florence, rejoining the Shelleys and Williamses on June 7. Claire and Jane Williams in this brief period of calm became close friends, and Claire was devoted to the children, Rosalind (Dina) and Edward Medwin (Meddy). On October 24 Claire looked back in a letter to Jane from Vienna: "I have lost *my dear den* that I had with you where I soothed and recovered my spirits by songs and thoughts which approached or drew me towards the world of imagination, so different from the real round substantial globe we inhabit" (unpublished letter, Abinger MSS.). See Appendix D for an anonymous fictionalized account, in a similar style, of this calm interlude before the storm that was to destroy or scatter them. On July 8 Shelley and Edward Williams were drowned off Viareggio. Through the rest of the summer the three women clung together. Then, on September 20, Claire began her long-planned journey to join her brother in Vienna. (For this interval, see Shelley, *Letters*, II, 413–445; *Mary Shelley's Journal*, pp. 177–180; Mary Shelley, *Letters*, I, 168–192; Gisborne and Williams, *Journals*, pp. 143–156; and *Shelley and Mary*, III, 800–869.)

[19] This date stands alone on an otherwise blank page, indicating a day of memorable happiness with Trelawny (see her recollection of it three years later in her entry of August 25 [September 6], 1825, below). Trelawny had fought Claire's departure from Italy and had implored her to stay and attach herself to him. His first letters to her contain violently emotional offers of friendship and love. On December 4 [1822?] he wrote, "I loved you from the first day, — nay before I saw you, — you loathed and heaped on me contumelies and neglect *till we were about to separate*" (Trelawny, *Letters*, p. 30; italics mine). On April 20, 1823, he wrote that though poverty, sickness, or sorrow should cling to her, there was one who "will receive you, and press you to his bosom with the same undiminished ardour he did when he first pressed you there" (unpublished passage in the British Museum, Ashley MSS. 5119). Forman, who omitted this and several similar passages from his edition of the letters, used to think that some one passage in the letters indicated that Claire had actually become Trelawny's mistress. None of the omitted passages in the Ashley MSS. seems to me to warrant this conclusion, though Claire has rendered several unreadable with crossing out, and certainly there was a brief but passionate interlude of

# Italy 1822

Thursday September. 19th.[20] Get up at seven. After breakfast call upon the Marchese Guadagni—go with him to Balzani's—Dine at Borelli's 1126 Porta Rossa. It comes on to rain in torrents about four o'clock, notwithstanding which I go with Mr. Borelli to Balzani's to sign the scrittura. Then to buy stockings. Go to bed at eleven.

Friday September 20th. Get up at five. Pack. Breakfast. It pours with rain. The carriage comes at ten with a Russian gentlemen and a fat Bolognese woman who looks to be a Jewess—⟨We⟩ and Giuseppe and Francesco for Vetturini. We set out for Bologna. During the first part of the road I was too occupied with my own thoughts to attend to the scenery. I remembered how hopelessly I had lingered on the Italian soil for five years, waiting ever for a favorable change ↑instead of which↓ ⟨and⟩ I was now leaving it, ⟨after⟩ having ⟨lost every object of⟩ buried there every thing that I loved. We stopped to dine at Tagliaferro, where we rested two hours and then again set forward. Notwithstanding the rain which came by fits very heavy, I walked up the steep hills, hoping by fatigue of body to dull the painful activity of mind with which I found myself troubled. The scenery was pretty of itself, but rendered to me beautiful by the dark & gloomy character ⟨th⟩ it had borrowed from the fast approaching wintry season. Small hills rise on every side, and the road winds mounting, through ⟨there⟩ ↑their↓ innumerable ↑⟨vallies⟩ & yet small vallies↓ ⟨may the eye⟩ whose

---

mutual attachment of some sort before Claire realized the futility of their relationship and fled. Rosalie Glynn Grylls, who has had access to the entire Forman collection, has found there no further evidence (see her *Trelawny*, p. 101). Claire summarized their relationship astutely in a letter to Mary, March 28, 1830: "There is a certain want of sympathy between us which makes writing to ⟨me⟩ him extremely disagreeable to me. I admire esteem and love him; some excellent qualities he possesses in a degree that is unsurpassed, but then it is exactly in another direction from my centre and my impetus. He likes a turbid and troubled life; I a quiet one; he is full of fine feelings and has no principles; I am full of fine principles but never had a feeling ⟨in my life⟩. He receives ⟨every⟩ all his impressions through his heart; I through my head. *Che vuole* ? *Le moyen de se rencontrer* when one is bound for the North Pole and the other for the South" (Abinger MSS.; printed, with some differences, in *Shelley and Mary*, IV, 1128).

[20] Claire was about to leave from Florence. See her letter to Mary, September 11 (Marshall, *Mary Shelley*, II, 29–30), and Mary's reply (Mary Shelley, *Letters*, I, 191–192).

# Fourth Journal

〈greatest charm consisted in their excessive variety of character〉 which sometimes widen into a plain, and whose greatest charm consists in the varied scenery they present. Platforms of green 〈an〉 fertility, and 〈little〉 groves of 〈the most bea〉 chesnut-trees mingled with the more tender green of poplars, ash and beech 〈are sprinkled clothe the sides of the hills〉 are sprinkled here & there over the almost immeasurable prospect & relieve the eye from the contemplation of its otherwise barren rocky soil. I saw one or two 〈conv〉 monasteries situated as is usual in the most choice spots. One near the road side ↑from which it was↓ separated only by a line of cypress trees of the most venerable appearance. To the left it looked across the road over an undulating plain richly cultivated and of the most varied appearance 〈whilst〉 ↑and↓ on the right 〈into a valley〉 over the heads of smaller hills heaped in masses around unto a boundary line of majestic Appenines darkened into the deepest 〈shade〉 ↑hue↓ by the ↑shadows of the↓ black clouds which hang〈ing〉 over ↑upon↓ their summits 〈threw their tremendous shades upon their sides.〉 We continued thus our journey untill about seven in the evening The 〈fo〉 white fog which as we mounted had been always encreasing now became so dense as to hide the road from our eyes. The 〈W〉 Vetturini got down & lead the horses step by step when we reached a cottage where we were obliged nay even glad to take up our night's rest. It was very poor and so dirty, the dark, 〈w〉 vaulted kitchen looked like a cavern of Hell. I did not attempt to go to bed but lent

*[here follow fourteen blank pages]*

## Indian Song.[21]

---

Mootrib i K'hoosh nuwa bigo, tazu bu tazu now bu now,
Badue dil Khoosha bidih, tazu bu tazu now bu now.
K'hoosh binusheen bu Kilwuter, chung nuwaz sa utee
Bosee sutam bu Kam uzo, tazu bu tazu now bu now.

[21] Gazel iii from the *Divan* of Hafiz. The first twelve lines, in Persian, are written sideways on the page, with the title along the left margin. On April 2, 1822, Shelley had written to Claire: "Mary will . . . send you the Indian air, either by this post or the next" (Shelley, *Letters*, II, 403). Medwin wrote of Jane Williams: "Shelley was particularly fond of music, and delighted in her simple airs, some of which she had brought with her, in memory, from the East. For her were composed the exquisite lines, 'I arise from dreams of thee,'

286

# Italy 1822

Bur zi hy at Ky K'horee? gur nu budam my K'horee?
Badu by Khoor bu zadi zo, tazu bu tazu now bu now.
Sag'ee sum sag'i mun, amudu ganib e' chumun
Zood Ki poor koonum sooboo, tazu bu tazu now bu now.
Shahid i dil Khoosha'e, mun; muckoonud uz fida'e, mun,
Nugsh i ze aub o rungi boo, tazu bu tazu now bu now
Badi suba choo būzzuree, bur suri Koee an puree
Quip'ee Hafiz ush bigo, tazu bu tazu now bu now —

---

⟨Indian Song⟩

---

*Mootrib i K'hoosh nuwa bigo, tazu*
— Songster sweet begin the lay
—      Ever fresh and ever gay
— Bring the joy inspiring wine
— Ever fresh and ever fine

2

With a heart alluring lass,
    Gaily let the moments pass,
Kisses stealing when you may;
Ever fresh and ever gay.

3.

Gentle Boy, whose silver feet
    Nimbly move to cadence sweet,
Fill as quick the gen'rous wine
    Ever fresh and ever fine.

4

How enjoy life's tedious ⟨pow⟩ hour
    Without wine's seducing pow'r?
These will make them pass away
    Ever fresh and ever gay.

adapted to the celebrated Persian air sung by the Knautch girls, '*Tazee be tazee no be no*' " (Medwin, *Shelley*, pp. 317–318). Just to hear the first chords of this song on the harp a year later in London was more than Mary could bear, so clearly did it call up the memory of Shelley's voice (Mary Shelley, *Letters*, I, 256). A verse translation and prose paraphrase of this ode may be found in *Persian Lyrics, or Scattered Poems, from the Diwan-i-Hafiz*, trans. Hindley (London, 1800), pp. 40–42, 82.

# Fourth Journal

### 5.

To me the sweet enchanting Maid
Charms devotes that never fade,
Charms to inspire her Poets song
Ever fresh and ever young.

### 6

Zephyr's while you gently move,
By the mansion of my love,
Softly Hafiz's strains repeat
Ever new and ever sweet.[22]

For an Ague ——————— Dr. Warren [23]

1 Oz of the best red Bark.
1 Nutmeg grated
1 Tablespoonful of beaten blk. Pepper.
1 ——————— of Coarse Sugar
To be mixed with Syrup of Poppies into an Electuary —
A large ↑Tea↓ Spoonful to be taken as Soon as the Fit is quite off
and to be repeated every half hour that the whole quantity may be
taken in 24 Hours — An Emetic is to be taken the Evening before
the Fit is expected —
Half the quantity for a Child —

-----

Wer hast gegeben der Saga [24]
diesse rosse.
Wie viel haare haben sie.
Ich freue mich sie wieder ↑zu↓ sehen
    Wir willen

                   No. 30 Sans peur et sans reproche
die Zeit ist verstrichen
die frau des hofzuckerbäckereygefühlen

[22] Sideways on the page beside the song are the numbers 13710 and 174,202.
[23] The following recipe in another hand is pasted into the journal.
[24] This and the following are on the inside of the back cover, clearly used
for scribbling. The German and the word "Head" are in German script. Some
suggested translations are as follows: "Who has given the saga of this horse."
"How many hairs have you." "I am happy to see you again." "We wish." "No.
30 Fearless and irreproachable." "The time has elapsed." "The woman of
court-confectioner's feelings." "Medical councillor's wife."

# Italy 1822

Head.

a Large

Medicinalräthin.      Alessandro Manzoni.

author of the Conte di Carmagnola.

Sunday May 27th. at three or four o'clock.

fiss — 1 fedelin

fidelin

Angella

# FIFTH
# JOURNAL
*May 12 (24), 1825, to January 2 (14), 1826*

# [1822-1825]

Life in the Austrian capital was friendly, and when Claire arrived, in October 1822, she was warmly received. The city was then at the height of the glory that present-day Viennese and tourists so sentimentally celebrate. In her brother Claire found perfect sympathy: "He is so quiet, good, and mild, that we quite suit one another; and then he allows me to be as wild, and extravagant as I please in my theories."[1] Claire stayed with Madame Jeannette de Henickstein, an extremely agreeable woman whom she had known in Pisa, probably the sister-in-law of the Orientalist Joseph Freiherr von Hammar-Purgstall.[2] All five of the other people who lived there wanted English lessons, and Claire found herself with more than enough to do. Nevertheless, as time went on she discovered more and more difficulties — all very real indeed — to deprive her of the security she had hoped to find in Vienna.

Her first problem was financial, since she was never able to procure a government license to teach. Charles was unable to support her, and the money sent by Mary and Trelawny she hated to accept. Godwin realized that Claire was much worse off than Mary, but to help her was beyond his power. Mr. Tighe and Lady Mount Cashell, living modestly on their small stipends, and with

[1] Abinger MSS., October 24, 1822. Trelawny, too, liked what he knew of Charles: "There is an honesty and romance about him mingled with just enough of worldliness and feeling and talent — I should like much to know him" (Trelawny, *Letters*, p. 23).

[2] Huscher, "Charles und Claire Clairmont," *Englische Studien*, 76:61 (1944).

two daughters approaching marriageable age, could not undertake the responsibility, much as they would have liked to. Lady Mount Cashell, however, had a practical idea. Sincerely worried about the possibility of Claire's starving in a strange land, she took it upon herself to write to Byron, whom she had never met, to suggest that he do something for the bereaved mother of his child.[3] Byron had been genuinely grieved by Allegra's death and had acceded to all of Claire's pitiful last requests. He had a certain amount of respect for Lady Mount Cashell's opinions, even without having met her, for in advising Mary Shelley against a trip to see about Shelley's will he had written, "You can consult Mrs. Mason, and regulate yourself by the mechanism of 'Claire's Minerva.'"[4] But in return for her good intentions Lady Mount Cashell received an insult: Byron wrote her a curt refusal with "a sting in its tail." Lady Mount Cashell wrote to Mary that she had thought until then that Byron had behaved wisely about Allegra: "I am an old woman & something of a philosopher — and I no more give full credit to the ravings of an angry Poet than I do to those of a disappointed girl — I thought better of Lord B— before I received his letter (or I should never have written to him) but a person who can lightly doubt of the *solemn assurance* of another, casts a reproach upon his own integrity."[5]

Lady Mount Cashell tried again to make her position clear to him, but with no better results. She then wrote to Mary: "No doubt you have heard from Lord B— of his having written to me again — As it is impossible that he should understand me, I will not trouble him with any more letters, but shall be much obliged to you if you will tell him *that I give full credit to his assurances of not meaning to offend me, that I thank him for his good opinion, & am glad we part in peace* — I see he totally mistakes my motives, looking on me as a mere partizan of C—, when in truth my first letter to him (the offspring of cool reflection) was produced as much by respect for genius, as by compassion for misfortune — Let C—'s conduct have been what it may, the story of A— is that which has published her imprudence to the world; & if she comes to any fatal end for want of means of subsistence, it will remain

[3] Marchand, *Byron*, III, 1049–1050.
[4] Abinger MSS., September 10, 1822.
[5] Abinger MSS., postmarked January 13 [1823].

an eternal reproach on the character of Lord B— Having heard of the furious letter from Lerici as well as others of a similar nature, had I not considered him as a high-minded man I should never have applied to him in her behalf — but I had some vague idea that a noble generosity, combined with a tender recollection of the departed babe, would have induced him to settle some small annuity on the Mother; who if she be what he asserts her, has even stronger claims on a benevolent heart than a person conscious of upright feelings & with no cause of self-reproach but weakness in conduct — As Lord B— has confided this affair to you, I hope with your aid he will yet be persuaded to do what he may one day rejoice to have done." [6]

There was apparently widespread discussion about Byron's obligation to Claire. Hogg wrote to Jane Williams, "I cannot doubt that the Giaour will do for C. what he promised: his evil Genius will compel him to do it with a bad grace; he will lose both the gain of a bad action & the credit of a good one." [7] The fact that Claire had been right about Allegra, when all reason and all reasonable friends had reassured him of the wisdom of his behavior toward the child, must have been insufferably bitter. What Byron "promised," possibly in a conversation with Mary, was never carried out.

Claire's troubles in Vienna were not only financial; she was also for a while desperately ill. Apparently when she looked back on it Claire decided that Vaccà had been right: the inflammation of her glands was tubercular. Years later she wrote to her sister-in-law: "Our family is consumptive and very delicate; our vivacity, our readiness to oblige, our energy gives us an appearance of strength which we do not possess. I was dying ten times from twenty to thirty-six. . . . I nearly died at Vienna when I was four-and-twenty — I grew skeleton thin — I had constant low fever — I could not eat — and this for months and my Brother wrote to Mrs. S[helley] that he did not think she would ever see me again." [8]

One must allow for exaggeration after thirty-four years, but it does appear that Claire was alarmingly ill in Vienna. Lady Mount

[6] Abinger MSS., January 14, 1823. See also McAleer, *The Sensitive Plant,* pp. 173–177.

[7] Hogg, *After Shelley,* ed. Norman, p. 10.

[8] Clairmont MSS., July 12, 1856.

# Fifth Journal

Cashell showed one of her letters to Vaccà and Tantini, and both were much disturbed. She wrote to Mary, "Tantini says her only chance, if she holds out till spring, is to go & live in the sea (which she is so fond of) like a mermaid — if Lord B— will supply her with the means of doing so comfortably, I shall forgive him every-thing."[9] Mary sent money for medical assistance immediately, and despite the dreary prognosis Claire managed to get through the winter.

The third horror of the Viennese winter was political. No sooner had Claire arrived than she and Charles were dogged by police spies, set on by an anonymous letter to the police reporting that these two English had been associated with the notorious sub-versives, Godwin and Shelley. Metternich's agents worked thor-oughly, and the tremendous quantity and detailed quality of the Dossier Clairmont are astonishing even by present-day standards of red tape and paper work.[10] Jane Williams heard from Mrs. God-win that, as Jane put it, Claire and Charles "had been ordered to quit Vienna in five days. This after her reception is an enigma I cannot solve. Poor girl, her bitter destiny still pursues her." Then before she had finished her letter to Mary, Jane had heard further from Mrs. Godwin that the orders had been revoked but that "the police were still annoying them: it seems that the Emperor has lately published an edict to prevent the establishment of foreign Instructors both male and female particularly the English, so that their prospects there are very gloomy."[11] Charles finally managed to get a license to teach, and he went on to a distinguished aca-demic career in Vienna.

For Claire, however, there seemed to be nothing but in-security. Even her sanctuary with Madame de Henickstein, where she lived on the footing of a friend of the house, lost what little security it had promised. Charles wrote to Mary: "The old grand-mother died; Mrs. H[enickstein]'s sister-in-law dying; one of the daughters extremely ill; the bridegroom of the other, to whom she was to have been married in a week, or two, changes his mind and

[9] Abinger MSS., postmarked February 6, 1823.

[10] Grylls has discussed this aspect of Claire's Viennese sojourn thoroughly in *Claire Clairmont*, pp. 165–175. See also Huscher, "Charles und Claire Clair-mont," *Englische Studien*, 76:61ff. (1944).

[11] Abinger MSS., December 22, 1822.

leaves the poor girl in the lurch." [12] Everything conspired to make the end of Claire's stay in Vienna as miserable as possible.

Claire's decision to go to Russia, in defiance of her poor health and the advice and entreaties of all her friends, seems suicidal until one realizes how uncomfortable she had been in Vienna. Even so, her departure was exactly what Trelawny called it: "Compulsive emigration to the North." Charles attempted to explain the decision to Mary: "She has . . . almost closed an agreement with the Countess Zotoff, daughter of Prince Kurakin one of the Russian Ministers, to go to Petersburg. She gives but about £75. The Countess pleases us both but you know the Russians are not much to be depended on. She has two beautiful daughters of 14 & 16 whose companion Claire is to be rather than Governess. But C[laire] is in great hopes that as the girls in Russia marry early, they will soon be off hand and that then, as the Countess' health is not robust, she may be tempted to go and fix in Italy or some warm climate." [13]

On March 22, 1823, Claire left Vienna and traveled north with the Countess. For nearly a year nobody heard from her. Mary was disturbed, but knowing Claire as well as she did she suspected that the silence was motivated by a love of mystery and suspense. By the spring of 1824 Claire was settled in Moscow as governess to the children of Zachar Nicolaivitch, a prosperous lawyer, and his strongminded wife, Marie Ivanovna. Life was a far cry from the companionship of the Shelleys which she had for so many years enjoyed, but it was not without its compensations. She undoubtedly believed herself miserable, and she certainly had the usual periods of depression and sometimes of ill health, but on the whole her journal for eight months of 1825 shows that she had a busy and entertaining life. While she constantly deplored the character of the Russian people, several of them became her lifelong friends.

Claire's letters and journals provide a vivid picture of the life of a governess in a wealthy Russian family. "Never any where," she wrote to Jane Williams, "did quarrelling flourish as in Russia — every house is in a state of civil war — as every child has its governess, and each governess is of a different nation: each pursues her own mode and method, and such a system affords no center of re-

[12] Abinger MSS., February 22, 1823.
[13] Abinger MSS., February 22, 1823.

pose to the eternal jarring of their ideas, manners, and languages." [14]
The educational principles of Mary Wollstonecraft, with their emphasis on reason and affection, had been taken for granted in the
Godwin household, and since Mary Wollstonecraft had been Lady
Mount Cashell's governess, Claire had recently had these principles
reaffirmed. Needless to say, they were not taken for granted in Russia. "A tutor is ten thousand times happier than a governess," Claire
wrote to Mary, "because boys may jump and play, but girls must
always be in a perpetual state of etiquette, which constraint spoils
their disposition, by forcing it from its natural channel into a narrow
space." She and the Russians were always at cross-purposes, she
continued, because "they pull one way, and I another — they edu-
cate a child by making the external work upon the internal, which
is, in fact, nothing but an education fit for monkies, and is a mere
system of imitation — I want the internal to work upon the external; that is to say, that my pupil should be left at liberty as
much as possible, and that her own reason should be the prompter
of her actions." [15] In the long run, Claire's methods were a distinct
success. Looking back in 1827 on her earlier career in Moscow,
Claire told Jane Williams: "I came here quite unknown, I was at
first ill-treated on that account, but I soon acquired a great reputation because all my pupils made much more progress in whatever
they undertook than those of other people." [16] The fortunate re-
cipient of Claire's attention and affection was the daughter of
Marie Ivanovna and Zachar Nicolaivitch, five-year-old Dunia,
just the age Allegra had been at her death.

Another solace to Claire in her years in Moscow was the warm
and faithful friendship of Chrétien-Hermann Gambs, tutor to
Dunia's brother John. In a letter to Jane, October 27, 1825, Claire
described him: "I have lately made acquaintance with a german
gentleman, who is a great resource to me; in such a country as
Russia, Where nothing but the vulgarest people are to be met, a
cultivated mind is the greatest treasure; his society recalls our former circle, for he is well versed in ancient & modern litterature

[14] Abinger MSS., September 11, 1824 (O.S.), from a copy of a transcript
in the hand of Mr. Gisborne.
[15] Abinger MSS., April 29, 1825, from a copy of a transcript in the hand of
Mr. Gisborne.
[16] Abinger MSS., postmarked January 22, 1827.

# Introduction

and has the same noble enlarged way of thinking. You may imagine
how delighted he was to find me, so different from every thing
around him and capable of understanding what had been sealed
up so long in his mind as treasures to precious to be wasted on the
coarse russian soil. I talk to you thus freely about him because I
know you will not believe that I am in love, or that I have any
other feeling but that of a most sincere & steady friendship for
him. What you felt for Shelley, I feel for him. I feel it also my duty
to tell you I have a real friend, because in case of sickness or death,
happening to me, you would at least feel the consolation of knowing that I had not died in the hands of strangers. I talk to him very
often of you, & of Mary ⟨&⟩ untill his desire to see you becomes
quite a passion; he is like all germans very sentimental, a very
sweet temper & uncommonly generous. His attachment to me is
extreme, but I have taken the very greatest care to explain to ⟨me⟩
him, that I cannot return it in the same degree; this does not make
him unhappy and therefore our friendship is of the utmost importance to both." [17]

Chrétien-Hermann Gambs was the eldest child of a Strasbourg
pastor, Karl Christian Gambs (1759–1822),[18] and Claire's journal
and letters provide an attractive picture of the young Hermann,
intellectual and poet, who reminded her in many ways of Shelley.
Her later letters give no hint of a continuation of their friendship,
however, so that it comes as quite a surpise to find, ten years later,
the poetry of Hermann Gambs appearing in considerable quantity under the pseudonym of "C. Clairmont." One can find three
of these volumes in the Bibliothèque Nationale in Paris, all under
the pseudonym of C. Clairmont.[19] Two further works, which I

---

[17] Abinger MSS., quoted in Marshall, *Mary Shelley*, II, 145–146.

[18] The senior Gambs was from 1784 to 1806 chaplain to the Swedish legation
in Paris, pastor of the Ansgariikirche in Bremen from 1807 to 1814, and from
the fall of Napoleon (1814) until his own death, September 12, 1822, *Pfarrer*
(minister) to the Aurelienkirche in his native Strasbourg (*Autobiographie des
Pfarrers Karl Christian Gambs* [1909]). After Hermann, who was of age at his
father's death, came two sisters, Ida, who later married C. Reichard, and Henriette, who married C. Frommel, father of the court preacher and enormously
popular author Emil Wilhelm Frommel (1828–1896). There was also a younger
brother, still a schoolboy in 1822.

[19] *Moïse* (Paris: C. Gosselin, 1836), an "epic in twelve cantos"; *Vladimir et
Zara, ou les Kirguises* (Paris: C. Gosselin, 1836), a "poem in four cantos, fol-

have not seen, are in the Bibliothèque Nationale et Universitaire, Strasbourg.[20] Standard references list C. Clairmont as a pseudonym for C. Gambs, and one can only speculate as to his motivation in presenting his creative work under this particular nom de plume. One possibility is suggested by the printing of a thesis by Chrétien-Hermann Gambs, to obtain a bachelor's degree in theology from the Université de France, Faculté de Théologie de Strasbourg.[21] It may well be that the publication of verses that expressed Shelleyan sympathies would have been indiscreet in a theological student (see for example the opening lines of *Moïse* in the note to Claire's journal of May 20 [June 1], 1825, below). One reads these poems, some of which were certainly written during his association with Claire in Moscow, with great attention, both for the Shelleyan parallels, of interest to the student of comparative literature, and for possible clues to the relationship between Claire and the poet. In the introductory verses to several of the poems there are references to a sensitive feminine reader and critic, and one may guess that she might be Claire. The introductory poem to *Vladimir et Zara* contains these lines:

> Je n'ose vous nommer du fond de ma retraite.
> Mon cœur est plein de vous, mais ma bouche est muette;
> Vous-même, par ma voix vous n'apprendrez jamais
> Que pour toujours ma muse a revêtu vos traits.[22]

Somewhat more explicit, and in the same vein, are the introductory verses to *Ismaïl*:

> Le monde est sourde à la voix du poète,
> Indifférent il écoute ses chants,
> Aime à juger; mais à regret se prête
> Au doux pouvoir de ses accords touchans.

---

lowed by some fugitive poems"; *Ismaïl* (Paris: C. Gosselin, 1836), a "poem in four cantos, followed by miscellanea."

[20] *Oeuvres poétiques de C. Clairmont*, 3 vols. (Paris: Renouard, 1834); *Poésies fugitives recueillis par Sesamis de Strasbourg* (Strasbourg: Dannbach, n. d.), with dedication dated January 7, 1838.

[21] *Vie et doctrines de Godescale* [a ninth-century bishop] (Strasbourg, 1837), 15 pp., quarto.

[22]
> From the depths of my retreat I dare not speak of you.
> My heart is full of you, but my lips are silent;
> You will never learn from my voice
> That my muse has forever donned your features.

# Introduction

Que de tourmens! Quand de la multitude
Il veut fixer le suffrage incertain;
Les longs travaux, les veilles et l'étude
N'ont pour tout fruit souvent que le dédain.
Quelques amis, leur language sincère,
Un cercle étroit de juges indulgens,
Et mieux encore le culte solitaire
De la beauté, trésor des cœurs aimans,
Tel est pour lui l'élément de la vie.
Mais si le sort, favorable à ses vœux,
Lui montre un être ému de sympathie,
Gardant encore un souvenir des cieux;
S'il a trouvé quelque femme sensible,
Noble, céleste; et si dans son regard
Pur et brillant d'une fierté paisible,
Il a pu lire un suffrage sans art;
Il est heureux d'un bonheur sans mélange.
Ce qu'elle approuve est l'œuvre de talent:
Elle a jugé comme peut juger l'ange,
Elle a senti; c'est là son élément.

Ma faible voix souvent parut vous plaire,
Vous qu'en ces vers je ne veux pas nommer.
Devinez-moi; mais laissez-moi me taire
Sur des attraits bien fait pour me charmer.
Ce calme heureux d'une âme sainte et belle,
Ce doux parler, qui vous gagne les cœurs,
Si j'en parlais, chacun dirait: C'est elle;
Et vous fuyez les éloges flatteurs.
C'est donc à vous que j'offre cet ouvrage.
Vous comprendrez ces vers mystérieux;
Et si vous-même en acceptez l'hommage,
Je saurai bien le lire dans vos yeux.[23]

[23] The world is deaf to the voice of the poet,
Indifferent it hears his songs,
Fond of judging; but yields unwillingly
To the gentle power of his moving harmonies.
What torment! As for the multitude
It wants to pin down the uncertain appraisal;
Long labors, wakefulness, study
Often earn only scorn as reward.
A few friends, their words sincere,
A narrow circle of indulgent critics,
And still better, the solitary cult

# Fifth Journal

Although this account fits perfectly with what we know of Claire at the time she and Gambs were friends (Claire made something of a joke of her fleeing "les éloges flatteurs"), the passage remains cryptic, and any suspected connection cannot be proved.

The *Ismaïl* volume contains one more bit of near evidence: an "esquisse dramatique" called "Le Choix d'une Amie," set in "une résidence du Nord," and exalting among the ladies of the cast "la Fauvette" named Clara, a paragon of virtues.[24]

The successful career of Hermann's nephew, Emil Frommel (1828–1896), has resulted in the preservation of several further glimpses of the uncle. From Frommel's biographer, his son Otto, we learn that Gambs was descended from an old Alsatian patrician family, elevated by Charles V to the hereditary nobility in 1549, an honor voluntarily renounced by the family during the Thirty Years' War. Frommel, who was to become a prolific and popular writer, as well as *Feldpropst* (chaplain general) to the Kaiser's army, spent several years before he was twenty in the home of his uncle Hermann and motherly aunt, Adèle (born Jeanette Adèle

---

Of beauty, treasure of loving hearts,
Such for the poet is the essence of life.
But if fate, smiling on his desires,
Reveals to him a being moved by sympathy,
Preserving still a memory of the heavens;
If he has found some woman of sensibility,
Noble, heavenly; and if in her eyes
Pure and shining with a quiet pride,
He has been able to read an artless appraisal;
He is blessed with an unmixed happiness.
What she approves is the work of talent:
She has judged as an angel could judge,
She has felt; in that is her element.

My feeble voice often has seemed to please you,
You whom I wish not to name in these lines.
Understand me; but let me be silent
About those enchantments well formed to charm me.
That happy calm of a holy and beautiful spirit,
That soft speech, that wins hearts to you,
If I were to speak of them, everyone would say: 'Tis she;
And you flee flattering praises.
It is therefore to you that I present this work.
You will understand these mysterious lines;
And if you do accept their homage,
I will be well able to read it in your eyes.

[24] *Ismaïl*, pp. 265–338; *fauvette* is a warbler, or singing bird.

Lewin), in their country parish in Alsace. He recalled his uncle as inheriting a fiery temperament and a French vivacity; a bilingual preacher who combined a passion for liberty and equality with a strong attachment to the land, despite his urban education and extensive travels. He had been a composer in his youth, especially noted for two books of waltzes for four hands, and his orchestral compositions were frequently performed in his birthplace, Paris. "Good Uncle" Gambs retired from the ministry in June 1886, spent the last few months of his life in Schwindratzheim, which had come to be his home, and died peacefully there in October. Only one son survived him; to this cousin, Emil Frommel wrote: "In my youth, adolescence, young manhood his image loomed before me, and I have him to thank for much of the best I have. What might have become of me had it not been for him and your good mother! He taught me to preach; he oversaw my schooling, guided freely and ungrudgingly my fate and my path in life, so that I have hardly encountered anyone so great hearted as he."[25]

In Moscow, as in Florence, Claire was associated with high-ranking Russian families, and her journal records much colorful gossip as well as news about the political events that were agitating the nation. Russia was in one of the most significant stages of its history, and Claire's account of the life of the time is of interest to students and historians of that period. Alexander I had become czar after the assassination of his father, Paul I, on March 24, 1801 (see Claire's entry for November 17, 1821, above). Educated by a Swiss tutor, Frédéric César de Laharpe, Alexander considered himself a republican, and in the early years of his reign he had reversed the xenophobic policies of his father, encouraged intellectual traffic with Europe and America, and taken steps toward alleviation of the distress of the serfs. After the defeat of Napoleon in 1812, Alexander emerged as one of the most powerful leaders in Europe. In 1815 he inaugurated the Holy Alliance, which, despite its idealistic-sounding premises, developed into an instrument

[25] Otto H. Frommel, *Emil Frommel: Ein Lebensbild* (Berlin, 1908), pp. 177-178. This is a reprint of *Frommels Lebensbild*, vols. I and II (1900-1901) in Emil Frommel, *Das Frommel-Gedenkwerk*, 7 vols. (Berlin, 1900-1904). Other information in this paragraph is from Otto H. Frommel, "Emil Wilhelm Frommel," in *Allgemeine Deutsche Biographie* (Leipzig, 1904), XLIX, 184-202, and from letters in 1967 from Otto Gambs of Ludwigshafen, Germany.

of despotism and tyranny. Alexander himself became more and more a reactionary ruler, retreating into mysticism and pietism, increasingly morbid and withdrawn. His death in 1825 produced a peculiar vacuum, since no one was prepared to succeed him. His brother the Grand Duke Constantine would have been the natural successor, but the rumor that he had resigned his right of succession — reported by Claire on December 15 (27), 1825 — was indeed true; he had secretly resigned in January 1823. His brother Nicholas, seventeen years his junior, had not been informed of the abdication (or else kept up a convincing front of ignorance), and the Russian people were treated to the spectacle of Constantine, in Warsaw as governor-general of Poland, proclaiming Nicholas czar, while Nicholas, at home, proclaimed Constantine. Nicholas I, as the new ruler, was far from popular. A reactionary with a strong affinity for Prussian militarism, he was described — as Claire reports — as a "rising Nero." Several liberal segments of the aristocracy, already organized into secret societies, chose the day on which the oath of loyalty to Nicholas was to be taken as a day of protest. On December 14 (26) — thus the term "Decembrist" — a group of army officers led a disorganized revolt (reported by Claire on December 18 [30]) that was swiftly put down. Because the leaders of this abortive coup were from some of the noblest families and the cream of the intelligentsia, their gesture — though it seemed to lead only to execution or Siberia — had a profound effect on the Russian consciousness and began a process that was to have its ultimate expression in 1917.

Although life in Russia had many discomforts and frustrations, Claire did not live in an atmosphere of unalleviated gloom, finding much to console and delight her. She had friends, above all the amiable and talented Hermann Gambs. She continued to respond to the changing face of nature, and when she reopened her journal, after a lapse of three years, she was about to go to Islavsky, the spacious summer home of her employers, in the country, on the Moskva Reca (Moscow River), where through her eyes we see life much as Tolstoy and Gogol have described it.

# Moscow 1825

Teusday May 12–24th[1] I have long resolved to recommence my Journal and provided myself accordingly to-day with a Book. My Life flows so swiftly away and so unobservedly that I have need of a Journal to mark a little its progress. Early in the morning I read Madame Roland[2] — then I called upon Princess Ouronsoff — She was as usual surrounded by a set of old ugly governesses, all ravenous and open-mouthed after places. When I came home I gave my lessons. Then walked in the garden and read Madame Roland. Then ⟨we got n⟩ M. Gambs,[3] M. Cornet and I we got into a long talk about Philosophy from which discourse we found nothing but to conclude that every chain of reasoning whatever ⟨begins upon⟩ is founded upon a supposition. The foundation of every system is always begged — for instance Mathematics ⟨begin⟩ set out from a point — What is this point? It has neither length, nor breadth nor consistence and is therefore nothing — Yet this is what this famous system is founded upon. You are begged to believe in a point which has neither length, breadth, nor substance and consequently is a thing without existence. Then they demonstrate that a line is an aggregate of points, and possesses length and breadth but no substance   then comes the square &c. &c. We then talked of Materialism and Immaterialism — M. Gambs proved that all colours were in the eye and not in the things we see — in short that our eye colours every thing with its own hues. He mentionned Lavoisier's system of Molecules and the experiment he tried with roses. A red rose being washed with muriatic acid, becomes perfectly white, and seen through a⟨glass⟩ microscope it will be plainly discovered that the molecules which had been lying one way when the rose was red have been ⟨disc⟩ decomposed ⟨are⟩ and in the white rose are lying another way. Every day confirms me more in my belief of Immaterialism and if my reason were not more convinced by this system than by any other yet I should yet be attached to it from its tendency to promote the belief of an organic

[1] Russia had not yet adopted the Gregorian calendar and was thus twelve days behind the English. Claire records both Old Style and New Style dates. Where I have referred to both dates, I have put the Russian date first, followed by the Gregorian date in parentheses or brackets.

[2] Saint Albin Berville and Jean François Barrière, *Mémoires de Madame Roland*, 2 vols. (Paris, 1821).

[3] Chrétien-Hermann Gambs. See the introduction to this journal, above. Unless noted otherwise, Claire's many references to G. are to him.

# Fifth Journal

devellopement instead of a mechanic one which Materialism preaches.

After dinner I go with Olga Michailovna[4] and the children to the Gorod [*the city*], to Hutchinson's Magazine and to Gualtier's. We return late to tea. Mr. Baxter there and all the Ka-KoschKine family.[5] Talk again with Mr. Baxter and Mr. Cornet upon Immaterialism. M. Cornet resits resolutely— he will believe that a Piano forte has a separate existence from the idea of it in his mind. Afterwards a little political talk with Mr. Baxter about the Milan Congress, now assembled, about the state of Russia — her armies. Russia has a million of soldiers fit for war — the mortality among these troops is dreadful from excess of fatigue and bad nourishment. At least ten and sometimes fifteen in every hundred die which is as great a mortality as in time of war — so Du Pin[6] proves, for he says in the war between ⟨Spain⟩ Napoleon and England, carried on in Spain, where there was at least one pitched battle every year the mortality was not greater. I learned a very curious circumstance. It is generally believed that the Russian people were always slaves. This is by no means the case. There were no slaves in Russia but such as became prisoners by the chance of war, and were given to their conquerors, untill three hundred years ago — ⟨the Czar used to receive⟩ every peasant paid a contribution or tax to the Czar but was else free and by no means attached to the Glebe; ⟨but⟩ the prisoners paid nothing, they only worked for their master and he was obliged to pay their tax for them. The Government found that the prisoners or slaves' tax was much more regularly paid than that of the peasants, and therefore reduced the latter into a state of bondage, by attaching them to the soil, and exacting the tax from the master to whom they were given. This is the origin of slavery in Russia, and this very slavery the Emperor is trying to destroy by every means in his power. So far were the Russians from being slaves, that there were even republics in the very heart of the state. Nisjni Novogorod was a republic, and defended its liberties against Ivan Vasilivitch

[4] Unmarried niece of Marie Ivanovna.

[5] Mr. Baxter, a Scotsman, was tutor to Alexis Kyrieff; the various spellings of the next name finally resolve on Kakoschkine.

[6] Probably André Marie Dupin, called Dupin the Elder (1783–1865), French magistrate and statesman.

surnamed the Grosnoï (or cruel) so desperately that it yielded not till that monster had caused eighty thousand of its inhabitants to perish in the space of three months. To the remnant engulphed by despair, and mute from consciousness of their mutilated state, he gave them their life, only ordering them to lay down their arms, and to pray for him. Afterwards M. Gambs repeated to us the frau Schnipps of Bürger, and the Bettler of Pfeffel.[7]

Wednesday May 13th. — 25th. Read Memoirs of Madame Roland. Give my lessons. A letter from Mr. Baxter. After dinner go with the children and Olga Michailovna and Catharine and Helene[8] to Madame Glinka's — from thence to the Promenade at Devichni Pol.[9] Finish the Memoirs of Madame Roland. Go to bed very early. The following stanzas are from the King's Quair written by James I whilst prisoner in the Round Tower of Windsor Castle and are descriptive of the Lady of his love.

> Of her array, the form, gif I shall write
> Toward her golden hair, and rich attire
> In fretwise, couched with pearlis ⟨whil⟩ white
> And greaté balas, lemyng as the fire.
> With many an emeraut, and fair sapphire
> And on her head, a chaplet fresh of hue
> Of plumys parted red and white & blue.

---

> About her neck white as the fire emaille
> A goodly chain of small orfe⟨y⟩yrie
> Whereby there hung a ruby without fail
> Like to a heart yshapen verily,
> That as a spark of love so wantonly
> Seemed burning upon her white throat
> Now gif there was good parly, God it wote.[10]

[7] "Frau Schnipps: Ein Mährlein, halb lustig, halb ernshaft, sammt ange-hängter Apologie," by Gottfried August Bürger (1747–1794), best known for his ballad "Lenore"; "Der Spieler und der Bettler," by Gottlieb Konrad Pfeffel (1736–1809), author of many popular fables and poems.

[8] Catharine and Helene Ivanovna received lessons from Claire.

[9] The Devitchei Pole was one of the most distinguished of Moscow's parks.

[10] James I, king of Scotland, The King's Quair, ed. Ebenezer Thomson (Edinburgh and London, 1815), canto ii, stanzas 28–29.

# Fifth Journal

Thursday May 14th. 26th. Learn my part in M. Gamb's comedy, and walk in the garden. English lesson to John.[11] Miss Hardorff [12]

[11] Son of Zachar Nicolaivitch and Marie Ivanovna. Claire described him and his mother in a letter to Mary: "The lady with whom I live is of such an extremely weak character, the only good she does me is to make me laugh a hundred times a day — Every minute she changes her opinion; and then she has such an adoration of instruction and Knowledge, that she can't possibly spend a minute without recalling some *souvenir historique*, and she crams her son's head with chronological, typographical and geographical facts to such a degree, that he told her the other day, 'sur mon honneur, Maman, si vous continuez à me persecuter avec la litterature, comme vous faites. Je vous jure ma parole que Je me fracassirai la tête contre la muraille' [on my honor, Mama, if you continue to persecute me with literature, as you are doing. I give you my word that I am going to smash my head against the wall]. The Tutor and I so reason with her, and as she is uncommon weak, she always finishes by declaring she will follow our ideas; but no sooner are our backs turned, than she gets the child into a corner, to teach him some important fact in Universal history — The boy is only nine years old, and a great favourite of mine, because he is so very frank but he is quite distorted by knowledge — he speaks four languages — Of these four, every day he reads, and writes and learns the grammar — by the time his lessons are over, his head is completely confused — to add to this, he has a very lively imagination, and he does not know enough of any language to express what he feels. he begins to relate something, but can find no words, yet the idea is so forcible, in his mind, and he wants so much to give it utterance, that in his embarrassment for want of words, he takes to pulling and tearing your clothes or his own. If you hold his hands, he cannot speak, if you offer to supply him with a word, it must be at hap-hazard as you cannot possibly imagine what word he is seeking for. He is a very amiable good boy, if he were only reasonably brought up — About two months ago, his mother left us to go to Petersburgh, about a lawsuit; she was much agitated at parting from him, and he, amiably seizing her by the shawl, and working as many holes, as he collected his whole strength of words together, by thrusting his fingers through the border every time he paused, he said; 'Je vous assure, Maman, que Je fais tout mon possible pour pleurer, mais Je ne puis pas' [I assure you, Mama, I am making every effort to cry, but I cannot]. the time she spent away was the only pleasant time I ever spent in Russia, as the children were entirely under my care — I wrote to her that I had diminished half John's lessons, and that notwithstanding the friendship I had for her, I was actually cruel enough to allow the poor boy to eat breakfast, without the aid of historical recollections, and that, in the space of two months, he had progressed so much from learning fewer words and thinking more, that I was happy to inform her, he could now say a sentence to the person opposite to him, without twisting all the buttons off his waistcoat, or breaking the first thing that might come to hand" (Abinger MSS., April 29, 1825, from a transcript in the hand of John Gisborne).

[12] There were two Misses Hardorff, one called Lise.

interrupts us—Afterwards lesson to Dunia.[13] Read Madame Roland. The Kakorchkine family at dinner. Play the Duett of Di Tanti Palpiti by Ries.[14] M. G— accompanies on the horn. Afterwards we repeat for the first time the comedy. The Prince Aerestoff calls in the Evening. Conversation till eleven. M. Gambs relates his early years—How with some other youths when a student at Strasburg, he concealed himself in the topmost ⟨to⟩ gallery of the great tower at Strasburgh and when mid-night struck, they began to play the most delightful harmony upon the music instruments they had brought with them which consisted in horns and tromboni's. The whole town slept, but awoke to this delightful music which heard from the distance of four hundred feet from the ground seemed to issue from the heavens. Also a duel he had with another student, who came up to him one morning at four o'clock in a garden where he was drinking milk and insulted him—Being asked the reason of such extraordinary conduct, he replied, that the colour of M. G's Pipe was not to his fancy—The consequence of this was a duel.

Friday May 15. ⟨16⟩ 27th. Walk in the garden and learn my part. This is the first fine day this spring—the wind tho' high ⟨was warm and⟩ blew⟨ing⟩ full from the South, was warm and balsamic —several showers fell during the day, but their soft pattering on the leaves and the avidity with which the Earth drank in the rain. I can compare the beauty of Summer to nothing but a prodigal, who throws ↑lavishes↓ his gifts in abundance every where, and showers down his wealth upon everyone around him. Winter on the contrary to a wretched miser who puts on the most forbidding aspect and shuts up his riches in his own bosom.

"gentle hills, whose rocky summits gave them the dignity and pride of mountains.

lent them the solemn air of mountains.

Give a lesson to John and Catherine. Madame Siminoff and her mother calls. After dinner read Die Cypressenkranze de la Ba-

[13] Dunia (Sophia), who was almost six at this time, was the daughter of Marie Ivanovna and Zachar Nicolaivitch. She was Claire's special charge.

[14] Ferdinand Ries (1784–1838), pianist and composer, piano pupil of Beethoven and author of a book about him. "Di Tanti Palpiti" consisted of variations on a cavatina from Rossini's opera *Tancredi*.

# Fifth Journal

ronne la Motte Fouqué.[15] Then ⟨we⟩ go to the bower in the garden with Miss Olga and Mr. Gambs reads to us his tale of Skiold. We drink tea on the balcony — Nicolai Ivanich comes and afterwards the Miss Aconloffs.

Saturday May 16th. — 28th. Learn my part and walk in the garden. Give lessons to John and Dunia. M. Gbs. brings the Opera of Le Nozzi di Figaro — which I play. After dinner Olga Michailovna and I concert with Mr. Gambs how we can get her ⟨to⟩ off from going in Miss Hawker's[16] box — We arrange to put the watches all half an hour too slow which we. Mr. and Mrs. Kitto call. After tea go to the Opera in the great theatre with O.M. Catherine ⟨Ina⟩ Stramiloff and Mr. Gambs. The Opera was Il Crociato in Egitto. Music by Meyerbier.[17] In coming out meet Miss Weston. The ride home was delightful  The sky overhead cloudless of a deep blue broken only by the mild moon—  all round the horizon ⟨the⟩ gleamed the pale Northern lights which ressembles the appearance of the clearest day break. No rough wind, the air was soft and balmy as in Italy. The weather was truly delightful. In such hours one⟨s⟩ feel what Göthe calls in Egmont die süsse Gewohnheit des Daseyns — or in english the sweet sentiment of existence.[18]

Sunday May 17th. ⟨19t⟩ 29th. Drive to Miss Trewin's — Her sister is arrived — Then to Madame Chateinzoff's — The weather is tolerably warm ⟨but the sky not clear from threatening black clo⟩ and the sky clear. The KakorchKine's come to dinner and ⟨Mr.⟩ the Countess Tolstoÿ and a frenchman of the name of Kello.[19] After dinner we assemble in the covered walk and ⟨repeat⟩ there is a rehearsal of the Improptu d'Islavsky at which we laughed very much. We drink tea in the covered walk — Madame du Monchelles and Miss Hardorff come also, Mr. Ebler and the Miss Aconloffs. The Night was beautiful — the heated atmosphere was succeeded

[15] A prose tale by F. H. Karl, Baron de La Motte-Fouqué.
[16] Another governess.
[17] Giacomo Meyerbeer; the first performance of this opera was in Venice, March 1824.
[18] Actually, "Süsses Leben! schöne freundliche Gewonheit des Daseyns und Würckens" ("Sweet life! Sweet, pleasant use of being and activity!") Goethe, *Egmont*, Act V (trans. A. D. Coleridge).
[19] Actually Quellot.

by the freshness of Evening. But I am always unhappy for I can enjoy nothing — for I am always surrounded by common people and their incessant squabblings frightens away every happy thought and every sublime meditation. In winter I do not feel their presence so much or rather their society ⟨afford⟩ gives a kind of life to the dead scene. But in ⟨low⟩ summer when Nature speaks in such full tones to the heart, when ⟨Mind⟩ the Imagination awakens under the magic touch of reviving nature, it is disgusting to come in contact with the beings by whom I am surrounded. The soft melancholy Nature inspires ⟨gives⟩ banished by their angry voices and vulgar manners, gives place to relentless pining after some more congenial mind, and the delicate fancies engendered by the sight of Nature's new born beauties fly away for ever from the wretched wanderer who is condemned to live with such tasteless animals. My whole heart turns to gall. I seek a corner in this tumultuous house where to enjoy a moments reverie, and I can only compare myself to some unfortunate miscreant pursued by a shouting rabble. I wish I could paint the hate and disgust these people inspire me with. I can compare them to nothing but crows, that having the whole atmosphere before them, leave the mountains and their peaks, leave the forests and their trees, leave the expanse of wide spreading fields over which the lark carols for hours, to perch ↑exulting↓ upon some carrion object, the very refuse of creation.

Monday May 18th. 30th. The whole scene is changed to-day — the smiling serenity of the heavens is replaced by dark clouds ⟨stretching⟩ stretching in massy ridges across the heavens. The rain falls between the gusts of wind. ⟨I⟩ Play the Opera of Figaro. Mr. Baxter calls — Walk with him in the garden, and ⟨sho⟩ the blossoms of the accacia trees fall in showers upon us as we pass under their boughs. The Kakosckine's dine and Mr. Pouchkine [20] and Madme. Simonoff a jolie mimandeuse de Tamboff and Mr. Kitto. After dinner Mr. Gambs reads aloud his tale of Skiöld. It pleases me very much — Its principal charm is the naturalness of ⟨his⟩ its descriptions, the novelty as well as naturalness of Skiöld's character, and the extreme vivacity of the style.

[20] This name appears spelled seven different ways. It is at any rate not the poet Alexander Pushkin, who was in Mickhaelovskoe at this time.

# Fifth Journal

The Countess Tolstoÿ said yesterday that she ⟨ha⟩ wanted to hire a tutor — a gentleman presented himself and the first question she addressed to him was, I hope Sir, you don't drink". and she expressed much indignation at the astonishing impudence of the man ⟨who⟩ because he declined having any further to do with a lady who could ask such a question.

Tuesday May 19th. 31st. Call early in the morning upon Mr. Butler — upon Miss Trewin. Come home and go with Miss Hardorff to the Princess Ouronsoff's and upon Miss Cournand in the Via Moff Doma. After dinner go on before on foot with Dunia and Nicholas [Michelofsky] and ⟨we⟩ the carriages overtake us and I proceed with Marie Ivanovna and Mr. ⟨Mr.⟩ Gambs and the two children to Islavsky where we arrive at ½ past eight and spend the rest of the evening in running over the grounds. I was much tired and retired to rest early, but all hopes of repose were at an end after spending ½ an hour in bed — Bugs the torment of Russia came in troops and I escaped only from them by sitting up the whole night in an arm-chair.[21] The night was northern, light black clouds were spread all over the heavens the air was cool and the moon shone only by intervals.

Wednesday May 20th. June 1st. I am not well to-day and feel stiff and chill from sitting up in the cool night air. After breakfast walk round the grounds with Catherine Stramiloff and Nicolas Michelofsky. The morning is cold and cloudy. ⟨Th⟩ I prefer the walk by the Mosca Reca to any in the garden — it is a pretty woodland scene animated only by flocks of rooks flying from the groves in our garden to the corn fields which lay on the other side of our garden. It began to rain during our walk and continued to do so without intermission the whole day. We were therefore confined to the house, yet I cannot express what pleasure I felt ⟨in⟩ when through the windows the green fields and the groves met my eye. It made my delight the whole day. I unpack and

[21] An anonymous Englishwoman who went to Russia in 1843 wrote: "A Russian lady whom I know once spoke to her peasants on the subject of cleanliness, and especially concerning the vermin. Their reply would have done honour to a Gentoo: 'Ah, Sudarina, it is a *sin to kill them, because God has given them to us!*'" (*The Englishwoman in Russia*, "By a Lady, Ten Years Resident in that Country," p. 34.)

arrange my things and read a little of Wilhelm Meister.[22] Marie Ivanovna is busily employed the whole day in scolding the steward and the starista [23] of the estate, in giving audience to all the peasants &c. After dinner M. Gambs reads aloud the 3, 4, 5, and 6th. Canto of Moses.[24] The third canto is extremely fine — the fourth is only not so fine because it treats of milder softer feelings, the fifth again is magnificent. His excellence seems to consist in presenting his subject to your attention in the most natural attitude, yet it ⟨is⟩ ↑has↓ by no means a careless air but on the contrary all the noble carriage which high philosophic thinking gives. I think he has great dramatic excellence for whenever his heroes speak⟨s⟩ the poem improves. A pretty comparison for this poem would be ⟨a fore⟩ its foreground is occupied ⟨and animated⟩ by heroes who animate the scene by impassioned thoughts and resolves, and ⟨its back ground is filled fills up the whole with pastoral descriptions and lyrical images.⟩ the pastoral scenes ⟨he⟩ described in lyric⟨al⟩ verses, and interspersed through the ⟨whole⟩ poem, form⟨s⟩ a back-ground and ⟨gives to the whole⟩ by ⟨linking⟩ ↑connecting↓ the different circumstances together, ⟨give form an enchanting pic⟩ presents the aspect ⟨of⟩ ↑may be likened to the contemplating↓ a picture, where the eye ↑tho' it↓ wanders from object to object, yet seems to ⟨catch⟩ ↑seize see↓ the whole ↑subject↓ at the first glance. In this poem Moses is not the Moses of the Genesis. ⟨Me⟩ true it is that he is a legislator; but the author represents him, as freeing an enslaved people, as ⟨having⟩ a reformer snatching them from their chains and plunging them again into the regenerating circle of a pastoral life, foreseing with that intuitive

[22] *Wilhelm Meister's Lehrjahre*, 4 vols. (Berlin, 1795-1796).

[23] A misspelling of *stárosta*, overseer.

[24] By Gambs. The opening lines illustrate the Shelleyan revolutionary spirit of the poem:

> Je chante le mortel qui de la tyrannie
> Osa briser le sceptre, et dont l'heureux génie,
> Près d'un peuple jouet d'un despote irrité,
> Le premier ramena la douce liberté.
> Vainement l'ennemi de la grandeur divine
> Des malheureux humains conspirait la ruine,
> En vaine de Pharaon les farouches soldats
> Contre un peuple opprimé s'excitaient aux combats,
> Et, pressant les Hébreux vers l'humide rivage,
> Semblaient crier à tous: La mort ou l'esclavage!
> *Moïse*, pp. 1–2

# Fifth Journal

knowledge which belongs to great mind, that ⟨in order one receeding step would⟩ a return to Nature would enable them ⟨to
pursue to begin their glorious course⟩ to ensure the glory of their
future course. Thus ⟨the⟩ he who prepares to jump, first redoubles
the ↑necessary↓ impulse by receeding. ⟨and gaining doubled activity from⟩ and joining concentration to dexterity accomplishes
fully his task.

Thursday May 21st. June 2nd. The weather is again fine but
very windy — Read Wilhelm Meister — After breakfast walk with
Dunia, John Mr. Gambs, Nicolas Catherine and Helene to the
Mills. The country round is only rurally pretty, yet it fills me with
delight, and I sat at my window this morning, and listened with
melancholy pleasure to the sound of the wind among the neighbouring trees — it recalled to my mind the breaking waves upon the
shores of Lerici. Our walk to the Mills was delightful, sometimes
the warm wind blew in such gusts we could scarcely keep our feet.
When we come home we lunch upon *prastagnasha,* and then we
sing Genichsta's music for the Impromptu of Islavsky.[25] Marie
Ivanovna does not dine at home — she is gone to Madame Zimmermann's. After dinner Dunia digs her garden and I read Wilhelm
Meister. Marie Ivanovna comes home — After tea some officers
come. Sing with Olga Michailovna and Mr. Gambs. Then walk

---

"I sing of the man who dares to break the scepter of tyranny, and whose happy
genius, close to a people who are the plaything of an inflamed despot, first
restored sweet liberty. In vain did the enemy of divine glory conspire the ruin
of unfortunate creatures, in vain the fierce soldiers of Pharaoh were incited to
combat against an oppressed people, and, pressing the Hebrews to the watery
shore, seemed to cry to all: Death or slavery!"

[25] The word *prastagnasha*, probably garbled, has eluded all efforts to identify it.

Joseph Genischta (1795–1853), of Czech origin, was at the beginning of
a distinguished career as pianist, violoncellist, composer, and conductor. By 1824
he was well known as a pianist and in 1837 became director of a singing society
in Moscow. Berlioz, rehearsing *Faust* in Moscow in 1847, referred to him as "a
very good German teacher" who acted as accompanist to the rehearsal (*Memoirs
of Hector Berlioz*, trans. R. and E. Holmes, p. 436). He was a prolific composer,
with a style influenced by Beethoven, extremely popular for his romances, such
as "Der schwarze Schal" and "Es erlosch des Tages Leuchte" (settings of poems
by Pushkin), both orchestrated by Glinka; for his comic operas; and for his
First Sonata for Piano and Violoncello. See Claire's description of him in her
entry of June 4 (16) below.

with Catherine on the bank of the river and climb up and down the Hills. After supper long talk with Marie Ivanovna and Mr. G. upon astronomy. He relates to us the newest discoveries in Astronomy — The immensity of this universe. Our sun with all its tributary planets ⟨revolves round⟩ and with 65 other suns and their attendant planets revolve round another sun, whose size can only be conceived by recollecting that by its power of attraction alone, it sustains the order of the innumerable planets, worlds, and suns revolving round him. A third sun exists so far from us (or to speak worldlily we are on the very confines of the system) that his light only reaches our hemisphere in seven years — it is probable therefore that ⟨the second sun⟩ this ⟨second⟩ ↑third↓ sun is the centre of attraction to the second, and draws it round it with all *its* revolving worlds. Carry this idea still further, multiply to infinity the ⟨sun⟩ solar systems and you will understand what Pascal said — that the centre of the universe was every-where but its circumference no where.

Plato said, if the colour of the sky had been scarlet instead of blue, ⟨our we should all have been of sanguinary dispositions⟩ the prevalent quality of man had been a sanguinary disposition.
Notes for S[helley]— His life was ⟨shot⟩ short but sweet — the life of a Poet — like a bird he glanced ↑floated↓ in a rapid passage over the world, ↑and his flight was too high to admit↓ too far removed ↑high exalted↓ to see ↑of his seeing↓ its defects, he saw only ⟨the⟩ its beauties. His nest was ever built in the sweetest spots ⟨fou⟩ far from men, and here he had gathered together the fairest fruits Life can give — Love & friendship were his boon companions and filled every moment of his Life ⟨w⟩ which was not devoted to Intellectual culture — His whole existance was a striving after virtue wisdom and he hurried on his course with such rapid eager steps he often overtook them. He tasted the ⟨Spr⟩ Summer of Life ⟨but knew not⟩ and took flight ere the arrival of its inevitable Winter.[26]

Friday May 22nd. June 3rd. Read Wilhelm Meister. Give lessons. Before dinner walk with the children and Marie Ivanovna and M. G. in the garden, in the theatre, to the dairy, and to the hot-

[26] Charles Clairmont expressed himself similarly in his letter to Mary Shelley on September 18, 1822 (Bloom, "A Letter of Consolation," *Yale University Library Gazette*, p. 36 [July 1958]).

houses. After dinner talk with M. G. about Women and sing our Music. Zachar Nicolaitch comes. After tea walk to the Sand Hill and on the banks of the River.

Saturday May 23rd. June 4th. Walk with Dunia and Olga Michailovna to the Sand Hill and the Church Yard. Give lessons. After dinner the children work in their garden and M. G. reads to me Schiller's Wallenstein. ⟨After tea⟩ ↑and then↓ cross the river with the children and run on the opposite banks and then come home to tea.

Sunday May 24th. June 5th. Go early with Catherine to the little wood beyond the church yard — Delightful warm morning — as we come back we meet M. Gambs and his pupils, and we return with them to the little wood. M. G. describes the life of the Court at Weimar, also the savage life he led at Saratoff for four years buried in the country, and the only amusement he allowed himself was now and then a day's hunting in the boundless Steppe's around. With his horse and his two dogs the day used to pass delightfully away — when tired of the chase, he used to repose under a tree and make verses or recite some aloud. He says it was the happiest time in his life. In the wood we hear the church bell ring for the mass and in the distance all the churches of the far off villages sounding also — this gave gave a meaning to the scene — ⟨savannah⟩ village replying to village with intelligible language. This sound beating over the wild savannah, and brought from many distant hills and ravines to the ear, told the little history of the day. When we come home, sit in the balcony and M. G. reads Wallenstein aloud. Dress for dinner and sing with O. M. and M. G. Officers at dinner. Go to the theatre where we rehearce a little. Then to the arbour in the english garden and M. G. reads aloud to me and Marie Ivanovna the ⟨with⟩ 9th. and 10th. Canto of Moses. In the 9th. death of Acora and the 10th. Episode of Razah and Amasis. The last very beautiful. We drink tea in the Arbour. The sun setting from beyond the river pierced ↑thro↓ the deep woods behind the arbour in lines of golden light, and every opening ⟨in the⟩ between each ⟨leaves⟩ leaf seemed to be filled up by a diamond or a gem radiant with every different hue. This was our cieling and underneath we saw the ground of a green and gold colour from the departing rays of day. Then go

and walk with John, Nicolas, and Catherine. The evening was
still, except a soft wind whispering in the ear and lightly lifting
every curl, but it seemed as if the movement of our bodies thro'
the still air produced the current for every tree was stirless. We
met the flocks straying ⟨over⟩ homeward over the common — the
villagers were playing on the green, and as we proceeded onward,
all these rural sounds melted ⟨into⟩ blended indistinctly into ⟨one⟩
a confused ↑distant↓ murmur, and ressembled the breathing of
the ⟨earth⟩ ↑Nature sinking into the arms of Repose.↓ rather than
the hum of distant ⟨m⟩ humanity. The western clouds ⟨still emitted
hung⟩ still floated upon the horizon, and penetrated by the brilliancy of the Sun they veiled, ⟨were masses of golden light⟩ ↑opened
like golden fleeces↓ — They also ⟨benigh benigh⟩ benignantly lent
⟨so⟩ some of their splendour to the landscape around and the
⟨distant⟩ windings of the river ⟨were rosy amid looks were⟩ red
⟨from the⟩ ↑with↓ borrowed light ⟨and⟩ ⟨illumined⟩ ↑seemed to↓
smile⟨d⟩ ⟨in⟩ tho' the greyness of Evening. This day has been in-
expressibly dear to me — I feel that I can still waken to the charms
of Nature and I do not utterly despair. Oh! that Destiny, now on
⟨its⟩ ↑her↓ road, remorseless pitiless as she is, would bring some
hour of happiness.

Monday May 25th. June 6th. After a very sleepless night rise at
½ past three — walk with Catherine to the little wood — Delightful
morning. Breakfast. Walk with Marie Ivanovna round her gardens.
Give Lessons. Work in the garden with Dunia. After dinner in our
garden with the children. John makes a door to our garden. Drink
tea on the Balcony. Then walk on the river side with the whole
household. ○ [27] Beautiful sunset. Light violet coloured clouds ⟨in⟩ surrounded by ⟨a buv brigh with⟩ golden edges, were reflected in the
still bosom of the river, and so truly so naturally, ⟨they⟩ the reflection could only be compared to Lover's hearts — Different yet
equally beautiful, it could not be said which was the most perfect.
If the sky ⟨had a look of brightness more than the water, the latter
was⟩ turned forth its clouds with more brightness yet ⟨they looked⟩
↑their fellows had a↓ deeper ↑stiller majesty↓ in the water especially
⟨with the yew grove⟩ backed by the dark green grove ⟨which whose

---

[27] Claire's symbol refers to the similarly marked expansion of this material
at the end of the entry for May 30 (June 11), p. 322 below.

shade casting its green shade upon the liquid surface, imaged on the clear wave⟩ which threw its image upon the wave and the image of its shade. I may exclaim with Mac Piccolomini — that I now enjoy the first leisure hour of my life; ⟨which⟩ grief consumed the tender bloom of youth; and the whole world was a scene of distress and struggling — but now I yield my soul up to all that surrounds me — at ease upon one point that the affection of my dear friend ↑Trelawny↓ is not changed for me, I dare to look upon Nature as a consoling friend.[28]

Tuesday May 26th. June 7th. **X** Walk at four with Catherine & Nicolas upon the high road — The country is hid by a white fog which promises a fine day. Breakfast. Read Wallenstein. A letter from Mr. Baxter. Give lessons. Mr. Gambs arranges our garden for us. Officers at dinner. M. G. reads aloud Wallenstein in our garden. Slight shower of rain with a few distant clap of thunder. We go to the House and ⟨vea⟩ read. Then ⟨Sit⟩ sit with Marie Ivanovna, and walk with Dunia in the garden and run over the Kakorchkine House. We drink tea in the under Balcony. Afterwards Mr. G. repeats some parts of his Ode to Urania.[29] I find it

---

[28] Max Piccolomini, in Schiller's *Die Piccolomini*, Act I, scene 4. Although Trelawny complained of the icy coldness of Claire's letters to him, it is clear from her journal that she was sincerely attached to him and deeply affected by all news of his danger or safety. See Note to September 6, 1822, above.

[29] "Uranie" appears in *Vladimir et Zara*, pp. 189–193. Its Shelleyan tone is clear in the following excerpt (the first two of seven stanzas):

> Toi que je cherche en vain dans tout ce qui respire,
> Mais dont les traits sacrés ennoblissent mon coeur,
> Qui presses mes esprits d'un délire enchanteur,
> Et par de doux transports signales ton empire;
> Source de la lumière et du céleste amour,
> Qui de tes favoris enflammes le génie,
>     Immortelle Uranie,
> Que ne puis-je te suivre au céleste séjour!
>
> Sur l'aile du désir mon ame impatiente
> Souvent aux champs des cieux s'élance sur tes pas,
> Contemple ton visage et tes chastes appas,
> Et les plis lumineux de ta robe flottante.
> Tu franchis d'un regard l'immensité des cieux,
> Et, répandant au loin sa splendeur solonnelle,
>     Ta couronne éternelle
> De divines clartés inonde tes cheveux.

# Islavsky 1825

strange that he should be born the 4th of August ⟨and write⟩ the very same day as our ever dear friend and write also on Intellectual Beauty.

Wednesday May 27th. June 8th. M. G. goes early to Moscow. I read Wallenstein and give my lessons. After dinner walk ⟨in the⟩ with the children and Mr. Rudolfski to the village over the river.

Thursday May 28th. June 9th. Read Wallenstein. Give my lessons. At two M. G. arrives from Moscow with Mr. Cornet. After dinner Marie Ivanovna goes with the children to visit Madame Alsufieff[30] We repeat L'Impromptu at the theatre and sing. M. G. reads aloud Wallenstein — The scene where he meditates upon the obligation in which he finds himself, of adopting measures because he had allowed his imagination to luxuriate in their contemplation. A letter from Mrs. Seymour.[31] After tea Marie Ivanovna returns. Talk with her upon the Balcony.

Friday May 29 — June 10th. Write to Mr. Baxter. Lessons in the morning — and repetition of music and Impromptu. Also after dinner. Go with O[lga]. M[ichaelovna]. Helene and Catherine à la rencontre of Zachar Nicolaivitch — On our return drink tea in the Balcony. M. G. reads aloud Ode to Urania.

Saturday May 30th. June 11th. Wash and Iron. Give lessons — Repetition both before and after dinner of the Impromptu. Towards

[You whom I seek in vain in all that breathes,
But whose blessed features ennoble my heart,
Who importune my senses with a delightful frenzy,
And by sweet raptures show your empire;
Source of light and of heavenly love,
Who ignite the genius of your favorites,
    Immortal Urania,
Could I but follow you to the heavenly regions!

On the wings of desire my impatient soul
Often on the fields of heaven flings itself in your path,
Contemplates your visage and your pure charms,
And the luminous folds of your floating gown.
With a glance you leap over the immensity of the heavens,
And, spreading afar its solemn splendor,
    Your eternal crown
Floods your hair with divine brilliance.]

[30] Later spelled Alsonfieff.

[31] A governess who had gone to Odessa to attempt to establish a boarding house. See entry of October 25 (November 6) and Note 86, below.

319

# Fifth Journal

Evening there came on a high cold wind — notwithstanding the Sun set gloriously — Unattended by clouds, he sunk ⟨beh⟩ beyond the horizon, and the whole western sky was a flood of golden light. Over our heads fleeces of ⟨pink⟩ rosy coloured clouds ⟨hu⟩ floated and paused as if ⟨in contempl⟩ immovable in admiration of the setting sun. M. G. read aloud Villars' preface to his translation of Kant, a very profound as well as amusing piece of writing.[32] He observes that french literature began by the Belles lettres — that the french had a literature long before they had any knowledge of the sciences — whereas the Germans were a most profoundly learned people before they possessed any thing of what is called literature. This may accound for the difference of taste ⟨in⟩ ↑between↓ the two nations. The German Belles lettres was born of Science and therefore highly ressembles its parent — its whole being is penetrated or ⟨marked⟩ modified by profound knowledge — the french on the contrary exists very well without the slightest reference to Science — it lives and breathes as if no such branch of litterature existed. Villars says the versatility of Kant's mind in the Sciencs is astonishing — He wrote upon Astronomy — and predicted 26 yrs before the ⟨dis⟩ existence of that star which Herschel afterwards discovered, and acknowledged he owed the idea of its existence to Kant. He wrote a profound treatise upon the Vital principle in Man, and many other scientific works which I cannot recollect. ⟨Kan⟩ but in all his innumerable works what is most to be admired is the total absence of every minor or personal question of her alone he treats in all his books, and his zeal in her pursuit never relaxes a minute — every ⟨part bears you on the to the great end⟩ passage every word is a step further on the road of Knowledge. What is admirable in Kant is the steady profoundness with which he pursued his object — with enthusiasm and fervent zeal he ⟨displays⟩ treats of and displays to mankind the remotest recesses of Knowledge, and never for a moment in any one of his numerous books, upon so many different branches of Science, does he admit ⟨the slightest inroad upon⟩ any minor question to ⟨diminish the ardour of his pursuit.⟩ break in upon the devoted unity of his subject.

[32] Charles Villers, *Philosophie de Kant: Ou Principes fondamentaux de la philosophie transcendentale* (Metz, 1801), pp. xii–xlvii. This is an explication rather than a translation of Kant.

# Islavsky 1825

This preface led to a great dispute upon the German and french theatre. Mrs. Ponikoff maintaining the superiority of the french theatres. She quoted Aristotle and his three Unities to which M. G. replied that Aristotle had ⟨no⟩ only mentionned the necessity of unity in the action: that the action chosen to be celebrated in a tragedy should of itself when devellopped form a whole. To me it seems — when I read a french tragedy as if I heard a very clever rhetorician declaiming upon the nature of the passions — and trying to prove more by the elegance and choice of his expressions the value of his own art than to give a picture of the passion on which he treats. There is to me one very clear reason why passion never can be touching upon the french boards — every thing there is according to rule — now Passion in every stage of life and in every ↑one of its↓ possible forms ⟨of life⟩ is nothing more than the throwing down of all barriers. Passion is the high tide of the mind — it overleaps all bounds, precipitates itself over all the barriers ⟨of decorum⟩ which Religion and Philosophy have multiplied upon its road. Passion while it lasts is free — how then can narrow rules imitate or present ⟨what knows no rules⟩ a subject ⟨that⟩ whose very first movement is to annihilate all rules. Passion in human nature is a Titan,* [*see Claire's expansion, p. 322*] on the french stage they imitate it upon ↑such↓ small⟨er⟩ proportions ⟨and⟩ that she becomes a dwarf; true it is of good and delicate proportions but still a dwarf. The German and english masters have dared to look upon their original Nature and have endeavoured to raise themselves to her standard rather than to degrade her to theirs; they have represent ⟨f st⟩ like faithful copiers, her ⟨large full⟩ limbs, ⟨the overflowing of a luxuriant coil [?] a temperament full even to repletion⟩ ↑soft↓ large and full like ⟨the soul which⟩ the generous soul which animates them, if there is a superfluity it is the superabundant health of a robust temperament, ⟨not⟩ but this fault ⟨renders⟩ renders the copy ↑still↓ more ressembling. ⟨whereas the french have allowed the sickly drawling tone of the confined movements of a small circle⟩ the smallness of the circle in which the french have shut themselves up, gives an extreme narrowness to all the movements of their tragedies. The drawling sickly tone of the french tragedians can no more represent the storming of the passions than the tinkling of a bell can ⟨rep⟩ imitate the ⟨thunders⟩ noise of thunder.

# Fifth Journal

⟨rising against⟩*⟨seeing only in the obstacles which oppose it⟩ ↑it↓
ris⟨ing⟩es against the obstacles which oppose it, as they did against
the Gods, and blind relentless in its force pours the whole rage of
a destructive war both upon itself and them.
∘ So have I seen an Autumnal Sunset — when the radiant heaven
pours the full glory of its presence upon the bosom of a deep lake;
the placid ⟨w⟩ surface kindles into beauty and expression (like a
gentle beauty animated by the ardent gaze of her lover) ⟨that in
the end has caught some of his fire, and finishes by reflecting
faithfully his feelings⟩ under the beaming eye of Heaven, and lake
and sky seem at last by gazing upon one another to lose their
⟨d distinc⟩ separate being and to melt insensibly into one.

Sunday May 31. June 12th. Run over the gardens with Dunia and
visit the church. M. G. reads aloud a little of Wallenstein, but
very little for we are interrupted by their coming back from church.
We then rehearce. Then dress for dinner. Madame Perecouloff
and her daughters, Mr. Tcherbachoff and Officers dine. After
dinner a rehearsal at the theatre. Madame Spiridoff and Madame
Alsonfieff arrive — Go a walk with Dunia alone all round the
gardens. ⟨D⟩ When we come back we find the Kakorchkine family
arrived. We drink tea in the Arbour in the english garden. Afterwards a rehearsal for the third time to-day. ⟨and then sit in⟩ Mr
Gbs. says — the disposition of the mind most favourable to high
thoughts is when tinged by a slight melancholy feeling, ⟨the⟩ our
thoughts approach towards and discover themselves to our consciousness ⟨in the⟩ as if they were sentiments.

Monday June 1st. — 13th   Give my lessons. Read Wallenstein. The
Piano comes. Call upon Miss Hawker. Walk in the Great Alley
with M. G. who reads aloud the plan of his discource. After dinner
unpack the Piano and sing. Repitition at the theatre — then drink
tea in the garden. They play at Garialki.[33]

Tuesday June 2nd. — 14th. Walk at four with Anna Vassilievna
and Catherine and Barbe [34] first to the Dairy and then to the little

[33] A misspelling of *gorélki* (pronounced garyélki); a game popular in
Russian villages, in which a person standing in front of a group catches other
participants who try to run away from him in pairs.
[34] There may be two Barbes, a Barbe Kakoschkine who was among the

# Islavsky 1825

wood. Delightful morning. The air soft and warm and yet there was but little Sun; and only by gleams as he traversed the white clouds that had assembled at his rising. The sides of the ravines are covered by cornfields, and the tender green of the corn now in its youth, shaded by the dark pine groves spread here and there form a most charming contrast of youth and maturity. After breakfast give lessons. At ½ past One, Mr. Gambs pronnounces his first discourse upon the Sublime and beautiful. ⟨After dinner, a rehearsal and then we all go to the Mills. Talk with M. G. the wh⟩ He looked very handsome — His ⟨open⟩ ↑broad↓ ⟨expansive ↑large↓⟩ white forehead; ⟨⟨ ⟨and his arched⟩ ↑⟨and dark ↑black↓ hair;⟩↓ his brows rather arched and broad.⟩⟩ The extreme ⟨brightness⟩ ↑fire↓ of his ⟨dak⟩ dark eyes, ⟨and the the smallness and⟩ ↑in↓ contrast⟨ed well⟩ with the ↑retiring↓ delic ↑acy↓ ⟨ate oval⟩ of the lower part of his face; ↑and ⟨his⟩ ↑the↓ varying colour of his cheek↓ ⟨⟨while he spoke his complexion was animated and ⟨the intellec⟩ one ⟨his⟩ contemplated only the predominancy of the intellect in his countenance concentrated the whole play of his countenance to ⟨des⟩ an expression of most predominant intellectuality. expressed enthusiasm sensibility and Intellect.⟩⟩ formed a countenance rich in expressive enthusiasm and Intellect. After dinner we rehearce at the theatre and then the whole society go to the Mills. Agreeable walk and talk with ⟨L'Envoné⟩ Diapason the whole way. At the Mills — we sit and contemplate the prospect and ⟨din⟩ drink milk and then return. I walk with Miss KakorchKine and Barbe and Nicolas — M. G. joins us and we come home thro' the gardens. Tea on the Balcony. Miss Hawker talks of the Princess Dachkoff.[35] She decided Catherine to mount on the throne by saying — If you don't I will. Then at ten go and walk with Miss Hawker and Mr. G— a little way on the high road — Before us the sky was clear and serene still faintly smiling as if yet lighted by the last rays of the Sun, but when we turned to go back, we perceeived the whole sky behind covered with the blackest clouds, stretching in enormous layers of black cloud across the whole breast of heaven, and hanging in heavy rolls between earth and heaven heavy black masses of

---

children in Claire's care and a Miss Barbe Acaroff who married a Mr. Kakoschkine (see August 27 [September 8], below).

[35] Catherine Romanovna Dashkov (1743–1810). See Fitzlyon, *Memoirs of Princess Dashkov.*

clouds ⟨suspended over the earth floating between Heaven and⟩ which seemed to have descended from Heaven and to ⟨float pa⟩ have paused and to brood over the unhappy Earth with dire mien, and aspects full of threatening destruction. Every step we advanced we seemed to enter deeper ⟨into the⟩ into a most gloomy darkness and ↑when↓ ⟨just⟩ ↑as we arrived↓ at home, the grove opposite our house ⟨agi⟩ shaken by a violent gust of wind seemed ⟨to bend driven before⟩ to yield the whole body of its innumerable trees and leaves and boughs before the fury of the tempest and bent its whole weight to ground — The rain instantly poured down from the swollen black clouds, ⟨and the lightning played darted here and there by fits over the whole and⟩ which vivid flashes of lightning illumined momentanuously the thunder mutterd amid the howling of the wind and the beating of the rain. This made me melancholy — every gust of wind recalls Lerici and those days of storm and rain when the wind seemed raving up and down that savage place and roaming round our desolate home, as if searching every corner for our lost friends, or ↑as if↓ ⟨breathing the⟩ venting the dreadful anguish of our hearts in widely wandering lamentations, and ⟨s⟩ breathing forth a requiem to their departed spirits.

Wednesday June 3rd. 15th. Rain. Read Wallenstein. Give my lessons — but I pass my morning very idly for M. G. is there and he makes me talk and sing with him. At one go to the Bath. Here I was very happy — reclining in ⟨a warm⟩ ↑the↓ warmth of the soft water; and listening alone to the ⟨wind amid⟩ wind amid the trees; the green shade which the ⟨wood⟩ surrounding grove thew upon the room; it seemed to me as if I had laid my head upon the very bosom of Nature and were listening to the beating of her pulses and the ⟨pantings of her respiration⟩ breathings of her breast. ⟨After din⟩ There is a General from Moscow at dinner. Afterwards a rehearsal. Then walk in the Great alley with Duninka [Dunia]. The weather is cloudy and the wind very cold  I sit upon the wooden terrace at the bottom of the alley, and lose my consciousness in gazing upon the scene before me. At last my ⟨pleasantly⟩ ↑pleasure↓ wearied eyes closed insensibly and I enjoyed a ⟨g⟩ few moments of the ⟨sweetest repose⟩ most soothing repose. We sup. M. G. sets out for Moscow to fetch M. Genichsta — but returns after an hour having met that gentleman and M. Kynil on the road.

# Islavsky 1825

Thursday June 4th. 16th. Rain in torrents and very cold. Write my Journal betimes and then dress. We all sing with M. Genichsta and then he plays. Rehearsal at the theatre. Then M. G. reads aloud a little of Wallinstein — After dinner the musicians arrive — It pours with rain — we go and rehearse. Then drink tea. Then I play Di tanti palpiti with Mr. Genichsta who then sits at the Piano and plays the ⟨old⟩ whole evening — he extemporizes and executes a quantity of his own compositions; among others an Ecossaise he composed of his sister's husband scolding her, and her answer. He is a divine musician, and ⟨almost⟩ the first that as a man pleased me — He seems a world of music he breathes he speaks on the piano, and his soul such as he expresses it there, seems composed of harmony and fire, nature and art. Imagination, electric touches, deep breathing melodies and ⟨a vary⟩ mellifluous accompaniments, ⟨mul⟩ multiplied to an almost endless variety, were mingled together in soft accord — We hung speechless upon his notes — Silence was enchanted to lose her being in such sweet sounds. His countenance is very original — his features hair and complexion truly feminine, an open forehead and a soft smile, a low gentle voice, and sensibility ⟨in ever⟩ trembling in every fibre render him truly interesting. At night I was as fatigued with listening to him as if I had lived a thousand years. When I came to my own room, all seemed a desert solitude, for there was no power in myself to keep alive ⟨all⟩ the exalted thoughts and feelings his music had awakened and I feel as it were from a commanding height, into ⟨a d pleasureless abyss⟩ a mean confined flat.

Friday June 5th. 17th. Marie Ivanovna's Birthday. The weather is cold and there are many clouds, yet it does not rain. ⟨I watch⟩ I sit in my room and watch the sun struggling to pierce the thick white clouds around him; and the long broad line of dark shadow receeding from the plain up the hill as ⟨th⟩ his sunny rays ⟨fall upon⟩ pierced the clouds and lightened the earth. Dress. Read Wallenstein. ⟨Rehearsal⟩ Grand Rehearsal at the theatre. Come home and dress for dinner. Madame Spiridoff, Miss Kasci, Miss Calloschine, Miss ⟨C⟩ Krouschoff and her father and governess, the Messieurs Tcherbaschoffs and Eugenie [Tcherbaschoff] and Miss Massy, Mr. Als⟨u⟩↑on↓fieff, a quantity of Officers whose names I do not know dine here. After dinner play the Impromptu d'Is-

# Fifth Journal

lavsky   Then we drink tea in the Orangerie, and dance   We return to the house thro' the gardens, with a Polonaise. The rest of the evening passes in dancing.

Saturday June 6th. 18th. Mr. Genichsta, Mr. Kynil and Mr. Cornet go to Moscow. Give lessons. After dinner play with Catherine and ⟨the Barber⟩ also the ⟨Barber of⟩ Marriage of Figaro. As I am going to Bed I receive a letter from the Countess Betsy Zotoff.[36] Terrible Rainy weather. ↑The first number of the Islavsky Gazette↓ appears.

Sunday June 7th. 19th. Rainy dull weather. Write to the Countess Betsy. Read the Revolt of Islam[37] with M. G. After dinner Marie Ivanovna goes with the General to Moscow. After tea we all walk upon the high road — The weather is dull and grey — The Sun shines by fits thro' the clouds and fall in golden gleams upon the far spreading landscape. The dark pine groves which skirt the prospect remain in shade and seem to issue from the sunny plain like a line of dark hills. Sing and play Figaro.

Monday June 8th. 20th. Give lessons. The weather is still uncertain. Read Islam with M. G. After dinner he reads Wallenstein. After tea we all take a long walk. When we return Marie Ivanovna arrives with Lilinka Dubosch.

Tuesday June 9th. 21st. Write account of Mr. G's first lecture. Give lessons. Rainy day. M. G. gives his second lecture. After dinner altho' it has begun to rain we all go out walking and are caught in a heavy shower, and wet thro'. After tea we all play at Hide and seek.

Wednesday June 10th. 22nd. Rainy weather. Write account of M. Gambs' discourse. from nine till four I am engaged in giving lessons. then dine. After dinner dispute in the Balcony about women which puts me in a very ill humour. Madame ⟨Te⟩ Tcherbaschoff, Eugenie and Miss Massy spend the evening. We go to

---

[36] One of Claire's first pupils, and a lifelong friend. See above, p. 297. In November 1842 Claire wrote to Mary that her former pupil, Betsy Zotoff, was married to Prince Czernicheff; two years later he was appointed governor-general of Warsaw (Abinger MSS.). After the marriage on September 16, 1825, Claire refers to her friend as "Madme. Tchernicheff."

[37] By Shelley.

the swings — We find a Bird with a lame leg. The whole Evening is very uncomfortable — They go out walking. I remain at home. Write a refusal of Colonel Griefsky to Mr. Butler. To bed early.

Thursday June 11th. 23rd. Rainy day. Give lessons. At ½ past one M. Gambs gives his lecture upon History. After dinner walk with Marie Ivanovna among the corn fields. The children gather corn flowers — a sweet calm evening. After tea we sit in the Balcony and Marie Ivanovna reads aloud Le Russe à Paris a Satire by Voltaire. also a satire upon the french ⟨G⟩ by Gilbert. When dying he wrote thus

> Au banquet de la vie, infortuné convive,
> J'apparus un jour et je meurs:
> Je meurs ⟨Je⟩; et ⟨ur⟩ sur la tombe où lentement j'arrive
> Nul ne viendra verser les pleurs.[38]

Friday June 12th. 24th. Early in the morning receive a letter from Mr. Baxter with a number of Blackwood's Magazine and some Edinburgh Newspapers. Read them all day. Give lessons. ⟨Af⟩ Rainy day. Then it is fine — Then a violent storm of wind and rain — Then fine again. Zachar Nicolaivitch comes and M. Rudolf-ski.

Saturday June 13th. 25th. Write an article for the Gazette. Write to Mr. Baxter. Give lessons. After dinner M. Gambs reads aloud the Gazette which is very amusing. We all then walk to a wood on the road to Iviniggorod. The road lay thro' corn fields — which on the ↑the left↓ ⟨right⟩ stretched far away to the skirts of a dark pine wood, and on the left descended by a gentle slope to the plain which leads to Moscow. We reached a wood, full of green openings to right and left and long level lines of ⟨shi⟩ sun shine pierced thro' them into the deep forest's shade. This was a most delightful walk.

---

[38]       At the banquet of life, unfortunate guest,
              I appeared one day and I die:
          I die; and on my tomb where slowly I am coming
              No one will come to shed tears.

Nicolas Joseph Laurent Gilbert (1751–1780) wrote two satires on the French: "Le Dix-huitième Siècle" and "Mon Apologie." The famous quatrain is quoted from his "Ode IX: Imitée de plusiers psaumes," composed eight days before his death (*Oeuvres complètes de Gilbert* [Paris, 1823], p. 133).

# Fifth Journal

Sunday June 14th. 26th. This is the first real Summer day we have had this fortnight. Read Wallenstein and ⟨Revolt⟩ Islam with M. Gambs. Then walk with him and Cathcrine, the children and Nicolas over the english garden. We get on the raft and ⟨row⟩ row round the islands. Come home and dress for dinner. Zachar Nicolavitch goes directly after for Moscow. We all walk to the Bridge which is the limit of Marie Ivanovna's territory. This bridge is built across a little stream which runs from ⟨right to left⟩ ↑left to right↓ thro' a little valley: close beside the bridge rises a large hill ⟨wt⟩ with a plain on its top covered with field flowers. On the platform which this hill affords, we sat — beyond the bridge the hills which turn their gentle sides to the valley are ⟨coverd⟩ covered with fir-groves — the stream ⟨round⟩ runs round the foot of the hill and after many windings becomes a a mill course. This is on the side ⟨with⟩ which leads to Moscow, and the high road is seen crossing an opposite hill, looking out between two borders of pine wood. Towards Islavsky the valley becomes wider; on the right is the high road under a cliff edged with wood — to the right, a green valley where the little river turns a thousand times like a snake upon itself — and gleams with its white breast thro' the ⟨ban⟩ meadows on its banks — ⟨its furthest side is⟩ gentle hills bound the meadows ⟨and⟩ clothed with wood; the whole valley is covered with innumerable flowers, and is streaked by their various colours in long lines like a rainbow. M. Gambs the children and I — cross the little bridge and penetrate into the woods beyond — a narrow path sunk in the soil and with grassy banks on each side, from which the pines spring up one behind and beside the other in countless gradations, runs straight thro' it upwards a long slip of blue sky seemed to repose upon the tops of the pine trees — the children run about, find vergissmin-nichts and strawberries. After tea in the   we return home on foot. The whole face of the country is now beautiful — The wide space around is ⟨coverned⟩ covered by the high green corn, beyond one sees on every side, the dark pine woods, stretching forwards, in a broken irregular line into the verdant plain; the Sun sets without a cloud, a quiet ocean of golden light — the ⟨troop of⟩ flocks eating their evening meal ⟨were⟩ proceeding with us on our return home, to the village, and each one by one turned in the village, at the well known ⟨door⟩ stable door. I spent a very agreeable evening — except that some of the people who were with me, fell into quarrels and ill-humours, that all the strict rules of etiquette were not followed in a country walk.

Monday June 15th. 27th. Beautiful Morning. Read and finish Wallenstein — The following character of Max I find very descriptive of our lost friend.

> Er machte mir das wirkliche zum Traum,
> Um die gemeine Deutlichkeit der Dinge
> Den goldnen Duft der Morgenröthe webend —
> Im feuer seines liebenden Gefühls
> Erhoben sich, mir selber zum erstaunen,
> Des Lebens flach alltägliche Gestalten.[39]

Give lessons till two — Then Mr. Gambs gives his fourth lecture upon History. Very interesting. After dinner lesson to Dunia. Then the weather changes and becomes very black and cloudy   we drive a little in the great charaban. then go to the Dairy — The clouds gather and gather, and some drops fall. We hurry home and a violent shower falls. After tea we play at Charades in action. M. G. is ill.

Tuesday June 16th. 28th. Beautiful warm day. Write a little of account of the lecture of yesterday. Give lessons till two o'clock. After dinner Lesson to Dunia and John. At six we go to the Stone Hill and wander about in the woods on the Banks of the Moscow River till nine o'clock. Lovely calm evening — At ½ past nine we return and drink tea in the Dairy. A note from Mr. Butler.

Wednesday June 17th. 29th. Fine Morning. Walk in the English garden. Begin Mendelsohn's translation of Plato's Phäedon.[40] and Memoirs of Marmontel.[41] After breakfast lessons till 2. Then M.

[39]
> he made reality
> Appear a dream, weaving the golden haze
> Of morning round the things that else had been
> So palpable and commonplace, till I
> Myself was fain to marvel how the glow
> Of his affection could so much enhance
> The flat and ev'ryday aspects of life.

Description by Wallenstein of Max Piccolomini in Schiller's *Wallenstein's Tod*, Act V, scene 3 (trans. J. A. W. Hunter, *Wallenstein: A Drama* [1885], p. 396).

[40] Moses Mendelssohn, *Phaedon, oder über die Unsterblichkeit der Seele in drey Gesprächen* (Berlin, 1767).

[41] *Memoirs of Marmontel, Written by Himself*, 4 vols. (London, 1805).

# Fifth Journal

G. gives his lecture upon the ⟨dif⟩ manner in which History should be treated. After dinner lesson to Varinka. Then walk with the children to the Sand Hill. Come home and sit in the ⟨Bel⟩ Balcony — M. G. reads alouds Wilhelm Tell by Schiller.

Thursday June 18th. 30th. Enormously high wind all day. Walk early in the morning upon the banks of the river, whose ripples break at my feet. All was silent around; the dark woods behind me reposed, and the river and ⟨its wide⟩ the plain on its opposite bank were buried in repose. Now and then a rook quitted the wood and flew high across the river to the opposite cornfields. The float was coming to Islavsky and moved so gently thro' the water, as swans without motion or noise. Give lessons till two — Tired to death and ill with the dreadful wind. M. G. reads a little of Wilhelm Tell. Miss Hardorff arrives in the evening. A letter from Mr. Baxter and Miss Cournand.

Friday June 19th. July 1st. Give lessons. Read Memoirs of Marmontel. Walk in the Evening to the Sand-Hill.

Saturday June 20. July 2nd. Read Marmontel. Give lessons. Rain in torrents the whole day. Write to Mrs. Seymour. Bathe in the ⟨Gar Hou⟩ House in the garden. It pours with rain as I come home. After dinner copy Gazette for M. G. Scene between Marie Ivan-ovna and Miss Hawker. Then M. G. reads aloud the Gazette. We talk on the Balcony untill Bed time. Write to Jane.

Sunday June 21st. July ⟨2⟩ 3rd  Finish letters to Jane, to Mrs. Seymour — Write to Colonel Griefsky and Mr. Butler. After break-fast M. Gambs reads aloud Islam. At dinner the General relates the following story of Mr. Kallagriev — He disguised himself as a Lady, and went to a masquerade — There he met a ⟨friend⟩ Baron from Livonia, and addressing him — told him he had known his father once in Livonia and enquired very particularly after his health — the Baron answered that he had had the misfortune to lose his father about two years ago, upon which the pretended lady immediately fell into his arms in a fainting fit. The whole company was in a consternation giving salts and water to the unhappy lady, who when she came to said she had only fainted to sustain her character. After dinner walk in the garden and laugh very much in the Pavillion opposite the island. Miss Hardorff calls M. G.

# Islavsky 1825

l'ingatable [*incorruptible*] M. Gambs. Then return and sing Duett from Figaro. After tea, M. Gambs reads aloud from L'Hermite de la Chaussee d'Antin [42] — Le Genre Sentimentale, L'homme insupportable   Les Enfans du Jour. I spend half the day in folding up letters.

⟨Saturday⟩ ↑Monday↓ June 22nd. July 4th. Write 2nd. Lecture. Rain ⟨to⟩ in torrents. Give lessons — at ½ past one M. G. gives his Lecture which I do not hear by his giddiness. I play on the piano, quite resolved to take my revenge. ⟨After dinner⟩ At ⟨dispute⟩ dinner dispute about the article of *Vergiss mein nicht*, in the last week's Gazette. I turn it adroitly upon Mr. Gambs. After dinner I said to M.G. I request your presence in Marie Ivanovna's cabinet — in a most serious cold tone — When there, I pointed to the chair he had occupied in his morning lecture, and sitting myself down in the place I always occupy, I said — If you have any sense of justice you will now repair the wrong you did me this morning, in depriving me of hearing your lecture by your want of thought in beginning ⟨at⟩ 5 minutes too soon." He readily consented but Marie Ivanovna was ⟨ca⟩ scandalized and declared it was *too violente*. I however insisted and his lecture lasted an hour. Then I gave lessons. At seven they went out a ride in the ligne, for the rain had ceased and the ⟨sh⟩ sun shone; ⟨in mild⟩ the horses however would not go — one side horse would absolutely drive his head in at the window of Afanassi Ivanich's house. Sing with M. G. Play with Mademoiselle Hardorff.

Tuesday June 23rd. July 5th. Write in the morning — reflections upon Women; the day is not rainy but very dark and cloudy and the ground very wet. Give lessons. After dinner Johnny goes out riding when ⟨we⟩ he comes home, we play at Base Ball, on the green before the door — Then drink tea in the Balcony below stairs. M. G. relates to us his flight from Paris to Germany with his friend

[42] Victor Joseph Étienne de Jouy, *L'Hermite de la Chaussée-d'Antin, ou observations sur les moeurs et les usages parisiens au commencement du XIXe siècle*, 5 vols. (Paris, 1812–1814). "Le Genre sentimentale" is in vol. II. "Les Enfans d'aujourd'hui" and "L'Homme insupportable" are in vols. I and II, respectively, of the same author's *L'Hermite de la Guiane, ou observations sur les moeurs et les usages français au commencement du XIXe siècle*, 3 vols. (Paris, 1816).

Stedmann and all their sufferings. Then sing from Figaro with Miss Hardorff.

Wednesday June 24th. July 6th **X** [43] Ill all day. It is St John's day in the Russian Church — They all go to Mass. Read Islam with M.G. The children have a holiday. Sing with Olga Michailovna. At ½ past one M. G. gives his lecture upon Æstethique. Very ⟨imter⟩ interesting. After dinner I lie down. At six they go out. A violent storm comes on and torrents of rain — They all return home wet through. Singing. M. G. reads aloud Schiller's poem to ⟨the⟩ Greece. I read in the Newspapers that Odysseus has been defeated four times near Atalandi by Gura, that he has given himself up prisoner and has been conveyed to Napoli: [44] What this means I cannot make out — I can not believe that the chief, Edward has chosen is one capable of betraying his country; but I am naturally extremely low spirited at this news, tho' I do my best to believe it is false.

Thursday June 25th. July 7th. Not well all day. Marie Ivanovna goes early in the morning to make visits. Give lessons. Read a little of Islam. Walk in the garden with the children. After dinner walk also in the garden    Sit in the Balcony near the swings. M. G. reads aloud a German poem he has composed and a piece of prose entitled Zweÿ Blicke in der Unendlichkeit which I think very good. We are caught in a violent shower and take refuge in the Green House. We drink tea there. When we come home — they talk over in the Balcony how to arrange the play of Esther. [45] Mr. Gambs is to act two parts — ⟨bu⟩ Aman and Mardoch — but scarcely is Aman sent to be hung, but Mardoch must come on the scene — there are only two lines to be repeated on the stage ⟨while⟩ and M.G. must transform himself in the meanwhile. Marie Ivanovna

[43] For three months Claire indicates the beginning of her menstrual period with an asterisk; then in September and October she changes to a diamond-shaped symbol before switching back in November to an asterisk. To avoid confusing the reader I have continued to use the large black **X**.

[44] Odysseus, betrayed by his unreliable colleague Ghouras, had been captured on April 6 and confined in the Venetian tower on the Acropolis. After some weeks' imprisonment he was found dead at the foot of the tower with an uncoiled rope; the report was given out that he had tried to escape (Grylls, *Trelawny*, p. 133).

[45] By Racine.

swore that five minutes was enough for the operation — he granted that, but added how can you drawl out two lines thro' five minutes. She said it was possible — he pulled out his watch, and she recited — and drawling them and putting as much false emphasis and making more pauses than the sense would permit, it only took a quarter of a minute. She said — I'll tell you what. The instant you quit the scene as Aman you shall find 6 valets waiting for you. ⟨In⟩ Un pour vous arracher le turban, un autre pour vous en remettre, un pour vous arracher la barbe, un autre pour la replacer, un pour arracher votre habit et un autre pour vous habiller de nouveau." In this way Mardoch will be dressed in a quarter of a minute and you can present yourself. There is nothing but spouting of verses heard all over the house — Miss Hardorff is the Zarés  L'epouse eploreé d'Aman and as she has le ver solitaire we call her L'epouse affamée.[46]

Friday June 26th. July 8th. Anniversary 3 yrs of our dear friend's death.[47] Write in the morning conversation between Man and Woman. Give lessons. At ½ past one M. G. gives his lecture upon History. The subject was a description of the Commerce of Asia — a description of their Caravans of the towns they met in — of the commerce of the Syrians. Some of these caravans came from so far they were three years on their road — With a cut of his finger across the map Mr. G. measured their road in three minutes — this is a pretty good idea of the quickness of his mode of proceeding. What takes others three years to do, he does in three minutes. After dinner go dawdling about till seven o'clock with the children and M. G. We sit in the Balcony — we gather strawberries, we go to the dairy and ⟨gather strawberries⟩ sit in the Balcony there. When we come home find the General Monsieur Basile and Mr. Cornet arrived. Johnny goes on horseback. Drink tea in the Balcony — then go downstairs, and write in the lower Balcony with M.G. Man and Woman for our Gazette. Miss Hardorff plays the whole ⟨whl⟩ while in her room. My whole day goes in a stroll from

[46] "One to pull off your turban, another to put on a second, one to pull off your beard, another to replace it, one to take off your coat and another to put on the new costume"; "Miss Hardorff is Zarès The suffering spouse of Aman and as she has tapeworm we call her The famished spouse" (Racine's actual phrase is *épouse alarmée* [the alarmed wife]).

[47] Shelley.

# Fifth Journal

Balcony to Balcony. I cannot count the number of Balconies there are in Islavsky, and I stroll delightfully from one to another and spend a little time in each contemplating its prospect. Marie Ivanovna is in low spirits to day, because ⟨When⟩ it is discovered that a woman was murdered in our village by her husband about a month ago. Her body was found to day, and buried in the Church yard upon the Hill. I do not know what kind of a strange feeling takes possession of one when such events occur — it is not fear and yet darkness and solitude after such an event become terrible. One feels ⟨af⟩ as if an evil principle were hovering about the place, and uncertain that one's self may not be its next victim — it seems as if the Penates of the place had been disturbed and had fled and with them the ⟨fel⟩ feeling of security, the repose and peace the country inspires. Happily the murderer is not one of Marie Ivanovna's peasants. He had come here to work, but belongs to Count Effimofsky.

Saturday ⟨July⟩ ↑June↓ 27 — July 9th. Give lessons — then write with M.G. Man & Woman for the Gazette. Lessons till three. then Lessons till five when they call me to read the Islavsky Gazette. Then we sing — then we play at holding a cord and giving one another taps [48] — then a fighting ⟨sen⟩ scene takes place between me, John and Mr. Gambs. Then we play at Homonymes. Then sup and to Bed.

Sunday June 28th. July 10th. Get up early — Go to walk with Miss Hardorff   John Sophy and M. Gambs. Miss H— is ill and so we are obliged to come home again. Then we go to the Dairy and breakfast there. Then the children go to church and M. G. tunes Miss H's Piano and then we read Islam and gather roses. Then lunch — Then we all go a walk to Tcherbaschoff's wood where we find a quantity of Strawberries and many field flowers — Return home and dress — ⟨D⟩ After dinner ⟨g⟩ wander about the garden till tea time. Madame Zimmermann and Miss Kalloschine pay a visit — Then we talk in the lower balcony and run with the chil-

---

[48] In a letter to Mary, May 2 (14) of the following year, Claire described this game ("the Ring") as a frequent Sunday evening game which was broken up violently by the lady of the house who insisted that it was shockingly indecent for a young lady to give a gentleman a tap on the hand (Abinger MSS., quoted in Grylls, *Claire Clairmont*, pp. 181–182).

dren. Mr. Pouchschine arrives. Riddles. Mon Premier est potable, mon second est potable, et mon tout est potable. Po et Tage. 2nd. Si vous ⟨l'a⟩ lavez, ne me le donnez pas, mais si vous ne lavez pas, donnez le moi. lavoir.[49]

Monday June 29th. July 11th. ⟨Walk⟩ St Peter and St Paul's day. Walk in the garden with the children. Read a little of Islam but very little. After Mass, we all go to the woods. When we get there, sit on the grass — the children bring us strawberries — Read Der ewige Jude by Schubart, the translation of which is in the Notes of Queen Mab.[50] It is very fine weather but the wind is very high. After dinner we all walk in the garden. Adventure with the raft as we go to the Island. Then we drink tea at the Dairy. When we come home ⟨every⟩ prepare my commissions for Moscow — Send letter to Miss Trewin.

Tuesday June 30th. July 12th. The General, M. Cornet, M. Pouchkine and M. Gambs to to Moscow. Give lessons. Dress. Monsieur and Mademoiselle Kaverin dine. After dinner Marie goes with them and John to pay a visit ten versts off.[51] Walk with the ⟨childr⟩ Dunia in the garden. Marie Ivanovna comes home late.

Wednesday ⟨June⟩ July 1st. 13th. Walk with Miss Hardorff on the banks of the River. Lovely calm morning — the green banks form a kind of promontory, by advancing ⟨low⟩ into the river as if to meet it, and their soft green sides are turned towards us. Give lessons. M.G. comes at two o'clock. After dinner we all go a long walk to the Banks of the River where they are making Hay. Clouds gather on every side, as if a storm was shortly approaching, and we hurry home. The sun however set on the far horizon clear and without a cloud, but the circle of his glory was curtailed by the

---

[49] "My First is potable, my second is potable, and my whole is potable. Po and Tage" (Tagus). The pun is on *potage*, soup. In the second riddle, the pun is on *lavez* (wash) and *l'avez* (have it). What sounds like "If you have it, don't give it to me, but if you don't have it, give it to me" can be read "If you're washing, don't give it to me, but if you are not washing, give it to me." The answer, *lavoir*, means wash-house, perhaps Claire's error for *savon*, soap.

[50] C. F. D. Schubart (1739–1791), "Der ewige Jude: Eine lyrische Rhapsodie," in *Sämtliche Gedichte* (Frankfort on the Main, 1787), II, 68–73; *Queen Mab* by Shelley.

[51] A *verst* and a half, plus six yards, is a mile.

massy black clouds which seemed hanging about impatient to stretch over even the little space his beams made clear.

Thursday July 2nd. 14th. Give Lessons. Beautiful day. After dinner we all go to Nazarievna the seat of the Prince ⟨Goll⟩ Galitzin.[52] It is six versts off — It is a little village ⟨al⟩ situated in a small plain surrounded by hills, and cut into islands by the windings of a little river that like a serpent turns with a hundred folds upon itself that flows thro' the little plain — The Hills are covered with pine wood, except one opening upon which the House of the Prince Galitzin is placed — behind it the woods join from right and left to form a bower over its head. before the hill descends ↑steeply↓ in a smooth shaven lawn to the banks of the little river, and ⟨beyon a wide horizon of⟩ the eye ranges over a wide prospect of corn fields, broken by clumps of dark green fir which seem to spot their brighter green. We come home at ten o'clock.

Friday July 3rd. 15th. Olga Michailovna's Birthday. Give lessons. Walk with Miss Hardorff and O. M. and Dunia to the island. M. G. gives at ½ past one his lecture on the Commerce of Asia. After dinner play on the Piano. Then go to the island to celebrate the fête. John tumbles and M. Ru⟨dof⟩dolfski tumbles. The General and M. Cornet arrive. A letter from M. Baxter. We drink tea on the island — Only one ray of light one round full beam penetrates thro' the trees upon the island — all else around was of the deepest shade and the eye following the ray of light to its source saw the sun small and almost a point between the trees. At our return walk a little in the Great Alley — M. G. reads Letters from his pupils and his friend and a little of Hymn to Intellectual Beauty. Send letter to Charles.

Saturday July 4th. 16th. Write article for the Gazette. Give lessons. Dinner. After dinner the Gazette is read aloud. Much laughing. Dispute with Marie Ivanovna & M. Cornet about who wrote the article upon the Balconies. Then we play at Charades. Paris, Souris, Sopha Pavie. Rain all day.

Sunday July 5th. 17th. Torrents of Rain. Write to Mr. Baxter. After Breakfast talk with M. Cornet and M. Gambs about the

[52] Probably Prince Paul Galitzin. See the introduction to the sixth journal, below.

Greeks. Then read Revolt of Islam. Dress and dine. After dinner
the General and Monsieur Bazile go to Moscow. Practice ⟨in⟩ the
Freÿschutz [53] — M. Cornet reads out Phoedre from Racine. After
tea 1st rehearsal of Esther.

### Monday July 6th. 18th.

---

### Tuesday July 7th. 19th

---

### Wednesday July 8th. 20

---

Thursday July 9th. 21st. These last three days I have been unhappy
and in low spirits. Mr. Gambs went to Moscow and when he
returned he told me that Mr. Harvey had a letter for me. Every
day I expect it and not knowing what news it may contain, I pass
my time in fear and anxiety. Marie Ivanovna has been ill all this
week with the rheumatism. Give lessons. After dinner we all walk
to the wood — A most lovely walk thro' rising corn fields, and the
dark green wood ⟨on⟩ bounds the horizon before us. Play the Freÿschutz a little. Letter from the Countess Betsy Zotoff requesting
to see me the 13th at Moscow.

Friday July 10th. 22nd. Cloudy weather. Give lessons. at ½ past
one lecture on History — the Assyrian Empire. M. Cornet and
Monsieur Basile arrives. The first brings Les Noces de Figaro.
Walk after dinner walk with the children on the road to Moscow.
After tea a rehearsal of Esther.

Saturday July 11th. 23. Rainy day. Give Lessons. After dinner the
Gazette is read — It is not good. Then Rehearsal of Esther — I amuse
myself with pining papers to the actors backs.

Sunday July 12th. 24th. Rain in torrents. Nothing but talking and
⟨ref⟩ rehearsals the whole day. Sit a little in the under Balcony and
read a stanza or two of Islam. The Rain comes on with such
violence that we are obliged to get in at Miss Hardorff's window
⟨and⟩ into her room. Letter from my mother. Their Business is

[53] By Carl Maria von Weber (1821).

# Fifth Journal

finished.[54] Mrs. Spiridoff and Madme. Mochanoff call after dinner. Rehearsal in the Evening. Then dancing. Prepare to go to Moscow.

Monday July 13th. 25th. Get up at three — Wait till seven — Then set out with Miss Hardorff and Olga for Moscow. The weather pretty good tho cloudy but the road detestable. Spend the day with the Countess Zotoff at Kopp's[55] in the Twerskoi. In the Evening walk ⟨at in the⟩ round the Ponds of Preshneje.

Tuesday. July 14th. 26th. Spend the morning at the Twerskoi. Walk with the Countess Betsy to Gaultier's and to Smith's Bridge. Dine at home with the General and Monsieur Bazile. After dinner return to Islavsky where we arrive at ½ past nine.

Wednesday July 15 — 27th. ⟨Do Nonsense⟩ Rainy day. Give lessons. Rehearsals all day. Lecture on Easthetique.

Thursday July 16th. 28th. Rain in torrents. Give lessons. Colonel Mack and an officer dine. After dinner singing and playing — Then give lessons. Then dancing. At ten o'clock a violent thunderstorm comes. Sheets of lightning flood the sky and the thunder is so loud all the windows tremble. It ceases in an hour — but during the night I heard many violent claps of thunder and the rain fell in torrents.

Friday July 17 29th. Write in the Morning for the Gazette. Read Travels in Germany.[56] Give lessons. Rainy day. ⟨After dinner⟩ Monsieur Basile and Mr. Cornet arrive from Moscow at dinner. Afterwards it clears up. ⟨Sit⟩ In the Morning Miss Kakorchkine gave the Lecture upon History instead of Monsieur Gambs. It was

[54] In 1822 Godwin had lost a lawsuit over the Skinner Street rents. Despite a public subscription in 1823, the Juvenile Library ceased publication, and Godwin was declared bankrupt (Grylls, *William Godwin*, p. 233). The final cataclysm should have come as no surprise. Because the title of the house in Skinner Street was disputable, Godwin had from 1808 paid no rent at all. When he was evicted in 1822 he was ordered to pay the rent for 1820–1822, and in 1825 a second judgment demanded rent for 1817–1819, in both cases with costs. To raise the new sum of over £400, Godwin was forced to sacrifice virtually all his copyrights (Brown, "Notes on 41 Skinner Street," *MLN*, 54:330–331 [May 1939]).

[55] An inn.

[56] Probably [Alexander Gordon], *Travels in Germany and the Illyrian Provinces* (Dublin [1825?]).

a review of his three first lectures upon History. After dinner they all go to rehearse at the theatre — Zachar Nicolaitch arrives. Play with Dunia and on the Piano. After tea *M. G. shews something about Mathematics upon Paper.* most remarcable.

Saturday July 18th. 30th. Fine day. the first for these three weeks. Give lessons. After dinner lessons. Then go in the garden to gather black currants. Then go to the Bath. Some gentlemen come to tea. Then they go. The Gazette is read aloud. Very amusing.

Sunday July 19th. 31st. Beautiful clear weather. Walk about the whole day enjoying the return of the fine weather. Begin in the morning the comedy of the *Governesses.* After church we all go to the Stone Mountain and climb up and down its ⟨precipices⟩ ravines. The path runs along the side of the hill and was so narrow there was only room ↑for↓ ⟨of⟩ one's foot — ⟨Tr⟩ The trees from above & below hang so closely over it we were sometimes obliged almost to creep on all all fours ere we could make our way thro'. On the brink of the cliffs the prospect is extremely pretty; at ⟨it⟩ their base the Muscova reca and ⟨in⟩ its lawny banks, and beyond the ⟨plain meadowy plain is spotted with⟩ green of the meadows beyond is broken by thick clumps of wood. Dress for Dinner. Mad Perecouloff and her Daughters and three Officers dine. After dinner walk in the garden and gather black currants. Then rehearsal at the theatre.

Monday July 20th. August 1st. Fine weather. Do nothing all day, for there is nothing to be heard, but ⟨exl⟩ exclamations and orders for the theatre and the rehearsal. Walk in the garden before dinner with the children. Dark clouds begin to assemble and cover the horizon. After dinner M. Cornet goes to Moscow. Walk in the garden with the children. Sit on the Balcony at the bottom of the great Alley.

Tuesday July 21 August 2nd. Fine weather. Give lessons. Rehearsals all day. M. Cornet arrives from Moscow. After dinner Mr. Corsicoff and Madme. Stramiloff and son arrive. Also Zachar Nicolaitch.

X Wednesday July 22nd. August 3rd. Marie Ivanovna's Birthday. Ill all day. Mr. Kakorchkine, Mr. Vassiltchikoff,[57] Platon Stepan-

[57] In a letter postmarked November 29, 1842, Claire told Mary that she was

itch arrive. Madme. Spiridoff, Madme. Monchanoff Mad. Percouleff and daughters, Eugenie Tcherbacheff and Miss Massy Colonel Mack and innumerable other officers at dinner in the Green House. After dinner — Esther is played and a russian piece by Prince Ichahafskoy which ends at nine o'clock. Then Dancing until supper.

Thursday July 23rd. August 4th. We all get up late and tired. Very fine weather. We all go a long walk to the Tcherbacheff wood and home by the Mills. After dinner Marie Ivanovna goes in the Ligne — read and finish 3rd Canto of Islam with M. G. The Ligne passes over the arm of a little girl — fortunately the arm is only a little bruised. We play after tea in the balcony at clapping our hands together.

Friday July 24th. August 5th. Fine weather. Give lessons. Read Life of Göthe, Lecture on Modern History by M. Gambs. After dinner walk to Nicolokoi Gara. We cross the river and follow its opposite bank to the foot of the mountain, we gain its steep thro' a path ⟨wh⟩ overshadowed by a thick grove on both sides. We repose in a grassy nook and make garlands with grass and try our luck with blades of grass in flower. Colonel Mack at tea. Singing.

Saturday July 25th. August 6th.

—— —— —— —— —— —— —— ——

Sunday July 26th. August 7th. Fine warm sunny weather. Walk in the garden, read Islam. Then to the Summer House on the Banks of the River ⟨and⟩ with Miss Hawker, and Miss Kakorchkine — ↑and M. Cornet↓ M.G. reads aloud two chapters of a Russian Tale he has composed. Russian Officers at dinner. After dinner we play at different games and drink tea in the Summer House on the River — then we dance.

Monday July 27th. August 8th. At nine we all set out for the seat of Prince Laponchkine — They go in ⟨t⟩ carriages — but M.G.   M. Cornet, Nicolas and I go the whole way on foot. The weather is fine and warm as in Italy. We sit in the woods and find Strawberries. The seat of Prince Laponkine is delightful — ⟨Fre⟩ We dine in a large stone balcony supported upon corinthian columns —

about to see Madame Vassiltchikoff, the aunt of one of her Moscow pupils (Abinger MSS.).

beneath is a wide terrace and then immediately the garden, one extent of wood descends to the river, which emerging from under the farthest grove, ⟨at⟩ is seen ⟨in a the dista⟩ traversing the distant valley — the body of the house consists in a large handsome saloon and in an antichamber — on each side is a colonnade ⟨at joining the wings⟩ which conducts to a wing — the intervening spaces between the house and the wings is planted with flowering shrubs which peep in between the columns of the colonnade and have a delightful appearance. There was also a portrait of Catherine II and her son Paul the first. Catherine has a remarkably look of penetration, and her mouth expresses an extremely placid disposition; but Paul has the wandering look of an imbecile; there is a silly ⟨smiling smile of⟩ smirking look in the little eyes particularly expressive of meanness an expression much inforced by a short cock up nose and the shortness of the lower part of his face in comparison with his ⟨a⟩ length of forehead, disorganizes his whole face and gives an expression of folly and strangeness to the whole countenance. After dinner walk thro the garden down to the River — here the view is beautiful when one looks towards the house. from the bank of the river an ⟨ampht⟩ amphitheatre of meadow its background is broken by woods ⟨which sweep in irregular clumps and the hills behind⟩ rising ⟨in⟩ one above the other upon the hills behind, and stretching ⟨over⟩ on both sides of the amphitheatre into the river, so that the space we stood on ressembled a little bay among the hills, ⟨whose⟩ and from among the woody height the white house peeped forth. Further upwards the river in a sudden bend disclosed the house of Tcherbachoff to our sight which altho' on the same bank as we were seemed by the bending of the river to be opposite. To the left on the opposite bank, stood the town of Ivinigorod ⟨an⟩ stretching out at the foot of its convent. As we contemplated this landscape the sky seemed to devide into two parts — that over our heads was of a bright blue which broken by a long line of dark grey which stretch ⟨all⟩ along its whole surface — all beyond of was of one unbroken dun colour every where in the distant country we perceived small vapours ⟨which concealed⟩ rising which concealed the ground. We concluded there would be a storm. The dark part of the Heaven which before ⟨had⟩ seemed only covered with a blackish mist, this mist seemed to thicken into clouds of massy size and thickness. We hurried to the carriages and went home.

# Fifth Journal

Notwithstanding that I had a most dreadful head-ach the whole day, yet this excursion amused me extremely.

Tuesday July 28th. August 9th. Give lessons. After dinner M. Cornet sets out for Moscow with Lise Hardorff. Finish Life of Göthe.

Wednesday July 29th. August 10th. Give lessons. Fine weather. After dinner we all go to Ivinigorod. First to the convent which is two miles beyond the town. Here we hear a Te Deum sung. ⟨The convent is of a square form⟩ The convent is surrounded by four white walls with a tower at each corner — ⟨it is⟩ the road is always mounting and half way up the ⟨whl⟩ hill ⟨h⟩ three paces from the road side and hid amid trees is the convent — beneath it the hill and its groves slope in a gentle descent to the river, and above it the hill is also covered with trees. ⟨Opposite the convent⟩ on the other side of the road, opposite the convent, is a little ⟨hot⟩ inn also hid among trees — behind the inn you descend the side of the hill and begin to mount another — at your side the ground descends into a plain, and never have I seen a prettier grove than that with which the descent is covered — no under wood intercepts the view, every trunk and stem of each tree was seen turned in a gentle bend towards the slope of the hill — and the ⟨lawny lawn⟩ mossy lawn was cut by little streams of light which the rays of the sun had made thro' each line of trees. We sit at the edge of the hill towards the town of Ivinigorod and Miss Kakoschkine sketches it. Return very late. From Axinievna walk home with M. G. Nicolas and John.

Thursday July 30th. August 11th. It is a dark warm day. Every instant we expect it to rain. Give lessons. Write for the Gazette. Letter from Miss Trewin enclosing ⟨a⟩ something from the News-paper.

Friday July 31st. August 12th. Torrents of rain. Give lessons. Write for the Newspaper⟨s⟩. Lecture upon Modern History. Spain — the war of Ferdinand of Arragon and his wife Isabel of Castille against the Moors. Conquest of Grenada — Establishment of the Inquisi-tion. Ferdinand freed himself so far from the power of the Pope, that since his reign not a single Bishop or Arch-bishop has ever been nominated except by the Crown. Oath of the Castillians to

# Islavsky 1825

Ferdinand — I swear to defend you, so long as you protect us and our rights and the holy Catholic Church. if not — not. And this is the oath which to this very day the Spanish nobles ⟨take⟩ make upon the Coronation of each King. Jeanne La folle daughter of Ferdinand & Isabelle, married to Philip le Beau of Austria — He dies at the age of 28 — and Jeanne goes mad and remains so fifty years untill the time of her death. Their Son Charles, succeeds to the throne of Castille under the regency of his grandfather Ferdinand and by the name of Charles the 5th. Officer at dinner. Walk in the great Alley with M. G. and the children  Zachar Nicolaitch arrives and Colonel Mack drinks tea. Sing ⟨in⟩ before Supper. I am melancholy because I have no news of my friends and fear they are not well.

Saturday August 1st. 13th. It is a holiday to day. Fine warm weather. Write all the morning for the Gazette. Colonel Mack & other officers at dinner. We dine in the Green House. At seven the Gazette is read. Scene. M. G. declares he will write no more. Before Supper we sing.

Sunday August 2nd. 14th. Fine day. Walk in the great Alley. Read Islam which makes me very melancholy. Colonel Mack at dinner. We dine in the Green House. Zachar Nicolaitch says — I am now perfectly happy — My son devotes himself to his Marmot, and my wife to a Colonel. Dancing in the Evening. Letter from M. Harvey enclosing one from Leopoldine and a letter from M. Baxter.

Monday August 3rd. 15th. Beautiful Weather. Give lessons. Lecture on Ancient History. Description of Babylon. Floating Garden. Asia Minor. The Kingdoms of Troy, Phrygia and Lydia. The Hatred between the Greeks and the Trojans a commercial hatred — when the Greeks dispatched the fleet of the Argonauts to reconnoitre the advantageous positions of the Black Sea, the Trojans did every thing in their Power to annoy and damage the expedition, feeling that it was the greatest attack against the prosperity of their commerce which had yet been made. Priam had in his youth, been captive in Greece — At the time Troy was destroyed, he reigned over almost the whole of Asia Minor; this province had at first peopled Greece, and afterwards received colonies from Greece  colonies which became far more rich, and more civilized than the mother

343

country. After dinner visit Vinerka and her two puppies. Then walk with Miss Hardorff, Catherine, M. Gambs  Nicolas and John, ↑to↓ Nazarievo — We sit on the grass and M. G. reads aloud Schubart's Poems The Prisoner to Liberity, to his Daughter Julia.[58]

Tuesday August 4th. 16th. M. G.'s Birthday. Fine weather. Give lessons. Write to M. Harvey. After dinner Zachar Nicolaivitch and ⟨Mons Ba⟩ Vassili Michailovitch go to Moscow. We all go a long walk beyond Nicolsky Gara — the top of the hill once gained our walk proceeded thro a straight road, bordered by pine woods on each side, which sometimes opening on our right we discovered steep precipices clothed with young oak, sloping to the river's side, and beyond ⟨a⟩ corn fields ⟨and⟩ bounded by new woods. As we return the sun was setting behind the forest on the left side of the road; sometimes ⟨a light⟩ his rays penetrating ⟨ob⟩ obliquely lighted up ↑softly with a tender golden gleam↓ every separate trunk, but left ⟨the top⟩ their tops in a dark green shade; then sinking lower the verge of the horizon seemed like a fire ⟨↑sending bright masses of↓ whose flames penetrate thro' the wood whose bright flames filled up every interstice of the wood.⟩ blazing beyond the wood, and its bright flames filled up the space between the stem of one tree to the other. The pine forest, ⟨even at with its dark green⟩ ↑almost black in the growing shade of Evening,↓ stretched ↑its dark mass↓ before us, and seemed in the distance to approach together from each side and to shut in the road, as if ⟨one⟩ ↑we were walking in an↓ amphitheatre of wood ⟨were before us⟩ M. G. reads aloud Schillers Poems.

Wednesday August 5th. 17th. Fine weather. Give lessons. Lecture on AEsthetique. We do not walk to day.

Thursday August 6th. 18th. Great Holiday. Walk in the morning to the Mill. The sky is dark and cloudy. Read Islam, before dinner and after dinner. The Evening is very fresh. Singing with Miss Hardorff — We sing so much that we all three lose our voices.

Friday August 7th. 19th. Give lessons. Read Le Distrait by Regnier.[59] Marie Ivanovna goes to Madame Zimmermann's. Lecture on

[58] Schubart, *Sämtliche Gedichte*, "Der gesangene Sänger," II, 154; "Meiner Julie," II, 245–248.
[59] Not Régnier, but Jean François Regnard (1656–1710), *Le Distrait*, verse

# Islavsky 1825

Modern History. This lecture began with the History of France under the reign of Charles VII. After he had succeeded in regaining his empire from the hands of the English, he did not display so great a character in peace as in war. He was on very ill terms with his son Louis XI, who after a rebellion against his father took refuge at the court of the Duc of Burgundy, a vassal of France. Here he passed some time, in daily relation with the son of the Duc, who afterwards became his enemy, when he succeeded to his father under the tittle of Charles Le Temeraire. Louis XI at last succeeded to his throne, and from that instant all his efforts were directed to the enlarging his power. He was cold, cruel and false, and from his love of plotting ⟨nd⟩ indirectly against others obtained the surname of Surnois. There were then no regular troops in france, and he established a guard of ⟨Sch⟩ Scotch, round his person; on great occasions he called them to aid to detirmine a battle, or to save him in retreat, and their heavy armour and their discipline always turned the balance in their favour. Louis XI lived in the most economical manner and spent all his treasure, in keeping spies at the other courts, whose ministers even he kept in his pay; so that he always knew ⟨was⟩ what was going forward and took his precautions accordingly. His great aim was to reduce his two vassals, the Duke of Burgundy and the Duke of Brittany whose territories were so large, they must either swallow up France or be swallowed up by her. Charles Le Temeraire was now duke of Burgundy, he had married the sister of Edward the 4th of England, and his bold enterprising hot character made him no unfit victim for the calculating prudence of Louis. War was declared between them – Both armies marched forward, but when on the field of battle both ↑armies↓ virtually without a stroke having been drawn, took flight; Louis fled with his troops but sought to recall them. Charles, remained alone on the field of battle, ready as he said, to maintain it ⟨a⟩ by his single arm against an army while his generals tried to respirit the frightened troops – this battle therefore was decided to have been gained by Charles. In another battle at          he also remaind victor – but at          Louis brought up his Scotch guard and Charles was vanquished. Louis then concluded a treaty with the town of Liege, a powerful free city that

comedy in five acts (1697), in *Théâtre des auteurs du premier ordre* (Paris, 1810), vol. XXIV.

they should send troops into the very centre of Burgundy while he should march to its frontiers Thus Charles would be attacked on both sides. In the meantime Charles sent a herald to Louis, demanding a conference, in hopes of settling every bout ↑by↓ a negotiation Louis consented to this, for wherever he could spare his armies he did, and besides he hoped, to gain more by a negotiation in which he was a profound master, and Charles, a most unsuspecting fool, than by arms where notwithstanding his successes, Charles was still his superior. He consented therefore, and dispatched a messenger to Liege to bid them delay untill they should hear further from him, ⟨and⟩ whilst he marched to Peronne, where Charles was, and where the conference was appointed. Their meeting was very amiable and every thing very nearly arranged between them, when Charles received news from his general stationned in the centre of Burgundy that the ⟨Lieg⟩ Ligeois had fallen upon him, and destroyed his regiment — that all the prisoners they had made they had cut the ⟨thum⟩ veins round the thumbs of their ⟨right⟩ right hand, in order to disable them from ever again taking up arms. ⟨This news and this⟩ It seems that the messenger Louis had sent, had been assassinated on the road by robbers, and therefore Liege had never received his message, had acted according to their first agreement. This news and this seeming want of faith, so exasperated Charles that he was on the point of stabbing Louis with his own hand; his nobles withheld him, bidding him recollect, that Louis was still his King and that they themselves were bound to protect Lewis's life, for in their oath to Charles they had bound themselves to obey him ⟨only⟩ in every thing sauf what was due to their King. Thus withheld, Charles suddenly seized upon the person of Lewis and shut him with ⟨th⟩ his court in the citadel of Peronne. Lewis had no other resource but to pray to his two Virgins, the one Notre Dame des Secours and the other Notre Dame de Clery, and to offer them all sorts of temptations in the guise of chapels and altars if they would only get him out of this scrape. Among his attendants was an astrologer an Italian of the name of ⟨Campo Baccio⟩ ↑Marchetti↓; Lewis who never began an undertaking without consulting him was furious that he had not warned him of what was to befall at Peronne. He plotted with Olivier le Dain (his barber, a man who served him in all his cruelties, and who by his riches and influence was equal to a minister⟩ and another, and said Send me ⟨Campo Baccio⟩ ↑Marchetti↓, if at the end of our conversation I say, que le ceil vous conduisse! stab him as he comes into the antichamber. He then sent for ⟨Campo Baccio⟩ ↑Marchetti↓ and reproached him with his want of skill, and asked him how he could possibly have overlooked such a principal event as this his captivity. ⟨Campo Baccio⟩ ↑Marchetti↓ replied, that he could not answer for every thing; true it was, he had observed an appearance of mystery in the stars which this event now accounted for. And pray said Lewis ironically have you any idea concerning your own Death, if it is near ⟨of⟩ ↑or↓ far off? ⟨Campo Baccio⟩ ↑Marchetti↓ without losing countenance replied; that as to the period he was not very certain, but one curious circumstance the stars had revealed to him, which was that his Death would ⟨precede⟩ preceed that of Lewis, about three time twenty fours hours. Lewis mused upon this, and then dismissed him, taking great care to say loudly at the door Que le bon Dieu vous conduisse! instead of Que le ciel vous conduisse. Thus ⟨Campo Baccio⟩ ↑Marchetti↓ was saved.

Charles then ⟨send⟩ sent two of his ministers to negotiate with Lewis for his freedom — one was Philip de Commines and the other                But Lewis faithful to his custom, began by corrupting them, and ⟨with his p⟩ by gold and persuasions he brought them over to his side. He accepted the hard conditions Charles imposed, but with the aid of the two ministers he placed under his seal with which he signed them a protestation to the contrary. Philip de Commines became afterwards minister to Lewis and has written the history of his time⟨s⟩. Charles conducted Lewis to Liege, and made him behold his own french troops attack and conquer the town of Leige; ⟨which⟩ which was razed to the ground and the plough passed over its streets; the King of France was then restored to Liberty. His first action, on arriving at Paris was to declare nul and void all he had signed, and ⟨a new war⟩ the materials for a new war, lay brewing between the houses of France and Burgundy. ⟨Lewis⟩ ◇ [notes continued under August 10th]

Saturday August 8th. 20th. ⟨Fine day.⟩ Give lessons. Monsieur Bazile arrives in the rain. After dinner M. Gambs goes to Moscow.

Sunday August 9th. 21st. Fine day. John remains in his room all day. I remain with him. Colonel Mack the Captain, Daniel Assipitch, Vassili Nicolavitch, Madme. Perecouloff and her daughters, dine. After dinner Miss Massy with Eugenie arrives. They dance in the Green House. After dinner dancing and we play at the Ring.

Monday August 10th. 22nd. Rain at intervals and high wind. Give lessons. We dine early — After dinner Marie Ivanovna goes to pay visits. M. Gambs comes home in the night.

◊ Lewis according to his custom, set about seeing, how much of the storm which hung over his head could be averted by nego-tiation. He ⟨bib⟩ bribed the go-between of Charles ⟨un⟩ of Bur-gundy & Edward of England who resided at Cherboug⟨h⟩, to remit him all the letters which passed by his medium between these two ⟨pof⟩ powers, and by ⟨there⟩ these he learned, that a confedaration had been entered into between Charles Edward, and the Duke of Brittany to attack France ⟨at the⟩ in the ensuing spring and from three different quarters. This plan which if it had been followed ⟨had brought⟩ would have brought almost inevitable ruin upon France failed however from the following cause⟨s⟩. Charles ⟨the⟩ le temeraire, finding he had nothing to do during the winter, and hating inactivity, led his troops to attack the city of Nuitz on the borders of the Rhine. Here however he lost so many men, and the siege was so long protracted that when Spring came, and with it Edward landed at Calais, Charles was obliged to send to tell him he could not come. Lewis seized this opportunity to negotiate with Edward, and in an interview he had with him upon a bridge each King separated from the other by a barrier draw across it, Lewis being well accompanied and Edward only by his brother Clarence, insinuated to Edward that Charles had only been playing with him; he further begged pardon of Edward for his having assisted Mar-guerite of Anjou against him, and expressed his desire that an alliance might be formed between them, which offer he seasoned by a proposal of an annuity of 50,000 markes a year to the English King. Edward acceeded to this willingly and withdrew his troops. The Duke of Brittany being left thus alone naturally ⟨allow⟩ re-mained quiet. When Charles returned from Nuitz, deprived as he was of his english ally, he found himself too weak to attack France, and therefore turned his arms against the Duke of Lorraine who was firmly supported by the Swiss. In this war the course of

# Islavsky 1825

Charles's victories had an end — the loss of the Burgundians was severe at Sempach and at Morat, so ⟨muc⟩ much so that at the last place, the whole field of battle was still strewn with their bones no later than fifty years ago. At last Charles lost his life at ⟨M⟩ Nanci; no one ever knew the manner of his Death; nor was his body found, but it is generally supposed his death was effectuated by his doctor ⟨who⟩ who was ⟨br⟩ bribed to it by Louis XI and what renders this circumstance the more probable is that the very day of his disappearance and of the battle of Nanci, his death was publicly known at Paris. He left only one daughter Marie de Bourgogne who was married to Maximilian ⟨Em⟩ Ist. Emperor of Germany and it is from this marriage that the wars for the succession of Burgundy which followed between France and Germany had their rise. ⟨Marie of⟩ Lewis found himself now delivered from his most formidable enemy, and turned his thoughts towards the establishment of his children, whom however he never could endure. His son Charles VIII had been brought up among peasants — Anne his eldest daughter, a woman of great beauty and merit was much loved by Louis of Orleans, then the first of the prince of blood and afterwards Louis XII. ⟨but⟩ a most amiable accomplished ⟨h⟩ handsome man, but for no reason whatever Lewis would not hear of the match, but married his daughter Anne to the Duke of Beaujeu and ⟨insisted that⟩ ↑made↓ Lewis ⟨should⟩ marry his second daughter Jeanne, who was little ⟨and⟩ ugly and difformed. This marriage made Louis d'Orleans extremely unhappy, and to rid himself of his wife, he fled shortly after his marriage to the court of the Duke of ⟨Burgundy⟩ Brittany where he remained many years, and during which time he became hopelessly altho' passionately attached to Anne of ⟨Brittay⟩ Brittany. ⟨When Louis⟩ After some years spent in the misery of suspicion and in the strictest retirement, Lewis XI expired. His daughter Anne de Beaujeu then shewed herself in her true colours: she declared herself regent untill her brother should be of age; she withdrew him from the humble vulgar life to which the suspicious character of his father had consigned him, and applied herself, to give him a princely education. She remitted half the taxes with which her father had aggrieved the people. ⟨⟨In the meantime Marie de Bourgogne wife of Maximilian Emperor of Germany died, leaving only two children, a daughter and one son Philip le Beau who after-

# Fifth Journal

wards married Jeanne La Folle, daughter of Isabel of Castille and Ferdinand of Arragon. Maximilian, who was a ⟨truly⟩ true fortune hunter among the Potentates of his day, manifested a desire of marrying Anne of Brittany, by ⟨which he would have united⟩ whom, as she was an only child, he would have united Brittany as well as Burgundy to his Empire. Shortly before this Brittany had declared war to France, and its army appoached the frontiers headed by Lewis d'Orleans. Anne's situation was difficult, her means were by no means brilliant; she looked round her court for a general to head her army and having fixed upon Tremouille she called him, and told him what a difficult desparing enterprize it would be against Brittany⟩⟩ Louis d'Orleans declared that the regency belonged to him as nearest male relation to the young King, and induced the Duke of Brittany to take up arms in his favour. Anne's situation was difficult, her means were very limited, and what was far worse she was surrounded by a nobility ⟨whom⟩ her enemies of her house, from the unjust tyranny her father had exercised over them. In this emergency she fixed upon a noble called La Tremouille ⟨and told him⟩ one of those who had most suffered under the late reign, and appointed him to command the ⟨a⟩ french army. He promised her not only to defeat the Duke of Brittany's troops, but to bring Louis d'Orleans prisoner — which he faithfully performed. Louis was condemned to a strict but honorable prison. In the meantime, Marie de Bourgogne, wife of Maximilian Emperor of Germany died leaving only two children a daughter and one son Philip le Beau, who married Jeanne la Folle daughter of Ferdinand of Arragon and Isabel of Castille. ⟨Ma⟩ Burgundy naturally fell to Philip le Beau, who was yet a minor; Maximilian, who was truly a fortune hunter among the Potentates of his day, cast his eyes upon Anne of Brittany, by whom as she was an only child, he would have added Brittany to his empire, and he succeeded so well that ⟨the⟩ he had already been affianced to her. Anne de Beaujeu beheld in this alliance, a danger of the newest & most pressing kind for France. Brittany and Burgundy united to the Empire of Germany became a most formidable power. She sent for Louis d'Orleans and promised him his liberty on one condition, that he should set out for Brittany and ⟨use⟩ use the power their mutual affection gave him over Anne's mind, to persuade her to ⟨bea⟩ annull her marriage with Maximilian and espouse the young King Charles

# Islavsky 1825

VIII. This Louis d'Orleans ⟨mot⟩ most faithfully promised and performed. Anne married Charles, ⟨an⟩ who dying young and leaving no children, Louis d'Orleans became heir to the throne, under the tittle of Louis XII, and divorced his first wife Jeanne to marry Anne. ⟨that thus    for thus⟩ which his long affection for her, and the interest of France required. They had one daughter ⟨Claudia⟩ Clotilde who was married to her cousin the Duc d'Angouleme, and afterwards Francis I. Their son Henry II was the first King of France, in whose person, Brittany became ⟨un⟩ legally and indisputably united to France.

Teusday August 11th. 23rd. Rain autumnal weather. Give lessons. In the Evening make a cake.

Wednesday August 12th. 24th. It is St Clara's day. I spend my last happy day. At tea under a cake the inside of which was hollow, I find a dove with the following verses.

> Bonnement, avec indulgence
> De l'amitie reçois les vœux
> Elle parle dans l'innocence
> D'un cœur sincere, affecteux.
> Loin de moi le projet frivole
> De t'encenser comme une idole,
> Que des sens profane l'erreur;
> Je suis le culte d'Uranie;
> Quand elle regne sur ma vie
> Ton nom peut vivre dans mon cœur.
>
> ~
>
> Je veux y graver ton image;
> Ton œil voilé de souvenirs.
> Ton âme enflammant ton visage
> De haine pour de vains plaisirs.
> Cette ame encor compatissante
> D'une creature souffrante
> Partageant l'angoisse et les maux;
> Et pour combattre l'injustice,
> Prête a partager le supplice
> Des Laons livrès aux bourreaux.
>
> ~

351

# Fifth Journal

Aprés les fureurs de l'orage
D'un lac, les Cygnes dispersés
S'Eloignent enfin du rivage,
À se reunir empressés.
Aprés de penibles allarmes
Ainsi tu peux gouter les charmes
D'Un bonheur aux vertus allié.
Et dans les champs de l'Hesperie
Consacrer les jours de ta vie
Aux doux loisirs de l'Amitie.[60]

Thursday August 13th. 25th. I do not know how I have the courage to trace the remembrance of this unhappy day in my Journal.

[60]

Truly, with the indulgence
Of friendship receive the vows
It speaks in the innocence
Of a heart sincere, affectionate.
I am far from the frivolous project
Of worshiping you like an idol,
A profane error of the senses;
I follow the cult of Urania;
While she reigns over my life
Your name can live in my heart.

I wish to engrave there your image;
Your eye veiled with memories.
Your soul igniting your face
With hatred for vain pleasures.
That soul still compassionate
For a suffering creature
Sharing anguish and evil;
And to combat injustice,
Ready to share the torture
Of Laons delivered to the executioners.

After the furies of the storm
On a lake, the scattered Swans
Finally leave the shore,
Eager to reunite.
After the painful alarms
You too can enjoy the charms
Of happiness allied to virtue.
And in the Hesperian fields
Devote the days of your life
To the sweet leisures of Friendship.

By Hermann Gambs, but not among the published poems that I have seen. Laon is a reference to Shelley's hero in *The Revolt of Islam*.

# Islavsky 1825

Give lessons in the morning. Then walk with John and Dunia Nicholas and M. Gambs towards Tcherbaschoff's wood. After dinner I take up the Newspaper by accident and read there an account of a duel between Trelawny and another englishman. In a moment my whole peace is destroyed. ⟨Yet I must⟩ They say he is dangerously wounded, but I must hope — what else have I left to choose, but to despair or hope, and hope I must, but I know despair will come.[61]

Friday August 14th. 26  Spend a most unhappy day. Give lessons. Mr. Armfeld comes.

Saturday August 15th. 27th. My spirits are extremely bad. It is Miss ⟨K⟩ Kakorchkine's birth-day. The House is full of company dancing singing and masking the whole day. In the universal joy around me, I seemed to be an exil from Hope and Happiness.

Sunday August 16th. 28th. Dreadful bad weather. Rain in torrents the whole day. There is a fair at Islavsky and our house is full of company. Singing, dancing and in the Evening masking. Read a little of Islam.

Monday August 17th. 29th. Rain in torrents and bleak cold wind. Give lessons. Read a little of Islam. In the Evening Mr. Cornet, Mr. Gambs and Mr. Armfeld repeat the Parody of Esther.

X Tuesday August 18th. 30th. I dreamt this night that I saw Inwalert — He was masked but spoke not. My spirits are very low and otherwise I am extremely indisposed. Mr. Cornet, Mr. Armfeld and Mr. Kassioff go to Moscow. Give lessons. After dinner read Islam. Colonel Mack and Daniel Assipitch at tea. Mr. Gambs relates to us the beginning of The Ring by La Motte Fouqué [62] and stories from the Arabian Nights.

Wednesday August 19 — 31st. Extremely Unwell the whole day and extremely depressed in spirits. Give lessons till eleven. Then walk with the children and Mr. Gambs to a new view he has

---

[61] This was the disabling but not fatal attack by Whitcombe on Trelawny in his cave stronghold on Mt. Parnassus (see Grylls, *Trelawny*, pp. 133–135). In a letter to Jane Williams, October 27, 1825, Claire describes the depression into which this news threw her (Abinger MSS.).

[62] *Der Zauberring: Ein Ritterroman*, 3 vols. (Nurenberg, 1812).

# Fifth Journal

found of the Moscow Reca. At ½ past one lecture upon Œsthetique. After dinner give lessons. After tea M. G. relates Arabian Nights. Mr. Cornet and Monsieur Bazile arrive. They bring me a letter from Mary. It is dated the 26th. of July and makes no mention of Odysseus's death — therefore I must hope that the whole is a false report. Were it otherwise Mary must have ⟨herd⟩ heard by the 26th. of July what had happened the 13th. of June.

Thursday August 20th. September 1st. My health is better. Give lessons. The weather is beautiful. At twelve we all set out for a long walk but we lose Miss Hardorff, Miss Kassioff, her brother & Mr. Cornet by the way. we continue our walk over the hill and across the meadow to the garden home. Marie Ivanovna dines at Madme. Zimmermann's. After dinner give lessons. Then read a little of Islam and Mr. G. reads aloud letters from his family. He relates also the Ring from La Motte Fouqué — and Marie Ivanovna comes homes at nine. Then long talk with Mr. Cornet and Mr. G. upon sentiment and thought. I say I cannot distinguish one from the other. They say they are two perfectly different things.

Friday August 21st. September 2nd. Fine weather. Walk in the great Alley. Again the sight of Nature rejoices me. I sit upon the Balcony at the bottom of the great Alley, and watch the wind among the trees of the little grove before me. Give lessons. Mr. Gambs gives his lecture upon Modern History at Miss Kakorch-kine's. England, Austria, the Porte and the Popes. After dinner we all go a walk to the wood to seek nuts. Miss Hardorff's three petticoats fall and she lags behind as usual — Dispute about the beauty of Men and Women. Mr. Gambs very disagreeable. As we come home we meet Ivan upon the full gallop, to tell us there is the scarlet fever in the village and that we must return by the garden. When we come home Marie Ivanovna is already gone to Madme. Zimmermann's to beg a lodging and when she comes home, she settles that the children shall go there. Sing Figaro and then to bed.

Saturday August 22nd. September 3rd. Fine weather. — Pack up. Call upon Miss Hawker cross the river with Mr. Cornet, Vassili Michailovitch and Mr. Gambs. Then go with Marie Ivanovna Dunia, Vania [Johnny], Madlle. Olga and Catherine Ivanovna to

## Islavsky 1825

Madame Zimmermann's. Very friendly reception. Walk three times in the glen by the side of the house, sometimes winding thro' the innumerable foot-paths which run like a river cut into a thousand channels thro' its narrow bottom, and sometimes on the edge of the hills which over look it. At one the General and Mr. Gambs arrive. They all go to dinner at Madame Tcherbascheff's. Sit in the Balcony and admire the prospect. Read Islam. Drink tea & talk in the balcony till eight in the Evening when Marie Ivanovna comes. They all go home. Happy, quiet day, when my spirit enjoys the beautiful plain before me, the quiet river gliding in serenest repose at the foot of the steep bank under the house, and quiveringly reflecting every hue of Heaven.

Sunday August 23rd. September 4th. Fine clear weather dry but rather cold. After breakfast walk on the balcony. Examine our habitation. It is an old wooden house built on the very verge of the cliff which descends steeply to the river — a bed of stones and sand extends from the cliffs foot to the river which in its riduced state flows thro' a deeper but very narrow channel in the middle of the spacious bed which is only covered in spring or Autumn. On the other side, is an extensive stretch of meadow land and Madme. Tcherbaschoff's house in the distance, and on both sides masses of dark forest stretch from her house to meet the banks of the river in its windings thro' distant vallies. By the side of our dwelling a little mountain river comes from inland and joins here the Moscow River. We follow it to its source thro' a wild ravine between two ⟨clif⟩ ridges of hills which its own impetuosity has separated and worked a deep channel at their feet. The sides of the hills are clothed with pines and verdure, or sometimes bare; the paths are narrow and intricate and so numerous and distinct when seen from above they look like a thousand little rills watering the ⟨wa⟩ valley below, and intersecting each other's path and running up and down, now higher now lower like a serpent's track.

Marie Ivanovna comes to see us at one o'clock. She takes Madme. Zimmermann home with her — After dinner walk with the children in the ravine. They run and climb ⟨a⟩ up and down its steep sides. Read Islam. and talk. Drink tea on the Balcony. Mad. Zimmermann comes home at ½ past eight. Talk with her till ½ past nine then to Bed. Write to my mother and send my letter.

355

# Fifth Journal

Monday August 24th. September 5th. Fine weather. Give lessons. Mrs. Spiridoff dines. Marie Ivanovna & Nicolas come after dinner. Go with Catherine Ivanovna, Mr. G. Dunia, John & Nicolas to a review in the plain beyond Ivinigorod. Beautiful afternoon.

Teusday August 25th. Septr. 6th. Lovely weather. I think a great deal of past times to-day and above all of this day three years. but the sentiments of that time are most likely long ago, vanished into air. This is life. So live to nothing but toil and trouble — all its sweets are like the day whose anniversay this is — more transitory than a shade — yet it had been otherwise if Inwalert had been different and I might have been as happy as I am now wretched.[63] Give lessons. After dinner walk with the children and Mr. G. to Dunina on the other side of the river.

Wednesday August 26th. Sept. 7th. Fine weather. Go early to the bath. Give ⟨breakfast⟩ ↑lessons↓. Marie Ivanovna goes home. Madme. Zimmermann goes ⟨hom⟩ to dine at Alsufieff's. M. I[vanovna]. comes with Olga Michailovna too late. so M. I[vanovna]. I & Dunia we go there after dinner. It is Natalie's name's day. Spend a very pleasant evening with Miss Sayce. As we return home meet Mr. G. Nicolas & John. At home, Mr. G. talks of his gaining three prizes at school. Letter from Mrs. Seymour.

Thursday August 27th. September 8th. After breakfast go a long walk with O.M. M.G. John & Dunia towards the House of Alsufieff — ⟨Come home & give lessons.⟩ during our walk concert with M. G. the plan of Gottingen. The wind is very high & the whole country before us is veiled by clouds of Dust. Come home give lessons. Nicolas comes. After dinner Marie Ivanovna & Olga Michailovna go home. M. G. begins to write his seventh canto. Go with Dunia & John & Annette & Lise on the road to Axinievna to conduct Nicolas home. On our return drink tea and spend the rest of the Evening with Madme. Zimmermann who relates to me the manner of the marriage of Miss Barbe Acaroff to Mr. Kakorchkine.

Friday August 28th. Sept. 9th. Rain during the night and in the morning — The whole meadow beyond seems veiled by a thin

[63] Claire has left only this entry to suggest the nature of her happiest relationship with Trelawny, on September 6, 1822.

# Islavsky 1825

white mist of falling rain. Breakfast. Walk a little in the balcony.
Give lessons. The day clears up. After dinner walk with the children & M.G. upon the high road to Axienievna. A servant comes
to tell us that Madme. Alsufieff is arrived. We hurry home. They
drink tea & then go. Letter from Mr. Baxter and two London
Monthly reviews.

Saturday August 29th. Sept. 10th. Fine day. It is a great holiday
being the day on which St John's head was cut off by Herod.
Mr. Cornet arrives shortly after breakfast. Spend the whole morning in talking and in walking upon the balcony. He goes before
dinner. Marie Ivanovna Zachar Nicolaitch and Madlle. Olga
come to dinner and some people from Ivinigorod and two Officers.
After dinner all our *marmaille* [64] arrive from Islavsky. After much
singing & jumping walk with John & Nicolas part of the way
home — They seated in their drochsky set off full gallop & leave
Nicolas with us to make the best of our way home, which we reach
at ½ past nine. Find all the maid servants in the drawing room
playing at Durac with the two Officers. Write to Mrs. Seymour &
Mr. Baxter.

Sunday August 30th. September 11th. Mr. Gambs sets off early
for Islavsky & Moscow   Set out with John & Nicolas on foot for
Islavsky. It is very warm. As we reach Axienievna the regiment is
just leaving it. Meet Captain Alexandroff. It was with pleasure
that I again greeted the woody banks of Islavsky — in the short
space of a week Autumn has changed their deep green hues to
the a withered brown. The green shade of the groves reflected on
the calm water at its feet, seemed an old familiar face. Colonel
Mack, Madme. Zimmermann, Daniel Assipitch pass the day.
Much dancing in the Evening. The two Officers take leave as their
regiment is already gone.

Monday August 31st. September 12th. Rain in torrents. Give lessons. Zachar Nicolaitch & Monsieur Basile go to Moscow. Play &
sing Figaro. Spend the Evening in Miss Hardorff's room, grumbling
after my lost music.

Tuesday September 1st. 13th. Rain in torrents. Give lessons. At

[64] Crowd of brats.

357

# Fifth Journal

two Mr. Gambs arrives from Moscow. Read a little after dinner with him in the Reviews.

Wednesday Sept. 2nd. 14th. Fine weather. ⟨G⟩ Marie Ivanovna & Olga Michailovna set off for Moscow. Give lessons and then walk with John Nicolas & Mr. Gambs on the road to ⟨Mosc⟩ Nazarievna. Very high wind. We talk always about Gottingen. After dinner play with the children, & read Rollin.[65] After tea play at Hot Cockles, & read Catholic deputation with Mr. Gambs in Hessey & Taylor's Monthly Review.[66]

Thursday Sept 4th. — 15th. I had a violent fever the whole night and ⟨was⟩ kept my bed untill the Evening. I then got up & went into Marie Ivanovna's cabinet where we read a little of Rollins. Marie Ivanovna comes at near nine o'clock. She tells us that ⟨Zachar'⟩ her husband's affair ⟨at B⟩ with Basskoff is finished to his satisfaction & that she is extremely happy. We all rejoice with her.

Friday September 5th. 16th. Fine clear but cold weather. Johnny has fallen ill of a high fever. I am yet far from well. The whole house is sad and uneasy. We wait the whole day for the Doctor who only comes at nine in the Evening.

Saturday September 6th. 17th. ⟨The b⟩ Zinai Ramanitch says Johnny has the scarlet fever. The weather is fine but cold.

---

Sunday September 13th. 25th. From Saturday September 6, to this day, I have neglected to write my Journal, for I have had a terrible relapse of melancholy inactivity, such as I used to experience at times when my mind was wholly devoted to Sorrow. But this happy day, all the clouds which have lately hung over my horizon disappeared. After breakfast, in a mood hopeless of good and careless utterly of my future fate, the newspapers were put by Catherine Ivanovna into my mind — I glanced over them hastily as is my custom to see if there is any thing about Greece. I saw my dear friend's name; I did not dare to read, yet notwithstanding with

[65] Charles Rollin, *Histoire ancienne des Égyptiens, des Carthaginois, des Assyriens, des Babyloniens, des Mèdes et des Perses, des Macédoniens, des Grecs*, 13 vols. (Paris, 1730–1738).
[66] A review of Shute, Lord Bishop of Sarum, *A Letter to the Clergy of the Diocese of Sarum*, appeared in *Monthly Review*, 1:175–178 (February 1790).

a horrible feeling of dread & yet hope — I read — that he was well and still in his cavern. Who shall describe the happiness I felt. This sudden relief from horrible inquietude ⟨& once⟩ to all the sweet certainty of his being well. I went then instantly into the garden and sat myself on the balcony to enjoy all the fullness of my happiness. The whole sky was dark and portentous; the grove was agitated by a rushing wind which poured thro' its bared form and shook the dying leaves to the ground in showers. Not a single bird was heard, ⟨they⟩ the whole grove was solitary its leaves abandonned it and were strewed on the plain. But I in this wasted scene was full of joy & life. I spent the whole day in silent happiness — Many people dined. Madame Zimmermann, Madame ⟨Po⟩ Percouroff & her daughters & many officers. I sat with Johnny afterwards. After tea they all went. I sung Figaro with M. G. ⟨A letter arrives⟩ At nine in the Evening a letter from Charles telling me of the birth of his little Pauline on the 28 of July,[67] enclosing one from Madame Moreau begging me to come to Vienna.[68]

Monday September 14th. 26th. Dreadful cold high wind. It is a great holiday. the children do no lessons. Walk in the great Alley & sit upon the Balcony. After dinner write to the Countess Betsy Zotoff & to Mr. Harvey. Read the story of the Basket Woman [69]

[67] Pauline Clairmont (1825–1891), known to her family as Plin, was to be the companion of Claire's last years in Florence. From 1870 to 1877 she lived with Claire as a paying guest; thereafter, until the death of her aunt in 1879, she remained as housekeeper without pay. She was the prototype of Tina in *The Aspern Papers* (1888), though far from being the retiring spinster imagined by Henry James.

[68] Claire described the two Moreaus in a letter to Jane Williams, September 11, 1824 (O.S.): "Nothing can exceed the friendship I met with from the Moreaus and the Henicksteins — the first you would like very much, as they are so liberal in their opinions, and notwithstanding their polite manners, 'a la francais,' truly romantic spirits, and associating very little with the world" (Abinger MSS., from a transcript in the hand of Mr. Gisborne). This may have been Mme. Jeanne Hulot Moreau, daughter of General Hulot d'Osery, and widow of General Jean Victor Moreau who had died in 1813 after returning from a nine years' exile in America to direct the forces of Russia, Austria, and Prussia against his native France. She had a daughter, who married the Vicomte de Courval.

[69] By Maria Edgeworth, in *The Parent's Assistant, or Stories for Children*, 6 vols. (3rd. ed.; London: J. Johnson, 1800), vol. V. Other stories read to

to Johnny. Captain Bault drinks tea. Sing Figaro with Mr. Gambs
& early to bed.

X Teusday September 15th. 27th. Great holiday. It is the anniversary of the Emperor's coronation.[70] Read all the morning Das
Bild von Houwald with Mr. G. It is a charming tragedy in the
romantic style and the novelty of the invention & yet its naturalness is delightful. The following description of the sun-rise in
Switzerland & its effects upon a ⟨youn⟩ youthful mind is beautiful.

Leonhard.

Mit meinem Meister, hatt'ich heute früh
Den nahen Fels erstiegen; finst⟨ra⟩re Schatten
⟨W⟩Verhüllten unserm Blick noch Berg und Thal.
Doch eines Riesengletschers stolzes haupt
Begann bald in dem dunkeln Meer der Nacht,
Wie eines Leuchthurms Kuppel zu erglühen. —
Was ist das ? rief ich ängstlich; öffnen sich
Auch hier der Erde grasse Feuerschlünde?
Hat der Vesuv hier seine Brüder steh'n?
"Sey ruhig," sprach der Meister, "jener Berg
Es ist die Jungfrau, die allmorgentlich
Ihr haupt mit frischen Feuerlilien schmuckt"!
Und seht, indess wir also sprachen, fingen
Auch and're Gletscher hoch an zu erglüh'n
Und standten leuchtend vor dem dunkeln Himmel. —
Da war es mir, als würde jetzt Frühmette
Im Dom des Herrn gehalten, und als eilten,
Die Sacristane zu den Hochaltären,
Um die geweihten Kerzen anzuzünden; —
Und nieder sank ich, innig mit zu bethen.[71]

---

Johnny from this work are "Tarlton," vol. I; "The Birth-Day Present," vol. II;
"The Barring Out," vol. VI; "Mademoiselle Panache," vol. IV; and "Simple
Susan," vol. II.

[70] Alexander I (1777–1825), czar of Russia 1801–1825.

[71] "Leonard. Early this morning I climbed the nearby crag with my master;
dark shadows obscured our view of mountain and valley. Yet the proud head of
a giant glacier began soon to glow in the dark sea of night like the lantern of a
lighthouse. — What is that? I called out anxiously; does a horrible fiery throat of
the earth open here as well? Has Vesuvius stationed his brother here? 'Be calm,'
said the master, 'that mountain is the Jungfrau, which every morning decks her

# Islavsky 1825

After dinner I had very bad spasms & was obliged to lie down.

Wednesday September 16th. 28th. Dark cold weather. Give lessons. Marie Ivanovna goes early with Olga Michailovna to dine at Madame Zimmermann's. Read with M. G. Das Bild. After dinner walk with him & Nicolas ten times up & down the great Alley. The groves are not yet bare, but its fresh countenance is changed to a deep brown except where the unchanging pine stretches its vigourous branches amid the fading beauties of its neighbours.

Thursday September 17th. 29th. Cloudy rainy weather. ⟨St⟩ It is St. Sophia's day — so Dunia has a holiday. Read Das Bild.

> MAHLER.
> Der Leidenschaften bin ich quitt! ich habe
> Als Mensch mit Thränen ihre Schuld bezahlt,
> Und sie zu Grab' getragen. Will jedoch
> Die Fantasie des Künstlers sie beschau'n,
> Heb' ich das Leichentuch noch ein Mahl auf.
> Da liegen sie, als wie von Traum befangen,
> Und grinsen furchtbar, oder lächeln still!
> Doch fürchtet nichts, sie steh'n nicht wieder auf.
> MAHLER.
> .   .   .   .   .   .   .   nur der Genius
> Der in ihm lebt, und immer neu erfindet,
> Dem keine Gegenwart die Bilder leiht,
> Der in sich ⟨selbst⟩ selbst der Ideale schafft,
> Und Kühn erdenkt, was noch kein Auge sah,
> Obgleich es wahr vor jedem blick erscheint,
> Der macht den Meister.
> idem.
> Für kalt, an Worten arm, wird sie mich halten;
> Die Stimme stockte, und was mir beredter
> Ins Auge trat, das konnte sie nicht seh'n.

---

head with fresh firelilies'! And behold, while we were thus speaking, another glacier high up began to glow and stand luminous against the dark heaven. — For me it was as though just now matins were being celebrated in the cathedral of the Lord, and as though the sacristans were hastening to the high altars to light the holy candles; — and down I sank, fervent to join in prayer." (Ernst Christoph von Houwald, *Das Bild: Trauerspiel in fünf Akten* [Leipzig, 1822], Act I, scene **5.**)

# Fifth Journal

idem.

Ich zog hinaus — dem raschen Strome gleich,
Der sich durch hain und Flur und Thäler windet,
In seinem Spiegel wechseln tausend Bilder,
Indess er nur das eine Bild, der Sonne,
Die ihn von seiner Quelle an erwärmt,
Treu mit sich fort hinab in's Weltmeer trägt.[72]

Friday September 18th. 30th. Fine weather. Give lessons. Go before dinner a walk on the high road with M. G. & Nicolas. After dinner read to Johnny the story of Tarlton. A letter from Mr. Baxter.

Saturday September 19th. October 1st. Fine weather — I have a severe cough therefore cannot go out. M. G. goes early to visit the German Doctor at Ilinsky, the seat of the Countess Ostermann. At dinner he returns & brings the news that the Turks & Egyptians ⟨have⟩ after a general assault have been obliged to raise the siege of Missolunghi and are retreating from every corner of Greece as fast as they can and that ⟨Lad⟩ Lord Cochrane is arrived ⟨in⟩ with two fregates to aid the Greeks. This news gives me the greatest spirits. Begin Voltaire's Life of Charles XII.[73] Zachar Nicolaitch arrives after dinner. Read Tarlton to Johnny in the Evening.

Sunday September 20th. October 2nd. Read the life of Charles

[72] "Mahler. I am free of passions! As a human being I have discharged their guilt with tears, and borne them to the grave. If the fantasy of an artist wishes to view them, once more I raise the shroud. There they lie, as though overcome by a dream, and grimace frightfully, or silently grin! But there's no cause for fear, they never again will rise." (*Das Bild*, Act I, scene 8.)

"Mahler . . . . it is only the genius which lives in him, and always invents anew, whose pictures borrow from nothing real, which in itself creates the ideal, and boldly imagines, what no eye has yet seen, although it appears true to every sight, that makes the master." (Act II, scene 1.)

"idem. From my poverty of words she will take me to be cold; my voice failed, and what convinced me, struck me in the eye, she could not see." (Act II, scene 2.)

"idem. I went on my way — like the swift stream, that winds through grove and field and valley, a thousand pictures interchanging in its mirror, while it carries only that one image, the sun, that has warmed it from its source, faithfully with it down into the ocean." (Act III, scene 5.)

[73] *Histoire de Charles XII, roi de Suède*, 2 vols. (Basel, 1731).

the XII. Walk in the great Alley with M. G. and Nicolas. The Perecouroffs and Officers at dinner. After dinner read Barring Out to Johnny and Mr. Gambs. Dunia falls sick after tea & goes to Bed.

Monday September 21st. October 3rd. Dunia has been ill all night. Zachar Nicolaitch goes to Moscow. Finish reading Charles XII. Walk with Nicolas & Mr. Gambs & Miss Hardorff & Miss Olga in the great Alley and then on the banks of the River — Fine weather. Read after dinner the Birthday Present to Johnny ⟨after dinner⟩.

Teusday September 22nd. Octbr. 4th   Very fine warm weather. Dunia is very ill. Write to Mr. Baxter. Begin reading the History of Charles ↑the↓ XII by Becker in German.[74] At Eleven we all go out a long walk over the meadow & home by the River side. We saw a ram all alone in a solitary field who did nothing but run round & round. Our walk was delightful — A wide plain at our feet, beyond the country gently rises and is thickly wooded as far as the eye can see; here & there in the distance the ⟨woo⟩ dark line of the woods is broken by uplands which look like lakes ⟨spread between the forests⟩ surrounded by forests. When we reach home, Mr. ⟨Gib⟩ Ilya Gibalich[75] arrives. After dinner sit with Johnny. At tea there are some officers & a gentleman from Pazkazoba. A parcel from Mr Baxter ⟨& a letter from the same⟩ containing a number of the Edinburgh Review & a letter in which he mentions that there is a general rumour of England's resolution of helping Greece. This idea cheers me greatly.

Wednesday September 23rd. October 5th. Dark cloudy weather. Dunia has spent a very bad night and in the morning a blister is applied to her throat. Receive after breakfast a long letter from Miss Weston at Penza. Read the Edinburgh Review. At one o'clock Mr. Gibalich goes away. Walk in the garden before dinner ten times up & down the great Alley with Nicolas & Mr. Gambs. ↑I receive a letter from Mrs. Mason & from the Countess Zotoff telling me the Countess Betsy was to be married the 16 Sept.↓ After

[74] In vol. IX of Carl Friedrich Becker, *Die Weltgeschichte, für Kinder und Kinderlehrer*, 9 vols. (Berlin, 1801–1805).

[75] In the journal here and in the following entry this name is in Russian script.

dinner we are alarmed at Dunia's state, one of perpetual restless list-lessness. No consciousness yet perpetually tossing from side to side. I went to her at eight o'clock & did not leave her till five the next morning when she expired. She lay in utter insensibility would taste nothing, her chest more oppressed at every moment; ⟨a⟩ her cheeks of a burning pink and all round her mouth of an ashy pale. At twelve o'clock at night call up Mr. Gambs & he sets out to fetch the German doctor at Ilinsky. ⟨Her⟩ The difficulty of breathing encreased every moment, & we were obliged to hold her up-right to prevent her from suffocation & it was thus he found us when he returned at five in the morning — he brought orders to apply leeches behind the ear and sinepismes of mustard on the legs. We did so but she gently expired while it was being applied. To describe the scene that followed would be impossible. The wretched mother threw herself on the ground & writhed there in an agony of grief, and the lovely child smiling & brilliant as a star lay ⟨in death before⟩ not in death but in a sweet stillness before us. A thousand wounds bled afresh in my heart.

Thursday September 24th. October 6th. At six in the midst of these terrible scenes Mr. Gambs departs for Moscow to announce this unhappy loss to Zachar Nicolaivitch. ⟨Pra⟩ Dunia is dressed in white & laid out upon a table and tapers in tall candalabras ⟨burn⟩ are burning around. The angelic ⟨beauty⟩ smile of death is soon lost, the brilliancy of her complexion as if animated by the sweetest pleasure, soon gives place to the yellowness of death, and a hollow leaden vacancy looks out from the once beaming countenance. Church service is performed — all the peasants come to take leave of her, and the whole morning was spent in weeping & wailing. Mr. Henkin the German doctor comes at eleven. He says she was lost by neglect; that the first drowsiness which succeeded to the restleness which ⟨succeeded to⟩ prevailed before, was the first sympton of inflammation ⟨of⟩ on the brain. Zinevai Ramanitch had left her, we did not know that we ought to apply leeches, & if her drowsiness still prevailed, ice upon the head, and the inflammation carried her off in twelve hours.[76] Mrs. Perecouroff

[76] Claire would have done well to recall Rousseau's cynical comment in *Émile* (book i) on the doctor's advantage: "If the child dies, he had been called in too late; if he recovers, it was he who saved the infant's life" (Nugent's trans.,

& her daughters dine. In the Evening Zachar Nicolaivitch arrives with Mr. G.

Friday September 25. October 7th. Half the night I sat up — the windows were open   I sat at one & looked out upon the night — all beyond the window was utterly dark & no sound was heard but the rustling of the trees which altho' so near were hidden by the gloom. ⟨In the room all was light but the⟩ Thus it is with the heart when it sees the object of its affections lying in death; a sudden gloom falls upon all the senses, the universe once so animated becomes black & dark like a hollow precipice; life yawns before one like a dark abyss. The wretched Zachar Nicolaivitch could find no rest for his sorrow; every moment he returned to look at his lost darling & then again hurried away unable to bear the sight.

After breakfast, write to the Countess Zotoff & to the Countess Betsy. At ⟨one⟩ twelve Mr. G. Johnny Nicolas, Lucheria & the two Hardorffs depart for Moscow. Dunia is carried to the church at Eleven. Walk in the great Alley with Olga Michailovna — All nature is faded, the dead leaves are stirless on their ⟨da⟩ branches; not a single bird in the grove that but a month ago resounded all day long with ↑⟨joy⟩ joyful notes.↓ warblers. ⟨After dinner Madme. Zimmermann comes⟩ At dinner Feodor, Feodorivitch [77] arrives & then Madame Zimmermann.

Saturday September 26th. Oct. 8th. Get up early & go to the Church where Catherine Ivanovna has spent the whole night. At eleven the funeral service began — after the mass, the priest gave a lighted taper to every & after singing the funeral anthem, every one in the church approached to kiss the departed — Marie Ivanovna & ⟨A⟩ Catherine Ivanovna fell to the ground in hysterics — Every one shrieked & wept as the body was lowered into the grave — the scene was so terrible I saw & felt nothing but the pressure of the people and the ⟨terrible⟩ whole atmosphere filled with shrieks & tears. Marie Ivanovna was carried home on a drochki. Foedor Feodoritch goes to Moscow. Very melancholy dinner & day. Read in the afternoon. Histoire de la Revolution française

---

pp. 35–36). Streptococcus pneumonia, a rapidly fulminating complication of scarlet fever, may well have been the cause of Dunia's death.

[77] Possibly Fedor Fedorovitch Matiouchkin, whose journal of travels in the north of Asia is discussed on December 9 (21), below.

# Fifth Journal

par Antoine Fantin Desodoards.[78] In the Evening letter from Mr. Gambs that Johnny is well.

Sunday September 27th. Oct. 9th. They go to mass in the morning. I pack up & read the whole day Memoirs of Madame Campan.[79] Madame Alsoufieff & Madme. Monchanoff call in the morning. Madme. Perecouroff & daughters & Captain Boult dine. After dinner Madame Zimmermann returns to Kasino. Captain Bault & another Officer from Axienievna spend the Evening with Marie Ivanovna.

Monday September ⟨29⟩ 28th. Oct 10 Pack up. Walk all round the gardens. All is solitude, silence & ruin. The wind sung dismally thro' the pines ⟨near the ruins⟩ and the ruins of the old house were stretched over the ground. The waters of the little lake were covered with dead leaves and ⟨the sum⟩ broken columns of Jupiter Pluvius ⟨were⟩ lay upon the ⟨hill⟩ sides of the hilly island before me. ⟨Never⟩ The whole scene was in harmony — ⟨⟨all nature seemed ⟨about⟩ to ⟨yield⟩ be fading in the arms of rough dismal winter — all spoke of charms, but charms long gone past.⟩⟩ the ruins of the ancient house, the broken columns of the temple strewed upon the side of the hill, the bosom of the lake disfigured by a covering of dead leaves which lay unmoved upon its stagnant waters, all spoke of former ⟨charms⟩ times & of ↑former↓ charms; the whole scene seemed to be sinking rapidly into the arms of desolate Winter. Madame Zimmerman arrives.

Tuesday September 29th. October 11th. we left Islavsky and ⟨came⟩ arrived in Moscow at three o'clock. We found Johnny ill of a nervous fever — The anxiety and misery prevented my writing my Journal & also the confusion, for there were neither chairs nor tables in the house — even now that Johnny is nearly recovered (Friday October 9th.) the ⟨h⟩ whole house is topsy-turvy. I sleep upon chairs every night there being no bed to be had & the only furniture I have in my room is a single chair.

[78] Antoine Étienne Nicolas Fantin des Odoards, *Histoire philosophique de la révolution de France*, 10 vols. (5th. ed.; Paris, 1807).

[79] Jeanne Louise Henriette Campan, *Mémoires sur le vie privée de Marie Antoinette, reine de France . . . suivis de souvenirs et anecdotes historiques sur les règnes de Louis XIV, de Louis XV et de Louis XVI*, 3 vols. (Paris, 1822).

# Moscow 1825

Thursday October 8th. 20th. Read in the morning German Gazettes. Write a note of excuse to the Princess Ouronsoff. Sit with Johnny all the morning. After dinner Mr. Demitrieff calls. Go with Catherine Ivanovna to fetch Catherine in the Tverskoi [*Boulevard*]. The Kakorchkine's spend the Evening.

Friday October 9th. 21st. Rainy weather. Go at eleven with Nicolas to the Princess Ouronsoffs. meet Madme. Kasairoff there who insists upon my coming to live at her house.[80] In the Evening Miss Aconloff calls. The days pass so miserably away they leave nothing but a blank trace of misery behind them.

Saturday October 10th. 22nd. Go with Catherine to Madme. Bielfeld's to see Miss Hardorff — It is so far off and the streets are so dirty that this jaunt takes up the whole morning. Madme. ⟨Spri⟩ Spiridoff calls before dinner. Mr. Ebler & Mr. Pouchechine dine. Mr. Gambs is out the whole day. The Kakosckine's spend the Evening. Read Tarlton to Johnny. Read the lives of the Saints.

Sunday October 11th. 23rd. Low spirits. Read Tarlton with Johnny. Write to Miss Weston. Mr. & Miss Kakorchkine dine and Mr. Pavloff. After dinner Mr Quellot spends the Evening & Miss Hawker calls late.

Monday October 12 — 24th. Extremely low spirits. Go early in the morning to Mrs. Harvey — She is preparing to christen her child & it is likewise the anniversary of her wedding. call afterwards upon Mrs. Kitto. Read Barring out with Johnny in the Evening & go to bed very early. In the lives of the Saints I remark one curious thing — like the Russian girls who protest against it to the very last moment when they are going to be married & who are esteemed in proportion to the obstinacy of their resistance, so the Saints invariably the moment they were invited to ⟨take pr⟩ become bishop always opposed a most violent resistance & only yielded when it was absolutely forced upon them. The longevity among them is remarkable. Notwithstanding the enthusiasm which must have prevailed in their minds, yet a suspicion of imposture & ⟨affect⟩ affectation forces itself upon my mind when I read all the numerous

[80] When Claire left Russia in 1828 it was in the company of Madame Kaisaroff and her ailing daughter Natalie, to whom Claire was both nurse and governess. See Miscellanea, below.

367

# Fifth Journal

penances they imposed upon themselves and all the exaggerated stories of the miracles they performed.

Tuesday October 13th. 25th. Write to Madme. Mason. Call with Helen upon Mrs. Kitto. Mr. Baxter & his pupil Alexy Kyrieff Miss Hawker & Miss Kakorchkine spend the Evening.

Wednesday October 14th. 26th. Dreadful, damp, rainy weather. Finish writing to Madme. Mason, but I am ill all day. ⟨M⟩ After dinner M.G. relates about Alaric King of the Longobardi and Theodolinda his wife. Madame Rajefsky and another Lady, Miss Kakorchkine & Miss Hawker spend the Evening.

X Thursday October 15th. 27 Very damp weather. I am ill all day. Read Schillers Ghost ⟨Sat⟩ Seer. Miss Hardorff & Sophy call to take leave for ⟨R⟩ Resan. The Kakorchkine's dine. After dinner Mr. Sommer & Genichsta call. Marie Ivanovna says to the latter — I have ↑had↓ the misfortune to lose my daughter a most interesting little creature — No doubt you remember her — ⟨Gen⟩ To which Genischsta said — No indeed I don't. Nicolai Ivanich Ivreneuf spends the Evening — ⟨Mary⟩ M[arie]. I[vanovna]. asks him to marry Miss Olga [Michailovna]. A man comes to Zachar Nicolaitch and cries & recommends his suit to him which is to be tried to-morrow & which will decide whether he is to be a beggar or no. The Russians have a most amazing facility of tears — a man would scarcely cry in England whilst telling his case to a lawyer.

Friday October 16th. 28th. Rainy cold disagreeable weather. Read the Ghost Seer — Mr. Pouchschine dines. After dinner read a little of Werner's Templers [81] with M. G. but not much for I am very stupid with a bad head-ach. Miss Hawker & Miss Kakorchkine drink tea.

Saturday October 17th. 29th. My new maid Palagaza comes. Pass the morning in looking over linnen &c. After dinner Mr. Gambs goes to the Opera for the first representation of Figaro. Alexis Kyrieff, Madme. Rajefsky and the Miss Aconloffs spend the Evening.

Sunday October 18 — 30th Dawdle about with Johnny almost

[81] Friedrich Ludwig Zacharias Werner, *Die Templer auf Cypern* (Berlin, 1803).

the whole morning. Read Paul & Virginia.[82] Mr. Kakorchkine & his daughter, Alona Antonievna, & Mr. Pouchschine ⟨dine⟩ & Mr. Ebler dine. ⟨A⟩ Mr. Armfeld, Mr. Baxter, & Mr. Quellot spent the Evening. We sung — They played at the Ring and I talked about the Catholic & Protestant Religion with Mr. Baxter.

Monday October 19th. 31st. A slight fall of snow. ⟨Pla⟩ Practise in the morning. A note from Mr. Baxter with Lingard's ⟨defence⟩ Reply to the attacks of Shute, Bishop of Durham against the Catholic Religion[83] which I read. Mr. Ebler & Mr. La Grenet[84] call — the latter brought a beautiful portrait of his wife. Mr. Volkoff calls. After dinner sing. Miss Hawker & Miss Kakorchkine call & the Countess Tolstoy.

Teusday October 20th. November 1st. Practised Genichsta's second Exercise. Read Lingard. After dinner Miss Hawker & Miss Kakorchkine came. Mr. Gambs read aloud Rollin. Genichsta came and gave me his first lesson. Afterwards he played & sang a prayer of his own composition the words by Mr. Vinivitinoff

Wednesday October 21st. November 2nd. Rainy bad weather. ⟨Af⟩ Give lessons. Practise. The old Madme. Afrasimoff called after dinner. also M. Du Vivier. A packet of Newspapers from Mr. Baxter. I sit in my room & read them all the evening.

Thursday October 22nd. Nov. 3rd. It is four weeks to day that Dunia died. Practise till eleven. Give lessons. Write to Madame Kaisareff a refusal. Carry my letter to the Princess Ouronssoff's. come home through a hard rain. Dress. Mr. Kay below — comic scene between him & Mrs. Pomikoff — he is so slow & she is so impatient. The Prince Wolchonsky calls. Miss Kakorchkine & Miss Hawker, Mr. Ebler, Mr. La Grennée the painter & his son Auguste dined. The two latter are thoroughly french, easy in their manners, flippant, vivacious and thinking of nothing but of making

---

[82] *Paul et Virginie* (1787) by Jacques Henri Bernardin de Saint-Pierre.

[83] John Lingard, *Tracts Occasioned by the Publication of a Charge Delivered to the Clergy of the Diocese of Durham by Shute, Bishop of Durham* (Newcastle, 1813), includes five of Lingard's anonymously published tracts in defense of the Catholic religion.

[84] François La Grennée (1774–1832), a painter, chiefly of miniatures, who went to Russia in 1823 to work in the school of fine arts founded by Elizabeth, wife of the Czar Alexander.

# Fifth Journal

l'aimable en societé. Mr. La G. told us that he had seen in the Imperial palace at Petersburgh a copy book of Louis the XIV written when he was a child. It ran thus. Les rois peuvent faire ce qu'ils veulent, les rois peuvent faire ce qu'ils veulent [85] — and so on down the whole page & signed for a whole ⟨lign⟩ line at bottom Louis, Louis, Louis. This is rather an extraordinary text for a pupil of Fenelon's. They all go at six & Mr. G. spends the Evening at Vinivitinoff's. Practise & give a music lesson to Helen.

Friday October 23rd. November 4th. Practise. Give lessons. Read the Newspapers. After dinner Mr. Genichsta comes & gives us a lesson. Miss Kakorchkine & Miss Hawker also call for a moment.

Saturday Octbr 24th. ⟨Mov⟩ Nov. 5th. Fine clear weather ⟨the⟩ for the first time these many weeks. ⟨P⟩ Get up at five. Practise. ⟨Call upon⟩ Walk to Mrs. Kitto's — Meet her in the Street — then call upon the Princess Ouronssoff. Miss Merrytt there. ⟨Read I⟩ On my return read the Newspapers. After dinner dispute with M.G. & Marie Ivanovna about Women. Mr. G. relates the history of Metka Schild & Ernest. Then sit upon the divan in Marie Ivanovna's cabinet & read Madlle. Panache to Johnny. Nikolai Ivanich, Platon Stepanitch, Miss Kakorchkine & Miss Hawker, & Mr. Pavloff drink tea. I am so fatigued with the walk I took that I retire very early to my room. I am besides in very low spirits because it is a very long while that I have had no news of my friends. I thought much of Shelley to-day, & I thought one might very well apply to him what Cicero said of Rome. Ungrateful England shall not possess my bones.

Sunday October 25th. Nov. 6th. Rainy bad weather. Practise. Miss Trewin called. Read the Newspapers. Mr. Pouschine, Mr. Ivanoff, & the Kakorchkines dine. The Princess Gortchakoff, Mr. Baxter, & Mr. Armfeld spend the Evening. Mr. Baxter told ⟨the⟩ me the bad news of Mrs. Seymour's death at Odessa.[86]

[85] "Kings can do what they will."

[86] Claire wrote to Jane Williams on October 27, 1825 (O.S.): "I had one english woman here to whom I was attached; a woman of the most generous heart and whom misfortune perhaps imprudence had driven to Russia. She thought with me that nothing can equal the misery of our situation, and accordingly she went last spring to Odessa, hoping to find some means of establishing a boarding house in order to have a home; if it succeeded she was to

# Moscow 1825

Monday October 26th. Nov. 7th. After a sleepless night rise early   practise. Go to the Princess Ouronssoff's who confirmed the news to me. then call upon Mrs. Kitto who was not at home. Very low spirits — After dinner talk with M. G. his conversation & society in the abandoned state in which I am in Russia is my only consolation. Then sit upon the divan & read Simple Susan with Johnny & M.G.   Madme. Monchanoff came & the Kakorchkine's — I played the sixth concert of Field.[87] When they were all gone sat with Marie Ivanovna who related an interview she had with the Bishop ⟨Phorphyry⟩ Porphyry; she was remarkably pious and always running after holy men hoping to benefit her soul thereby; ⟨she⟩ no sooner did she hear of Porphyry's arrival, than she ran to see him at the monastery where he was lodged with her niece Miss Olga — ⟨the holy⟩ Porphyry a man of about thirty and very handsome seemed very little flattered by her hurry to seek his society; but began to grumble rather uncourteously — ⟨that⟩ after listening to her apology for intruding upon his solitude upon the score of the benefit his pious ⟨counn⟩ counsels would be of to her soul; "this is the way," replied he, this is just the way with the women," ⟨always running after   because it happens to be the fashion to run after pious men⟩ you only run after us because it is the fashion; just ⟨at⟩ as it is at the Smith's Bridge, one day ⟨blue⟩ ↑pink↓ is the fashion, the next blue, so one day the ⟨Bas⟩ Bishop Eugene is ⟨the mode⟩ ↑all the rage↓ and the next Porphyry. We are truly much obliged to you — you come here pretending to seek the salvation of your souls; all I know of the affair is that you make us lose our's — such a crowd of women, pretty ugly, old & young   good ones, bad ones,

have sent for me; but however she wrote to me that after well considering every thing, she found such a plan would not succeed, and that I might expect her shortly in Moscow to resume her old manner of life. I expected her arrival daily, and began to grow uneasy — and at length some one wrote to another acquaintance of her's here, that she had destroyed herself. I who knew her thoughts have no doubt the horror of entering again as governess, made her resolve upon this as the only means to escape it" (Abinger MSS.).

[87] John Field, *Sixième Concerto pour le pianoforte avec accompagnement de grand orchestre* (Moscow: Charles Louis Lenhold, n.d.). Field (1782–1837), the Dublin-born virtuoso performer, teacher, and composer, had gone to live in St. Petersburg in 1803 and then settled in Moscow in 1822, where he remained, giving many concerts, throughout the period Claire was there. He is best known today for his influence on Chopin, through his invention of the keyboard nocturne. See Flood, *John Field of Dublin* (Dublin, 1921).

⟨fre⟩ prudes, coquettes, & we must hear all they ⟨make   take it ple⟩ have to confess, and I would like to know how it is possible for us to be pious with all the folly of the beau monde pouring ⟨into veri⟩ at every instant into our ears. Be pleased when you come, not to bring your pretty young niece with you at least. After this exordium he allowed her to explain the doubtful state of her soul, ⟨the difficulty⟩ its wavering state between her love of religion and its perpetual yieldings to wordly vanities & pleasures. "Above all" said she what most distresses me, is the pleasure the transport I feel when the Emperor ⟨honores⟩ honours us with a visit—Bah! said Porphyry interrupting her, do you think I don't perceive you ⟨in order you⟩ tell me all this in order to find an opportunity of letting me know the Emperor comes sometimes to see you."

Teusday October 27th. Nov. 8   Got up early & ⟨breakfast⟩ practised. At nine went to Mrs. Kitto's. Come home & give lessons. After dinner read Simple Susan to Johnny & Mr. G.   then the latter read a little of Rollin aloud. We begin to be a little more comfortable for the Sopha is ready in Marie Ivanovna cabinet and we established ourselves there for the first time. Nicolai Ivanitch, the Count Tolstoÿ, the Prince Dolgarouky  Miss Hawker & Miss Kakoschkine spent the Evening. Genichsta came & gave us a lesson. Then he played ⟨the most⟩ his own Solo & various other pieces. John asked him to represent Mr. Gamb's scolding on the piano— and he immediately ⟨in⟩ extemporized a piece to that effect. A note from Mr. Baxter enclosing a fable of Rossi's L'Acqua fra Sassi.

Plato said, the Spartans knew how to die for their country, ⟨but⟩ & the Athenians how to live for her.

Wednesday October 28th. Nov. 9th. Practise. Very bad weather. ⟨Write⟩ Give lesson, write to Jane. After dinner Mr. Johnson & Mr. Parkinson call then ⟨read⟩ Mr. G.— reads aloud Werner's Martin Luther.[88]

Thursday Octobr. 29th. Novr. 10th. Get up early. Practice. It is Miss Kakorchkine's name's day. Go with Catherine ↑Ivanovna↓ to congratulate her. Then to Mrs. Kitto's. Mr. Johnson there. Write with Mr. K. letter to Attwood & Co. Return to dinner—They all dine at Kakoschkine's—After dinner read Simple Susan aloud

---

[88] *Martin Luther, oder die Weihe der Kraft* (Berlin, 1807).

Then sleep a little & then M. G. reads aloud Martin Luther. I admire the scene between him & his parents extremely; it is an extremely happy defence of the Protestant religion and the abuses of the Catholic Church, are pointed out in an allegory full of point and yet very natural. Mr. G. related the following story to me. Tetzlar, the Pope Nuncio came to Juterbo⟨c⟩k in Saxony where he remained some time to sell indulgences. When his purse was grown very heavy and he was preparing to depart ⟨Tron Tr⟩ Fronsberg a partizan of Luther, came to him and begged to purchase an indulgence for a very heavy crime that he intended to commit; the Nuncio sold it him at a very high price but without the smallest scruple, so entirely lost to shame was the ⟨Pop⟩ Romish Church. Then Tetzlar departed, but at about twenty versts from the city was attacked by ⟨ro⟩ Fronsberg at the head of a troop of armed men; they plundered his carriage & Fronsberg got hold of his strong box & carried it off in triumph, at the same time exclaiming to Tetzlar, ⟨This⟩ that ⟨it was⟩ this was the intended crime for which he had previously purchased absolution. The principal trait in Luther's character seems to ↑be↓ an overbearing power of bending all his energies to one purpose; ⟨Melanet⟩ Melanchton goes further in depth of design, but his timid ↑gentle↓ character is a ⟨perpetual⟩ drawback ⟨to the execution⟩ & perpetually steps between his conceptions and the realizing them. Theobald is a perfect sketch of youthful enthusiasm which subdues all things to its own colour.

Friday October 30th. Novbr. 11th. Get up early & Practise. At eleven give my english lesson. M.G. has a new coat & admires himself in the glass. After dinner read Simple Susan. Copy & send Letter to Attwood & Co. We read Rollin also. Write to Mr. Baxter & send back newspapers. Mr. Genichsta came & we took our lessons.

Saturday October 31st. Nov. 12. Get up early & practise. Then walk to Miss Trewin's she is just going out — Call at Chateinzoff's, they are full of the plan of following the Princess Gartchakoff to Germany. Come home. Mr. Sobolefsky the drawing master gives me a letter from Mr. Baxter. Mr. Gambs dines at Kakorchkine's, they all come at six.

Sunday Nov 1st. 13th. Wet detestable weather. Get up early &

practise. Then go at nine o'clock thro' a drizzling rain to Miss Trewin's. Chat with her an hour & then return home   Meet Mr. G. ↑Mad. Gerard calls.↓ Feodor ⟨Feodoritch⟩ Feodorovitch, Mr. ⟨Acolo⟩ Aconloff, Mr. Mansouroff, Nicolai Ivanovitch, Alexander Simonovitch ⟨& Mr⟩ Mr. Pavloff & a very fat General called   Pavil Ivanovitch & the Kakorchkine's dine. After dinner read Simple Susan. Miss Aconloff, Miss ⟨Walt⟩ Volkoff, the two Mr. Joli's, Mr. Armfeld & Modeste Aconloff spent the evening. We played at Vingt-un. Write to Mr. Baxter & Miss Feldhausen.

Monday Novbr. 2nd. 14th. Get up early & practise. Then give english lesson⟨s⟩; then dress and read Martin Luther with M. G. His prayer just before presenting himself before the council at Worms is fine & full of energetic simplicity; what I chiefly remark is that in this piece, ⟨as in⟩ there are no passages of surpassing beauty as in Houwald, but the interest & vigour never relaxes for a moment either into indifference or feebleness. After dinner read Simple Susan aloud. Then sleep for half an hour. Then Mr. Baxter comes — he tells me of a lesson at Doctor Jenish's. also that the chairs of anatomy & astronomy have been suppressed as impious at the University of Casan. A letter from Mr. Cornet.

Teusday Nov. 3rd. 15th. Get up early & practise. Then give lessons. Mr. Butler calls. Write to Jane. After dinner read aloud & finished Simple Susan. Mr. Genichsta & gave us lessons. Miss Kakorchkine, Miss Hawker, & Anna Vassilievna & Miss Barbe spent the evening. When they are gone, sit by the frame where Miss Olga was at work and Mr. Gambs reads aloud Martin Luther. But I am very sleepy and go to bed.

Wednesday Nov. 4th. 16th. Get up & practise. Then give english lesson. Then dress and give Helen a lesson. After dinner, begin to ⟨Mar⟩ write the course of lectures. Nicolai Ivanovitch and Miss Hawker & Miss Kakorchkine drink tea. Read a little of Martin Luther. Catherina prayer which is beautiful, beyond description natural & beautiful. Then practise. & go to bed very early.

Thursday Nov. 5th. 17th. Get up early & practise. Then give lessons. Then walk to Zuchari Baschnik. The ⟨sr⟩ streets are in the most horrid state & there is a slight fall of snow. The Kakorchkines dine. Read after dinner Rosamond[89] to the children. Then write a little. Then practise.

Friday Novbr. 6th. 18th. Get up early — practise. Give lessons. Then go to Zuchari Baschnik & call upon Doctor Jenish in the Pomeran⟨z⟩sevoi Doma. Come after dinner. It is very dirty cold weather. Mr. Genichsta comes & gives ⟨up⟩ us our lesson. ↑Mr. Baxter drank tea.↓ I am very tired in the Evening.

Saturday Nov. 7th. 19th. Get up early. Practise. I finished yesterday with Genichsta Hummel Variations of La Sentinelle, & I began with him Variations ⟨to an⟩ of a March in the Cenerentola of Rossini by the same author.[90] At eleven go to Zuchari Bashnick and give my first lesson to the Jenish's. After dinner Marie Ivanovna ⟨and⟩ goes to Kakorchkine to hear Schulz play. Give a lesson to Katherine. Read a little of Martin Luther with M. G. The scene between Catherine & the Abbess wherein the former relates the death of Theresa is uncommonly weak — ⟨The⟩ In the first place Theresa being but a secondary ⟨ca⟩ character in the piece & in no ways necessary to the devellopping of either of the principal ones, has no right whatever to have such a long scene devoted to her, for the anxiety of Luther's fate is now at its highest pitch, and the reader in the midst of his impatience is obliged to listen to Catherine's most ⟨ve⟩ wearisome explanations of an ⟨ev⟩ event that seems almost indifferent to the piece. If this production of Werner's had been called a poetic novel instead of a tragedy, it would have been perfect in its kind, then the episodes of Theresa, Theobald &c &c might very well have been introduced. Theresa in herself is a sweet creation and of a class that belongs almost wholly to German literature — a ⟨peci⟩ peculiar character which now half hides itself now is half discovered, that seems to flit around the principal personnages & ⟨yet to have a very decided & strong sentiment of her own,⟩ breaks in upon the action of the piece by some half broken expression or some ⟨action⟩ striking jest, and who murmurs in half ⟨bo⟩ broken phrases, the allegory of the whole piece which is sometimes extremely evident & prettily introduced and sometimes as wide from the purpose . . . . . . . .

[89] Maria Edgeworth, *Rosamond: A Sequel to Early Lessons*, 2 vols. (London, 1821). "The Nine Days' Wonder" is in vol. I; "The Black Lane" in vol. II.

[90] Johann Nepomuk Hummel (1778–1837).

# Fifth Journal

Then Mr. Volkoff called & Madame Armfeld. Talked with M. G. of Mad. Mason.

Sunday Nov. 8th. 20th. Most dismal weather. Get up early & practise. Then dress. Madame Simionoff calls. Write to M. Cornet. Read to John Nine day's wonder. Begin reading Segur[91] upon women. Miss Kakorchkine   Anna Vassilievna, Mr. Kakouchkine, Mr. Pouschschine, Mr. Simionoff dine. ⟨Mr. M. G.⟩ Midge[92] comes home after dinner. Mr. Quellot had come in the morning and ⟨tell⟩ told him that there was a letter with a black seal ⟨by⟩ from his mother lying at Visar's — So away flies Midge but it was a hoax for instead of bad news it was a present from his sister of a watch key with a ⟨lon⟩ nosegay worked ⟨in⟩ with the hair of the family. Then he spends the evening at the Princess Zeneide Wolchonsky's.[93] Mrs. Rajefsky calls. Mr. Armfeld spent the Evening. He ⟨imitating⟩ imitated Lodi ⟨a⟩ which was excessively droll. We played also at Garialki.

Monday Nov. 9th. 21st. Wretched weather. Get up early & practise. Give lessons. Then read Der Handschuh and Pegasus im Joche by Schiller with M.G. Then dress. After dinner Midge reads aloud a letter from his sister. Then I ⟨si⟩ sit in my room & read Segur upon Women. Mr. Schultz the great Harp player called — he is a very vulgar young man & speaks very vulgar english — he says he makes nearly 60,000 roubles a year here; ⟨Mr.⟩ M. Ivanovna ⟨m⟩ loaded him him with compliments, called him the model of ⟨bothers⟩ sons & of brothers, asked him to come to Islavsky next summer & assured him she would try every thing in her power to render his stay there agreeable, entreated him to bring his sister

[91] Alexandre Joseph Pierre de Ségur, *Les Femmes, leur condition et leur influence dans l'ordre social chez différents peuples anciens et modernes*, 3 vols. (Paris, 1803).

[92] Mr. Gambs.

[93] The Princess Zenaide (or Zinaide) Wolkonski (1792–1862), who held a salon in Moscow, had been in Paris in 1823, where Mary Berry describes her: "La Zeneide began reading to us a novel of her writing in which there was much imagination; but the MS. was so confused that she could not even continue it herself" (*Journals and Correspondence of Miss Berry*, III, 344). In the 1830's the Princess was "relegated to a convent and deprived of her lands" because she was accused of "wanting to convert her *valet de chambre* to Catholicism" after her own conversion (C. de Grunwald, *Tsar Nicholas I*, p. 208n.).

with him, as country air would do her health good, in short laid herself out to the best advantage. Then she said — You must know M. Schulz Miss C— is no great admirer of the harp — to which I did not know what to reply, after she had been shewing herself of such an amiable disposition, for me to appear an enemy of his superior talent, was quite a contrast. Mr. Evrainoff & Madme. Tcherbashoff called & likewise Miss Kakorchkine.

Teusday Nov. 10th. 22nd   Get up early and practise. Give lessons. Write a little of Introduction to History. After dinner read with ⟨G⟩ Midge a little of 1st Canto of Paradise lost by the side of the fire which is lighted in the great drawing room. Genichsta comes & gives his lessons. Miss Hawker & Miss Kakorchkine drink tea. ⟨Midge at⟩ When they are gone sit with M. Ivanovna at her embroidery frame — Helen overturns the lamp & there is a very comic scene.

X Wednesday Nov. 11th. 23rd   Get up later than usual — Practise. The weather is wretchedly bad — every body is surprized that this foggy rainy weather should last so long. Give lessons. Then I sleep a little for I am far from well. Then dress and read Ségur. Nicolai Ivanovitch Evrainoff dined. After dinner walk up & down the great hall — then Midge read aloud Rollin & ⟨begin a beg⟩ began a novel of Hoffmann[94] — but we read but little for Mr. Baxter & Alexy came. They spent the Evening as well as Miss Kakorchkine & Miss Hawker.

It is impossible to describe the appearance of the sky that we have had for the last two months. ⟨The it⟩ It is one dark mass from one end of the horizon to the other, which seems as if fixed like a ceiling over head. for there is not the slightest movement in the clouds — and they present the same forms one day as another — I can compare it to nothing but a muddy pool whose waters ⟨are never renewed⟩ and ⟨which⟩ seem⟨s⟩ to sleep away ⟨its whole life⟩ their whole existence in stagnation.

---

We read Rollin — about Sesostris — he cut canals every where to protect Egypt from the inroads of the enemy's cavalry. ⟨Midge Tentyre or now Dendera upon the Nile⟩ Crocodiles were wor-

[94] Ernst Theodor Wilhelm Hoffmann (1776–1822).

# Fifth Journal

shipped in Egypt because when the Arabs used to make incursions upon the country, they destroyed them in great quantities. The Egyptians on the contrary were accustomed to combat that animal and were generally its conquerors. The inhabitants of Tentyra now Dendera, on the Nile were so famous for destroying crocodiles that it was said the moment that animal smelt a Tentyrian he would immediately retreat. The men of Tentyra used to cover their arm with the thickest leather, and plunging it down the animal's ⟨openened⟩ opened jaws, stuck a sharp knife with the other behind his ear which caused instantaneous death.

Thursday Nov 12th. 24th. Very unwell. Get up early and practise. Then give lessons. Then I am obliged to lie down. Dress for dinner. Nicolai Ivanovitch Evrainoff & Miss Kakoschkine & Miss Hawker, Miss Varinka & Anna Vassilievna dine. After dinner Midge reads aloud Der Majorat a tale by Hoffmann.[95] Then we read Rollin. Then a letter came from Mr. Baxter with english books for John. Read a little of the Black Lane in Rosamond to him. Played again on the Piano forte & then went to Bed. Sent letter to Mr. Cornet. In Rollin we read about Psammeticus who was one of the twelve Kings who ruled over Egypt at once and who built the famous twelve palaces ⟨at⟩ and labyrinth of Lake Moeris; he was banished by the other eleven ⟨to⟩ & wandered ⟨much a long while⟩ ↑many years↓ about the marshes — there he begged the assistance of some Carian⟨s⟩ and Ionian troops whom a tempest had thrown on the Egyptian shores. By their assistance he became sole master of Egypt; he established these Carians & Ionians in Egypt & assigned lands for their subsistence; the children of these Greeks ⟨were distinguished⟩ formed a separate caste known by the name of Interpreters because they spoke both⟨e⟩ the Egyptian & Greek language.

Friday Novbr. 13th. 25th.

———  ———  ———

Saturday Nov. 14th. 26th. This was one of the most disagreeable days I ever spent. The weather was dreadfully bad and I spent almost the whole day in the streets. At nine I went to the Princess Ouronssoff's then to Zuchari Baschnik where I staid till 2 — and it

[95] "Das Majorat," in E. T. W. Hoffmann's *Nachtstücke*, 2 vols. (Berlin, 1817), vol. II.

378

took three hours before I got home, the streets were almost impassable from mud and ↑so↓ slippery from the half frost half thaw of the night before, that I was near falling twenty times. When I got home I took tea & went to bed for I was dreadfully tired.

Sunday Nov 15th. 27th. Get up early & practise. I cannot describe the state of low spirits I have been in now for three weeks. All occupation is hateful; it seems to me as if I were one of those miserable fag horses who have scarce strength to stand and yet are made to toil from morning till night. I have no enjoyment of any kind and yet I work harder than any one. Every trace of Nature has disappeared in this dreadful season — it is as if she had never existed — one looks around for trees & verdure and the blue sky and one sees with horror an interminable white plain and a dun lowering sky unbroken by the slightest strip of white or blue.

I was far from well — M.G. read aloud Martin Luther — the perpetual striving after allegories in this piece makes a most wearisome performance. Martin is the only really well sustained character in the piece — his energy is not over strained always the same. Mr⟨s⟩. & Mrs. Simionoff ⟨dined⟩ Mr Aconloff & Mr. Pouschine & the Count Tolstoy dined. Mr. Armfeld & the little Bielfeld spent the Evening — we read Wordsworth's Ballad of Simon Lee & then we talked.

Monday Novbr. 16th. 28th. Got up early & practised. Go at nine to the Princess Ouronssoff's  then call on Madame Babarikin. This latter came to me in all her night gear — a black mantle hanging from her shoulders, her night cap half aside, and four ⟨p⟩ curl papers with peaked twisted points ornamented her forehead; ⟨this neg⟩ she is old and her ⟨nos⟩ mouth quite fallen in & toothless and her whole person presented a most singular contrast to the enthusiasm of her manners. She declared herself quite delighted enchanted with Mr. Evans. When I came home I wrote a little of History. After dinner read Ibycus & Die Kraniche [96] with Midge. Then slept till tea. Then Miss Hawker  Miss Kakorchkine & Mr. Glinka & his son Walodi called. I practised.
Analysis of Ibycus and the Cranes.
The epic ballad is employed to treat those minor narrative subjects

[96] Schiller, "Die Kraniche des Ibykus."

which are not ample enough to fill an epic poem. It was evidently Schiller's intention to represent in the ballad of Ibycus & the Cranes the idea entertained by the ancients of Nemesis, or that secret power which forced a criminal to become his own accuser even at the very moment that he thought himself ⟨safest from dis⟩ furthest from discovery.

Ibycus on his Journey to Corinth is murdered in the sacred wood of Poseidon; abandonned by Gods and men he invokes a flock of cranes flying over his head & calls upon them to bear witness against his assassins. The news of his death filled every breast with sorrow. During the Isthmian games, ⟨the Eu⟩ Eschylus's tragedy of the Eumenides was performed and at the very instant of the horrible imprecations uttered by the chorus against the unhappy wretch who should spill the blood of his fellow, a flock of cranes flew past over the heads of the spectators & one of the audience was heard to say to another — Behold Timotheus, the very cranes of Ibycus! This exclamation betrayed the authors of his death who were accordingly punished.

One of the chief charms of this ballad ⟨in⟩ consists in the simplicity & truth with which the poet has described the grecian manners. The address to Jupiter, the account of the grief which the news of Ibycus's death spread at Corinth, the inimitable description of the Theatre which may be said to surpass every other attempt of the Kind, all breathe the very spirit of the Grecian times. Can any thing be more sublime or more perfectly classic⟨al⟩ than the chorus of the Eumenides? In short to such a pitch ⟨d⟩ of deception has Schiller carried the illusion that the murderer's exclamation seems the ⟨cry of Nature.⟩ revealing cry of Nature.

With regard to the form of the Poem it is composed in Iambic stanzas.

Tuesday November 17th. 29th. Got up early & practised. Then gave lessons. Then wrote the Analysis of Ibycus. Then translated. untill dinner. Mr. Pushkin [97] dined. Olga Michailovna went to the theatre with Helen. I practised and Mr. Genichsta came & gave me a lesson. Talk afterwards with M.G. about Materialism. Then give a lesson to Catherine. The weather is still dreadful — I cannot describe the feelings which the complete change in all

[97] This name is in Russian script.

around produces; ⟨one asks every where⟩ one asks every where what is become of Nature, why has she utterly disappeared — Nothing answers and ⟨it is⟩ the same mournful feeling is felt as when silence is the only answer given to our enquiries after a lost friend. ⟨Then⟩ In both cases a mysterious melancholy takes possession of the mind and the craving after that knowledge which could interpret the strange change to us, is the only feelings which prevents the soul from sinking into utter despair.

Wednesday Nov. 18th. 30th. Get up early & practise. Then gave a lesson & wrote my Journal. Then ⟨translated⟩ untill dinner wrote History. After dinner finished Martin Luther with M. G. Then I slept. ⟨Then drank tea⟩ or rather dozed for my spirits are so horribly oppressed, I become incapable of repose the moment my mind is unoccupied. I am pursued by a horrible sense of evil and nothing but the laborious life I am now leading ⟨keeps me⟩ sustains me. After tea ⟨re⟩ begin Müllner's Schuld [98] with M. G. We are interrupted by M. Baxter who spends the Evening. We talked of Ast's latin translation of Plato. [99]

Thursday Nov. 19th. December 1st. Get up early & practise. Then give lessons. Then go to Babarikin's and give my first lesson. Come home to dinner  Mr. Kitto dines. Marie Ivanovna dines in her room as she is preparing to take the sacrament & Zachar Nicolaitch was not at home. Then slept. Then read Die Schuld with M. G. The priest comes & stays the whole evening with Marie Ivanovna who confesses. Mr. Harvey calls and brings a letter from Jane. Write to Mr. Baxter and Mad Leon.

Friday Novbr 20th. December 2nd. Get up early & practise — Heavy fall of snow. Then gave lessons and afterwards a lesson of english ⟨grammar⟩ grammar ⟨N⟩ then dress for dinner. Mr. Sobolefsky dined. Read a little of ⟨the⟩ Die Schuld. Mr. Genichsta came & gave us a lesson. Then read the Schuld. Miss Hawker & Miss Kakorchkine called. Then I played on the piano untill bed time & gave lessons to Helen & Katherine.

[98] Amand Gottfried Adolph Müllner, *Die Schuld: Trauerspiel in vier Acten* (Vienna, [1815]). About five years before, Claire had read an attack on this melodramatic play in Hare's article "On the German Drama" in *Olliers Literary Miscellany*, no. 1, pp. 95–104. See Note 10 to entry of January 26, 1821, above.

[99] D. Fridericus Astius, *Platonis Phaedrus* (Leipzig, 1810).

# Fifth Journal

Saturday Novbr. 21st. December 3rd. Get up early & practise till eleven. Then go in a sledge to Pomeransavoi Doma and return to dinner. The wind was bitter cold but the sky for the first time these three months was clear and cloudless and ressembled a clear day break in Italy it was so ⟨cold⟩ still & clear. Mr. Gambs dined at Kakorchkine's. A note from Mr. Baxter. I went to bed early for I was very tired.

Sunday November 22nd. Dec. 4th. Get up late & dress. Practise a little. Read Robertson's History of Charles V.[1] Miss Trewin & Miss Gottman called. Miss Kakorchkine and her father, the Count Tolstoÿ Mr. Pouschine, Mr. Pavloff, General Evrainoff Mrs. Glincka & her children, Miss Rosen and Mr. Armfeld dined. After dinner Mr. Armfeld began talking of operations which made me almost faint. then Mr. Sommer came in in ⟨hus⟩ his usual wild hurried manner, set himself down to the Piano but declared he was too agitated to play — We asked him what agitated him — he replied it was a Kleinikeit [trifle] — then running over the Piano in every direction untill he had not left a note untouched he at last consented to play a Sonata of ⟨Beth⟩ Beethoven's and M.G. accompanied him on the horn. Then after inveighing against every thing in Moscow, pavement, lights, houses & the women he caught up his hat and departed. to our great relief. They played at the Cat & the Mouse and I read Robertson.

Monday Novbr. 23rd. Decbr 5th. Get up early & practise. Call upon the Princess Ouronssoff. ⟨Then come⟩ Heavy fall of Snow Then come home and give lessons. Then dress and write History till dinner time. After dinner a long talk with Marie Ivanovna. Then read Evenings at Home[2] with John. Then drink tea and Mr. Baxter comes & stays till ten. ⟨and then went to Bed.⟩ Miss Hawker and Miss Kakorchkine called also a bridal visit from Mr. Bibikoff and his wife. The snow has fallen between the bare branches of the trees and filled up every interstice, so that once

---

[1] William Robertson, *The History of the Reign of the Emperor Charles V. with a View of the Progress of Society in Europe, from the Subversion of the Roman Empire, to the Beginning of the Sixteenth Century*, 3 vols. (London, 1769).
[2] John Aiken and Anna Letitia Barbauld, *Evenings at Home; or, the Juvenile Budget Opened*, 6 vols. (London: J. Johnson, 1792–1796).

there was an overarching canopy of leaves now presents a roof of snow & frost work.

Tuesday Nov 24th. Dec. 6th. Get up early & practise — then give lessons — then walked to Mrs. Kitto's — She was not at home. On my return Miss Hawker & Miss Kakorchkine were here; read till dinner time Die Schuld which we begin over again — After dinner go to sleep. Then read Evenings at Home to Johnny. Then practise — then read Die Schuld & Robertson untill twelve o'clock. It was St Catherine's day, and therefore ↑⟨Wednesday Nov. 25th⟩↓ Mr. Genichsta did not come.

Wednesday Nov. 25th. Dec. 7th. Get up early and practise. Mr. Dolfini calls & invites me to come and see the princess Volchonsky. The following passages are from Die Schuld.

Jerta.
Singend zieht der weisse Schwan,
In der brust den tiefen frieden,
Wenn der Winter kommt, nach Süden
Durch der Lüfte freie Bahn;
Und mit glänzendem gefieder,
Singend, wie er ist geschieden
Kehrt er aus der fremde wieder.
Nicht so Hugo: — Fortgezogen
Ist er auf dem Segelkahn,
Durch das reich der blauen wogen,
Heiter wie der weisse Schwan⟨n⟩
Kräftig, wie der junge Aar;
Aber was er scheidend war,
Ist nicht wieder heimgekehrt,
Zu dem väterlichen herd.

Wie in eurem Busen, rasen
Stürme wilder Leidenschaft
In dem ⟨eu⟩ seinigen, und blasen
Aus die fackel seiner Kraft.
Seine fest verschloss'ne Brust
Bei dem Drang' nach wilder Lust;
Seine scheuen, düstern Blicke

# Fifth Journal

Die, wenn sie in *eure* sehn
Glut in Glut untergehn —
Ach! sie zeugen nicht von Glücke!
    Gluck ist ohne frieden nicht.

-----

Einer Leiche gleich, die mit
Offnen Augen ist gestorben,
Sah sie drein . . . . . . . .
    Hugo.
. . . . . . . . Geuss aus dein Gift, dass es
Seine schale nicht zerfresse!
    Hugo.
Wenn er käme — käm' in dieser
Bösen Stunde, wo die Liebe —
Ausgebrannt, wie diese Kerzen,
Aufgezehrt von Sinnentriebe —
    Nicht mehr leuchtet in den herzen [3]

[3] With inward peace his bosom deeply fill'd,
And singing as he goes, when winter comes,
To southern realms the white swan hies away.
Thence duly he returns, with clearer voice,
And plumage more resplendent. — *Not so*, Hugo!
Borne through the azure kindgoms of the main,
Gaily he went, unruffled as the swan,
Strong as the mountain-eagle. But, alas!
As he went forth, not so did he return
To his paternal hearth and anxious friends.
    As in your bosom, so in his prevails
A storm of passions fierce that blaze away
The torch of his internal energy. —
His lock'd up bosom that but ill conceals
The impulse to wild pleasure; and his looks
Retiring, dark, — that when they meet in yours,
Gleam after gleam of self-destroying fire —
    Ah, these are not the signs of happiness!
*That* cannot live, unless where it is fed
By calm repose and peace.
                 (*Guilt*, Act I, scene 6)

For almost like a corse with open eyes,
So hagard [sic], and so pale she look'd
                 (Act II, scene 1)

. . . . pour thy poison forth, lest it corrode
The cup that holds it —
                 (Act II, scene 4)

# Moscow 1825

⟨Thursday Nov. Dec 26th. Dec. 8th. Get up early & practise. Then give lessons. Then write History⟩
then give lessons—then write History. After dinner sleep. then give lessons to Helen & Catherine—then practise till eleven. then ⟨wit⟩ write a sentence or two, then read Robertson untill one o'clock.

Thursday Nov 26th. Decbr 8th. Get up early & practise. Then give lessons. then go to Baborikin's and give a lesson. It snows the whole way. come home and read Robertson. Miss Hawker and Miss Kakorchkine, Varinka, and Anna Vassilievna dined. After dinner sleep. Then read ⟨with J⟩ Tarlton with Johnny. Then practise till ten—read Robertson till eleven & then to-bed.

Friday Nov 27th. Dec. 9th. Get up early & practise. Then give lesson. Then write history. After dinner Mr. Genichsta comes. Practise.

Saturday Nov 28th. Dec 10th. Get up early & practise. Then call upon the Princess Ouronssoff—she sends me to call upon another Princess Ouronssoff in Garden Street—then took a sledge and went to Zuchari Baschnik—gave lesson at Jaenisch's. Return to dinner. Then sleep. then read Robertson then gave lessons to Helen & Catherine till 10 o'clock. Send my letter to Mad. Mason.

⟨Saturday⟩

Sunday Novbr. 29th. Dec. 11th. Get up late and dress. Then go to Miss Trewin's—and then Miss Gottman comes to fetch us. ⟨Th⟩ to Church; the first thing she said was—Do you know the Emperor is dead at Taganroj! Every body of course was lost in grief and astonishment. At church I saw Mr. & Mrs. Harvey, Miss Sayce and Mrs. Leon; the latter told me to call at Madme Melianofsky's. Return to dinner. Feodor Feodoritch, Mr. Poushchine, Mr. Ivanoff, Mr. Aconloff, Miss Kakorchkine, Varinka and Anna Vassilievna dined. At seven Madame Rajefsky came and Mr.

---

If *now* he were to come, at this dark hour,
When love at last, by its own fire consumed,
Burnt out even like those candles, laughs no more
In either heart

(Act II, scene 4)

Müllner, *Guilt*, trans. R. P. Gillies (Edinburgh, 1819).

# Fifth Journal

Gambs came home and brought Mr. Armfeld with him who spent the Evening. Nothing was talked of but the death of the Emperor, and nothing was heard but lamentations for his loss. The Count Arakcheeff has inscribed over the tomb of his murdered mistress — Ici repose mon amie et l'epouse de mon cocher.[4] Letter from Miss Henriette with a hundred roubles which I enclosed to Miss Hawker.

Monday Novembr. 30th. Dec. 12th. Get up early & practise. Then give lessons. Then go in a sledge to Sheremeteef's hospital. Call upon Madme. Melianofsky. Return & read Robertson. Then dine. then sleep. then write to Mr. Cornet and Madme. Polen. Then drink tea & read some of Schiller's riddles — then practise Beethoven's ⟨17t⟩ seventeenth sonata where there are triolets and semiquavers that almost drive me mad.

Tuesday Dec 1st. ⟨Dec.⟩ 13th. Get up early & practise ⟨my l⟩ Then give lessons. Then I spend a long while in having my hair combed. Then read Robertson. After dinner Nicolai Ivanovitch comes and Miss Hawker & her pupil. Mr. Genichsta comes. after the lessons were over he played his ballad of Der Ring des Polycrates and Mr. Gambs sung it. There was a violent scene between Miss Hawker & Marie Ivanovna. Letter from Madme. Tchernicheff from Taganroj dated the 13th. of November but she makes no mention of the Emperor's sickness.

Wednesday Dec. 2nd. 14th. Get up early & practise. Then give lesson. Madame Spicchinsky comes. Then dress and give Helen a lesson. Mr. Gambs had the tooth-ache, so he went to Joly's and had his tooth drawn. Read Robertson and Milton's Paradise Lost. After dinner give a lesson to Catherine. Then Mr. Baxter drank tea with his pupil Alexy. We talked of Political Justice and Academical

---

[4] "Here lies my love and the wife of my coachman." General Count Alexis Andreievitch Araktcheif (1769–1834) was a person of obscure origin, promoted by Alexander I to minister of war in 1808. Although talented as an administrator, he had no military capacity and had a reputation for cruelty and brutality (Waliszewski, in notes to *Souvenirs de la Comtesse Golovine née Princesse Galitzine, 1766–1821*, p. 131). He was also a sentimentalist of sorts. He was so fond of the nightingale's song that to protect the birds he ordered in 1817 that all the cats in his village be hanged (Mazour, *The First Russian Revolution*, p. 42).

# Moscow 1825

Questions[5] and of Mrs. Prater. Marie Ivanovna received a letter from her sister at Petersburgh in which she tells her the late Emperor has left a will declaring his brother Nicolas his successor.[6] A letter from Mr. Cornet.

Thursday Dec. 3rd. 15th. Get up early & practise. Then give english lesson. Then Dr. Jaenisch called and informed of his intended departure for Petersburgh. Then went to Miss Baborikin & gave a lesson. Come home at ½ past two & read Robertson. After dinner slept. After tea practised ⟨till⟩ sung with M.G. Then practised till ten, Then read Robertson till ½ past twelve. Finish the 1st Volume & begin the History of Charles the 5th.

Friday Dec. 4th. 16th. Get up early & practise. It is Saint Barbara's day I went ⟨thererofe⟩ therefore to call upon the Princess Ouronssoff to congratulate her. She was not at home. Meet Miss Merrytt there. Return & give english lesson. Then put all my thing to rights which took me till dinner time and an hour afterwards. Then dress. Genichsta comes and gives lessons. Then he plays ⟨and⟩ a funeral march he has composed on the death of Prince Cavansky's son, and the Ring des Polycrates, die Grösse der Welt, die Würde der Frauen and several other poems of ⟨sich⟩ Schillers which he has set to music. There is a peculiar character in his music, unlike the compositions of the present day; sentiment seems to float along ⟨gen⟩ in the gentlest undulations from the first note to the last, ⟨all is so smooth⟩ the changes are so smooth so naturally brought about that scarcely any one of them makes a more decided impression on the hearer⟨s⟩ than the others, and the effect can only be described by the feeling of noble exaltation of mind which his music produces. When he ceased to play, all seemed dull flat and void; the air seemed empty to which before he had given a soul⟨d⟩.

Afterwards talked with Marie Ivanovna till twelve o'clock — then read a little of Robertson and then to-bed.

Saturday Dec. 5th. 17th. Got up early & practised till eleven. Then wrote History till three. Then dined. Then Johnny wrote a note to ⟨Mr. Baxter⟩ Alexy. Then I gave lessons till ½ past eight to ⟨Che⟩ Catherine & Helen. My eyes were then so painful I could

---

[5] By William Godwin and William Drummond, respectively.
[6] Nicholas I (1796–1855), czar of Russia 1825–1855.

do no more. Mr. Pouschine called — after he went, talked with Marie Ivanovna & Mr. Gambs till eleven — Then went to bed.

Sunday December 6th. 18th. Get up late. Dress. Write to Madame Tchernicheff. Then walk with Nicolas & Catherine ⟨of⟩ to Mrs. Kitto's — Sit there an hour. Come home and dress. Feodor Feodorovitch, his daughter, Mr. Galavine & General Kappenko & his son dine. Mr. Baxter  the Miss Aconloffs, Alexy Kyrieff, & Modeste drink tea. Talked about the Poets of the present day  about Walter Scott with Mr. B. Midge after being out the whole day comes home at eight to bring me a present from Genichsta of all his compositions. Mr. Kitto told us to-day that Mr. Quasdoff went to Gualtier's and told how he wished to buy an english book for his children. Gualtier recommended him Glass's cookery-book as very entertaining and that ⟨gne⟩ gentleman accordingly bought it.[7]

Monday Dec. 7th. 19th. Got up early & practised. Then wrote History till three o'clock. It was Miss Hawker's name's day  Mr. G. dined there and the young ladies spent the Evening. After tea I practised till eleven.

Tuesday Dec. 8th. 20th. Got up early and practised. Then wrote till three. Letter from Mr. Baxter and Forsyth's Travels in Italy.[8] After dinner I read it. The following is a description of a view from ⟨Fies⟩ Fiesole.

> Monti superbi, la cui fronte Alpina
> Fa di se contro i venti, argine e sponda!
> Valli beate, per cui d'onda in onda
> L'Arno con passo signoril cammina.

Give a lesson to Johnny. Mr. Genichsta came  After his lessons were over, he played and Mr. Gambs sang Der Ring des Poly-

[7] Hannah Glasse, *The Art of Cookery Made Plain and Easy* (London, 1824).

[8] Joseph Forsyth, *Remarks on Antiquities, Arts, and Letters*, which she had read with the Shelleys in 1819. The quatrain quoted in this entry is from p. 83 and may be translated:

> Proud hills, whose Alpine brow
> Serves as dyke and parapet against the winds!
> Blessed valleys, through which wave by wave
> The Arno makes its stately way.

crates. Then Mr. Armfeld ⟨called⟩ came and staid till ten o'clock Read Robertson.

Wednesday Dec 9th. 21st   Got up early & practised. Then wrote ⟨on⟩ history. Mr. Baxter & Alexy spent the Evening. Talked with him upon english litterature, ⟨upon⟩ about Lyall's History of Moscow[9] about Matouschkin's Journal of his travels in the north of Asia.[10]

X Thursday Dec 10th. 22nd. Got up early and practised. Bad headach the whole day. Went to Baborikin's and gave my lesson. Called in my way upon the Princess Ouronssoff's. Come home at two — Doctor Jenken was there. Mr. Kakorchkine and his daughter and Alona Antonievna dined — the two first went away early, the latter and Mr. Evrainoff spent the evening. After dinner I had so severe a head I was obliged to lie down ⟨ate⟩ — at eight I got up & read Forsyth a little.

Friday Decbr. 11th. 23rd. Extremely unwell the whole day. Got up & practiced  then gave lesson to Johnny, then went to bed again and remained there the whole day. Mr. Genichsta came but I did not take my lesson. Read Robertson.

Origin of the Jesuits. At the siege of Pampeluna carried on by L'Espaire in Francis the 1st.'s name against Charles the 5th. Ignatio Loyola was dangerously wounded — During the progress of a lingering cure he occupied himself in reading the lives of the Romish Saints; the effect of this on his mind naturally enthusiastic was to inspire him with an ardent desire of imitating these fabulous worthies of the Roman Church and he was led at last to institute the Society of the Jesuits.

Charles the 5th. visited England on his way to Spain in the year 1522, and made a residence of six weeks there.

Saturday Dec. 12th. 24th. Got up early and practised. Then wrote till three. After dinner lay down. After tea read Forsyth with Mr. Gambs.

[9] Robert Lyall, *The Character of the Russians, and a Detailed History of Moscow* (London, 1823).

[10] Possibly Fedor Fedorovitch Matiouchkin, *Le Nord de la Sibérie, voyage parmi les peuplades de la Russie asiatique et dans la mer glaciale . . .* , trans. from the Russian by Prince Emmanuel Galitzin, 2 vols. (Paris, 1843). This might be the Feodor Feodorovitch whose regular visits Claire recorded.

# Fifth Journal

Inscription from the gate of an Italian Villa.
Amicis
Et, ne paucis pateat
Etiam fictis.[11]

Of Arezzo whose peasants Dante calls Bottoli from their surly character and of the sudden turn the Arno makes near its walls Dante says,

> Bottoli trova poi venendo giuso
> Ringhiosi piu che non chiede lor possa
> E a lor disdegnoso torce 'l muso.[12]

The chesnuts of Bibbiena are famous for their size and sweetness and are thus described by Burchiello.

> Ogni castagna in camiscia e'n pelliccia
> Scoppia e salta pe'l caldo e fa trictracche
> Nasce in mezzo del mondo in cioppa riccia;
> Secca, lessa e arsiccia
> Si da per frutte a desinar e a cena
> Questi sono i confetti di Bibbiena.[13]

At La Verna they shew the spot where St Francis received the five wounds of Christ and this described by Dante.

> Nel crudo sasso infra Tever ed Arno
> Da Christo prese l'ultimo sigillo;
> Che ⟨due⟩ le sue membra due anni portarno.[14]

[11] Claire quoted Forsyth often inaccurately and probably from memory. The inscription (*Remarks on Antiquities*, p. 27) may be translated:

> For friends
> And, lest it open for few,
> Even for the false.

[12] This passage (Forsyth, p. 102) is from *Purgatorio*, canto xiv, lines 46–48: "Anon in its downward course it meets with curs, disposed to snarl more than their strength demands, and at them in contempt it twists its muzzle" (Tozer's trans.).

[13] Burchiello's lines (Forsyth, p. 101): "Every chestnut in chemise and fur coat bursts and leaps for the heat, goes *tap-tap*, and appears amidst the world in a curly hood. Parched, boiled, and roasted, they are served for fruit at dinner and supper; these are the sweetmeats of Bibbiena."

[14] The lines about La Verna (Forsyth, p. 97) are from *Paradiso*, canto xi, lines 106–108: "O mid the rude rocks between the Tiber and the Arno he

# Moscow 1825

Description by the same of Camaldoli under the heights of Falterona which is called the giant of the Apennines and from which both the surrounding seas of Italy may be discovered.

> Fra due liti d'Italia surgon sassi,
> E fann'un gibbo che si chiama Latria;
> Dissott'al quale è conservato un Ermo,
>     Che suol esser disposto à sola latria,[15]

And further

> Come Apennin sopre il mar schiavo e'l Tosco
> Dal giogo onde a Camaldoli si viene.[16]

Sunday Dec. 13th. 25. English Christmas day. Unwell the whole day. Write from 12 till 5 in the Afternoon, yet I did little for I was much interrupted by Johnny and by a visit from the two Miss Trewin's and Miss Gottman. I dined in my room. After dinner slept — then went down stairs to drink tea. and practised till ten. Modest Aconloff was there. Then read Robertson till twelve.

Monday Dec. 14th. 26th. Got up early and practised till eleven. Then wrote a note to Mr. Baxter — a new door was put to my room which prevented my writing. The following is the beginning of a philosophical lecture delivered by a professor at Gottingen. Es ist ⟨wh⟩ wohl bequem für ein faules Gemüth zu glauben. and this of another upon History. Es war einmal ein mann der hiess Jesus.[17] Mr. Kaverine dined — at dinner he said to Marie Ivanovna As for you, you are fond of the cross, because the court is religious — we all know when Augustus used to drink all Poland ⟨were w⟩ got

---

received from Christ his final seal, which two years long his limbs did bear" (Tozer's trans.).

[15] The description of Camaldoli (Forsyth, p. 92) is a garbled version of *Paradiso*, canto xxi, lines 106–111: "Between [*Tra*, not *Fra*] the two shores of Italy rocks arise . . . and make a hump that is called Catria, beneath which a hermitage is consecrated [*consecrato*], which was once devoted solely to the worship of God."

[16] The final quotation is not in Forsyth. Claire has recalled it from Ariosto, *Orlando furioso*, canto iv, stanza xi, lines 85–86: "Just as Apennine shows the Slavic Sea and the Tuscan Sea from the ridge by which one goes to Camaldoli" (Gilbert's trans.).

[17] "It is most fitting for an indolent spirit to believe." "Once upon a time there was a man called Jesus."

drunk. There is a general report that Constantine will not accept the russian crown but means to resign his rights. After dinner read Forsyth with Midge. Then give a lesson to Johnny. Nicolai Ivanovitch drank tea. Practised. Madme. Gerardoff called and disputed so loud upon holy subjects with Marie Ivanovna there was no staying in the room. ⟨Her shrieks and⟩ Each tried by raising her voice to make the other listen and as neither yielded, the noise went on rapidly encreasing to the very highest pitch of alto. When remonstrated on ⟨&⟩ for this unchristian violence they declared ⟨they were⟩ it was only an ejaculatory moment. Read a little more of Forsyth. Then talked of Trelawny which put me into such low spirits I could not sleep the whole night. I fear a thousand things for him — the impetuosity of his temper, the difficulty of his situation, the want of a sober friend entirely devoted to his welfare, whose attachment would inspire him with sufficient confidence to yield the direction of his actions to him.

Tuesday Dec. 15th. 27th. Got up early and practised till eleven. Then dressed and read Robertson. Then gave a lesson to Miss Helen. Then dined. After dinner read Forsyth with Ya-Yan.[18] Then gave Johnny an english lesson. Mr. Genichsta came and gave his lesson. Then he played the music he has composed for Schillers Taüscher, der Ring des Polycrates &c. &c. After he was gone read Forsyth with Ya-Yan.

Wednesday Dec. 16 — 28th. Got up early and practised. Then wrote a little but very little for I was not disposed and could not conquer my disenclination. After dinner lay down. Then gave a lesson to Johnny, then to Katherine the chair upon which I sat broke and I fell and hurt myself. After tea read Forsyth — but I suffered a good deal and was in low spirits and went early to bed.

Thursday Dec. 17 — 29th. Got up early and practised till eleven. Then wrote ⟨a⟩ notes to Mr. Baxter, to Miss Trewin & to Miss Sayce. Then go to Boborikin's and give a lesson. ⟨It was⟩ There were twenty degrees of cold — the sky was clear and without the trace of a cloud; only the smoke reflecting the bright yet cold rays of the sun ⟨spread like golden⟩ mounted like golden fleeces and

[18] Another pet name for Gambs.

spread athwart the blue heaven. After dinner lay down. Then gave an english lesson. Nicolai Ivanovitch drank tea. Then practised till eleven — then went to bed. It is said in the Evening that Nicolas Ukase is come declaring his brother's renounciation and his succession to the throne.

Friday Dec. 18 — 30th. Got up early and practised till eleven. Then read Forsyth — I found it impossible to write — my mind is so unsettled and my spirits so low — every thing disgusts me. The Senator went to day to swear allegiance to Nicolas. There was bad news from Petersburgh where the soldiers have made a serious opposition to the succession of Nicolas and Miloradovitch was ⟨kull⟩ killed by a common soldier as he was haranguing them to obedience.[19] The Count Tolstoÿ and Mr. Galavine called and talked in whispers — Mrs. Pomikoff calls Nicolas a rising Nero. ⟨She told us⟩ but as she always passes with the most surprising quickness in the midst of her grief for Russia's state governed as she says only by a name and a coffin, her alarm for the future and her determination to fly to another land for safety on the slightest appearance of ⟨an⟩ public commotion, she recollected a most amusing story which took place at the entry of Alexander the first into Moscow shortly after his being declared Emperor. They had a slave in their family who was a hair dresser, a man who was always drunk from morning to night. Mrs. Acaroff used to punish him with the greatest severity. She went with her two daughters to a house in the Twerskoi to see the Emperor ⟨p⟩ make his public entry. The procession was very fine; ⟨an⟩ acclamations rent the air the moment the Emperor appeared; he went slowly by on horse back and his bridle was held by their drunken slave who was crying Long live Alexander with all his might & main; the moment however his eye met his mistress's posted in an open window he let go the bridle of the Emperor's horse and took to his heels as quick as he could.

　　After dinner Mrs. Pomikoff went with Johnny to visit Mad Zimmermann so there was no english lesson. Genischsta came as usual. He played the Taucher, ⟨his own Varr⟩ Variations, Russian

[19] General Count Mikhail Andreevich Miloradovich (1771–1825), governor of St. Petersburg. This hero of the war of 1812 was the first victim of the Decembrist uprising (see Grunwald, *Tsar Nicholas I*, p. 7).

# Fifth Journal

elegy from ⟨Pouschine⟩ Poushkine,[20] the Copack by the same, Fingal and Malvina of his own Composing. I then practised till eleven and went to bed.

Saturday Dec. 19 — 31st. Got up early and practised till eleven. Then dawdled the whole morning away. Went out an airing with Johnny. There is a russian lady from Ionla [?] at dinner. She remained untill ten at night and not one single moment was her mouth shut. After dinner I slept. Then gave Helen a lesson. Then practised till eleven.

## [1826 N.S.]

Sunday Dec 20th. January 1st. Got up late & practised a little. Went out in the sledge with Johnny to Madame Zimmerman's — non c'era — then to Mrs. Kitto's. The usual people dined. Mr. Baxter & Mr. Armfeld spent the Evening. All the guests are as usual full of consternation and surmises. Different arrests have taken place. Some say Poland is in a state of revolt; others that Wittengstein with his army has moved towards Poland in order to force Constantine to mount the throne.

Monday Dec. 21st. January 2nd. The cold is intense. Got up early & practised. A letter came from the Countess Zotoff announcing her arrival and that of her two daughters and inviting me ⟨there⟩ to dine with her to-morrow. I am delighted at the idea of seeing Betsy again. Read Charles the 5th.

Tuesday Dec. 22nd. January 3rd. Got up early and practised. The cold was intense. Then dressed and read Forsyth. The carriage came at ½ past two  Went to the Countess's. Dined with Betsy & Natalie, the Count, Miss Elizabeth, Cecile, Helen, and Madme. Paris. Prince Paul ⟨Gall⟩ Galitzin came at seven. He said the cold was intolerable, and as it seemed to encreasing at every instant, I departed. Not a word was said of Petersburgh. Betsy is expecting either her husband's arrival, or a letter to tell her where to go — ⟨Wh⟩ The cold returning home was intense one's breath seemed chilled in one's breast and scarcely able to force a passage against

[20] This setting of Pushkin's "Elegie" may be found in *Sammlung russischer Romanzen und Volkslieder für eine Singstimme mit Begleitung des Pianoforte*, Russian text with German trans. by Bruno (Hamburg: Fritz Schuberth, n.d.), in the British Museum.

the cold. When I came home found Mr. Genischta still there, but he could not give me a lesson. Also Miss Hawker & Miss Kakorch-kine.

Wednesday December 23rd. January 4th. Unwell with the cold. Notwithstanding went in a sledge & breakfasted with Madame Czernicheff and her father. Then Natalie came and we all went to the Countess Zotoff's. Then I came home. The cold was very severe but the ⟨shon⟩ sun shone brightly and the atmosphere was so clear that every thing sparkled in his rays; frost ice, spires and steeples, all seemed gay and dazzling with a thousand beams. After dinner I was completely ill with a bad rheumatick headach & obliged to go to bed.

Thursday Dec. 24th. January 5th. Completely ill all day. I was obliged to lie down the whole day my head-ach was so bad. There was an examination in the morning of the children and Barbe Kakoschkine won the prize.

Friday Dec. 25th. January 6th. Xmas day. I was ill the whole day and confined to my room. Many people dined amonsgt others Miss Henrietta Feldhausen and she paid me a visit in my room. In the evening I drank tea downstairs but was soon obliged to go to bed again.

Saturday Dec. 26th. January 7th. I am somewhat better. Practised in the morning. Write a note to Madme. Tchernicheff. Mrs. Spiri-doff & Miss Sayce drink tea. Begin reading Göthe's translation of Benvenuto Cellini's Memoirs.[21]

Sunday Dec. 27th. January 8th. Got up late. It was still extremely cold. Go with Johnny in a sledge and call upon Madme. Tcherni-cheff. When we come home read ⟨M⟩ Cellini with Ya-Yan. Then dress for dinner. Mr. ⟨Genishsta⟩ Genichsta, Mr. Armfeld and the usual people dined.

Monday Dec. 28th. January 9th. Got up early & practised. It is very cold. After dinner slept & then practised till eleven at night.

[21] Benvenuto Cellini, *Eine Geschichte des XVI Jahrhunderts*, trans. from the Italian by Goethe, 3 vols. (Brunswick, 1798).

# Fifth Journal

Tuesday Dec. 29th. January 10th. Got up early and practised. Read Charles the 5th. After dinner Mr. Genischta came. Miss Hawker, Miss Kakoschkine & Nicolai Ivanovitch Evrainoff drank tea.

Wednesday Dec 30th. January 11th. Got up early and practised. Dressed. Began writing a note to Mr. Baxter. Marie Ivanovna begged me to go out. Went to Stanisfield's Magazine, to Gnathers and called on Carolina Carlovna at Chateinzoff's. Madame Zimmermann dined and spent the Evening. After dinner slept. The Prince Jean Labanoff drank tea. Read Ritter Gluck by Hoffman [22] with Mr. Gambs. Then finished writing to Mr. Baxter and read Robertson till one o'clock.

Thursday December 31st. January 12th. Got up early and practised till one. Then dressed and read Hoffman's phantasicen Stücke in dem Callot's manier with M.G. ⟨After⟩ Marie Ivanovna & her husband dined at Madme. Zimmermann's. After dinner slept. The Priests come & sing. Madame Stramiloff and her son & daughter drink tea. Then read Hoffman (Kreussleriana) [23] untill bed-time. Another year is gone but it has been fortunate in one respect for me. I have gained a real devotedly attached friend.

## [1826 O.S.]

⟨Thursday⟩ ↑Friday↓ January 1st. 12th [13th]. Got up early and practised. Low spirits the whole day. Went with Johnny in the sledge to Madme. Czernicheff's to Madme. Alsonfieff's & Madame Zimmerman. The usual people dined. Just before dinner Miss Trewin called. After dinner read Hoffman.

Saturday January 2nd. 13th [14th]. Got up early and practised. Then called upon the Princess Ouronssoff, Miss Boborikin, Miss Trewin & Mrs. Harvey. Come home tired and late. After dinner ⟨slep⟩ they all went to drink tea at Kakouchkine's—I slept a little and read Hoffman with M. G. The Senator Dourassoff & his brother called.

The Thaumatrope; being rounds of Amusement, or how to please and surpri⟨z⟩se by turns at 10s and 6d.

[22] "Ritter Gluck: Eine Erinnerung aus dem Jahre 1809," in E. T. W. Hoffmann's *Fantasiestücke in Callot's Manier*, 2 vols. (Bamberg, 1819), vol. I.
[23] "Kreisleriana," in *Fantasiestücke*, vol. I.

By Boosey and Sons Bond Street, Papyro-plastics; or the art of modelling in Paper an instructive amusement for young people. 5s.[24] I humbly beg you to convey.[25]

Mavali puram.

12 Mortimer Terrace⟨t⟩

To send my fur tippet to be mended —
    to look for music.

Kentish Town.[26]

Get my concerto from
Chateinzoff's. also a

5. Bartholomew Place
Kentish Town.[27]

Receipt to make a cake. call
on the Kitto's, the Butler's.
Ask for Books every where.    Mrs.
Buy a slate for Dunia and
for John.

Parents Assistant

⟨32 & 75 copecks.⟩
⟨To M. G. I owe 129 roubles    5 roubles⟩
⟨for Net.⟩ To M.G. I owe 157   ,,   75 copecks in
                                23   ,,   45    Paper.
J. C. Hudson Esq, Legacy Office, Somerset House.
    Mr. Harvey, in Bachmeetieff's House in the Sdvijenka.
    Messrs. J. H. Attwood & Co. Odessa.

[24] The thaumatrope, or "wonder-turner," was made by placing cardboard discs back to back and whirling them on strings so that the images on the two sides merged into one (a parrot into a cage, a ship into a bottle, etc.). This forerunner of the early moving-picture devices illustrates the principle of persistence of vision. Kits for the construction of thaumatropes and similar boons to governesses are still published by the Rumbold Gallery, Midhurst, Sussex, at five shillings each.
    Bernard Heinrich Blasche, *Papyro-Plastics; or the Art of Modelling in Paper*, trans. from the German by Daniel Boileau (London, 1824), went through at least three editions, each enlarged. It explained the construction of model furniture and buildings from cardboard.
[25] This phrase is in Russian script.
[26] Address of Jane Williams.
[27] Address of Mary Shelley.

# SIXTH
# JOURNAL
## December 21, 1826, to February 2, 1827

with omissions

# [1826]

For almost a year — January to December 1826 — Claire neglected her journal. When she resumed it she was with a different family in Moscow, the death of Dunia having left her with no position in that household. She was probably in charge of several children in the family of Prince Paul Galitzin, who had two brothers, Prince Alexander and Prince Peter. In a letter to Jane Williams she gives an account of her normal day: "From eleven till four I teach my children, then we dine — at five we rise from table — they have half an hour's dawdling for play it cannot be called, as they are in the drawing room and then they learn two hours more. At eight we drink tea, and then they go to bed which is never over till eleven because all must have their hair curled which takes up an enormous time." [1]

Although Claire had friends with whom she could enjoy conversation, there was no one, since the departure of Hermann Gambs, to whom she could talk freely of her family and closest friends — of Shelley and Godwin, of Mary and Jane. "I had few acquaintance among the english," she wrote to Jane in the same letter, "to those I had never mentioned a single circumstance of myself or fortunes but took care on the contrary to appear content and happy as if I had never known or seen any other society all my days." She went on to explain that when her friend Miss Trewin went to England, she had sent with her a letter to Jane, confident that the name of Williams would excite no suspicions.

---

[1] Abinger MSS., postmarked January 22, 1827.

# Sixth Journal

"But it seems my mother got hold of Miss T—," Claire explained, "sought her out and has thereby done me a most incalculable mischief.[2] Miss T— has come back full of my story here, and though she is very friendly to me, yet others who are not so have already done me injury. The Professor at the University here, is a man of a good deal of talent and was in close connection with Lockhart the son in law of Sir Walter Scott and all that party; he has a great deal of friendship for me because as he says very truly, I am the only person here besides himself who knows how to speak english. He professes the most rigid principles and is come to that age when it is useless to endeavour to change them; I however took care not to get upon the subject of principles and as he was of infinite use to me both by counselling and by protecting me with the weight of his high approbation. You may imagine this man's horror when he heard who I was; what [*that*] the charming Miss Clairmont, the model of good sense accomplishments and good taste was brought up, issued from the very den of freethinkers. I see that he is in a complete puzzle on my account, he cannot explain to himself how I can be so extremely delightful and yet so detestable; the inveteracy of his objections is shaken    this however has not hindered him from doing me serious mischief; I was to have undertaken this winter the education of an only daughter, the child of a very rich family, where the Professor reigns despotic; because he always settles every little dispute with some unintelligible quotation or reference to a Latin or Greek author. I am extremely interested in the child, he used to say, and no one can give her the education she ought to have but Miss C. The mother and the father have been running after me these two yrs to persuade me to enter when the child should be old enough. I consented, when now all is broken off, because the scruples of my Professor do not allow of it. God knows he says what Godwinish principles she might not instil. You may therefore think how teized I have been. More so from the uncertainty of my position as I do not know how far this may extend. If this is only the beginning what may be the end!"

Thus sensitive to the precariousness of her position, Claire begins a new section of her journal.

[2] Godwin's diary records on August 21, 1826, "Miss Trewen dines" (Abinger MSS.).

# Moscow 1826

Dec. 21st  My Journal had been a long while interrupted, every-day I have put off writing it, tired of having nothing to say and because I was overwhelmed with work. Now I am a little quieter, I am at the Princess Galitzin's[1] in Dmitrieff's home opposite the Strastnova Monastery on the Tverskoi Boulevard. The Prince and Princess, Helen and Miss Harriett are all in the country. So I am as quiet as a bird roosting for the night . . .

Dec. 26th  Got up early. Miss Weston came to fetch me and I went to church. We came late and sat next Mr. Baxter who was so pious and devout that he looked very severe. He sighed most profoundly . . .
     The parson preached against infidelity as is natural on Christmas Day, and Harriet said she was sure it was meant at me. Came home and practised.

Dec. 27th . . . The Prince Alexander[2] and the Count Rastop-shin[3] dined. It was very disagreeable for me. The latter praised Albè up to the skies and reviled our dearest Shelley — I would not bear this and defended him. — Among other things he said that this paragon of generosity had pensioned Shelley's widow. Oh my God, the lies there are in the world. They all went to the Opera . . . I played the rest of the evening, but I was out of sorts for I am far from well.

Dec. 28th . . . Found a note from M. de Villeneuve. Wrote to

[1] "On a later page of the Journal Princess Galítzin is repeatedly called by Mme. de Villeneuve *La troppo bella e troppo buona* [too beautiful and too good]" (Huscher, "Claire Clairmont's Lost Russian Journal and Some Further Glimpses of Her Later Life," *KSMB* 6:47n. [1955]).
[2] Galitzin.
[3] "Perhaps a close relation of Count Fedor Vasiljevitsh Rostópchin (1765–1826), Governor-General of Moscow, and reputed to be the instigator of the burning of the City in 1812. Professor Max Vasmer, Berlin, suggests that the Count Vasiljevitsch [sic] mentioned here was Andrei, a son of the Governor-General. Andrei Rostopchin took a lively interest in romantic literature and sought the society of poets. His wife, Yevdokia, née Sushkova, who died in Moscow in 1858, was herself a poet. In her four volumes of collected poems she chose no less than thirty-eight mottoes from Byron. The motto to a poem published between 1838 and 1843 was taken from Shelley's 'Autumn, a Dirge'" (Huscher, *KSMB* 6:47n.).

beg he would come and dine with us. . . Then dressed for dinner. Mr. Villeneuve dined. I am more and more enchanted with him. He talked the whole time and it was like reading the most entertaining book or seeing a series of pictures. He described the Grecian valleys, mountains and rivers, the Grecian ruins, the dress of men, the women, the characters of all the principal heroes of that reviving country and their actions and Samos and Chios and Hydra and Navarino. Lately a young princess called Mavrogenia [4] brought up at Vienna has much distinguished herself. The exertions to serve her country have been indefatigable, and she is always armed at the head of her own band of followers. She is only two and twenty and extremely beautiful and many sued for her hand, but she answers: "I will only marry a freeman. Fight and gain your liberty and we will see." After a defeat she came to Mavrokordato to beg for arms and supplies —. He began to compliment her on her deeds and her beauty. She cut the conversation short — "No compliment, Mavrocordato, give me the arms and the help I am come to entreat and let me return to the defence of my country." Happy the country where heroism and virtue seem natural, easy and unaffected as if it were the affair of every day.

Mr. de Villeneuve saw a Grecian woman flying from the Turks — a well lay in her path — she cast a look back and saw her pursuers near — she took the child and threw him in, and then leaped in herself.

Four hundred Greeks rescued the body of their dead chief Marco Bozzaris [5] from an army of sixteen thousand Turks and carried it off in triumph to Missolunghi where he was buried. Yet the greater part of the Greeks are utterly ignorant of the deeds and actions of their pagan forefathers, and when they behold strangers transported at the sight of Marathon or weep over tombs of their ancient heroes, they ask: "What is the matter?"

He was also at Smirna and saw there an ancient statue of the founder of that town, an Amazon called Smirna. The Amazons were always believed to have lived on the northern borders of the

---

[4] "In 1821 Modena Mavrogenia helped to prepare and to spread the rising among the inhabitants of the Greek Islands" (Huscher, *KSMB* 6:47n.).

[5] Marco Botzaris, leader of the gallant Suliotes, was killed in action on August 21, 1823, just before Byron was to join him in the fighting north of Missolonghi (Marchand, *Byron*, III, 1114-1115).

# Moscow 1827

Black Sea, and Smirna in Russian means gentle.[6] Everybody was
delighted with M. de Villeneuve. I was quite enchanted at a dinner
in which not a word of indecent was uttered, for it is the first time
in a Russian home. His forehead is broad and high and shaded by
long flowing locks of dark brown hair, his eyes are steady and
piercing and tranquil, his nose long, his cheeks rather sunken and
his mouth and chin smaller in proportion than the upper part of
his face. He is tall, very broad-shouldered but otherwise remarkably
slightly built. He went away at seven.

Wednesday, December 29th  I walked home. It snowed or rather
sleeted hard. I heard faint sounds of military music in the distance
which produced a most striking effect when contrasted with the
grey sky charged with snow and the desolate appearence of everything around . . . Dined at Labanoffs. The Prince was out. Our
conversation at table was very amusing—We agreed to form a state
upon the Turkish model, only that the tables should be turned and
the men shut up in harems and kept by the women.

[1827]

Saturday, January 1st, 1827. The Prince and Princess dined out.
I was very unwell and lay down. They came home and went to
sleep. I also went to sleep for I was frightened to think I had
another year to run like the last . . .

January 2nd . . . Then came home and dressed for dinner. Monsieur and Madame de Villeneuve dined. We had a very gay dinner.
As for him—he is an apparition in my life which lies stagnant from
inactivity, he like a clear rivulet come fresh from the mountains,
and liberty runs through our stagnant marsh and enlivens what
before was dead.

Monday, January 3rd  I got into my sledge and went to Pomikoffs. It was about five in the afternoon—the moon was up and
shining with a white light upon the white snow—we went thro'
narrow by-streets—the window-shutters of the houses were all
shut, the yard-doors likewise, not a soul was to be seen, not even
a dog baying the moon or seeking stray morsels among the heaps

---

[6] "Russian *smirnyi*, quiet, peaceful, from *mir*, peace. Claire's etymology is,
of course, a mere fanciful combination, but the idea of a gentle amazon is
characteristic of her romantic mind" (Huscher, *KSMB* 6:47n.).

of rubbish — all seemed at this early hour buried in repose. We glided along this scene like ghosts at midnight with the utmost swiftness and silence. Our motion was noiseless. I amused myself very much at Pomikoffs. I thumped all the boys, which they bore with great patience. We jumped up and down on the sofa. — I jogged Johnny's arm as he was drinking his tea; it was spilt over him, and he was furious. The tall Nicola opened his mouth and said: "Oh! My God, Miss Clairmont, how you are funny!"

Tuesday, January 4th . . . Called upon Madame de Villeneuve. I was beginning to write a note to her husband when in he came. We chatted a long while about Men and Women. I said Sex ought to be abolished — He was of my opinion, she not. They want me to go with them to Greece. — How much I should like it, but I dare not for fear of being a burthen. And yet once more to feel the sweet air of the South, to see its deep blue sky and feel its fervid Sun is indeed a temptation.

Wednesday Jan. 5th . . . Then we went a-shopping. I called at Lehnhold's [7] and found a letter from Mary. Got into the carriage and read it. There were two lines from Percino: [8] "My dear Aunt. When will you come over here? I have seen your portrait and want to see you. Yours affectionately . . ." Darling boy! Thank Heaven they are all well. This made me gay the whole day. We went to Levy's Magazine. I read my letter whilst the Princess walked round the shop. — In came a tall man rather common-looking with a blue Carbonaro mantle hanging from his shoulders lined with yellow. He stared at the Princess and then at my letter — its black seal seemed to startle him. Everywhere we turned he turned and could not get on in his speech to the showman for staring. I do not know whether it was my letter or the Princess's beauty which struck him. She as usual was frightened.

Thursday, Jan. 6th . . . We dined at Kaisaroff's. — Mr. Baxter, Alexis and the Prince Peter Galitzin were also there. The conversation was as usual animated and about Greece. After dinner we attacked Mr. Baxter about his aristocracy. He said equality was a chimera; I said: Certainly it would be so so long as it were believed to be one, but that we had only to alter our faith upon that point,

[7] The music publisher at whose shop Claire received all her mail.
[8] Percy Florence Shelley, by now seven years old.

# Moscow 1827

and the result would come of itself. I told him the greatest fault in his character was his hopelessness of anything good. He said he had always been reproached for his sanguine character.

Then I ran home to dress. The Princess related to me the conversation which had taken place at dinner about me. The Prince Alexander and the Count Rastopchin said my dislike to men was affected, that they were sure I was always falling in love and that either one or the other had only to make love to me for a day or two and I should become *amoureuse folle!* Amiable delightful creatures! I must really take great care of my poor heart lest I should not only fall in love with one but perhaps with both at once . . .

Friday, January 7th  Got up early and ran away to breakfast at Kaisaroff's. The moon was shining bright and cold in a clear grey sky. — There were fifteen degrees of frost. Breakfasted with Natasha. Mrs. Kaisaroff, like me, is enchanted with Mr. de Villeneuve. — "Where shall we look", said she, "for such a countenance among the Russians!" Then we talked of the weather. — "You may be sure it is excessively cold because the sun shines." — My God, what a country where the sign of severe cold is sunshine and where one sees its rays without feeling them . . .

. . . Then talked with the Prince about Mr. de Villeneuve's journal. — He does not think much of it. — As far as I can judge there is not much erudition, but a feeling of enthusiasm for liberty and in general for the beautiful predominates through the whole, and the display of this feeling, when natural, is always agreeable . . .

Saturday, January 8th  Got up late and ran off to Kaisaroff's. The moon was up quite round and still no troop of clouds attendant. All alone in the blue vault of heaven she looked as solitary as our sledge, which slid over the white floor of snow, and no other stirring thing was to be seen. Breakfasted with Natasha. We were very happy as usual — happy living things; every trifle amuses us for life runs over in our veins . . .

I told Mr. de Villeneuve what I thought of his journal — that there was too much love in it. — He offered me some verses which he had written for me. — I knocked them out of his hand and would not read them for I am tired of learning that I am charming . . .

407

# Sixth Journal

Dressed for dinner. The Princess Alexy and her husband, the Prince Alexander and Mr. R[astopshin]. dined. It was a most tiresome dinner. The conversation as is usual in Russia turned upon love, for it is the only subject upon which they can speak their minds, and they make use of their freedom until it becomes licence. The men talked the usual nonsense about infidelity being unpardonable in women but very pardonable in men. After dinner Mr. de Villeneuve came. He presented some verses to the Princess. They played at cards. She went to the theatre, and I sat and talked with him an hour. — How different the conversation! We talked of the necessity of Women's being free that Man may walk, unencumbered by his fair clog, more freely towards a noble destiny — then upon religion. — He is a materialist — a conclusion which would seem impossible to so ardent a mind as his seems to be. — How believe a heavy lumpy substance like our body can produce such a thing as thought which is without limit or form. — At any rate they ought to keep to their own reasoning of cause and effect. I never heard yet of an effect of totally different nature to its cause.

Thursday, Jan. 11th    The cold was excessive. We talked upon that subject. It struck us as very strange the Russians should believe in a hell of fire and flame which must rather be a temptation than a scarecrow to poor wretches shivering with bitter cold — a hell of ice and snow and the bitter blasts they produce would be ten thousand times more frightful — but the flames and fire with which Hell is adorned stamp that place as an imagination of the South where heat and burning are the torments of the inhabitants . . .

Friday, January 28th    Got up early. Gave my lesson at Kaisaroff's and at Pomikoff's. — Then home and gave Lenska a lesson. — The Princess told me she intended to set out for Petersburgh to morrow — everything was in a bustle packing up.

I read Medwin's book upon Lord Byron.[9] — My God, what

[9] *Journal of the Conversations of Lord Byron: Noted during a Residence with His Lordship at Pisa, in the Years 1821 and 1822* (London, 1824). For Claire's further reaction to this book, see the second leaflet of Miscellanea below. On hearing of the forthcoming publication of Medwin's book, T. J. Hogg wrote to Jane Williams, in a letter postmarked September 28, 1824 (British Museum, Add. MSS. 41,686): "I rejoice that M. is to have £500, because he is a good 'tempered fellow, & I dare say wants it: but I wish he cod get it in a more

lies that book contains! Poor Shelley is made to play quite a secondary part, and I particularly admire the patronizing tone which L.B. assumed, the more so when I recalled how he sneered at his talents at Geneva and thought him quite a dabbler in verses. This death-bed scene as related by Fletcher is quite proper and edifying, but one does not know how to settle his extreme tenderness for the Guiccioli in the first half of the work with his utter forgetfulness of her when dying except indeed that at that awful moment nothing less legitimate than a wife and a daughter born in lawful wedlock could enter the mind of a man who respected the world's prejudices so much as he did. What is very droll, is that Fletcher who declared publicly that he talked of nothing but his wife and child, declared to Mary privately that he talked of me and seemed uneasy at my fate and anxious if possible to repair it.[10] But this I always thought was a lie, invented by the tenderness of Fletcher's heart. — I knew the man too well to suspect he was ever sorry for the mischief he had done me. He planned that mischief in cold blood, executed it in cold blood and rejoiced at it in cold blood.

We dined very late. — The Prince Alexander was there. — As usual, the character of their eldest brother Peter fell under animadversion . . .

When I was in bed, I wept a great deal because my reading of to-day had brought back Shelley vividly to my mind. — It is cruel to think how his merit was lost upon the world, how that impostor Byron was admired for his imposture, how tenderly they relate of him that he declared he could not leave his monkeys behind because

---

reputable manner. Selling the memory of a friend to a bookseller is to me a resurrectionlike measure & ressembles selling his body to the Surgeons for dissection. . . . A life is nothing without a portrait, the noble Poet was fond of fancy dresses, what cod be more fanciful than a likeness of one of the garments all torn and rent? [Jane had apparently told Hogg that the Guiccioli's two faults were thick ankles and her having torn Byron's nightshirts.] Claire no doubt can draw; let her draw it, & show her taste by a judicious disposition of the shreds of calico; Colborne will give her, at least, £500, & we shall see advertised 'Memoirs of the Rt. Hon. Ld Byron by Captn. Medwin, his bosom friend, with a striking likeness in a favorite fancy dress by C. C., governess to the Hon. Countess Kut-off' " [for Zotoff?].

   [10] Mary Shelley corroborated this statement in a letter to Trelawny, dated July 28, 1824 (see Mary Shelley, Letters, I, 298).

strangers could not take care of them, whilst he left his daughter to the care of ignorant bigoted mercenaries and let her die for want of care. How mean and detestable is the world — even those who knew this licked his hand and soothed him with soft words of praise because he had the world's voice with him.

Saturday, January 29th . . . I was excessively unwell. The pain in my chest was intolerable.

Sunday, January 30th   I was excessively unwell. I stayed in bed and wrote to Hermann [11] and arranged various papers . . . walked to Kaisaroff's. I was so weak I could scarce go.

Found Mr. Baxter, Bolivanoff and Mr. Ichebaiff there. — After dinner I and Mr. Baxter as usual had a long dispute. He said Schlegel had proved that no nation could civilize itself, that civilization had penetrated from country to country in a direct line from the East. How the first country had received it, no one knew, but he supposed from God. I saw very well at what he was tending to prove; that God had delivered civilization to the nations on the Mount Sinai. I maintained that it was man's natural tendency to become civilized. He said I could not bring a single proof of a nation's making a single step towards civilization without having received it from some people more advanced than itself. I said I did not know what he meant by a single step in civilization. Were not the Britons to a certain degree civilized when they were found by Julius Caesar? They had fortified towers, they had a rude kind of chariot and they had a rude kind of warfare; they had a religion of their own. I considered them as as civilized as the Hebrews under Moses from whom he pretended we had all received our civilization; and yet certainly they had had no intercourse with any other nation. This he denied and raked up an old story of the Phoenicians visiting Thule and further protested that no nation could be called civilized who did not know how to write and read, which the Hebrews certainly did, and that in proof of his theory: ask whatever savage of whatever country you chose where his fathers came from, he would always point to the East etc. etc. I shall write to Hermann on this subject . . .

[11] Gambs had left Moscow the preceding spring for five years in the country, according to Claire's letter to Jane Williams, postmarked January 22, 1827 (Abinger MSS., printed in part in Marshall, *Mary Shelley*, II, 160).

# Moscow 1827

I was very ill myself. I had such a pain in my chest with talking to Mr. Baxter that I soon after went to bed quite worn out. I have moved to-day to Kaisaroff's. They are extremely kind.

Wednesday, Feb. 2nd . . . . . . . .

> [Tu] proverai siccome sa di sale
> Lo pane altrui e come è dure calle
> Lo scendere e 'l salir per l'altrui scale.[12]

How true! Little did I think when I wrote these lines some years ago in my Journal book at Florence that I should feel their bitterness to the quick. None can know like me what it is to mount daily a stranger's stairs and to feel with every step that a solitary room and faces filled with strange indifference await us. The world is closed in silence to me. It is four years that I have lived among strangers. The voices that spoke to my youth, the faces that were then around me, are almost forgotten; and not to be able to remember them augments what I feel. — The last consolation is torn away . . .

[12] "Thou wilt learn by experience how bitter is the taste of another's bread, and how hard a path it is to ascend and descend another's stairs" (Dante, *Paradiso*, canto xvii, lines 58–60; Tozer's trans.). Claire had earlier entered the passage on April 13, 1821, above.

# MISCELLANEA
## (Two Leaflets)
### 1828 - 1830

# [1828 - 1830]

In May of 1828 Claire left the cold of Russia forever behind her, but still eating the bread of strangers she departed as companion to Madame Kaisaroff, the wife of a personally formidable general, and their ailing over-indulged twelve-year-old daughter Natalie. Claire had arranged to go as English tutor to the girl in return for traveling expenses, but despite the hopeful tone of her letters to Mary Shelley and Jane Williams she must have foreseen the problems of the arrangement, to judge from the description of Natalie in Miscellanea — a description apparently written before the departure from Moscow (below, pp. 425–426). Her account of the actual trip, which appears as a draft of a letter to a slight acquaintance (below, pp. 419–421), tells only part of the story; in a letter to Mary (July 22, 1828), she reported that the Kaisaroffs "behaved so ill upon the road" that she was forced to quit them en route.[1] Despite the quarrel, Madame Kaisaroff saw to it that Claire got as far as the Baths of Tuplitz, near Dresden, where she could consult a doctor about her weakness and the pain in her side, and where she stayed long enough to take the much-needed *Kur*. Claire's intention, however, was to get to England as soon as possible in order to join Charles during his visit there with his Austrian wife, Antonie, and their two little girls, Pauline and Clara. She eventually found a traveling companion in Miss Esperance Sylvestre, one of the governesses of the Duchess of

[1] Abinger MSS.

# Miscellanea

Saxe-Weimar,[2] and on October 16 she reached London, three months after her brother's arrival.[3]

Almost as soon as Claire arrived Godwin set to work on a new novel, a paraphrase of the old ballad of the babes in the woods, to be called *Cloudesley*. As he progressed in age, Godwin found more and more difficulty in producing new ideas and relied to an ever increasing extent on the suggestions of others.[4] The fresh influences of 1828 and 1829 are apparent in this, his fifth novel. Claire's arrival, with her colorful tales of her travels, inspired Godwin to work on the opening chapters, which are set in Russia. Trelawny had called on Godwin on May 21, 1828, and he stalks through *Cloudesley* in the person of Borromeo.[5] The book is distinguished by vivid firsthand descriptions of scenes near Vienna, in Russia, and in Italy. One of these passages, the stunning description of the waterfall of Terni, was lifted verbatim from a letter from Shelley to Peacock,[6] and it is not surprising that Mary has been held responsible for some of the direct description.[7] While Godwin undoubtedly took whatever he could get from anyone who was willing to help, Mary had been back in England for years, and it was not until Claire landed that Godwin had the incentive to begin the work. It is not necessary to assume that Claire (or Charles) actually wrote the descriptions of Vienna and St. Petersburg, but there can be no doubt that they provided Godwin with the material. Nevertheless, it is not at all impossible that Claire took a real hand in the writing. She resumed her attempts at authorship at about this time, and it is clear from her attitude about her short story, "The Pole," published two years later as by the author of *Frankenstein*, that she was not averse to having her work appear over the name of another. Her 1830 letters bear witness to her particular and eager interest in the reception of the book; she wrote

[2] Clairmont MSS., July 26, 1856.

[3] Godwin diary, Abinger MSS.

[4] For a letter from Godwin to Mary, April 13, 1832, begging her for help in finishing a work on which he had run out of ideas, see Marshall, *Mary Shelley*, II, 241–242.

[5] Mary too included Trelawny in the novel begun about that time and published in 1830, the same year as *Cloudesley*: he appears as Hernan de Faro in *Perkin Warbeck*.

[6] Shelley, *Letters*, II, 55–56, and *Cloudesley*, III, 138–139.

[7] See Woodcock, *William Godwin*, pp. 230–231.

to Mary, "You may imagine how anxious I am to hear how you like Cloudesley and what reception it meets with from the public." [8] She wrote to Jane Williams, also, for her opinion of the book, which fortunately had a good critical reception.

Claire stayed a year in England, visiting with Godwin and Mary. She admired Percy Florence excessively, although he seems not to have liked her.[9] She renewed her acquaintance with Jane Williams, now living as Jane Hogg and the mother of a baby girl called Prudentia. She got to know her amiable but conventional sister-in-law, Tonie, and the young Clairmonts. And again she saw Trelawny. The flame which he had been nursing with a certain fidelity for more than six years received a sudden dousing with cold water. Six years had changed Claire — she herself had complained in her journal of the steady deterioration that was the result of the living death of being a governess. The role of good respectable maiden aunt which she had adopted had become fixed, alas, all too firmly ever to be abandoned. Trelawny preferred her letters to actual conversation because "you are becoming so horridly prudish — and sister-like insensible." His tone was jocular, but the implications were melancholy: "I consider you very fish-like — bloodless — and insensible — you are the counterpart of Werter — a sort of bread butter and worsted stockings — like Charlotte fit for 'suckling fools and chronicling small beer.' Adieu old Aunt." [10] In a letter to Mary he expressed his discontent: "She talked of nothing but worsted stockings and marrying — the only doubt to my mind is which is worse — but if I am condemned to one — I think I must take the former." [11]

[8] Abinger MSS., March 28, 1830. For some reason Mrs. Marshall omitted this sentence when she published the letter (*Mary Shelley*, II, 199–203). It shows beyond the shadow of a doubt that Claire, not Mary, was intimately familiar with the novel during the period it was being written.

[9] She wrote back to Mary after her departure: "How delighted I was with the news of Percy's health as also with his letter though I am afraid it was written unwillingly and cost him a world of pains. Poor child he little thinks how much I am attached to him. When I first saw him, I thought him cold; but afterwards he discovered so much intellect in all his speeches, and so much originality in his doings that I willingly pardoned him for not being interested in anything but himself" (Abinger MSS., March 28, 1830).

[10] Trelawny, *Letters*, p. 116.

[11] Abinger MSS., not seen; quoted by Grylls, *Trelawny*, p. 153. Miss Grylls reads this as though the worsted stockings and potential marriage were Claire's.

# Miscellanea

On September 18, 1829, Claire returned to the Kaisaroffs in Dresden. Charles went back to Vienna alone on November 14, his family following on March 30, 1830.[12] Trelawny wrote Claire asking her to come to Italy to help take care of his daughter Zella (by the sister of his companion Odysseus) who was arriving soon from Greece, but Claire missed her chance. For some reason she had a horror of returning to Italy just then and even threatened to break with Madame Kaisaroff when it was suggested that they spend the next winter there.[13] It was decided instead to go to Nice, to which Claire had no objection. There is no way of knowing why, later in the year, Claire changed her mind and wrote suggesting that at last she join Trelawny and take over the education of Zella. On January 4, 1831, he wrote to reject her offer.[14] She was too late: although she had nearly half a century to live, the tide was at the ebb.

*[The first leaflet begins without a heading]*

I am not a Mrs. Killinger or a Madame du Bois[1] — I cannot send you my whole being in a letter; ↑Je ne puis pas rendre mon dernier soupir ni verser tout mon etre et rendre mon dernier soupir dans une billet d'invitation:↓[2] so great a quantity of sensations assail me when I take the pen in my hand, all entreating to be listened to and to see themselves written down in black and ⟨wr⟩ white that I am perfectly confounded between the claimants and know⟨n⟩ not which to choose. [If you would allow me to write you a novel in nine volumes like Richardson perhaps I could ⟨g⟩ then lay before

---

Undoubtedly they were Claire's recommendations for Trelawny. He was notorious for never wearing stockings, even in extreme old age, and almost as soon as Claire heard that Trelawny was returning to England she wrote to Jane to see that he did not get his feet wet and fall ill (Abinger MSS., postmarked January 22, 1827).

[12] Godwin diary, Abinger MSS.

[13] Abinger MSS., March 28, 1830. This interesting letter, describing the winter in Dresden, is almost complete in Marshall, *Mary Shelley*, II, 199–203.

[14] Trelawny, *Letters*, pp. 137–139.

[1] *Histoire de Madame Dubois, écrite par elle-même. Nouvelle anglaise* (Amsterdam, 1769).

[2] "I cannot give up my last gasp, nor pour out all my being and give up my last gasp in a letter of invitation."

# First Leaflet

you a part of ⟨all I feel⟩. the enormous whole that I feel.] [3] My own nature, the integral part of me, the intimate construction of my soul, prompts me to listen to the pleasurable part of my being but then the painful sensations ↑in order to revenge themselves for my neglect↓ press themselves forward with such additional vehemence and so countlessly, ⟨that⟩ that I am obliged to listen to them, in order to get rid of them. I see no chance therefore dear Madame, of my being able to give you any other than the above account of myself, and certainly a most embroiled and confused one it is, now joyous and now desolate, unless indeed you would allow me to write you a novel in nine volumes ⟨like Richard⟩ long and detailed like Richardson's, and then perhaps I should be able to ⟨lay before you with some order the various movements of my soul⟩ reduce into something like order the various elements of which my sensations are composed, and the various movements of soul which they produce. One little resumé of the whole, however I must venture on, which is: that I have through the whole journey been able to discern in myself, the distinct and peculiar workings of two rival powers; one a principle of happiness, it is the integral part of my nature which leads me to welcome all that happens with an aspect of joy; I have been able to discern two distinct states of being that have been surrounding me; the first ⟨is that of my own peculiar nature; belongs to me⟩ ↑state is internal and belongs entirely to me↓ an exceeding desire to be happy and to welcome whatever befalls pleasant or unpleasant with a joyous aspect: ⟨⟨the second is external and in direct contradiction; it seems as every circumstance ⟨made war upon me, in⟩ conspired against this principle of Life and Joy, and made war upon it;⟩⟩ but I was not allowed to do so, in short I never am. Instantly as If an evil power pursued me invisibly and ⟨insp⟩ breathed his own ↑⟨ho⟩↓ spirit into all that surrounded me, instantly every circumstance, every incident of every moment, the faces of those around, in short that mass of accidental impressions which we are accustomed to denominate circumstances ⟨by⟩ became hostile to me, and forced me to be sad and sour as themselves.

I wished excessively to be gay; I was in a humour to be pleased with every thing; ⟨had I been alone⟩ the roads, the woods, the mountains, the seasons of the year ⟨seemed⟩ all to my stupid and

[3] The square brackets throughout this leaflet are thus in the manuscript. It is clear that Claire was revising her text as she went along.

419

childish mind seemed to promise joy; had I been alone I should
have skipped and played and been lost the whole way in a trance of
pleasure. but this state was too childish to please the wise Natalie;
⟨in⟩ so she set about correcting me by demonstrating, the absurdity
of my delight, the wretchedness of every thing that surrounded
us; ⟨↑every pretty or pleasing thing she refused to recognise; if I
pressed the↓ [every discomfort she carefully picked up, and insisted
upon my inspecting it; she made disquisitions about it that lasted
two hours; she did not even give me any hope for the future, but
promised to recollect the bad inns, the bad beds, the bad food, the
bad voiturier, and the bad horses to the last day of her life; in short
she never rested till she had turned my poor dear Arcadia in which
I so much delighted into a wild and desert heath, without a flower
or a blossom or even a blade of grass, or the slightest ornament to
recreate the mind and the spirits.⟩ [Every pretty or pleasing thing
she refused to recognise ⟨she⟩ if I pressed it upon her attention,
she denied its existence absolutely with as much boldness as most
would have asserted it; every discomfort on the contrary she carefully picked up and not ⟨only⟩ content with cherishing it herself
insisted upon my doing so likewise; she made disquisitions ⟨and⟩
about it, that lasted two two hours; she dissected it to the very last
particles; she made it the God of the present moment; the sole
thought of her mind; nor did she give me any hope for the future
for she promised in the most exalted and heroic way, to remember
the bad inns, the bad beds, the bad carriage, the bad coachman
and the bad horses, ↑and my most hateful and disagreeable self↓
to the last day of her life. ⟨If people would⟩ in short she never
rested till she had turned my poor dear Arcadia, in which I so much
delighted into a ⟨desert⟩ flat wide desert steppe, devoid of flowers,
blossoms or grass, or in short of any ornament that Nature lends
to charm the heart of Man. In short dear Madam, can you imagine
any thing more horrid than us two travelling; my only recourse was
to ⟨joke up⟩ make jokes about the whole affair. [In short dear
Madam if you can imagine the Comic Muse and the Tragic Music
seated side by side in a Diligence you will have some idea of us:
or if you can imagine ⟨a picture of the Universe upon a small scale⟩
two eternal Dissonances struggling in vain to mingle in unison you
will have some idea, both of the Vast Universe we inhabit, and,
of the little Universe of a John Ruticher's carriage which we then

# First Leaflet

inhabited.] I stuffed ⟨up⟩ my ears full of cotton; I wound up my nerves to the proper Narcissean state of utter insensibility; I braced my heart in a case of armour and ⟨setting spurs⟩ giving the reins to my Imagination, dashed right through the middle of the whole, and through utter despair began to make jokes upon the whole. ⟨I compared ourselves to the⟩ Natalie I called the ⟨comic Muse, m⟩ tragic Muse, myself the Comic, and laughed ready to kill myself at ⟨this⟩ the combination of circumstances that made these two ⟨be seated side⟩ travel side by side in the Diligence from Carlsbaad to Mù. By this short cut I regained my dear delightful ⟨hl⟩ hilarity that I prize so much, but which some are pleased to call unnatural. Though what they mean by this term, I confess I am at a loss to understand, since in Nature ⟨I defy them to shew me a single melancholy thing. A⟩ Inanimate Nature that is to say, I defy them to shew me a single melancholy thing.

To hope against hope; ⟨to⟩ with subdued manners to keep my soul invincible in its purposes, that is my cue. This reserve adds double ⟨f⟩ effect to the beauty of the object. It is the same principle as that treated of in Lessing's Dramaturgie,[4] where he says the artist whether poet, painter or musician must always keep within the line of Absolute Beauty. This reserve, this retreat within the line of demarcation renders doubly striking the effects which the author or the actor intends to produce.

Un Shakespeare, comme dans Lear, ou un Dieu comme dans l'Univers, aurait pu unir ces deux choses, et en les unissant meme etendre ↑jusqu'à l'infini↓ le cercle des ⟨ses⟩ ↑fleurs↓ pouvoirs; ↑par cette union↓ mais je ne suis ni l'un ni l'autre, et je n'eus pour toute resource que de me jetter ⟨im⟩ dans les badinages J'ai plaisanté donc, et cela impitoyablement tout le chemin.[5]

I have not talked much of you, but entirely of myself; because I know nothing of you ⟨and should only be fighting in the dark⟩ and to talk of ⟨w⟩ what one knows nothing about, is pretty much the

---

[4] Gotthold Ephraim Lessing, *Hamburgische Dramaturgie*, 2 vols. (Hamburg, 1767–1768).

[5] "A Shakespeare, as in Lear, or a God as in the Universe, could have united these two things, and in uniting them even extend to infinity the circle of their powers by that union; but I am neither the one nor the other, and the only resource I had was to throw myself into raillery I joked therefore, and I did it mercilessly all the way."

same thing as to fight in the dark. but being quite au fait de moi meme j'ai ⟨voulu⟩ traitu de ce sujet, esperant que mes connoissances l'a dessùs sera l'excuse de mon egoisme.[6] For myself I cannot bear when a person writes to me from a distance that they should talk of me; I want to hear of them in the same way that is very disagreeable at a french dinner that the first thing they give you to satisfy your hunger is ⟨some thin⟩ a plate of soup.

To hope against hope — this is the key of the secret intelligence that reigns between me and Mrs. Kaisaroff. She met with me when I was a solitary and uncertain wanderer upon the face of the earth; a branch cut off from the plantation where it had grown and abandoned amid strangers; my mind was in that state of destitution and misery which ⟨are but too often⟩ are the surest roads to Vice. I met her in the lucky hour; she gave me a home, she gave me consideration and kindness, and beyond all these sympathy in my thoughts and feelings. [I was cut off for ever as I considered from the list of human beings; I might exist but ⟨that existence was doomed to incurable to be barren of all joy⟩ the joys the honours, the pleasures of existence were not to be allowed to me in the least portion. I belonged to an outcast race; our name was one of utter reprobation; it lived in my heart, but was never in these many long years pronounced by my lips. The most unworthy conduct, the most unworthy principles were attributed to the beings whom I belonged to, and whom I looked upon as sacred; the principles that I looked upon as saced were objects of execration to ⟨these as⟩ the rest of mankind; the persons whom I cherished and revered were the objects of scorn and blame whenever they were mentioned. Every ⟨thing⟩ ↑quality↓ that can disgrace ⟨the⟩ human nature was attributed to them; how unjustly I well knew, though none beside did know; their race ⟨was⟩ was cursed, their name one of utter reprobation; and so forbidden that though deeply graven in my heart, it never passed my lips. In this state of destitution and misery ⟨th⟩ Mrs. K. found me; an outcast from society, an uncertain and solitary wanderer, sullen from the sense of unmerited sufferings, in hatred with all mankind; [except these one or two individuals who yet survived the destruction that has been made of us,

---

[6] But being quite "an authority on myself I have treated this subject, hoping that my insights into it will excuse my egotism."

but these were too far] who that knows human nature but know that this state of mental ⟨vice is⟩ solitude, this state of incesenbility [*insensibility?*] to all ⟨the be⟩ social claims, is the surest forunner of Vice. In this state I was. One or two individuals yet ⟨lived⟩, there were, who still lived having ⟨survive⟩ survived the destruction that had been heaped upon us, but these were too far from me to afford me succour. I looked upon them with suppliant eyes, as the drowning mariner may look upon the distant ⟨clouds⟩ ↑heaven↓ that are ⟨gathered in the h⟩ congregated in the horizon. but whilst I admired and adored, I expected no help. In this state I met Mrs. K. She selected me from the crowd ⟨among whom I was⟩ where I was lost and overlooked; raised me from the state of despondency into which I had fallen, gave me a home and a sister in herself, and far more than these, ⟨made me⟩ restored to me, that which I had been accustomed to and which of all my losses seemed the heaviest, sympathy for my thoughts and opinions. Once more they breathed the light of day; once more my lips revealed the workings of my mind; once more I received and gave ⟨all that is noble⟩ noble aspirations. By how many pledges therefore am I not bound to her. By the honour of the sect to whom I belong; by my duty to prove ↑by my actions that↓ these calumniated persons, ⟨in my own person⟩ are worthy of a better name and better fate. My whole soul is bent upon preserving this friendship; ⟨I will⟩ my first thought when I rise in the morning, my last at night, is ⟨how can I best preserve without reproach, the affection⟩ how shall I guard our affection from ↑these blights of↓ coldness distrust, or misunderstanding ⟨or any of these⟩ which are the reproach of commoner affections; how may I preserve it as it now is inviolate, untouched by Time or the World's abuse, that to the end it may last in all its present perfection. To this my being is dedicated.

Leave me to expiate my virtues in misery.

S—[7] was beautiful that kind of beauty which Bacon says is the best — "that which a picture cannot express." It dwelt upon his countenance. it enshrined his person, and seemed to be a perpetual ⟨emati⟩ emanation from himself, rather than any union of exquisite

---

[7] Shelley. The following quotation is from Bacon's "Of Beauty" in *The Essayes or Counsels, Civill and Morall* (1625).

proportions either in form or figure. The beholder saw that he was beautiful ↑preeminent in beauty↓ but could not discover in what ↑that preeminence↓ it consisted. Other men had as fair open and commanding foreheads and as dark and ⟨lex⟩ luxuriant brown hair to shade them, eyes as full of poetic ⟨and⟩ fire and lips as ⟨soft and⟩ expressive of gentle serenity, but they wanted that nameless something which touched the heart at every glance ⟨m⟩ subdued it to silent homage. [*rest of this page blank*]

An excess of tenderness is a fatal error in education. The love ⟨one feels⟩ a parent feels for its offspring though it be felt with passion, ⟨but never shows to the⟩ ↑should never be shown but with↓ extreme moderation to the object or objects of it. The intellect of a child is too weak to understand ⟨you⟩ ↑an enthusiastic↓ devotion — he has too little experience to be aware that the self sacrifices you practise are rare and should therefore be highly prized — He looks upon them as things of course, tributes due to his merit that belong to him by right and not as benefits and blessings that emanate entirely from the overflowing goodness of his parents  The inexhaustible love, the never sleeping zeal ⟨of Mrs.⟩ to procure her pleasures which Mrs. C— exercised towards her daughter had already begun to produce in the latter seeds of selfishness. ⟨W⟩ Under a less tender mother this would not have been the case; but she had accustomed Maimonna to ⟨profit by all⟩ expect from her every sacrifice and all sacrifices and to profit by them. The mother seemed only to exist in order to create and establish the happiness of the daughter, and the daughter naturally soon learned to look upon ⟨it as⟩ her own satisfaction ↑as an object of the utmost importance↓ with the same ardent feelings. Because the mother ⟨thought herself made to preserve Maimonna from disappointment and⟩ was ever ready to immolate her own wishes to ⟨that object the child⟩ ↑hers, the child↓ soon began to ⟨live⟩ ↑expect everyone else to do so;↓ as if she were the only being extant or at least had an internal feeling; ⟨⟨perhaps⟩ scarcely well defined in so young a mind, but yet not less producing the most detirminate result in her mien and actions⟩ that every one was to yield to her. Of course in ↑the mind of↓ so young a creature this feeling ⟨was not⟩ ↑could not be very↓ well defined ⟨in her mind as to have become a law or a guide to her conduct⟩, but had ⟨it been⟩ she had the strongest sense the most apprehended ⟨know⟩ consciousness of it, the results it

produced in her conduct and mien could not have been more
detirminate.

⟨she seemed to live as if she were the only being extant⟩, all her
thoughts ⟨were about herself⟩ were engrossed by herself; in the
most innocent ↑unaffected↓ manner she seemed to live as if she
were the only being extant, or if other beings crossed her path,
great indeed was her surprize and gloomy and morbid her dis-
satisfaction if they did not immediately yield to her. This proud
desire of domination was certainly not yet well defined in the mind
of so young a creature, but had it been a strong sense, ↑the most↓
apprehended of all ideas, it could not have produced more decided
effects of selfishness in her mien and conduct.

[*thirty-four blank pages follow and then three pages upside down
beginning with "Natalie"*]

Natalie.

She neglects no opportunity of saying every thing she conceives to
be most disagreeable to me. I was regretting not hearing from M.
Miltz because I had written requesting him to furnish him with
⟨recomm⟩ letters of introduction — she instantly thrust herself into
the discourse with a toss of the head. I wonder you are always
writing for letters of introduction, you who pretend to be so fond
of solitude ⟨do not want⟩ have no need for letters in order to make
acquaintainces. This is one of a hundred instances — in future I
shall note them down. But I remark with the greatest pain the
excessive malice of her disposition. This is the principle upon which
she proceeds; as I ⟨cannot make⟩ am not loved by so, so I am
detirmined to make myself hated. This is the object of her solici-
tude, the object which employs her thoughts night and day. Every
preparative that I make for the journey she blames: I cannot stir
a step but she throws ridicule and scorn and ineffable contempt
upon my proceedings. There is no end to the predictions she makes
as to the accidents we are to meet with in the journey. We are to roll
down the hill, or fall over the precipice, or be blown over by the
wind or be struck dead by a flash of lightning and assassinated by
robbers: ⟨we⟩ these are the great evils; when her tongue is tired of
expatiating upon thise, then she sinks into an enumeration of all
the evils which are to befall us; we shall find no beds, or if we do,
such as cannot be slept upon, we shall have nothing to eat, ⟨and⟩

or only *Schwein's Carre*. What these Schwein's Carre are I know not, nor how they got into her head, unless by a that peculiar sympathy which attracts ⟨certain⟩ ↑noble↓ thoughts to ⟨certain⟩ ↑noble↓ minds, and ⟨certain⟩ mean thoughts to ⟨other⟩ mean minds. She pays not the slightest attention to my representations. I beg her to think that the roads we go over, are at the very moment we speak, being traversed by hundreds of individuals, some rich, most of them poor, and that of these hundreds and hundreds, it is rare that a slight accident should happen, and a mortal one almost impossible. I point out to her Major Milner who has travelled like fifty thousand other people all over Europe alone, Mr. and Mrs. Carlen who have been wandering in every county except Russia and Poland for these many years, quite unattended and nothing ever happened to them; ⟨M⟩ finally Miss de Lally and Miss Sabine who though of high birth travel quite alone. She has seen all these ⟨thm⟩ people and has heard their accounts and must know that what they say is true. It has all no effect upon her; her mind is too narrow to take it in; there is one idea there and that is Schwein's Carre and that is all it will hold. Or perhaps she does not choose to give up her position, because if she did, she must give up at the same time, her pretext for tormenting me. So now she goes on in this way for three weeks, the same stupid arguments repeated every ↑moment↓ till at length I am as wearied of them, as of the ⟨noise⟩ ↑clack↓ of a water-mill.

Another scene. Mrs. Levarcheff came. She talked to me. Natalie thrust herself forward in the most useless manner and contradicted me in every opinion I advanced. Mrs. Levacheff stared at her sulky look and impertinent arrogant tone, but was naturally too well bred to take any notice of it.

*[Here begins the second leaflet of miscellanea.]*

Anecdotes, Remembrances &c &c.

I was once invited when very young to spend an evening with three very devout old maids. It has always appeared to me that those ladies having suspected by my simplicity of manner and various marks of ingenuous surprise I gave, when some religious ceremonies had fallen under my observation by chance, that I must be very ignorant indeed upon these subjects and this visit was intended to sound me upon this affair, for scarcely had I entered before they fell unanimously to sighing and groaning upon the wickedness of the times. Woful days we are fallen upon indeed said one! Worse than those of Sodom and Gomorrah says another! Sin cries from every corner of the earth said the third, and we may shortly expect that the anger of the Lord will be stirred to destroy us ⟨as⟩ ↑even as↓ he ⟨↑has↓ promised by fire and the sword!⟩ faithfully promised ⟨us⟩ to do by fire and the sword. It is awful to think of that day what suffering, what ⟨gn⟩ gnashing of ⟨teath⟩ teeth, what hot tears ⟨from⟩ of repentence from us miserabl⟨l⟩e sinners and all too late! ⟨Eternal damnat⟩ Heigh-ho! said the oldest rocking herself backwards and forwards, what miserable creatures we are! Conceived in sin — —

And born in sin sighed out the third

Bred up in wickedness said the second

A prey to all the lusts of the flesh and the devil ⟨said the⟩ continued the first —

Sinning in ⟨word⟩ ↑word↓ and deed every hour, ⟨eve nay   every minute⟩ of the day!

Oh! ⟨rather far⟩ ↑Worse↓ worse, sinning in thought every minute —

Who can can count the corruptions of our hearts! exclaimed the first

Or number the filthy abominations which harbour at the bottom of our souls — —

This was enough for me — my blood grew colder in my veins at every instant. The horrid account these three thin women gave of themselves, of their origin and their present life, of their future destination so different from the God-like pure beings to whom I had been accustumed filled me with astonishment and horror. ⟨⟨Nothing came before my mind but the wierd sisters ⟨of⟩ ↑in↓ Macbeth dancing about a cauldron⟩⟩ ⟨B⟩ "Conceived in Sin, born in Sin, bred up in wickedness, ⟨reserved for future eternal ever consuming fl⟩ plotting mischief every hour of the day and sinning in thought every minute, ⟨who for I⟩ who for heaven's sake can they be thought I. Nothing came to answer that thought but the image of the wierd sisters in Macbeth dancing about the cauldron and reciting their horrid exploits, and with a childish instinctive horror of evil I fled out of the room back to my home. I found

427

# Miscellanea

X X X[8] playing at chess — notwithstanding the calm attention she was giving to the game, ⟨my agitated⟩ the slight agitation in my countenance did not escape her and she asked the cause. My explanation drew a smile — They are people said she, who think to please God, by exaggerating ⟨un⟩ even unto horror the load of their ⟨faults⟩ faults and by crouching before him in the dust as beggars ⟨do to us when we enter our carriage⟩ fall before us when we go out, and hiding their heads upon the pavement multiply to infinity the number⟨s⟩ of their sores ⟨and⟩ ↑or their↓ misfortunes. Strange error that which makes people think the nearest road to God is by lowering their souls instead of striving to elevate our minds as near to him as possible.

---

The subject on which he was speaking was beautiful and his countenance and manner the whole while was to his subject, ⟨what⟩ like a beautiful accompaniment to a beautiful melody.

---

The history of Noah was related to [*a name, quite clearly not "Allegra," crossed out with the letter A. over it, apparently in Claire's hand, and "Allegra" written above in Dowden's hand*] — how everyone was drowned because they were wicked and he alone was saved because he was honest; I'll never be honest — said the child — Why not? Because I would not like to be left alone!! Honesty has the same effect in our days as in the time of Noah, its possessor may count upon a perfect solitude.

---

I read Medwin's Conversations[9] with disgust — What an idol has he chosen to fall upon his knees before, we have all read that the Mussulmen worship the black stone at Mecca and attribute a thousand ⟨vit⟩ virtues to it, ⟨⟨so ⟨we cannot call Mr. Medwin's admiration⟩ as this instance of absurdity is upon record ⟨we⟩ to keep the world in countenance we dare not call the public admiration of L.B. by its real real name a piece of gross imbecility.⟩⟩ in

[8] Claire made these X's of dotted lines. I have not been able to guess to whom they refer.

[9] *Journal of the Conversations of Lord Byron* (1824). See also entry for January 28, 1827, above.

428

# Second Leaflet

the same manner this modern Mussulman has made himself a God as far as morality is concerned ⟨of of⟩ out of the most worthless piece of humanity he could find and attributes a thousand qualities to it which were neither inherent in its nature nor could by any means find a place in it. According to M— he was a model of humanity his heart a "charitable asylum" for the unfortunate ⟨who⟩ and he apologizes for travelling with a train of dumb animals because he was afraid ⟨they⟩ had he left them with strangers, sufficient attention would not have been paid them, yet he left his child, notwithstanding the earnest representations of all his friends, the prayers the entreaties of her mother to die of neglect and confinement among mercernaries without a single human being to watch over her helpless infancy. Did ⟨Hypocrisy want a name⟩ we want a proverb for Hypocrisy this mournful contrast of a dying child ↑unnoticed↓ kept in the background and the pampered Monkey kept for shew in the front, might supply it — Virtue loses her healthy glow, she sickens and wastes to nothing ⟨before⟩ when she sees Vice so triumphant.

———————

Shelley is passed over in a note, ⟨just mentioned⟩ honoured with a mention because he was a star a little twinkling star that happened to be shining while the great Luminary ⟨gave light⟩ was rolling his round

The death of a child is like an interrupted revel where consternation and despair succeed to the buoyant dance of Life. We prepared ourselves a long pleasure but its enjoyment was dashed from us.

My soul seems to have been regenerated in the fountains of adversity into which it fell; there is a vigour and elasticity in my spirit which it never knew even in the spring of life. Before I seemed to breathe an atmosphere of Pain, every pulse of my being seemed a weary load that I was impatient to be quit of but now the whole earth seems tingling with pleasure and ⟨pleasurable sensation⟩ ↑joy.↓ — I look upon the sun the moon and the stars ↑as if they were new to me,↓ the ⟨blue⟩ face of heaven whether it be smiling or wrapt in dark tempestuous clouds, ⟨cold⟩ snow and verdure the frozen lake and the rippling brook, the bare rock or the cliff covered with waving woods, winter and summer spring and autumn ⟨keep up a perpetual succession of pleasure in my bosom.⟩ all these varied objects ⟨have only⟩ awake only one chord in my bosom, pleasure. It seems to me as if Nature was holding a Jubilee and I was invited to the banquet.

In the middle ages Europe ⟨who⟩ was alarmed by a whisper which ran thro' every state and which announced the appearance of a wonderful and mysterious book of a nature too horrible to admit of its being talked of publickly. Every state, every town every little village talked of "the book"; [10] ⟨Germa⟩ no one had ever seen it tho' all knew that its contents were of the most horrible description, a dispute arose as to in what nation it had first made its appearance Germany France Italy and Switzerland all brought great and convincing proofs of their separate claims to its possession    Refutations were written against it tho' no one knew what it contained. Thro' all Europe "the Book" its probable contents, its author was the universal theme of mysterious conversation carried on in more mysterious whispers, every body was dying to see it, yet no one had ever seen it, neither could any one tell where it was, Germany France ⟨and⟩ Switzerland and Italy each swore to their being in possession of it yet neither could produce it in testimony. Not a single line of its contents could ever be got at yet innumerable refutations loading it with ignomiy and shame appeared against this terrible incognito "the Book." So about this time ⟨thro' all Engl⟩ nothing was to be heard talked of but a terrible book called Queen Titania, no one had seen it tho' every body knew its author and knew what it contained; one said it was full of blasphemous doctrine whilst another persisted it was only ⟨a late⟩ squib against ministers, the young ⟨men⟩ ↑men↓ swore it was Spinosa turned into ⟨verse⟩ blank verse ⟨and the old that it was a parody upon the Bible⟩ the young ladies supposed it was something Anacreontic which caused so much scandal whilst the old with a ⟨sg⟩ sigh and nod agreed with one common accord that it was no doubt a parody upon the Bible. ⟨The Booksellers were questioned    put to the torture ↑by their customers↓, bribes carresses flattery were lavished on them in vain    they could not give what they had not got.⟩ The philosophers believed it was a refutation of vulgar errors, physicians

---

[10] This notorious nonexistent work sounds like *The Three Impostors*, referred to by Sir Thomas Browne in his *Religio Medici*, part I, sect. xx. Claire seems to be developing a fanciful analogy to the ignorant reaction to Shelley's *Queen Mab*.

# Second Leaflet

⟨a series⟩ An essay in favour of Materialism drawn from a new
course of Surgical experiments, ⟨Lawyers trembled lest it should
be⟩ tho' at variance upon the subject yet there was but one opinion
upon its contents that it was horrible too horrible to be talked of
as any thing but a profound secret. Irritated by ⟨curiosity⟩ unsatisfied
curiosity speculations were formed upon the probable contents of
this horrid productions; ⟨and it was then⟩ dire and terrible was
the war of words one protesting to his belief it was only a squib
against ministers, another that it was Spinosa turned into blank
verse, a third that it was Anacreontic and a fourth that it was a
parody upon the Bible; a physician knew from the best authority
that it was an Essay upon Materilism containing
                    [*rest of page left blank*]

> Life is a waste of wearisome hours
> Which seldom the rose of Enjoyment adorns
> And the heart that is soonest awake to the flowers
> Is always the first to be touched by the thorns.

———

> Fame that vain echo of an empty blast
> That rainbow symbol of a tempest past
> Which when the storm has sealed the sufferer's doom
> Extends its arch of beauty o'er the tomb.

[*"Mrs. Shelley" is written in Dowden's hand above the following
description*]
Mary's hair is light brown, of a sunny and burnished brightness
like the autumnal foliage when played upon by the rays of the
setting sun; / [11] it sets in round her face and falls upon her shoulders in gauzy wavings and is so fine it looks as if the wind had
tangled it together into golden network/ she wore it in its natural
state, flowing in gauzy wavings round her face and throat, and
upon her shoulders ⟨as if it had been tangled by the wind into a
golden network⟩. and it was so fine the slightest wind or motion
tangled it into a golden network/ it was rather short and she ⟨wore
it⟩ let it fall into its natural state like golden network ⟨about⟩
↑round↓ her face and throat, and half way down her shoulders and
it was so fine, one feared /to disturb ↑the beauty of↓ its gauzy

---

[11] This and the following slash marks are Claire's.

431

wavings with a breath/lest the slightest breath should disturb the beauty of ⟨lo⟩ its gauzy wavings.

She has given up every hope of imaginary excellence, and has compromised all the nobler parts of her nature ⟨for the pitiful pleasure of trifling with triflers⟩, and has sneaked in upon any terms she could get into ⟨the depraved condition of⟩ society although she full well knew she could meet with nothing there but depravity. Others still cling round the image and memory of Shelley — ⟨with her it ought to be the sole thought of her being⟩ his ardent mouth [*end of page*]

Tete à Tete avec une fleur.[12]

his exalted being, his simplicity and enthusiasm are the sole thought of their being, but she has forsaken even their memory for the pitiful pleasure of trifling with triflers, and ⟨for a share⟩ has exchanged the sole thought of his being for a share in the corruptions of society. Would to God she could perish without note or remembrance, so the brightness of his name might not be darkened by the corruptions she sheds upon it. What low ambition is that, that seeks for tinsil and gaudiness when the reality of all that is noble and worthy has passed away. ⟨It will perhaps be objected to these⟩ The only ⟨alliev⟩ palliation I have to offer to these meanesses of conduct and heart, is the surpassing beauty of her mind; every sentiment of her's is so glowing and beautiful, it is worth the actions of another person.

She is a mixture of vanity and good-nature.

Recollecting her conduct at Pisa I can never help feeling horror even in only looking at her — the instant she appears I feel ⟨the⟩ not as if I had blood in my veins, but in its stead the sickening crawling motion of the Death Worm.

What would one say of a Woman ⟨who should go⟩ how would feel towards her who should go and gaze upon the spectacle of a Child le⟨a⟩d to the scaffold, one would turn from her with horror — yet she did so, she looked coolly on, rejoiced in the comfortable place

---

[12] This line, perhaps the title of a song, is centered at the top of the page, suggesting that Claire may have used the leaflet originally for copying poems or songs, such as the one beginning "Life is a waste," at the top of the preceding page, facing it.

# Second Leaflet

she had got in the shew, chatted with her neighbours, ⟨and after all⟩ never winced once during the exhibition and after all was over, went up and claimed acquaintance with the executioner and shook hands with him.

I never saw her afterwards without feeling as if the sickening crawling motion of a Deathworm ⟨were in⟩ had replaced the usual flow of my Blood in my veins.

Shelley on the contrary acted like himself—it was his principle never to refuse his countenance even to the most guilty; he could not therefore now that he was touched withdraw; but his sad countenance betrayed how painful was the duty imposed upon him.

*[the following sentence is at the top of an otherwise blank page]*
He lies like a porcupine in my way; his prickles disturb at every instant my feet as they wander thro' the flowery path.

Of Dresden. About two months and a half ago we had falls of snow for many days.[13] It was dry and crisp, not wet and powdery as it usually is in the beginning of winter, and one tripped as lightly over it as over a new shaven lawn. Since then alternate frosts and ⟨thews⟩ thaws have turned the snow into ice and every street seems paved as in chrystal. The houses rise on both sides like tall grey ramparts ⟨patched⟩ with snow patched summits. Dresden is as unfit for Germany and Winter, as Naples or Burgos would be for the North Pole if transported there; ⟨shut out the sun, keep in the shade it is suited for Spain or Italy and puts you constantly in mind of them and looks as if it had been built by architects who bring or repeated⟩—Heaven knows what the good architect was ⟨about⟩ thinking about when he built it; Göthe sang I should think of
Kennst du das Land wo die Citronen blüh'n

> Im dunkeln Laub die gold Orangen glühn
> Ein sanfter Luft von blauen himmel weht
> Die Myrte still, und hoch der Lorbeer steht.[14]

[13] This reference helps date this entry as late 1829 or early 1830, since Claire spent that winter in Dresden with Natalie Kaisaroff.

[14]     Know you the land where the lemon trees bloom?
    In dark foliage the gold oranges glow
    A soft wind blows from the blue heavens
    The myrtle stands silent, and the bay tree tall.

"Mignon," from *Wilhelm Meister* (1795–1796).

# Miscellanea

The streets are southern and the houses are southern but alas the soft air and the blue heaven are wanting   instead of these we have a dun grey sky and an atmosphere of falling snow. The streets are very narrow the homes of massy dark coloured stones and built so high they shut out the sky, the sun and the wind. Their fronts are very small, but if you look down the narrow lanes which run by their sides and divide them into sets of threes and fours, you will see that they extend in a dead wall to a vast depth backwards. You can look into these lateral lanes, but I don't believe any body ever ⟨y⟩ went into them; they are so close a dog could scarcely creep in and though I have looked down very often, I never saw any thing there besides snow and rubbish. The interiors of the houses are also constructed upon the same southern plan of getting as much shade and keeping in as much cold as possible. The street door is a massy portal barred with iron and studded with the largest iron nails; the entry is underground, is paved with flag stones and vast and damp and dark as a cellar; at the opposite end is another door generally open (a poet would say swinging to the breeze, if ⟨there⟩ the massy walls around would let any in to swing to) through which is seen a small gloomy court enclosed between the four tall sides of the house ⟨and full of snow⟩ a heap of snow in one corner and a water butt in the other; By the side of the back door is the staircase; it is of stone and pitch dark at noon day; when you have groped up the first flight your head gets a good knock from a bulky corner which ⟨projets⟩ projects like the buttress of some sea washed castle and you catch a glimpse of light straggling down ⟨fom⟩ from a window or sometimes an open grating above; ⟨mounting⟩ as you mount past this you see through it the snowy court I made mention of below and enter upon the other side into the apartments which look upon the street. These are but one or two in number and the more lofty and spacious the more dusky; the nearness and tallness of the opposite houses precludes ⟨muc⟩ much light from entering; what little there is of it lies in patches upon the floor and ceiling near the window, while the ⟨rest of the apartment⟩ back of the chamber and three parts of its sides are covered with a thick shadow. The rest of the rooms including kitchen and offices, are built round the court and are small and uninhabitable from want of light and air. In summer however it must be pleasant to sit in these shaded rooms, and with both front

434

# Second Leaflet

and back windows thrown open, hear through one the busy hum of the market place and through the other the singing of the birds perched in the trees of the neighbouring terrace, or the flowing of the Elbe, if you happen to live near it. But in this season of the year, the whole house seems to me like an ice cellar and you may think how I long for one glimpse of sun to cheer the darkness and damp, and lighten the gloom of our cavern. ⟨and A burning sun,⟩ I know not how the architect who built the city could justify the precautious mode ⟨of⟩ he has adopted in the edifices. If you except two market places, the bridge and the planted walks which run between the city and the suburbs the whole town is skyless, sunless windless. It always seems to me that I am wandering in the corridors of an ancient palace; I expect every moment they will termi [15]

P.B.S. His whole existence was visionary, and there breathed in his actions in his looks and in his manners that high and super-human tone which we can only conceive to belong to a superior being to whom any moment of weakness or change is unknow. his life was a pictured dream, ⟨a visionary existence⟩ his existence ↑a vision↓ visionary, his thoughts lofty supreme and powerful, and his actions dropped balm and peace every where like the wings of an angel. Through all his beauty and splendour, and even through that gay air of careless loveliness which was his usual presence, there peeped ⟨a⟩ slight traces of melancholy and dejection, as if almost unconsciously he were longing for a brighter home than Earth could afford him. His virtue which never flagged a moment, his undying spirit, the ⟨beautiful⟩ ↑contempt of pain and Death his carelessness of riches↓ ⟨smooth current⟩ harmony of his actions with his words, the calm majesty of a constant communion with high thoughts ⟨m all these things⟩ spread over all his being, sometimes won me to think him immortal had not a certain delicacy of ⟨form⟩, complexion, a fragility of form and shape a certain grace of imperfection in his outward nature ⟨recalled⟩ the man ↑assured one he was human↓. ⟨In his⟩ You felt that ⟨in his⟩ there was a ↑spell a↓ silent agency in his presence, which opened a new world of nobleness and wisdom to one's gaze.

[15] Continued below the sketch of Shelley, which follows. It appears that the paragraph about Shelley was written first, on the top two-thirds of a right-hand page, and the description of Dresden was filled in around it later.

-nate in an open court where I may view the building to advantage; at last one comes to the market place so open and clear one takes the light of the blue sky for a sky light; on the other side you plunge again into a labyrinthe of dark avenues. Notwithstanding this, Dresden is a very cheerful city; the streets gloomy as they are are full of passengers and men working all day long at their trades in the free air. All day long I hear below my window the saw of the wood cutter, the gossip of the women at their stalls, the creaking of sledges over the snow the fiddle of an opposite musician, the hammering of a cooper and the morning and evening hymn of the scholars of a neighbouring school. The sides of the streets are lined with shops, rich and showy, and full of articles of classic taste or fashionable elegance, and the foot paths has a row of stalls where even now the prettiest garlands of ⟨flowers⟩ roses and other flowers, and the choicest fruit is displayed. To me Dresden offers an eternal field for amusement. Even the houses though the same in their general character, yet differ much in their parts, and being so vast always afford scope for novelty. You cannot say of them as of those of London, when you have seen one, you have seen all; Scratch off the paint from the London houses, what remains? a long brick wall as shallow and as pierced with holes as the slice of raw potato which has been played upon by the pop gun of an idle boy: nothing can change the solid character of a Dresden building; even in ruins its massy walls lofty portals and gloomy recesses would inspire curiosity and awe.

*[rest of page left blank]* [16]

At Lerici I know not how it was — I had a stern tranquillity in me suited to the time — ⟨I looked with⟩ the flame of a deep sullen resentment ⟨burned⟩ for unmerited misfortunes burned within me and I bid defiance to the dark visitings of misfortune and to the

[16] At this point, fourteen leaves have been cut from the middle of the leaflet. The remaining edges of six of these pages show traces of Claire's writing. The mutilation obviously occurred after Dowden had marked several passages in pencil and suggested identifications, for some of that penciling shows on one of the cut pages. Since, after the cutting, as many as nine letters remain on the lines at the inner margin, the pages were probably removed to be destroyed, not to be given away or sold.

# Second Leaflet

disastrous hauntings of Fate. I said, You cannot inflict more than I will proudly bear.[17]

---

⟨the visit⟩ I went to Russia that I might forget the visitings of my dark and wayward Fate, the disastrous hauntings that seemed inseparable with my name.

---

I have trodden life alone without a guide and without a companion and before I depart for ever I would willingly leave with another, what my tongue has never yet ventured to tell. I would willingly think that my memory may not be lost in oblivion as my life has been.

---

Amid the thousand thousand lines of human life, branching and intersecting in endless and infinite directions, there was not one I could choose that would lead to safety.

---

All is love in the universe — the silver showers of the fountain, the quiet life of the leaves, ⟨the evening face of Heaven strewn with silver blossoms or⟩ the ↑flowery↓ path in May even the deep night of Heaven is strewn with golden blossoms ⟨while the wretched an⟩ ↑Man alone is a↓ disastrous and discordant atom amid these elements of harmony and love.
↑In↓ The Architecture of the Greeks and Romans there is a strong taste of their love of pleasure; at home and in the countries they conquered the superb theatres temples and baths were all dedicated to pleasure in one way or another — ⟨in the Gothic⟩ its ranges of columns and gigantic arches admit every where the cheerful light and sun streaming through them into the interior of the building and uniting it with the surrounding landscape and ⟨with pre⟩ permeable every where to the eye of man; compare with this the Gothic, Norman or Moorish architecture in which nothing is ⟨m⟩ visible beside the love and rage of power; fortresses, embattled castellated, fortified from top to bottom, a heavy mass, no light playing between the impermeable walls, only some few straggling

---

[17] This is confirmed by Shelley's report to Byron of Claire's fortitude, after the first shock, at the news of Allegra's death (Shelley, *Letters*, II, 420).

437

rays fall through the loop-holes intended for the arrows, a true picture of the image of power, dark isolated and impenetrable.

[*rest of page blank*]

Naples.

The woody windings of the shore reveal in their deep recisses the glimmering marble fragments of the abodes of ancient heroes — the verdurous and lovely hues of the promontories mingle with the grey upright columns of a shattered temple, or clothe with the voluptuous pomp of life the pale funereal urn of a departed God ⟨w to whose manes the⟩ ↑whilst↓ foliage and the fountains ⟨around, murmur⟩ with invisible minstrelsy, ↑murmur around↓ a requiem of joy and gladness. ⟨The air on that beautiful warm coast⟩ Earth, Sea and Sky blaze like three Gods, with animated, but tranquil loveliness, with a splendour that does not dazzle, with a richness that cannot satiate. The air on that beautiful warm coast is a field of fragrance; the refreshing sea-breeze seems to blow from Paradise, quickning the senses and bringing to them the odour of a thousand unknown blossoms. In that enchanted garden, Morning is a Rose, Day a tulip, Night a lily, and Evening like Morning again a rose, and Life is a ceaseless song ↑of beautiful and glowing sentiments.↓ that one goes singing to oneself, ↑as one↓ wanders ⟨ing like a Bee or a Butterfly⟩ along ⟨a⟩ ↑this↓ perpetual chain of Flowers.

# APPENDICES

# APPENDIX A

## Mary Shelley's Review, "The English in Italy"

[from the *Westminster Review*, October 1826]

1. *The English in Italy*. 3 vols. London. 1826.
2. *Continental Adventures. A Novel*. 3 vols. London. 1826.
3. *Diary of an Ennuyée*. London. 1826.

When peace came, after many long years of war, when our island prison was opened to us, and our watery exit from it was declared practicable, it was the paramount wish of every English heart, ever addicted to vagabondizing, to hasten to the continent, and to imitate our forefathers in their almost forgotten custom, of spending the greater part of their lives and fortunes in their carriages on the post-roads of the continent. With the brief and luckless exception of the peace of Amiens, the continent had not been open for the space of more than one-and-twenty years; a new generation had sprung up, and the whole of this, who had money and time at command, poured, in one vast stream, across the Pas de Calais into France: in their numbers, and their eagerness to proceed forward, they might be compared to the Norwegian rats, who always go right on, and when they come to an opposing stream, still pursue their route, till a bridge is formed of the bodies of the drowned, over which the living pass in safety. The simile holds good in more ways than one: the first emigrants, it is true, were not wholly killed, but the miseries they endured, of dirty packets and wretched inns, were the substratum from which has arisen the elegant steam-packet, and the improved state of the continental hotels. But in those early days of

441

# Appendix A

migration, in the summer of 1814, every inconvenience was hailed as a new chapter in the romance of our travels; the worst annoyance of all, the Custom-house, was amusing as a novelty; we saw with extasy the strange costume of the French women, read with delight our own descriptions in the passport, looked with curiosity on every *plât*, fancying that the fried-leaves of artichokes were frogs; we saw shepherds in opera-hats, and post-boys in jack-boots; and (*pour comble de merveille*) heard little boys and girls talk French: it was acting a novel, being an incarnate romance. But these days are now vanished: frequent landings at Calais have deprived it of its captivating novelty. Many of our children, under the guidance of foreign nursery-maids, lisp French as well as any little wood-shod urchin among the natives. We have learned to curse the *douane*, and denounce passports as tyrannical and insufferable impediments to our free progress.

When France palled on our travelled appetites, which always crave for something new, Italy came into vogue. As preparatives for our pilgrimage to that country, whose charm is undying, we devoured the fabulous descriptions of Eustace, and well-poised sentences of Forsyth, and a traveller from Italy inspired us almost with devotional respect. We do not think that we are guilty of any exaggeration when we affirm, that even now that the English are almost cloyed with foreign travel, a journey to Italy is still regarded with enthusiastic transport, and when visited, that country is quitted with greater regret than any other, and the peculiarity of its situation accounts for this. We all wish to burst our watery bound, and to wander in search of a more genial climate than that enjoyed (according to the vulgarism, *he enjoys a very bad state of health*) by our native land. Neither France, Germany, nor Switzerland, content the swallow English. La belle France is now acknowledged to be the most unpicturesque, dull, miserable-looking country in the world. The name of Germany is sufficient in itself to inspire a kind of metaphysical gloom, enlightened only by meteoric flashes from the Hartz or the Elbe. Passing the Jura, surrounded by the mighty Alps, we ramble delightedly over Switzerland, till the snow and ice, ushered in by the chilling Biz, cause us to escape from the approach of a winter more severe than our own. We fly to Italy; we eat the lotus; we cannot tear ourselves away. It is the land of romance, and therefore pleases the young; of classic lore, and thus possesses charms for the learned. Its petty states and tiny courts, with all the numerous titles enjoyed by their frequenters, gild it for the worldly. The man of peace and domesticity finds in its fertile soil, and the happiness of its peasantry, an ameliorated likeness of beloved but starving England. The society is facile; the towns illustrious by the reliques they contain of the arts of ancient times, or the middle ages;

442

# Mary Shelley's Review

while its rural districts attach us, through the prosperity they exhibit, their plenteous harvests, the picturesque arrangement of their farms, the active life every where apparent, the novelty of their modes of culture, the grace which a sunny sky sheds over labours which in this country are toilsome and unproductive.

This preference accorded to Italy by the greater part of the emigrant English has given rise to a new race or sect among our countrymen, who have lately been dubbed Anglo-Italians. The Anglo-Italian has many peculiar marks which distinguish him from the mere traveller, or true John Bull. First, he understands Italian, and thus rescues himself from a thousand ludicrous mishaps which occur to those who fancy that a little Anglo-French will suffice to convey intelligence of their wants and wishes to the natives of Italy; the record of his travels is no longer confined, according to lord Normanby's vivid description, to how he had been "starved here, upset there, and robbed every where" [*English in Italy*, vol. ii. p. 229]. Your Anglo-Italian ceases to visit the churches and palaces, guide-book in hand; anxious, not to see, but to say that he has seen. Without attempting to adopt the customs of the natives, he attaches himself to some of the most refined among them, and appreciates their native talent and simple manners; he has lost the critical mania in a real taste for the beautiful, acquired by a frequent sight of the best models of ancient and modern art.

Upon the whole, the Anglo-Italians may be pronounced a well-informed, clever, and active race; they pity greatly those of their un-Italianized countrymen, who are endowed with Spurzheim's bump, denominated stayathomeativeness; and in compassion of their narrow experience have erected a literature calculated to disseminate among them a portion of that taste and knowledge acquired in the Peninsula. Lord Byron may be considered the father of the Anglo-Italian literature, and Beppo as being the first product of that school; lord Normanby brings up the rear. The plan of his work, entitled, "The English in Italy," is excellent. It is difficult, after a long residence in a foreign country, to collect one's variety of experience into one focus. The detached anecdotes and observations on manners, made at various periods and places, are grouped in the mind, while it is impossible to select any form of journal, letter, or narrative, which will combine the mass in an intelligible form, and cause the reader to seize, as the author did, the conclusions to be drawn from such multifarious materials. Besides, though mere travellers are culpably negligent on this score, the resident Anglo-Italian is withheld by honour, from the exposition of facts and names. Lord Normanby has hit upon a medium both novel and entertaining. He has given a series of tales, in which the English and Italians alike figure; the contrast between the two nations adds to the

443

interest of these sketches, while the colouring of fiction is thrown over truths, which it would be difficult to convey in any other manner. It is impossible to read "The English in Italy" without being struck at every page with the verity of the delineations of character and manners, and without admiring the skill with which the noble author has seized and expressed the slight shadowings, and evanescent lights, peculiar to the complicated form of Italian society, which must have escaped a ruder pen. We frequently, it is true, dissent from his lordship's opinions and conclusions, but we always assent to the truth of his facts.

The first (and it is the best) of his longer stories is entitled L'Amoroso. It is the tale of a high-bred English girl, who, enchanted with the beauty of Naples, the softness of its climate, the vivacious and easy tone of society, and the ardour of her Italian lover, sacrifices her first *half* love (first loves are, for the most part, we fear, half loves), and gives her hand to a Neapolitan count. The gradual development of her Italian husband's feelings, her awakening to the truth of her situation, and the growth of her despair, is admirably managed; yet in all this there is something besides the comparative merits of English and Italian domestic customs. We can none of us attempt, with impunity, to engraft ourselves on foreign stocks: the habits of our childhood cling to us, and we seek in vain for sympathy from those who have travelled life quite on a different road from that which we have followed. We are far from advocating the Italian conjugal system, which puts the axe to domestic happiness, and deeply embitters the childhood of the offspring of the divided parents; nevertheless, we must observe, that the misery suffered by the English girl in Italy would on other accounts, but in no minor degree, become the lot of an Italian married to an Englishman. Let us imagine the daughter of a Neapolitan noble, dragged from her beautiful country and sunny clime, deprived of her box at the opera, her ride on the Corso, her cortège of devoted servants, her circle of complaisant friends, her *dolce far niente*; to the toils and dulness of an English home — to the cares of housekeeping — a charge not imposed on Italian females — her snug, but monotonous, fire-side, her sentry-box of a house; to our cloudy sky; to the labour of giving dinners and entertaining evening parties; to those numerous etiquettes easy to the natives, unattainable by foreigners; to the *sotto voce* tone (if the metaphor be admissible) which characterizes our social intercourse, to the necessity of for ever wearing that thick and ample veil of propriety which we throw over every act and word: introduce the ardent, simple-hearted, undisguising Italian to this world, so opposite to her own, and she would experience the same heart-sickening disappointment that visited the heart of the heroine of the Amoroso. To us, and particularly to our females, these laws of constraint are the music, the accompaniment by which they regulate their steps until they cannot walk without it; and the veil before spoken of is as necessary to their sense of decency as their very habiliments. It is natural, therefore, that the English girl of the tale should be transfixed with grief at the request from her husband to conform with Italian customs; and it is also inevitable that the first step she takes in compliance with this request must sin against Italian etiquette, and, though liberty is offered her, that she should find that even the excess of freedom does not permit her the exact liberty she wants.

The "Politico" contains a rapid but masterly sketch of the Piedmontese revolution. The author, it is true, judging only from the apparent effects, blames this sudden burst of impatience on the part of Italians any longer to bear their galling chains. He says, that they had better have waited a few years, as if the capacity of waiting did not engender a callousness to the evils of tyranny, incompatible with a generous love of liberty. The revolution ended unfortunately, it is true; but, most certainly, if the attempt had not been made, the Italians would have lost their characteristic of being slaves "ognor frementi," and have sunk into as degraded an existence as that of the Fanariotes of Constantinople. From the smothered fire of this crushed revolt a brighter flame will hereafter rise: it was a glimmer, a flash, a reflection, sent back from the blaze just then kindled by the Spaniards: both are quenched now, but not for ever.

If the Italians could have viewed the Spanish struggle, and still submitted uncontending to the Austrian, they could never more have lifted their heads as a nation, nor possessed any claim to our commiseration. One of the chief causes, indeed, of the failure of the revolt of 1820–21 was political despair. This despair originated in the disarmed state of the natives, and the terror engendered by the Austrian bayonets. In every Italian state, except Tuscany, this fear was joined to a never-dying hatred of their oppressive rulers; which made them on the alert to seize every opportunity to rebel against their tyrants. While the flame of revolt spread from the Alps to Brundusium, Tuscany alone was tranquil. They talked of liberty, but their enthusiasm began and ended in talk. The grand duke appreciated so well the quiescence of his loving subjects, that when the Austrian minister presented him with a list of sixty-seven Carbonari worthy of incarceration, Ferdinand refused to look at it. He did not believe, he said, that these men were Carbonari, but he was sure if he imprisoned them they would become so. Who, indeed, were to form the patriotic band? Not the peasants: the idea of political liberty never entered their heads. They work hard, and their genial climate lightens their labour of all the misery which renders the peasant's life so irksome in this country; yet still, from the utter want

# Appendix A

of money and traffic, their hardest labour only enables them to labour on. In the cities neither the rich nor the poor are willing to risk their wealth or their safety. There is another class of persons, the men of letters and students at the universities. The first are peacefully inclined, the second unprincipled: they are ready for riot, but they are little fitted for any commotion which has for its aim a noble and enlightened purpose. Yet we do not think the emancipation of Italy far off. In one circumstance, Italy is far better situated than Spain — in case of a revolution. Religion is here no enemy of political liberty. Napoleon gave a blow to Italian superstition, from which it will never recover. By destroying the wealth of the priests, he has destroyed their influence. The higher classes are liberal in their opinions, and the little bigotry that subsists among the lower orders is wholly untinged by the spirit of persecution. The great and immoveable foundation stone, the boundary mark of Italian liberty, which still subsists, though no superstructure is thereto added, is their natural talent. In spite of college restrictions, in spite of almost universal ignorance, their native genius flourishes; their untaught courtesy, their love for the fine arts, the poetry with which their sunny sky endows them, prevent their being brutified; and thus Italy possesses in her own bosom the germs of regeneration, which, in spite of their late overthrow, will in the end give birth to their emancipation.

But to return to "The English in Italy" The "Sbarbuto" approaches nearest to a failure of any of the sketches; the hero is a kind of ideal of lord Byron. The "dear Corsair expression," now going out of fashion, is introduced, and the mixed character of bandit and dandy is carried to its height. Truth of description and liveliness of narrative, two chief characteristics of this author, render even this strange anomaly interesting. The conclusion of the tale is singularly abrupt, but it may be observed that all lord Normanby's catastrophes are faulty; that of "Matilda" has been justly censured. The author wished to pourtray the evils resulting from certain modes of action, and yet the tragic conclusion of the tale is entirely independent of the chain of unhappy events which were to appear of necessity to arise from the heroine's departure from the moral laws of her country. The conclusion of the "Sbarbuto" is still worse, and our imagination received a most disagreeable baulk, when, on turning the last page of this tale, we found that was indeed the last.

The sketches called the "Zingari," which detail a variety of adventures which have befallen the gipsy English in Italy, are perhaps the best part of the book. There is nothing outré, nothing of caricature in any of these portraits. We recognize many well-known faces, and at each successive narration remember a *pendant* that has come within

446

# Mary Shelley's Review

our own experience. Utter ignorance of the Italian language is the source of many of the ludicrous situations in which the English get involved. French does not, as has been said, carry the traveller through Italy; those who depend on it, will find their support fail them at the first Italian town they enter. Besides, the Italians speak French with peculiar awkwardness; they are unable to accentuate its unutterable consonants and slip-shod vowels. When an Italian has welcomed a foreigner with gravity, and even with sulkiness, answering their introduction with a few mispronounced French phrases, if replied to in their own language, their ease of manner returns, and they become as graceful and facile in conversation as before they were repulsive.* The tales of the "Zingari" may serve as so many lessons to all future travellers as to what they may seek and what they may shun in Italy. We may learn the perils of Vetturino travelling from "The Economist," assured that the details are by no means caricatured; and we may reap still more serious profit from the sketches entitled, "Change of Air," and "Boyhood Abroad." And yet, as is frequently the case, further experience overthrows the minor one, and the discomforts and dangers which are the lot of an invalid traveller in Italy will change to comforts and safety, if he becomes a resident there. If, indeed, the invalid travel, like lord Normanby's hero, from one town to another, from one bad inn and cold lodging to another a match for the last, he may certainly return from such pursuit of health worse than he went. But let him fix on some city for a constant residence: Pisa we recommend as most equable in climate; let him get his English comforts about him, as he may with ease and cheapness from the free port of Leghorn, not twelve miles distant, and he will then find the advantage of a southern residence. The streets of Pisa are quiet, and the whole town wears a sober,

* Innumerable are the anecdotes that might be related of the ridiculous mistakes of the un-Italianized English in Italy. A gentleman at Rome said to us one day, "These Italians have no idea of morality or virtue; the fine arts are the only things they think worth praising. I was speaking to signora D————— of a young lady whom I described as, Di gran genio, bella, amabile, e poi virtuosissima, on which the signora asked with vivacity, Davvero si conosce forse nella musica?" We were near the same gentleman at a conversazione, he was looking over some pieces of music, when an Italian lady, apropos of his occupation, asked, "È virtuoso lei?" — "Lo spero," replied the astonished Englishman, and then turned to us to remark on the oddity of catechising a gentleman concerning his virtue; forgetful that even with us virtù is not virtue. Foreigners may murder English, but an Englishman's assassination of French and Italian is even more entire and remorseless. We heard one of our countrymen in Paris, in felicitous Anglo-French, ask the driver of a fiacre, "Pouvez-vous aller à rue Saint Honoré dans vingt cinq minuits?"

# Appendix A

scholastic aspect. The north side of the Lung Arno, looking towards the south, is warm at mid-winter, and always presents a delightful promenade. The rides round the town are beautiful; you have your choice of the pine forest of the Cascina, or the road along the plain that skirts the neighbouring hills, which, covered with olives, chesnuts, and last, toward their summit, with pines, are, though not high, remarkably picturesque. The whole road from Vico Pisano to Lucca, some twenty or thirty miles, presenting successive pictures of fertility in the plain, and of the view of ravine or precipice in the mountains, is within four miles of one or other of the gates of Pisa. The neighbourhood to the sea is an advantage not to be omitted. Let an invalid do this, and he will speedily acquire the health and spirits, the promise of which drew him from his home.*

We are surprised that lord Normanby has not introduced more of the country life of Italy, which bears a peculiar stamp, and which is pregnant with interest and beauty. Generally speaking, our countrymen see only the surface of the country, and are unaware of the minutiae of the peasants' life, and their mode of agriculture. They are connoisseurs in paintings, and frequenters of drawing-rooms; but the inferior classes of their fellow beings possess no interest for them: and yet it is in the country of Italy that you see most of the true Italian character, and most enjoy the exhaustless delights of that sunny clime. The very aspect of the country to a cursory observer will prove this assertion. The use of oxen in their agricultural labours is seemingly a small, and yet, in truth, a great improvement to the picturesque of the rural scene. The oxen of Italy surpass, in beauty of form, in the sleekness of their dove-coloured skin, and the soft expression of their large eyes, all other animals of their species. In every part of Italy we encounter, during our walks, in lanes bordered by elms and sallows, to which the vines are trained and festooned, frequent wains drawn by these animals, yoked by the neck; and the dark-eyed driver, with his sun-burnt limbs, in no manner detracts from the beauty of the picture. It is curious in Italy to observe the great advantage the peasants possess as to personal appearance, over the town's-people. The inhabitants of the cities, whether rich or poor, are for the most part low in stature, sallow-complexioned, bent shouldered; but if while you are induced, by the appearance of the citizens, to lament the degeneracy of Italian beauty,

* We were about to add that in the Professor Vaccà he would find an able substitute for any English medical aid; but alas! this estimable man is now dead, and we can do no more than consecrate this note to his memory. His talents were of the highest order, and as a practical surgeon he stood in the first rank of his profession. His private virtues secured for him universal esteem; he was gentle, yet full of enthusiasm; a select specimen of Italian virtue and genius.

448

# Mary Shelley's Review

you wander in the country, or enter the market-place, to which, on certain days, the country people resort, you are immediately convinced that you now behold the models of the Italian painters. You are struck by groups resembling those fine fellows represented in the paintings of the Adoration of the Shepherds. Their very occupation adds to their pictorial appearance. They are employed among the vines, or following the oxen-drawn plough, whose rough mechanism is such as Virgil describes; frequently in summer they work merely in a shirt, and the white colour of the linen contrasts well with limbs whose veins seem to flow with dark wine. The women, less hard-worked than the French *paysannes*, perform the lighter labours of the farm, and, notwithstanding the shade of their large straw-hats, soon acquire a deep but healthy hue; in an evening they are seen returning from fetching water at the spring, bearing their pitchers of an antique shape on their heads, stepping freely under the burthen. Of course we do not pretend to say that all, or even that the greater part of them, are handsome; but they have, for the most part, pleasing expressions of countenance, and the beauty you do encounter is of a high character; their brows are finely moulded, their eyes soft and large; the cheeks sink gently towards the chin, and their lips remind you of those chiselled by Greek sculptors. Such we have seen in the evening emerging from the trellised *pergole*, or vine-walks, singing in perfect tune, and with clear, though loud voices, the simple but beautiful melodies peculiar to the Italian peasantry.

It is true that, in thus eulogizing the country of Italy, our remarks must be understood as being principally confined to Tuscany. In Lombardy the abundance of pasture-land is inimical to the happiness of the peasantry: nor are we sufficiently acquainted with the rural districts of the Roman and Neapolitan states, to speak with precision concerning their inhabitants. In Tuscany the farms are usually small, and held at long leases; the rent is often paid in kind, and the landlord receives as his share one half of the produce. The expenses are also shared between the landholder and the cultivator, the former providing the heavy stock, cattle, ploughs, out-houses, wine-presses, &c.; the peasantry the lighter utensils, and repairs of hedges, sluices, &c. The smallness of the farms renders the farmer almost always the labourer; a hired workman is rare among them; and the cottager, we should almost call him, with a farm of twelve acres, whose family is sufficiently large to cultivate the land, and whose share of corn and wine suffices to maintain that family without extra purchase, considers himself rich; for, then, the superfluous money he obtains by the sale of vegetables, fruit, and the better kind of wine, clothes his family, and keeps his farm and house in repair. Their lives would be deemed, and justly deemed, hard in Eng-

449

# Appendix A

land, for our unbenign climate would render painful the continual out-door work, which is light to them.

The Tuscan name for their small farms is *podere*, and in appearance they resemble what we imagine to have been the first attempts at agriculture, every thing being cultivated in patches. A podere generally contains six or eight acres; they are hedged in; in the neighbourhood of Leghorn the hedges are of myrtle, which, like all evergreens, are fragrant even when out of bloom; and when in flower, their spicy odour gives a taste of Indian climes. Little hay is raised, for the Indian corn is much used in its stead; so after the spring-labour of pruning the vines, the wheat is the first harvest. The wheat-fields are planted with rows of trees, to which the vines cling; and the shade, far from being detrimental, is considered a shelter for the crops. When the wheat is gathered in, and threshed on the threshing-floor, constructed in the open air, with all the care Virgil advises, the land is again sown with Indian corn. This is a beautiful harvest. The men cut it down, and the women and children sit round the threshing-floor, taking the grain from the pod, loosening it from the stalk, and spreading it in the sun, till its paler orange hue deepens to a fiery glow. The vintage follows — an universal feast. The men pluck the fruit from the trees, which is received and deposited in the vats by the women and children. The plucking of the olives brings up the rear of their *raccolte*. But it is not the mere sowing, and the harvests that demand labour; the long droughts force them to construct sluices through every part of the podere, and the water-wheel is for ever at work to irrigate the land; nature the while is busy and noisy. During the day the loud cicale, with ceaseless chirp, fill the air with sound, and in the evening the fire-flies come out from the myrtle hedges, and form a thousand changing and flashing constellations on the green corn-fields, which is their favourite resort. Meanwhile the *contadini* cheer themselves with songs, either singly, in harmony, or in response. One of the favourite games among the Tuscan peasants (we have forgotten the name of it), especially during the time of the vintage, is singularly poetic. A man on one tree, will challenge another perched afar off, calling out the name of a flower; the challenged responds with an extempore couplet, sometimes founded on the metaphoric meaning attached, of the flower's name, sometimes given at random, and then returns the challenge by naming another flower, which is replied to in the same manner. We have unluckily preserved but two of these impromptus, and they are both on the same flower: —

Fior di cent' erbe!
Non bimbi voglion bene a loro mamma,
Quanto io alla speranza mia.

# Mary Shelley's Review

Fior di cent' erbe!
Se un sospiro avesse la parola,
Quanto bell' ambasciator sarebbe.

It is this exhaustless fertility that makes Italy a paradise, and affords never-ending variety of object to the residents. With us nature is parsimonious, if not frugal; her very magnificence is that of a well-regulated mansion, where, though great show is made, there is no waste. In Italy she superabounds, overflows, and, like a prodigal, casts immense treasures to the winds. This abundance is not displayed alone in inanimate nature; but among the Italians themselves there exist rich stores of talent, useless it is true, in the general sense of the term, which are displayed to the delight of their countrymen and astonishment of travellers. We cannot give a better idea of what we mean than by instancing their improvisatori, who pour out, as a cataract does water, poetic imagery and language; but except that the genial moisture somewhat fertilizes the near bordering banks, it reaches the ocean of oblivion, leaving no trace behind. Sgricci may be given as an example. He is well read, and profoundly versed in the works of the Greek metaphysicians and historians, as well as their poets. The mode of his improvisation is wonderful, and different from the usual style of these exhibitions. When he comes on the stage, his personal appearance, animated countenance, and regular features, lost in his daily costume, strike you with admiration. It is the custom for those who choose, to leave at the door of the theatre a slip of paper, on which is written a subject for a tragic drama. We were present at three of these performances. The subject of the first was "Ifegenia in Tauride;" the plan of the tragedy was closely copied from Euripides; but the words and poetry were his own, and we were continually startled by images of dazzling beauty, and a flow of language which never degenerated into mere words, but, on the contrary, was instinct with energy and pathos.

Inez de Castro was a tragedy he gave at Lucca, the subject being imposed on him by the arch-duchess, who was in the theatre. When towards the end, he caused the audience to understand that the prince, Don Pedro, husband of Inez, drawing a curtain, suddenly displays to his father the bodies of his murdered wife and children, the same thrill was felt, nay, far greater than if the real mock bodies (the implied bull must be excused) had been brought forward. His words were so living, that you saw them, not decked out with stage trickery, but in the true livery of death, livid, stiff, and cold. The last tragedy we heard was the Death of Hector.* In it you were transported within the walls

* The same subject was subsequently given him at Turin, and a

# Appendix A

of Troy, and heard mad Cassandra denouncing its fall. Speaking afterwards to the poet, he said that he did not remember much about any other part; but he had a vivid recollection that when he poured forth the ravings of the prophetess, he no longer saw the theatre; Troy was around him; Troy burning; Priam stabbed at his altar, and the women dragged lamenting away in chains. From all this magical creation of talent, what resulted? The poet himself forgets all his former imaginations, and is hurried on to create fresh imagery, while the effects of his former inspirations are borne away with the breath that uttered them, never again to be recalled —

"Nec revocare situs, aut jungere carmina curat."

For the rest, he acquires the enthusiastic praises of some few of the more refined of his countrymen — for Sgricci's poetry is of too classic and elevated a nature to please the multitude — and the animated recollection of those few English who understand sufficient Italian to appreciate his genius.

Italy is an exhaustless theme to those who, having been long residents there, are familiar with its novel and beauteous aspect. But our limits warn us not to pursue our digression, and oblige us to turn our attention to those other works whose titles head our article. We shall not dilate much upon them; for the scope of our present writing is to treat of Italy, and as these volumes do not bear the same perfect Italian stamp as those of lord Normanby, they may be passed more cursorily over.

"Continental Adventures" are the production of the very clever authoress of "Rome in the Nineteenth Century." This latter publication is an inestimable guide to all who visit the Eternal City, and even to those at home, more than any other work on the same subject, gives a faithful account of the wonders of that metropolis of the world. "Continental Adventures" is on another and a worse plan. It mixes real scenes with fictitious ones, not in the style of the "English in Italy," where the manners of the natives form the ground-work of the tales, but in the mode of a common novel — a novel of the day: a lady and her lover, the baulks to love, the rival, and the denouement, all English:

---

shorthand writer took it down, and it was published. The plot resembled the one we heard, otherwise it struck us as inferior in poetry, and was certainly a very different production. The plot is not the least admirable part of these impromptu dramas. When a novel subject is given, it is of course arranged during the heat of inspiration and delivery; it never lags; the interest is continually increasing, and the scenes grow naturally from each other. They are shorter than our five-act plays, being, on the Greek plan, interspersed with choruses.

# Mary Shelley's Review

and the "Continental Adventures" are merely, that while the hero and heroine are *progressing* towards the fulfilment of their hopes, they ramble about Switzerland, and the lady, in particular, endures so many perils, that we really think that no female in real life could have undergone them without becoming prematurely grey. She commences by breaking her collar-bone and two of her fingers; is twice in imminent danger of perishing in snow-drifts; narrowly escapes tumbling down a precipice; is nearly shot by a robber in one of the Alpine Ravines; and last, is carried away by Italian banditti, at whose hands death was the least evil she expected, and from whom she saves herself by the administration of a piece of opium, which she had fortunately put into her *pocket* the day before. The story of the novel is commonplace enough, and the gordian knot, tied just at the end, then to be cut, is confused, and even displeasing. The discovery of relationship in a forbidden degree between lovers is always disagreeable; and the mode by which these lovers are found to be related, disfiguring the sacred associations always blended with a mother's name, is even revolting. The authoress is evidently nearly related to Scotland, though we believe she is not Scotch. She has a taste for humour, and her comedy is generally very entertaining, though she too often falls into a comedian's worst fault, of wire-drawing a comic scene, till it becomes tedious; and once or twice she is guilty of giving them for their foundation subjects hardly admissible on the score of propriety. The book is, however, written with great spirit, and is very entertaining. Some of the scenes of real life are sketched with fidelity and true humour. The Côche-d'Eau on the Rhone is one of these, and the Reverend Saunders M'Muckleman is throughout a genuine comic character. Her descriptions of scenery are, however, the best part of the book; they are varied and faithful. We select one, as a specimen of the style in which they are executed: —

'The glaciers of the Aar, which we visited from the Grimsel, present a scene which I am convinced the world cannot equal; which none who have beheld it can ever forget, and none who have not seen it can ever conceive. I will not mock you with a futile attempt at description. You cannot picture the scene; but you can form some idea of the awestruck astonishment which filled our minds, when, after surmounting all the difficulties of the way, we found ourselves standing amidst a world of ice, extending around, beneath, above us; far beyond where the straining sight, in every direction, vainly sought to follow the interminable frozen leagues of glaciers, propped up in towering pyramids or shapeless heaps, or opening into yawning gulphs and unfathomable fissures. The tremendous barren rocks and moun-

453

tains of the impenetrable Alps, amidst which the terrific Finster-aarhorn reared his granitic pyramid of fourteen thousand feet, appeared alone amidst this world of desolation. Eternal and boundless wastes of ice, naked and inaccessible mountains of rock, which had stood unchanged and untrodden from creation, were the only objects which met our view. Hitherto, with all we had seen of desolation and horror, there was some contrast, some relief. The glaciers of Chamouni are bordered by glowing harvests; the glaciers of Grindelwald are bounded by its romantic vale; the glaciers of the Schiedeck shine forth amidst its majestic woods. Even among the savage rocks and torrents of the Grimsel, though animated life is seen no more, the drooping birch and feathery larch protrude their storm-beaten branches from the crevices of the precipices; and the lonely pine-tree is seen on high, where no hand can ever reach it. But here there is no trace of vegetation, no blade of grass, no bush, no tree; no spreading weed or creeping lichen invades the cold still desolation of the icy desert. It is the death of nature. We seemed placed in a creation in which there is no principle of life; translated to another orb, where existence is extinct, and where death, unresisted, holds his terrific reign. The only sound which meets the ear is that of the loud detonation of the ice, as it burst open into new abysses, with the crash of thunder, and reverberates from the wild rocks like the voice of the mountain storms.'
— Vol. ii. p. 134.

These volumes contain the best description and guide to Switzerland that we have ever seen, but Italy makes only a small portion of them. We have some animated scenes on the romantic lake of Como, and visit, with the personages of the novel, the galleries and palaces of Florence; but a guide-book and a romance form an incongruous mixture, and we certainly wish that they should be separated in future.

"The Diary of an Ennuyée," is a very well written and interesting imposture. Well written and interesting it is true, but still an imposture, and that not of a kind which is admissible. The very laws of *cavaliere serventeism* in Italy are not more delicate, subtle, and yet strict, than those of fiction, and they are transgressed in the volume before us. A fiction must contain no glaring improbability, and yet it must never divest itself of a certain idealism, which forms its chief beauty. Once in Italy we saw a drama, which was any thing but dramatic, and we were reminded of it by the pages of the book before us. The hero was an English Milord who had a diseased arm; no medical attendant was able to afford him any relief; one doctor, one alone could cure this otherwise mortal disorder; but this doctor refused to exert his skill until

454

# Mary Shelley's Review

his friend *Jenkisson,* who was imprisoned in the Tower under suspicion of treasonable practices, should be liberated by the sick Milord, who was also a secretary of state; but Milord was too patriotic to sacrifice public good to his private advantage. Miledi, in the mean time, ran from her husband to the doctor, adjuring the one and supplicating the other, while Milord, with his bound-up arm, groaning when on the stage, and shrieking while behind it, formed a most distressing foreground to the picture. You actually felt for the poor man; and a greater verity of scenic illusion (such as it was) was produced by that bandaged arm, and the moaning and crippled action of the patient than Kean or Pasta usually effect in their portentous identifications with ideal woe. That our readers may not be left in a painful suspense, we proceed to inform them, that when Milord was at his last gasp, and the doctor stood unmoved in the midst of his kneeling and supplicating relatives, Jenkisson himself, whose innocence had been discovered, appeared; a general reconciliation took place; and the doctor was proceeding to work a cure, when the curtain fell.

We do not wish to cast an air of ridicule over the volume before us, which we read, really believing in it as we read, with great interest; but having discovered that the sensitive, heartbroken, dying, dead diarist is a fictitious personage, we are angry at the trick of art that excited our real sympathy; and we were led to a conviction that the circumstances that demand our deepest interest as a reality, are, when feigned, not of an high order of idealism, and conseqently the fraud being discovered, the fictitious part of the book falls below the usual rate of novel interest.

But to leave this criticism, or hypercriticism, let us advert to the real merits of the work. It is written with great spirit and great enthusiasm: the descriptions are vivid, the anecdotes entertaining, and the whole style displays intelligence and feeling. The few traits recorded of Italian manners are felicitously seized, and the English party is well sketched, from the quiet, retiring, suffering, ideal authoress, to the blundering and vivacious L———, who may stand as a specimen of a whole tribe of English rovers in Italy. We turn over the pages to find an extract, which our limits will not permit us to make long. We hesitated between the account of the eruption of Vesuvius, the description of the improvisatore Sestini, the Capanna and Gesu Bambino, always exhibited in the convents during Christmas, the Diarist's Adventure with the Governor of Lerici — between these and the following one, which we have fixed upon as one of the most interesting anecdotes in the book: —

'Last night we had a numerous party, and Signor P———

# Appendix A

and his daughter came to sing. *She* is a private singer of great
talent, and came attended by her lover, or her *fiancé*, who, according to the Italian custom, attends his mistress every where during
the few weeks which precede their marriage. He is a young artist,
a favourite pupil of Camuccini, and of very quiet, unobtrusive
manners. La P. has the misfortune to be plain; her features are
irregular, her complexion of a sickly paleness, and though her eyes
are large and dark, they appeared totally devoid of lustre and expression. Her plainness, the bad taste of her dress, her awkward
figure, and her timid and embarrassed deportment, all furnished
matter of amusement and observation to some young people (English of course), whose propensities for *quizzing* exceeded their good
breeding and good nature. Though La P. does not understand a
word of either French or English, I thought she could not mistake
the significant looks and whispers of which she was the object,
and I was in pain for her and for her modest lover. I drew my chair
to the piano, and tried to divert her attention, by keeping her in
conversation, but could get no farther than a few questions, which
were answered in monosyllables. At length she sang, and sang
divinely; I found the pale automaton had a soul as well as a voice.
After giving us with faultless execution, as well as great expression,
some of Rossini's finest songs, she sang the beautiful and difficult
cavatina in Otello, *"Assisa al piè d' un salice,"* with the most enchanting style and pathos, and then stood as unmoved as a statue,
while the company applauded loud and long. A moment afterwards,
as she stooped to take up a music-book, her lover, who had edged
himself by degrees from the door to the piano, bent his head too,
and murmured, in a low voice, but with the most passionate accent, "O, brava, brava, cara!" She replied only by a look, but it
was such a look! I never saw a human countenance so entirely, so
instantaneously changed in character: the vacant eyes kindled and
beamed with tenderness: the pale cheek glowed, and a bright smile
playing round her mouth, just parted her lips sufficiently to discover a set of teeth like pearls. I could have called her at that moment beautiful; but the change was as transient as sudden; it
passed like a gleam of light over her face, and vanished, and by
the time the book was placed on the desk, she looked as plain, as
stupid, and statue-like as ever. I was the only person who witnessed this little bye-scene, and it gave me pleasant thoughts and
interest for the rest of the evening." — p. 207.

We hope to heaven all this is true, and not false as the Ennuyée
herself. One thing alone at all atones for her deception. We longed,

456

while reading her work, to thank the fair authoress for reviving many a half-forgotten Italian scene, and for shedding a beautiful light over many a favourite spot; we regretted that our gratitude was due to the dead; but since the writer lives, we no longer have this painful debt heavy at our hearts, and we pay it with the praise she entirely merits.

We shall hail with pleasure any new production from the pen of any one of the writers of these works; and we were not a little gratified at the announcement of Lord Normanby's "Historiettes." We hope that in these he has a little abated an offensive display of superiority of rank. It is unworthy of the enlightened heir of a peerage thus to prize himself above nine-tenths of his readers on account of his adventitious advantages, and very absurd to shew it. We remember, in former times, that this nobleman had a warm love for talent, though its possessor was unendowed either with rank or fashion; we hope the generous feeling is not dead. His lordship has too much real talent not to feel and appreciate the nobility of nature as well as that of birth, and some indication of such a feeling would give a grace to his productions, in which, at present, they are deficient.

# APPENDIX B

## Some Reviews of Theatrical Productions Attended by the Shelleys and Claire Clairmont in 1818

### I

"Harlequin Gulliver, or the Flying Island," as reviewed in the *Examiner*, no. 524, p. 26 (January 12, 1818)

The Covent Garden pantomime, *Harlequin Gulliver, or the Flying Island*, is much better [*than that at Sadlers Wells*]; — and the scenery very beautiful. It is founded on Gulliver's Travels. The island of Laputa comes sailing through the air, and takes up by a ladder an English sailor, who runs away with a fair captive in possession of the king, — the king and his chancellor afterwards becoming *Pantaloon* and *Clown*, and the sailor and his mistress *Harlequin* and *Columbine*. The Laputians are a very queer old womanish sort of people, with long, monstrous faces, and a hopping gait. The lovers fly from them into Liliput, where the little men and women are well performed by boys and girls; which, by the way, may be tolerated in an occasional pantomime; but to make children act in plays, as it has lately been attempted to do again, and to bring them in general on the stage, is what we always protested against, and always shall, as a thing in its nature incompetent to the task required, and above all, extremely hurtful to the health, simplicity, and present if not future happiness of the children. It is destroying all

458

# Theatrical Productions

the unconsciousness and best bloom of their time of life. The Brobdingnagians are excellently managed by men built up into huge dolls,
as least quite as well as it appears possible to manage them, unless
perhaps the men could be placed at the top part of the figure instead of
below, so as to move the arms better. But their good-natured huge faces
are quite taking, though not altogether so intelligent as they appear in
Swift. The scene in which the lovers first make their appearance in
Brobdingnag, is the corn-fields mentioned in *Gulliver*; and the enormous
golden corn cuts a beautiful magnificent figure, and makes us see for
an instant as we may suppose insects to see; who, if they do so, must
live in a glorious world indeed, of colours, and shapes, and over-topping
splendours. It is almost impossible indeed for a spectator of this pantomime not to feel the *best* part of the lesson which is read us in
*Gulliver*, and see how comparative things are, and how little human
nature has to value itself exclusively. The astonishment of the Laputans
at what appear to them our ugly face and manners; the pride and
passions of the little Liliputians; the gentleness and beauty of the huge
Brobdingnagians in spite of the coarse detail perceptible to minuter
eyes; the smallness or largeness of ourselves, in proportion as we are
measured with others; and the magnificent *size* as well as shape and
colour of the commonest vegetables and weeds, when our sight is
reduced to that of millions and millions of living creatures, — all help to
impress upon us a strong sense of the force of ideas and of circumstances, to abate pride and exclusiveness of every sort, and to open our
eyes to those infinite treasures, beauties, and blessings of Nature, which
are *not* to be found in poetry alone, though poetry unfortunately is
almost the only thing that finds *them*.

## II

"Acis and Galatea" and "Zephyr: Or, the Return of Spring," as
reviewed in the *Examiner*, no. 531, pp. 138–139 (March 2,
1818)

They have had two very pleasing new ballets here, *Acis and
Galatea*, and the *Return of Spring*. It is curious that the French, who
are not at all so imaginative a people as the English and other neighbours, at least as the poetical individuals of those nations, should yet be
the only persons to keep alive a public taste for the beauties of Greek
poetry and mythology. It shews the natural grace and cheerfulness of
the ancient imagination; for the French are, at any rate, a graceful and
chearful people, — so chearful indeed, that the only apparent reason,

459

# Appendix B

why they at once keep these things alive and yet go no further with them, is, that although they have taste enough to seek for elegant pleasure, they are somewhat too easily satisfied both with it and themselves, to search into its depths and sentiment. They go dancing over the surface, and are contented.

It is on this account, that the ballet of *Acis and Galatea* is not so good a thing as the *Return of Spring*, and did not so well succeed. There was some beautiful scenery and dancing in it; and it is impossible not to pity *Polyphemus*, when his love and his hopeless deformity ever come before one; but the charm of this story is in the depth and simplicity of the sentiment; even Ovid has spoilt it compared with Theocritus; and what was to be expected from the still greater and irrelevant conceits, the twists, and twirls, and pretty ostentations of a French ballet? *Polyphemus*, who promises well at first, goes off into a mere desperado, and then repents and joins the lover's hands, like a conscience-smitten old guardian in a play.

The *Return of Spring* is another matter. Here even the defects of the French school of dancing might be turned to account, by the license of the renovated spirits of Nature, and the fluttering and whisking of *Zephyr*. And so they are. The twirls are not overdone; and the gracefulness as well as coquettishness of the volatile Deity is preserved. We do not know which performs better, — M. Baptiste as *Zephyr*, or Mademoiselle Milanie as *Chloris*: nor are we anxious to find out, for it is much better to be delighted with both. The only defect in M. Baptiste, besides a little too much French twirling, which however he scarcely practices too much in the present piece, is one which he has in common with most if not all other male dancers, — a too great laxity of air when he is not immediately dancing. But when he is, nothing can be more elegant, alert, powerful, and full of meaning. The scene in which he endeavours to *carry off* or to *whisk* the rose out of *Chloris's* hand was truly enchanting, and as complete an embodying of the idea of a spring air as possible. He went close round her at times, stooping, and fawning with his head; then glanced hither and thither; then floated in a circle; then stopped and threw his limbs about, like little shoots of a breeze; then darted at her hand again, and missed the rose, which in the meanwhile she carried about in all sorts of graceful attitudes, sometimes with hands downwards, sometimes holding it up on each side of her in the air and gazing at it. We never saw a lovelier scene on the stage. The masques of Ben Jonson could not suggest any thing more beautiful and aerial. — Such entertainments revive the finest associations of our youth, keep the beauty of the external world before us, and remind us of the elements of grace and enjoyment we have in

460

our natures. It is instructive as well as curious to see how the utmost refinement in the more polished part of society comes round for it's [sic] entertainment to the pastoral pleasures, — to music, dancing, and poetry.

## III

"Zephyr: Or, the Return of Spring," as reviewed in the *Courier* (February 23, 1818)

On Saturday night, after the very popular Opera of *Don Giovanni,* a new Ballet Pantomime, entitled *Zephyr: or, The Return of Spring,* was performed for the first time, and received with universal applause. We have not of late seen any thing more delightful, from its airy and tasteful elegance, than this *bluette.* It is the composition of Mons. DUPORT, the brother of Madame BAPTISTE, and has been got up here with admirable fidelity by Mons. GUILLET, who is the accomplished Director of the School of Dancing established at the Opera-house. It is a pretty little allegory, in which the amorous *Zephyr,* or the western wind, is personified. On the return of Spring, he enters, and seems to float in the air, and to kiss the various flowers that are opening to his refreshing breath. The Nymphs represent the different flowers — the rose, the lily, &c. and the inconstant *Zephyr* flies from Nymph to Nymph, till at length *Cupid* touches his heart, and he settles on the Rose. The lightness and brevity of the fable make it rather a Divertisement than a Ballet; but the exquisite charm with which the opening scene between *Zephyr* and *Chloris* was danced by M. BAPTISTE and Madamoiselle MILANE gave the spectators so lively a sensation of pleasure, that the whole was rapturously applauded. The evolutions of *Zephyr* and the coquetry of the Nymph were in what the French call *le bon genre,* and gave us a high idea of M. GUILLET's taste as a Master. We trust that this is only the first of many things of his selection.

# APPENDIX C

## Biographical Sketches

### Marianna Candida Dionigi

The Signora Marianna Candida Dionigi was born in Rome in 1756 to distinguished parents: her father the physician Giuseppe Candidi, and her mother, gifted both as historian and mathematician, Maddalena Scilla, last of a noted family of Massina. From her earliest years Marianna studied music seriously; she was thoroughly schooled in dancing and singing, and as harpist and pianist was admired by Anfossi, Paisiello, and Cimarosa. She studied first Latin and Greek, which were to bring her to proficiency as a classical scholar and to great honor as an archaeologist, and later French and English.

She turned when still very young to landscape painting, studying under the director of the Academy of Perugia, Carlo Labruzzi, and she amazed her contemporaries with the persistence and the *animo virile* that kept her for months at a time buried in the country studying with brush in hand the various changes in nature. She worked in tempera, watercolor, and encaustic (having found herself allergic to the varnish necessary to work in oils), and she generously gave to her friends her original works and sent her copies of such masters as Claude Lorraine, Salvator Rosa, and Nicolas Poussin to various galleries, as far afield as America. She was so famous when still a child that she was invited to the court of France to supervise the education of a princess, an invitation she refused.

At the age of fifteen Marianna was married to Domenico Dionigi, of a noble family of Ferrara, a man well versed in letters and juris-

462

prudence. Seven children were born before Domenico's death in 1801, and their mother supervised their education. Of these, Enrichetta was at the age of ten inscribed with Goethe in the Accademia dei Arcadi for precocity in poetry, and another daughter, Carolina, acquired *una erudizione vastissima* in history. Of her two sons one learns only that Alessandro had four children, none of whom lived to perpetuate the name, and that Ottavio, the one child mentioned by Claire, died unmarried.

Early in her married life Marianna Dionigi watched her home become the meeting place of the great men in archaeology and art — D'Agincourt, Visconti, Canova. She herself was an honored member of no less than ten academies, including the most important, the Accademia di San Luca. This academy lent the full force of its authority to her critical work *Precetti elementari sulla pittura de' paesi* (Rome, 1816), otherwise known as *Prospettiva e regole di paesaggio*. Her other work was also authoritative: *Viaggi in alcune città del Lazio che diconsi fondate dal re Saturno* (Rome, 1809–1812). In carrying out the archaeological research for this impressive folio volume she watched every measurement made by the architect, supervised every step which she did not take herself, collected inscriptions, and made her own drawings of the excavations.

When the Shelleys arrived in Rome they became close neighbors of this distinguished woman, who lived at 310 Corso. Claire and Shelley found her *conversazione,* or musical evenings, very much to their taste. Lady Murray, wife of the publisher, visited Rome two years later and described the quiet meetings of the literary set, quite apart from the nobility, with no attempt to dress, and no refreshment but cold water. Typical was the soiree of the Signora Dionigi, "a very agreeable elderly lady, who lived up two pairs of stairs, which her friends crept up in the dark, and then entered a room lighted by a common lamp with three burners, and one wax taper. She received company every evening" (Lady Murray, *Journal*, III, 80–81). Mary Shelley considered her "very old, very miserly & very mean" (Mary Shelley, *Letters*, I, 69); Claire, however, with her excellent command of Italian, was delighted to climb the dark stairs on nearly half of the evenings between their arrival and the Signora's departure on April 27. For Shelley and Claire she opened the door to the magnificent church music of Rome.

A few years after Shelley's visit she took her paintings and her famous collection of autograph letters and retired to her little villa near Cività Lavinia, where she died at the age of seventy in 1826. After her death one of the broad streets in the new section of Rome was named for her — the Via Marianna Dionigi, running from the Piazza Cavour to the Tiber. (The preceding account is drawn from Tipaldo, *Biografia,*

# Appendix C

V, 37–39; and Nicola Marcone, *Marianna Dionigi e le sue opere* [Rome, 1896]. There is also a biography by Luigi Cardinali, which I have not seen.)

### Andrea Vaccà Berlinghieri

Andrea Vaccà Berlinghieri (1772–1826) was the son and grandson of distinguished physicians. His father, Francesco Vaccà Berlinghieri (1732–1812), had written more than a dozen medical works and was associated with the University of Pisa, where his three sons later distinguished themselves in their various fields.

Andrea, having indicated very early in his career an interest in surgery, journeyed to Paris in 1787 to study at the best medical institutions in Europe. When still only fifteen years old he managed to convince the prince of French surgeons, Pierre Joseph Dessault, to take him as a student. The young Vaccà succeeded brilliantly and before returning to Italy made a trip to England in the company of his elder brother, the experimental physicist Leopoldo, to pay homage to Hunter, Bell, and Cullen.

Like the rest of his family Andrea was infected with the revolutionary spirit, and he assisted at the storming of the Bastille when he was seventeen. Then in 1791 he returned to Pisa, where under his own father he complemented his excellent surgical training by studying the medical aspects of his profession. In 1793, his studies complete, he was awarded *la laurea dottorale* by the University of Pisa. Immediately, while still in his twenty-first year, he published his first work, *Osservazione sulla chirurgia di Beniamino Bell*, which was so remarkably mature that it was taken for the work of his father and widely praised.

The French invasion of 1799 was a summons to the young man who had helped take the Bastille, and Andrea joined the French forces, becoming attached to General Olivier, who shortly thereafter was desperately wounded at the battle of Trebbia. Vaccà followed the general to Paris and gained much acclaim by the almost miraculous cure which he worked. While in France he renewed and extended his acquaintance among the leading medical scientists, and challenging some of the most firmly established surgeons he saw his techniques supersede theirs. He read a paper before a learned society and published, in French, the treatise which provided the final assurance of his reputation, *Traité des maladies vénériennes*.

Andrea Vaccà returned to his native Pisa in 1800 and was offered a professorship at the university, where he became a colleague of his father and his two brothers — one in science and the other in law. In 1803, just after he turned thirty, he was further honored by the endowment of a new chair of medicine, the *Cattedra di Clinica*, established for him in recognition of his achievement in revolutionizing the medical profession, so long in disrepute in Italy. In 1804 he was offered the *Cattedra di Scarpa* at the University of Pavia, one of the highest honors possible in his native land, but he declined it, pleading his great attachment to his father. As a team, one in medicine and the other in surgery, they made Pisa the capital of their profession in Italy.

As a teacher he was often compared to Hippocrates, and as a physician he was firm and gentle, inspiring confidence in his patients. He was particularly good with children. Men and women came from all parts of Europe, including St. Petersburg, and even from Egypt, to consult him. He continued to experiment and to write; like his father he published thirteen books of great value to his colleagues. He invented four new instruments and perfected four already in use.

In 1809 his elder brother Leopoldo died, and after five years, by special dispensation, Andrea married his widow, the excellent Sofia Cauderon. Having been a model son, he became a gentle and devoted husband and father. Nearly everyone who has written about him has paid tribute to the quality of his family life.

When Shelley came to him in 1820, Vaccà was in the prime of life. He was described in the spring of 1814 as riding a horse with an air that gave one the impression that he would be perfectly at home on the battlefield. He lived a full and varied life: his mornings were devoted to study; the afternoons were divided, two hours to teaching and four to consulting and practice. He found time for the study of agriculture (a favorite subject of Mr. Tighe), and on his estates he was known to go into the fields and work like a brother among the laborers.

The doctor was also interested in literature and particularly appreciated the works of Lucian, Molière, Cervantes, and Swift. He joined enthusiastically in the salon of Madame de Staël when she was in Pisa in 1816, and his vigorous differences of opinion, his spontaneous laughter, and his improvised sketches provided the salt and pepper of these conversations.

All these aspects of Vaccà's character and personality appealed to Shelley, but most important of all the doctor was a humanitarian after the poet's own heart. Three hours every day Vaccà set aside for medical service to the poor of the community. During the famine of 1817 he had almost single-handed provided food for the starving population of Montefoscoli. He was gracious to strangers, in 1816 taking Byron's erstwhile physician Polidori into his home (*Diary of Dr. John William Polidori*, pp. 205–206). It was little wonder that he was called by an Austrian colonel "Dio della Medicina," and by Byron one of the great men of his day (*Works of Lord Byron*, ed. E. H. Coleridge, II, 324), or that when he died, in 1826, a monument was erected to him, designed and executed by Thorwaldsen. Claire's miserable health in the year 1820, and her persistent trouble with glands, which from time to time needed to be opened, suggest that her condition may indeed have been the tubercular one diagnosed by Vaccà. He had at once wisely diagnosed Shelley's ill health as nervous in origin, recommending the relaxation of the baths and a relief from medicines.

That Andrea Vaccà reciprocated Shelley's admiration is clear from a letter from T. J. Hogg to Jane Williams, from Florence, postmarked November 15, 1825 (British Museum, Add. MSS. 41,686). Hogg was on a tour of Italy, the first of a long stream of pilgrims to the Byron and Shelley shrines there. He was warmly received by the Countess Guiccioli and by Lady Mount Cashell and her family, and on one day he met Vaccà, whom he quotes as saying "that the English were a strange people; that they were never tired of speaking ill of Shelley & of Ld. Byron, but that no man was ever so much loved by his friends as S., & that the English used to run out with telescopes to see Ld. B. pass at a distance." At this Hogg commented, "I thought this the remark of a clever man."

(This account, except as otherwise noted, is based on Laura Vaccà Giusti, *Andrea Vaccà e la sua famiglia* [Pisa, 1878], with a few details from Pozzolini, *Miscellanea di prose e poesie italiane* [Florence, 1845]. See also Angeli, *Shelley and His Friends in Italy*, pp. 110–112, although it is inaccurate in some details.)

### Elizabeth Parker ("Suora Ancilla" or Betsy, the English Nun)

In her very old age Claire looked back on her friendship with Betsy, the English nun, as a very intimate and important one. About the year 1870 Claire spent much of her time in writing lengthy letters to Trelawny about her life and recollections (which were apt to be two different matters), and in those letters she cited Betsy as a witness that in 1822 Claire's friends considered Byron's behavior about Allegra brutal. Claire maintained that Betsy had recommended the most drastic measures, saying that if she were in Claire's position she would stab or shoot Byron and thereby save the child, even at the cost of her own life (Grylls, *Claire Clairmont*, p. 141). Dowden's statement that Elizabeth Parker, or Sister Ancilla, was an orphan sent by Mrs. Godwin to live with Mrs. Mason (Lady Mount Cashell), who had later (i.e., after 1822, the year Dowden was writing about) entered the convent, must also stem from Claire's letters to Trelawny, which are no longer available to scholars (Dowden, *Shelley*, II, 486–487).

# Biographical Sketches

A major source of evidence about Elizabeth Parker appeared among Claire's papers after her death: a copy in Claire's hand of a supposed letter from Miss Parker to Claire, describing in vivid detail a scene at Casa Silva, in which Shelley flew into a passion about Byron's treatment of Allegra, and in which the possible effect of horsewhipping was discussed. Dowden has printed a long excerpt from this letter, with the essential caveat that it is known only from Claire's copy (*ibid.*, II, 487). What Claire could not guess, when fifty years after the occasion she "copied" the letter which expressed so vividly her own point of view, was that Lady Mount Cashell had left an account of Elizabeth Parker's history in a letter to Mary Shelley (Abinger MSS., undated, but written early in her acquaintance with Mary). This letter explains that when she left England for Italy she picked up the girl at the house where she was lodging in London and took her abroad with her as a servant. The girl proved honest, faithful, and intelligent, but unfortunately in Pisa she picked up "the itch." During a stay at the hospital, where she had been sent by Vaccà, Miss Parker came under the influence of an old Capuchine and the nun with whom she lived, who resolved to save her soul. "To shorten my story," continued Lady Mount Cashell, "she abjured the errors of the Church of England & found rich friends in consequence who paid all the necessary expenses to make her a Nun of St. Clare & she has now been above four years in the Hospital where she is highly respected."

In the light of this undeniably authentic account, many of the details of Claire's later story appear distorted. That Elizabeth Parker was an uneducated girl of the servant class, and not a poor orphaned friend of Mrs. Godwin, makes it improbable that she was, in Claire's words, "my best, firmest and most affectionate friend — and has ever been so" (Grylls, *Claire Clairmont*, p. 141). It is strange that her dearest friend should be mentioned only four times (all in 1820) and never again in all the journals and letters. Further, it was necessary for Claire to postpone the entrance of the Parker girl into the convent until after 1822 to render plausible the story of her intimacy at Casa Silva during the most confidential family scenes. It is easy, however, to understand the wishful thinking, working in Claire's memory over half a century, that created a sympathetic support against Byron at a time when she felt most persecuted.

## Lega Zambelli

The recent acquisition by the British Museum of the Zambelli papers (Add. MSS. 46871–46882; 12 vols.) helps round out the picture of this man who made himself so useful to Byron.

# Appendix C

Two notes by Ethel Lega-Weekes (Add. MSS. 46878, last leaf) are worth quoting; they accompany miniature portraits of Lega Zambelli in his seventy-seventh year and of his daughter Aspatia, wife of William Fletcher, Byron's valet, whom she married in 1838. Also on this page are a photograph of Giovanni Battista Falcieri, Byron's servant "Tita," in old age, and coats of arms of the Zambelli and Fletcher families.

Antonio tommaso Lega Zambelli, l.l.d. (full title — de'zambelli della lega, di varnello.)

Born at brisighella, in the Province of ravenna, c. 1770–1771, died in London as a Political Exile, 1867. Son of giovanni lega [zambelli] & Paola n. lama. Was destined for the Priesthood, the Living of lugo being bequeathed to him by his uncle lorenzo lega, but on the Conquest of the Papal States by napoleon, took secular offices under him. Either this Conquest or its reconquest by Austrian & Papal Forces ruined his family, who lost their ancestral (since 1250) Castle of varnello, (the last stones of which were removed only about 1923)

Antonio was a Patriot, was a Carbonaro, became private Secretary and Legal adviser to lord byron in Venice and in Greece. Antonio's wife francesca silvestrini, and her sister Maria (Contessa de rossi) were daus. of andriana pasta domenichini, heiress of zero, near treviso, and descendant of soranzo & cornaro patrician families. Antonio was gt. gd. father of Ethel Lega-Weekes now (1930) of exeter, england.

Aspatia Andriana, daughter of Antonio Lega Zambelli, l.l.d., borne in Parish of Ste. Maria Carmine venice by his wife Francesca nata silvestrini 15 March, 1817. Died in London 1890.
Francesca & her sister Maria Antonia (wife of Conte Antonio de'rossi, architect at Court of alex. 1 of russia) — were daughters of Giacomo Benedetto silvestrini, by his wife andriana giovanna pata domenichini, heiress of the Palazzo & township of zero near treviso, and descendant of the Patrician families of soranzo and cornaro, lineally from Giorgio brother of catterina cornaro queen of cyprus. aspasia m. 1838 fredk Wm. fletcher & had clelia born 1841, d. 1924 married ansel weekes of mattapoisett mass, usa, & had Ethel Lega-Weekes of exeter.

## Henry Willey Reveley

Henry Willey Reveley (1788?–1875) was the son of Maria Gisborne and her first husband, Willey Reveley, the distinguished architect

468

# Biographical Sketches

and editor of the third volume of a standard work on Greek architecture, James Stuart's *Antiquities of Athens*. Reveley died when his son was ten, and his widow soon remarried. Henry appeared to the Shelleys as "the pattern of good boys." Mary wrote to Marianne Hunt: "He is only thirty years of age and always does as he is bid — this is no exageration although that age he is under as complete a subordination as few boys of twelve are — this however is all to his praise for he is very clever" (Mary Shelley, *Letters*, I, 77). Henry had studied under John Rennie, architect and engineer of Waterloo Bridge, and had had the best engineering training Italy could offer. Shelley invested heavily in Henry's project to build a steamboat to ply between Leghorn and Marseilles (see Claire's account of the casting of the cylinder, July 22, 1820, above), but this project, so dear to Shelley's heart because it would allow him to serve his fellow man in some practical way, eventually collapsed when the Gisbornes left for England. Shelley's verse "Letter to Maria Gisborne" bears witness to this ill-fated enthusiasm. Henry appears to have proposed marriage to Claire during 1820, and the scanty evidence suggests that the Gisbornes were not pleased at this unseemly independence. Mary wrote to Maria on October 5, 1820, inviting them to call, and adding, "Claire is on a visit, and therefore your H[enry] would meet with no temptations" (Jones, "Mary Shelley to Maria Gisborne," SP 52:67 [January 1955]). In 1824 Henry married a sister of Copley Fielding, the painter, and took her with him to Capetown in 1826, where he was civil engineer and superintendent of works and buildings, at a salary of £500 a year. His inadequacies as an administrator, however, resulted in his dismissal two years later, though he had remained long enough to leave a strong classical influence on Capetown church architecture.

Henry and his wife left South Africa in 1829, accompanying Captain James Sterling, the leader of a party that called at the Cape of Good Hope in May of that year, in his expedition to found a colony at the Swan River, Western Australia, later to become the city of Perth. Henry thus became the first engineer and architect in Western Australia, taking charge of all public works and building the first barracks, government offices, jail, and courthouse. In 1956 the latter two buildings were still standing, the oldest surviving public buildings in Western Australia: the jail, a twelve-sided building known as the Round House, on Arthur's Head, Fremantle; and the old courthouse adjacent to the Supreme Court in Perth. A private venture, the first water mill in Perth, seems to have been unsuccessful, and in 1838 he left Perth for New Bedford, where he disappears from the record until his death on January 27, 1875, at Reading, Berkshire, England. *The Modern Encyclopaedia of Australia and New Zealand* (1964) identifies him as

# Appendix C

"First Civil Engineer in W A" and concludes: "A friend of Percy Bysshe Shelley; spent most of his life in Italy and Greece and had great difficulty in writing English" (p. 857).

(The preceding account is drawn from Dowden, *Shelley*, II, 209n.; D. H. Varley, "Henry Willey Reveley — First Colonial Civil Engineer at the Cape," *Quarterly Bulletin of the South African Library*, 12:118–121 [March 1958]; Neville Rogers, *Shelley at Work* [Oxford, 1956], appendix iv; and *The Australian Encyclopaedia*, VII, 412.)

### Antonio Bojti

Professor Antonio Bojti, or Boïti (1778–1827), was a physician and surgeon. To be ready at a moment's call from his friend and patron, the Grand Duke Ferdinand III, Dr. Bojti lived in one of the tall houses opposite the Palazzo Pitti, in the same block as the house which later gained fame as Casa Guidi. He has been described as an excellent citizen, an affectionate husband, and a tender father, active and enthusiastic in the education of his children. He was a Roman who at the age of eleven had passed an examination to enroll for the study of surgery in the Arcispedale di S. Spirito in Rome. Having gained three silver medals and one gold, he entered the Flaiani clinic and was rector of the school of anatomy. His rise among Roman surgeons was rapid, and by 1805 he had been called to the court of the Grand Duke Ferdinand, then duke of Salzburg. He became at that time particularly interested in obstetrics, and following the Grand Duke was welcomed to the medical faculties of Salzburg, Wurzburg, and finally Florence, there he was practically the founder and certainly the main support of the Medical–Surgical academy of that city. His *Osservazioni ad un nuovo metodo di amministrare il decotto di corteccia di melograno contro il verme tenia* was published in 1826 (see St. Grottanelli de' Santi, in Tipaldo, *Biografia*, III, 93). In 1822 Dr. Bojti, with Vaccà, advised and treated Byron's mistress, Teresa Guiccioli. On March 9, 1827, Lady Mount Cashell wrote to Mary, "Doctor Boïti (Claire's friend) died suddenly just after he assisted the Grand Duchesses *accouchement*, being scarcely out of the room when he dropped down dead" (Abinger MSS.).

### Tommaso Sgricci

Tommaso Sgricci was born in 1789, the son of a surgeon who died when Tommasso was only two, leaving him to be brought up by his mother, Claire's friend Madame Martini. The boy received training in law at the Collegio Ferdinando di Pisa and was graduated in 1810. He was appointed to a six-year post of legal practice by the city of Florence, under an agreement binding him to continue his legal studies and present an annual certificate of his accomplishment, and these certificates of his assiduous scholarship and moral probity were preserved in the files of the Archivo di Fraternità in Florence.

By 1812, however, Sgricci had discovered his talent for improvisation, and during his vacations he was often invited into the homes of the nobility to deliver his lyric impromptus. On October 9, 1813, he gave his first full-dress *accademia* in his home town of Arezzo, where the mingled tears and applause of his audience gave him the feeling of a most satisfying power over their sentiments. By the time his legal studies were completed in 1816 the drudgery of the law courts had become insupportable to him, and he launched out boldly into the more colorful and more immediately rewarding career in which he was already practiced, proficient, and much in demand.

From January to April he spent in Siena, giving occasional performances, and here for the first time had to face the full strength of his mother's disappointment and disapproval. To her he seemed to be deserting an honorable profession for the trappings of a mountebank. But he continued, via Arezzo and Perugia, to Rome, his "Capitale del Mondo," where he met with intoxicating success, and his letters to his mother contain elated accounts of swelling gate receipts and the plaudits of the newspapers. Most biographers of Sgricci agree that success went to his head and that he lost the respect of several of his close friends while in Rome.

After a few months he moved north, stopping at Pesaro as the guest of Conte Perticare, who, Sgricci announced, adored him. He also received the adoration of the Contessa Costanza, daughter of the renowned scholar Vincenzo Monti of Milan and one of the most beautiful women in Italy. Costanza accompanied Sgricci on his tour north to triumphs in Bologna and Milan, where her father joined her in her patronage of the Muses.

Polidori describes an unsatisfactory performance in Milan (*Diary*, pp. 183–186), at which Sgricci found one excuse after another not to treat the subjects suggested by the audience and drawn from a glass vase at the beginning of the performance, and in which, when he finally settled on one to his taste, the only bearable parts were those that he appeared to have memorized beforehand. The newspapers support Polidori's account, but Sgricci's advance publicity, spiced with gossip about the daughter of Monti, filled the house repeatedly. Despite his expression of utter boredom, even Polidori went twice to hear him.

At the end of 1816 the critic and scholar Pietro Giordani entered the dispute which was raging passionately over the merits and demerits of the *improvvisatore*. His hostile article, "Dello Sgricci e degli im-

# Appendix C

provvisatore in Italia," damning the art as *ludus impudentiae*, would have crushed a man less devoted to his career, but Sgricci survived the blow and went on his way. He repeated his three-part program — one selection in blank verse (*sciolti*), one in terza rima, and a tragedy — throughout Italy, alternately quarreling and making his peace with Vincenzo Monti. At the beginning of 1818 he fulfilled his ambition to return to Rome, but he was at once arrested and exiled from that city, possibly for unguarded statements about the Prince Corsini.

Early in 1820 Sgricci was in Ravenna, where he encountered Byron, who wrote to Hobhouse that he was improvising with great success: "He is also a celebrated Sodomite," reported Byron rather surprisingly, "a character by no means so much respected in Italy as it should be; but they laugh instead of burning, and the women talk of it as a pity in a man of talent, but with greater tolerance than could be expected, and only express their hopes that he may yet be converted to adultery" (Marchand, *Byron*, II, 844n.).

When Shelley met him, Sgricci was approaching the height of his career. He could produce on the spot a full two-and-a-half-hour tragedy on the Greek plan from a story outline, on a subject with which he was not familiar, suggested by the audience. He had a prodigious memory and could draw names, dates, and facts from his head as from a library; he had a minute knowledge of the Greek and Italian classics; and he was a natural showman. Sgricci and the *tragedie sgricciane* had a strong impact on the Shelleys (Mary Shelley, *Letters*, I, 117, 122–124, 126–128, and 132–133; Mary's opinion remained enthusiastic, as can be seen from her account of these performances in her article "The English in Italy" [see Appendix A, above]. See also H. Buxton Forman, "The Improvvisatore Sgricci in Relation to Shelley," *Gentleman's Magazine*, 246:115–123 [January 1880]). He appealed to Shelley by his eloquent defense of freedom (and rumored Carbonarism). More importantly he appeared, by his talent for spontaneous creation, to be the medium of true inspiration, according with Shelley's analogy between the poet and the aeolian lyre ("A Defense of Poetry," Shelley, *Works*, VII, 109) and the concept of the inspired poet in Plato's *Ion* (trans. Shelley, *ibid.*, VII, 233–248). Shelley was not blind, however, to Sgricci's faults, such as a snobbery that fitted poorly with his political liberalism. He referred to a large group of his fellow poets as *canaglia letterata* (literary rabble), provoking Shelley to write: "I hate the cowardly envy which prompts such base stories as Sgricci's about the Neapolitans: a set of slaves who dare not to imitate the high example of clasping even the shadow of Freedom" (Shelley, *Letters*, II, 266).

Early in 1821 Sgricci stayed in the general neighborhood of Pisa and Lucca, giving one *accademia* after another. He spent much time in

# Biographical Sketches

Florence with his mother, the Signora Martini, and with their old friend the Marchesa Orlandini. When Claire returned to Florence at the end of December she was introduced to both women, called on them regularly, and often met Sgricci on her calls.

The greatest triumphs of Sgricci's career lay ahead of him. In 1823 he was hailed in Paris, where several of his tragedies were stenographically transcribed and printed. In 1825, on his return to Florence, he was offered a pension by the Grand Duke Ferdinand. In 1826 he again visited Paris and Rome and spent three months in England. In the next year he performed a diplomatic mission for Vittorio Fossombrone in Rome, was summoned to the court of the king of Naples, and was honored with a medal and a special publication of one of his tragedies in Arezzo.

Many of his works found their way into print toward the end of his career: there are fifty items in his bibliography, many of them made up of several works (Ugo Viviani, *Un Genio Aretino: Tommaso Sgricci: Poeta tragico improvvisatore* [Arezzo, 1928], pp. 203–205). But the published works lack the fire of the performances — Mary Shelley found the transcription of the "Death of Hector" vastly inferior poetry to what she remembered. As his career drew to a close Sgricci tried to perform with a pen what he had been accustomed to improvise on the stage, but whenever he tried he was overcome by a violent nausea, the counterpart of the fever which afflicted him during his most impassioned tragedies — an indication of the emotional (and eventually hysterical) intensity with which the impromptus were wrenched from him. After 1827 he found the strain too heavy and quit the stage. He died in 1836 in Arezzo, after a long illness. (Except as otherwise noted, the preceding sketch is drawn from Viviani, *Sgricci*, and Luigi Carrer, in Tipaldo, *Biografia*, III, 404–410. In his account of Sgricci, Medwin [*Shelley*, pp. 265–266] outdid himself in inaccuracy.)

### Alexander Mavrocordato

[The following account of Alexander Mavrocordato is from Julius Millingen, *Memoirs of the Affairs of Greece; Containing an Account of the Military and Political Events, Which Occurred in 1823 and Following Years. With Various Anecdotes Relating to Lord Byron, and an Account of His Last Illness and Death* (London: John Rodwell, 1831), pp. 64–68. Millingen had gone to Greece in 1823 to assist the Greek cause, and there he became personal physician to Lord Byron. He served as surgeon in the Greek army, was taken prisoner by the Turks, and — adjusting his allegiance accordingly — had a successful career as physician to several

# Appendix C

sultans in Constantinople. It was he who introduced the Turkish bath to England.]

The day after my arrival, I presented myself to the Governor-General of Western Greece, Mavrocordato; anxious to see a man who had such a reputation in Europe. He had arrived a few days before on board the Greek vessels, that were engaged in the late action off Ithaca; being there as passenger with his suite; not, as Sir Thomas Maitland supposed in his proclamation, in the character of Commander. On the appearance of the Turkish fleet in June, the inhabitants of Mesolonghi, mindful of his services, and how he had, in 1822, contributed to the preservation of their town, began to feel the necessity of his presence; and at the same time, that they petitioned the senate to send the fleet to their assistance, they requested, that Mavrocordato might be appointed their eparch, instead of Constantino Metaxà; a Cephaloniot nobleman, whose arrogancy, they asserted, was equalled only by his incapacity.

When the petition arrived, Mavrocordato was at Hydra; where he had taken refuge; happy to escape the vengeance of Colocotrone, who had twice attempted to assassinate him. Although president of the legislative body, he willingly accepted the proposal of the Mesolongiots; not only because it placed him beyond the attempts of his numerous enemies; but because he hoped to add fresh laurels to the crown, which Greece had there bestowed upon him. The fleet did not second his impatience, nor that of the Mesolonghiots; for several weeks elapsed before the sailors could be prevailed upon to put to sea; refusing to depart, till they received three months' pay in advance. Not one of the wealthy capitani or primates of Peloponnesus, or of the islands, notwithstanding the danger which threatened Mesolonghi, would advance the 20,000 dollars which were required. Seeing this, a foreigner, Lord Byron, more alive than themselves to their own interests, supplied the sum upon his own credit.

I found the prince on a divan, on which sat, cross-legged, several of the Roumeliot capitani; whom, immediately after his arrival, he had convoked to a general assembly. Numerous servants, armed with silver pistols and yataghans, waited on the company. They presented them with coffee and pipes, observing precisely the same ceremonial as the Turks; or with the hand, folded on the breast, they stood expecting their masters' commands. As Mavrocordato was busily occupied in conversation with the capitani, I had leisure to observe his physiognomy. The ensemble of his head was excessively fine, being very large in proportion to his body; and its bulk was not a little increased by his bushy jet black hair and prodigious whiskers. His thick eye-brows and huge mustachios gave a wild, romantic, expression to his features, which could not but produce a striking effect on a stranger. The expression of his physiognomy was that of a clever, penetrating, ambitious man. His large Asiatic eyes, full of fire and wit, were tempered by an expression of goodness. His looks had not, perhaps, sufficient dignity; for they had a kind of indecision, and timid flutter, which prevented him from looking any one stedfastly in the face. His stature was much below the usual size; and his carriage altogether too unmartial to impart much confidence to a half-civilized people, who prize external appearance so much, and are more, perhaps, than others, influenced by an awe-commanding countenance. The prince also paid too little regard to dress; insomuch that even the Franks could not refrain from remarking how much to his disadvantage the contrast was between his plain European attire and travelling-cap, and the splendid, highly graceful, Albanian costume, worn by the other chiefs.

If nature had neglected Mavrocordato's exterior, she amply compensated him for such omission by the lavish manner, in which she had endowed his mind. Educated at Constantinople, he had devoted his earlier years to the study of Oriental languages. Few persons were more intimately acquainted with Persian and Arabic, of which the court language of the Turks is, in great part, formed. He was an excellent Greek scholar, spoke and wrote French like a native of France, and was tolerably well acquainted with English and Italian. Setting aside his wit and other qualities, which, in private life, rendered him the charm of society, we have only to consider him as a public character, belonging to history. He was, perhaps, the only man in Greece, who united, in an eminent degree, unadulterated patriotism, and the talents which form a statesman. He alone was capable of organizing and giving a proper direction to civil administration. This he showed shortly after his arrival in Peloponnesus, when he drew up a form of government out of the chaos, in which every thing then lay. He gave constant proofs of his genius for order, whenever he had the lead of affairs; and few, in any country, ever possessed, more than he did, the talent of simplifying the most complicated questions, and rendering them intelligible to the most illiterate. The rapidity and precision, with which he despatched business, was surprising; and no doubt, the extensive practice he had had, when secretary to Caradja Hospodar of Wallachia, was now of no small assistance to him. He had been repeatedly accused of retaining too much the principles of a Fanariot education. Incapable of a plain, bold, open conduct, it has been said, that he could only advance by crooked ways, and obtain his ends by tricks and cunning. The untractable, suspicious, and deceitful character of those, he had daily to deal with, might render this necessary. It was the current money of the country. No other would pass.

# Appendix C

Indeed, it was fortunate for Greece, that Mavrocordato was so well acquainted with the character of those he had to deal with; since it contributed to the preservation of Mesolonghi, till the arrival of reinforcements enabled it to sustain Omer Pasha's assault. The reproach would be justified, if it could be shown, that he ever pursued any other object, than the good of his country; or that he sacrificed her interests to the prosecution of his own private views. But in every foreign relation, even his bitterest enemies confessed his superiority, by constantly having recourse to his assistance, to settle their disputes; the different naval officers, employed in those transactions, repeatedly rendered justice to his merits as a diplomate, and to his qualities as a gentleman, by refusing to transact business with any other person. Happy would it have been, had Mavrocordato known the extent of his qualifications. He would then not have aspired to military command. Transported however by the desire of serving his country, he often placed himself at the head of troops; but as often, partly through his incapacity, and partly owing to the jealousy of others, he met with the severest repulses. Perhaps, he might, considering their profound ignorance, combine the plan of a campaign better than most capitani: yet he was, certainly, the worst man to execute it. The greatest fault in his character, and the cause of incalculable evils both to his country and to himself, was a total want of firmness. He was incapable of pronouncing "*no.*" Had the inflexible sternness, the bold unalterable resolution of a Cromwell, made part of his character, how many just reproaches might he have avoided! Indiscriminately liberal in promises, his performance was as invariably nothing. This changed many of his friends into enemies. Whatever deficiencies, however, may be laid to his charge, it must in justice be conceded, that, unlike most of his countrymen and foreigners, who came to Greece in quest of wealth and distinction, he sacrificed the whole of his fortune in the service of his country. He was, indeed, occasionally so distressed, as to be unable to provide for his daily expenses. In the most favourable circumstances he displayed the greatest disinterestedness; his patience and resignation in the most trying situations were exemplary; a constant friend to good order, he invariably pursued what he believed to be most advantageous to the general welfare; so that if he erred, his errors are, in no instance, to be attributed to sordid ambition or badness of heart. How often, too, has he been disappointed in his best endeavours by the lawlessness of barbarians; and even by the jealousy of the more enlightened Greeks and Phil-hellenes themselves; on whom he relied most for the execution of his plans, and the success of his efforts!

# APPENDIX  D

## "A fragment—"

The following fragment is to be found among the papers of Thomas Jefferson Hogg, presented to the British Museum by J. W. Williams in 1934 (Add. MSS. 43,805). Accompanying it is a letter from Richard Garnett to Mr. Williams, dated November 8, 1900, which says, "I really think that 'Ianthe' is in Claire Clairmont's writing, though I cannot be sure, as the only specimen with which I can compare it is a much later date. Still, I think it is Claire's." The manuscript experts at the British Museum are convinced that Garnett was mistaken, and indeed the handwriting — which varies from one section of the manuscript to another — and the spelling differ slightly from Claire's practice.

In content, the fragment appears to be a thinly disguised, conventionally romantic portrayal of Jane Williams (Ianthe) and her love for Edward Ellerker Williams and their children. The close friends, Alastor and Marian, are Shelley and Mary. Since a disaster for the boat is hinted at in the fragment (which would seem to have been begun as an attempt at a novel), I should place its composition not long after the drowning of Shelley and Edward Williams in 1822. The epitaph at the end is in the same hand but bears no relation to the narrative.

The manuscript is on two sheets of paper, the first 8¼ x

# Appendix D

5¾ inches; the second folded in half to give four sides, each
8¼ x 5¾. "A fragment—" is written on both sides of the first
leaf and on the first two pages of the folded leaf. The third page
of the folded leaf is blank, and the epitaph is written on the
fourth, or back, page.

### A fragment —

Ianthe sat alone and desolate in her deserted bower — her face leaned
upon her hand and her eyes were bent to the earth whose flowers
woo'ed her in vain with their sweetness: she gazed but ↑on the beautiful
scene around her↓ a mist seemed to overshadow it altho' the Sun's last
rays glittered on the panes of her ↑own↓ bright home and the deep was
so clear it seemed that one might penetrate immensity. she took up her
guitar but and struck a few chords but tears followed their vibrations.
she called on him but he answered not! so swiftly the wild waves bore
him away. There was a rock sheltered by a single tree whose ample
branches gave a welcome shade; stretched beneath this she would
oftimes watch their little bark as it sped across the bay now hoping now
despairing as its veering course bore them towards or from their home.
thither now she went full of sad thoughts for the light of her life had
fled and she knew that many suns must rise and set ere they should
watch his departing beams together. But who was the light of her life?
and why had he fled, did his frail bark ever return? You shall hear —
Edward was the Idol of his Ianthe from him she first learnt the deep
mysteries of that divine love ⟨which⟩ ↑that↓ filled her whole being with
its essence ⟨and⟩ ↑to her seemed to↓ diffuse⟨d⟩ into all things ⟨around⟩
a portion of its own exquisite loveliness. Her only wish was immortality
for her golden dreams were realized; ⟨Her chosen⟩ The object of her
souls worship was beside her. The fruit of his love was at her feet their
paradise was fair Italy their home at the foot of the wild Appenines —
Ianthe ⟨whose light form seemed upborne by her lighter spirit⟩ loved
to climb their preciptous sides and garlanding her head with wild
flowers she sped along like youth pursued by hope & love the happy
genius of that sweet solitude. Her favorite spot was one of difficult
access whose pathway up the steep mountain's side wound thro' tangled
thickets where the loose gravel scarcely gave a resting place to her
daring foot but well did its loveliness repay her toil. ⟨The summits of⟩
↑Above her head the↓ mountain summits were clad with intermingled
foliage from the darkest pine to the bright chesnut  At her feet the
myrtle shed its ↑odorous↓ blossoms  To the right ⟨were⟩ ↑old↓ Towers
⟨clad [?]⟩ the mountain tops whose thick walls ⟨elegance[?]⟩ stood in

478

# "A fragment"

proud defiance ⟨of⟩ ↑to↓ time and tyranny — The smoothe and treah-
erous sea rolled in the distance streaking the horizon with a bright
silvery line while the intermediate plain glowing with luxuriant profusion gave ↑to the eye↓ every variety of tint — The wandering Serchio
↑with its many windings↓ flowed silently ⟨thro the valley⟩ ↑along↓ and
here and there gleamed the white cottages of the happy peasants
Ianthe gazed on these scenes and thought of her own unequalled
happiness till her heart seemed too small for the ⟨excess of the⟩ many
feelings centred there and she felt as if she should die of their very
excess. "What am I" she would say "Oh thou beautiful giver of all that
is good and lovely what am I that thou shouldst have made my destiny
thy peculiar care? Thou hast given me a heart to feel, adore, and
worship the divinity of love and an object who will receive and return
my offerings. Thou hast imbued me with a deep sense of the loveliness
of creation of the beauty and order of the universe and in this divine
country I can enjoy with those I love a life of innocence and peace"
then casting her eyes towards her home she saw her ⟨beloved one in⟩
beloved garden in ↑all↓ its flowering pride her arbour twined with many
a sweet plant that beloved form stretched on the grass in merry sport
with his babes: she gazed on the scene for a moment and the thought
passed across her, "What if he were not!" swift as lightening she
descended nor paused till she folded him in her arms ⟨then⟩ ↑while he↓
laughing ⟨he⟩ ↑at her vision↓ would dry her tears with a kiss — There
were two dear friends whose prescence shed delight and gladness in the
halls of Pugnano Alastor and his Marian. She was delicately fair and
"beautiful in her young wisdom" and her warm and vivid imagination
decked all things with its own bright hues. while on her expansive
brow sat reason triumph⟨ing⟩ant over youth

[*one page blank*]

Beneath this stone to worms a prey
Himself as poor & vile as they
Eugenio lies in hope of rest
Who deemed further hope a jest
Who ne'er on fancy's wings could rise
To heaven built domes above the skies
Content from whence he sprung to lie
Nor wished to live nor feared to die —

479

# Genealogical Chart I  The Godwin and Shelley Families

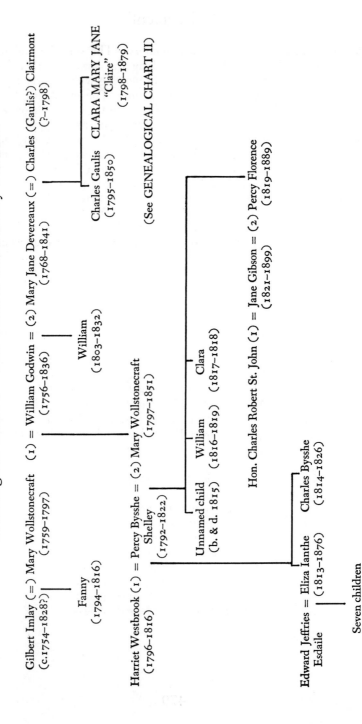

# Genealogical Chart II   The Clairmont and Byron Families

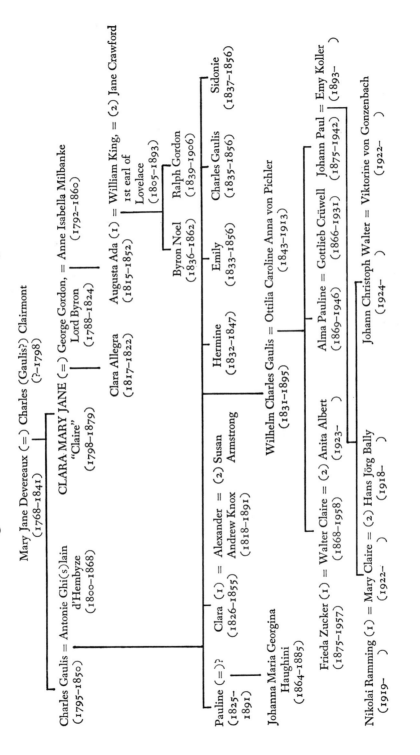

# Bibliography
# and Manuscript Sources

I have read and pored over countless books, newspapers, travel guides, magazines, maps, diaries, and letters in the editing of Claire Clairmont's journals. In the following list I have included only works that I consulted continually and works to which I have specifically referred.

## Selected Bibliography

| | |
|---|---|
| KSJ | *Keats-Shelley Journal* |
| KSMB | *Keats-Shelley Memorial Bulletin* |
| MLN | *Modern Language Notes* |
| MLR | *Modern Language Review* |
| PMLA | *[Publications of the Modern Language Association of America]* |
| PQ | *Philological Quarterly* |
| SP | *Studies in Philology* |

Anderson Galleries. *The Library of the Late H. Buxton Forman.* Parts I–III. New York, 1920.

Angeli, Helen Rossetti. *Shelley and His Friends in Italy.* London: Methuen & Co., Ltd., 1911.

*The Annual Register, or a View of the History, Politics, and Literature,* for the years 1814–1822. London: Baldwin, Cradock, and Joy, et al., 1815–1823.

Ariosto, Ludovico. *Orlando furioso,* trans. Allan Gilbert. New York: Vanni, 1954.

*The Australian Encyclopaedia.* 10 vols. Sydney: Angus and Robertson, 1958.

Barber, Giles. "Galignani's and the Publication of English Books in

# Selected Bibliography

France from 1800 to 1852," *Library* (London), 16:267–286 (1961).

Beavan, Arthur H. *James and Horace Smith, Joint Authors of "Rejected Addresses": A Family Narrative.* London: Hurst and Blackett, Ltd., 1899.

Bell, John. *Observations on Italy.* London: T. Cadell, 1825. Dr. Bell, Fellow of the Royal College of Surgeons, Edinburgh, was the Shelleys' physician in Rome in 1819. His book, published posthumously, was written in 1817. It contains some interesting illustrations by the author.

Berlioz, Hector. *Memoirs of Hector Berlioz from 1803 to 1865 Comprising His Travels in Germany, Italy, Russia, and England,* trans. Rachel (Scott Russell) Holmes and Eleanor Holmes, annotated and the translation revised by Ernest Newman. New York: Alfred A. Knopf, 1932.

Berry, Mary. *Extracts of the Journals and Correspondence of Miss Berry from the Year 1783 to 1852,* ed. Lady Theresa Lewis. 3 vols. London: Longmans, Green, 1865.

Beyle, Marie Henri (Stendhal). *Journal d'Italie,* ed. Paul Arbelet. Paris: Calmann-Lévy, 1911.

—— *Rome, Naples et Florence, en 1817, ou esquisses sur l'état actuel de le société, des moeurs, des arts, de la littérature, etc. de ces villes célèbres.* Paris: Delaunay, and London: Colburn, 1817.

—— *Rome, Naples, and Florence, in 1817: Sketches of the Present State of Society, Manners, Arts, Literature, etc. in These Celebrated Cities.* London: Colburn, 1818.

Blessington, Lady. See Marguerite Gardiner.

Bloom, Harold. "A Letter of Consolation to Mary Shelley," *Yale University Library Gazette,* 33:35–40 (July 1958).

Brand, C. P. "A Bibliography of Travel-Books Describing Italy Published in England 1800–1850," *Italian Studies* (Manchester, England), 11:108–117 (1956).

Brown, Ford K. *The Life of William Godwin.* London: J. M. Dent & Sons, 1926.

—— "Notes on 41 Skinner Street," *MLN,* 54:326–332 (May 1939).

Bürger, Gottfried August. *Sämmtliche Werke.* Göttingen: Dieterischen Buchhandlung, 1835.

Burr, Aaron. *Correspondence of Aaron Burr and His Daughter Theodosia,* ed. Mark Van Doren. New York: Covici-Friede, 1929.

—— *The Private Journal of Aaron Burr: Reprinted in Full from the Original Manuscript in the Library of Mr. William K. Bixby, of St. Louis, Mo.,* ed. William Holland Samson. 2 vols. Rochester, N.Y.: The Post Express Printing Co., 1903.

Byron, George Gordon, Lord. *Lord Byron's Correspondence, Chiefly*

*with Lady Melbourne, Mr. Hobhouse, the Hon. Douglas Kin-
naird, and P. B. Shelley,* ed. John Murray. 2 vols. London: John
Murray, 1922.

———— *The Works of Lord Byron. Letters and Journals,* ed. Rowland
E. Prothero. 6 vols. London: John Murray, 1898–1901. References
to Byron, *Works,* are to these volumes.

———— *The Works of Lord Byron. Poetry,* ed. Ernest Hartley Coleridge. 7 vols. London: John Murray, 1898–1904.

Campbell, Thomas. *The Complete Poetical Works,* ed. J. Logie Robertson. London: Oxford University Press, 1907.

Charles d'Orléans. *Poësies de Charles d'Orléans.* Grenoble: J. L. A.
Giroud, 1803.

Cicognara, Leopoldo. *Storia della scultura dal suo risorgimento in Italia
sino al secolo di Napoleone.* 3 vols. Venice: Picotti, 1813–1818.

Clairmont, C. See Chrétien-Hermann Gambs.

[Clairmont, Claire]. "Italy in 1832," *Metropolitan Magazine,* 4:165–
173 (June 1832).

[————] "The Pole" ("by the author of 'Frankenstein'"), *Court
Magazine, and Belle Assemblée* (London), n.s., 1:64–71, 129–136
(August, September 1832).

Cline, Clarence Lee. *Byron, Shelley and Their Pisan Circle.* Cambridge: Harvard University Press, 1952.

C[okayne]., G. E., *et al. The Complete Peerage or a History of the
House of Lords and All Its Members from the Earliest Times,* ed.
H. A. Doubleday and Lord Howard de Walden. 11 vols. and sup-
plement. London: The St. Catherine Press, 1910–1949.

[Coleridge, John Taylor]. "Shelley's *Revolt of Islam,*" *Quarterly Review,* 21:460–471 (April 1819).

Constable, Thomas. *Memoir of the Reverend Charles A. Chastel de
Boinville, Compiled from His Journal and His Letters.* London:
James Nisbet & Co., 1880.

Cottin, Madame Sophie Ristaud. *Claire d'Albe.* Paris: L. Tentré, 1820.
Trans. as *Clara; a Novel.* 2 vols. London: Henry Colburn, 1808.
While all the sources cite 1798 as the date of original publication,
the only edition I have found is the 1820 one.

*The Courier* (London). October 14, 1814; February 14 and 23, 1818.

Coxe, Henry. *Picture of Italy; Being a Guide to the Antiquities and
Curiosities of That Classical and Interesting Country. . . .* London: Sherwood, Neely & Jones, 1815.

Dante Alighieri. *Dante's Divina Commedia,* trans. H. F. Tozer. Oxford: Clarendon Press, 1904.

De Beer, Gavin. "An 'Atheist' in the Alps," *KSMB,* 9:1–15 (1968).

Delli, Giulio. *Un Poeta dimenticato: Pietro Bagnoli samminiatese 1767–*

# Selected Bibliography

*1847*, in *Miscellanea storica della Valdesa*. Castelfiorentino: Giovannelli e Carpitelli, 1919.

*Dictionary of National Biography*, ed. Leslie Stephen. 63 vols. with supplements. London: Smith, Elder & Co., 1885–1900.

Dionigi, Marianna Candida. *Precetti elementari sulla pittura de' paesi*. Rome: Romanis, 1816.

—— *Viaggi in alcune città del Lazio che diconsi fondate dal re Saturno*. Rome: L. P. Salvioni, 1809–1812.

Dowden, Edward. *The Life of Percy Bysshe Shelley*. 2 vols. London: Kegan Paul, Trench & Co., 1886.

Drummond, Sir William. *Academical Questions*, vol. I (no more published). London: W. Bulmer, 1805.

[Ducos, B.]. *Itinéraire et souvenirs d'un voyage en Italie en 1819 et 1820*. 4 vols. Paris: Dondey-Dupré, 1829.

*Encyclopédie de la musique*. 3 vols. Paris: Fasquelle, 1958–1961.

*The Englishwoman in Russia; Impressions of the Society and Manners of the Russians at Home*. "By a Lady, Ten Years Resident in that Country." London: John Murray, 1855.

Farina Cini, Neri. *La Famiglia Cini e la carteriera della Lima (1807–1943)*. Florence: Le Monnier, 1947.

Fétis, F. J. *Biographie universelle des musiciens*, 2nd. ed. Paris: Firmin Dodot, 1860–1863.

Field, Kate. "Last Days of Walter Savage Landor," *Atlantic Monthly*, 17:385–395 (April 1866), 540–551 (May 1866), 684–705 (June 1866).

Finberg, A. J., ed., for the National Gallery. *A Complete Inventory of the Drawings of the Turner Bequest*. 2 vols. London: His Majesty's Stationery Office, 1909. Joseph Mallord William Turner's sketchbooks for his first three trips to the Continent provide voluminous illustrations of many of the places visited by Claire and the Shelleys. The 1802 sketchbooks, particularly the one numbered LXXIX, and the 1817 books, particularly CLX and CLXI, portray the Rhine. The 1819 sketchbooks, particularly CLXXII–CLXXIX and CLXXXII–CLXXXVII, show in detail the Italian scenes mentioned in Claire's journal and the letters and journals of the Shelleys. The drawings are preserved in the Department of Prints and Drawings of the British Museum.

Fitzlyon, Kyril, ed. *The Memoirs of Princess Dashkov*. London: John Calder, 1958.

Flood, W. H. Grattan. *John Field of Dublin: Inventor of the Nocturne*. Dublin: Martin Lester, 1921.

Forman, H. Buxton. "The Improvvisatore Sgricci in Relation to Shelley," *Gentleman's Magazine*, 246:115–123 (January 1880).

# Selected Bibliography

Frommel, Otto H. *Emil Frommel: Ein Lebensbild.* Berlin: E. S. Mittler & Son, 1908.

———— "Emil Wilhelm Frommel" in *Allgemeine deutsche Biographie,* vol. XLIX. Leipzig: Duncker and Humblot, 1904.

———— *Frommels Lebensbild.* Vols. I and II (1900–1901) of Emil Frommel, *Das Frommel-Gedenkwerk.* 7 vols. Berlin: E. S. Mittler & Son, 1900–1904.

Gambs, Karl Christian. *Autobiographie des Pfarrers Karl Christian Gambs (1759–1783), mit einem Anhang.* Strasbourg: J. Singer, 1909.

[Gambs, Chrétien-Hermann]. *Ismaïl, poème en quatre chants, suivi de mélanges,* "par C. Clairmont." Paris: C. Gosselin, 1836.

[————] *Moïse, épopée en douze chants,* "par C. Clairmont." Paris: C. Gosselin, 1836.

Gambs, Chrétien-Hermann. *Vie et doctrines de Godescale* [a ninth-century bishop]. Strasbourg: G. Silbermann, 1837, 15 pp., quarto. A thesis to obtain a bachelor's degree in theology from the Université de France, Faculté de Théologie de Strasbourg.

[————] *Vladimir et Zara, ou les Kirguises, poème en quatre chants, suivis de quelques poésies fugitives,* "par C. Clairmont." Paris: C. Gosselin, 1836.

Gardiner, Marguerite (Countess of Blessington). *Conversations of Lord Byron with the Countess of Blessington.* London: Henry Colburn, 1834. See also under R. R. Madden.

Garnett, R. S., ed. *Letters about Shelley Interchanged by Three Friends — Edward Dowden, Richard Garnett and Wm. Michael Rossetti.* London: Hodder and Stoughton, 1917.

Gates, Eunice Joiner. "Shelley and Calderon," *PQ,* 16:49–58 (January 1937).

George, Mary Dorothy. *Catalogue of Political and Personal Satires Preserved in the Department of Prints and Drawings in the British Museum,* vols. IX (1811–1819), X (1820–1827). London: Trustees of the British Museum, 1949, 1952.

Gillman, James. *The Life of Samuel Taylor Coleridge,* vol. I (no more published). London: William Pickering, 1838.

Giordani, Pietro. "Dello Sgricci, e degl'improvvisatori in Italia" (1816), in *Opere.* 3 vols. Florence: Le Monnier, 1846 (I, 446–459).

[Gisborne and Williams]. *Maria Gisborne and Edward E. Williams, Shelley's Friends: Their Journals and Letters,* ed. Frederick L. Jones. Norman: University of Oklahoma Press, 1951.

Giusti, Laura Vaccà. *Andrea Vaccà e la sua famiglia: Biografie e memorie.* Pisa: Francesco Mariotti & Co., 1878.

487

# Selected Bibliography

[Godwin, William]. *Cloudesley: A Tale.* 3 vols. London: Henry Colburn and Richard Bentley, 1830.

Godwin, William, Jr. *Transfusion; or the Orphans of Unwalden.* 3 vols. London: John Macrone, 1835.

Goethe, Johann Wolfgang von. *Egmont: A Tragedy,* trans. Arthur Duke Coleridge. London: Chapman & Hall, 1868.

—— *Goethe's Faust, Parts I and II,* trans. Louis Macneice (an abridged version). London: Faber and Faber, 1951.

—— *Memoirs of Goëthe: Written by Himself.* 2 vols. London: Henry Colburn, 1824.

Gonnelli, Giuseppe. *Elogio di Lorenzo Ghiberti.* Florence: Guglielmo Piatti, 1822.

Gower, Lord Granville Leveson (first Earl Granville). *Private Correspondence 1781–1821,* ed. Castalia Countess Granville. 2 vols. London: John Murray, 1916.

Graham, William. *Last Links with Byron, Shelley, and Keats.* London: Leonard Smithers & Co., 1898.

*The Greek Anthology,* trans. William R. Paton. 5 vols. Loeb Classical Library. London: William Heinemann, 1916–1918.

Griffith, Ben W., Jr. "An Unpublished Shelley Reading List," *MLN,* 69:254–255 (April 1954).

—— "The Writing of *The Revolt of Islam*: A Study in Percy Bysshe Shelley's Methods of Composition from the Genesis of the Idea through the Final Publication," unpub. diss. Northwestern University, 1952. Contains a typescript of the Shelley-Rolls Collection (MS. Shelley adds. e. 14) presented to the Bodleian Library, Oxford, in 1946.

*Grove's Dictionary of Music and Musicians,* 5th ed., ed. Eric Blom. 9 vols. London: Macmillan, 1954.

Grunwald, Constantin de. *Tsar Nicholas I,* trans. Brigit Patmore. London: Douglas Saunders, MacGibbon & Kee, 1954.

Grylls, Rosalie Glynn. *Claire Clairmont: Mother of Byron's Allegra.* London: John Murray, 1939.

—— *Mary Shelley.* London: Oxford University Press, 1938.

—— *Trelawny.* London: Constable & Co., 1950.

—— *William Godwin and His World.* London: Odham's Press, 1953.

Hafiz Shirazi. *Persian Lyrics, or Scattered Poems, from the Diwan-i-Hafiz: With Paraphrases in Verse and Prose . . . ,* trans. John Haddon Hindley. London: E. Harding, J. Debrett, and West and Hughes, 1800.

Hale, J. R. See Samuel Rogers.

Hamilton, Otho William Hawtrey. "Recollections of a Tour [through

# Selected Bibliography

France, Switzerland, and Italy] in the Summer and Autumn of 1822." 3 vols. British Museum Additional MSS., 44836–44838. Vol. I, France (Calais — Paris — Lyons) and Switzerland (Geneva to Milan); vol. II, Milan, Venice, Bologna, Florence, etc.; vol. III, Rome and Naples. This manuscript, elegantly written out by a copyist under Hamilton's direction, with many watercolor drawings (by the author and others), engravings, lithographs, and maps, illustrates scenery, costumes, antiquities, etc. as Claire and the Shelleys would have seen them.

Hare, Augustus J. C. *Memorials of a Quiet Life.* 2 vols. London: Strahan & Co., 1872. Supplementary volume, with 52 mounted photographs. London: Daldy, Isbister & Co., 1876.

Haumant, Émile. *La Culture français en Russie* (1700–1900). Paris: Hachette, 1910.

Hogg, Thomas Jefferson. *After Shelley: The Letters of Thomas Jefferson Hogg to Jane Williams,* ed. Sylva Norman. London: Oxford University Press, 1934.

Holcroft, Thomas. *Travels from Hamburg, through Westphalia, Holland, and the Netherlands, to Paris.* 2 vols. London: Richard Phillips, 1804.

Hort, G. M. "Firstborn of Ariel," *Contemporary Review,* 169:362–366 (June 1946).

Hunt, James Henry Leigh. *The Autobiography of Leigh Hunt,* ed. J. E. Morpurgo. London: The Cresset Press, 1949.

—— *The Correspondence of Leigh Hunt,* ed. Thornton Leigh Hunt. 2 vols. London: Smith, Elder & Co., 1862.

—— ed. *Examiner,* nos. 500–531 (July 27, 1817–March 2, 1818).

—— ed. *Indicator,* vols. I–LXXVI (October 13, 1819–March 21, 1821).

—— *Leigh Hunt's Dramatic Criticism, 1818–1831,* ed. Lawrence Huston Houtchens and Carolyn Washburn Houtchens. New York: Columbia University Press, 1949.

—— ed. *The Liberal. Verse and Prose from the South.* 2 vols. London: John Hunt, 1822–1823.

—— *The Literary Pocket-Book; or, Companion for the Lover of Nature and Art.* 5 vols. London: C. & J. Ollier, 1819–1823.

—— *Lord Byron and Some of His Contemporaries; with Recollections of the Author's Life, and of His Visit to Italy.* London: Henry Colburn, 1828.

Hunt, Thornton Leigh. "Shelley: By One Who Knew Him," *Atlantic Monthly,* 11:184–204 (February 1863).

Huscher, Herbert. "Alexander Mavrocordato, Friend of the Shelleys," *KSMB,* 16:29–38 (1965).

# Selected Bibliography

———— "Charles und Claire Clairmont," *Englische Studien* (Leipzig), 76:55–117 (1944).

———— "Charles Gaulis Clairmont," *KSMB*, 8:9–19 (1957).

———— "Claire Clairmont's Lost Russian Journal and Some Further Glimpses of Her Later Life," *KSMB*, 6:35–47 (1955).

———— "The Clairmont Enigma," *KSMB*, 11:13–20 (1960).

———— "A New Viviani Letter," *KSMB*, 14:30–33 (1963).

Ingpen, Roger. *Shelley in England: New Facts and Letters from the Shelley-Whitton Papers*. London: Kegan Paul, Trench, Trubner & Co., 1917.

James, Henry. *The Aspern Papers*. New York: Charles Scribner's Sons, 1908. (Vol. XII of the New York Edition.)

Johnstone, Andrew. *Johnstone's London Commercial Guide, and Street Directory*. London: Barnard and Farley, 1817.

Jones, David L. "Hazlitt and Hunt at the Opera House," *Symposium*, 16:5–16 (Spring 1962).

Jones, Frederick L. "Mary Shelley to Maria Gisborne: New Letters, 1818–1822," *SP*, 52:39–74 (January 1955). See also under Shelley; Gisborne and Williams.

Jouy, Victor Joseph Étienne (*called* de). *The Hermit in Italy, or Observations on the Manners and Customs of Italy*. 3 vols. London: George B. Whittaker, 1825.

[Kent, Elizabeth]. *Flora Domestica, or the Portable Flower-Garden; with Directions for the Treatment of Plants in Pots; and Illustrations from the Works of the Poets*. London: Taylor and Hessey, 1823.

[————] *Sylvan Sketches; or, a Companion to the Parks and the Shrubbery; with Illustrations from the Works of the Poets*. London: Taylor and Hessey, 1825.

Kessel, Marcel. "The Mark of X in Claire Clairmont's Journal," *PMLA*, 66:1180–1183 (December 1951).

———— "Shelley's 'To Constantia Singing,'" *Times Literary Supplement* (London), January 17, 1935, p. 33.

Kingston, Marion. "Notes on Three Shelley Letters," *KSMB*, 6:13–17 (1955).

Koszul, André. "Notes and Corrections to Shelley's 'History of a Six Weeks' Tour' (1817)," *MLR*, 2:61–62 (October 1906).

Lamb, Charles. *The Letters of Charles Lamb to Which Are Added Those of His Sister Mary Lamb*, ed. E. V. Lucas. 3 vols. London: J. M. Dent & Sons, 1935.

[————] "Tom Pry's Wife," in the "Lepus Papers," printed in *The Avon Booklet*, vol. III. London: J. Thomson, 1905.

Lecky, William Edward Hartpole. *A History of England in the Eigh-*

*teenth Century*. 8 vols. London: Longmans, Green & Co., 1878–1890.

Lovell, Ernest J., Jr. *Captain Medwin: Friend of Byron and Shelley*. London: Macdonald, 1963.

Luigi, P. daGatteo. *Un 'Oasi nel deserto: Storia del monastero di S. Giovanni Battista in Bagnacavallo*. Faenza, 1935.

Lyall, Robert. *The Character of the Russians, and a Detailed History of Moscow*. London: T. Cadell, 1823.

McAleer, Edward C. *The Sensitive Plant: A Life of Lady Mount Cashell*. Chapel Hill: University of North Carolina Press, 1958.

McKerrow, Ronald B. *An Introduction to Bibliography for Literary Students*. Oxford: Clarendon Press, 1951.

Madden, R. R. *The Literary Life and Correspondence of the Countess of Blessington*. 3 vols. London: T. C. Newby, 1855.

Male, Roy R., and James A. Notopoulos. "Shelley's Copy of Diogenes Laertius," *MLR*, 54:10–21 (January 1959).

Marchand, Leslie. *Byron: A Biography*. 3 vols. New York: Alfred A. Knopf, 1957.

Marcone, Nicola. *Marianna Dionigi e le sue opere*. Rome: Claudio Stracca, 1896.

Marshall, Mrs. Julian (Florence A.). *The Life and Letters of Mary Wollstonecraft Shelley*. 2 vols. London: Richard Bentley & Sons, 1889.

Marshall, William H. *Byron, Shelley, Hunt, and "The Liberal."* Philadelphia: University of Pennsylvania Press, 1960.

Mazour, Anatole G. *The First Russian Revolution: 1825: The Decembrist Movement: Its Origins, Development, and Significance*, 2nd. ed. Stanford, California: Stanford University Press, 1961.

Medwin, Thomas. *The Angler in Wales, or Days and Nights of Sportsmen*. 2 vols. London: Richard Bentley, 1834.

―――― "Canova: Leaves from the Autobiography of an Amateur," *Fraser's Magazine*, 20:370–375 (September 1839).

―――― *Conversations of Lord Byron*, ed. Ernest J. Lovell, Jr. Princeton, New Jersey: Princeton University Press, 1966.

―――― *Journal of the Conversations of Lord Byron: Noted during a Residence with His Lordship at Pisa, in the Years 1821 and 1822*. London: Henry Colburn, 1824.

―――― *The Life of Percy Bysshe Shelley: A New Edition*, ed. H. Buxton Forman. London: Oxford University Press, 1913.

*Memoirs of the Secret Societies of the South of Italy, Particularly the Carbonari*. London: John Murray, 1821.

Millingen, Julius. *Memoirs of the Affairs of Greece; Containing an Account of the Military and Political Events, Which Occurred in*

# Selected Bibliography

*1823 and Following Years. With Various Anecdotes Relating to Lord Byron, and an Account of His Last Illness and Death.* London: John Rodwell, 1831.

*The Modern Encyclopaedia of Australia and New Zealand,* ed. Victor S. Barnes. Sydney and Melbourne: Horowitz-Grahame, 1964.

[Moore, Margaret King, Countess Mount Cashell]. *Advice to Young Mothers on the Physical Education of Children,* "By a Grandmother." London: Longman, Hurst, Rees, Orme, & Brown, 1823.

[———] *Continuation of the Stories of Old Daniel: Or Tales of Wonder and Delight. Containing Narratives of Foreign Countries and Manners, and Designed as an Introduction to the Study of Voyages, Travels, and History in General.* London: M. J. Godwin and Co. at the City Juvenile Library, no. 41 Skinner Street, 1820.

[———] *Simple Stories, in Words of One Syllable, for Little Boys and Girls,* "By the Author of *Stories of Old Daniel.*" London: J. Harris & Son, 1824.

[———] *Stories of Old Daniel: Or Tales of Wonder and Delight.* London: M. J. Godwin, 1807.

[Moore, Thomas]. *The Fudge Family in Paris,* "Edited by Thomas Brown, the Younger." London: Longman, Hurst, Rees, Orme, & Brown, 1818.

Moore, Thomas. *The Life and Death of Lord Edward Fitzgerald.* 2 vols. London: Longman, Rees, Orme, Brown, & Green, 1831.

Morgan, Lady Sydney. See Sydney Owenson.

Mount Cashell, Lady. See Margaret King Moore, Countess Mount Cashell.

Müllner, Amand Gottfried Adolph. *Guilt; or the Anniversary,* trans. R. P. Gillies. Edinburgh: James Ballantyne & Co., 1819.

[Murray, Lady]. *A Journal of a Tour in Italy.* 5 vols. London: Privately printed, [1836].

[Napier], Lady Sarah (Lennox) Bunbury. *The Life and Letters of Lady Sarah Lennox: 1745–1826.* 2 vols. London: John Murray, 1901.

Negri, Giovanni. *Luigi Calamai, ceraiolo e naturalista fiorentino.* Florence: Società Columbaria, 1932.

Nesselrode, Karl Robert von. *Lettres et papiers du chancelier comte de Nesselrode: 1760–1850.* 11 vols. Paris: A. Lahure, 1904–1911.

Nicoll, Allardyce. *A History of English Drama: 1660–1900.* 6 vols. Cambridge: Cambridge University Press, 1952–1959.

Nitchie, Elizabeth. *The Reverend Colonel Finch.* New York: Columbia University Press, 1940.

Norman, Sylva. *Flight of the Skylark: The Development of Shelley's Reputation.* Norman: University of Oklahoma Press, 1954.

# Selected Bibliography

Notopoulos, James A. "New Texts of Shelley's Plato," *KSJ*, 15:99–115 (Winter 1966).

—— *The Platonism of Shelley: A Study of Platonism and the Poetic Mind.* Durham, North Carolina: Duke University Press, 1949.

*Olliers Literary Miscellany in Prose and Verse*, no. 1 (no more published). London: C. and J. Ollier, 1820.

Orange, Ursula. "Elise: Nursemaid to the Shelleys," *KSMB*, 6:24–34 (1955).

Origo, Iris. *The Last Attachment.* London: Jonathan Cape & John Murray, 1949.

—— *A Measure of Love.* London: Jonathan Cape, 1957.

Owenson, Sydney, Lady Morgan. *Italy.* 2 vols. London: Henry Colburn, 1821.

—— *Lady Morgan's Memoirs: Autobiography, Diaries and Correspondence.* 2 vols. London: Wm. H. Allen & Co., 1862.

Pacchiani, Francesco. *Alcune Lettere inedite offerte ai novelli coniugi Italo Martelli — Ernesta Pacchiani.* Prato: Ranieri Guasti, 1875.

—— *In Morte di Ferdinando Terzo, granduca di Toscana: Canto.* Pistoia: Cino, n.d.

Pacini, Giovanni. *Le Mie Memorie artistiche*, ed. Ferdinando Magnani. Florence: Le Monnier, 1875.

Paston, George [Emily Moise Symonds]. "New Light on Byron's Loves. V. Claire Clairmont: A Rebel Maid," *Cornhill Magazine*, 150:129–144 (August 1934); "New Light on Byron's Loves. VI. Claire Clairmont: The Struggle for Allegra," *ibid.*, 150:257–276 (September 1934).

—— and Peter Quennell. *"To Lord Byron": Feminine Profiles Based on Unpublished Letters, 1807–1824.* London: John Murray, 1939.

Patton, Lewis. "The Shelley-Godwin Collection of Lord Abinger," *Library Notes: A Bulletin Issued for the Friends of Duke University Library*, no. 27, pp. 11–17 (April 1953).

Paul, Charles Kegan. *William Godwin: His Friends and Contemporaries.* 2 vols. London: Henry S. King & Co., 1876.

Peacock, Thomas Love. "French Comic Romances," *London Review*, 2:69–84 (July 1835).

—— *Letters to Edward Hookham and Percy B. Shelley with Fragments of Unpublished Mss.*, ed. Richard Garnett. Boston: The Bibliophile Society, 1910.

—— *Memoirs of Percy Bysshe Shelley* [with Hogg's *Life of Shelley* and Trelawny's *Recollections of Shelley and Byron*] in *The Life of Percy Bysshe Shelley*, ed. Humbert Wolfe. 2 vols. London: J. M. Dent & Sons, 1933.

# Selected Bibliography

────── *The Novels of Thomas Love Peacock*, ed. David Garnett. London: Rupert Hart-Davis, 1948.

Peck, Walter Edwin. "The Biographical Element in the Novels of Mary Wollstonecraft Shelley," *PMLA*, 38:196–219 (March 1923).

────── *Shelley: His Life and Work.* 2 vols. Boston and New York: Houghton Mifflin Company, 1927.

Pfeffel, Gottlieb Konrad. *Poetische Versuche.* 3 vols. Vienna: F. A. Schraembl, 1791.

Polidori, John William. *The Diary of Dr. John William Polidori, 1816, Relating to Byron, Shelley, etc.*, ed. William Michael Rossetti. London: Elkin Mathews, 1911.

Potocka, Countess Anna. "Voyage d'Italie (1826–1827)," *La Revue hebdomadaire*, 6:457–477 (May 1898); 7:33–58, 172–190, 319–336, 458–478 (June 1898).

Pozzolini, Luigi. *Miscellanea di prose e poesie italiane.* Florence: Bencini, 1845.

*Rambles in Italy; In the Years 1816 . . . 17*, "By an American." Baltimore: N. G. Maxwell, 1818.

*The Retrospective Review*, vol. II. London: Charles and Henry Baldwin, 1820.

Rieger, James. "Lord Byron as 'Albè'," *KSJ*, 14:6–7 (Winter 1965).

Riemann, Hugo. *Musik Lexicon*, 11th ed., ed. Alfred Einstein. 2 vols. Berlin: Max Hesse, 1929.

Robertson, Lorraine. "The Journal and Notebooks of Claire Clairmont: Unpublished Passages," *KSMB*, 4:35–47 (1952).

────── "Unpublished Verses by Shelley," *MLR*, 48:181–184 (April 1953).

Robinson, Henry Crabb. *Henry Crabb Robinson on Books and Their Writers*, ed. Edith J. Morley. 3 vols. London: J. M. Dent & Sons, 1938.

Rogers, Neville. "Music at Marlow," *KSMB*, 5:20–25 (1953).

────── *Shelley at Work.* London: Oxford University Press, 1956.

Rogers, Samuel. *The Italian Journals of Samuel Rogers, Edited with an Account of Rogers' Life and Travel in Italy in 1814–1821*, ed. J. R. Hale. London: Faber and Faber, 1956.

Rolleston, Maud. *Talks with Lady Shelley.* London: George G. Harrap & Co., 1925.

[Romanelli, L.]. *Alcune Poesie di F. Pacchiani e T. Sgricci.* Arezzo: Belloti, 1885.

[Rose, W. S.]. *Letters from the North of Italy. Addressed to Henry Hallam, Esq.* 2 vols. London: John Murray, 1819.

Ross, Janet, and Nelly Erichsen. *The Story of Lucca.* London: J. M. Dent & Sons, 1912.

# Selected Bibliography

Rousseau, Jean-Jacques. *Emilius: Or an Essay on Education*, trans. Nugent. 2 vols. London: J. Nourse & P. Vaillant, 1763.

Salvioli, Giovanni, and Carlo Salvioli. *Bibliografia universale del teatro drammatico italiano*, vol. I (no more published). Venice: Carlo Ferrari, 1903.

Schiller, Johann Christoph Friedrich von. *The Poems of Schiller*, trans. Edgar A. Bowring. London: John W. Parker & Son, 1851.

—— *Wallenstein: A Drama*, trans. J. A. W. Hunter. London: Kegan Paul, Trench & Co., 1885.

Scott, Walter Sidney, ed. *Harriet and Mary: Being the Relations between Percy Bysshe Shelley, Harriet Shelley, Mary Shelley, and Thomas Jefferson Hogg.* London: The Golden Cockerel Press, 1944.

Shaw, J. Thomas, ed. *The Letters of Alexander Pushkin.* 3 vols. Bloomington: Indiana University Press, and Philadelphia: University of Pennsylvania Press, 1963.

Shelley, Lady [Jane]. *Shelley Memorials: From Authentic Sources.* London: Smith, Elder & Co., 1859.

[Shelley, Mary Wollstonecraft]. "The English in Italy," *Westminster Review*, 6:325–341 (October 1826).

[——] *The Fortunes of Perkin Warbeck.* 3 vols. London: Henry Colburn, 1830.

Shelley, Mary Wollstonecraft. *The Letters of Mary W. Shelley*, ed. Frederick L. Jones. 2 vols. Norman: University of Oklahoma Press, 1944.

—— *Mary Shelley's Journal*, ed. Frederick L. Jones. Norman: University of Oklahoma Press, 1947.

—— *Rambles in Germany and Italy, in 1840, 1842, and 1843.* 2 vols. London: Edward Moxon, 1844.

—— *Tales and Stories by Mary Wollstonecraft Shelley*, ed. Richard Garnett. London: William Patterson, 1891.

[——] *Valperga: Or, the Life and Adventures of Castruccio, Prince of Lucca.* 3 vols. London: G. & W. B. Whittaker, 1823.

[—— and Percy Bysshe Shelley]. *History of a Six Weeks' Tour through a Part of France, Switzerland, Germany, and Holland: With Letters Descriptive of a Sail Round the Lake of Geneva, and of the Glaciers of Chamouni.* London: T. Hookham, Jun. and C. and J. Ollier, 1817.

Shelley, Percy Bysshe. *The Complete Works of Percy Bysshe Shelley*, ed. Roger Ingpen and Walter E. Peck. 10 vols. London: Ernest Benn Ltd., 1926–1930 (the Julian edition).

—— *The Esdaile Notebook: A Volume of Early Poems by Percy*

*Bysshe Shelley*, ed. Kenneth Neill Cameron. New York: Alfred A. Knopf, 1964.

—— *The Esdaile Poems: Early Minor Poems from the "Esdaile Notebook,"* ed. Neville Rogers. Oxford: Clarendon Press, 1966.

—— *The Letters of Percy Bysshe Shelley*, ed. Frederick L. Jones. 2 vols. Oxford: Clarendon Press, 1964.

—— *The Prose Works of Percy Bysshe Shelley*, ed. H. Buxton Forman. 4 vols. London: Reeves and Turner, 1880.

*Shelley and His Circle* (The Carl H. Pforzheimer Library). Vols. I and II, ed. Kenneth Neill Cameron. Cambridge: Harvard University Press, 1961.

*Shelley — Leigh Hunt: How Friendship Made History*, ed. R. Brimley Johnson. London: Ingpen and Grant, 1928.

Shelley, Sir Percy Florence and Lady [Jane]. *Shelley and Mary.* 4 vols. Privately printed, [1882]. Edward Dowden's annotated copy, in the British Museum, Ashley 4088, includes notes from Claire Clairmont's papers, from the period when they were in Forman's collection. A typescript made from this copy is in the Manuscript Room of the Duke University Library.

[Smith, Horace, and James Smith]. *Rejected Addresses, or the New Theatrum Poetarum.* London: John Miller, 1812.

Sotheby and Company. *Catalogue of Valuable English Printed Books, Autograph Letters and Historical Documents Comprising the Property of Signor Neri Farina Cini, et al.* For sale November 9 and 10, 1964.

—— *Catalogue of Valuable Printed Books, Autograph Letters and Historical Documents.* For sale March 14, 1967. Includes further materials from the property of Neri Farina Cini.

Southey, Robert. *The Correspondence of Robert Southey with Caroline Bowles to Which Are Added: Correspondence with Shelley, and Southey's Dreams*, ed. Edward Dowden. Dublin: Hodges, Figgis, & Co., 1881.

Spohr, Louis. *Louis Spohr's Autobiography.* 2 vols. London: Longman, Green, Longman, Roberts, & Green, 1865.

Staël-Holstein, Anne Louise Germaine de. *Germany.* 3 vols. London: John Murray, 1813.

Starke, Mariana. *Travels on the Continent: Written for the Use and Particular Information of Travellers.* London: John Murray, 1820.

Stendhal. See Marie Henri Beyle.

*Storia genealogica delle famiglie illustri italiane*, ed. Ulisse Diligenti. 2 vols. Florence, 1891–1893.

Summers, Montague. *A Gothic Bibliography.* London: The Fortune Press, [1940].

# Selected Bibliography

Tantini, Francesco. *Opuscoli scientifici*. 3 vols. Pisa: Nistri, 1812–1830.

—— *Pensieri, reminiscenze ed elogi del Professore Francesco Tantini*. Hamburg: Augusto Campe, 1833.

Tighe, George William. "Memoria intorno a una nuova varietà di patata con alcune esperienze riguardo alla coltura ed all' uso delle patate in generale," *Giornalo agrario toscano*, nos. 11–14. Florence, 1829–1830.

Timbs, John. *Curiosities of London*. London: David Bogue, 1855.

Tipaldo, Emilio de, ed. *Biografia degli italiani illustri nelle scienze, lettere ed arti del secolo XVIII, e de' contemporanei compilata da letterati italiani di ogni provincia*. 10 vols. Venice: Alvisopoli, 1834–1845.

Trelawny, Edward John. *Letters of Edward John Trelawny*, ed. H. Buxton Forman. London: Henry Frowde, Oxford University Press, 1910.

Turner, J. M. W., sketchbooks. See Finberg.

Varley, D. H. "Henry Willey Reveley — First Colonial Civil Engineer at the Cape," *Quarterly Bulletin of the South African Library*, 12:118–121 (March 1958).

Viviani, Ugo. *Un Genio aretino: Tommaso Sgricci: Poeta tragico improvvisatore*. No. 26 of *Collana di publicazioni storiche e letterarie aretine*. Arezzo: 1928.

Viviani Della Robbia, Enrica. *Vita di una donna (l'Emily di Shelley)*. Florence: G. C. Sansoni, 1936.

[Waldie, Jane]. *Sketches Descriptive of Italy in the Years 1816 and 1817 with a Brief Account of Travels in Various Parts of France and Switzerland in the Same Years*. 4 vols. London: John Murray, 1820.

Waliszewski, Kazimierz, ed. *Souvenirs de la Comtesse Golovine née Princesse Galitzine, 1766–1821*. Paris: Plon-Nourrit, 1910.

White, Newman Ivey. *Shelley*. 2 vols. New York: Alfred A. Knopf, 1940.

—— *The Unextinguished Hearth: Shelley and His Contemporary Critics*. Durham, North Carolina: Duke University Press, 1938.

Wilmot, Catherine. *An Irish Peer on the Continent (1801–1803): Being a Narrative of the Tour of Stephen, 2nd Earl Mount Cashell, through France, Italy, etc., as Related by Catherine Wilmot*, ed. Thomas U. Sadleir. London: Williams and Norgate, 1920.

Wilmot, Martha (Mrs. W. Bradford). *The Russian Journals of Martha and Catherine Wilmot; Being an Account by Two Irish Ladies of Their Adventures in Russia as Guests of the Celebrated Princess Daschkaw, Containing Vivid Descriptions of Contemporary Court*

# Manuscript Sources

*Life and Society, and Lively Anecdotes of Many Interesting Historical Characters, 1803–1808,* ed. Marchioness of Londonderry and H. M. Hyde. London: Macmillan & Co., Ltd., 1934.

Wilson, Harriette. *The Memoirs of Harriette Wilson, Written by Herself.* 2 vols. London: Privately printed for the Navarre Society, Ltd., 1924.

Wise, Thomas James. *The Ashley Catalogue.* 11 vols. London: Privately printed, 1922–1936.

—— *A Shelley Library.* London: Privately printed, 1924.

Wollstonecraft, Mary. *A Vindication of the Rights of Woman,* Vol. I (no more published). London: J. Johnson, 1792.

Woodcock, George. *William Godwin: A Biographical Study.* London: The Porcupine Press, 1946.

# *Manuscript Sources*

Abinger Manuscripts: The papers of William Godwin, Mary Wollstonecraft, and the Shelleys, in the collection of James Richard Scarlett, eighth Baron Abinger.

> Lord Abinger's grandmother, Bessie Florence Gibson, was adopted as an infant by Sir Percy Florence Shelley and Lady Shelley, who had no children of their own. I have consulted both the original collection and the microfilm copy of the manuscripts on twenty-six reels in the Duke University Library. The materials I have chiefly used are the journal of Shelley and Mary, the diary of William Godwin, and the letters of Claire Clairmont, Ralou d'Argyropoulo, Fanny Imlay, Horace Smith, and Lady Mount Cashell.

British Museum

Journals of Claire Clairmont (Ashley 394, Ashley 2819).

Two leaflets of miscellanea by Claire Clairmont (Ashley 2820).

Two letters by Claire Clairmont in "The Story of Allegra: Comprised in a Series of Letters Written by Byron, Claire and Their Friend Trelawny, with Portraits and Three Locks of Hair" [Byron's, Allegra's, and Claire's] (Ashley 4752).

Twelve letters from Edward John Trelawny to Claire Clairmont, 1822–1829 (Ashley 5119).

Letters of Thomas Jefferson Hogg to Jane Williams, 1822–1851 (Additional MSS. 41,686).

Papers of Jane Williams, 1819–1875 (Additional MSS. 43,805).

Papers of Lega Zambelli (Additional MSS. 46,871–46,882).

Clairmont Family Papers: The papers of Claire Clairmont and Charles

# Manuscript Sources

Gaulis Clairmont and his descendants, inherited by Mary Claire Bally-Clairmont and Christoph W. Clairmont-von Gonzenbach.

This collection has suffered some losses since World War II. The short Russian journal was lost before I first studied the collection in 1949; two portraits and most of the journals of Pauline Clairmont have been lost since then. The rest has survived virtually intact, including twenty-seven letters by Claire Clairmont, 1850–1879, and a large number of letters by Charles Gaulis Clairmont and his family. There are also family portraits and documents.

Duke University Library: Notebooks and correspondence of Newman Ivey White.

Farina Cini Papers: The papers of Lady Mount Cashell and her family, inherited by Mr. Neri Farina Cini.

I consulted these papers, as well as the books surviving from Lady Mount Cashell's library, on a visit to San Marcello Pistoiese, in 1952. The collection has since been broken up, by private and public sale. A partial inventory is in McAleer, *The Sensitive Plant*, pp. 233–235. See also Sotheby and Company catalogues for sales on November 10, 1964, and March 14, 1967.

Harvard University, Houghton Library: Letter from Percy Bysshe Shelley to Claire Clairmont, postmarked "8 AGOSTO" [1821] (MS Eng 258 F).

Murray Manuscripts: Thirty-five letters from Claire Clairmont to Byron, 1816–1820, in the collection of Sir John Murray.

New York Public Library, Henry W. and Albert A. Berg Collection: Letters of Pauline Clairmont, Charles Fairfax Murray, and Henry Roderick Newman about the sale of Claire Clairmont's estate (1879–1890).

Oxford University, Bodleian Library:
Papers of Robert Finch (MS. Finch d. 9, 21).
Letters of Charles Gaulis Clairmont to Claire Clairmont and Mary Shelley (Shelley Adds. d. 5).

University of California at Berkeley, Library: Papers of Roger Ingpen.

University of Texas, Library: Letter from Claire Clairmont to Dina Williams, December 31, 1862.

Vienna State Archives: Dossier Clairmont, 1822; described and illustrated in Grylls, *Claire Clairmont*, pp. 170–171.

# Claire Clairmont's Reading List
## and List of Performances Attended

Included here are an alphabetized list of the reading Claire mentions in her journals, and a list of the performances, theatrical and musical, that she attended or in which she herself took part. Their wide range demonstrates the remarkable extent of her interests and her continuing self-education. Claire's journals show that she studied languages systematically until she could read French, Italian, and German fluently. She was able to read Spanish literature and to translate Latin; she studied Greek and made some attempt at Russian.

The two most obvious influences on Claire's education were her stepfather, William Godwin, and Percy Bysshe Shelley. Godwin's radical humanitarianism directed her early intellectual development, but Shelley, from 1814 until his death in 1822, was her principal mentor, reinforcing, broadening, and deepening her range of reading. A third major influence began in 1820 when she arrived with the Shelleys in Pisa, met Lady Mount Cashell, and immersing herself in the library at Casa Silva organized it and read extensively in the rich collection of Irish and political works she found there. After Shelley's death and Claire's removal to Russia, a fourth impact on her reading came from her fellow tutor, Hermann Gambs, and the strong element of German romanticism he provided.

## Reading List

This list includes not only the works Claire said she read but also works that were read aloud to her and, appropriately noted, works and writers (Aristotle's *Poetics* for example) that she alludes to and presumably did read. When there is reason to believe she used a particular edition, I have cited that publication date; otherwise the date given is usually of the first edition.

# Claire's Reading List

The relation between Claire's reading and that of the Shelleys may be studied by comparing the list below with the catalogue of Shelley's reading compiled by Frederick L. Jones (Shelley, *Letters*, II, 467–488) and with the reading lists and indexes in his editions of *Mary Shelley's Journal* and *The Letters of Mary W. Shelley*. I have inserted an S. or an M. after the journal date in the entries below when there is evidence that Shelley or Mary also read the work.

Aarenstein. *See* "Ditmar von Aarenstein"

Aeschylus: *Prometheus Bound*, in Greek and English. (1820: end of Third Journal, and December 20; S., M.)

Aikin, John, and Anna Letitia Barbauld: *Evenings at Home; or, the Juvenile Budget Opened*, 6 vols., 1792–1796 (1825: November 23–24 [December 5–6]; S.)

Alfieri, Count Vittorio: *Memoirs of the Life and Writings of Victor Alfieri: Written by Himself*, 2 vols., 1810 (1814: October 20; S., M.); *Myrrha, a Tragedy*, in vol. III of *The Tragedies of Alfieri*, trans. Charles Lloyd, 3 vols., 1815 (1819: May 18; S., M.)

Anacreon (in Greek; 1814: September 23; S., M.); "Ode to the Cicala" (ode no. 43), translated (1820: July 12); *see also* Moore, Thomas

Antiphilus of Byzantium: "Epigram upon Julius Agricola," *Anthologia Palatina*, in Latin (1820: end of Third Journal)

*Arabian Nights*, stories told by Gambs (1825: August 18–19 [30–31]; M.)

Ariosto, Lodovico: *Orlando furioso* (1825: December 12 [24]; S., M.)

Aristotle: *Poetics*, referred to (1820: end of Third Journal; 1825; May 30 [June 11])

Arnstein (or Arnsteiner), Benedict David. *See* "Ditmar von Aarenstein"

Astius, D. Fridericus: *Platonis Phaedrus*, 1810, talked of (1825: November 18 [30])

Bacon, Francis: *De augmentis scientiarum*, 1623 (1820: March 25); *The Essayes or Counsels, Civill and Morall*, 1625 – "Of Beauty" (*ca.* 1828: Miscellanea, p. 423), "Of Riches" (1821: April 14)

Baker, David Erskine: *Biographia dramatica; or, a Companion to the Playhouse* . . . , 3 vols., 1812 (1820: March 13–14, 21–22)

Barbauld, Anna Letitia. *See* Aikin, John

[Barbé-Marbois, Marquis F. de]. See *Lettres de Madame la Marquise de Pompadour.*

Barnard, Mrs. Caroline: *The Parent's Offering; or Tales for Children*, 2 vols., 1813 (1820: August 19)

Barrière, Jean François. *See* Berville, Saint Albin

Barruel, l'Abbé (Augustin): *Mémoires pour servir à l'histoire du jacobinisme*, 4 vols., 1797–98 (1814: August 24–26, October 9, 11–12; S., M.)

[Barthélemy, Abbé Jean Jacques]: *Voyage du jeune Anacharsis en Grèce*,

*dans le milieu du quatrième siècle avant l'ère vulgaire,* 5 vols.,
1788 (1818: January 22–24, 28; S., M.)

Beaumarchais, P.-A. Caron de: *Le Barbier de Séville,* 1775 (1820:
July 16)

Beaumont, Francis, and John Fletcher (also Philip Massinger, Thomas
Middleton, and William Rowley): *The Beggars Bush* (1820:
March 17–18); *The Elder Brother* (1820: April 30); *The Noble
Gentleman* (1820: April 27); *The Tragedy of Thierry King of
France, and His Brother Theodoret* (1820: May 10; S., M.); *Wit
at Several Weapons* (1820: April 22); *Wit without Money* (1820:
April 22); *The Woman Hater* (1820: March 18–19); *Woman
Pleased* (1820: May 10); *The Woman's Prize, or the Tamer
Tam'd* (1820: April 19, 22)

Becker, Carl Friedrich: Vol. IX of *Die Weltgeschichte, für Kinder und
Kinderlehrer,* 9 vols., 1801–05 (1825: September 22 [October 4])

Belloy. *See* Buirette de Belloy

Berington, Joseph: *A Literary History of the Middle Ages,* 1814 (1818:
February 22)

Berville, Saint Albin, and Jean François Barrière: *Mémoires de Madame
Roland,* 2 vols., 1821 (1825: May 12–14 [24–26])

Bible, The: Gospel According to St. Matthew (1820: January 8; S., M.)

*Bibliothèque universelle des dames,* 20 vols., 1785–88 (M.): "Cléomades
et Claremonde" (1819: May 2); "La Fleur des Batailles" (1819:
April 17); "Flores et Blanche-fleur" (1819: May 2); "Guérin de
Montglave" (1819: April 23); "Histoire de Rigda et de Regner
Lodbrog" (1819: April 18); "Huon de Bordeaux" (1819: April
20, 22; M.); "Le Petit Jehan de Saintré" (1819: May 4); "Pierre
de Provence et la belle Maguelone, fille du roi de Naples" (1819:
May 2)

*Bibliothèque universelle des sciences, belles-lettres, et arts,* 120 vols.,
1816–35 (1821: February 23)

Birkbeck, Morris: *Letters from Illinois,* 1818, and *Notes on a Journey
in America, from the Coast of Virginia to the Territory of Illinois,*
1818 (1819: June 10; S.) It is not clear whether Claire read one
or both of the Birkbeck books.

*Blackwood's Magazine* (1825: June 12 [24])

Blasche, Bernard Heinrich: *Papyro-Plastics; or the Art of Modelling in
Paper,* trans. Daniel Boileau, 1824 (1826: end of Fifth Journal)

Boccaccio, Giovanni: *Decameron* (1819: May 10–11, 19, 21–23, 25–
26, 30–31, June 1; 1820: June 30; S., M.)

Bock, Baron Félix de: *Les Chevaliers des sept montagnes . . . ,* trans.
from the German, 3 vols., 1800 (1820: April 9)

Bolingbroke, Viscount. *See* St. John, Henry

Bondi, Clemente: "Le Conversazioni: Poemetto, in *Poemetti italiani,* 12
vols., 1797 (1820: November 19)

Boswell, James: *The Life of Samuel Johnson,* 2 vols., 1791 (1820:
May 23–28; S., M.)

# Claire's Reading List

[Bret, Antoine]: *Mémoires sur la vie de Mademoiselle de Lenclos*, 2 vols., 1750–51 (1819: March 17)

Brooke, Charlotte: *Reliques of Irish Poetry* . . . , 1789 (1820: September 15, 20, 24)

Brotier, Gabriel. *See* Tacitus

Brown, Charles Brockden: *Ormond; or, the Secret Witness*, 1799 (1820: September 1; S.)

Brydone, Patrick: *A Tour through Sicily and Malta, in a Series of Letters to William Beckford* . . . , 2 vols., 1773 (1820: April 23–26; M.)

Buirette de Belloy, Pierre-Laurent: *Gabrielle de Vergy, tragédie*, 1770 (1821: December 22)

Bürger, Gottfried August: "Frau Schnipps: Ein Mährlein, halb lustig, halb ernsthaft, sammt angehängter Apologie" (1825: May 12 [24])

Burns, Robert: "Lament for James Earl of Glencairn" (1821: November 18); "Tam O'Shanter" (1821: November 18; S.)

Byrom, John: "Epigram on the Feuds between Handel and Bononcini," (falsely attributed by Claire to Swift), in *Miscellaneous Poems*, 2 vols., 1773 (1820: July 9)

Byron, Lord: *Childe Harold's Pilgrimage*, canto iii, 1816 (1820: October 30; S., M.); *Don Juan*, cantos i–ii, 1819 (1820: January 3; S., M.); "Fare Thee Well," parodied by Claire (1821: November 28); *Lara*, 1814 (1814: September 17; S., M.); *Mazeppa*, 1819 (1820: January 5; M.)

Calderón de la Barca, Pedro: *La Cisma de Ingalaterra* (1820: February 11–12, 16, 19, 21, 23–25; S.); *Los Cabellos de Absalón* (1820: January 2, 6; S.); *Guárdate del agua mansa* (1820: December 12); *La Vida es sueño* (1820: January 7–9); *La Virgen del Sagrario* (1820: May 6–11)

Campan, Jeanne Louise Henriette: *Mémoires sur la vie privée de Marie Antoinette, reine de France* . . . *suivis de souvenirs et anecdotes historiques sur les règnes de Louis XIV, de Louis XV et de Louis XVI*, 3 vols., 1822 (1825: September 27 [October 9])

Campbell, Thomas [the poet]: "Lines Written on Visiting a Scene in Argyleshire," 1800 (1821: October 28)

Campbell, Thomas: *A Philosophical Survey of the South of Ireland, in a Series of Letters to John Watkinson, M.D.*, 1777 (1820: September 9–10, 12)

Caritat, Marie Jean Antoine Nicolo, Marquis de Condorcet: *Vie de Voltaire par le Marquis de Condorcet; suivie des mémoires de Voltaire, écrits par lui-même*, 1789 (1820: March 26, 29, April 5, 12; S., M.)

Castlehaven, Earl of. *See* Touchet, James

*Cause célèbre: Procès des prévenus de l'assassinat de M.* [Antoine Bernardin] *Fualdès* . . . , 1817 (1820: May 12–13; S., M.)

Cellini, Benvenuto: *Eine Geschichte des XVI Jahrhunderts*, trans. J. W.

# Claire's Reading List

von Goethe, 3 vols., 1798 (1825: December 26–27 [1826: January 7–8])

Cenci family, manuscript of (1819: May 14; S., M.)

Charles d'Orléans: "Rondeau" (1822: January 17)

Chateaubriand, François René de: *De Buonaparte, des Bourbons, et de la nécessité de se rallier à nos princes légitimes* . . . , 1814 (1820: January 29)

Cobbett, William (1819: March 13–14); *Cobbett's Weekly Political Register* (1818: January 19; 1820: June 9, 14); *A Year's Residence in the United States of America*, 1818 (1819: after June 17)

Coleridge, Samuel Taylor: "Christabel" (1820: August 16; S., M.); "France: an Ode" (1820: end of Third Journal; S., M.); "The Rime of the Ancient Mariner" (1814: August 30, September 15, October 5; S., M.)

Condorcet, Marquis de. *See* Caritat, M. J. A.

Coxe, Henry: *Picture of Italy: Being a Guide to the Antiquities and Curiosities of That Classical and Interesting Country* . . . , 1815 (1820: December 17)

Crébillon, Prosper Jolyot de, *Rhadamisthe et Zénobie*, 1711 (1821: December 29). *See also Lettres de Madame la Marquise de Pompadour*

Cuoco, Vincenzo: *Saggio storico sulla rivoluzione di Napoli*, 3 vols., 1800 (1820: May 6, 20, June 5–7, 28–29, July 3, 5–8, 11, 24, 26–27, 29, August 10, 16)

Curran, William Henry: *The Life of the Right Honourable John Philpot Curran, Late Master of the Rolls in Ireland*, 2 vols., 1819 (1820: March 15)

Dante Alighieri: discussed (1814: October 18); *Inferno* (1814: end of First Journal; 1820: December 9; 1821: April 12; S., M.); *Purgatorio* (1819: May 15–20, December 2, 6; S., M.); *Paradiso* (1819: May 1; 1827: January 30; S.)

Da Ponte, Lorenzo: *Così fan tutte*, Mozart's libretto, 1790 (1818: February 26); *Le Mariage de Figaro* (after Beaumarchais), Mozart's libretto, 1786 (1818: February 15)

Davanzati Bostichi. *See* Tacitus

Davy, Sir Humphrey (1820: April 8; S., M.)

Day, Thomas: *The History of Sandford and Merton*, 3 vols., 1783–89 (1821: July 25; M.)

De Beaunoir [pseudonym of Alexandre Louis Bertrand Robineau]: *Jérome Pointu: Comédie*, 1781 (1820: July 16)

Demosthenes: Latin speeches, translated by Claire (1820: July 28, 31, August 10, 14, 18; S.)

Desodoards. *See* Fantin des Odoards

Diogenes Laertius: *Diogenes Laertii de vitis, dogmatibus et apophthegmatibus clarorum philosophorum libri decem, graece et latine*, 1759 (1820: June 30; S.)

"Ditmar von Aarenstein," unidentified, possibly a work by Benedict David

# Claire's Reading List

Arnstein or Arnsteiner (1821: December 31; 1822: January 3, 9, 13)

Drummond, Sir William: *Academical Questions*, 1805, discussed (1825: December 2 [14]; S., M.)

Dubois, Madame: *Histoire de Madame Dubois, écrite par elle-même,* 1769 (*ca.* 1828: Miscellanea, p. 418)

[Du Bois, Edward]: *St. Godwin: A Tale of the Sixteenth, Seventeenth, and Eighteenth Century,* by "Count Reginald De St. Leon," 1800 (1814: October 6; S., M.)

Dureau de La Malle. *See* Tacitus

Edgeworth, Maria: *Comic Dramas, in Three Acts,* 1817 (1820: July 19; M.); *The Parent's Assistant, or Stories for Children,* 3rd. ed., 6 vols., 1800 (1825: September 14 [26], 18–21 [30–October 3], October 10–12 [22–24], 24 [November 5], 26–27 [November 7–8], 29–30 [November 10–11], November 1–3 [13–15], 26 [December 8]); *Rosamond: A Sequel to Early Lessons,* 2 vols, 1821 (1825: November 5 [17], 8 [20], 12 [24])

Edgeworth, Maria, and Richard Lovell Edgeworth: *Essay on Irish Bulls,* 1802 (1820: July 19, 21)

Edgeworth, Richard Lovell: *Memoirs of Richard Lovell Edgeworth . . . Concluded by . . . Maria Edgeworth,* 2 vols., 1820 (1821: July 11–12; M.)

Edinburgh newspapers (1825: June 12 [24])

*Edinburgh Review, The* (1818: January 22; 1819: March 7; 1820: June 11, 14, 25, 27; 1825: September 22–23 [October 4–5]; S., M.)

Encyclopedia, The, probably *Encyclopaedia Britannica,* 5th ed., 20 vols., 1814–17 (1820: April 28; S., M.)

*Examiner, The. See* Hunt, Leigh

Fantin des Odoards, Antoine Étienne Nicolas: *Histoire philosophique de la révolution de France,* 10 vols., 1807 (1825: September 26 [October 8])

Farquhar, George: *Love and a Bottle* (1820: April 13); *Plays* (1820: May 16)

Fletcher, John. *See* Beaumont, Francis

Forsyth, Joseph: *Remarks on Antiquities, Arts, and Letters during an Excursion in Italy in the Years 1802 and 1803,* 1813 (1819: April 10; 1825: December 8 [20], 10 [22], 12 [24], 14–16 [26–28], 18 [30], 22 [1826: January 4]; S., M.)

[Forteguerri, Niccolò]: *Il Ricciardetto di Niccolò Carteromaco,* 1738 (1819: April 21, 23–30; S., M.)

Fualdès, Antoine Bernardin. See *Cause célèbre*

*Galignani's Messenger* (Paris) (1822: January 7; S., M.)

Gambs, Chrétien-Hermann: *Moïse,* 1836 (1825: May 20 [June 1], May 24 [June 5]); *A Russian tale* (1825: July 26 [August 7]); "Skiöld" (1825: May 15 [27], 18 [30]); "Uranie" (1825: May 26 [June 7], May 29 [June 10]); Verses to Claire on her name-day

# Claire's Reading List

(1825: August 12 [24]); "Zwey Blicke in der Unendlichkeit"
(1825: June 25 [July 7])

Genlis, Stéphanie Félicité Brulart, Countess de: *La Duchesse de la
Vallière*, 2 vols., 1804 (1822: March 27)

German Gazettes (1825: October 8 [20])

Gerning, Johann Isaac von: *Reise durch Oesterreich und Italien*, 3 vols.,
1802 (1821: May 5–7, 10–11, 21–22)

Giannone, Pietro: *Dell' Istoria civile del regno di Napoli*, 4 vols., 1723
(1820: October 27, November 3–4, 6, 8–9, 13–14)

Gilbert, Nicolas Joseph Laurent: A satire upon the French, and "Ode
IX: Imitée de plusieurs psaumes" (1825: June 11 [23])

Godwin, William: *An Enquiry Concerning the Principles of Political
Justice*, 2 vols., 1793 (1814: September 19, October 4–7, 9–11,
13, 19–20, 24, November 2–3, 7–8; talk of, 1825: December 2
[14]; S., M.); *Memoirs of the Author of a Vindication of the Rights
of Woman*, 1798 (1814: September 3; M.); *St. Leon: A Tale of
the Sixteenth Century*, 3 vols., 1799 (1814: October 6, 14; S.,
M.); *Things as They Are: Or the Adventures of Caleb Williams*,
3 vols., 1794 (1820: August 8–10; S., M.)

Goethe, Johann Wolfgang von, Life of (1825: July 24 [August 5], 28
[August 9])

Goethe, Johann Wolfgang von: *Aus meinem Leben. Dichtung und Wahrheit*, 4 vols., 1811–22 (1822: March 9, 11–18, 21–26, April
3, 7–10; S.); *Egmont*, 1788 (1825: May 16 [28]); *Faust*, 1808
(1821: October 17–19, 21, 23; S.); *Die Leiden des jungen
Werther*, 1774 (1821: May 29, 31, June 1–5, 7, 9–10; S., M.);
*Wilhelm Meisters Lehrjahre*, 4 vols., 1795–96 (1825: May 20–22
[June 1–3]; S.); "Mignon" (*ca.* 1829/30, Miscellanea, p. 433)

Goldoni, Carlo: (1821: April 28; 1822: February 20); *L'Adulatore*
(1821: May 20); *L'Avaro fastoso* (1821: March 29); *La Buona
Moglie* (1821: May 2); *La Cameriera brillante* (1821: April 29);
*Il Cavaliere di buon gusto* (1821: June 18); *La Donna volubile*
(1821: May 18); *Le Donne curiose* (1822: March 26); *I Due
Pantaloni o i mercatanti* (1822: March 26); *La Famiglia dell'
antiquario* (1821: April 27); *Le Femmine puntigliose* (1821:
May 13); *Il Feudatario* (1821: April 30); *Gli Innamorati* (1821:
May 13); *Il Matrimonio per concorso* (1822: March 31); *La
Moglie saggia* (1821: April 30); *Il Poeta fanatico* (1822: March
29); *Il Tutore* (1821: May 13); *La Vedova scaltra* (1821: April
27)

Goldsmith, Oliver: *The History of Greece, from the Earliest State, to the
Death of Alexander the Great*, 2 vols., 1812 (1818: January 24);
*She Stoops to Conquer* (1814: October 24; M.); *The Vicar of
Wakefield*, 2 vols., 1766 (1820: June 15; M.)

[Gordon, Alexander]: *Travels in Germany and the Illyrian Provinces*
[1825?], probably the book Claire read (1825: July 17 [29])

Grévin, Jacques: *La Mort de César*, 1560 (1822: January 17)

# Claire's Reading List

Hafiz Shirazi: *Divan*, gazel iii (1822: end of Fourth Journal)

[Hare, Julius Charles]: "On the German Drama: No. 1, Oehlenschlaeger," in *Olliers Literary Miscellany in Prose and Verse*, 1820 (1821: January 26; S.)

"History of England, written in french by a Jew after the manner of the Bible," unidentified (1820: June 25)

Hoffmann, Ernst Theodor Wilhelm (1826: January 1–2 [13–14]); A novel (1825: November 11 [23]); *Fantasiestücke in Callot's Manier*, 2 vols., 1819 — "Kreisleriana" (1825: December 31 [1826: January 12]), "Ritter Gluck" (1825: December 30 [1826: January 11]); *Nachtstücke*, 2 vols., 1817 — "Das Majorat" (1825: November 12 [24])

[Hogg, Thomas Jefferson]: *Memoirs of Prince Alexy Haimatoff*, by "John Brown," 1813 (1814: October 3 [?], 4, 19, 29, November 6; S., M.)

[Holberg, Ludvig]: *A Journey to the World Under-Ground. By Nicholas Klimius*, 1742, possibly the work referred to by Claire (1814: October 7. M.)

Homer: *Iliad*, see Pope, Alexander; *Odyssey* (1820: August 19–20; S., M.)

Hope, Thomas: *Anastasius: Or, Memoirs of a Greek*, 3 vols., 1819 (1821: August 30–31, September 1–2; S., M.)

Houwald, Ernst Christoph von: *Das Bild: Trauerspiel in fünf Akten*, 1822 (1825: September 15–17 [27–29])

Hume, David: "An Enquiry Concerning Human Understanding," in *Essays and Treatises*, 2 vols., 1809 (1820: December 15; S., M.)

Hunt, Leigh: "The Daughter of Hippocrates," *Indicator*, June 14, 1820 (1820: December 12)

—— ed.: *The Examiner* (1820: June 9; S., M.); *The Indicator*, 1819–1821 (1820: December 12–13, 15–16; S., M.)

Hutchinson, Mrs. Lucy: *Memoirs of the Life of Colonel Hutchinson . . . to Which Is Prefixed the Life of Mrs. Hutchinson, Written by Herself, a Fragment*, 1806 (1821: August 7, 15; M.)

*Indicator, The.* See Hunt, Leigh

"Inno di Guerra," by a Neapolitan, unidentified (1821: March 7)

Irish Pamphlets, probably including [Margaret King Moore, Countess Mount Cashell]: *A Few Words in Favour of Ireland by Way of a Reply to a Pamphlet Called "An Impartial View of the Causes Leading This Country to the Necessity of an UNION,"* by No Lawyer, 1799; *A Hint to the Inhabitants of Ireland by a Native*, 1800; and *Reply to a Ministerial Pamphlet, Entitled "Considerations upon the State of Public Affairs in the Year 1799, Ireland,"* by a Philanthropist, 1799 (1820: January 27–29)

[Irumberry, Charles-Marie, d']: *Voyage à Constantinople, en Italie et aux îles de l'Archipel, par l'Allemagne et la Hongrie*, 1799 (reference may be to Martin, q. v.; 1819: March 10)

"Islavsky Gazette," written by Claire, Gambs, etc. (1825: June 6 [18],

# Claire's Reading List

20 [July 2], 22 [July 4], 27 [July 9], July 4 [16], 11 [23], 18 [30], August 1 [13])

James I: *The King's Quair* (1825: May 13 [25])

Johnson, Samuel: *The History of Rasselas*, 2 vols., 1759 (1814: September 16; M.)

Jonson, Ben: *Sejanus His Fall* (1820: April 16, 18–19; S., M.)

Jouy, Victor Joseph Étienne (*called* de): *L'Hermite de la Chaussée-d'Antin, ou observations sur les moeurs et les usages parisiens au commencement du XIXe siècle*, 5 vols., 1812–14 (1825: June 21 [July 3]); *L'Hermite de la Guiane, ou observations sur les moeurs et les usages français au commencement du XIXe siècle*, 3 vols., 1816 (1825: June 22 [July 4])

Kant. *See* Villers, Charles

Keats, John: *Endymion*, 1818 (1820: September 26–27; 1821: April 14–15; S.); *Lamia, Isabella, the Eve of St. Agnes, and Other Poems*, 1820 — "Hyperion" (1820: November 10; 1821: February 27; S., M.), "Isabella; or, the Pot of Basil" (1820: October 15; S., M.), "Lamia" (1820: November 8; S., M.)

Kelly, Hugh: *False Delicacy, ou La Fausse Délicatesse*, trans. Marie Jeanne Riccoboni, 1818 (1821: December 22)

Klinger, Friedrich Maximilian von: *Travels before the Flood* . . . , 2 vols., 1796 (1820: January 28, February 5, 7; S., M.)

Kotzebue, August Friedrich Ferdinand von: "Geschichten" (1821: June 27); *Possen, die Zeit beachtend, bey Gelegenheit des Rückzugs der Franzosen. Seitenstück zum Flussgott Nieman* . . . , 1813 (1821: May 16, 20)

La Boétie, Étienne de: *Discours de la servitude volontaire*, also known as *Le Contre-un, ca.* 1553 (1820: Claire translates, March 1, 3, 5, 10, 15–22; she transcribes, March 24–25, 27–31, April 1–3)

La Motte-Fouqué, Friedrich Heinrich Karl, Baron de: *Die Cypressenkranze* (1825: May 15 [27]); *Sintram and His Companions: A Romance*, trans. Julius C. Hare, 1820 (1821: January 10; S., M.); *Der Zauberring: Ein Ritterroman*, 3 vols., 1812 (1825: August 18 [30], 20 [September 1])

Lawrence, Sir James Henry: *The Empire of the Nairs; or, the Rights of Women*, 4 vols., 1811 (1814: September 26; S., M.)

Lefanu, Alicia: *Helen Monteagle*, 3 vols., 1818 (1818: February 8; M.)

Lemierre, Antoine Marin: *Hypermnestre*, 1758 (1821: December 29)

Lenclos. *See* Bret, Antoine

Lessing, Gotthold Ephraim: *Hamburgische Dramaturgie*, 2 vols., 1767–68 (ca. 1828: Miscellanea, p. 421)

*Lettres de Madame la Marquise de Pompadour; depuis 1753 jusqu'à 1762 inclusivement* . . . , 2 vols., London, 1771 — fictitious correspondence attributed to the Marquis F. de Barbé-Marbois or to Prosper Jolyot de Crébillon (1819: April 1, 4)

Lewis, Matthew Gregory: *The Monk: A Romance*, 3 vols., 1796 (1814:

# Claire's Reading List

September 22–23; S., M.); *Tales of Wonder*, 2 vols., 1801 (1814: September 24; M. [?])

*Life of Joanna Southcott* . . . , 1814 (1814: September 23)

Lingard, John: *Tracts Occasioned by the Publication of a Charge Delivered to the Clergy of the Diocese of Durham by Shute, Bishop of Durham*, 1813 (1825: October 19–20 [31–November 1])

Lives of the Saints (1825: October 10 [22], 12 [24])

Locke, John: *An Essay Concerning Human Understanding*, 2 vols., 19th ed., 1793 (1820: February 13, 17–18, 21, 24, April 14–15, 17–19, 22, 29, May 9; S., M.)

*London Monthly Review* (1825: August 28 [September 9], September 1 [13]); review of Shute, *A Letter to the Clergy of the Diocese of Sarum*, issue of February 1790 (1825: September 2 [14])

Louvet de Couvray, Jean-Baptiste: *Narrative of the Dangers to Which I Have Been Exposed, since the 31st of May, 1793*, 1795 (1814: October 31–November 1; S., M.)

Lucas, Charles: *The Infernal Quixote: A Tale of the Day*, 4 vols., 1801 (1819: May 24)

"Lunatic Asylums," in *The Edinburgh Review*, August 1817 (1818: January 22)

Lyall, Robert: *The Character of the Russians, and a Detailed History of Moscow*, 1823, discussed (1825: December 9 [21])

Machiavelli, Niccolò: *Belfagor*, first published as *Novella piacevolissima*, 1545 (1820: November 30); *Discorsi . . . sopra la prima deca di Tito Livio* . . . , 1531 (1820: December 11)

MacKenzie, Henry: *The Man of Feeling*, 1771 (1814: November 8)

Marmontel, Jean François: *Memoirs of Marmontel, Written by Himself*, 4 vols., 1805 (1825: June 17 [29], 19–20 [July 1–2])

[Martin, Abbé Guillaume]: *Voyage à Constantinople, fait à l'occasion de l'ambassade de M. le Comte de Choiseul-Gouffier à la Porte ottomane*, 1819 — reference may be to C.-M. d'Irumberry, *q. v.* (1819: March 10)

Massinger, Philip. See Beaumont, Francis

Matiouchkin, Fedor Fedorovitch: *Le Nord de la Sibérie, voyage parmi les peuplades de la Russie asiatique et dans la mer glaciale* . . . , 2 vols., 1843, discussed (1825: December 9 [21])

Medwin, Thomas: *Journal of the Conversations of Lord Byron: Noted during a Residence with His Lordship at Pisa, in the Years 1821 and 1822*, 1824 (1827: January 28; *ca.* 1828: Miscellanea, pp. 428–429)

*Mémoires de Madame la Marquise de Pompadour . . . écrits par elle-même* [or rather by an unknown writer], 2 vols., 1766 (1819: March 22–23, 26)

Mendelssohn, Moses: *Phaedon, oder über die Unsterblichkeit der Seele in drey Gesprächen*, 1767 (1825: June 17 [29])

Mendes Pinto, Fernando: *Voyages and Adventures of Fernand Mendez Pinto*, 1653 (1821: December 9, 16–17, 19–20)

# Claire's Reading List

Mercier, Louis Sébastien: *Mon Bonnet de nuit,* 2 vols., 1784 (1819: May 7)

Michaud, Joseph François: *Histoire des croisades,* 7 vols., 1819–22 (1821: March 13)

Middleton, Thomas. *See* Beaumont, Francis

Milanese Gazettes (1821: March 22)

Milton, John: *Comus* (1814: October 28–30; S., M.); *Paradise Lost* (1825: November 10 [22], December 2 [14]; S., M.)

Molière (pseud. of Jean Baptiste Poquelin): *L'Amour médecin* (1818: April 10); *Amphitryon* (1818: April 17); *L'Avare* (1818: April 9); *Le Bourgeois Gentilhomme* (1818: April 10); *La Comtess d'Escarbargnas* (1818: April 11); *Le Dépit amoureux* (1818: April 15–16); *Don Juan; ou, le festin de pierre* (1818: April 10); *L'Étourdi* (1818: April 13–14); *Les Fourberies de Scapin* (1818: April 10); *George Dandin; ou, le mari confondu* (1818: April 9; M.); *Le Malade imaginaire* (1818: April 11); *Le Mariage forcé* (1818: April 10); *Le Médecin malgré lui* (1818: April 11); *Monsieur de Pourceaugnac* (1818: April 9); *Les Précieuses ridicules* (1818: April 16); *Le Tartuffe; ou, l'imposteur* (1818: April 9)

Montpensier, Anne Mary Louisa, Duchess of: *Mémoires de Mademoiselle de Montpensier, fille de M. Gaston d'Orléans, frère de Louis XIII* . . . , 6 vols., 1728 (1819: March 11)

Moore, Dr. John: *Edward: Various Views of Human Nature, Taken from Life and Manners, Chiefly in England,* 2 vols., 1796 (1820: July 21–22)

[Moore, Margaret King, Countess Mount Cashell]: *Continuation of the Stories of Old Daniel: Or Tales of Wonder and Delight* . . . , 1820 (1820: July 18). *See also* Irish Pamphlets

Moore, Thomas: *Odes of Anacreon, Translated into English Verse, with Notes,* 1800 (1818: January 23)

[————] *Tom Crib's Memorial to Congress,* 1819 (1821: July 29)

Morgan, Lady. *See* Owenson, Sydney

Mount Cashell, Lady. *See* Moore, Margaret King

Mozart, Wolfgang Amadeus. *See* Da Ponte, Lorenzo

Müllner, Amand Gottfried Adolph: *Die Schuld: Trauerspiel in vier Acten,* 1815 (1825: November 18–20 [30–December 2], 24–25 [December 6–7])

Nicholson, William: *An Introduction to Natural Philosophy,* 2 vols., 1782 (1820: June 28)

O'Connor, Arthur (afterwards Condorcet), T. A. Emmett, W. J. McNevin: *Memoir on the Objects of the Societies of United Irishmen* [1798] (1820: October 13)

"Oh, Cara Memoria," perhaps a song (1821: July 13)

*Olliers Literary Miscellany in Prose and Verse,* 1820 (1821: January 26; S.)

Otway, Thomas: *The Orphan* (1820: March 22)

# Claire's Reading List

Overbury, Sir Thomas: Character of "A Fair and Happy Milkmaid," quoted in the *Retrospective Review*, 1820 (1821: January 26; S.)

Owenson, Sydney, Lady Morgan: *Florence Macarthy: An Irish Tale*, 4 vols., 1818 (1820: July 23; M.); *France* (probably error for *Italy, q. v.*), 1817 (1821: December 14; S., M.); *Italy*, 2 vols., 1821 (1821: September 1–3, December 9–10, 12, 14 [?], 15, 25, 27–28)

Paine, Thomas: *The Age of Reason*, 1794–95 (1820: February 14–17; S., M.); *The American Crisis*, 1776–83 (1820: January 31, February 1–2, 4); *Common Sense*, 1776 (1820: January 31; M.); *A Letter Addressed to the Abbé Raynal on the Affairs of North America*, 1782 (1820: February 5, 7; M.); *Rights of Man*, 1791–92 (1820: February 8–9, 11–12; S.). See also *Trial of Thomas Paine*

Pananti, Filippo: *Avventure e osservazione sopra le coste di Barberia*, 2 vols., 1817 (1821: April 11–13)

Peacock, Thomas Love: *Melincourt*, 1817 (1821: June 25; S.); *Nightmare Abbey*, 1818 (1819: June 17; S.)

*Petit Charles ou neveu de mon oncle, Le*, unidentified (1819: June 2)

Petrarch (Francesco Petrarca) (1819: May 3; S., M.); *Sonnets* — an old edition (1820: December 14)

Pfeffel, Gottlieb Konrad: "Der Spieler und der Bettler" (1825: May 12 [24])

Phaedrus: *Fables* (1820: October 23–24, 26–28, 30–31, November 7, 9, 13–14, 16–17)

Pichler, Carolina, a book by (1821: April 7)

*Piffari di montagna, ossia cenno estemporaneo sulla congiura del principe di Canosa, é sopra i carbonari*, I, 1820 (1821: April 16)

Pigault-Lebrun, Charles Antoine Guillaume, discussed (1814: October 5); *Tableaux de société* (1819: May 29)

Pindemonte, Ippolito: *Le Prose e poesie campestri d'Ippolito Pindemonte*, 1817 (1821: February 26, March 5, 8)

Plato. *See* Mendelssohn, Moses; Shelley, P. B.

Plutarch: *Plutarch's Lives*, 6 vols., 1770 (1820: January 3, 5–9, 11–18, 21; S., M.)

Pompadour, Madame de: see *Lettres de Madame . . . de Pompadour* and *Mémoires de Madame . . . de Pompadour*

Pope, Alexander: *The Iliad of Homer, translated by Alexander Pope*, 1808 (1820: July 26, 28–31; M.)

Pradt, Dominique Dufour de: *Du Congrès de Vienne*, 2 vols., 1815 (1821: May 27–28, June 3)

*Quarterly Review, The* (1819: March 7; 1820: June 11, 13–14; S., M.); review of Robert Southey, *The Life of Wesley*, October 1820 (1821: June 29)

Quevedo y Villegas, Francisco Gómez de: *Les Visions (Sueños)*, 1627 (1819: May 7; M.)

# Claire's Reading List

Racine, Jean: *Esther*, see Performance List; *Phèdre* (1825: July 5 [17])

Radcliffe, Mary-Anne: *Manfroné; or, the One-handed Monk*, 1809 (1814: November 4)

Ravle on [?], unidentified song translation (1820: March 19)

Reeve, Clara: *The Old English Baron: A Gothic Story*, 1808 (1820: August 7)

Regnard, Jean François: *Le Distrait*, 1697 (1825: August 7 [19])

*Retrospective Review, The*, 1820 (1821: January 26, 28; S.). *See also* Overbury, Sir Thomas; Sydney, Sir Philip

Riccoboni, Marie Jeanne. *See* Kelly, Hugh

Richardson, Samuel: *Clarissa; or, the History of a Young Lady*, 7 vols., 1747–48 (1818: April 16–17, 22; 1820: September 3–7, 12–14; S., M.)

Robertson, William: *The History of the Reign of the Emperor Charles V. with a View of the Progress of Society in Europe, from the Subversion of the Roman Empire, to the Beginning of the Sixteenth Century*, 3 vols., 1769 (1825: November 22 [December 4], 24–26 [December 6–8], 28 [December 10], 30 [December 12], December 1–4 [13–16], 8 [20], 11 [23], 13 [25], 15 [27], 21 [1826: January 2], 29–30 [January 10–11]; S.)

Rollin, Charles: *Histoire ancienne des Égyptiens, des Carthaginois, des Assyriens, des Babyloniens, des Mèdes et des Perses, des Macédoniens, des Grecs*, 13 vols., 1730–38 (1825: September 2–3 [14–15], October 20 [November 1], 27 [November 8], 30 [November 11], November 11–12 [23–24]; S.)

Rossi, Giovanni Gherardo de: Fable nine, "L'Acqua fra' sassi" (1825: October 27 [November 8])

Rousseau, Jean Jacques (1814: August 20); *Discours qui a remporté le prix à l'Académie de Dijon, en l'année 1750: . . . si le rétablissement des sciences et des arts a contribué à épurer les moeurs*, 1750 (1820: January 30; S.); *Discours sur l'origine de l'inégalité parmi les hommes*, 1755 (1814: September 16); *Émile*, 1762 (1814: September 9–10, 15, 18–20; 1821: June 5, 7–10; S., M.); *Pigmalion: Scène lyrique*, quoted in the *Indicator*, May 10, 1820 (1820: December 12)

Rowley, William. *See* Beaumont, Francis

St. Augustine: *Confessions*, one line quoted (1814: end of First Journal; S.)

St. John, Henry, Viscount Bolingbroke: *A Collection of Political Tracts*, "By the Author of the Dissertation upon Parties." 1788, or possibly *The Works of the Late Right Honourable Henry St. John, Lord Viscount Bolingbroke*, 7 vols., 1754–98 (1820: October 24)

Saint-Pierre, Jacques Henri Bernardin de: *Paul et Virginie*, 1787 (1825: October 18 [30]). Trans. H. M. Williams, 1795 (1814: November 8)

Schiller, Johann Christoph Friedrich von: "Der Gang nach dem Eisen-

# Claire's Reading List

hammer" (1821: March 23, 26–27); "Das Geheimniss" (1821: February 9); *Der Geisterseher*, 1787–89 (1825: October 15–16 [27–28]; M.); "Das Gluck" (1821: February 9–10); "Der Handschuh" (1825: November 9 [21]); *Hero und Leander*, 1801 (1821: March 15, 18, 21); *Die Jungfrau von Orleans* [Johanna D'Arc], 1802 (1821: October 6–8, 11, 13, 15; S.); *Kabale und Liebe*, 1784 (1821: August 5–6, 10–13); "Der Kampf mit dem Drachen" (1820: inside front cover of Fourth Journal; 1821: April 5, 7–9); "Die Kraniche des Ibykus" (1825: November 16 [28]); "Das Lied von der Glocke" (1821: February 11, 13, 15–16, March 13–14); "Pegasus im Joche" (1825: November 9 [21]); Poem to Greece (1825: June 24 [July 6]); Poems (1825: August 4[16]); Riddles (1825: November 30 [December 12]); "Der Ring des Polykrates" (1821: April 2); *Wallenstein: Ein dramatische Gedicht*, 2 vols., 1800 (1825: May 23–28 [June 4–9], 31 [June 12], June 1 [13], 3–5 [15–17], 8 [20], 14–15 [26–27]); *Wilhelm Tell*, 1804 (1825: June 17–18 [29–30]); "Die Zerstörung von Troja, freie übersetzung der zweiten Buchs der Aeneide" (1821: April 14, 18, 21–24)

Schlegel, August Wilhelm von: probably *A Course of Lectures on Dramatic Art and Literature*, trans. John Black, 2 vols., 1815 (1819: March 19, 27, 30; 1820: January 28; S., M.)

Schlegel, Friedrich, as quoted by Hare (*q. v.*) in *Olliers Literary Miscellany*

Schubart, Christian Friedrich Daniel: "Der ewige Jude: Eine lyrische Rhapsodie" (1825: June 29 [July 11]; S.); "Der gesangene Sänger" and "Meiner Julie" (1825: August 3 [15])

Scott, Sir Walter: *The Abbot*, 1820 (1821: June 24; M.); *The Bride of Lammermoor*, 1819 (1820: June 16; M.); *The Heart of Midlothian*, 1818 (1819: June 17); *Ivanhoe*, 1819 (1820: June 8–10; 1821: October 4; M.); *Kenilworth*, 1821 (1821: August 28–30; M.); *A Legend of Montrose*, 1819 (1820: June 17; M.); *Rob Roy*, 3 vols., 1818 (1818: February 6–7; S., M.)

Ségur, Alexandre Joseph Pierre de: *Les Femmes, leur condition et leur influence dans l'ordre social chez différents peuples anciens et modernes*, 3 vols., 1803 (1825: November 8–9 [20–21], 11 [23])

Serassi, Pietro Antonio: *La Vita di Torquato Tasso*, 1785 (1818: April 10–11, 14–15, 18, 20)

Shakespeare, William (1822: January 7, March 8); *All's Well That Ends Well* (1822: January 27; S., M.); *As You Like It* (1814: August 17; M.); *Cymbeline* (1821: December 30; S., M.); *Hamlet* (1818: April 18; 1822: March 3; S.); *Henry IV* (1820: January 20; 1821: December 30; S., M.); *Julius Caesar* (1821: December 2; S., M.); *King Lear* (1814: August 27, 31; 1818: April 18; 1822: January 17; S., M.); *Macbeth*, referred to (*ca.* 1828: Miscellanea, p. 427; S., M.); *Pericles, Prince of Tyre* (1821: December 2); *Richard III* (1814: August 27, November

514

# Claire's Reading List

6–7; S., M.); *Romeo and Juliet* (1822: March 10; S., M.); *Titus Andronicus* (1821: December 30; S.)

Shelley, Percy Bysshe: *Adonais*, 1821 (1821: July 24); "The Assassins," 1814 (1814: August 25); "Hymn to Intellectual Beauty," 1816 (1825: July 3[15]); "Ode to Naples," 1820 (1820: September 3); Translation of Plato's *Symposium*, 1818 (1819: April 14–16; 1820: August 10–11, 14); *Prometheus Unbound*, 1820 (1820: November 8, 11); *Queen Mab*, 1813 (1814: September 16, October 30–31; *ca.* 1828: Miscellanea, pp. 430–31); *The Revolt of Islam*, 1818 (1825: June 7–8 [19–20], 14 [26], 21 [July 3], 24–25 [July 6–7], 28–29 [July 10–11], July 5 [17], 12 [24], 23 [August 4], 26 [August 7], August 2 [14], 6 [18], 16–18 [28–30], 20 [September 1], 22–23 [September 3–4]); "To Constantia Singing," 1817 (1818: January 19); *Zastrozzi*, 1810 (1814: October 10)

Smellie, William: *The Philosophy of Natural History*, 2 vols., 1790, 1799 (1814: September 24–29)

Smith, Adam: *Essays on Philosophical Subjects*, 1795, with an introduction by Dugald Stewart (1820: March 16)

Sophocles: *Oedipus Rex* (1820: December 9; S., M.)

Southcott, Joanna. See *Life of Joanna Southcott.* . .

Southey, Robert: *The Curse of Kehama*, 1810 (1814: September 17, 19; S., M.); *Letters Written during a Short Residence in Spain and Portugal*, 1797 (1820: February 11); *Life of Wesley* . . . , 2 vols., 1820, as reviewed by *Quarterly Review* (*q. v.*); *Thalaba the Destroyer*, 2 vols., 1801 (1814: September 20, 23–24; S., M.)

*Spectator, The* (1819: July 1)

Staël-Holstein, Anne Louise Germaine de: *De l'Allemagne*, 3 vols., 1810 (1820: December 26–29; 1821: January 3, 5; M.); *Corinne; ou l'Italie*, 2 vols., 1807 (1819: May 6; S., M.)

Sterbini, Cesare (after Beaumarchais, *q.v.*): *Il Barbiere di Seviglia* (Rossini's libretto), 1816 (1818: February 11, 13)

Sterne, Laurence: *The Life and Opinions of Tristram Shandy, Gentleman*, 9 vols., 1760–67 (1818: February 27; S., M.)

Stewart, Dugald: *See* Smith, Adam

Swift, Jonathan. *See* Byrom, John

Sydney, Sir Philip: *Arcadia*, quoted in the *Retrospective Review*, 1820 (1821: January 28; S.)

Tacitus, Cornelius (S., M.): *Annals*, in Bernardo Davanzati Bostichi, *Tacito volgarizzato*, 3 vols., 1804 (1820: February 19, 21–22, 24–27, March 1–5, 7, 10, 12, 15, 17–19); *De oratoribus*, in Dureau de La Malle, *Tacite*, 6 vols., 1818 (1820: April 11–12); *Germania*, in Dureau de La Malle (1820: April 9–10); *Historiae*, in Dureau de La Malle (1820: *ca.* March 21–22, 24–31, April 1–4); Brotier's chronological supplement to book v of *Historiae*, in Dureau de La Malle (1820: March 17, April 4–6, 9); *Life of Agricola*, in Dureau de La Malle (1820: April 10–11)

# Claire's Reading List

Tasso, Torquato, discussed (1814: October 18); *La Gerusalemme liberata* (1830: December 17; S., M.)

Tegrimi, Niccolò: *Vita di Castruccio Castracani de gl' Antelmi nelli principe di Lucca*, 1496 (1820: August 13; M.)

Touchet, James, Lord Audley, third earl of Castlehaven: *The Memoir's of James Lord Audley Earl of Castlehaven, His Engagement and Carriage in the Wars of Ireland, from the Year 1642 to the Year 1651*, 1680 (1820: September 17)

*Trial, The, of Thomas Paine, for Certain False, Wicked, Scandalous and Seditious Libels. . . , 1793?* (1820: February 14)

*Trials, The, of Arthur Thistlewood, James Ings, John Thomas Brunt, Richard Tidd, William Davidson and Others, for High Treason . . . , 2 vols., 1820* (1821: October 29)

Vallancey, Charles: *A Grammar of the Iberno-Celtic, or Irish Language*, 1773 (1820: September 20)

Vanbrugh, Sir John: *Plays*, 2 vols., 1719 (1820: May 17)

Villeneuve, de: "Journal" (1827: January 7)

Villers, Charles: *Philosophie de Kant: Ou Principes fondamentaux de la philosophie transcendentale*, 1801 (1825: May 30 [June 11])

Virgil (Publius Vergilius Maro): *Aenead* (1820: July 2, 4–12, 14, 27, 29–30, September 27; 1822: March 7; S., M.)

[Voltaire (François Marie Arouet)]: *Histoire de Charles XII, roi de Suède*, 2 vols., 1731 (1825: September 19–21 [October 1–3]; S., M.)

Voltaire: *Mémoires de M. de Voltaire écrits par lui-même*, bound with its translation, *Memoirs of the Life of Voltaire, Written by Himself*, 1784 (1814: October 17, 19–20; S., M.) *See also* Caritat, M. J. A; "Le Russe à Paris," 1760 (1825: June 11 [23])

Walpole, Horace: *The Castle of Otranto*, 1808 (1820: August 8)

Weber, Veit (pseudonym of George Philipp Waechter): *The Sorcerer: A Tale from the German*, trans. Robert Huish (?), 1795 (1814: September 19; S., M.)

[Werner, Friedrich Ludwig Zacharias]: *Martin Luther, oder die Weihe der Kraft*, 1807 (1825: October 28–29 [November 9–10], November 2–4 [14–16], 7 [19], 15 [27], 18 [30])

Werner, Friedrich Ludwig Zacharias: *Die Templer auf Cypern*, 1803 (1825: October 16 [28])

Wieland, Christoph Martin: *Aristipp und einige seiner Zeitgenossen*, 4 vols., 1812 (perhaps in translation; 1820: July 4–6, 8–12, 14; S., M.); *Menander und Glycerion*, 1812 (1821: November 3–6, 8, 23, 25, December 7–8)

Winckelmann, Johann Joachim: *Histoire de l'art chez les anciens*, trans. H. J. Jansen, 2 vols., 1790, 1803 (1819: May 2, 11; S., M.)

Wohlzogen, Mme. Caroline: *Agnès de Lilien*, 1802 (1820: May 3–5)

Wollstonecraft, Mary: *Letters Written during a Short Residence in Sweden, Norway, and Denmark*, 1796 (1814: August 30–31,

# Performance List

September 1; 1820: June 1–2, 4; S., M.); *A Vindication of the Rights of Woman*, 1792 (1820: May 29–31, June 2–4; S., M.)

Wordsworth, William (1819: March 16); *The Excursion*, 1814 (1814: September 15; S., M.); *Lyrical Ballads*, 1798 — "The Mad Mother" (1814: October 5; S., M.); "Simon Lee, the Old Huntsman" (1825: November 15 [27])

Wyss, Johann David: *The Family Robinson Crusoe: Or, Journal of a Father Shipwrecked, with his Wife and Children, on an Uninhabited Island*, 2 vols., 1814 (1820: August 20)

## *Performance List*

(Theatrical and musical performances
attended or participated in by Claire Clairmont)

*Agamemnon*, ballet at the Pergola, Florence (1821: January 19)

"The Astrologer," farce at the Pergola, Florence (1822: March 27)

"Bacchettona" [bigot]: a farce on this subject at the Cocomero, Florence (1821: December 5)

Beethoven, Ludwig van: Sonatas (1825: November 22 [December 4], November 30 [December 12])

Bonfio, Giacomo: *Il Viaggio d'una donna di spirite*, play at the Cocomero, Florence (1822: February 15)

Bouilly, Jean Nicolas: *L'Abbé de l'épée, comédie historique*, play at the Cocomero, Florence (1821: December 5)

Buonavoglia, L. G.: *Il Ciarlatano, ossia i finti savojardi*, play in Pisa (reference may be to Goldoni, *q.v.*; 1820: December 8; M.)

"Cyanippe and his daughter," ballet at the Teatro Goldoni, Florence (1821: June 12)

D'Aste, Ippolito Tito: *Luigia de la Valliere*, play at the Teatro Goldoni, Florence (1821: March 18)

Duport (choreographer): *Zephyr: Or, the Return of Spring*, ballet at the Opera (Covent Garden Theatre), London (1818: February 21, 24, 28; S., M.)

Favier (choreographer): *Acis et Galathe*, ballet at the Opera (Covent Garden Theatre), London (1818: February 10; S., M.)

Field, John: *Sixième Concerto pour le pianoforte avec accompagnement de grand orchestre*, played by Claire in Russia (1825: October 26 [November 7])

Gambs, Chrétien-Hermann: "Impromptu d'Islavsky" (*q.v.*)

Genischta, Joseph: "The Copack," words by Pushkin (1825: December 18 [30]); "Écossaise" (1825: June 4 [16]); "Elegie," words by Pushkin (1825: December 18 [30]); "Fingal" (1825: December 18 [30]); Funeral march on the death of Prince Cavansky's son (1825: December 4 [16]); "Die Grösse der Welt," words by

517

# Performance List

Schiller (1825: December 4 [16]); "Impromptu d'Islavsky" (*q.v.*); "Malvina" (1825: December 18 [30]); Prayer, words by Viniviti-noff (1825: October 20 [November 1]); "Der Ring des Polykrates," words by Schiller (1825: December 1 [13], 4 [16], 8 [20], 15 [27]); "Der Taucher," words by Schiller (1825: December 15 [27], 18 [30]); "Die Würde der Frauen," words by Schiller (1825: December 4 [16])

Goldoni, Carlo: *Il Ciarlatano*, play in Pisa (reference may be to Buona-voglia, *q.v.*); *Il Matrimonio per concorso*, play at the Pergola, Florence (1822: March 27)

Guglielmi, Pietro: *Miserere*, heard in part in Rome (1819: April 9)

*Harlequin Gulliver, or the Flying Island*, pantomime at the Covent Garden Theatre, London (1818: February 16; S., M.)

*L'Homme gris et le physiognomiste*, unidentified play or plays seen in Lyons (1818: March 23; S., M.)

Hummel, Johann Nepomuk: Variations on *La Sentinelle* (op. 34, no. 2) and variations on a march from Rossini's *Cenerentola*, played by Claire and Genischta (1825: November 7 [19])

Ichahafskoy, Prince: A Russian piece, performed in Russia (1825: July 22 [August 3])

"Impromptu d'Islavsky," words by C.-H. Gambs, music by Joseph Gen-ischta, performed in Russia (1825: May 17 [29], 21 [June 2], May 28–June 5 [June 9–17])

"Italians in Algiers," ballet by children, Teatro Borgo Ogni Santi, Florence (1821: March 5)

Marcello, Benedetto: *Psalmi*, heard in Rome and Florence (1819: May 27; 1821: December 11; S.)

Mazzei, Lucretia, *improvvisatrice*, heard in Florence (1821: February 8, March 31)

Metastasio, Pietro: *La Clemenza di Tito*, play at the Teatro Goldoni, Florence (1821: March 30)

Meyerbeer, Giacomo: *Il Crociato in Egitto*, opera in Moscow (1825: May 16 [28])

Milman, Henry Hart: *Fazio*, play at the Covent Garden Theatre, London (1818: February 16; S., M.)

*Miserere*, heard in Rome (1819: March 29; S.)

Morlacchi, Francesco: *Il Barbiere di Seviglia*, first act of the opera, at the Cocomero, Florence (possibly Rossini's *Il Barbiere di Seviglia*, *q.v.*, or an error for Mozart, *Le Nozze di Figaro*, *q.v.*; 1820: November 7); *Il Corradino*, first act of the opera, at the Cocomero, Florence (falsely attributed by Claire to Rossini; 1820: November 7)

Mozart, Wolfgang Amadeus: *La Clemenza di Tito*, overture played by Claire, in Florence (1822: January 10); *Don Giovanni*, opera in London (1818: February 10, 14, 21, 24; S., M.); *Le Nozze di Figaro*, opera at the Covent Garden Theatre, London (1818: February 4; S. [?]); *Le Nozze di Figaro*, performed by Claire in

Russia (1825: May 16 [28], 18 [30], June 6 [18], 21 [July 3], June 23 [July 5], August 21 [September 2], August 31 [September 12], September 13–14 [25–26], October 17 [29]). *See also under* Morlacchi, *above*

*Orfanello*, afterpiece at the Cocomero, Florence, possibly by Zinelli (1822: February 15)

Pacini, Giovanni: *Il Falegname di Livonia*, opera at Teatro Goldoni, Florence (1821: June 12); *La Sposa fedele*, opera at Teatro Goldoni, Florence (1821: May 17)

Paër, Ferdinando: *Griselda*, opera at Covent Garden Theatre, London (1818: February 28; S., M.)

Paisiello, Giovanni: *La Molinara*, opera mentioned in London (1818: January 29)

"Pappagalli" [parrots], farce at the Cocomero, Florence (1822: January 14)

*Il Pittore per amore*, ballet at the Cocomero, Florence (1820: November 7)

Racine, Jean Baptiste: *Esther*, performed in Russia (1825: June 27 [July 7], July 5 [17], 10–12 [22–24], 15 [27], 17 [29], 19–22 [July 31–August 3]); *Esther*, parodied (1825: August 17 [25])

Ries, Ferdinand: "Di Tanti Palpiti," duet played by Claire in Russia (1825: May 14 [26], June 4 [16])

Romani, Felice: *L'Amante e l'impostore*, play at the Cocomero, Florence (1822: January 14)

Rossini, Gioacchino: *Aureliano in Palmira*, opera in Pisa (1820: March 11); *Il Barbiere di Seviglia*, opera in Florence (possibly by Morlacci or Mozart *qq.v.*; 1820: November 7); *Il Barbiere di Seviglia*, opera in Leghorn (1821: August 15); *La Cenerentola; ossia, la bontà in trionfo*, opera in Pisa (1820: February 8; S.); *Edoardo e Cristina*, opera at the Cocomero, Florence (1821: November 16); "Languir per una bella," from *L'Italiana in Algerie*, transposed by Claire (1821: December 23); *Mosè in Egitto*, opera at the Pergola, Florence (1818: April 3); "Mi manca la voce," quartet from *Mosè in Egitto*, heard in Florence (1821: December 11); *Ricciardo e Zoraide*, opera at the Pergola, Florence (1821: June 6). *See also under* Hummel *and* Morlacchi, *above*

*Sacente* (or *Lacente*), play at the Cocomero, Florence (1822: January 30)

Sampieri, Francesco: *Emilia o la vestale*, opera at the Pergola, Florence (1821: February 28)

Sgricci, Tommaso, *improvvisatore*, heard in Pisa (1820: December 1, 21)

Shakespeare, William: *Hamlet*, at Drury Lane Theatre, London (1814: October 13)

Sografi, Simone: *Il Cavalier Woender*, play at the Teatro Goldoni, Florence (1821: March 22)

# Performance List

"The Three Gobbi," ballet at the Pergola, Florence (1821: February 28)

Viganò, Salvator (choreographer): *Otello ossia il moro di Venezia*, ballet in Milan (1818: April 8; S., M.)

Weber, Carl Maria von: *Der Freischütz*, practiced by Claire in Russia (1825: July 5 [17], 9 [21])

Zinelli. See *Orfanello*

# Index

The abbreviations R.L. and P.L. below indicate entries in the Reading List and the Performance List respectively. In the Reading List I have designated with S. or M. each work I have reason to believe that either Shelley or Mary read, but this index includes under their names only their reading as mentioned in this book. Some names of persons and places mentioned only once or twice are omitted, and also many of the names referred to in Claire's reading notes and in the lectures she heard in Russia. Painters are listed, but not the subjects of their paintings. I have included references to sources cited in my notes and introductions, but for full bibliographical information the reader should consult the Bibliography. Several sources cited very frequently, such as the journals and letters of Shelley and Mary, are indexed only when they contain a quotation of six or more words. When Claire or the Shelleys used obsolete, inaccurate, or varying spellings of names, the most conspicuous of the variants are given in parentheses after the main heading, with cross-references where they seem useful. The following abbreviations are used:

CC   Claire Clairmont      P.L.   Performance List
Lady M   Lady Mount Cashell      R.L.   Reading List
MWS   Mary Wollstonecraft      m.   other mention
    Shelley      q   quotation
PBS   Percy Bysshe Shelley      n   note

# Index

Godwin, William, diaries; Shelley, P.B. and Mary, journals

Acaroff, Mrs. (Moscow), 393

Acaroff (later Kakoschkine), Barbe (Russia), 323n, 356

*Accademia*, described, 131n

Accademia dei Arcadi, 463

Accademia di San Luca, 463

Achilles, 153

*Acis et Galathe* (ballet), *see* Favier

Aconloff, the Misses (Moscow), 310, 367–68, 374, 388

Aconloff, Mr., 374, 379, 385

Aconloff, Modeste, 374, 388, 391

Acropolis, Athens, 332n

Acton, John, 218

Adam and Eve, 181–82

Addison, Joseph: *Cato*, anecdote from Baker, 133

Aerestoff, Prince (Moscow), 309

Aeschylus, *Prometheus Bound*, 161–62q, 198q, R.L.

Aesop, 17, 180n

Afrasimoff, Mme. (Moscow), 369

*Agamemnon* (ballet) Florence, 204, P.L.

Aigue-belle, 88

Aikin, John, and Mrs. Barbauld, *Evenings at Home*, 382–83, R.L.

Aimèe (Elise's daughter), 88

Alba, *see* Clairmont, Clara Allegra

Albano, PBS goes to, 112

Albé (nickname for Byron), 76. *See also* Byron, Lord

Alberti, Signora (daughter of Countess Tolomei, Florence), 212n, 268–69

Albion House, Marlow (residence of Shelleys and CC), 76

Alcibiades, 153

Aldersgate st., London, 56

Alessandria, 216

Alexander I, czar of Russia: anecdote of, 393; dies, 385–86; m. 257n, 303–04, 306, 360, 369n, 372, 468

Alexandroff, Capt. (Russia), 357

Alexy, Princess, and husband (Moscow), 408

Alfieri, Vittorio: *Memoirs*, 52; *Myrrha*, 112; R.L.

Allegra, *see* Clairmont, Clara Allegra

Allegri (priest at Florence), 211, 227

Allegri, casa, 215

Allodi family (Florence), 271, 275

Allsops Buildings, Marylebone, London, 167

Aloi, M. and Mme. (Florence), 208

Alps, 27, 29, 88–89, 442, 453–54

Alsace, 303

Alsonfieff (Alsoufieff), Mme. (Russia), 319, 322, 356–57, 366, 396

Alsonfieff, Mr., 325

Ambrogetti (basso), 83n

America, in De Staël, 200

Amorone, Signor (Rome), 101

Amory, Mr. (PBS's solicitor), 46

Anacreon: in Greek, 45; "Ode to the Cicala," translation quoted, 155; R.L.

Anfossi, Pasquale, 462

Angeli, H. R., 117n, 205n, 466

Angrisani (basso), 83n

*Ania*, Hindu book, in Pananti, 221

Anna Marie, 167

Annette (niece of Countesses Waronzoff and Boutourlin in Florence), 210

Annette (Russia), 356

Antelminelli family (Lucca), 169–70

Antiphilus of Byzantium, epigram from *Anthologia Palatina*, 161q; R.L.

Antonelli, Count (Florence), 269, 277

Antonievna, Alona (Moscow), 369, 389

Antrodoco, 216

Apennines, 174, 286, 391

Appollonicon, in London, 82, 85

Aquila, 216

Aquila Nera (inn in Leghorn), 114

*Arabian Nights*, 353–54; R.L.

Araktcheif, General Count A. A., 386

Archivo di Fraternità, Florence, 471

Arcispedale di S. Spirito, Rome, 470

Arco di San Piero, Florence, 259

Ardenza, the, Leghorn, 242, 244–45

Arena theater, Florence, 237

Aretino, Pietro, 226–27

Arezzo, 390, 471, 473

522

# Index

Argine, Pisa, 120–23, 126, 129, 178, 188
Argyropoulo, George, 190n, 191
Argyropoulo, Princess Ralou: letter to MWS, 190n; m. 190–91, 193, 198, 279
Ariosto, Lodovico: *Orlando furioso,* 391q, R.L.
Aristophanes, 172n
Aristotle: on comedy, 161; on unities, 321; R.L.
Armfeld, Mr. (Russia), 353, 369–70, 374, 376, 379, 382, 386, 389, 394–95
Armfeld, Mme., 396
Armstrong, Susan, 481
Arno River, 118, 119n, 121–22, 133n, 140, 203n
Arnstein (or Arnsteiner), B. D., 267n
Arpino, 107–09
Arquinto, Count (Leghorn), 243
Artois, 87
Aruntian family tomb, Rome, 101
Asciano, road to, 171–72
Ashley Library, British Museum, 3–4, 7–9, 275n, 284n. *See also* Wise, T. J.
Assipitch, Daniel (Russia), 347–48, 353, 357
Astius, D. F.: *Platonis Phaedrus,* 381; R.L.
Aston, Harvey, 213
"Astrologer, The" (farce), Florence, 281, P.L.
Atalandi, 332
Attwood and Co., Odessa: CC and Mr. Kitto write to, 372–73; m. 397
Auber's, Everitt st., London, 53, 57
Aufrere (Aufer), Mme. (Florence), 236, 262
Au Grand Cerf (inn in Calais), 87
Aurelian, Aqueduct of, Rome, 101
Auspitz, Edoardo (CC's German teacher, Florence): CC pays, 280; m. 231, 274–75, 277, 279–81, 283
Aust, Mme. (Pisa), 189
Austen, Jane, 68
Austin, Col. (cousin of Miss Farhill, Florence), 255, 262
*Australian Encyclopaedia,* 470
Austria: currency of, 174–75; troops,

209–10, 215–18, 229, 264; m. 180n, 468
Austria, Emperor of, 104, 172
Aversa, 218
Axinievna, 342, 356–57, 366

Baborikin, Mme. (Moscow): CC teaches her daughter, 381, 385, 387, 389, 392; described, 379
Baborikin, Miss, 396
"Bacchettona" (farce), Florence, 262, P.L.
Bacciocchi (Baccocchi, Basciocchi), family (Florence), 230n
Bacciocchi, Count (Signor), 237, 262, 271
Bacciocchi, Signora, 228, 261
Bacciocchi, M. and Mme., 230, 234, 269
Bacciocchi, Elisa Bonaparte (eldest sister of Napoleon, Pisa), 190n, 230n
Bacciocchi, Count Felice, 230n
Bachmeetieff's House, Moscow, 397
Backler, Mr. (painter on glass), 84n
Bacon, Francis: *De augmentis scientiarum,* 136; *Essayes,* "Of Beauty," 423, "Of Riches," 224; m. 184; R.L.
Bagnacavallo, Convent of: Allegra placed there, 216; Allegra's death there, 284n; m. 227, 230n
Bagnese, Count (Florence), 204, 212–13, 219, 231, 234, 277, 280
Bagnese, Countess, 204, 212, 230, 233–34
Bagnetti, Leghorn, 176, 178, 240–42
Bagni di Lucca, *see* Baths of Lucca
Bagni di Pisa, *see* Baths of Pisa
Bagni di San Giuliano, *see* Baths of Pisa
Bagnoli, Professor Pietro (University of Pisa): *Il Cadmo,* 226n; m. 226–27
Baiae, 96
Baker (historian), 151
Baker, D. E., *Biographia dramatica,* 133 (summarized), 136 (summarized); R.L.
Baldi, Giuseppe (Florence), 219, 221, 227, 235, 237, 260–62, 265,

# Index

269, 273, 275, 277, 279–80, 282–83

Balestrucci, the (Florence), 271

Ballachey, G. B. (money lender), 20, 44–47, 51–52

Bally, Hans Jörg, 481

Bally-Clairmont, Mary Claire, x, 481

Balzani's (Florence), 285

Balzani (little boy, Pisa), 199

Bandelloni, Signor (CC's singing teacher, Rome), 105, 110

Bani, Miss (Florence), 255, 281, 283

Baptiste, Mme. (sister of choreographer Duport), 461

Baptiste, M. (dancer), 460–61

Barraca (Leghorn), 241–42

Bar-sur-Aube, 22, 24

Barbauld, Mrs., *see* Aikin, John

Barbe (Russia), 322–23, 374

Barbé-Marbois, Marquis F. de, *see* Pompadour

Barnard, Mrs. Caroline: *Parent's Offering*, 171; R.L.

Barrière, J. F., *see* Berville, S. A.

Barruel, L'Abbé, *Mémoires du jacobinisme*: 29–31; PBS reads aloud, 49–50; R.L.

Barthélemy, J.J., *Anacharsis*, 80–81q, 102n; R.L.

Bartlett's Buildings, London, 55

Bartolini, Marchese (Florence and Leghorn), 213, 217, 244–45

Bartolini, Professor Antonio (Florence), 213n

Bartolini, Bartolino (banker, Florence), 213n, 261

Bartolini, Signora Laura (Florence), 219, 231, 233–34, 236

Bartolini, Lorenzo (sculptor, Florence), 189n, 213n

Basciocchi, *see* Bacciocchi

Basel, 32–33

Basile (Bazile), M. (Russia), 333, 337–38, 347, 354, 357

Bassanti (Pisa), 189

Basskoff (Russia), 358

Bastille, the, 464

Bath, 73

Bath, earl of, anecdote of, 256

Baths of Lucca, 96, 105n, 107n

Baths of Pisa (Baths of San Giuliano): CC visits, 178, 237, 243, 247–52; Lady M and children visit, 172; Shelleys and CC move there, 168; m. 173n, 230n

Baths of St. Jacopo, Leghorn, 238–39, 244, 246, 248

Bault (Boult), Capt. (Russia), 360, 366

Baum, Paull Franklin, x

Baxter, Mr. (tutor to Alexis Kyrieff, Russia): letters to CC, 307, 318, 327, 330, 336, 343, 357, 362–63, 369, 372–73, 378, 382, 388; mentioned, 306, 311, 368–70, 374–75, 377, 381–82, 386, 388–89, 394, 403, 406, 410–11. *See also under CC, letters*

Baxter, Mrs. (Florence), 115

Baxter, Christy (school friend of MWS), 20

Baxter, Isabel, *see* Booth, Mrs. David

Baxter, Margaret (first wife of David Booth), 57n

Baxter, W. T. (father of Isabel Baxter Booth), 86

Beauclerc, Mrs. and daughters (Leghorn), 240–41n, 244, 260, 283n

Beauclerc, Charles George, 241n

Beauclerc, Georgianna ("Gee," friend of MWS), marriage to Sir John Dean Paul and subsequent separation, 241n

Beaufort, Charlotte, duchess of, 264. *See also* Strozzi

Beaumarchais, P.-A. C. de: *Le Barbier de Séville*, 156, R.L.

Beaumont, Francis, and John Fletcher (also Philip Massinger, Thomas Middleton, and William Rowley): *Beggars Bush*, 135; *Elder Brother*, 145q; *Noble Gentleman*, 144; *Thierry and Theodoret*, 147; *Wit at Several Weapons*, 143; *Wit without Money*, 143; *Woman Hater*, 135–36; *Woman Pleased*, 147; *Woman's Prize*, 141, 143; R.L.

Becker, C. F., *Weltgeschichte*, 363, R.L.

Becket, St. Thomas à, 151

Beethoven, L. von: Sonatas, 382, 386; m. 309n, 314n; P.L.

# Index

Belgioioso (Bel Jojoso), Prince, of Milan (Leghorn), 244-45

Bell, Dr. Benjamin, 464

Bell, Dr. John (British physician in Rome): attends William Shelley, 113; m. 98, 102-03, 105, 108-11

Bell, Mrs. John, 103, 108, 111

Bello Squardo, Florence, 255, 263, 282

Belloy, *see* Buirette de Belloy

Belvidera, Principessa (Rome), 107

Benci, Signor (Florence), 232, 235, 260, 273, 277, 279-80

Benini, Mme. (Florence), gives CC dancing lessons, 254

Benvenuti, Signor (Florence), 217, 219, 266, 273-74, 276

Berg Collection, N.Y.P.L., 3

Berington, Joseph, *Literary History of the Middle Ages*, 85, R.L.

Berlioz, Hector, *Faust*, 314n

Berry, C. F. de B., Duc de, assassination reported, 129

Berry le Bac, 87

Berry, Mary, 129, 202n, 376n(q)

Bertini (*cavaliere servente* of Signora Gerini), 116

Berville, S. A., and J. F. Barrière, *Mémoires de Madame Roland*, 305, 307, 309, R.L.

Besançon, 25

Béthune, 87

Betsy, the English nun, *see* Parker, Elizabeth

Beyle, M. H., *see* Stendhal

Bianchi (music teacher in Florence), 167n, 208, 279

Bianchi, casa, 167n, 207

Bianchi, Maddalena, 167

Bibbiena, 390

Bibikoff, Mr. and Mrs. (Moscow), 382

Bible Society, 143

Bible, The: PBS reads St. Matthew aloud, 116; referred to in Paine, 126-27; m. 430; R.L.

Bibliothèque Nationale, Paris, 299

Bibliothèque Nationale et Universitaire, Strasbourg, 300

*Bibliothèque universelle des dames*: "Cléomades et Claremonde," 110; "La Fleur des Batailles," 107;

"Flores et Blanche-fleur," 110; "Guérin de Montglave, 108; "Histoire de Rigda et de Regner Lodbrog," 107; "Huon de Bordeaux," 108; "Le Petit Jehan de Saintré," 110; "Pierre de Provence et la belle Maguelone," 110; m. 107n; R.L.

*Bibliothèque universelle des sciences, belles-lettres, et arts*, 211, R.L.

Bickerstaff (Lady Oxford's accoucheur), 130

Bicknell, Mrs. (friend of Mrs. Godwin), 68

Biddulph, Mr. (Florence), 266

Bielfeld, Mme. (Moscow), 367

Bielfeld, "the little," 379

Bingen, 36

Bini, Domenico (Pisa), 276

Biondi, Carlo (lawyer, brother of Luigi Biondi), 229-30, 232, 235

Biondi, Francesco (father of Carlo and Luigi Biondi), 229n

Biondi, Luigi (married Theresa Emilia Viviani), 229n

Biondi, Maria Bertolini (mother of Carlo and Luigi Biondi), 229n

Birkbeck, Morris: *Letters from Illinois*, 114; *Notes on a Journey in America* 114n; R.L.

Biron, in Richardson's *Clarissa*, 173

Black Sea, 405

Blackwall, 42

*Blackwood's Magazine*, 327, R.L.

Blamire, 60

Blarnis, M. (Florence), 216

Blasche, B. H., *Papyro-Plastics*, 396-97n, R.L.

Blessington, Marguerite, Lady, 247n, 254n

Bloom, Harold, 315n

Boboli (or Buboli) Gardens, Florence, 173n-74n, 180, 204, 206, 210, 218, 223-25, 228, 259

Boborikin, *see* Baborikin

Boccaccio: *Decameron*, 111-13, 153; m. 101n; R.L.

Bochdamm (Bochdann), Countess (Florence), 212, 219, 229

Bock, Félix de, *Chevaliers des sept montagnes*, 140q, R.L.

Bodleian Library, Oxford, 7, 123n,

525

# Index

# Index

Bramley (moneylender), 52
Bramsen (Bransen), Mr. (London), 83–84
Brandi, the Misses (Leghorn), 238
Brandi, Signor (Leghorn), 240–42, 246–48
Braubach, 36
Breisach (Brissac), 33
Bremen, 299n
Bret, Antoine: *Mémoires sur la vie de Mademoiselle de Lenclos*, 101, R.L.
*Bride of Abydos, The* (play based on Byron's poem), 85
Brie, 22
Brighton, 281
Brisighella, 468
Brissac, *see* Breisach
Brissot de Warville, J. P., 56
Bristol, 13n
British Institution, London, 82
British Museum, CC visits, 82
British Museum Add. MSS., 408n, 09n(q), 467–68q, 477–79q
British West Indies, 145
Bronzoli, Signora (Pisa), 179
Brooke, Charlotte: *Reliques of Irish Poetry*, 174–75, 176–77q, R.L.
Brotier, Gabriel, *see* Tacitus
Brown, C. B., *Ormond*, 172; source of name Constantia, 172n; R.L.
Brown, F. K., 17n, 125n, 338n
Brown, Baron Sigismund (Florence), *accademia* of, 206
Browne, Sir Thomas: *Religio Medici*, 430n
Brownlow st., London, 55
Brunnen, CC and Shelleys take lodgings there, 30; leave, 31; m. 29
Brunt, J. T., executed for treason, 148
Brutus, in Tacitus, 131
Brydone, Patrick, *A Tour through Sicily and Malta*, 144, R.L.
Buboli (Baths of Pisa), 171, 173
Buirette de Belloy, P.-L.: *Gabrielle de Vergy*, 266, R.L.
Buonavoglia, L. G.(?): *Il Ciarlatano*, 192, P.L.
Buoncompagni, Abate (Florence), 261
Burchiello, quoted by Forsyth, 390

Buree (Büren), 29
Bürger, G. A.: "Frau Schnipps," 307; "Lenore," 307n; R.L.
Burghersh, Lord (British minister in Florence), 236
Burgos, 433
Burke, Edmund, in Paine, 124
Burney, Dr. Charles, 113n
Burns, Robert: "Lament for Glencairn," 258q; "Tam O'Shanter," 258q; R.L.
Burr, Aaron: and Mrs. Godwin, 16–18q; describes visits to Godwins, 18–19; and Amelia Curran, 18, 108n(q); on MWS, 19
Butler, Mr. (Russia): CC writes to, 327, 330; letter to CC, 329; m. 312, 374
Butlers, the (Russia), 397
Butterlin, *see* Boutourlin
Byrom, John: epigram, 154–55n(q)
Byron, Lady, 481
Byron, Augusta Ada, 481
Byron, George Gordon, Lord:
  CHRONOLOGICAL: CC begins liaison, 69–71; lack of affection for CC, 72–75; view of PBS's poetry, 409; thirtieth birthday, 81; Venetian gossip about, 95; Allegra brought to him in Venice, 95; visit from Shelley, 96; credits gossip about CC, 97n; compared by CC to Count Cenci, 111n; goes to Ravenna, 116; vows to keep Allegra, 145; rumored to be in England, 172; on Sgricci, 472q; Sgricci imitates, 190; on Vaccà, 465; Vaccà on, 466; CC dreams of, 227–28; CC passes on road near Empoli, 253; squabble with Southey, 274; commissions translation of Goethe, 278; refuses Lady M's appeal for CC, 294–95; Elizabeth Parker on, 466; in Greek war of independence, 473–74; mentioned, vii–viii, 6, 40–41n, 61n, 74, 78, 80, 92, 107n, 109n, 113n, 115n, 130n, 144, 155n, 171, 176, 187n, 189n, 191, 192n, 198n, 200, 247, 281n, 284, 296, 403, 404n, 408–10, 437n, 443, 446, 467–68, 481

527

# Index

# Index

ence), 260–61, 265, 271, 273–74, 279–81, 283
Carrara, 248
Carter, Mr., 86
Carvoisin d'Achy, Anne de, duchess of Clermont-Tonnerre (Rome), 103
Cary, Mr. (English vice-consul in Rome), 111
Casa Aquinta, Pisa, 149
Casa Baldini, Florence, 168, 205
Casa Bertini (Shelleys' lodging at Baths of Lucca), 96, 105n
Casa Dori, Florence, 199
Casa Frasi (Frassi) (Shelleys' residence, Pisa), 120, 133
Casa Frilli, Via Chiara, Florence, 267
Casa Galetti (Shelleys' residence, Pisa), 189n
Casa Gerini, Florence, 115
Casa Giacour, 167
Casa Giorgi, Florence, 215
Casa Guidi, Florence, 470
Casa Lazzarini, Florence, 277
Casa Lozzi, 118
Casa Majotti, Florence, 211–12, 218
Casa Marucelli, Florence, 219
Casa Peruzzi (Princess Argyropoulo's house, Florence), 279
Casa Poschi, Pugnano, 150
Casa Prinni (Shelleys' residence, Baths of Pisa), 168
Casa Ricci (Gisbornes' house, Leghorn): Shelleys and CC move there, 151; CC spends month there, 172–78
Casa Schwaloff, Florence, 203, 210
Casa Seratti dietro San Remigi, Florence, 212n, 268, 273, 277
Casa Silva (Lady M's house, Pisa): CC arranges library, 148; m. 119n, 122–51 passim, 156, 172, 174, 178, 198, 243, 247, 249, 251, 253, 276, 467
Casa Spannocchi, Leghorn, 240. See other houses under the names of their owners
Casan, University of, 374
Casciana (Casciano), 147–51
Cascina, Florence: described, 203n; m. 185, 187, 199, 203–07, 209–10, 213, 218–19, 228–29, 233–34
Cascina, Pisa, 129, 448

Cascina dei Ricci, Florence, 280
Cassandra, 204
Cassius, in Tacitus, 131
Castel St. Angelo, Rome, 106
Casting of cylinder (Leghorn), 157–58
Castle and Falcon (inn in London), 57
Castlehaven, earl of, see Touchet, James
Castracani, Signor (Florence), 262, 269
Castruccio Castracani: MWS and CC visit tomb and copy inscriptions, 169–70q; subject of MWS novel Valperga, 169n; CC meets descendant of, 262
Catalani, Angelica (Adelina? prima donna, Pisa), 133
Caterina (Shelleys' servant), 174
Catherine (Russia), 367
Catherine II of Russia, 323, 341
Cato Street Conspiracy, 148, 252–53
Cause célèbre: Procès . . . Fualdès, 147, R.L.
Cavallegeri (Leghorn), 248–49
Cecile (Moscow), 394
Cellini, Benvenuto: Geschichte des XVI Jahrhunderts, trans. Goethe, 395, R.L.
Cenci, Count: Byron compared to, 111n
Cenci, Beatrice: portrait in Palazzo Colonna, Rome, 108; Theresa Emilia Viviani compared to, 190n; m. 111n
Cenci family, manuscript of, 111, R.L.
Ceprano, 217
Ceresa, Mme. (Florence), 206, 212
Cervantes, 465
Châlons-sur-Marne, 87
Chalons sur Seine (CC error for Châlons-sur-Marne, q.v.)
Champlitte, 24
Chapeau Rouge, Le (inn in Dijon), 87
Chapel st., Grosvenor Square (Westbrook residence), 42, 54
Charelli, see Sciarelli
Charenton, 22
Charlemagne, 269

529

# Index

Charles V of Germany, 226, 302

Charles VI of Germany, anecdote in Condorcet, 138

Charles d'Orléans, "Rondeau," 270q, R.L.

Charleville, Lady (Florence), 129

Charlotte (Leghorn), 175

Charlotte, Princess, 83n

Charlton st. (London), 56

Charrière, M. de la (Florence), 266, 268

Charters (Chartres), Thomas (coachmaker, PBS's creditor), 53–54

Chateau, Comte de (Florence), 212. *See also* Du Chateau

Chateaubriand, F. R. de: *De Buonaparte et des Bourbons*, 120q, R.L.

Chateinzoff, Mme. (Moscow), 310, 373, 396

Chateinzoffs, 397

Chatham, 42, 86

Chatham Place, London, 54

Chaumont, 24, 87

Cheval Blanc, Le (inn in Lucerne), 31

Chiappa, G. B. del (Shelleys' landlord at Baths of Lucca), 96, 105, 107

Chios, 404

Chiroplast, great fuss over, 123

Chopin, F. F., 371n

Christianity (includes references to Christ), 41, 90, 108n, 155, 184–86, 205, 391

Christ's Hospital, London, 14

*Ciarlatano, Il,* see Buonavoglia *and* Goldoni

Cibber, Theophilus (son of Colley Cibber), in Baker, 133

Cicalas, 155–56

Cicognara, Count Leopoldo (Florence), 213

Cimarosa, Domenico, 462

Cini family papers, 130

Cina, Giovanni Cosimo (CC's executor), 3

Cirillo, Domenichino (Neapolitan patriot), 147

Città Lavinia, 463

Clairmont, Alma Pauline, see Crüwell-Clairmont

Clairmont, Anita Albert, 481

Clairmont, Antonie Ghi(s)lain ("Tonie"), C. G. Clairmont's wife, 14, 415, 417, 481

"Clairmont, C.," pseudonym of C.-H. Gambs (*q.v.*)

Clairmont, Charles (unidentified father of CC), 15, 28n, 480–81

Clairmont, Charles Gaulis (CC's brother): birth and parentage, 13n, 14–15; works for Constable (Edinburgh), 18; relations with CC and Shelleys in *1814*, 43–44, 53, 55, 57, 59; to Ireland, 69; moves from Spain to Florence to Vienna, 114n; letters to MWS, 122, 123n(q), 296–97q, 315n; letters to CC, 122, 132q, 149, 174–75 (summarized), 241, 269, 275, 359; love for Louisa du Plantis, 122n; joined by CC in Vienna, 284n, 285; career in Vienna, 293, 296; described by CC and Trelawny, 293; visits England, 415; returns to Vienna, 418; m. 295, 480–81. *See also under* CC, letters

Clairmont, Charles Gaulis (CC's nephew), 481

Clairmont, Claire (Clara Mary Jane, also called Jane, Clara, and Clare)
CHRONOLOGICAL: antecedents and early life, 13–20, 28, 480–81; varying forms of name, 13n; accompanies PBS and MWS on elopement, 20–22; begins journal, 23; returns to England, 42; fits of horrors, 31, 48–49; involved in PBS's London troubles, 42–59; letter from Godwin, 51; quarrels with PBS and MWS, 50–52, 54, 58; goes to Lynmouth, 68–69; to Ireland, 69; begins liaison with Byron, 69–71; Byron's "Stanzas for Music" thought to be addressed to her, ix, xiii; pregnancy, 72; lodges in Bath, 73–74; birth of Allegra, 76; at Marlow, 76–78; PBS's "To Constantia Singing" written for her, ix, xiv–xv, 13n, 79, 172n; sightseeing and visiting in London, 82–86; trip to Italy with Shelleys and Allegra, 87–95;

# Index

caricatures, 182–84; attacks Medwin's characterization, 408–10, 428–29

OPINIONS ON PBS: and Allegra, 433; attacks Medwin's view of, 409, 429; caricature, 184; and Cicero, 370; eulogies, 315, 423–24, 435; Max Piccolomini compared to, 329

MISCELLANEOUS OPINIONS (not exhaustive) on: architecture, 437; brutality related to madness, 80; civilization, 410; drama, 321–22; education, 298, 424–25; equality, 406–07; German licentiousness, 36–37, 39; hunting, 59; love and the sexes, 406–08; marriage, 116–17, 367–68; nature and romantic scenery, 25–28, 30, 89, 311, 317–18, 322–24, 354, 359, 381, 421, 429–30; philosophy, 305–06, 320, 408; poets, 194–95, 225–26; religion, 90, 154–55, 367, 408, 426–28; reviewers, 138–39; ruins, 24, 27, 37, 100; Russia, 207, 408; sentiments and thought, 354

WRITINGS: "Beggar's Bush"(?), 135; *Cloudesley* (possibly assisted Godwin), 416–17; Common Place Book, 43; "Gertrude," 58; "Hints for Don Juan," *see under* CC, opinions on Byron; "Ideot," 40, 43–44, 48; "Introduction to History," 377, 381, 387–88; Islavsky Gazette, 327, 331, 333–34, 336, 338, 342–43; journals — compared to those of PBS and MWS, 6–7, description of manuscripts, 7–9, previous use by scholars, vii–viii, 3; letters — to be edited, ix, m. 297, 416, *see also* CC, letters, below; "Letters from Italy" — writes, 98–99, 138, 140–41, 156, 159, copies, 154–55, 159–60; "Notes for S[helley]," 315; novel, rough draft shown to Byron, 75; novel unsuccessfully offered by PBS to publisher, 77; "The Pole," 416

LETTERS: to Atwood & Co., 372–73; Mr. Baxter, 319, 327, 336, 357, 363, 373–74, 381, 391–92, 396; Madame Bojti, 191, 193, 238, 240–41, 244, 251, 259, 262, 267, 269, 271, 273; Miss Boutourlin, 283; Countess Maria Boutourlin, 251, 273; Mr. Butler, 327, 330; Byron, 13n(q), 14–17, 28n, 40n–41n(q), 61n(q), 70q, 71q, 72–73, 74–75q, 78–79q, 92, 95q, 97n(q), 111n(q), 112, 115n(q), 127, 135n, 144–46, 149, 171, 191, 193, 197n(q), 205, 217–18, 275–76n(q); C. G. Clairmont, 44, 53, 57, 122, 264, 269, 276–77, 336; Mr. Cornet, 376, 378, 386; Miss Farhill, 239–40; Henrietta Feldhausen, 374; Maria Gisborne, 102n(q), 113n, 153; M. J. Godwin (includes "Skinner Street"): 52–53, 238, 275, 277, 355; Colonel Griefsky, 330; Mr. Harvey, 344, 359; Mrs. Hoppner, 105, 111, 127, 130–31, 135, 144–45, 152; Dina Williams Hunt 143n(q); Fanny Imlay, 57q; Mme. Ivanoff, 259, 263, 268, 271, 274, 277, 282–83; Mrs. Kaisaroff, 369; Mrs. Leon, 381; James Marshal, 50–51; Mme. Martini, 205; Lady M, 153, 156, 173–74, 178, 180–82, 185, 199, 201–04, 206–07, 209–10, 212, 215, 218, 220–21, 224, 228–31, 233, 238, 244, 246, 253, 255, 259, 261, 263–64, 266, 269, 271–78, 280–81, 296, 368, 385; Princess Ouronsoff, 367; Mme. du Plantis, 123; Louisa du Plantis, 122, 123n; Mme. Polen, 386; Mrs. Pollok, 120, 124, 127, 130, 137; Miss Sayce, 392; Mrs. Seymour, 330, 357; Harriet Shelley, 54; MWS, 14, 69q, 174, 178, 179n(q), 182, 199–204, 206–11, 215, 218–20, 228, 230–32, 240, 242, 247, 249, 253, 255, 259, 262, 264, 268, 273–74, 276–77, 279, 279n(q), 280–83, 285n(q), 298q, 299q, 308n(q), 326n, 334n, 339n–40n, 415q, 417q, 417n(q); PBS, 56, 180–82, 186, 203, 205–07, 210, 217, 219, 224, 228–30, 232–33,

# Index

# Index

Shakespeare, 272; writing assertion of the Christian religion, 272; m. 68; R.L.

Coliseum, Rome, 97, 99–100, 103–05

Collegio Ferdinando di Pisa, 470

Collini, Pisa, 188

Colocotrone, 475

Cologne, 36–37

Colombani, Count, of Forli (Florence), 269

Como, Lake, 89, 91, 454

Condorcet, Marquis de, see Caritat

Constable, Archibald (Godwin's publisher, employer of C. G. Clairmont), 18

Constantia, name assumed by CC, ix, xiv–xv, 13n, 79, 172n

Constantine, Grand Duke, 257, 304, 392, 394

Constantine, arch of, Rome, 100

Constantinople, 474–75

*Constitutionel* (French newspaper), 191n(q)

*Continental Adventures*, 441, 452–54

*Conversazione*, described, 103

Cooper, Mr. (Shelley's creditor), 44

Cordella, Giacomo (?), 192n

Cornaro, Catterina, Queen of Cyprus, 468

Cornaro family, 468

Cornaro, Giorgio, 468

Cornaro, Luigi, on Venice, 215q

Cornet, Mr. (Russia): CC writes to, 376, 378, 386; letters to CC 374, 387; m. 305–06, 319, 326, 333, 335–40, 342, 353–54, 357

Corsi, Mr., 46

Corsicoff, Mr. (Russia), 339

Corsini, Prince Nero: children of, 263; offended by Sgricci, 472

Corso, Florence, 211, 213

Corso, Rome, 99, 110, 162

Cosimo di Medici, 186n

Cottin, Sophie, *Claire d'Albe*, 76n

*Courier* (London newspaper): review of ballet *Zephyr* reprinted, 461; m. 19n, 50n, 83n

Cournand, Miss (Russia): writes to CC, 330; m. 312

Court Chapel, Florence, 227

Courval, Vicomte de, 359n

Covent Garden Theatre, 50, 84, 458

Coveri (Florence), 204

Coxe, Henry, *Picture of Italy*, 197, R.L.

Crawford, Jane, 481

Crébillon, P. J. de, *Rhadamisthe et Zénobie*, 267, R.L. *See also* Pompadour

Crespino, near Pisa, 243

Croce di Malta (inn at Lucca), 169

Croft, Sir Richard, news of his death, 83

Cross Keys, St. John st., London, 57

Crüwell, Gottlieb, 481

Crüwell-Clairmont, Alma Pauline, 4, 9, 481

Cullen, Dr. William, 464

Cuoco, Vincenzo: *Saggio storico sulla rivoluzione di Napoli*, 146–48, 150, 152–55, 158–60, 168, 171, R.L.

Curran, Amelia: visitor at Godwin's, 16; friend of Aaron Burr, 18, 108n; association with Shelleys and CC in Rome, 108–13; paints portraits of CC and Shelleys, 109n, 110–11; MWS writes to, 109n(q)

Curran, J. P.: visitor at Godwin's, 16; *Life*, 134; m. 180n

Curran, W. H., *Life of J. P. Curran*, 134, R.L.

Cuvier, George, 188n

"Cyanippe and his daughter" (ballet), Florence, 236, P.L.

Czernicheff, Prince, 326n, 394

Czernicheff, Princess, *see* Zotoff, Betsy

D'Agincourt, 463

Daltons (or Doltons, Florence), 115

Dante Alighieri: CC and PBS discuss, 52; *Divina Commedia*, 222; *Inferno*, in hand of PBS, 61–62q, 192q, 222q; *Paradiso*, 110, 223q, 224n, 390–91q, 411q; *Purgatorio*, 111–12, 191, 390q; m. 115n, 189n, 195, 208n; R.L.

DaPonte, Lorenzo: *Così fan tutte* (Mozart's libretto), 85; *Le Mariage de Figaro* (Mozart's libretto), 84; R.L.

Dartford, 86

534

# Index

# Index

# Index

# Index

Florence: CC and Shelleys there, 114-18; CC goes there to live, 179; CC returns to, from Pisa, 199, 253; CC departs from, for Vienna, 284n, 285; m. 96, 102, 173n-74n, 187n, 193, 199, 201, 202n, 203n, 205n, 209, 215-16, 220n, 223n, 230n, 255n, 411, 454, 466, 470-71, 473, and many more, too numerous to list
Florence road (from Pisa), 149
Flower, Desmond, of Cassell & Co., 5
Fodor (soprano), 83n
Foggi, Elise (Swiss nursemaid to Shelley children): conducts Allegra to Byron, 95; meets Paolo Foggi, 96; gossips about Shelleys and CC to Hoppners, 97, 274; letters from, 104, 204; meets with CC in Florence, 275, 277-80, 282-83; writes Mrs. Hoppner, 279, 283; m. 73n, 76, 87n, 118, 176
Foggi, Professor Ferdinando ("Fudge," Pisa): description by Finch, 189q; m. 190, 192
Foggi, Paolo (Shelleys' servant): meets Elise, 96; attempts to blackmail PBS, 97, 150n; m. 279
Fontana (inn in Florence), 179
Fontebuoni, two (Florence), 213, 236
Forli, 269
Forman, H. B.: purchaser of CC's journals, 3, 7, 9; m. 62n, 199n, 284n, 285n, 472
"Fornara, the," see Cogni, Margarita
Forsyth, Joseph: Remarks on Antiquities, Arts, and Letters, 105-06n, 388q, 389, 390-91q, 392-94, 442, R.L.
Forteguerri, Niccolò: Il Ricciardetto, 108-09, R.L.
Forum, Rome, 99-100, 103-04, 109
Fossombrone, Vittorio, 473
France, history of, 344-351
Franceschini, La (Florence), 271
Francesco (vetturino, Florence), 285
Francis I of Austria, 296
Francis, Mr., on Cobbett, 80
Fraser, Mr. (Florence), 229
Frederick of Prussia, anecdote of, 138
Frederiga (Florence), 215

Frederigo (Florence), 234
Fremantle, W. Australia, 469
French Revolution: in de Staël, 200; and Andrea Vaccà, 464
Freycavalli (Fricavalli, Frecavalli), Count (Leghorn), 240, 243-45, 247
Freyre, General, 134
Friend, W., 79-80
Frimont, General, 209n
Frommel, C., 299n
Frommel, Emil Wilhelm, 299n, 302, 303q
Frommel, Henriette Gambs, 299n, 376
Frommel, Otto H., 302-03n
Fualdès, A. B.: Godwin meets, 147n; see also Cause célèbre: Procès . . . Fualdès
Funzioni at St. Peter's, Rome, 106n
Furso, see Viersen

Galavine, Mr. (Moscow), 388, 393
Galignani's Messenger, 274, R.L.
Galimberti, lawyer and wife (Rome), 108
Galitzin, Princess (Moscow): employs CC, 401; m. 403, 405-08
Galitzin, Prince Alexander, 401, 403, 407-09
Galitzin, Helen ("Lenska") 403, 408
Galitzin, Prince Paul, 336, 394, 403, 405, 407
Galitzin, Prince Peter, 401, 406, 409
Gall, Dr. F. J., 44
Galli, Signor (Florence), 255
Gambs, Chrétien-Hermann ("M.G.," "Midge," "Ya Yan"):
CHRONOLOGICAL: CC describes, 298-99, 323; compared to PBS, 299-300, 313n, 318n-19; his family, 299, 302-03; plays the horn, 309, 382; anecdotes of student days, 309; anecdotes of country life, 316; on astronomy, 315, 320; in amateur theatricals, 332-33; birthday, 344; letter to CC, 366; anecdote of Tetzlar, 373; leaves Moscow, 410n; publication under pseudonym "C. Clairmont," 299-300; degree in theology, 300;

538

# Index

# Index

Gillman, James, 19n

Ginora (*fabbrica*), in San Lorenzo, Florence, 223, 228

Giordani, Pietro, 471–72

Giorgi, Signor (Florence), 275

Giovanni, Signor (Florence), 273

*Girandola* at Castel St. Angelo, Rome, described, 106

Gisborne and Williams, *Journals*, 157n, 171n, 180n, 251n, 253n, 272n, 284n

Gisborne, John: described, 114n; atheistical conversation, 142; letters from, 149–50, 154, 171; m. 95, 114, 130, 144, 220n, 249n, 298n, 308n, 359n

Gisborne, Maria (Mrs. John Gisborne, formerly Mrs. Reveley): CC writes to, 102n(q), 113n, 153; Godwin writes to, 272q; PBS writes to, 139n(q), 249n(q); atheistical conversation, 142; leaves for England, 144; on return offends Shelleys, 179n; letters to MWS, 179, 143n(q), 272q, 280; m. 76n, 95, 98, 101n, 104n, 105n, 109n, 113n, 114, 116n, 130, 132, 139n, 151n, 153, 155n 189n, 194n, 220n, 255n, 468–69. *See also under* MWS, letters

Gisbornes, the, *see* Gisborne, Maria

Giulia, Signora (Leghorn), 177

Giuliani, Signor (Florence), 233

Giunto-tardi (language-master, Rome), 143

Giuseppe (*vetturino*, Florence), 285

Giusti, Laura Vaccà, 466

Glaive (?), *see* Grevenbroich

Glasse, Hannah, cookbook, 388

Glinka, Mme. (Moscow): and her children, 382; m. 307

Glinka, Mr., 379

Glinka, M. I., 314n

Glinka, Walodi, 379

Godwin, Fanny, *see* Imlay, Fanny

Godwin, M. J., and Co., Juvenile Library: founded, 17; books published by, 45n, 157n, 171n; ceases publication, 338n

Godwin, Mary Jane (Mrs. William Godwin, CC's mother): ambiguous history, 13–15, 28n; marriage to Godwin, 14–15; as hostess and mother, 15–19; and flight of CC with Shelleys, 20–21; persecution of Fanny Imlay, 75; letter to MWS, 56; letter from Godwin to, 79q; letters to Jane Williams, 296; letter to CC, 337–38; meets Miss Trewin, 401–02; m. 20, 43, 45n, 50, 52–53, 56, 68, 73, 75–77, 171, 238, 275, 277, 467, 480. *See also under* CC, letters; Godwin, M. J., Juvenile Library

Godwin, Mary Wollstonecraft, *see* Wollstonecraft, Mary

Godwin, William:

CHRONOLOGICAL: courtship and marriage to Mrs. Clairmont, 14–15; described by Lamb, 15; meets Fualdès, 147n; financial distress, 16, 20, 59, 153n, 337–38; moves from Somers Town to Skinner st., 17; family life, 16–20; Shelley writes to, 43–44, 151n; alienated from CC and Shelleys, 20, 52, 59; reconciled to them, 76; visits them in Marlow, 76, 80; description of CC, 77; visited by CC and Charles, 416; m., 43n, 44, 53, 55–56, 69n, 73, 75–77, 95, 114n, 119n, 156n, 293, 296, 298, 401–02, 417, 480. *See also* Skinner st.

WRITINGS: *Caleb Williams*, 168; *Cloudesley*, 416–17; diaries, 15q, 16, 18, 19n, 35n, 47n, 69n, 76n, 78n, 147n, 402n, 416n, 418n; *Memoirs of the Author of the Rights of Woman*, 35; pamphlet defending Horne Tooke *et al.*, 124n–25n; *Political Justice*, 44–45, 47–50, 52, 54, 57–59, 386; *St. Leon*, 48, 51; R.L.

LETTERS (exclusive of many references without quotation in footnotes): to CC, 51; Maria Gisborne, 272q; Mrs. Godwin, 79q; MWS and PBS, 22, 45; Taylor of Norwich, 55n(q)

Godwin, William, Jr.: born, 15; gives lectures in imitation of Coleridge, 19; to school, 20; visits Shelleys and CC in Marlow, 80; m. 18, 480

540

# Index

# Index

# Index

Hookham, Thomas, Jr. (publisher): PBS writes to, 43; mediator between PBS and Harriet, 42–49, 51–52; his "treachery," 53; m. 56–57, 61n

Hope, Thomas: *Anastasius*, 247, 248q, R.L.

Hoppner, R. B. (British consul general at Venice): kindness to Shelleys, 96; hears scandalous gossip from Elise, 97, 274–75; letter from Byron to, 145n

Hoppner, Mrs. R. B.: Elise writes to, 279, 283; MWS writes to, 118, 127; letters from, 106, 116, 134, 145 ("concerning green fruit and God"), 145, 149; m. 96. See also *under* CC, letters

Hôtel de l'Europe (inn in Lyons), 87

Houtchens, L. H. and C. W., 83n

Houwald, E. C. von: *Das Bild*, 360–62q, R.L.

Hudson, J. C. (Somerset House), 397

Hugford, Mrs. (schoolmistress): PBS writes to, 48; m. 46n, 47

Hulot d'Osery, General, 359n

Humboldt, F. H. A. von, 188n

Hume, David: "Enquiry Concerning Human Understanding," 196; letter to Adam Smith; 134q; R.L.

Hummel, J. N.: variations on *La Sentinelle* and on a march from *Cenerentola*, 375, P.L.

Hunt, John (son of Leigh Hunt), 77

Hunt, Leigh (includes "the Hunts"): CC and Allegra visit, 76; association with CC and Shelleys in London, 81–86; MWS writes to, 76q, 472; PBS writes to, 108n(q), 111, 119n(q), 133q; letter to Shelleys, 105; CC criticises, 200; m. 89n, 154n, 169, 234n

 WRITINGS: "Daughter of Hippocrates," in *Indicator* (1820), 194q; *Examiner*, 82n, 83n, 84n, 150, reviews of ballets reprinted, 458–61; *Indicator*, 193–94, 196; R.L.

Hunt, Marianne (wife of Leigh Hunt): MWS writes to, 469q; m. 76–77, 81, 85

Hunt, Mary (daughter of Leigh Hunt), 77

Hunt, Rosalind (Dina) Williams (daughter of Jane and E. E. Williams): CC letter to, 143n(q); m. 284n

Hunt, Swynburne (son of Leigh Hunt), 77

Hunt, Thornton (son of Leigh Hunt), description of CC, 77

Hunter, Dr. John, 464

Huscher, Herbert, 4, 13n–15n, 28n, 190n, 191n, 231n, 241n, 293n, 296n, 303n–05n

Hutchinson, Mrs. Lucy: *Memoirs of Col. Hutchinson*, 245q, 246, R.L.

Hutchinson's Magazine (shop in Moscow), 306

Hyde Park, London, 203n

Hydra, 404, 474

Ichebaiff, Mr. (Moscow), 410

Ichahafskoy, Prince: a Russian piece by, 340, P.L.

Ile de Barbe, L' (Lyons), 87

Ilinski (Russia), 362, 364

Imlay, Fanny (daughter of Mary Wollstonecraft and Gilbert Imlay): parentage, 15; entertains Aaron Burr, 18–19; dines with Shelley and Harriet, 19; goes to Pentredevy, Wales, 20; difficult relations with CC and Shelleys, 43, 53, 55, 57; CC writes to, 57q; *Man of Feeling* ideal husband for her, 59, 75; persecution by Mrs. Godwin, 75; her suicide, 74–75; letters to MWS quoted, 75; m. 68, 480

Imlay, Gilbert (common-law husband of Mary Wollstonecraft), 15, 480

"Impromptu d'Islavsky," *see under* Gambs, C.-H.; Genischta, Joseph

India, 135n

India House Library, visited, 83

Indian Song, see Hafiz Shirazi

*Indicator, The,* see Hunt, Leigh

Inez de Castro, Sgricci improvises on, 451

Ingpen, Roger: plans for editing CC's journals, 4–5q, 6; m. 3, 55n, 60n

Ings, J., executed for treason, 148

# Index

# Index

# Index

Koutouzoff, Princess (Florence), 256, 259, 263–64

Krouschoff, Miss (Russia), 325

Krouschoff, Mr., 325

Kurakin, Prince (father of Countess Zotoff), 297

"Kut-off," Countess (Zotoff?), in Hogg's caricature, 409n

Kynil, M. (Russia), 324, 326

Kyrieff, Alexis (pupil to Mr. Baxter, Moscow), 306n, 368, 377, 386–89, 406

Labanoff, Prince Jean (Moscow), 396, 405

La Boétie, Étienne de, *Discours de la servitude volontaire*: CC translates, 131–32, 134–36; CC transcribes, 136–37; R.L.

Labruzzi, Carlo (Perugia), 462

*Lacente*, see *Sacente*

*Lady Castlereigh* (Dover-Calais ship), 86

La Fère, 87

Lagesward (Lagesworth), Mme. (Florence), 234, 266

Lagesward (Lagesworth), M., 234, 266, 273

La Grennée (La Grenet), Auguste (Moscow), 369

La Grennée, François (painter, Moscow), 369–70

La Harpe, F. C., tutor to Czar Alexander I, 303

Lally, Miss de, 426

Lamb, Charles, attacks on Mrs. Godwin, 15q, 17

Lamb, Charles and Mary, and the Godwins, 16–18

Lambe, Mary (daughter of Dr. William Lambe), 86

Lambe, Dr. William (physician and vegetarian), 86n

Lambert (Godwin's creditor), 59

La Motte-Fouqué, Baron de: *Die Cypressenkranze*, 309–10; *Sintram*, 202, 206n; *Der Zauberring*, 353–54; R.L.

Landor, W. S. (Pisa): refuses to see English, 146; on PBS, 146n

Langhorne, John and William (translators of Plutarch), 115n

Langres, 24, 87

Lanslebourg, 88

L'Antinori, Marchesa (Leghorn), 242, 268

Lanz, Miss Caroline (Swiss, Florence), 261–64, 267–69, 273, 276

Laon, France, 87

Laponchkine (Laponkine), Prince (Russia), 340

Lattin (Latin), Miss (Florence), 206, 215, 228, 230, 233–34

Laufenbourg (Luffenbourg), 32–33

La Verna, 390

Lavoisier, A. L., 305

La Vrine (L'Avrine), 26

Lawrence, J. H.: *Empire of the Nairs*, 46, R.L.

Lazzarettos, Leghorn, 157

Leadenhall street, London, 42

Lecky, W. E. H., 129n

Lefanu, Alicia: *Helen Monteagle*, 82, R.L.

Lega, Lorenzo, 468

Lega-Weekes, Ethel, 468

Legerino (probably CC's dancing master in Pisa), 141–42, 144–48, 178

Leghorn (Livorno): described, 177–78, 242, 450; CC and Shelleys there, 113–14; PBS visits, 120–21, 131–32, 142, 144; CC visits coral manufactories, 160; CC and Shelleys move there for summer, 151; they leave for Baths of Pisa, 168; CC's extended stays there, 172–78, 237–49; m. 95, 153, 156–57, 159–60, 172, 174, 179, 188, 198–99, 201, 235n, 244–45n, 247–48, 447, 450, 469

Lehnhold's (music publisher, Moscow), 406

Leinster, duchess of, 240n

Lemierre, A. M.: *Hypermnestre*, 267, R.L.

Lenclos, *see* Bret, Antoine

Leon, Mrs. (Russia): CC writes to, 381; m. 385

Leopoldine (Russia), letter to CC, 343

Lerici: Shelleys, Williamses, and CC there, 284n; recalled in Islavsky, 314, 324; m. 295, 436, 454

546

# Index

# Index

Mannucci, Signor (Florence), 264
Manso, G. B.: *Vita di Torquato Tasso*, 90–91n
Manson, Mme., 147n
Mansouroff, Mr. (Moscow), 374
Mantua, 227
Manzoni, Alessandro: *Conte di Carmagnola*, 289
Marathon, 404
Marchand, Leslie, vii, 70n, 71n, 73n, 76n, 107n, 294n, 404n, 472
Marchatti, Mme. (Florence), 256
Marcello, Benedetto: *Psalmi*: heard in Rome, 113; in Florence, 264; P.L.
Marcone, Nicola, 464
Maremma, 158
Margaret st., Cavendish Square, Shelleys' lodgings, 43, 46, 55
Margate, CC there, probably in boarding school, 18
Maria Ferdinanda, Princess, of Saxony: marries grand duke of Tuscany, 230; her wardrobe, 271; her *accouchement*, 470
Marignolle, 265
Mariti, in Pananti, 273
Marlow: "To Constantia Singing" composed there, ix; Shelleys and CC live there, 76–78; leave, 81–82; m. 86, 124
Marmontel, J. F.: *Memoirs*, 329–30, R.L.
Marseilles, 469
Marshal (Marshall), James (Godwin's assistant): CC corresponds with, 50–51; m. 20, 55
Marshall, Mrs. Julian (biographer of MWS), 68n, 72n, 222n, 410n, 416n–18n
Martin, Abbé Guillaume (?): *Voyage à Constantinople*, 99, R.L.
Martin and Call (Shelley's bankers), 42
Martini, Mme. (mother of Sgricci, Florence): and her nephew, 205; CC writes to, 205; letter to CC, 205; m. 119, 201–02, 204, 206–09, 218, 230, 236, 256, 470, 473
Masi incident, 189n
Mason, Mrs., see Mount Cashell, Lady
Massa: epigram on, 158; m. 248

Massina, 462
Massinger, Philip, see Beaumont, Francis
Massy, Miss (Russia), 325–26, 340, 348
Matiouchkin, Feodor Feodorovitch (Russia): his daughter, 388; *Le Nord de la Sibérie*, 389; m. 365, 374, 385, 388; R.L.
Matravers (Maltravers?), 60
Mattapoisett, Massachusetts, 468
Mavrocordato, Prince Alexander: account of by Millingen, reprinted, 473–76; anecdote of, 404; described by Bessie Kent, 77n; m. 190n, 191, 193, 198–99, 261
Mavrogenia, Modena (Greek heroine), anecdote of, 404
Mayntz (Mayence), see Mainz
Mazimsky, Mme. (Russian, in Florence), 263
Mazour, A. G., 386n
Mazzei, casa, Florence, 208
Mazzei, Lucrezia (*improvvisatrice*): heard in Florence, 208, 219; described by Lady Murray, 208n(q); P.L.
Mazzoni Collection, Duke University Library, x
Meadows, Mr. and Mrs. (Florence), 114–18
Medici, Cavaliere, ex-minister of Naples (Florence), 271
Medwin, Thomas, Jr. (PBS's second cousin): believed CC would have been successful actress, 17n; bores the Shelleys, 187n; description of CC, 187n(q); description of Theresa Emilia Viviani, 189n–90n(q); letters from, 135, 154; on hypnosis of PBS, 196n; on PBS and Oriental music, 286n–87n(q); on Sgricci, 473; visits CC, 212, 215, 233; visits Theresa Emilia Viviani, 191; m. 187, 192n, 199n, 213, 276, 283n
  WRITINGS: "Canova," *Fraser's Magazine* (1839), 103n; *Conversations of Lord Byron* (CC criticises, 408–10, 428–29), 198n(q), 278n(q); *Shelley*, 187n(q),

548

# Index

189n–90n(q), 196n, 286n–78n(q), 473; R.L.
Meheux (Switzerland?), 60
Melianofsky, Mme. (Moscow), 385–86
Menander, *Arrephoren*, 254
Mendelssohn, Moses: Plato's *Phaedon*, 329, R.L.
Mendes Pinto, Fernando: *Voyages and Adventures*, 263, 265–66, R.L.
Mercato nuovo (Florence), 253, 256, 262, 268, 282–83
Mercier, L. S.: *Mon Bonnet de nuit*, 110, R.L.
Mericourt, Theroigne de, 80
Merrytt, Miss (Moscow), 370, 387
Merryweather, Mr. (Milan), 92
Metastasio, Pietro: *La Clemenza di Tito*, 218–19; m. 208n; P.L.
Metaxà, Constantine (Greek nobleman), 474
Metka Schild and Ernest, story of, 370
Metternich, 296
Mettingen, 32
Meyerbeer, Giacomo: *Il Crociato in Egitto*, 310, P.L.
Miccale (Florence), 212
Michailovitch, Vassili (Russia), 344–354
Michailovna, Olga (niece of Marie Ivanovna, Russia): her birthday, 336; m. 306–07, 310, 314, 316, 319, 332, 338, 354, 356–58, 361, 363, 365, 368, 374, 380
Michaud, J. F.: *Histoire du croisades*, 215, R.L.
Michelofsky, Nicholas (Russia), 312, 314, 317–18, 323, 325, 328, 340, 342, 344, 353, 356–58, 361–63, 365, 367, 388
Micher Boden (promontory on Lake Lucerne), 29, 60
Mickhaelovskoe, 311n
Middleton, Thomas, *see* Beaumont, Francis
Milan: Cathedral, 90; Corso, 90–92; opera, 89, 92, 234n; public gardens, 72; Theater of the Marionetti, 91; m. 87, 89, 471
Milan, Congress of, 306
Milanese Gazettes, 217, R.L.

Milani (painter, Rome), 102
Milanie, Mlle. (prima ballerina): impact on PBS, 85n; PBS compares Jungfrau to, 88; m. 460–61
Millingen, Julius: *Memoirs of the Affairs of Greece*, extract reprinted, 473–76
Milman, H. H.: *Fazio*, 84, P.L.
Milner, Major, 426
Miloradovich, General Count M. A., 393
Milton, John: CC visits grave, 19; *Comus*, 56; *Paradise Lost*, 377, 386; R.L.
Miltz, Mr. 425
Minerva Medica, temple of, Rome, 101
Minerva Press, 112n
*Miserere*, heard in Rome, 104, P.L.
Missolonghi, 362, 404, 474, 476
Modane (Modène), 88
*Modern Encyclopaedia of Australia and New Zealand*, 469–70
"Moira Borb," in Brooke, *Reliques*, 176q
Mole, The (Leghorn), 239–42
Molière: *L'Amour médicin*, 90; *Amphitryon*, 92; *L'Avare*, 90; *Le Bourgeois Gentilhomme*, 90; *La Comtess d'Escarbargnas*, 91; *Le Dépit Amoureux*, 91–92; *Don Juan; ou, le festin de pierre*, 90; *L'Étourdi*, 91; *Les Fourberies de Scapin*, 90; *George Dandin*, 90; *Le Malade imaginaire*, 91; *Le Mariage forcé*, 90; *Le Médecin malgré lui*, 91; *M. de Pourceaugnac*, 90; *Les Précieuses ridicules*, 92; *Le Tartuffe*, 90q; m. 465; R.L.
Molini (Florence), 274
Molino, Leghorn, 157
Mombelli, Mlle. (prima donna, Florence), 204n
Monchanoff, Mme. (Russia), 338, 340, 366, 371
Monchelles, Mme. du (Moscow), 310
Monboddo, Lord, 124
Monff, *see* Mumph
Montague, Lady Mary Wortley, 38n
Montaigne, M. E. de, 131n
Montain du Rhin (inn at Cologne), 37

549

# Index

# Index

119n; *Stories of Old Daniel*, 45n, 157n; R.L.

LETTERS: to Byron, 294; CC, 173–75, 201–02, 204, 206–07, 209–10, 212, 216, 218, 220–21, 224, 226, 228–31, 233, 235, 242–44, 246, 249, 254–56, 260, 262–63, 266, 268–69, 271–75, 277–79, 281–82, 363; MWS, 143n(q), 294–95q, 296q, 467q, 470q; Shelleys and CC, 156. *See also under* Casa Silva; CC, letters

Mount Cashell, Lord, *see* Moore, Stephen

Mozart, W. A.: anecdote of, in Gerning, 232; *La Clemenza di Tito*, overture, 268; *Don Giovanni*, 83, 85, 461; *Le Nozze di Figaro*, 82n, 182(?), 310–11, 326, 331–32, 337, 354, 357, 359–60, 368; P.L. *See also* Da Ponte

Mozzi, Marchesa, 244

Mù, 421

Mugnai (lawyer, Florence), 209n

Mugnaj, Luisa (CC's German teacher in Florence): CC pays, 230; m. 209, 216–17, 219, 227, 236. *See also* Borgo Pinti

Müller, Mme. (Swiss in Florence), 281

Müllner, A. G. A.: *Die Schuld*, 381, 383–85n(q), R.L.

Mumph (Monff), 32

Murgantal, 29, 60

Murray, Lady, 203n, 308n–12n, 216n, 259n, 462q

Murray, Sir John (Byron's friend and publisher), 148, 183

Murray, Sir John (editor of Byron letters), 76n, 279n

Murray, Sir John: owner of Byron papers, x; *see also* Murray MSS

Murray MSS, 13n, 70n–72n, 75n, 79n, 95n, 97n, 111n

Muro Rotto, Leghorn, 238, 241, 244, 246

Mutii, Capt. and Signora (Florence): 115; nephew of Capt. M., 116

Naldi (baritone), 83n

Naples: described, 438; Elise and Neapolitan mystery, 274, 278; Neapolitan war hymn, 213–15n (q); PBS on, 214n; revolution, 156, 159, 172, 196, 199, 203n, 207–10, 215–18, 332, 433, 444; m. 96–98, 108n, 126, 218, 229, 264, 268

Naples, King of, 156, 159, 196, 198–99, 215–16, 473

Naples, King and Queen, epigram on, 218

Napoleon Bonaparte, 22, 36–37, 39, 87–88, 103, 230n, 242, 257, 299n, 303, 306, 446, 468

Nash, Andrew John and George Augustus (moneylenders), 20

Nasi, the Misses (Florence), 258

Natalie (Russia), 356

Natalie (Zotoff?), 394–95

Navarino, 404

Nazarievna (seat of Prince Galitzin), 336, 344, 358

Necker, Jacques, in Pananti, 224

Negri, G., 211n

Nelson's Square, London, 59

"Nerina," *see* Tighe, Catherine

Nero: house of, Rome, 100; in Pananti, 221

Nesselrode, C. R. von 202n

Neuchâtel, 27–28

New Bedford, Henry Reveley there, 469

New Bond st., Bath (CC's residence), 73n

Newgate st., London, auctioneer in, 50

New Hummums Family Hotel (Peacock's residence, London), 82

Newman, H. R. (agent for H. B. Forman), 3

New Orleans, Louisiana, in De Staël, 200

Newspapers, 152, 187, 205, 212

Newstead Abbey, Curran portrait of CC there, 109n

Newton, Isaac, 239

Nice, 418

Nicholas I, czar of Russia, 304, 387, 393

Nicholson, William, *Introduction to Natural Philosophy*, 152, R.L.

Nicolaivitch (Nicolaitch), Zachar (lawyer, Moscow; husband of

# Index

Marie Ivanovna): reaction to Dunia's death, 365; m. 297–98, 308n, 316, 319, 327–28, 339, 343–44, 357–58, 362–64, 368, 381, 396
Nicolavitch, Vassili (Russia), 348
Nicolskoi, Gara, 340, 344
Nijmegen (Nimeguen), 38, 40
Nitchie, Elizabeth, 109n, 114
Nizhni Novgorod, 306
Noah, 428
Nodz (Noë), 26
Nogent, 22
Nore, The, 42
Norfolk, duke of, 88
Norfolk st., 46
Normanby, Lord: *English in Italy*, review by MWS reprinted, 441, 443–52, 457
North Pole, 256, 433
Notopoulos, James, 153n, 198n
Novello, Vincent: obtains piano for CC, 78
Novelluccia, Lino (Florence), 219
Nugent, Catherine: Harriet Shelley's letters to, 16n
Numa, in Plutarch, 116–17
Nuova, Abate (Florence), 216
Nuti, Signor and Signora (Florence), 218
Nutzolini, Mme. (and "the Nutzolinis," Leghorn), 249

O'Connor, Arthur, T. A. Emmett, and W. J. McNevin, *Memoir of United Irishmen*, 178, R.L.
Odessa, 319n, 370
Odysseus (Greek chieftain), 332, 354
"Oh, Cara Memoria," 242, R.L.
Old Bailey, London, 17
Olivier, General, 464
Olivieri, Mme. (Florence), 228
Ollier, Charles and James (booksellers and publishers): books published by, 202n, 205n, 206n; PBS writes to, 205n(q); m. 6, 83–84
*Olliers Literary Miscellany*, 205n, 381, R.L.
Omer Pasha, 476
O'Neill, Miss, in CC's dream, 228
O'Neill, Miss (actress), 84n

Oppizzoni, Count (Florence), 202, 212
Orange, Ursula, 97n
*Orfanello* (afterpiece), Florence, 275, P.L.
Origo, Iris, 86n, 155n
Orlandini, Marchesa (Florence): granddaughters described by Lady Murray, 209n(q); m. 199, 204–06, 208–13, 215–19, 221, 223, 227–34, 236, 241–42, 258, 274–75, 279, 473
Orlandini, Signora Anna (Florence), 256
Orlandini, casa, 204–09, 215, 219, 230, 232, 268
Orlandini, Ferdinando, 210, 212, 227, 229
Orlandini, Giulia, 210
Orsi (banker, Florence), 236
Ospedale Annunziata (Naples), files examined, 97n
Ospringe, 86
Ostermann, Countess (Russia), 362
Otway, Thomas: anecdote in Baker, 136; *Orphan*, CC comments on, 136, R.L.
Ouronssoff, Princess (Moscow), 385
Ouronssoff, Princess Barbara: 305, 312, 367, 369–71, 378–79, 382, 385, 387, 389, 396; *see also under* CC, letters
Overbury, Sir Thomas, in *Retrospective Review*, 205q, R.L.
Ovid, 460
Owenson, Sydney, Lady Morgan: description of Amelia Curran, 108n(q); *Florence Macarthy*, 158; *France* (error for *Italy?*), 264; *Italy*, 218n, 248, 263–64, 266–67, R.L.
Oxford, countess of (Jane Elizabeth Scott): anecdote of, 129–30; news of her daughter, 213
Oxford st., London, 49

Pacchiani, Francesco (Pisa, Florence): described, 187–88; inquisitive and indelicate, 193–94; Mme. Tantini's anecdote of, 192–93; witty remarks, 189–90, 199; m. 186n, 197–201, 206–08, 220n

552

# Index

# Index

# Index

Pisa: anonymous love letters from, 212, 216; CC visits, 172–74, 237, 243, 247, 249–53, 276, 284n; described by MWS, 447–48; odd English there, 146; Shelleys and CC live there, 119–51; m. 95, 118, 135, 142, 156–57, 159–60, 168, 188n–89n, 198n, 201, 205, 220n, 231–32, 259–60, 268, 283n, 293, 432, 464–67, 470, 472

Pisa, University of, 188n–89n, 220n, 226n, 464

Pitti, Cavaliere (Florence), 213, 234, 273

Pitti, Camilla, 273

Pittman, Major, 196

*Pittore per amore, Il* (ballet), Florence, 182, P.L.

Place, Francis, 69n

Plantis, Louisa du: CC writes to, 122, 123n; C. G. Clairmont in love with, 122–23n; letter from, 136; m. 114n, 116–17

Plantis, Mme. Merveilleux du (Shelleys' landlady in Florence): CC writes to, 123; furious letter to C. G. Clairmont, 122n–23; letter to CC, 136; m. 114n, 115

Plantis, Zoide du, 114n–18n, 159n

Plato: *Ion*, 198n; *Phaedon*, 329; *Symposium* (trans. PBS), 107, 168–69, 171; m. 184, 315, 372

Plich (Plick), M. (piano teacher, Florence): CC takes lessons from, 264–69, 271–76; CC pays, 269, 275

*Plutarch's Lives*, 115, 116–17q, 118, R.L.

*Podere*, described, 154n; m. 243, 450

Poggio Imperiale, Florence, 186, 204, 255–56, 259, 264, 280

Poland: rumored in revolt, 394; m. 391

Polen, Mme., CC writes to, 386

Polidori, Dr. J. W. (Byron's physician), 465, 471

Polish colony, Florence, CC's introduction to, 201

Pollok (Pollak), Mrs. (Florence): and her children, 115; letters from, 120, 129, 133; m. 114–16, 118, 120, 124, 127, 130, 137. *See also under* CC, letters

Pomerance, 229n

Pomeransevoi Doma (home of Dr. Jenish, Moscow), 375, 382

Pompadour, Mme. de: *Lettres*, 104–05; *Mémoires*, 101n, 102–03; R.L.

Pomikoff (Ponikoff) Mrs. (includes "the Pomikoffs," Russia), 321, 369, 393, 405–06, 408

Pomikoff, Johnny, 406

Pomikoff, Nicola, 406

Pompeii, 96

Pompey, statue of, Rome, 102

Pontarlier, 26

Pont Beau Voisin, 88

Ponte Molle (formerly Milow), Rome, 104

Ponte St. Trinita, Florence, 280

Pope, Alexander: *Dunciad*, in Baker, 133; *Iliad of Homer*, 159–60q; R.L.

Pope Pius VII, 100, 103

Poplicola, in Plutarch, 117

Popoli, duchess of, anecdote in Pananti, 222

Porphyry, Bishop, Marie Ivanovna's interview with, 371–72

Porta Colonella, Leghorn, 240, 242, 246, 248

Porta del Popolo, Rome 111

Porta delle Spiazze (Masi incident, Pisa), 281

Porta di Mare, Pisa, 179, 190

Porta Ferrajo, Elba, 217

Porta Fiorentina (Firenze), Pisa, 179, 190

Porta Lucca, Pisa, 178, 188

Porta Maggiore, Rome, 101

Porta Nuova, Pisa, 178, 188

Porta Pancrazio, Rome, 101

Porta Piaggi, Pisa, 149

Porta Pisa, Florence, 204

Porta Pisa, Leghorn, 238, 240, 242, 246–48

Porta Romana, Florence, 186n, 204, 210, 219, 259n, 260, 263–64, 280

Porta Rossa, Florence, 259, 285

Porta Salaria, Rome, 107–08

555

# Index

# Index

"Miserable Opera" *Emilia*, 212, P.L.
Samplach, Lake, *see* Sempach
Sand Hill, Islavsky, 316, 330
San Felice, church, Florence, 265
San Francesco, church, Lucca, 169
San Frediano, church, Lucca, 169
San Mateo, Florence: convent of, 205; spedale of, 206
San Niccolo, church, Pisa, 189
Sandt, Charles (Kotzebue's assassin), 150
Sant Ambrogio, convent, Florence, 206
Santa Margherita, Florence, 280
Santa Maria Maggiore, Florence, 168
Santa Maria Novella, theater, Florence, 212
Santa Maria sopra Minerva, church, Rome, 103
Santarelli, Signor (Florence), 234, 266, 280, 283–84
Santa Trinita, church, Florence, 236
Santi-Farina, Margherita, x
Saône River, 87
Saratov (Russia), 316
Sardinian Minister (Florence), 269
Savi (Professor of Botany, Pisa), 188n
Savoy, 88
Saxe-Weimar, duchess of, 415–16
Sayce, Miss (Russia): CC writes to, 392; m. 356, 385, 395
Schiedam (Skidam), Holland, 40
Schiller, J. C. F. von: "Der Gang nach dem Eisenhammer," 217–18; "Das Geheimniss," 208; *Der Geisterseher*, 368; "Das Gluck," 209q; "Die Grösse der Welt," 387; "Der Handschuh," 376; *Hero und Leander*, 216, 217q; *Die Jungfrau von Orleans* (Johanna D'Arc), 249–50; *Kabale und Liebe*, 245–46; "Der Kampf mit dem Drachen," 167, 220–21; "Die Kraniche des Ibykus," 379–80 (analyzed); "Das Lied von der Glocke," 209–10, 215–16; "Pegasus im Joche," 376; *Die Piccolomini*, 318; poem to Greece, 332; poems, 344; riddles, 386; "Der Ring des Polykrates," 219, 386–89; "Der Taucher," 392; *Wallenstein*, 316, 318–19, 322, 324–26, 328, 329q; *Wilhelm Tell*, 330; "Die Würde der Frauen," 387; *Die Zerstörung von Troja*, 224q, 227q, 228; m. 145, 380; P.L., R.L.
Schlegel, mentioned, 410
Schlegel, A. W. von: *Lectures on Dramatic Art and Literature*, 101, 103–04, 119, R.L.
Schlegel, Friedrich, in *Olliers Literary Miscellany*, 205q, R.L.
Schneider (Strasbourg University student), 34–35
Schoff Hock (Shauphane), 34
Schouwaloff, *see* Schwaloff
Schriwtz (or Schwitz, Strasbourg University student), 34–35
Schubart, C. F. D.: "Der ewige Jude," 335; "Der gesangene Sänger," 344; "Meiner Julie," 344; R.L.
Schuhbard, Baron, 227
Schultz, M. (harpist, Moscow), 375–77
Schwaloff (Schouwaloff), Countess (Florence), 203, 212–13
Schwindratzheim, 303
Sciarelli (Charelli), casa, Florence, 221, 259
Sciarelli, Mrs. (Florence), 232, 255, 259, 261, 263, 268, 271, 273–75
Sciarelli (?), Penelope, 261, 271, 273–75
Sciarellis, the, 233–34, 236, 260
Scilla Ruffo, Prince and Princess, 217
*Scipio* (English man-of-war), 159
Scolari, Giuseppe (?), 192n
Scota's Garden, Pisa, 128
Scott, W. S., 70n, 388, 402
Scott, Walter: *The Abbott*, 238; *Bride of Lammermoor*, 151; *Heart of Midlothian*, 114; *Ivanhoe*, 150, 249; *Kenilworth*, 247; *Legend of Montrose*, 151; *Rob Roy*, 82; R.L.
Scuola delle belle arti, Florence, 165
Sdvijenka, Moscow, 397
Ségur, A. J. P. de: *Les Femmes*, 376–77, R.L.
Sekendorff, anecdote of, in Condorcet, 138
Sempach (Samplach), Lake, 29

# Index

Semplere, Baroness (from Gorizia; in Florence), 233

Seneca, in Pananti, 221

Serassi, P. A.: *La Vita di Torquato Tasso*, 90–92; R.L.

Serchio, river, 250, 479

Servia, Greece, 219

Seymour, Mrs. (Russia): CC writes to, 330, 357; letters to CC, 319, 356; death, 370–71

Seymour's Court, 81

Sforzi (music teacher in Pisa), 148–50, 157

Sgricci, Tommaso (*improvvisatore*): biographical sketch, 470–73; improvises on Italian independence and on Byron, 190; on Pyramus and Thisbe, 198; on Iphegenia in Tauris, 198–99, 451; on Inez de Castro, 451; on death of Hector, 451–52; m. 131n, 191, 193, 205–07, 216, 218, 228–31, 262, 451–52; P.L.

Shakespeare, William: Coleridge on, 272; *All's Well That Ends Well*, 273q; *As You Like It*, 25; *Cymbeline*, 267; *Hamlet*, at Drury Lane, 50, m. 92, 277; *Henry IV*, 118, Parts I and II, 267; *Julius Caesar*, 261–62q; *King Lear*, CC's reading causes her "horrors," 31, m. 34, 92, 206n, 269, 271q, 421; *Macbeth*, 427; *Othello*, 206n; *Pericles*, 262q; *Richard III*, 31, 58, 206n; *Romeo and Juliet*, 278q; *Titus Andronicus*, 267; m. 133, 206n, 268, 278; P.L., R.L.

Shaw, J. T., 257n

*Shelley and Mary*, 7, 71n, 75n, 198n, 279n, 283n-85n

*Shelley and His Circle*, viii, 4, 15n, 58n

Shelley, Charles Bysshe (son of PBS and Harriet): Shelley loses custody of, 76; m. 74, 480

Shelley, Clara (daughter of PBS and MWS): christened, 86; death, 96, 97n; m. 87n, 480

Shelley, Elena Adelaide (PBS's Neapolitan charge): mysterious parentage, 97; occasion of blackmail attempt by Foggi, 97

Shelley, Eliza (PBS's sister): PBS plans abduction, 46–48. *See also* Eliza

Shelley, Eliza Ianthe (daughter of PBS and Harriet): birth of, 20; Shelley loses custody of, 76; m. 74, 480

Shelley, Harriet Westbrook: liked and then disliked Mrs. Godwin, 16q; dedication of *Queen Mab* to, 20; birth of daughter, 20; in Bath, 20; writes to Mary about subduing Mary's love for Shelley, 22; relations with Shelley in *1814*, 42–45, 47n, 48, 50, 54, 61n; illness, 49; CC writes to, 54; "plan to ruin Godwin," 56; her suicide, 75; Landor on, 146n; m. 68, 74, 76, 480. *See also under* PBS, letters

Shelley, Hellen (PBS's sister), PBS plans abduction of, 46–48

Shelley, Lady Jane (née Gibson; wife of Shelleys' son Percy), printed *Shelley and Mary*, 7; m. 206n, 480

Shelley, Mary Wollstonecraft (née Godwin):

CHRONOLOGY: childhood and schooling, 15–20; visited by Christy Baxter, 20; elopement with PBS, 20–21; letters from Godwin, 22, 45; shows PBS her papers, 22; crossing France, 22; her birthday, 34; rough passage back to England, 41; quarrels and tension with CC, 52, 67–68, 73–74, 150n, 153, 237n; death of first child, 67; to Geneva, 71; to Bath, 73–74; marriage to PBS, 76; at Marlow, 76, 78; sightseeing, visiting, and opera in London, 83–86; crosses France, 87–89; in Milan, 89, 91–92; with PBS to Como, 89, 91; death of Clara at Este, 96; fatigue and depression at Naples, 96; recorded as mother of Elena Adelaide Shelley, 97; recovers spirits in Rome, 97; takes up painting, 98; her pregnancy, 98; sightseeing in Rome, 104–05, 108–09; portrait by Amelia Curran, 109n; leaves Rome for Leghorn after death of William, 113–14; resides in Flor-

# Index

Byron, 74–75, 78, 95, 148n; loses custody of children by Harriet, 76; marriage to MWS, 76; moves with family to Marlow, 76–78; decides to go to Italy, 77; eye trouble, 81; sightseeing, visiting, and opera in London, 82–86; crosses France, 87–89; trouble over his books at Chambery, 88; sings climbing Mt. Cenis, 88; in Milan, 89, 91–92; enthusiasm for ballet, 89n; with Mary to Como, 89, 91; adventure with pistol, 91; escorts CC to visit Allegra at Este, 96; death of daughter Clara, 96; at Naples, takes responsibility for Elena Adelaide Shelley, 97; blackmailed by Foggi, 97; in Rome begins his *annis mirabilis*, 97; sightseeing in Rome, 100, 102–03, 110; delighted by *Miserere*, 104; portrait by Amelia Curran, 109n, 110–11; adventure at Post Office, 110; goes to Albano, 112; leaves Rome for Leghorn after death of William, 113–14; resides in Florence, 114–18; sketched by Tomkyns, 115–16; ill, 116; goes to live in Pisa, 119; attends opera, 122; visits Leghorn, 120–21, 131–32, 142–44; and Reveley steamboat project, 469; and Sgricci, 198n, 472; and Vaccà, 465; atheistical conversation, 142; sees Gisbornes off from Leghorn, 144; reading Encyclopedia in public, 146; and Landor in Pisa, 146n; visits Casciana, 148–50; moves family to Leghorn, 151; walks out with CC, 153–56, 171, 173; visits Pisa, 156, 157, 159–60, 168; moves family to Baths of Pisa, 168; visits Lucca, 169; goes to Monte San Pellegrino, 169, 171; escorts CC to Leghorn, 172; returns to Pisa, 173, 179; escorts CC to Florence, 179; visits Theresa Emilia Viviani, 191, 197, 237; is hypnotized, 196; concern for CC's prospects, 229n; escorts CC to Leghorn, 237; visits CC in Leghorn, 238, 245; visits Pisa, 243; his twenty-ninth birthday, 245;

goes to Ravenna, 247; his portrait painted by Williams, 247n; visit with MWS and CC to Spezzia, 248; visits Leghorn, 249; visits Pugnano, 250; praises CC's translation of Goethe, 278; invites CC to spend summer of 1822 with them, 283n; drowned off Viareggio, 284n; "Alastor" in "A fragment —," 477–79; m. (including "the Shelleys"), vii–ix, 6, 16, 18n, 35, 38, 41, 72, 77, 99, 114, 118, 122, 131, 150n, 153–54, 156, 159, 163, 188, 191, 198, 202n, 228, 251, 253, 274, 276, 294, 296–97, 299, 333, 401, 403, 409, 437n, 463, 470, 480

READING: Barruel, *Memoirs Illustrating the History of Jacobinism*, 30n, 49–50; *Bible*, St. Matthew, 116; Boccaccio, *Decameron*, 111n; C. B. Brown, *Ormond*, 172n; Burns, "Tam O'Shanter," 258n; Calderón, *Los Cabellos de Absalón*, 114–15n; *Cause célèbre: Procès . . . Fualdès*, 147n; Coleridge, "Ancient Mariner," 43, 47; Condorcet, *Vie de Voltaire*, 137n; Diogenes Laertius, 153n; Du Bois, *St. Godwin*, 48; Fletcher, *Thierry and Theodoret*, 147n; Forteguerri, *Il Ricciardetto*, 108n; *Galignani's Messenger*, 274n; Hope, *Anastasius*, 247n; Lucy Hutchinson, *Memoirs of Col. Hutchinson*, 245n; Irish pamphlets, 119n; Jonson, *Sejanus*, 141n; Klinger, *Travels before the Flood*, 120n; Lewis, *The Monk*, 45n; Manso, *Vita di Torquato Tasso*, 90n–91n; *Olliers Literary Miscellany*, 205n; Overbury, in *Retrospective Review*, 205n; Rousseau, *Discours sur les arts et les sciences*, 120n; Schiller, *Jungfrau von Orleans*, 249n; A. W. von Schlegel, *Lectures on Dramatic Art and Literature*, 101n; Shakespeare, *Hamlet*, 92, *Henry IV*, 118; Southey, *Curse of Kehama*, 44, *Thalaba*, 45–46; Sydney, in *Retrospective Review*, 206n; Tacitus, *Historiae*, 30; Wieland, *Aristipp*, 154n; Winckel-

# Index

mann, *Histoire de l'art chez les anciens*, 110n; Wollstonecraft, *Letters from Norway*, 33–34; Wordsworth, *The Excursion*, 43, "Mad Mother," 47–48. *See also* Reading List and Performance List

WRITINGS: *Adonais*, 243; *Alastor*, 61n; "The Assassins," 30, 40n; "Autumn, a Dirge," 403n; "The Boat on the Serchio," 276n; *The Cenci*, 111n–12n, reviews, 139n, Hare "review" of, 206n(q); "Defence of Poetry," 194n, 472; *Epipsychidion*, ix, 189n; *Esdaile Notebook*, 61n; *Hellas*, 190–91n; "Hymn to Intellectual Beauty," 319, 336; "Indian Serenade," 286n–87n; inscription in Chamonix visitors' book, 13n; *Laon and Cythna*, 68n; "Letter to Maria Gisborne," 469; notes and drafts in CC's First Journal, 8, 60–63; "Notes on Sculptures," 62n; "Ode to Liberty," 142n, 172n; "Ode to Naples," 173q; "Ode to the West Wind," 203n; *Oedipus Tyrannus; or, Swellfoot the Tyrant*, 172n; "Peter Bell the Third," 139n; *Prometheus Unbound*, 78n, 184–85; *Queen Mab*, 20, 56, 83, CC's allegory of, 430–31; notes to, 44, 196n, 335; *Revolt of Islam*, 108n, 326, 328, 330, 332, 334–35, 337, 340, 343–44, 352n, 353–55, attacked by *Quarterly*, 139n; song on ascending Mt. Cenis, 88; "To Constantia Singing," 77, 79, reprinted, xiv–xv, written for CC, ix, 13n; translations of Aeschylus, *Prometheus Bound* (by PBS?), 161–62n, of Plato's *Ion*, 198n, 472, of Plato's *Symposium*, 107, 168–69, 171; *Zastrozzi*, 49; R.L. *See also* Shelley, P. B. and Mary, journals

LETTERS (exclusive of many references without quotations in footnotes): to Amory, 46; Byron, 74q, 92n(q), 148n(q); C. G. Clairmont, 43; Claire Clairmont, 55–58, 175, 179n(q), 181q, 182, 184, 186, 201n(q), 203n(q),

204–07, 209–10, 216q, 217, 219, 224, 228–29, 231–33, 235, 246, 249, 249n(q), 259, 261–62, 264q, 267, 273–75, 278n(q), 279–80, 281n(q), 282–83, 286n(q), 472q; Gisbornes, 139n(q), 249n(q); Godwin, 43–44, 151n; Elizabeth Hitchener, 129n(q); Hogg, 43q, 47, 154n(q); Thomas Hookham, 43; Mrs. Hugford, 48; Hunt, 108n(q), 111, 119n(q), 133q; Ollier, 205n(q); Peacock, 88n(q), 89n(q), 102n, 106n, 114n(q), 213n(q), 416; Harriet Shelley, 44n(q), 46, 49, 54n(q); MWS, 57; Southey, 168n, 171; Trelawny, 134n(q); Henry Voisey, 43. *See also under* CC, letters, *and* CC, opinions

Shelley, P. B. and Harriet, 19–20, 70

Shelley, P. B. and Mary: *History of a Six Weeks' Tour*, 4, 21, 22q, 26n, 28n(q), 34n(q), 38n, 40n

Shelley, P. B. and Mary, journals: begun, 21; compared to CC's, 6–7; publication and use, 7; quoted or used as source of previously unpublished information, 22, 67–68, 95, and notes to pages 23–26, 29–31, 35, 41, 43–52, 54, 57–58, 60, 83, 86–88, 107–08, 111, 113, 115, 129, 150–51, 178, 181, 187, 191, 196, 198, 237, 241, 247, 274, 280

Shelley, P. B. and Mary, reading: compared to CC's, 6, R.L.

Shelley, Sir Percy Florence (son of PBS and MWS): birth, 114n; baptism, 118; illness, 132, 151; coldness to CC, 417; letter to CC, 406q; printed *Shelley and Mary*, 7; m. 178, 237, 480

Shelley, Sir Timothy (father of PBS), 68n, 88, 117n

Shelley, unnamed child, 480

Shelley, William (son of PBS and MWS): second birthday, 81; christened, 86; portrait by Amelia Curran, 109n, 111; illness and death in Rome, 112–13; m. 71, 73n, 74, 76, 83, 87n, 102n, 480

# Index

Sheremeteef's Hospital, Moscow, 386
Sherlock, Miss (Florence), 115, 118
Shepherd, Mr. (Florence), 118
Shields, Amelia ("Milly," Shelleys' servant), 82, 87n, 96
Shoreditch Church, Godwin's wedding there, 14
Shorf Bach (?), 32
Shute, Bishop, 358n, 369
Siberia, 257–59, 304
Sicard, Abbé, 262n
Siena, 253, 471
Silsbee, Capt. E. A., obtained Shelley notebook from Claire, ix
Silvestrini, Andriana Giovanna Pata (Pasta) Domenichini, 468
Silvestrini, Francesca (Fanny), see Zambelli
Silvestrini, Giacomo Benedetto, 468
Silvestrini, Maria Antonia (countess of Rossi), 468
Simionoff (Siminoff, Simonoff) Mme. (Moscow): and her mother, 309; m. 311, 376, 379
Simionoff, Mr., 376, 379
Simonovitch, Alexander (Moscow), 374
Sims, Miss (London), 49
Sims, Dr. J. (Harriet Shelley's physician), 49
Skidam, see Schiedam
Skinner Street, London (home of Godwins): life there described, 17–18; PBS visits, 20, 53; closed to CC, 67; CC visits, 69, 78n; CC dreams of, 119; letters from, 246, 274; lawsuit over, lost, 338n; m. 238, 277
Sky-ball, old and young (Pisa), 147
Sloane, Mr. (Leghorn), 244, 256, 262
Sloane st., London, 59
Smellie, William: Philosophy of Natural History, 46, R.L.
Smirna, 404–05
Smith, Adam: Essays on Philosophical Subjects, 134, R.L.
Smith, H. B., sale of his collection, 79
Smith, Horace: letters from, 129, 142, 159; Shelleys dine with, 84; Rejected Addresses, 84n

Smith, James (brother of Horace Smith), 84n
Smith, Maria: CC writes to, 43
Smith's Bridge, Moscow, 338, 371
Smollett, Tobias, 240n
Sobolefsky, Mr. (Moscow), 381
Socrates, 81, 153
Sografi, Simone: Il Cavalier Woender, 217, P.L.
Soleure, 29n
Solomon, 205, 282
Solon, in Plutarch, 117
Somerset House (Legacy Office), 80, 397
Somers Town: Godwin's residence, 14–15; Godwins leave, 17; Shelleys and CC move there, 46; m. 57
Sommer, Mr. (pianist, Moscow), 368, 382
Sophocles: Oedipus Rex, 192q; m. 102n, R.L.
Sophy (Moscow), 368
Soranzo family, 468
Southampton Buildings (Peacock's residence), 50–55, 58–59
Southcott, Joanna, Life of, 45, R.L.
Southend, 42
Southey, Robert: Curse of Kehama, 44; squabble with Byron, 274; letter to PBS, 168; PBS writes to, 168n, 171; Letters Written in Spain and Portugal, 124q; Life of Wesley, reviewed by Quarterly, 238–39q; Thalaba, 45–46; R.L.
Spain: C. G. Clairmont there, 114n; history of, 306, 342–43; revolution, 134, 142, 154, 156, 445–46
Spanish Consul in Pisa, 142
Specora, Garden of the, Florence, 216
Spectator, The, 114, R.L.
Specula, Florence, 261
Spezzia, Gulf of: CC and Shelleys visit, 248; summer of 1822 there, 284n
Spicchinsky, Mme. (Moscow), 386
Spinosa, 430–31
Spiridoff, Mme. (Russia), 322, 325, 338, 340, 356, 367, 395
Spohr, Louis, 113n
Spring Gardens, 80
Sproni, Signor (Leghorn), 247
Spurzheim, J. C., 44n, 443

564

# Index

# Index

# Index

# Index

# Index

# Index

Wieland, C. M.: *Aristipp*, 154–56; *Menander und Glycerion*, 253, 254q, 255, 259, 260q, 263q; R.L.

Wilkie (painter), 82n

Williams, Edward Ellerker (includes "the Williamses" and "Casa Williams"): his journal, viii; CC meets, 237; anecdote of, 243; goes to Leghorn, 247; at Pugnano, 247n; goes to Baths of Pisa, 247, 251; to Pisa, 253; CC dreams of, 260; and CC in summer of 1822, 284n; drowned off Viareggio, 284n; "Edward" in "A fragment —," 477–79; m. 171n, 251, 276, 280n

Williams, Edward Medwin ("Meddy," son of Jane and E. E. Williams): CC dreams of, 265; m. 284n

Williams, Helen Maria: letter to Lady M, 156

Williams, J. W., 477

Williams, Jane (later Mrs. T. J. Hogg): to Pisa with CC, 250; CC dreams of, 260, 265; letter to CC, 274, 381; close friendship with CC, 284n; and Asian music, 286n–87n; letter to MWS, 296q; her feeling for PBS, 299; London address of, 397; "Ianthe" in "A fragment—," 477–79; m. 72, 237n, 251–53, 280, 295, 298–99, 353n, 359n, 370n, 401–02, 408–09n, 415, 417. *See also under* CC, letters

Williams, Rosalind ("Dina"), *see* Hunt, Rosalind

Wilmot, Catherine: description of Princess Montemiletto, 203n(q); m. 120n, 142n, 156n

Winckelmann, J. J.: *Histoire de l'art chez les anciens*, 110–11, R.L.

Windsor Castle, 307

Wirtemberg, duchess of: CC dreams she is dead, 265

Wirtemberg, duke of (Florence), 266

Wise, T. J., 3, 7n, 9

Wittgenstein, L. A. P. (Russian general), 394

Wohlzogen, Caroline: *Agnès de Lilien*, 145–46, R.L.

Wolchonsky (Wolkonski), Prince (Moscow), 369

Wolchonsky, Princess Zeneide (Zinaide), 376, 383

Wolff (banker, Florence) and Mme. Wolff, 281

Wollshtoff, on Lake Lucerne, 29

Wollstonecraft, Mary (mother of Fanny Imlay and Mary W. Godwin): governess to Lady M, 119n; *Letters from Norway*, 33–34, 48(?), 149, CC's admiration of, 33; *Vindication of the Rights of Woman*, 112n, 149; m. 15, 57n–58n, 95, 156n, 271, 298, 480; R.L.

Woodcock, George, 125n, 416n

Wordsworth, William: at Godwin's, 16; *Excursion*, 43; *Lyrical Ballads*, "Mad Mother," 47–48, "Simon Lee," 379; m. 68, 101; R.L.

Wright, Mr. (London), 86

Wurzburg, 470

Wycombe (and Wycombe Road), London, 79, 81

Wyss, J. D., [Swiss] *Family Robinson Crusoe*, 171, R.L.

Xenophon, in Diogenes Laertius, 153

Xerxes, 118

York, duchess of, letter to, 51

York House (inn in Dover), 86

"Z., A.," *pseud.* of CC, 67

Zacharovitch, Ivan (Johnny, Vanya; son of Zachar Nicholaivitch and Marie Ivanovna): CC describes, 308n; has scarlet fever, 358–59; m. 298, 309–10, 312, 314, 316–17, 328–29, 331, 333–36, 342–44, 347, 353–57, 360, 362–63, 365–78, 382, 385, 387–89, 391–97

Zacharovna, Sophia (Dunia, CC's charge in Russia; daughter of Zachar Nicholaivitch and Marie Ivanovna): name-day, 361; fatal illness, 363; death, 364–65; m. 298, 309–10, 312, 314, 316–18, 322, 324, 328–29, 334–36, 339, 343, 353–56, 368–69, 397, 401

# Index